Essential C# 12.0

T0293077

Mark Michaelis
with Kevin Bost, Technical Editor

Addison-Wesley
Hoboken, New Jersey

Cover image: Iam_Anuphone/Shutterstock

For information about buying this title in bulk quantities, or for special sales opportunities (which may include electronic versions; custom cover designs; and content particular to your business, training goals, marketing focus, or branding interests), please contact our corporate sales department at corpsales@pearsoned.com or (800) 382-3419.

For government sales inquiries, please contact governmentsales@pearsoned.com.

For questions about sales outside the U.S., please contact intlcs@pearson.com.

Visit us on the Web: informit.com/aw

Library of Congress Control Number: 2023941980

ISBN-13: 978-0-13-821951-2
ISBN-10: 0-13-821951-6
5 2024

To my family: Elisabeth, Benjamin, Hanna, and Abigail. You have sacrificed a husband and daddy for countless hours of writing, frequently at times when he was needed most.

Thanks!

Also, to my friends and colleagues at IntelliTect. Thanks for filling in for me when I was writing rather than doing my job and for helping with the myriad of details to improve the content and keep a code base like this running smoothly. Thanks especially for making the EssentialCSharp.com website a reality.

Pearson's Commitment to Diversity, Equity, and Inclusion

Pearson is dedicated to creating bias-free content that reflects the diversity of all learners. We embrace the many dimensions of diversity, including but not limited to race, ethnicity, gender, socioeconomic status, ability, age, sexual orientation, and religious or political beliefs.

Education is a powerful force for equity and change in our world. It has the potential to deliver opportunities that improve lives and enable economic mobility. As we work with authors to create content for every product and service, we acknowledge our responsibility to demonstrate inclusivity and incorporate diverse scholarship so that everyone can achieve their potential through learning. As the world's leading learning company, we have a duty to help drive change and live up to our purpose to help more people create a better life for themselves and to create a better world.

Our ambition is to purposefully contribute to a world where:

- Everyone has an equitable and lifelong opportunity to succeed through learning.
- Our educational products and services are inclusive and represent the rich diversity of learners.
- Our educational content accurately reflects the histories and experiences of the learners we serve.
- Our educational content prompts deeper discussions with learners and motivates them to expand their own learning (and worldview).

While we work hard to present unbiased content, we want to hear from you about any concerns or needs with this Pearson product so that we can investigate and address them.

- Please contact us with concerns about any potential bias at https://www.pearson.com/report-bias.html.

Contents at a Glance

Contents

Foreword

Welcome to one of the most venerable and trusted franchises you could dream of in the world of C# books—and probably far beyond! Mark Michaelis's *Essential C#* book has been a classic for years, but it was yet to see the light of day when I first got to know Mark.

In 2005, when LINQ (Language Integrated Query) was disclosed, I had only just joined Microsoft, and I got to tag along to the PDC conference for the big reveal. Despite my almost total lack of contribution to the technology, I thoroughly enjoyed the hype. The talks were overflowing, the printed leaflets were flying off the tables like hotcakes: It was a big day for C# and .NET, and I was having a great time.

It was pretty quiet in the hands-on labs area, though, where people could try out the technology preview themselves with nice scripted walkthroughs. That's where I ran into Mark. Needless to say, he wasn't following the script. He was doing his own experiments, combing through the docs, talking to other folks, busily pulling together his own picture.

As a newcomer to the C# community, I may have met a lot of people for the first time at that conference—people with whom I have since formed great relationships. But to be honest, I don't remember them—it's all a blur. The only one I remember is Mark. Here is why: When I asked him if he was liking the new stuff, he didn't just join the rave. He was totally level-headed: *"I don't know yet. I haven't made up my mind about it."* He wanted to absorb and understand the full package, and until then he wasn't going to let anyone tell him what to think.

So instead of the quick sugar rush of affirmation I might have expected, I got to have a frank and wholesome conversation, the first of many over the years, about details, consequences, and concerns with this new technology. And so it remains: Mark is an incredibly valuable community member for us language designers to have, because he is super smart, insists on understanding everything to the core, and has phenomenal insight into how things affect real developers. But perhaps most of all, he is forthright and never afraid to speak his mind. If something passes the Mark Test, then we know we can start feeling pretty good about it!

These are the same qualities that make Mark such a great writer. He goes right to the essence and communicates with great integrity, no sugarcoating, and a keen eye for practical value and real-world problems. Mark has a great gift of providing clarity and elucidation, and no one will help you get C# 12.0 like he does.

Enjoy!

—Mads Torgersen
Principal Architect, Microsoft

Preface

Throughout the history of software engineering, the methodology used to write computer programs has undergone several paradigm shifts, each building on the foundation of the former by increasing code organization and decreasing complexity. This book takes you through these same paradigm shifts.

The beginning chapters take you through sequential programming structure, in which statements are executed in the order in which they are written. The problem with this model is that complexity increases exponentially as the requirements increase. To reduce this complexity, code blocks are moved into methods, creating a structured programming model. This allows you to call the same code block from multiple locations within a program, without duplicating code. Even with this construct, however, programs quickly become unwieldy and require further abstraction. Object-oriented programming, introduced in Chapter 6, was the response. In subsequent chapters, you will learn about additional methodologies, such as interface-based programming, LINQ (and the transformation it makes to the collection API), and eventually rudimentary forms of declarative programming (in Chapter 18) via attributes.

This book has three main functions.

- It provides comprehensive coverage of the C# language, going beyond a tutorial and offering a foundation upon which you can begin effective software development projects.
- For readers already familiar with C#, this book provides insight into some of the more complex programming paradigms and provides in-depth coverage of the features introduced in the latest version of the language, C# 12.0 and .NET 8.
- It serves as a timeless reference even after you gain proficiency with the language.

The key to successfully learning C# is to start coding as soon as possible. Don't wait until you are an "expert" in theory; start writing software immediately. As a believer in iterative development, I hope this book enables even a novice programmer to begin writing basic C# code by the end of Chapter 2.

Many topics are not covered in this book. You won't find coverage of topics such as ASP.NET, Entity Framework, Maui, smart client development, distributed programming, and so on. Although these topics are relevant to .NET, to do them justice requires books of their own. Fortunately, *Essential C# 12.0* focuses on C# and the types within the Base Class Library. Reading this book will prepare you to focus on and develop expertise in any of the more advanced areas, given a strong foundation in the C# langauge.

Target Audience for This Book

My challenge with this book was to keep advanced developers awake while not abandoning beginners by using words such as *assembly*, *link*, *chain*, *thread*, and *fusion*, as though the topic was more appropriate for blacksmiths than for programmers. This book's primary audience is experienced developers looking to add another language to their quiver. However, I have carefully assembled this book to provide significant value to developers at all levels.

- *Beginners:* If you are new to programming, this book serves as a resource to help transition you from an entry-level programmer to a C# developer who is comfortable with any C# programming task that's thrown your way. This book not only teaches you syntax but also trains you in good programming practices that will serve you throughout your programming career.
- *Structured programmers:* Just as it's best to learn a foreign language through immersion, learning a computer language is most effective when you begin using it before you know all the intricacies. In this vein, the book begins with a tutorial that will be comfortable for those familiar with structured programming, and by the end of Chapter 5, developers in this category should feel at home writing basic control flow programs. However, the key to excellence for C# developers is not memorizing syntax. To transition from simple programs to enterprise development, the C# developer must think natively in terms of objects and their relationships. To this end, Chapter 6's

Beginner Topics introduce classes and object-oriented development. The role of historically structured programming languages such as C, COBOL, and FORTRAN is still significant but shrinking, so it behooves software engineers to become familiar with object-oriented development. C# is an ideal language for making this transition because it was designed with object-oriented development as one of its core tenets.

- *Object-based and object-oriented developers:* C++, Java, Python, TypeScript, and Visual Basic programmers fall into this category. Many of you are already completely comfortable with semicolons and curly braces. A brief glance at the code in Chapter 1 reveals that, at its core, C# is like other C- and C++-style languages that you already know.
- *C# professionals:* For those already versed in C#, this book provides a convenient reference for less frequently encountered syntax. Furthermore, it provides insight into language details and subtleties that are seldom addressed. Most important, it presents the guidelines and patterns for programming robust and maintainable code. This book also aids in the task of teaching C# to others. With the emergence of C# 3.0 through 12.0, some of the most prominent enhancements are

    1. String interpolation (see Chapter 2)
    2. Implicitly typed variables (see Chapter 3)
    3. Tuples (see Chapter 3)
    4. Nullable reference types (see Chapter 3)
    5. Pattern matching (see Chapter 4)
    6. Extension methods (see Chapter 6)
    7. Partial methods (see Chapter 6)
    8. Default interface members (see Chapter 8)
    9. Anonymous types (see Chapter 12)
    10. Generics (see Chapter 12)

11. Lambda statements and expressions (see Chapter 13)
12. Expression trees (see Chapter 13)
13. Standard query operators (see Chapter 15)
14. Query expressions (see Chapter 16)
15. Dynamic programming (Chapter 18)
16. Multithreaded programming with the Task Programming Library and `async` (Chapter 20)
17. Parallel query processing with PLINQ (Chapter 21)
18. Concurrent collections (Chapter 22)

These topics are covered in detail for those not already familiar with them. Also pertinent to advanced C# development is the subject of pointers, covered in Chapter 23. Even experienced C# developers often do not understand this topic well.

Features of This Book

Essential C# 12.0 is a language book that adheres to the core C# Language Specification. To help you understand the various C# constructs, it provides numerous examples demonstrating each feature. Accompanying each concept are guidelines and best practices, ensuring that code compiles, avoids likely pitfalls, and achieves maximum maintainability.

To improve readability, code is specially formatted and chapters are outlined using mind maps.

Website

The interactive website for the book, available at https://essentialcsharp.com, provides the online chapters, which allows full text search. Shortly after this writing, I expect the website to provide interactive code editing and client-side compilation of many of the code listings. This will allow you to focus on the language rather than getting distracted by installations or dotnet setup issues.

Source Code Download

In addition to the EssentialCSharp.com website, all the source code is available on GitHub at https://github.com/IntelliTect/EssentialCSharp so it can be downloaded or cloned locally to your computer. This enables you to work through the code samples as is or modify them and see the effects. This is a great way to learn the intricacies of the language.

C# Coding Guidelines

One of the more significant enhancements included in *Essential C# 12.0* is the C# coding guidelines, as shown in the following example taken from Chapter 17:

Guidelines

DO ensure that equal objects have equal hash codes.

DO ensure that the hash code of an object never changes while it is in a hash table.

DO ensure that the hashing algorithm quickly produces a well-distributed hash.

DO ensure that the hashing algorithm is robust in any possible object state.

These guidelines are the key to differentiating a programmer who knows the syntax from an expert who can discern the most effective code to write based on the circumstances. Such an expert not only gets the code to compile but does so while following best practices that minimize bugs and enable maintenance well into the future. The coding guidelines highlight some of the key principles that readers will want to be sure to incorporate into their development. Visit https://intellitect.com/Guidelines for a current list of all the guidelines.

Code Samples

The code snippets in most of this text can run on most implementations of the Common Language Infrastructure (CLI), but the focus is on the .NET implementation. Platform- or vendor-specific libraries are seldom used except when communicating important concepts relevant only to those platforms (e.g., appropriately handling the single-threaded user interface of Windows). Any code that specifically relates to C# 8.0, 9.0, 10.0, 11.0, or 12.0 is called out in the C# version indexes at the end of the book.

Here is a sample code listing.

Listing 1.21: Commenting Your Code

```
public class CommentSamples
{
    public static void Main()
    {
        string firstName; // Variable for storing the first name
        string lastName;  // Variable for storing the last name

        Console.WriteLine("Hey you!");

        Console.Write /* No new line */ ("Enter your first name: ");
        firstName = Console.ReadLine();

        Console.Write /* No new line */ ("Enter your last name: ");
        lastName = Console.ReadLine();

        /* Display a greeting to the console
          using composite formatting. */

        Console.WriteLine("Your full name is {1}, {0}.",
            firstName, lastName);
        // This is the end
        // of the program listing
    }
}
```

The formatting is as follows:

- Comments are shown in italics.

```
/* Display a greeting to the console */
```

```
Console.Write /* No new line */ ("Enter your first name: ");
```

- Keywords are shown in bold.

```
static void Main() { }
```

- Highlighted code calls out specific code snippets that may have changed from an earlier listing, or demonstrates the concept described in the text.

Listing 2.23: Error; `string` Is Immutable

```
Console.Write("Enter text: ");
string text = Console.ReadLine();

// UNEXPECTED: Does not convert text to uppercase
text.ToUpper();

Console.WriteLine(text);
```

- Incomplete listings contain an ellipsis to denote irrelevant code that has been omitted.

```
// ...
```

Output 1.7

```
Hey you!
Enter your first name: Inigo
Enter your last name: Montoya

Your full name is Inigo Montoya.
```

- Console output is the output from a particular listing that appears following the listing. User input for the program appears in boldface.

Although it might have been convenient to provide full code samples that you could copy into your own programs, doing so would detract from your learning a particular topic. Therefore, you need to modify the code samples before you can incorporate them into your programs. The core omission is error checking, such as exception handling. Also, code samples do not explicitly include using System statements. You need to assume the statement throughout all samples.

Mind Maps

Each chapter's introduction includes a **mind map**, which serves as an outline that provides an at-a-glance reference to each chapter's content. Here is an example (taken from Chapter 6).

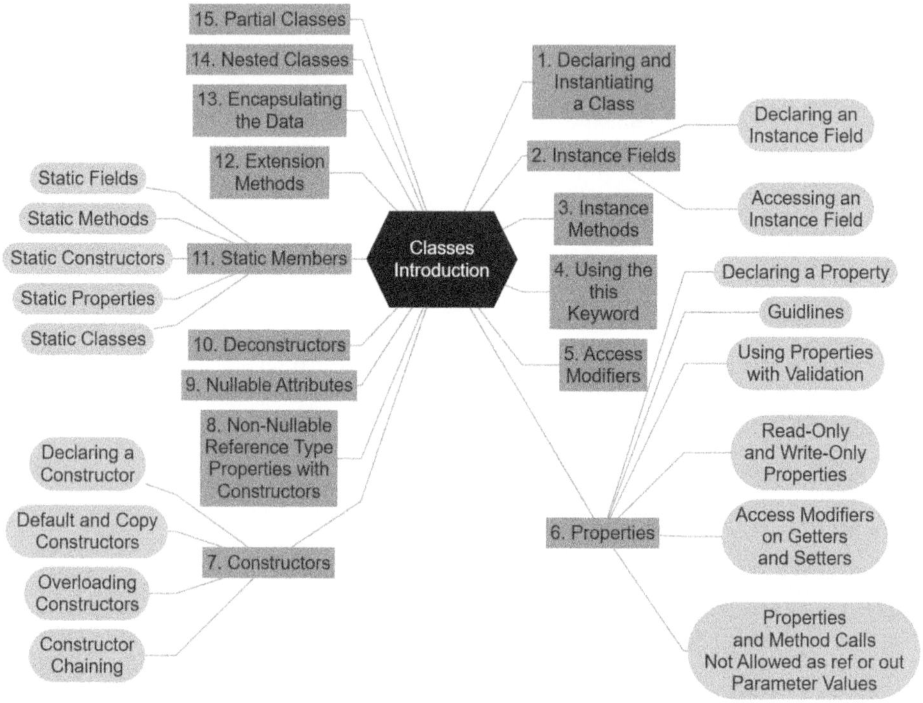

The theme of each chapter appears in the mind map's center. High-level topics spread out from the core. Mind maps allow you to absorb the flow from high-level to more detailed concepts easily, with less chance of encountering very specific knowledge that you might not be looking for.

Helpful Notes

Depending on your level of experience, special features will help you navigate through the text.

- Beginner Topics provide definitions or explanations targeted specifically toward entry-level programmers.
- Advanced Topics enable experienced developers to focus on the material that is most relevant to them.
- Callout notes highlight key principles in boxes so that readers easily recognize their significance.
- Language Contrast sidebars identify key differences between C# and its predecessors to aid those familiar with other languages.

How This Book Is Organized

At a high level, software engineering is about managing complexity, and it is toward this end that I have organized *Essential C# 12.0*. Chapters 1–5 introduce structured programming, which enable you to start writing simple functioning code immediately. Chapters 6–10 present the object-oriented constructs of C#. Novice readers should focus on fully understanding this section before they proceed to the more advanced topics found in the remainder of this book. Chapters 12–14 introduce additional complexity-reducing constructs, handling common patterns needed by virtually all modern programs. This leads to dynamic programming with reflection and attributes, which is used extensively for threading and interoperability in the chapters that follow.

The book ends with Chapter 24 on the Common Language Infrastructure, which describes C# within the context of the development platform in which it operates. This chapter appears at the end because it is not C# specific and it departs from the syntax and programming style in the rest of the book. However, this chapter is suitable for reading at any time, perhaps most appropriately immediately following Chapter 1.

Here is a description of each chapter (in this list, chapter numbers shown in **bold** indicate the presence of C# 10.0–12.0 material).

- ***Chapter 1***, *Introducing C#:* After presenting the C# "Hello World" program, this chapter proceeds to dissect it. This should familiarize readers with the look and feel of a C# program and provide details on how to compile and debug their own programs. It also touches on the context of a C# program's execution and its intermediate language.

- *Chapter 2, Data Types:* Functioning programs manipulate data, and this chapter introduces the primitive data types of C#.
- *Chapter 3, More with Data Types:* This chapter includes coverage of two type categories: value types and reference types. From there, it delves into implicitly typed local variables, tuples, the nullable modifier, and the C# 8.0–introduced feature, nullable reference types. It concludes with an in-depth look at a primitive array structure.
- *Chapter 4, Operators and Control Flow:* To take advantage of the iterative capabilities in a computer, you need to know how to include loops and conditional logic within your program. This chapter also covers the C# operators, data conversion, and preprocessor directives.
- ***Chapter 5**, Methods and Parameters:* This chapter investigates the details of methods and their parameters. It includes passing by value, passing by reference, and returning data via an out parameter. In C# 4.0, default parameter support was added, and this chapter explains how to use default parameters.
- ***Chapter 6**, Classes:* Given the basic building blocks of a class, this chapter combines these constructs to form fully functional types. Classes form the core of object-oriented technology by defining the template for an object.
- *Chapter 7, Inheritance:* Although inheritance is a programming fundamental to many developers, C# provides some unique constructs, such as the new modifier. This chapter discusses the details of the inheritance syntax, including overriding.
- ***Chapter 8**, Interfaces:* This chapter demonstrates how interfaces are used to define the versionable interaction contract between classes. C# includes both explicit and implicit interface member implementation, enabling an additional encapsulation level not supported by most other languages. With the introduction of default interface members, there is a section on interface versioning in C# 8.0.
- ***Chapter 9**, Introducing Structs and Records:* C# 9.0 introduced the concepts of records for structs and expanded it to reference types in C# 10. Although not as prevalent as defining reference types, it is sometimes necessary to define value types that behave in a fashion similar to the primitive types built into C#. In defining how to create custom structures, this chapter also describes the idiosyncrasies they may introduce.

- *Chapter 10, Well-Formed Types:* This chapter discusses more advanced type definition. It explains how to implement operators, such as + and casts, and describes how to encapsulate multiple classes into a single library. In addition, the chapter demonstrates defining namespaces and XML comments and discusses how to design classes for garbage collection.
- *Chapter 11, Exception Handling:* This chapter expands on the exception-handling introduction from Chapter 5 and describes how exceptions follow a hierarchy that enables creating custom exceptions. It also includes some best practices on exception handling.
- *Chapter 12, Generics:* Generics are perhaps the core feature missing from C# 1.0. This chapter fully covers this 2.0 feature. In addition, C# 4.0 added support for covariance and contravariance—something covered in the context of generics in this chapter.
- ***Chapter** 13, Delegates and Lambda Expressions:* Delegates begin clearly distinguishing C# from its predecessors by defining patterns for handling events within code. This virtually eliminates the need for writing routines that poll. Lambda expressions are the key concept that make C# 3.0's LINQ possible. This chapter explains how lambda expressions build on the delegate construct by providing a more elegant and succinct syntax. This chapter forms the foundation for the collection API discussed next.
- *Chapter 14, Events:* Encapsulated delegates, known as events, are a core construct of the Common Language Runtime. Anonymous methods, another C# 2.0 feature, are also presented here.
- *Chapter 15, Collection Interfaces with Standard Query Operators:* The simple and yet elegantly powerful changes introduced in C# 3.0 begin to shine in this chapter as we take a look at the extension methods of the Enumerable class. This class makes available a collection API known as the standard query operators, which is discussed in detail here.
- *Chapter 16, LINQ with Query Expressions:* Using standard query operators alone results in some long statements that are hard to decipher. However, query expressions provide an alternative syntax that matches closely with SQL, as described in this chapter.
- *Chapter 17, Building Custom Collections:* In building custom APIs that work against business objects, it is sometimes necessary to create custom collections. This chapter details how to do this and in the process introduces contextual keywords that make custom collection building easier.

- ***Chapter 18**, Reflection, Attributes, and Dynamic Programming:* Object-oriented programming formed the basis for a paradigm shift in program structure in the late 1980s. In a similar way, attributes facilitate declarative programming and embedded metadata, ushering in a new paradigm. This chapter looks at attributes and discusses how to retrieve them via reflection. It also covers file input and output via the serialization framework within the Base Class Library. In C# 4.0, a new keyword, *dynamic*, was added to the language. This removed all type checking until runtime, a significant expansion of what can be done with C#.

- *Chapter 19, Introducing Multithreading:* Most modern programs require the use of threads to execute long-running tasks while ensuring active response to simultaneous events. As programs become more sophisticated, they must take additional precautions to protect data in these advanced environments. Programming multithreaded applications is complex. This chapter introduces how to work with tasks, including canceling them, and how to handle exceptions executing in the task context.

- *Chapter 20, Programming the Task-Based Asynchronous Pattern:* This chapter delves into the task-based asynchronous pattern with its accompanying async/await syntax. It provides a significantly simplified approach to multithreaded programming. In addition, the C# 8.0 concept of asynchronous streams is included.

- *Chapter 21, Iterating in Parallel:* One easy way to introduce performance improvements is by iterating through data in parallel using a Parallel object or with the Parallel LINQ library.

- *Chapter 22, Thread Synchronization:* Building on the preceding chapter, this chapter demonstrates some of the built-in threading pattern support that can simplify the explicit control of multithreaded code.

- ***Chapter 23**, Platform Interoperability and Unsafe Code:* Given that C# is a relatively young language, far more code is written in other languages than in C#. To take advantage of this preexisting code, C# supports interoperability—the calling of unmanaged code—through P/Invoke. In addition, C# provides for the use of pointers and direct memory manipulation. Although code with pointers requires special privileges to run, it provides the power to interoperate fully with traditional C-based application programming interfaces.

- *Chapter 24, The Common Language Infrastructure:* Fundamentally, C# is the syntax that was designed as the most effective programming language on top of the underlying Common Language Infrastructure. This chapter delves into how C# programs relate to the underlying runtime and its specifications.

- *Indexes of C# 8.0-12.0:* These indexes provide quick references for the features added in C# 8.0 through 12.0. They are specifically designed to help programmers quickly update their language skills to a more recent version.

I hope you find this book to be a great resource in establishing your C# expertise and that you continue to reference it for those areas that you use less frequently well after you are proficient in C#.

—Mark Michaelis

IntelliTect.com/mark, mark.michaelis.net

X (formerly Twitter): @Intellitect, @MarkMichaelis

Register your copy of *Essential C# 12.0* on the InformIT site for convenient access to updates and/or corrections as they become available. To start the registration process, go to informit.com/register and log in or create an account. Enter the product ISBN (9780138219512) and click Submit. Look on the Registered Products tab for an Access Bonus Content link next to this product, and follow that link to access any available bonus materials. If you would like to be notified of exclusive offers on new editions and updates, please check the box to receive email from us.

Acknowledgments

No book can be published by the author alone, and I am extremely grateful for the multitude of people who helped me with this one. The order in which I thank people is not significant, except for those who come first. Given that this is now the eighth edition of the book, you can only imagine how much my family has sacrificed to allow me to write over the last 18 years (not to mention the books before that). Benjamin, Hanna, and Abigail often had a Daddy distracted by this book, but Elisabeth suffered even more so. She was often left to take care of things, holding the family's world together on her own. (While on vacation in 2017, I spent days indoors writing while they would much have preferred to go to the beach.)

In writing *Essential C# 12.0,* I am very grateful that Pearson gave permission for IntelliTect to host the manuscript on the website, essentialcsharp.com. I could never have done this without the IntelliTect team, however. I am so grateful to be surrounded by such amazing software engineers who produce such excellence autonomously from me. Many, many hours were spent parsing the manuscript, formatting it, editing the content, and creating both the website output and the manuscript for print. Thanks so much to the following contributors that made this edition possible: Benjamin Michaelis, Kevin Bost, Daniel Olvera, Jenny Curry, Mikaella Croskrey, Grant Woods, Zack Ward, Josh Willis, Andrew Scott, Anré "Ray" Tanner, Artem Chetverikov, Casey White, Austen Frostad, Tom Clark, Joseph Riddles, John Evans, Kelsey McMahon, Casey Schadewitz, Cameron J. Osborn, Nicole Glidden, and Elizabeth Pauley. Special thanks to Kevin Bost and my son Benjamin Michaelis. In addition to their code contributions, they helped manage the entire web tooling project, making the website a reality.

I have worked with Kevin Bost at IntelliTect since 2013, and he continues to surprise me with his incredible aptitude for software development. Not only is the depth of his C# knowledge phenomenal, but he is a level-10 expert in so many additional development technologies. For all this and more, I asked Kevin Bost to review the book as an official technical editor this year, and I am truly grateful. He brought insights and improvements to content that has been in the book since the early editions, which no one else thought to mention. This attention to detail, combined with his unswerving demand for excellence, truly establishes *Essential C# 12.0* as a quintessential C# book for those looking to focus on the language.

Of course, Eric Lippert is no less amazing as well. His grasp of C# is truly astounding, and I am very appreciative of his edits, especially when he pushed for perfection in terminology. His improvements to the C# 3.0 chapters were incredibly significant, and in the second edition my only regret was that I didn't have him review all the chapters. However, that regret has since been mitigated: Eric painstakingly reviewed every *Essential C# 4.0* chapter and even served as a contributing author for *Essential C# 5.0* and *Essential C# 6.0*. I am extremely grateful for his role as a technical editor in the editions leading up to *Essential C# 12.0*. Thanks, Eric! I can't imagine anyone better for the job. You deserve all the credit for raising the bar from good to great.

As is the case with Eric and C#, there are fewer than a handful of people who know .NET multithreading as well as Stephen Toub. Accordingly, Stephen concentrated on the two rewritten (for a third time) multithreading chapters and their new focus on async support in C# 5.0. Thanks, Stephen!

Over the years, many other technical editors have reviewed each chapter in minute detail to ensure technical accuracy. I was often amazed by the subtle errors these folks still managed to catch: Paul Bramsman, Kody Brown, Andrew Comb, Ian Davis, Doug Dechow, Gerard Frantz, Dan Haley, Thomas Heavey, Anson Horton, Brian Jones, Shane Kercheval, Angelika Langer, Neal Lundby, John Michaelis, Jason Morse, Nicholas Paldino, Jason Peterson, Jon Skeet, Michael Stokesbary, Robert Stokesbary, and John Timney.

Thanks to everyone at Pearson/Addison-Wesley for their patience in working with me in spite of my frequent focus on everything else except the manuscript. Thanks also to Malobika Chakraborty and Julie Nahil for helping me through the entire process from proposal to production.

About the Author

Mark Michaelis is the founder of IntelliTect, an innovative software architecture and development firm where he serves as the chief technical architect and trainer. Mark leads his successful company while flying around the world delivering conference sessions on leadership or technology and conducting speaking engagements on behalf of Microsoft or other clients. He has also written numerous articles and books, and is an adjunct professor at Eastern Washington University, founder of the Spokane .NET Users Group, and co-organizer of the annual TEDx Coeur d'Alene events.

A world-class C# expert, Mark has been a Microsoft Regional Director since 2007 and a Microsoft MVP for more than 25 years.

Mark holds a bachelor of arts in philosophy from the University of Illinois and a master's degree in computer science from the Illinois Institute of Technology.

When not bonding with his computer, Mark is busy showing his kids real life in other countries or playing racquetball (having suspended competing in Ironman competitions back in 2016). Mark lives in Spokane, Washington, with his wife, Elisabeth, and three children, Benjamin, Hanna, and Abigail.

About the Technical Editor

Kevin Bost is a successful Microsoft MVP and senior software architect at IntelliTect. He has been instrumental in building several innovative products, including System.CommandLine, Moq.AutoMocker, and ShowMeTheXAML. When not at work, Kevin can be found online, mentoring other developers on YouTube (youtube.keboo.dev) and maintaining the popular Material Design in XAML toolkit (http://materialdesigninxaml.net/). He also enjoys board games, Ultimate Frisbee, and riding his motorcycle.

1

Introducing C#

The C# programming language can be used to build software components and applications that run on a wide variety of operating systems (platforms)—including mobile devices, game consoles, web applications, Internet of Things (IoT), microservices, and desktop applications. Furthermore, C# is free; in fact, it is entirely open source, so you can view, modify, redistribute, and contribute back any improvements you make. As a language, C# is built on features found in its predecessor C-style languages (C, C++, and Java), making it immediately familiar to many experienced programmers.[1]

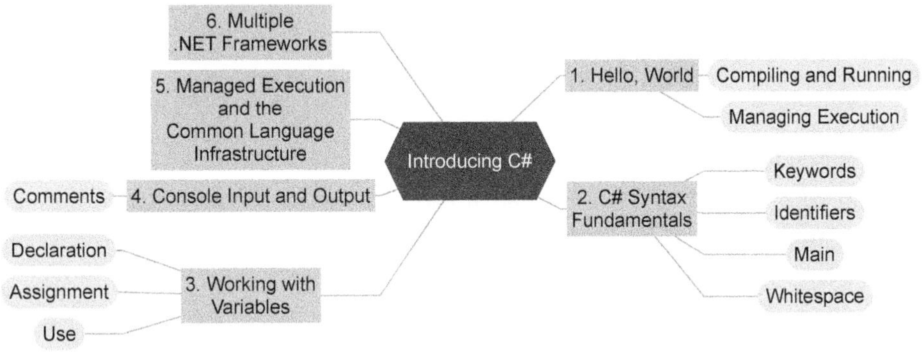

1. The first C# design meeting took place in 1998.

This chapter introduces C# using the traditional `HelloWorld` program. It focuses on C# syntax fundamentals, including defining an entry point into the C# program, which will familiarize you with the C# syntax style and structure and enable you to produce the simplest of C# programs. Prior to the discussion of C# syntax fundamentals is a summary of managed execution context, which explains how a C# program executes at runtime. This chapter ends with a discussion of variable declaration, writing and retrieving data from the console, and the basics of commenting code in C#.

Hello, World

The best way to learn a new programming language is to write code. The first example is the classic `HelloWorld` program. In this program, you will display some text to the screen.

Listing 1.1 shows the complete HelloWorld program; in the following sections, you will compile and run the code.

Begin 9.0

Listing 1.1: HelloWorld in C#[2]

```
Console.WriteLine("Hello. My name is Inigo Montoya.");
```

(A listing this simple requires a feature—**top-level statements**—enabled in C# 9.0 to help with learning C#. An alternative listing—arguably a more typical listing—is shown later in Listing 1.6. See Chapter 4 for more information about top-level statements.)

End 9.0

BEGINNER TOPIC

Basic Compilation Terms

A compiler acts like a translator, changing code from one language to another. Generally, the compiler is responsible for converting from a higher level language, like C#, to a lower level language that a computer understands directly. In the case of

2. Refer to the movie *The Princess Bride* if you're confused about the Inigo Montoya references.

C#, the compiler output is an intermediate language that a second compiler translates to machine language. This is discussed further in the "Managed Execution and the Common Language Infrastructure" section later in this chapter. Source code is simply the text that makes up a program, so Listing 1.1 is considered source code to our HelloWorld Program. The word *code* is often used interchangeably with *source code*.

Creating, Editing, Compiling, and Running C# Source Code

Once you have written your C# code, it is time to compile and run it. Based on your operating system, you have a choice of which compiler to download. Generally, the implementation is packaged into a **software development kit (SDK)**. The SDK includes the compiler, the runtime execution engine, the framework of pragmatically accessible functionality that the runtime can access (see "Application Programming Interface" later in the chapter), and any added tooling (such as a build engine for automating build steps) that might be bundled with the SDK. Given that there are compilers available for multiple platforms and that C# has been publicly available since 2000 (see "Multiple .NET Frameworks" later in the chapter), there are several options to choose from.

For each operating system the installation instructions vary. For this reason, we recommend you visit https://dotnet.microsoft.com/download for download and installation instructions, selecting the package to download based on which operating system you will be developing on. Furthermore, you have a choice of which .NET implementation(s) to use—sometimes referred to as the **.NET framework**(s). While we could provide further details here, the .NET download site has the most updated instructions for each combination supported. While there are multiple framework versions available, the easiest is to download the default one, which corresponds to the latest fully released version.

There are also numerous ways to edit your source code, including the most rudimentary of tools, such as Notepad on Windows, TextEdit on Mac/macOS, or vi on Linux. However, you're likely to want something more advanced so that at least your code is colorized. Any programming editor that supports C# will suffice. If developing on Linux, we recommend you consider the open source editor Visual

Studio Code (https://code.visualstudio.com). To optimize working with C# in Visual Studio Code, you will want to install the C# extension, as shown in Figure 1.1. However, if you are working on Windows or Mac, consider the corresponding version of Microsoft Visual Studio 2022 (or later)—see https://visualstudio.microsoft.com/. All are available free of charge.

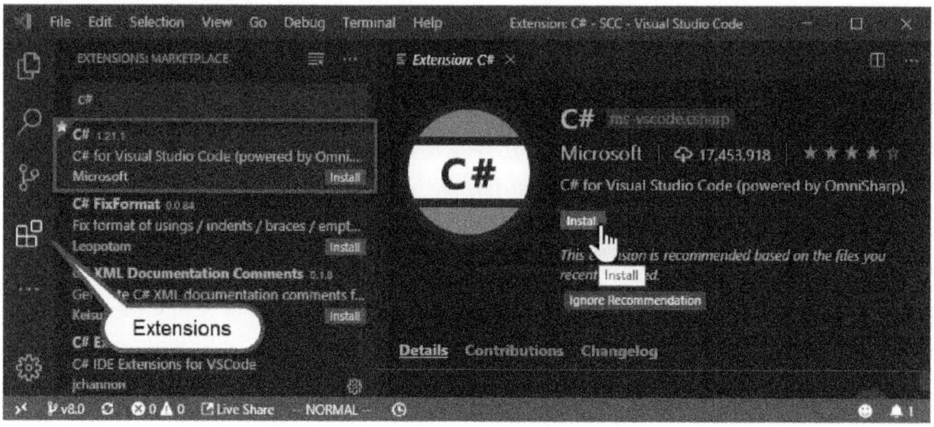

FIGURE 1.1: Installing the C# extension for Visual Studio Code

In the remainder of this section, we provide instructions for these editors. For Visual Studio Code, we rely on the command-line interface (CLI) tool **dotnet CLI** for creating the initial C# program in addition to compiling and running the program. For Windows and Mac, we focus on using the platform-specific version of Visual Studio 2022.

Begin 9.0

With Dotnet CLI

The dotnet command, `dotnet`, is the dotnet command-line interface, or dotnet CLI, and it may be used to generate the initial code base for a C# program in addition to compiling and running the program.[3] (To avoid ambiguity between CLI referring to the Common Language Infrastructure or the command-line interface, throughout the

3. This tool was released around the same time as C# 7.0, and it eclipsed compiling directly with the C# compiler, csc.exe.

book we will prefix CLI with dotnet when referring to the dotnet CLI. CLI without the dotnet prefix refers to Common Language Infrastructure.) Once you have completed the installation, verify that `dotnet` is an available command from the terminal—thus verifying your installation.

Following are the instructions for creating, compiling, and executing the `HelloWorld` program from a terminal on Windows, macOS, or Linux:

1. Open the terminal. (Optionally, consider using the cross-platform command-line interface PowerShell by running the command **pwsh**.[4])

2. Create a new directory where you want to place the code. Consider a name such as `HelloWorld` or `EssentialCSharp/HelloWorld`. From the command line, use

   ```
   mkdir HelloWorld
   ```

3. Navigate into the new directory so that it is the terminal's current location.

   ```
   cd HelloWorld
   ```

4. Execute `dotnet new console` to generate the initial scaffolding (or project) for your program. While several files are generated, the two main files are `Program.cs` and the project file `HelloWorld.csproj`:

   ```
   dotnet new console
   ```

5. Run the generated program. This compiles and runs the code created by the `dotnet new console` command. The content of `Program.cs` is similar to Listing 1.1 but it outputs "Hello World!" instead.

   ```
   dotnet run
   ```

6. Even though we don't explicitly request the project to compile (or build)—via the `dotnet build` command, that step still occurs implicitly.

---

4. https://github.com/PowerShell/PowerShell

7. Edit the `Program.cs` file and modify the code to match what is shown in Listing 1.1. If you use one of the editors mentioned to open and edit `Program.cs`, you will see the advantage of a C#-aware editor, as the code will be colorized to indicate the different types of constructs in your program. To open and edit using Visual Studio Code, use the following command or start Visual Studio Code and open the `Program.cs` file.

   ```
   code .
   ```

8. (Alternatively, Output 1.1 shows an approach using only the command line that works for Bash and PowerShell.)

9. Rerun the program:

   ```
   dotnet run
   ```

Output 1.1 shows the output following the preceding steps.[5]

Output 1.1

```
1>
2> mkdir ./HelloWorld
3> cd ./HelloWorld/
4> dotnet new console
The template "Console Application" was created successfully.

Processing post-creation actions...
Running 'dotnet restore' on C:
\EssentialCSharp\HelloWorld\HelloWorld.csproj...
  Restore completed in 100.38 ms for
C:\EssentialCSharp\HelloWorld\HelloWorld.csproj.
Restore succeeded.
5> dotnet run
Hello World!
6> echo '
Console.WriteLine("Hello. My name is Inigo Montoya.");
' > Program.cs
7> dotnet run
Hello. My name is Inigo Montoya.
```

5. The bold formatting in an Output indicates the user-entered content.

With Visual Studio 2022 (Windows or Mac)

With Visual Studio 2022, which runs only on Microsoft Windows or Mac, the procedure is similar, but instead of using the command line, you use an **integrated development environment (IDE)**, which has menus you can choose from rather than executing everything from the command line:

1. Launch Visual Studio 2022.
2. Click the **Create a new project** button. (If the Start Window is not visible, you can open it from the **File->Start Window** menu or jump directly to create the project via the **File->New Project** (Ctrl+Shift+N) menu.)
3. From the **Search box** (Alt+S), type *Console App* and select the **Console App** item (see Figure 1.2). (You can optionally select C# to reduce the options count if other languages are installed.)
4. For the **Project name** text box, use *HelloWorld*, and for **Location**, select a working directory of your choosing (see Figure 1.3).
5. At the **Additional information** dialog, choose .NET 7.0 in the Framework dropdown. (Leave the **Do not use top-level statements** checkbox unchecked.)
6. Once the project is created, you should see a `Program.cs` file, as shown in Figure 1.4.

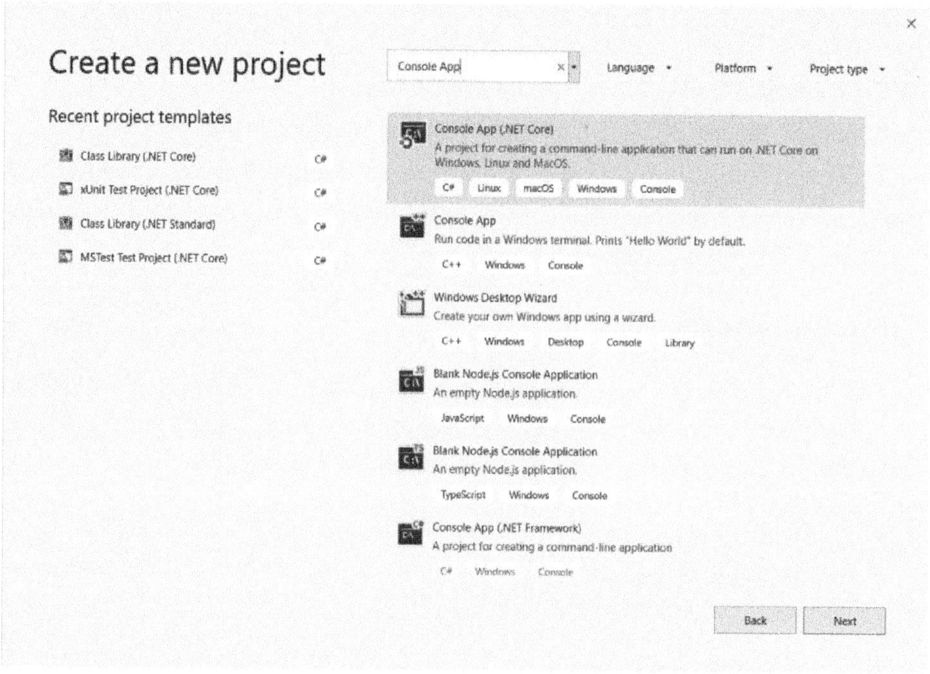

FIGURE 1.2: The Create a new project dialog

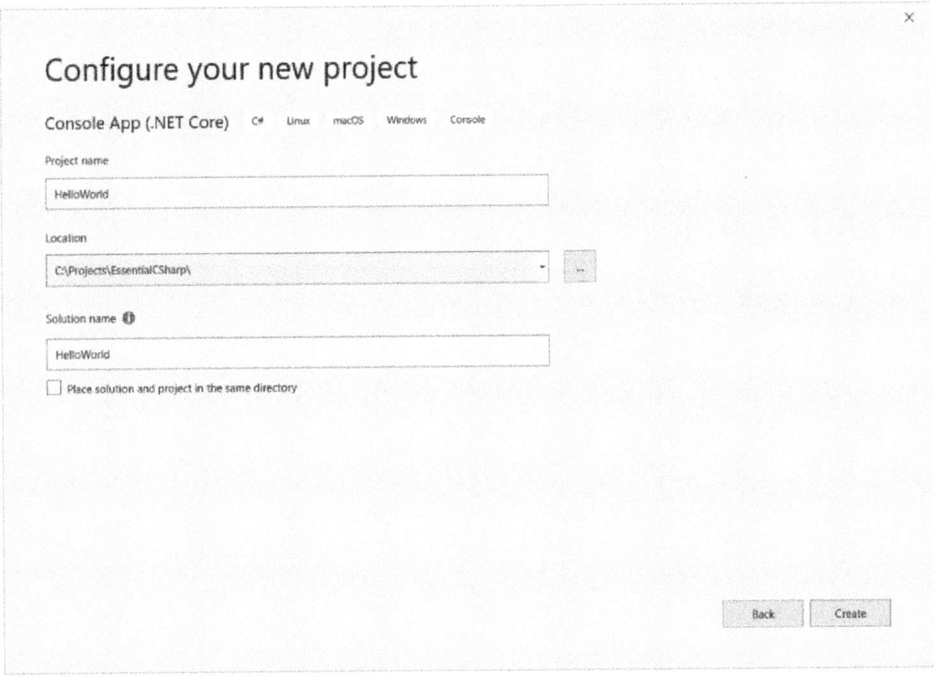

Figure 1.3: The Configure your new project dialog

7. Run the generated program using the **Debug->Start Without Debugging** (Ctrl+F5) menu. This displays the terminal with the text shown in Output 1.2 except the first line displays "Hello World!" only.

Output 1.2

```
Hello. My name is Inigo Montoya.

...\HelloWorld.exe (process 11856) exited with code 0.
Press any key to close this window . . .
```

8. Modify `Program.cs` to match Listing 1.1. Rerun the program to see the output shown in Output 1.2.

End 9.0

Begin 8.0

Begin 10.0

Understanding a Project

Whether using dotnet CLI or Visual Studio, there are several files created. The first file is a C# file with the name `Program.cs` by convention. The name *Program* is

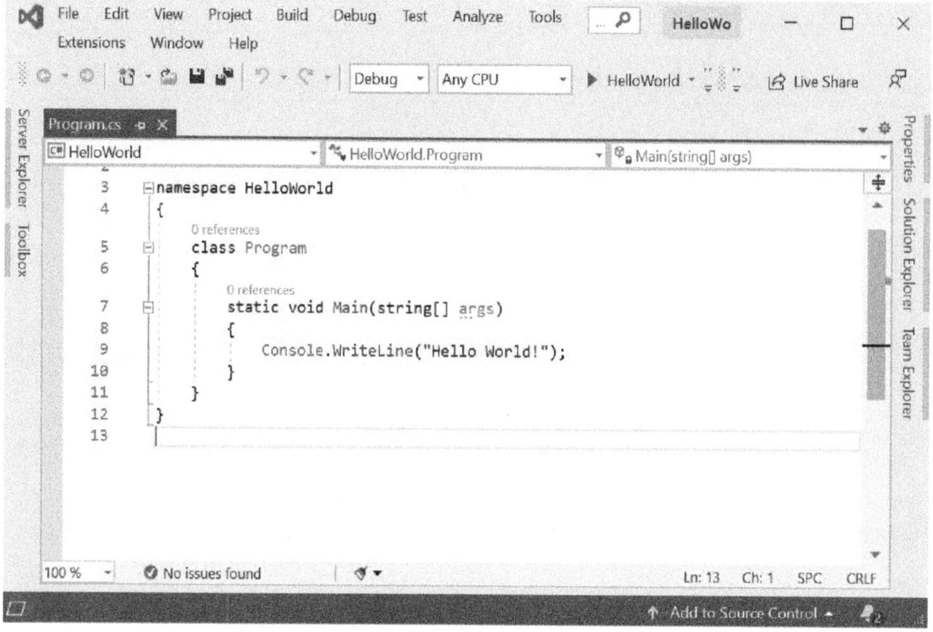

FIGURE 1.4: Dialog that shows the `Program.cs` file

commonly used as the starting point for a console program, even though any name could be used. The `.cs` extension is the standard convention for all C# files and what the compiler expects to compile into the final program by default. To use the code shown in Listing 1.1, open the `Program.cs` file and replace its content with Listing 1.1. Before saving the updated file, observe that the only functional difference between Listing 1.1 and what was generated by default is the text between the double quotes.

A configuration file called a **project file** is included as part of the generated source code of your C# project. The project file content varies from one application type and .NET framework to the next. However, at a minimum, it generally identifies what application type to build (console, web, library, etc.), which .NET framework(s) to support, compiler settings, and which potential settings are needed to launch the application, along with other dependencies the code may rely on (called *libraries*). For example, the simple .NET console application project file created in the previous section appears in Listing 1.2.

Listing 1.2: Sample .NET Console Project File

```
<Project Sdk="Microsoft.NET.Sdk">
  <PropertyGroup>
    <OutputType>Exe</OutputType>
    <TargetFramework>net7.0</TargetFramework>
    <ImplicitUsings>enable</ImplicitUsings>
    <Nullable>enable</Nullable>
  </PropertyGroup>
</Project>
```

In Listing 1.2, the application type is identified as a .NET 8.0 (`net8.0`) console application (`Exe`). The two other elements, `Nullable` (C# 8.0) and `ImplicitUsings` (C# 10.0) , will be discussed in "Declaring Types That Allow Null" in Chapter 3 and "Using Directives" (https://essentialcsharp.com/using-directives) in Chapter 5, respectively. All other settings (such as which C# files to compile) are identified by convention. For example, by default, all `*.cs`[6] files in the same directory (or subdirectory) as the project file are included in the compile.

End 8.0

End 10.0

Compilation and Execution

When you execute `dotnet run`, it first implicitly runs `dotnet build` to compile the code. The compiled output created by the `dotnet build` command is an **assembly** called `HelloWorld.dll`.[7] Assemblies contain a set of instructions specifying how a program will behave. The extension stands for dynamic link library (DLL), and with .NET, assemblies have a `.dll` extension even if they are console

6. The "*" in *.cs is called a wildcard character, and matches any number of characters including none. In this instance, this identifies that any file ending in .cs will be included. If it was i*.cs it would include any files starting with an i and ending in .cs.
7. Note that if you use the Microsoft .NET Framework to create a console program, the compiled code is placed into a `HelloWorld.exe` file that you can execute directly assuming the Microsoft .NET Framework is installed on the computer.

programs, as this one is. (On Windows, an `.exe` file is also created.) By default, the compiled output for a .NET application is placed into a subdirectory according to the `TargetFramework` identified in the project file, as shown in Listing 1.2 (`./bin/Debug/net7.0/`). The `Debug` directory is used because the default configuration is debug. This configuration causes the output to be optimized for debugging rather than for performance. The compiled output does not execute on its own. Rather, it needs the CLI to host the code. For .NET applications, this requires using the `dotnet.exe` (`dotnet` on Linux and Mac) process as a host process for the application. Hence why the program is executed with the `dotnet run` command. That said, there is a way to generate a stand-alone executable that includes the necessary runtime files so that installing the dotnet runtime is not required—see the "Advanced Topic: Publishing a Stand-Alone Executable" (On Windows, the `.exe` file can be used directly, if the dotnet runtime is installed, rather than using `dotnet run`.)

Essential C# Source Code

Both the source code and the manuscript text are available at https://essentialcsharp.com. Alternatively, the source code for this book is available for download on GitHub directly at https://github.com/IntelliTect/EssentialCSharp. Instructions for compiling and running the code are available in the `README.md` file at the same location.

An alternative approach is to paste the source code into the `HelloWorld` program created earlier in the chapter and then execute the source code.

C# Syntax Fundamentals

Once you successfully compile and run the `HelloWorld` program, you are ready to start dissecting the code to learn its individual parts. Of course, Listing 1.1 is the simplest of C# programs with only a single statement.

Statements and Statement Delimiters

The single statement is `Console.WriteLine()`, which is used to write a line of text to the console. C# generally uses a semicolon to indicate the end of a **statement**, where a statement comprises one or more actions that the code will perform. Declaring a variable, controlling the program flow, and calling a method are typical uses of statements.

ADVANCED TOPIC

Statements without Semicolons

Many programming elements in C# end with a semicolon. One example that does not include the semicolon is a `switch` statement. Because curly braces are always included in a `switch` statement, C# does not require a semicolon following the statement. In fact, code blocks themselves are considered statements (they are also composed of statements), and they don't require ending with a semicolon. Similarly, there are cases, such as the `using` declaration, in which a semicolon appears as a postfix, but it is not a statement.

Since creation of a newline does not separate statements, you can place multiple statements on the same line, and the C# compiler will interpret the line as having multiple instructions. For example, Listing 1.3 contains two statements on a single line that, in combination, display `Up` and `Down` on two separate lines.

LISTING 1.3: Multiple Statements on One Line

```
Console.WriteLine("Up"); Console.WriteLine("Down");
```

Similarly, each statement can be placed on its own line, as shown in Listing 1.4.

LISTING 1.4: Multiple Statements Each on Separate Lines

```
Console.WriteLine("Down");
Console.WriteLine("Side");
Console.WriteLine("Up");
```

C# also allows the splitting of a statement across multiple lines. Again, the C# compiler looks for a semicolon to indicate the end of a statement. In Listing 1.5, for example, the original `WriteLine()` statement from the `HelloWorld` program is split across multiple lines.

Listing 1.5: Splitting a Single Statement across Multiple Lines

```
Console.WriteLine(
    "Hello. My name is Inigo Montoya.");
```

Introducing a Class and a Method

In the listings shown so far, the statements are independent of any other C# constructs and appear this way in only a single file. The previous listings are the simplest of C# programs, a HelloWorld program, after all. Programs can, however, get vastly more complicated, and structure can be added to organize the code. The simplest structure is to add methods and to place those methods within classes. Listing 1.6 provides an example.

Listing 1.6: HelloWorld with Class and Method

```
public class Program
{
    public static void Main()
    {
        System.Console.WriteLine("Hello. My name is Inigo Montoya.");
    }
}
```

In this listing, the HelloWorld statement is placed into a method called `Main`, which is placed into a class called `Program`.

Those experienced in programming with Java, C, or C++ will immediately see similarities. Like Java, C# inherits its basic syntax from C and C++.[8] Syntactic punctuation (such as semicolons and curly braces), features (such as case sensitivity), and keywords (such as `class`, `public`, and `void`) are familiar to programmers experienced in these languages.

8. When creating C#, the language creators reviewed the specifications for C/C++, literally crossing out the features they didn't like and creating a list of the ones they did like. The group also included designers with strong backgrounds in other languages.

NOTE

C# is a case-sensitive language: Incorrect case prevents the code from compiling successfully.

Language Contrast: Java—Filename Must Match Class Name

In Java, the filename must follow the name of the class. In C#, this convention is frequently followed but is not required. In C#, it is possible to have two classes in one file, and even to have a single class span multiple files, with a feature called a **partial class**.

BEGINNER TOPIC

Keywords

To enable the compiler to interpret the code, certain words within C# have special status and meaning. Known as **keywords**, they provide the concrete syntax that the compiler uses to interpret the expressions the programmer writes. In the `HelloWorld` program, `class`, `static`, and `void` are examples of keywords.

The compiler uses the keywords to identify the structure and organization of the code. Because the compiler interprets these words with elevated significance, C# requires that developers place keywords only in certain locations. When programmers violate these rules, the compiler issues errors.

C# Keywords

Keywords are another construct common to other programming languages. Table 1.1 shows the C# keywords.

Begin 8.0

Begin 9.0

Begin 10.0

Begin 11.0

TABLE 1.1: C# Keywords

abstract	add*(1)	alias*(2)	and*
args*	as	ascending*(3)	async*(5)
await*(5)	base	bool	break
by*(3)	byte	case	catch
char	checked	class	const
continue	decimal	default	delegate
descending*(3)	do	double	dynamic*(4)
else	enum	equals*(3)	event
explicit	extern	false	file*
finally	fixed	float	for
foreach	from*(3)	get*(1)	global*(2)
goto	group*(3)	if	implicit
in	init*(9)	int	interface
internal	into*(3)	is	join*(3)
let*(3)	lock	long	nameof*(6)
namespace	new	nint*(9)	not*
notnull*(8)	null	nunit*(9)	object
on*(3)	operator	or*	orderby*(3)
out	override	params	partial*(2)
private	protected	public	readonly
record*	ref	remove*(1)	required*(11)
return	sbyte	scoped*	sealed
select*(3)	set*(1)	short	sizeof
stackalloc	static	string	struct
switch	this	throw	TRUE
try	typeof	uint	ulong
unchecked	unmanaged*(7.3)	unsafe	ushort

* Contextual keyword. Numbers in parentheses (*n*) identify in which version the contextual keyword was added.

After C# 1.0, no new **reserved keywords** were introduced to C#. However, some constructs in later versions use **contextual keywords**, which are significant only in specific locations. Outside these designated locations, contextual keywords have no

End 8.0

End 9.0

End 10.0

End 11.0

special significance.[9] By this method, even C# 1.0 code is compatible with the later standards.[10]

Identifiers

Like other languages, C# includes **identifiers** to identify constructs that the programmer codes. In Listing 1.6, `HelloWorld` and `Main` are examples of identifiers. The identifiers assigned to a construct are used to refer to the construct later, so it is important that the names the developer assigns are meaningful rather than arbitrary.

> **NOTE**
>
> A keen ability to select succinct and indicative names is an important characteristic of a strong programmer because it means the resultant code will be easier to understand and reuse.

Clarity coupled with consistency is important enough that the Framework Design Guidelines (http://bit.ly/dotnetguidelines) advise against the use of abbreviations or contractions in identifier names and even recommend avoiding acronyms that are not widely accepted. If an acronym is sufficiently well established (e.g., HTML), you should use it consistently. Avoid spelling out the accepted acronym in some cases but not in others. Generally, adding the constraint that all acronyms be included in a glossary of terms places enough overhead on the use of acronyms that they are not

---

9. For example, early in the design of C# 2.0, the language designers designated `yield` as a keyword, and Microsoft released alpha versions of the C# 2.0 compiler, with `yield` as a designated keyword, to thousands of developers. However, the language designers eventually determined that by using `yield return` rather than `yield`, they could ultimately avoid adding `yield` as a keyword because it would have no special significance outside its proximity to `return`.

10. There are some rare and unfortunate incompatibilities, such as the following: C# 2.0 requires implementation of `IDisposable` with the using statement rather than simply using a `Dispose()` method. Some rare generic expressions are different between versions. For example, `F(G<A,B>(7))` means `F((G<A), (B>7))` in C# 1.0, but in C# 2.0, it means to call generic method `G<A,B>` with argument 7 and pass the result to `F`.

used flippantly. Ultimately, select clear, possibly even verbose names—especially when working on a team or when developing a library that other developers will use.

There are two basic casing formats for an identifier. **Pascal case** (henceforth **PascalCase**), as the .NET framework creators refer to it because of its popularity in the Pascal programming language, capitalizes the first letter of each word in an identifier name; examples include `ComponentModel`, `Configuration`, and `HttpFileCollection`. As `HttpFileCollection` demonstrates with HTTP, when using acronyms that are more than two letters long, only the first letter is capitalized. The second format, **camel case** (henceforth **camelCase**), follows the same convention except that the first letter is lowercase; examples include `quotient`, `firstName`, `httpFileCollection`, `ioStream`, and `theDreadPirateRoberts`.

Guidelines

DO favor clarity over brevity when naming identifiers.

DO NOT use abbreviations or contractions within identifier names.

DO NOT use any acronyms unless they are widely accepted, in which case use them consistently.

Notice that although underscores are legal, generally there are no underscores, hyphens, or other nonalphanumeric characters in identifier names. Furthermore, C# doesn't follow its predecessors in that Hungarian notation (prefixing a name with a data type abbreviation) is not used. This convention avoids the variable rename that is necessary when data types change, or the inconsistency introduced due to failure to adjust the data type prefix when using Hungarian notation.

In rare cases, some identifiers, such as `Main`, can have a special meaning in the C# language.

While naming guidelines may seem relatively trivial, especially when coming from other languages where such guidelines are ambiguous or missing entirely, violations of these guidelines will be glaring to an experienced C#/.NET programmer and indicate poor quality or inexperience. To avoid this, learn the guidelines, and follow them religiously.

Guidelines

DO capitalize both characters in two-character acronyms, except for the first word of a camelCased identifier.

DO capitalize only the first character in acronyms with three or more characters, except for the first word of a camelCased identifier.

DO NOT capitalize any of the characters in acronyms at the beginning of a camelCased identifier.

DO NOT use Hungarian notation (that is, do not encode the type of a variable in its name).

ADVANCED TOPIC

Keywords

Although it is rare, keywords may be used as identifiers if they include `@` as a prefix. For example, you could name a local variable `@return`. Similarly (although it doesn't conform to the casing standards of C# coding standards), it is possible to name a method `@throw`, with parentheses following: `@throw()`.

There are also four undocumented reserved keywords in the Microsoft implementation: `__arglist`, `__makeref`, `__reftype`, and `__refvalue`. These are required only in rare interop scenarios, and you can ignore them for all practical purposes. Note that these four special keywords begin with two underscores. The designers of C# reserve the right to make any identifier that begins with two underscores into a keyword in a future version; for safety, avoid ever creating such an identifier yourself.

Type Definition

A class definition is the section of code that generally begins with `class <identifier> { ... }`, as shown in Listing 1.7, where `HelloWorld` is the identifier.

Listing 1.7: Basic Class Declaration

```
public class HelloWorld
{
    // ...
}
```

The name used for the type (in this case, `HelloWorld`) can vary, but by convention, it must be PascalCased. For this example, therefore, other possible names are `Greetings`, `HelloInigoMontoya`, `Hello`, or simply `Program`. (`Program` is a good convention to follow when the class contains the `Main()` method, described next.)

Guidelines

DO name classes with nouns or noun phrases.

DO use PascalCasing for all class names.

Generally, programs contain multiple types, each containing multiple methods.

BEGINNER TOPIC

What Is a Method?

Syntactically, a **method** in C# is a named block of code introduced by a method declaration (e.g., `static void Main()`) and (usually) followed by zero or more statements within curly braces. Methods perform computations and/or actions. Like paragraphs in written languages, methods provide a means of structuring and organizing code so that it is more readable. More important, methods can be reused and called from multiple places and so avoid the need to duplicate code. The method declaration introduces the method and defines the method name along with the data passed to and from the method. In Listing 1.8, `Main()` followed by `{ ... }` is an example of a C# method.

Main Method

The location where C# programs begin execution is the **Main method**, which begins with `static void Main()`. When you execute the program by typing `dotnet run` on the terminal, the program starts with the Main method and begins executing the first statement, as identified in Listing 1.8.

LISTING 1.8: Breaking Apart `HelloWorld`

```
public class Program                // BEGIN Class definition
{
    public static void Main()       // Method declaration
    {                               // BEGIN method implementation
        Console.WriteLine(          // This statement spans 2 lines
            "Hello, My name is Inigo Montoya");
    }                               // END method implementation
}                                   // END class definition
```

Although the Main method declaration can vary to some degree, `static` and the method name, `Main`, are always required for a program (see "Advanced Topic: Declaration of the Main Method").

The **comments**, text that begins with // in Listing 1.8, are explained later in the chapter. They are included to identify the various constructs in the listing.

ADVANCED TOPIC

Declaration of the Main Method

C# requires that the Main method return either `void` or `int` and that it take either no parameters or a single array of strings. Listing 1.9 shows the full declaration of the Main method. The `args` parameter is an array of strings corresponding to the command-line arguments. The executable name is not included in the `args` array (unlike in C and C++). To retrieve the full command used to execute the program, including the program name, use `Environment.CommandLine`.

LISTING 1.9: The Main Method with Parameters and a Return

```
public static int Main(string[] args)
{
```

```
    // ...
}
```

The `int` returned from `Main()` is the status code, and it indicates the success of the program's execution. A return of a nonzero value generally indicates an error.

C# 7.1 also added support for `async/await` on the Main method, in which case you would use `Task`-based types in the return.

> **NOTE**
>
> **All Lowercase**
>
> Unlike its C-style predecessors, C# uses an uppercase *M* for the Main method to be consistent with the PascalCased naming conventions of C#.

The designation of the Main method as `static` indicates that other methods may call it directly off the class definition. Without the `static` designation, the terminal that started the program would need to perform additional work (known as **instantiation**) before calling the method. (Chapter 6 contains an entire section devoted to the topic of static members.)

Placing `void` prior to `Main()` indicates that this method does not return any data. (This is explained further in Chapter 2.)

One distinctive C/C++-style characteristic followed by C# is the use of curly braces for the body of a construct, such as the class or the method. For example, the Main method contains curly braces that surround its implementation; in this case, only one statement appears in the method.

BEGINNER TOPIC

What Is Whitespace?

Whitespace is the combination of one or more consecutive formatting characters such as tab, space, and newline characters. Eliminating all whitespace between words is obviously significant, as is including whitespace within a quoted string.

Whitespace

The semicolon makes it possible for the C# compiler to ignore whitespace in code. Apart from a few exceptions, C# allows developers to insert whitespace throughout the code without altering its semantic meaning. In Listing 1.8 and Listing 1.9, it didn't matter whether a newline was inserted within a statement, between statements, or eliminated entirely, and doing so had no effect on the resultant executable created by the compiler.

Frequently, programmers use whitespace to indent code for greater readability. Consider the two variations on `HelloWorld` shown in Listing 1.10 and Listing 1.11. Although these two examples look significantly different from the original program, the C# compiler sees them as semantically equivalent.

Listing 1.10: No Indentation Formatting

```
public class HelloWorld
{
public static void Main()
{
Console.WriteLine("Hello Inigo Montoya");
}
}
```

Listing 1.11: Removing Whitespace

```
public class HelloWorld{public static void Main()
{Console.WriteLine("Hello Inigo Montoya");}}
```

BEGINNER TOPIC

Formatting Code with Whitespace

Indenting the code using whitespace is important for greater readability. As you begin writing code, you need to follow established coding standards and conventions to enhance code readability.

The convention used in this book is to place curly braces on their own line and to indent the code contained between the curly brace pair. If another curly brace pair appears within the first pair, all the code within the second set of braces is also indented.

This is not a uniform C# standard but a stylistic preference.

Working with Variables

Now that you've been introduced to the most basic C# program, it's time to declare a local variable. Once a variable is declared, you can assign it a value, replace that value with a new value, and use it in calculations, output, and so on. However, you cannot change the data type of the variable. In Listing 1.12, `string max` is a variable declaration.

LISTING 1.12: Declaring and Assigning a Variable

```
public class MiracleMax
{
    public static void Main()
    {
        string max;       // "string" identifies the data type
                          // "max" is the variable
        max = "Have fun storming the castle!";
        Console.WriteLine(max);
    }
}
```

BEGINNER TOPIC

Local Variables

A **variable** is a name that refers to a value that can change over time. *Local* indicates that the programmer **declared** the variable within a method.

To declare a variable is to define it, which you do by

- Specifying the type of data which the variable will contain
- Assigning it an identifier (name)

Introducing Data Types

Listing 1.12 declares a variable with the data type `string`. Other common data types used in this chapter are `int` and `char`.

- `int` is the C# designation of an integer type that is 32 bits in size.
- `char` is used for a character type. It is 16 bits, large enough for (nonsurrogate) Unicode characters.

The next chapter looks at these and other common data types in more detail.

BEGINNER TOPIC

What Is a Data Type?

The type of data that a variable declaration specifies is called a **data type** (or object type). A data type, or simply **type**, is a classification of things that share similar characteristics and behavior. For example, *animal* is a type. It classifies all things (monkeys, warthogs, and platypuses) that have animal characteristics (multicellular, capacity for locomotion, and so on). Similarly, in programming languages, a type is a definition for several items endowed with similar qualities.

Declaring a Variable

In Listing 1.12, `string max` is a variable declaration of a string type whose name is `max`. It is possible to declare multiple variables within the same statement by specifying the data type once and separating each identifier with a comma. Listing 1.13 demonstrates such a declaration.

LISTING 1.13: Declaring Two Variables within One Statement

```
string message1, message2;
```

Because a multivariable declaration statement allows developers to provide the data type only once within a declaration, all variables will be of the same type.

In C#, the name of the variable may begin with any letter or an underscore (_), followed by any number of letters, numbers, and/or underscores. By convention, however, local variable names are camelCased (the first letter in each word is capitalized, except for the first word) and do not include underscores.

> **Guidelines**
>
> **DO** use camelCasing for local variable names.

Assigning a Variable

After declaring a local variable, you must assign it a value before reading from it. One way to do this is to use the = **operator**, also known as the **simple assignment operator**. Operators are symbols used to identify the function the code is to perform. Listing 1.14 demonstrates how to use the assignment operator to designate the string values to which the variables `miracleMax` and `valerie` will point.

LISTING 1.14: Changing the Value of a Variable

```
public class StormingTheCastle
{
    public static void Main()
    {
        string valerie;
        string miracleMax = "Have fun storming the castle!";
```

```
        valerie = "Think it will work?";

        Console.WriteLine(miracleMax);
        Console.WriteLine(valerie);

        miracleMax = "It would take a miracle.";
        Console.WriteLine(miracleMax);
    }
}
```

From this listing, observe that it is possible to assign a variable as part of the variable declaration (as it was for `miracleMax`) or afterward in a separate statement (as with the variable `valerie`). The value assigned must always be on the right side of the declaration.

Running the compiled program produces the code shown in Output 1.3.

Output 1.3

```
>dotnet run
Have fun storming the castle!
Think it will work?
It would take a miracle.
```

In this example, we show the command `dotnet run` explicitly. In future output listings, we will omit this line unless there is something special about the command used to execute the program.

C# requires that local variables be (as determined by the compiler) "definitely assigned" before they are read. Additionally, an assignment results in a value. Therefore, C# allows two assignments within the same statement, as demonstrated in Listing 1.15.

Listing 1.15: Assignment Returning a Value That Can Be Assigned Again

```
public class StormingTheCastle
{
    public static void Main()
    {
        // ...
        string requirements, miracleMax;
        requirements = miracleMax = "It would take a miracle.";
        // ...
```

```
    }
}
```

Using a Variable

The result of the assignment, of course, is that you can then refer to the value using the variable identifier. Therefore, when you use the variable `miracleMax` within the `Console.WriteLine(miracleMax)` statement, the program displays "Have fun storming the castle!"—the value of `miracleMax`—on the console. Changing the value of `miracleMax` and executing the same `Console.WriteLine(miracleMax)` statement displays the new `miracleMax` value, "It would take a miracle."

ADVANCED TOPIC

Strings Are Immutable

All values of type `string`, whether string literals or otherwise, are immutable (or unmodifiable). For example, it is not possible to change the string `Come As You Are.` to `Come As You Age.` A change such as this requires that you reassign the variable instead of modifying the data to which the variable originally referred.

Console Input and Output

This chapter already used `Console.WriteLine` repeatedly for writing out text to the command console. In addition to being able to write out data, a program needs to be able to accept data that a user may enter.

Getting Input from the Console

One way to retrieve text that is entered at the console is to use `Console.ReadLine()`. This method stops the program execution so that the user can enter characters. When the user presses the Enter key, creating a newline, the program continues. The output, also known as the **return**, from the `Console.ReadLine()`

method is the string of text that was entered. Consider Listing 1.16 and the corresponding output shown in Output 1.4.

Listing 1.16: Using `Console.ReadLine()`

```
public class HeyYou
{
    public static void Main()
    {
        string firstName;
        string lastName;

        Console.WriteLine("Hey you!");

        Console.Write("Enter your first name: ");
        firstName = Console.ReadLine();

        Console.Write("Enter your last name: ");
        lastName = Console.ReadLine();
    }
}
```

Output 1.4

```
Hey you!
Enter your first name: Inigo
Enter your last name: Montoya
```

After each prompt, this program uses the `Console.ReadLine()` method to retrieve the text the user entered and assign it to an appropriate variable. By the time the second `Console.ReadLine()` assignment completes, `firstName` refers to the value `Inigo` and `lastName` refers to the value `Montoya`.

If you encounter a CS8600, "Converting null literal or possible null value to non-nullable type," warning when assigning `Console.ReadLine()`, you can safely ignore it until Chapter 2. Alternatively, use `string?` rather than `string` when declaring the `firstName` and `lastName` variables to address the warning. You can also disable the nullable-related warnings entirely by disabling them, setting the `Nullable` element in your project file to disable (`<Nullable>disable</Nullable>`) within the `PropertyGroup` element of the `.csproj` file.

ADVANCED TOPIC

System.Console.Read()

In addition to the `System.Console.ReadLine()` method, there is a `System.Console.Read()` method. However, the data type returned by the `System.Console.Read()` method is an integer corresponding to the character value read, or `-1` if no more characters are available. To retrieve the actual character, it is necessary to first cast the integer to a character, as shown in Listing 1.17.

LISTING 1.17: Using `System.Console.Read()`

```
int readValue;
char character;
readValue = Console.Read();
character = (char) readValue;
Console.Write(character);
```

The `Console.Read()` method does not return the input until the user presses the Enter key; no processing of characters will begin, even if the user types multiple characters before pressing the Enter key.

You can use `Console.ReadKey()`,[11] which, in contrast to `Console.Read()`, returns the input after a single keystroke. It allows the developer to intercept the keystroke and perform actions such as key validation or to restrict the characters to numerics.

Writing Output to the Console

Listing 1.16 prompted the user for their first and last names using the method `Console.Write()` rather than `Console.WriteLine()`. Instead of placing a newline character after displaying the text, the `Console.Write()` method leaves the current position on the same line. In this way, any text the user enters will be on the same line as the prompt for input. The output from Listing 1.16 demonstrates the effect of `Console.Write()`.

11. In C# 2.0 and above.

The next step is to write the values retrieved using `Console.ReadLine()` back to the console. In the case of Listing 1.18, the program writes out the user's full name. However, instead of using `Console.WriteLine()` as before, this code uses a slight variation that leverages **string interpolation.**[12] Notice in Listing 1.18, the dollar sign preceding the string literal in the call to `Console.WriteLine`; it indicates that string interpolation will be used. Output 1.5 shows the corresponding output.

LISTING 1.18: Formatting Using String Interpolation

```
public class HeyYou
{
    public static void Main()
    {
        string firstName;
        string lastName;

        Console.WriteLine("Hey you!");

        Console.Write("Enter your first name: ");
        firstName = Console.ReadLine();

        Console.Write("Enter your last name: ");
        lastName = Console.ReadLine();

        Console.WriteLine(
            $"Your full name is { firstName } { lastName }.");
    }
}
```

OUTPUT 1.5

```
Hey you!
Enter your first name: Inigo
Enter your last name: Montoya

Your full name is Inigo Montoya.
```

Instead of writing out "Your full name is" followed by another `Write` statement for `firstName`, a third `Write` statement for the space, and finally a `WriteLine`

12. A C# 6.0 feature.

statement for `lastName`, Listing 1.18 writes out the entire output string interpolation. With string interpolation, the compiler interprets the interior of the curly brackets within the string as regions in which you can embed code (expressions) that the compiler will evaluate and convert to strings. Rather than executing lots of code snippets individually and combining the results as a string at the end, string interpolation allows you to do this in a single step. This makes the code easier to understand.

Prior to C# 6.0, C# used a different approach, that of **composite formatting**. With composite formatting, the code first supplies a **format string** to define the output format—see Listing 1.19.

Listing 1.19: Formatting Using `Console.WriteLine()`'s Composite Formatting

```
public class HeyYou
{
    public static void Main()
    {
        string firstName;
        string lastName;

        Console.WriteLine("Hey you!");

        Console.Write("Enter your first name: ");
        firstName = Console.ReadLine();

        Console.Write("Enter your last name: ");
        lastName = Console.ReadLine();

        Console.WriteLine(
            "Your full name is {0} {1}.", firstName, lastName);
    }
}
```

In this example, the format string is `Your full name is {0} {1}.` It identifies two indexed placeholders for data insertion in the string. Each placeholder corresponds to the order of the arguments that appear after the format string.

Note that the index value begins at zero. Each inserted argument (known as a **format item**) appears after the format string in the order corresponding to the index value. In this example, since `firstName` is the first argument to follow immediately after the format string, it corresponds to index value `0`. Similarly, `lastName` corresponds to index value `1`.

Note that the placeholders within the format string need not appear in order. For example, Listing 1.20 switches the order of the indexed placeholders and adds a comma, which changes the way the name is displayed (see Output 1.6).

LISTING 1.20: Swapping the Indexed Placeholders and Corresponding Variables

```
Console.WriteLine("Your full name is {1}, {0}.", firstName, lastName);
```

OUTPUT 1.6

```
Hey you!
Enter your first name: Inigo
Enter your last name: Montoya

Your full name is Montoya, Inigo
```

In addition to not having the placeholders appear consecutively within the format string, it is possible to use the same placeholder multiple times within a format string. Furthermore, it is possible to omit a placeholder. It is not possible, however, to have placeholders that do not have a corresponding argument.

> **NOTE**
>
> Since string interpolation is almost always easier to understand than the alternative composite string approach, throughout the remainder of the book we use string interpolation by default.

Comments

In this section, we modify the program in Listing 1.19 by adding comments. In no way does this modification change the execution of the program; rather, providing comments within the code can simply make the code more understandable in areas where it isn't inherently clear. Listing 1.21 shows the new code, and Output 1.7 shows the corresponding output.

LISTING 1.21: Commenting Your Code

```
public class CommentSamples
{
    public static void Main()
    {
        string firstName; // Variable for storing the first name
        string lastName;  // Variable for storing the last name

        Console.WriteLine("Hey you!");

        Console.Write /* No new line */ ("Enter your first name: ");
        firstName = Console.ReadLine();

        Console.Write /* No new line */ ("Enter your last name: ");
        lastName = Console.ReadLine();

        /* Display a greeting to the console
          using composite formatting. */

        Console.WriteLine("Your full name is {1}, {0}.",
            firstName, lastName);
        // This is the end
        // of the program listing
    }
}
```

OUTPUT 1.7

```
Hey you!
Enter your first name: Inigo
Enter your last name: Montoya

Your full name is Inigo Montoya.
```

Despite the inserted comments, compiling and executing the new program produces the same output as before.

Programmers use comments to describe and explain the code they are writing, especially where the syntax itself is difficult to understand, or perhaps a particular algorithm implementation is surprising. Since comments are pertinent only to the programmer reviewing the code, the compiler ignores comments and generates an assembly that is devoid of any trace that comments were part of the original source code.

Table 1.2 shows four different C# comment types. The program in Listing 1.21 includes three of these.

TABLE 1.2: C# Comment Types

Comment Type	Description	Example
Delimited comments	A forward slash followed by an asterisk, `/*`, identifies the beginning of a delimited comment. To end the comment, use an asterisk followed by a forward slash: `*/`. Comments of this form may span multiple lines in the code file or appear embedded within a line of code. The asterisks that appear at the beginning of the lines but within the delimiters are simply for formatting.	`/*comment*/`
Single-line comments	Comments may be declared with a delimiter comprising two consecutive forward slash characters: `//`. The compiler treats all text from the delimiter to the end of the line as a comment. Comments of this form are considered a single line. It is possible, however, to place sequential single-line comments one after another, as is the case with the last comment in Listing 1.19.	`//comment`
XML delimited comments	Comments that begin with `/**` and end with `**/` are called *XML delimited comments*. They have the same characteristics as regular delimited comments, except that instead of ignoring XML comments entirely, the compiler can place them into a separate text file.[13]	`/**comment**/`
XML single-line comments	XML single-line comments begin with `///` and continue to the end of the line. In addition, the compiler can save single-line comments into a separate file with the XML delimited comments.	`///comment`

A more comprehensive discussion of the XML comments and how they are leveraged to generate API documentation appears in Chapter 10, where we further discuss the various XML tags.

13. XML delimited comments were explicitly added only in C# 2.0, but the syntax is compatible with C# 1.0.

There was a period in programming history when a prolific set of comments implied a disciplined and experienced programmer. This is no longer the case. Instead, code that is readable without comments is more valuable than that which requires comments to clarify what it does. If developers find it necessary to enter comments to clarify what a block of code is doing, they should favor rewriting the code more clearly over commenting it. Writing comments that simply repeat what the code clearly shows serves only to clutter the code, decrease its readability, and increase the likelihood of the comments going out of date because the code changes without the comments getting updated.

Guidelines

DO NOT use comments unless they describe something that is not obvious to someone other than the developer who wrote the code.

DO favor writing clearer code over entering comments to clarify a complicated algorithm.

BEGINNER TOPIC

Extensible Markup Language

The Extensible Markup Language (XML) is a simple and flexible hierarchical text format. XML is extensible because included within an XML document is information that describes the data, known as **metadata**. Here is a sample XML file:

```
<?xml version="1.0" encoding="utf-8" ?>
<body>
<book title="Essential C# 11.0">
<chapters>
<chapter title="Introducing C#"/>
<chapter title="Data Types"/>
...
</chapters>
</book>
</body>
```

The file starts with a header indicating the version and character encoding of the XML file, after which appears one main "book" element. Elements begin with a word in angle brackets, such as `<body>`. To end an element, place the same word in angle brackets and add a forward slash to prefix the word, as in `</body>`. In addition to elements, XML supports attributes. `title="Essential C#"` is an example of an XML attribute. Note that the metadata (book title, chapter, and so on) describing the data ("Essential C#," "Data Types") is included in the XML file. This can result in rather bloated files, but it offers the advantage that the data includes a description to aid in interpreting it.

Debugging

One significant feature of using an IDE is its support for debugging. To try it, follow these additional steps in either operating system version of Visual Studio or in Visual Studio Code:

1. With the latest version of `Program.cs` open (Listing 1.9), put your cursor on the last `Console.WriteLine` line and click the **Debug->Toggle Breakpoint** (F9) menu item to activate a breakpoint on that line.

2. In Visual Studio, click the **Debug->Start Debugging** (F5) menu to relaunch the application but this time with debugging activated.

3. Visual Studio Code is similar except the menu is **Run->Start Debugging** (F5). Visual Studio Code also displays a notification to create the build and debug assets, the `launch.json` and `tasks.json` files, if you haven't created them already. Because of the `Console.ReadLine` statement, you will also need to change the `console` line in the `launch.json` file to use "integratedTerminal" rather than "internalConsole." Now, when debugging, be sure to switch to the **TERMINAL** output window to respond to your program's prompts.

4. Once debugging starts, execution will stop on the line where you set the breakpoint. You can then hover your cursor over a variable (e.g., `firstName`) to see its value.

5. In Visual Studio, you can even move the execution of the program from the current line to another line within the method by dragging the yellow arrow in the left margin of the file window.

6. To continue the program execution, use the **Continue** button for either IDE (or the **Debug->Continue** (F5) menu in Visual Studio or **Run->Continue** (F5) in Visual Studio Code).

For more information about debugging, see the links corresponding to each version:

- Visual Studio: https://learn.microsoft.com/visualstudio/debugger/debugger-feature-tour
- Visual Studio 2022 for Mac: https://learn.microsoft.com/visualstudio/mac/debugging
- Visual Studio Code: https://code.visualstudio.com/Docs/editor/debugging

Managed Execution and the Common Language Infrastructure

The processor cannot directly interpret an assembly. .NET assemblies consist mainly of a second language known as **Common Intermediate Language (CIL)**, or **IL** for short.[14] The C# compiler transforms the C# source file into this intermediate language. An additional step, usually performed at execution time, is required to change the CIL code into **machine code** that the processor can understand. This involves an important element in the execution of a C# program: the **Virtual Execution System (VES)**. The VES, also casually referred to as the **runtime**, compiles CIL code as needed (a process known as **just-in-time** compilation or **jitting**). The code that executes under the context of an agent such as the runtime is termed **managed code**, and the process of executing under control of the runtime is called **managed execution**. The code is “managed” because the runtime controls

14. A third term for CIL is Microsoft IL (MSIL). This book uses the term CIL because it is the term adopted by the CLI standard. IL is prevalent in conversation among people writing C# code because they assume that IL refers to CIL rather than other types of intermediate languages.

significant portions of the program's behavior by managing aspects such as memory allocation, security, and just-in-time compilation. Code that does not require the runtime to execute is called **native code** (or **unmanaged code**).

The specification for a runtime is included in a broader specification known as the **Common Language Infrastructure (CLI)** specification.[15] An international standard, the CLI includes specifications for the following:

> **NOTE**
>
> The term *runtime* can refer to either execution time or the VES. To help clarify the intended meaning, this book uses the term *execution time* to indicate when the program is executing, and it uses the term *runtime* when discussing the agent responsible for managing the execution of a C# program while it executes.

- The VES or runtime
- The CIL
- A type system that supports language interoperability, known as the **Common Type System (CTS)**
- Guidance on how to write libraries that are accessible from CLI-compatible languages (available in the **Common Language Specification** [**CLS**])
- Metadata that enables many of the services identified by the CLI (including specifications for the layout or file format of assemblies)

Running within the context of a runtime execution engine enables support for several services and features that programmers do not need to code for directly, including the following:

---

15. Miller, J., and S. Ragsdale. 2004. *The Common Language Infrastructure Annotated Standard.* Boston: Addison-Wesley.

> **NOTE**
>
> This section provides a brief synopsis of the CLI to familiarize you with the context in which a C# program executes. It also provides a summary of some of the terms that appear throughout this book. Chapter 24 is devoted to the topic of the CLI and its relevance to C# developers. Although the chapter appears last in the book, it does not depend on any earlier chapters, so if you are eager to become more familiar with the CLI, you can jump to it at any time.

- *Language interoperability:* Interoperability between different source languages. This is possible because the language compilers translate each source language to the same intermediate language (CIL).
- *Type safety:* Checks for conversion between types, ensuring that only conversions between compatible types occurs. This helps prevent the occurrence of buffer overruns, a leading cause of security vulnerabilities.
- *Code access security:* Certification that the assembly developer's code has permission to execute on the computer.
- *Garbage collection:* Memory management that automatically de-allocates memory previously allocated by the runtime.
- *Platform portability:* Support for running the same assembly on a variety of operating systems.
- *Base Class Library (BCL):* Provides a foundation of code that developers can depend on so that they do not have to develop the code themselves.

Common Intermediate Language and Ildasm

As mentioned in the introduction of this section, the C# compiler converts C# code to CIL code and not to machine code. The processor can directly understand machine code; therefore, CIL code needs to be converted before the processor can execute it. Given an assembly, it is possible to view the CIL code using a CIL disassembler utility to deconstruct the assembly into its CIL representation. (The CIL disassembler is affectionately referred to by its Microsoft .NET Framework–specific filename,

Ildasm, which stands for IL Disassembler.) Ildasm disassembles an assembly and extracts the CIL generated by the C# compiler into text.

The output that results from disassembling a .NET assembly is significantly easier to understand than machine code. For many developers, this may raise a concern because it is easier for programs to be decompiled and algorithms understood without explicitly redistributing the source code. As with any program, CLI based or not, the only foolproof way of preventing disassembly is to disallow access to the compiled program altogether (e.g., hosting a program only on a website instead of distributing it to a user's machine). However, if decreased accessibility to the source code is all that is required, there are several obfuscators available. Obfuscators read the IL code and transform it so that it does the same thing but in a way that is much more difficult to understand. This technique prevents the casual developer from accessing the code and creates assemblies that are much more difficult and tedious to decompile into comprehensible code. Unless a program requires a high degree of algorithm security, obfuscators are generally sufficient.

ADVANCED TOPIC

CIL Output for `HelloWorld.exe`

The exact command used for the CIL disassembler depends on which implementation of the CLI is used. Instructions are available at http://itl.tc/ildasm. Listing 1.22 shows the CIL code created from running Ildasm.

Listing 1.22: Sample CIL Output

```
.assembly extern System.Runtime
{
  .publickeytoken = (B0 3F 5F 7F 11 D5 0A 3A )
  .ver 4:2:0:1
}


.assembly extern System.Console
{
  .publickeytoken = (B0 3F 5F 7F 11 D5 0A 3A )
  .ver 4:1:0:1
}
```

```
.assembly 'HelloWorld'
{
  .custom instance void [System.Runtime]System.Runtime.CompilerServices.
↪CompilationRelaxationsAttribute::.ctor(int32) = (01 00 08 00 00 00 00
↪00 )
  .custom instance void [System.Runtime]System.Runtime.CompilerServices.
↪RuntimeCompatibilityAttribute::.ctor() = (01 00 01 00 54 02 16 57 72 61
↪70 4E 6F 6E 45 78 63 65 70 74 69 6F 6E 54 68 72 6F 77 73 01 )
  .custom instance void [System.Runtime]System.Runtime.Versioning.
↪TargetFrameworkAttribute::.ctor(string) = (01 00 18 2E 4E 45 54 43 6F
↪72 65 41 70 70 2C 56 65 72 73 69 6F 6E 3D 76 33 2E 30 01 00 54 0E 14 46
↪72 61 6D 65 77 6F 72 6B 44 69 73 70 6C 61 79 4E 61 6D 65 00 )
  .custom instance void [System.Runtime]System.Reflection.
↪AssemblyCompanyAttribute::.ctor(string) = (01 00 0A 48 65 6C 6C 6F 57
↪6F 72 6C 64 00 00 )
  .custom instance void [System.Runtime]System.Reflection.
↪AssemblyConfigurationAttribute::.ctor(string) = (01 00 05 44 65 62 75
↪67 00 00 )
  .custom instance void [System.Runtime]System.Reflection.
↪AssemblyFileVersionAttribute::.ctor(string) = (01 00 07 31 2E 30 2E 30
↪2E 30 00 00 )
  .custom instance void [System.Runtime]System.Reflection.
↪AssemblyInformationalVersionAttribute::.ctor(string) = (01 00 05 31 2E
↪30 2E 30 00 00 )
  .custom instance void [System.Runtime]System.Reflection.
↪AssemblyProductAttribute::.ctor(string) = (01 00 0A 48 65 6C 6C 6F 57
↪6F 72 6C 64 00 00 )
  .custom instance void [System.Runtime]System.Reflection.
↪AssemblyTitleAttribute::.ctor(string) = (01 00 0A 48 65 6C 6C 6F 57 6F
↪72 6C 64 00 00 )
  .hash algorithm 0x00008004
  .ver 1:0:0:0
}


.module 'HelloWorld.dll'
// MVID: {05b2d1a7-c150-4f20-bd96-c065e4f97a31}
.imagebase 0x00400000
.file alignment 0x00000200
.stackreserve 0x00100000
.subsystem 0x0003  // WindowsCui
.corflags 0x00000001  // ILOnly


.class private auto ansi beforefieldinit HelloWorld.Program
↪extends[System.Runtime] System.Object
```

```
{

  .method private hidebysig static void Main(string[] args) cil managed
        {
    .entrypoint
    // Code size 13
    .maxstack 8
    IL_0000: nop
    IL_0001: ldstr "Hello. My name is Inigo Montoya."
    IL_0006: call void
↪ System.Console]System.Console::WriteLine(string)
    IL_000b: nop
    IL_000c: ret
    } // End of method System.Void
      // HelloWorld.Program::Main(System.String[])

  .method public hidebysig specialname rtspecialname instance void
↪.ctor() cil managed
    {
    // Code size 8
    .maxstack 8
    IL_0000: ldarg.0
    IL_0001: call instance void [System.Runtime]
        System.Object::.ctor()
    IL_0006: nop
    IL_0007: ret
    } // End of method System.Void HelloWorld.Program::.ctor()
} // End of class HelloWorld.Program
```

The beginning of the listing is the manifest information. It includes not only the full name of the disassembled module (`HelloWorld.dll`) but also all the assemblies it depends on, along with their version information.

Perhaps the most interesting thing that you can glean from such a listing is how relatively easy it is to follow what the program is doing compared to trying to read and understand machine code (assembler). In the listing, an explicit reference to `Console.WriteLine()` appears. There is a lot of peripheral information to the CIL code listing, but if a developer wanted to understand the inner workings of a C# assembly (or any CLI-based program) without having access to the original source code, it would be relatively easy unless an obfuscator is used. In fact, several free tools are available (such as Red Gate's Reflector, ILSpy, JustDecompile, dotPeek, and CodeReflect) that can decompile from CIL to C# automatically.

Multiple .NET Frameworks

As briefly mentioned earlier in the chapter, there are multiple .NET frameworks. The large number of offerings is driven mainly by the desire to provide .NET implementations across multiple operating systems and, potentially, even different hardware platforms. Table 1.3 shows those that are predominant.

TABLE 1.3: Predominant .NET Framework Implementations

Comment Type	Description
NET 6 and later	Starting with NET 6 (following .NET Core 5.0), the Core suffix was dropped to indicate .NET Core and the .NET Framework have essentially unified into one framework.
.NET Core	A truly cross-platform and open source .NET framework that supports a highly modularized set of APIs for both the server and command-line applications.
Microsoft .NET Framework	The first of the .NET frameworks—slowly being supplanted by .NET.
Xamarin	With the release of NET 6.0, this effectively becomes a legacy mobile platform implementation of .NET that works with both iOS and Android and enables the development of mobile applications from a single code base while still enabling access to native platform APIs.
Mono	The oldest open source implementation of .NET that formed the foundation upon which Xamarin and Unity were built. Mono has been replaced by .NET Core for new development.
Unity	A cross-platform game engine used to develop video games for game consoles, PCs, mobile devices, and even websites. (The Unity engine is the first public implementation to support projections into the Microsoft Hololens augmented reality realm.)

All the samples in the book work for .NET, at a minimum, unless they specifically indicate otherwise.

> **NOTE**
>
> Throughout the book, *.NET framework* (lowercase) refers to the framework supported by .NET implementations in general. In contrast, *Microsoft .NET Framework* refers to the specific .NET framework implementation that runs only on Microsoft Windows and was *first* released by Microsoft in 2001.

Application Programming Interface

All the methods (or more generically, the members) found on a data type such as `Console` are what define the `Console`'s **application programming interface (API)**. The API defines how a software program interacts with a component. As such, it is found not just with a single data type, but more generically; the combination of all the APIs for a set of data types is said to create an API for the collective set of components. In .NET, for example, all the types (and the members within those types) in an assembly are said to form the assembly's API. Likewise, given a combination of assemblies, such as those found in .NET, the collective group of assemblies forms a larger API. Often, this larger group of APIs is referred to as the **framework**—hence the term .NET *framework* in reference to the APIs exposed by all the assemblies included with the .NET. Generically, the API comprises the set of interfaces and protocols (or instructions) for programming against a set of components. In fact, with .NET, the protocols themselves are the rules for how .NET assemblies execute.

C# and .NET Versioning

Historically, the development life cycle of .NET frameworks has not always been consistent with that of the C# language; therefore, the version of the underlying .NET framework and the corresponding version of the C# language end up with different numbers. This means if you compile with the C# 11.0 compiler, it will, by default, compile against the .NET 7.0, for example. Table 1.4 is a brief overview of the C# and .NET releases for the Microsoft .NET Framework and .NET Core.

Begin 8.0

Begin 9.0

Begin 10.0

Begin 11.0

Table 1.4: C# and .NET Versions

Comment Type	Description
C# 1.0 with Microsoft .NET Framework 1.0/1.1 (Visual Studio 2002 and 2003)	The initial release of C#. A language built from the ground up to support .NET programming.
C# 2.0 with Microsoft .NET Framework 2.0 (Visual Studio 2005)	Added generics to the C# language and libraries that supported generics to the Microsoft .NET Framework 2.0.
Microsoft .NET Framework 3.0	An additional set of APIs for distributed communications (Windows Communication Foundation [WCF]), rich client presentation (Windows Presentation Foundation [WPF]), workflow (Windows Workflow [WF]), and Web authentication (Cardspaces).
C# 3.0 with Microsoft .NET Framework 3.5 (Visual Studio 2008)	Added support for LINQ, a significant improvement to the APIs used for programming collections. The Microsoft .NET Framework 3.5 provided libraries that extended existing APIs to make LINQ possible.
C# 4.0 with Microsoft .NET Framework 4 (Visual Studio 2010)	Added support for dynamic typing along with significant improvements in the API for writing multithreaded programs that capitalized on multiple processors and cores within those processors.
C# 5.0 with Microsoft .NET Framework 4.5 (Visual Studio 2012) and WinRT integration	Added support for asynchronous method invocation without the explicit registration of a delegate callback. An additional change in the framework was support for interoperability with the Windows Runtime (WinRT).
C# 6.0 with Microsoft .NET Framework 4.6 and .NET Core 1.X (Visual Studio 2015)	Added string interpolation, null propagating member access, exception filters, dictionary initializers, and numerous other features.
C# 7.0 with Microsoft .NET Framework 4.7 and .NET Core 1.1 or 2.0 (Visual Studio 2017)	Added tuples, deconstructors, pattern matching, local functions, return by reference, and more.

Table 1.4: C# and .NET Versions (continued)

Comment Type	Description
C# 8.0 with Microsoft .NET Framework 4.8 and .NET Core 3.0	Added support for nullable reference types, advanced pattern matching, using declarations, static local functions, disposable ref structs, ranges and indices, and async streams (although Microsoft .NET Framework 4.8 does not support the last two features).
C# 9.0 with Microsoft .NET 5.0 (most of the .NET Framework functionality was merged into .NET Core)	Added support for records, relational pattern matching, top-level statements, source generators, and function pointers.
C# 10.0 with .NET 6.0	Added simplifications included record structs, global using directives, file-scoped namespaces, extended property patterns. In addition, caller argument expressions and more were added.
C# 11 with .NET 7.0	Added support for file-scoped types, generic math support, default struct initialization, raw literal strings, generic attributes, list patterns, required members, and more.
C# with .NET 8.0	Extended use of primary constructors beyond records, and the using alias directive to any type. Added optional parameters in lambda expressions, and more.

Perhaps the most important framework feature add occurred alongside C# 6.0—that is, cross-platform compilation. In other words, not only would the Microsoft .NET Framework run on Windows, but Microsoft also provided the .NET Core implementation that would run on Windows, Linux, and macOS. This means that with the same code base it is possible to compile and execute applications that run across multiple platforms. .NET Core, renamed to simply .NET with version 5.0, is an entire SDK with everything from the .NET Compiler Platform ("Roslyn"), which itself executes on Linux and macOS, to the .NET runtime, along with tools such as the dotnet command-line utility, dotnet CLI (which was introduced around the time of C# 7.0).

End 8.0

End 9.0

End 10.0

Summary

End 11.0

This chapter served as a rudimentary introduction to C#. It provided a means of familiarizing you with basic C# syntax. Because of C#'s similarity to C++-style languages, much of this chapter's content might not have been new material to you. However, C# and managed code do have some distinct characteristics, such as compilation down to CIL. Although it is not unique, another key characteristic of C# is its full support for object-oriented programming. Even tasks such as reading and writing data to the console are object oriented. Object orientation is foundational to C#, as you will see throughout this book.

The next chapter examines the fundamental data types that are part of the C# language and discusses how you can use these data types with operands to form expressions.

2

Data Types

From Chapter 1's HelloWorld program, you got a feel for the C# language, its structure, basic syntax characteristics, and how to write the simplest of programs. This chapter continues to discuss the C# basics by investigating the fundamental C# types.

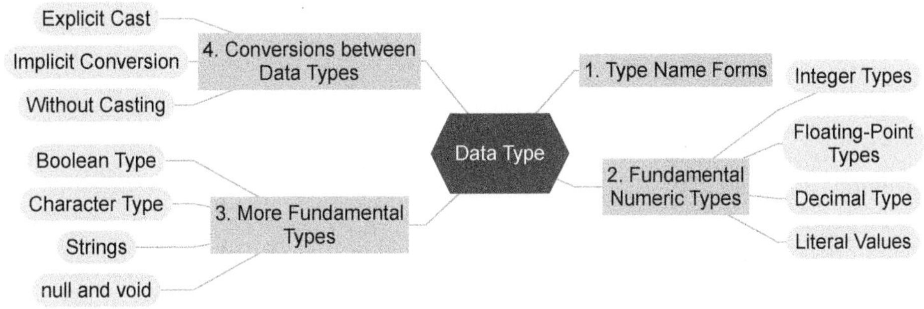

Begin 10.0

Until now, you have worked with only a few built-in data types, with little explanation. In C# thousands of types exist, and you can combine types to create new types. A few types in C#, however, are relatively simple and are considered the building blocks of all other types. These types are the **predefined types**. The C# language's predefined types include 10 integer types, two binary floating-point types for scientific calculations and one decimal float for financial calculations, one Boolean type, and a character type. This chapter investigates these types and looks more closely at the `string` type.

End 10.0

Type Name Forms

All built-in types have essentially three name forms. Consider the `string` type, for example. There is the full name (i.e., `System.String`), the implied or simplified name (i.e., `String`), and the keyword (i.e., `string`).

The full name provides all the context and disambiguates the type from all other types. This is the name used in the underlying CIL code into which C# compiles. The full name is comprised of the namespace (everything in the fully qualified type's name before the last period) followed by the type name (the final part of the name after the last period). If it wasn't for some C# conveniences, all types within C# would be referenced by their full name. All the predefined types themselves are part of the Base Class Library (BCL)—the name given to the set of APIs that comprise the underlying framework. The full name of the types included in the BCL, therefore, is also the BCL name.

The conveniences are shortcuts that allow the compiler to resolve a type's namespace implicitly rather than providing the namespace with each reference. Types with long namespaces such as `System.Text.RegularExpressions.RegEx` benefit a lot from the shortcut of avoiding the namespace qualifier (i.e., `RegEx`). See "Using Directives" (https://essentialcsharp.com/using-directives) in Chapter 5 for more information about the shortcuts and how the compiler can infer namespaces.

The keyword is a shortcut built into the C# language specifically for the predefined types. Types that are not predefined don't have a keyword. `Console` from Chapter 1, for example, has only the full name (i.e., `System.Console`) and simpler non-qualified name (`Console`) with the namespace inferred. Similarly, any of the custom types that you define (such as `Program`) don't have a keyword shortcut.

Developers have a choice of which of the three name forms to use when. Rather than switching back and forth, it is better to use one consistently. While there is seemingly little difference between using the unqualified name versus the keyword, C# developers generally use the C# keyword form (when available)—choosing, for example, `string` rather than `String` or `System.String` and `int` rather than `Int32` or `System.Int32`. Using the fully qualified name from within C# code is rare and generally reserved to disambiguate types with the same unqualified name (such as `System.Timers.Timer` and `System.Threading.Timer`).

Guidelines

DO use the C# keyword rather than the unqualified name when specifying a data type (e.g., `string` rather than `String`).

DO favor consistency rather than variety within your code.

The choice for consistency often may be at odds with other guidelines. For example, given the guideline to use the C# keyword in place of the full name, there may be occasions when you find yourself maintaining a file (or library of files) with the opposite style. In these cases, it would be better to stay consistent with the previous style than to inject a new style and inconsistencies in the conventions. Even so, if the "style" was a bad coding practice that was likely to introduce bugs and obstruct successful maintenance, by all means correct the issue throughout.

Begin 11.0

ADVANCED TOPIC

Using Directive and Global Using Static Directive

The full name of the `Console` class that we have used for reading and writing content from the command line is `System.Console`. The `System` portion of the name is the namespace. Namespaces provide a hierarchical grouping of types. For example, the `RegEx` class (used for parsing text with regular expressions) is located in the `System.Text.RegularExpressions` namespace. Each period in the namespace represents a different level within the hierarchy.

For example, you can place a using directive at the top of a file, `using System`, for example, thereby eliminating the need to prefix a type with the namespace because the compiler can assume the namespace from the using directives.

C# 10 also includes a global using directive such that the using directive is required only once for the entire project, instead of repeatedly within each file that leverages types within the namespace. To identify a using directive as global, you can prefix the statement with `global` as in `global using System`.

In addition, C# 10 generates a default set of global using statements. A lookback at the `enable` value of the `ImplicitUsings` element from Listing 1.2 turns this on. Once enabled, it is no longer necessary to provide using directives or fully qualified names for any types in the generated set including `System`. Specifically, the C# compiler generates a `.cs` file that contains a set of global using statements.

End 11.0

Fundamental Numeric Types

The basic numeric types in C# have keywords associated with them. These types include integer types, floating-point types, and a special floating-point type called `decimal` to store large numbers with no representation error.

Begin 10.0

Integer Types

There are 10 C# integer types, as shown in Table 2.1. This variety allows you to select a data type large enough to hold its intended range of values without wasting resources.

TABLE 2.1: Integer Types

Type	Size	Range (Inclusive)	BCL Name	Signed	Literal Suffix
`sbyte`	8 bits	–128 to 127	`System.SByte`	Yes	
`byte`	8 bits	0 to 255	`System.Byte`	No	
`short`	16 bits	–32,768 to 32,767	`System.Int16`	Yes	
`ushort`	16 bits	0 to 65,535	`System.UInt16`	No	
`int`	32 bits	–2,147,483,648 to 2,147,483,647	`System.Int32`	Yes	
`uint`	32 bits	0 to 4,294,967,295	`System.UInt32`	No	`U` or `u`
`Long`	64 bits	–9,223,372,036,854,775,808 to 9,223,372,036,854,775,807	`System.Int64`	Yes	`L` or `l`
`ulong`	64 bits	0 to 18,446,744,073,709,551,615	`System.UInt64`	No	`UL` or `ul`

TABLE 2.1: Integer Types (continued)

Type	Size	Range (Inclusive)	BCL Name	Signed	Literal Suffix
`nint`	Signed 32-bit or 64-bit integer is a [depends on platform]	Depends on platform where the code is executing. Use `sizeof(nint)` to retrieve size.	`System.IntPtr`	Yes	
`nuint`	Unsigned 32-bit or 64-bit integer is a [depends on platform]	Depends on platform where the code is executing. Use `sizeof(nuint)` to retrieve size.	`System.UIntPtr`	No	

End 10.0

Included in Table 2.1 (and all the type tables within this section) is a column for the full name of each type; we discuss the literal suffix later in the chapter. All the fundamental types in C# have both a short name and a full name. The full name corresponds to the type as it is named in the BCL. This name, which is the same across all languages, uniquely identifies the type within an assembly. Because of the fundamental nature of these types, C# also supplies keywords as short names or abbreviations for the full names of fundamental types. From the compiler's perspective, both names refer to the same type, producing identical code. In fact, an examination of the resultant Common Intermediate Language (CIL) code would provide no indication of which name was used.

Language Contrast: C++—`short` Data Type

In C/C++, the `short` data type is an abbreviation for `short int`. In C#, `short` on its own is the actual data type.

Begin 8.0

Floating-Point Types (`float`, `double`)

Floating-point numbers have varying degrees of precision, and binary floating-point types can represent numbers exactly only if they are a fraction with a power of 2 as the denominator. If you were to set the value of a floating-point variable to be 0.1, it could very easily be represented as 0.0999999999999999 or 0.1000000000000001 or some other number very close to 0.1. Similarly, setting a variable to a large number such as Avogadro's number, 6.02×10^{23}, could lead to a representation error of approximately 10^8, which after all is a tiny fraction of that number. The accuracy of a floating-point number is in proportion to the magnitude of the number it represents. A floating-point number is precise to a certain number of digits of precision, not by a fixed value such as ±0.01. There are at most 17 significant digits for a `double` and 9 significant digits for a `float`[1] (assuming the number wasn't converted from a string as described in the "Advanced Topic: Floating-Point Types Dissected"). [2]

C# supports the two binary floating-point number types listed in Table 2.2. Binary numbers appear as base 10 (denary) numbers for human readability. While there are additional floating-point types beyond the scope of this book (see https://learn.microsoft.com/dotnet/standard/numerics), they are not built-in types with associated keywords.

TABLE 2.2: Floating-Point Types

Type	Size	Significant Digits	BCL Name	Significant Digits	Literal Suffix
`float`	32 bits	$\pm 1.5 \times 10^{-45}$ to $\pm 3.4 \times 10^{38}$	`System.Single`	7	`F` or `f`
`double`	64 bits	$\pm 5.0 \times 10^{-324}$ to $\pm 1.7 \times 10^{308}$	`System.Double`	15–16	`D` or `d`

End 8.0

ADVANCED TOPIC

Floating-Point Types Dissected

1. Starting with .NET Core 3.0.
2. Prior to .NET Core 3.0, the number of bits (binary digits) converts to 15 decimal digits, with a remainder that contributes to a sixteenth decimal digit as expressed in Table 2.2. Specifically, numbers between 1.7×10^{307} and less than 1×10^{308} have only 15 significant digits. However, numbers ranging from 1×10^{308} to 1.7×10^{308} will have 16 significant digits. A similar range of significant digits occurs with the decimal type as well.

Denary numbers within the range and precision limits of the `decimal` type are represented exactly. In contrast, the binary floating-point representation of many denary numbers introduces a rounding error. Just as ⅓ cannot be represented exactly in any finite number of decimal digits, so $^{11}/_{10}$ cannot be represented exactly in any finite number of binary digits (the binary representation being 1.0001100110011001101…). In both cases, we end up with a rounding error of some kind.

A `decimal` is represented by `±N * 10k` where the following is true:

- `N`, the mantissa, is a positive 96-bit integer.
- `k`, the exponent, is given by `-28 <= k <= 0`.

In contrast, a binary float is any number `±N * 2k` where the following is true:

- `N` is a positive 24-bit (for `float`) or 53-bit (for `double`) integer.
- `k` is an integer ranging from `-149` to `+104` for `float` and from `-1074` to `+970` for `double`.

Decimal Type

C# also provides a decimal floating-point type with 128-bit precision (see Table 2.3). This type is suitable for financial calculations.

TABLE 2.3: Decimal Type

Type	Size	Range (Inclusive)	BCL Name	Significant Digits	Literal Suffix
`decimal`	128 bits	1.0×10^{-28} to approximately 7.9×10^{28}	`System.Decimal`	28–29	`M` or `m`

Unlike binary floating-point numbers, the `decimal` type maintains exact accuracy for all denary numbers within its range. With the `decimal` type, therefore, a value of 0.1 is exactly 0.1. However, while the `decimal` type has greater precision than the floating-point types, it has a smaller range. Thus, conversions from floating-point types to the `decimal` type may result in overflow errors. Also, calculations with `decimal` are slightly (generally imperceptibly) slower.

Begin 9.0

Begin 11.0

ADVANCED TOPIC

Native-Sized Integers

C# 9.0 added new contextual keywords to represent native-sized signed and unsigned integers, specifically `nint` and `nuint` respectively starting in C# 11. (See Table 2.4.) Unlike the other numeric types that are the same size regardless of the underlying operating system, the native sized integer types will vary depending on what platform the code is executing. A `nint`, for example, will be 32-bits on a 32-bit platform and 64-bit on a 64-bit platform. These types are designed to match the size of a pointer within the system on which they are executing. They are a more advanced type because they are generally only useful when working with pointers and memory in the underlying operating system rather than memory within the managed execution context of .NET.

TABLE 2.4: Native Integer Types[3]

Type	Size	Range (Inclusive)	BCL Name	Significant Digits	Literal Suffix
`nint`	Matches Operating System (OS)	Variable but available at runtime via `nint.MinValue` and `nint.MaxValue`	`System.IntPtr`	Matches OS	none
`nuint`	Matches Operating System (OS)	Variable but available at runtime via `unint.MinValue` and `unint.MaxValue`	`System.UIntPtr`	Matches OS	none

See Chapter 23 for more information on `nint` and `nuint`.

3. The exact BCL type varies based on context.

End 11.0

End 9.0

Literal Values

A **literal value** is a representation of a constant value within source code. For example, if you want to have `Console.WriteLine()` print out the integer value `42` and the `double` value `1.618034`, you could use the code shown in Listing 2.1 with Output 2.1.

Listing 2.1: Specifying Literal Values

```
Console.WriteLine(42);

Console.WriteLine(1.618034);
```

Output 2.1

```
42
1.618034
```

BEGINNER TOPIC

Use Caution When Hardcoding Values

The practice of placing a value directly into source code is called **hardcoding**, because changing the values requires recompiling the code. Developers must carefully consider the choice between hardcoding values within their code and retrieving them from an external source, such as a configuration file, so that the values are modifiable without recompiling.

By default, when you specify a literal number with a decimal point, the compiler interprets it as a `double` type. Conversely, a literal value with no decimal point generally defaults to an `int`, assuming the value is not too large to be stored in a 32-bit integer. If the value is too large, the compiler interprets it as a `long`. Furthermore, the C# compiler allows assignment to a numeric type other than an `int`, assuming the literal value is appropriate for the target data type. `short s = 42` and `byte b = 77` are allowed, for example. However, this is appropriate only for constant values; `b = s` is not allowed without additional syntax, as discussed in the section "Conversions between Data Types" later in this chapter.

As previously discussed in this section, there are many different numeric types in C#. In Listing 2.2, a literal value is passed to the `WriteLine` method. Since numbers with a decimal point will default to the `double` data type, the output, shown in Output 2.2, is `1.618033988749895` (the last two digits, 48, are now 5), corresponding to the expected accuracy of a `double`.

LISTING 2.2: Specifying a Literal `double`

```
Console.WriteLine(1.6180339887498948);
```

OUTPUT 2.2

```
1.618033988749895
```

To view the intended number with its full accuracy, you must declare explicitly the literal value as a `decimal` type by appending an `M` (or `m`) (see Listing 2.3 and Output 2.3).

LISTING 2.3: Specifying a Literal `decimal`

```
Console.WriteLine(1.6180339887498948M);
```

OUTPUT 2.3

```
1.6180339887498948
```

Now the output of Listing 2.3 is as expected: `1.618033988749895`. Note that `d` is the abbreviation for `double`. To remember that `M` should be used to identify a `decimal`, remember that "`m` is for monetary calculations."

You can also add a suffix to a value to explicitly declare a literal as a `float` or `double` by using the `F` (or `f`) and `D` (or `d`) suffixes, respectively. For integer data types, the suffixes are `U`, `L`, `LU`, and `UL`. The type of an integer literal can be determined as follows:

- Numeric literals with no suffix resolve to the first data type that can store the value, in this order: `int`, `uint`, `long`, and `ulong`.
- Numeric literals with the suffix `U` resolve to the first data type that can store the value, in the order `uint` and then `ulong`.
- Numeric literals with the suffix `L` resolve to the first data type that can store the value, in the order `long` and then `ulong`.
- If the numeric literal has the suffix `UL` or `LU`, it is of type `ulong`.

Note that suffixes for literals are case insensitive. However, uppercase is generally preferred to avoid any ambiguity between the lowercase letter `l` and the digit `1`.

Guidelines

DO use uppercase literal suffixes (e.g., `1.618033988749895M`).

On occasion, numbers can get quite large and difficult to read. To overcome the readability problem, C# 7.0 added support for a **digit separator**, an underscore (_), when expressing a numeric literal, as shown in Listing 2.4.

LISTING 2.4: Specifying Digit Separator

```
Console.WriteLine(9_814_072_356M);
```

In this case, we separate the digits into thousands (threes), but this is not required by C#. You can use the digit separator to create whatever grouping you like as long as the underscore occurs between the first and last digits. In fact, you can even have multiple underscores side by side—with no digit between them.

In addition, you may wish to use exponential notation instead of writing out several zeroes before or after the decimal point (whether using a digit separator or not). To use exponential notation, supply the `e` or `E` infix, follow the infix character with a positive or negative integer number, and complete the literal with the appropriate data type suffix. For example, you could print out Avogadro's number as a `float`, as shown in Listing 2.5 and Output 2.4.

Listing 2.5: Exponential Notation

```
Console.WriteLine(6.023E23F);
```

Output 2.4

```
6.023E+23
```

BEGINNER TOPIC

Hexadecimal Notation

Usually, you work with numbers that are represented with a base of 10, meaning there are 10 symbols (0–9) for each place value in the number. If a number is displayed with hexadecimal notation, it is displayed with a base of 16 numbers, meaning 16 symbols are used: 0–9, A–F (or in lowercase). Therefore, 0x000A corresponds to the decimal value 10 and 0x002A corresponds to the decimal value 42, being $2 \times 16 + 10$. The actual number is the same. Switching from hexadecimal to decimal, or vice versa, does not change the number itself—just the representation of the number.

Each hex digit is four bits, so a byte can represent two hex digits.

In all discussions of literal numeric values so far, we have covered only base 10 type values. C# also supports the ability to specify hexadecimal values. To specify a hexadecimal value, prefix the value with `0x` and then use any hexadecimal series of digits, as shown in Listing 2.6.

Listing 2.6: Hexadecimal Literal Value

```
//Display the value 42 using a hexadecimal literal
Console.WriteLine(0x002A);
```

Output 2.5 shows the results of Listing 2.6. Note that this code still displays `42`, not `0x002A`.

Starting with C# 7.0, you can also represent numbers as binary values (see Listing 2.7).

OUTPUT 2.5

```
42
```

LISTING 2.7: Binary Literal Value

```
// Display the value 42 using a binary literal
Console.WriteLine(0b101010);
```

The syntax is like the hexadecimal syntax except with `0b` as the prefix (an uppercase `B` is also allowed). See "Beginner Topic: Bits and Bytes" in Chapter 4 for an explanation of binary notation and the conversion between binary and decimal.

Note that starting with C# 7.2, you can place the digit separator after the `x` for a hexadecimal literal or the `b` for a binary literal.

ADVANCED TOPIC

Formatting Numbers as Hexadecimal

To display a numeric value in its hexadecimal format, it is necessary to use the `x` or `X` numeric formatting specifier. The casing determines whether the hexadecimal letters appear in lowercase or uppercase. Listing 2.8 with Output 2.6 shows an example of how to do this.

LISTING 2.8: Example of a Hexadecimal Format Specifier

```
//Displays "0x2A"
Console.WriteLine($"0x{42:X}");
```

OUTPUT 2.6

```
0x2A
```

Note that the numeric literal (`42`) can be in decimal or hexadecimal form. The result will be the same. Also, to achieve the hexadecimal formatting, we rely on the formatting specifier, separated from the string interpolation expression with a colon.

ADVANCED TOPIC

Round-Trip Formatting

By default, `Console.WriteLine(1.618033988749895);` displays `1.61803398874989`, with the last digit missing. To more accurately identify the string representation of the double value, it is possible to convert it using a format string and the round-trip format specifier, `R` (or `r`). For example, `Console.WriteLine($"{1.618033988749895:R}")` will display `1.6180339887498949`.

The round-trip format specifier returns a string that, if converted back into a numeric value, will always result in the original value. Listing 2.9 with Output 2.7 shows the numbers are not equal without the use of the round-trip format.

LISTING 2.9: Formatting Using the R Format Specifier

```
// ...
const double number = 1.618033988749895;
double result;
string text;

text = $"{number}";
result = double.Parse(text);
Console.WriteLine($"{result == number}: {result} == {number}");

text = $"{number:R}";
result = double.Parse(text);
Console.WriteLine($"{result == number}: {result} == {number}");

// ...
```

OUTPUT 2.7

```
False: result == number
True: result == number
```

When assigning `text` the first time, there is no round-trip format specifier; as a result, the value returned by `double.Parse(text)` is not the same as the original `number` value. In contrast, when the round-trip format specifier is used, `double.Parse(text)` returns the original value.

For those readers who are unfamiliar with the `==` syntax from C-based languages, `result == number` evaluates to `true` if `result` is equal to `number`, while `result != number` does the opposite. Both assignment and equality operators are discussed in the next chapter.

More Fundamental Types

The fundamental types discussed so far are numeric types. C# includes some additional types as well: `bool`, `char`, and `string`.

Boolean Type (`bool`)

Another C# primitive is a Boolean or conditional type, `bool`, which represents true or false in conditional statements and expressions. Allowable values are the keywords `true` and `false`. The BCL name for `bool` is `System.Boolean`. For example, to compare two strings in a case-insensitive manner, you call the `string.Compare()` method and pass a `bool` literal `true` (see Listing 2.10).

LISTING 2.10: A Case-Insensitive Comparison of Two Strings

```
bool ignoreCase = true;
string option = "/help";
// ...
int comparison = string.Compare(option, "/Help", ignoreCase);
bool isHelpRequested = (comparison == 0);
// Displays: Help Requested: True
Console.WriteLine($"Help Requested: {isHelpRequested}");
```

In this case, you make a case-insensitive comparison of the contents of the variable `option` with the literal text `/Help` and assign the result to `comparison`.

Although theoretically a single bit could hold the value of a Boolean, the size of `bool` is 1 byte.

Character Type (`char`)

A `char` type represents 16-bit characters whose set of possible values are drawn from the Unicode character set's UTF-16 encoding. A `char` is the same size as a 16-bit unsigned integer (`ushort`), which represents values between 0 and 65,535. However, `char` is a unique type in C# and code should treat it as such.

The BCL name for `char` is `System.Char`.

BEGINNER TOPIC

The Unicode Standard

Unicode is an international standard for representing characters found in most human languages. It provides computer systems with functionality for building **localized** applications—that is, applications that display the appropriate language and culture characteristics for different cultures.

ADVANCED TOPIC

16 Bits Is Too Small for All Unicode Characters

Unfortunately, not all Unicode characters can be represented by just one 16-bit `char`. The original Unicode designers believed that 16 bits would be enough, but as more languages were supported, it was realized that this assumption was incorrect. As a result, some (rarely used) Unicode characters are composed of "surrogate pairs" of two `char` values.

To construct a literal `char`, place the character within single quotes, as in `'A'`. Allowable characters comprise the full range of ANSI keyboard characters, including letters, numbers, and special symbols.

Some characters cannot be placed directly into the source code and instead require special handling. These characters are prefixed with a backslash (\) followed by a special character code. In combination, the backslash and special character code constitute an **escape sequence**. For example, `\n` represents a newline and `\t` represents a tab. Since a backslash indicates the beginning of an escape sequence, it can no longer identify a simple backslash; instead, you need to use `\\` to represent a single backslash character.

Listing 2.11 writes out one single quote because the character represented by `\'` corresponds to a single quote.

Listing 2.11: Displaying a Single Quote Using an Escape Sequence

```
public class SingleQuote
{
    public static void Main()
    {
        Console.WriteLine('\'');
    }
}
```

In addition to showing the escape sequences, Table 2.5 includes the Unicode representation of characters.

Table 2.5: Escape Characters

Escape Sequence	Character Name	Unicode Encoding
`\'`	Single quote	`\u0027`
`\"`	Double quote	`\u0022`
`\\`	Backslash	`\u005C`
`\0`	Null character	`\u0000`
`\a`	Alert (system beep)	`\u0007`
`\b`	Backspace	`\u0008`
`\f`	Form feed	`\u000C`
`\n`	Line feed (often referred to as a newline)	`\u000A`
`\r`	Carriage return	`\u000D`
`\t`	Horizontal tab	`\u0009`
`\v`	Vertical tab	`\u000B`

Table 2.5: Escape Characters (continued)

Escape Sequence	Character Name	Unicode Encoding
`\uxxxx`	Unicode character in hexadecimal	`\u0029`
`\x[n][n][n]n`	Unicode character in hex (first three placeholders are optional); variable-length version of `\uxxxx`	`\u3A`
\U00xxxxxx,	Unicode escape sequence for creating surrogate pairs (max supported sequence is \U0010FFFF)	\U00020100 (𠄀)
\uxxxx\uxxxx	Unicode escape sequence for creating surrogate pairs beyond \U0010FFFF	\uD83D\uDE00 (😀)

You can represent any character using Unicode encoding. To do so, prefix the Unicode value with `\u`. You represent Unicode characters in hexadecimal notation. The letter `A`, for example, is the hexadecimal value `0x41`. Listing 2.12 uses Unicode characters to display a smiley face (`:)`), and Output 2.8 shows the results.

Listing 2.12: Using Unicode Encoding to Display a Smiley Face

```
Console.Write('\u003A');

Console.WriteLine('\u0029');
```

Output 2.8

```
:)
```

Strings

A finite sequence of zero or more characters is called a **string**. The C# keyword is `string`, whose BCL name is `System.String`. The string type includes some special characteristics that may be unexpected to developers familiar with other programming languages. In addition to the string literal format discussed in Chapter 1, strings include a "verbatim string" prefix character of `@`, support for string interpolation with the $ prefix character, and the potentially surprising fact that strings are immutable. In C# 11, raw string literals were also added to the language.

Literals

You can enter a literal string into code by placing the text in double quotes ("), as you saw in the `HelloWorld` program. Strings are composed of characters, and consequently, character escape sequences can be embedded within a string.

In Listing 2.13, for example, two lines of text are displayed. However, instead of using `Console.WriteLine()`, the code listing shows `Console.Write()` with the newline character, `\n`. Output 2.9 shows the results.

LISTING 2.13: Using the `\n` Character to Insert a Newline

```
Console.Write(
    "\"Truly, you have a dizzying intellect.\"");
Console.Write("\n\"Wait 'til I get going!\"\n");
```

OUTPUT 2.9

```
"Truly, you have a dizzying intellect."
"Wait 'til I get going!"
```

The escape sequence for double quotes differentiates the printed double quotes from the double quotes that define the beginning and end of the string.

In C#, you can use the `@` symbol in front of a string to signify that a backslash should not be interpreted as the beginning of an escape sequence. The resultant **verbatim string literal** does not reinterpret just the backslash character. Whitespace is also taken verbatim when using the `@` string syntax. The triangle in Listing 2.14, for example, appears in the console exactly as typed, including the backslashes, newlines, and indentation. Output 2.10 shows the results.

Listing 2.14: Displaying a Triangle Using a Verbatim String Literal

```
Console.Write(@"Begin
          /\
         /  \
        /    \
       /      \
      /________\
End");
```

Output 2.10

```
Begin
          /\
         /  \
        /    \
       /      \
      /________\
End
```

Without the @ character, this code would not even compile. In fact, even if you changed the shape to a square, eliminating the backslashes, the code still would not compile because a newline cannot be placed directly within a string literal that is not prefaced with the @ symbol.

The only escape sequence the verbatim string does support is `""`, which signifies a single set of double quotes and does not terminate the string.

Language Contrast: C++—String Concatenation at Compile Time

Unlike C++, C# does not automatically concatenate literal strings. You cannot, for example, specify a string literal as follows:

```
"Major Strasser has been shot."
"Round up the usual suspects."
```

Rather, concatenation requires the use of the addition operator (+). (If the compiler can calculate the result at compile time, however, the resultant CIL code will be a single string.)

If the same literal string appears within an assembly multiple times, the compiler will define the string only once within the assembly and all variables will refer to the same string. That way, if the same string literal containing thousands of characters was placed multiple times into the code, the resultant assembly would reflect the size of only one of them.

Begin 11.0

ADVANCED TOPIC

UTF-8 String Literals

Earlier in the chapter, we mentioned that characters in .NET are all Unicode. Specifically, they are UTF-16 and requiring two bytes per character (or symbol). Therefore, the strings that are comprised of characters are all Unicode (UTF-16) as well.

Occasionally, especially working with externally defined formats, it will be necessary to work with UTF-8 stings. C# 11 allows specification of UTF-8 string literals with a suffix following a string's closing quote—u8. However, the data type is not a .NET string (`System.String`). Rather the data type is a generic `ReadOnlySpan<byte>`. An example of such a string declaration and assignment, therefore, would be:

```
ReadOnlySpan<byte> rates = "€ rates"u8;
```

End 11.0

String Interpolation

As discussed in Chapter 1, strings can support embedded expressions when using the string interpolation format.[4] The string interpolation syntax prefixes a string literal with a dollar symbol and then embeds the expressions within curly brackets. Listing 2.15 is an example in which `firstName` and `lastName` are simple expressions that refer to variables.

LISTING 2.15: String Interpolation

```
Console.WriteLine($"Your full name is {firstName} {lastName}.");
```

4. Starting in C# 6.0

Begin 11.0

Starting in C# 11, you can place new lines between the curly braces (Listing 2.16). In fact, any valid C# expression (where a single value is returned) is allowed. Prior to that, new lines were only support in verbatim interpolated strings.

LISTING 2.16: New Lines within String Interpolation

```
Console.WriteLine($@"Your full name is: {firstName} {lastName}");
```

End 11.0

Begin 8.0

Note that verbatim string literals can be combined with string interpolation by specifying the $ prior to the @ symbol (or `@$"..."` starting in C# 8.0), as in Listing 2.17:

LISTING 2.17: Combining String Literals with Interpolation

```
Console.WriteLine($@"Your full name is:
{firstName} {lastName}");
```

End 8.0

Since this is a verbatim string literal, the text is output on two lines. You can, however, make a similar line break in the code without incurring a line break in the output by placing the line feeds inside the curly braces in a verbatim string (even prior to C# 11). The problem with verbatim strings, however, is that the whitespace on all lines outside of the expression is significant. Therefore, you have to outdent the code to avoid extraneous indention within the code from appearing in the output. To resolve this problem formatting idiosyncrasy, however, C# 11 introduced raw string literals.

Raw String Literals

Begin 11.0

Similar to string literals, raw string literals were added in C# 11. Like string literals, raw string literals enable embedding any arbitrary text, including whitespace, newlines, additional quotes, and other special characters, without requiring escape sequences. However, there are some important differences. The simpler form is a single line raw string literal, such as in Listing 2.18.

The distinguishing characteristic, of course, is that the both the begin and end sets of quotes appear on the same line.

Notice that we don't need to escape the quotes embedded within the string. However, there is a space after the closing quotes of the chocolates quotation because

LISTING 2.18: Single Line Raw String Literal[5]

```
Console.WriteLine(
    """Mama said, "Life was just a box of chocolates..." """);
```

we can't end the string with four double quotes when it begins with only three. The ending quote count must match the begin quote count, and if they don't match, the compiler issues an error. (The solution to avoiding the extra space is provided by multiline raw string literals later in the section.)

The reason that raw string literals allow for more than three double quotes to delineate the raw string literal is to allow placement of three (or more) consecutive double quotes within the text. With five double quotes at the start and end of the raw string literal, for example, you can place four consecutive double quotes within the text and have them be interpreted literally as four consecutive double quotes.

You also can include interpolation as in Listing 2.19 with raw string literals.

LISTING 2.19: Raw String Literals with Interpolation

```
Console.WriteLine(
    $"""Hello, I'm {firstName}. {firstName} {lastName}""");
```

However, an additional complexity is that the curly brace count into which you place the expression must match the number of dollar symbols ($) you place at the beginning of the string. For example, two dollar symbols would require each expression to be surrounded by two curly braces. Listing 2.20 provides an example such that curly braces surround `mobius` in Output 2.11. (Two dollar symbols require two curly braces to render the `name` expression, resulting in a curly brace pair in the output because there are three curly brace pairs used in the code.)

Additionally, Listing 2.20 demonstrates a multiline version of raw string literals (multiline raw string literals).

LISTING 2.20: Displaying Mobius Strip Using Raw String Literal

```
string name = "mobius";
Console.Write(
    $$"""
```

5. Refer to the movie *Forrest Gump* if you're confused about the dialogue found in this section.

```
Begin
           ----
          /   /\
         /   /  \
        /   /   /\
       /   /   /  \
      /   /   /\   \
     /   /   /  \   \
    /   /   /\   \   \
   /   /   /  \   \   \
  /___/___/____\   \   \
 /     {{{name}}} \   \   \
/________________\   \   \
\                 \   \  /
 \_________________\___\/
End
""");
```

Output 2.11

```
Begin
           ----
          /   /\
         /   /  \
        /   /   /\
       /   /   /  \
      /   /   /\   \
     /   /   /  \   \
    /   /   /\   \   \
   /   /   /  \   \   \
  /___/___/____\   \   \
 /     {mobius} \   \   \
/________________\   \   \
\                 \   \  /
 \_________________\___\/
End
```

Note that even though the code is indented in Listing 2.20, the output is not indented. All whitespace to the left of the closing triple quotes—for all lines of the raw string literal—is removed. The start of the closing triple quotes, therefore, establishes the character column that will be leftmost in the output. For this reason, there can be nothing but whitespace to the left of the first quote of the closing triple quotes column or else the complier will emit a compile warning.

Also, with multiline raw string literals, there can be no characters following the initial set of double quotes or text prior to the closing set of double quotes. Anything other than white space following the `$$"""` opening sequence or prior to the closing `"""` will result in a compile error.

By using a multiline raw string literal, you can avoid the problematic final quote within your text as shown in the assignment of `mamaSaid` variable in Listing 2.21.

Listing 2.21: Displaying Mobius Strip Using Raw String Literal

```
string firstName = "Forest";

// Single-line raw string literal.
string lastName = """Gump""";

// Single-line raw string literal with interpolation.
string greeting =
$"""Hello, I'm {firstName}. {firstName} {lastName}""";

string proposal = "Do you want a chocolate?"
    + "I could eat about a million and a half of these.";

string mamaSaid = // Multi-line raw string literal.
    """
        Mama said, "Life was just a box of chocolates..."
        """;

string jsonDialogue =

    // Multi-line raw string literal with interpolation.

    $$"""
        {
            "quote": {
                "character": "The MAN",
                "dialogue": "{{greeting}}"
            },
            "description" : "She nods, not much interested. He...",
            "quote": {
                "character": "The MAN",
                "dialogue": "{{proposal}}"
            },
            "description" : "She shakes \"no\" He unwraps it...",
            "quote": {
                "character": "The MAN",
                "dialogue": "{{mamaSaid.Replace("\"", "\\\"")}}"
```

```
            }
        }
        """;

Console.WriteLine(jsonDialogue);
```

The text for the `jsonDialogue` variable in Listing 2.21 is, in fact, a special text format called JSON. The text is a collection of hierarchical name value pairs that is compatible with JavaScript. Initially it was only prevalent when programming for the web but the format is now a common means (at a minimum) for transferring data. Support for raw string literals is especially important for JSON because it allows direct placement of JSON strings into C# programs without complex and error-prone escape sequences.

The backslashes within the raw string literal assigned to `jsonDialogue` have no C# significance. Each string, both the name and the value within JSON, is surrounded by quotes. Therefore, JSON text within the value is escaped with a backslash. However, because the text within the entire string value is a raw string literal in which backslashes have no special significance, backslashes are just normal characters within the represented JSON string. This is a huge advantage to using raw string literals for placing JSON within C#. (Representing regular expressions within C# is another format where raw string literals prove extremely helpful.)

End 11.0

In addition, there is the invocation of the `Replace()` method embedded in the JSON. A list of the common string methods appears in the next section.

ADVANCED TOPIC

Understanding the Internals of String Interpolation

String interpolation is shorthand for invoking the `string.Format()` method. For example, a statement such as

```
Console.WriteLine(
    $"Your full name is {firstName} {lastName}.");
```

will be transformed into the C# equivalent of

```
object[] args = new object[] { firstName, lastName };
```

```
Console.WriteLine(string.Format("Your full name is {0} {1}.",
args));
```

This leaves in place support for localization in the same way it works with composite strings and doesn't introduce any post-compile injection of code via strings.

String Methods

The `string` type, like the `Console` type, includes several methods. There are methods, for example, for formatting, concatenating, and comparing strings.

Begin 11.0

The `Format()` method in Table 2.6 behaves similarly to the `Console.Write()` and `Console.WriteLine()` methods, except that instead of displaying the result in the console window, `string.Format()` returns the result to the caller. Of course, with string interpolation, the need for `string.Format()` is significantly reduced (except for localization support). Under the covers, however, string interpolation compiles down a CIL combination of constants (C# 11) plus `string.Concat()` and `string.Format()` invocations whenever the string combination is not made of string literals.

End 11.0

All of the methods in Table 2.6 are **static**. This means that, to call the method, it is necessary to prefix the method name (e.g., `Concat`) with the type that contains the method (e.g., `string`). As illustrated later in this chapter, however, some of the methods in the string class are **instance** methods. Instead of prefixing the method with the type, instance methods use the variable name (or some other reference to an instance). Table 2.7 shows a few of these methods, along with examples of their use.

TABLE 2.6: `string` Static Methods

Statement	Example

`static string`
`string.Format(`
`string format,`
`...)`
	`string text, firstName, lastName;`
	`//...`
	`text = string.Format("Your full name is {0} {1}.",`
	`firstName, lastName);`
	`// Display`
	`// "Your full name is <firstName> <lastName>."`
	`Console.WriteLine(text);`

Table 2.6: string Static Methods (continued)

Statement	Example
static string **string**.Concat(**string** str0, **string** str1)	**string** text, firstName, lastName; *//...* text = string.Concat(firstName, lastName); *// Display "<firstName><lastName>", notice* *// that there is no space between names* Console.WriteLine(text);
static int string.Compare(**string** str0, **string** str1)	*// 1.* **string** option; *//...* *// String comparison in which case matters* **int** result = **string**.Compare(option, "/help"); *// Display:* *// 0 if equal* *// negative if option < /help* *// positive if option > /help* Console.WriteLine(result); *// 2.* **string** option; *//...* *// Case-insensitive string comparison* **int** result = **string**.Compare(option, "/Help", **true**); *// Display:* *// 0 if equal* *// < 0 if option < /help* *// > 0 if option > /help* Console.WriteLine(result);

Table 2.7: string Methods

Statement	Example
bool StartsWith(**string** value) **bool** EndsWith(**string** value)	**string** lastName *//...* **bool** isPhd = lastName.EndsWith("Ph.D."); **bool** isDr = lastName.StartsWith("Dr.");
string ToLower() **string** ToUpper()	**string** severity = "warning"; *// Display the severity in uppercase* Console.WriteLine(severity.ToUpper());

TABLE 2.7: `string` Methods (continued)

Statement	Example

`string Trim()`
`string Trim(...)`
`string TrimEnd()`
`string TrimStart()`
	`// 1.`
	`// Remove any whitespace from`
	`// both the start and end`
	`username = username.Trim();`
	`// 2.`
	`string text =`
	`"indiscriminate bulletin";`
	`// Remove 'i' and 'n' from both the start or end`
	`text = text.Trim("in".ToCharArray());`
	`// Display: discriminate bullet`
	`Console.WriteLine(text);`

`string Replace(`
`string oldValue,`
`string newValue)`
	`string filename;`
	`//...`
	`// Remove ?'s from anywhere in the string`
	`filename = filename.Replace("?", "");;`

String Formatting

Whether you use `string.Format()` or string interpolation to construct complex formatting strings, a rich and complex set of composite formatting patterns is available to display numbers, dates, times, time spans, and so on. For example, if `price` is a variable of type `decimal`, then `string.Format("{0,20:C2}", price)` and the equivalent interpolation `$"{price,20:C2}"` both convert the decimal value to a string using the default currency formatting rules, rounded to two figures after the decimal place and right-justified in a 20-character-wide string. Space does not permit a detailed discussion of all the possible formatting strings; consult the MSDN documentation on composite formatting (http://itl.tc/CompositeFormatting) for a complete listing of possibilities.

If you want an actual left or right curly brace inside an interpolated string or formatted string, you can double the brace to indicate that it is not introducing a pattern. For example, the interpolated string `$"{{ {price:C2} }}"` might produce the string `"{ $1,234.56 }"`.

Newline

When writing out a newline, the exact characters for the newline depend on the operating system on which you are executing. On Microsoft Windows operating systems, the newline is the combination of both the carriage return (`\r`) and newline (`\n`) characters, while a single line feed is used on UNIX. One way to overcome the discrepancy between operating systems is simply to use `Console.WriteLine()` to output a blank line. Another approach, which is almost essential for working with newlines from the same code base on multiple operating systems, is to use `System.Environment.NewLine`. In other words, `Console.WriteLine("Hello World")` and `Console.Write($"Hello World{Environment.NewLine}")` are equivalent. However, on Windows, `WriteLine()` and `Console.Write(Environment.NewLine)` are equivalent to `Console.Write("\r\n")`—not `Console.Write("\n")`. In summary, rely on `WriteLine()` and `Environment.NewLine` rather than `\n` to accommodate Windows-specific operating system idiosyncrasies with the same code that runs on Linux and macOS.

Guidelines

DO rely on `System.Console.WriteLine()` and `System.Environment.NewLine` rather than `\n` to accommodate Windows-specific operating system idiosyncrasies with the same code that runs on Linux and macOS.

ADVANCED TOPIC

C# Properties

The `Length` member referred to in the following section is not actually a method, as indicated by the fact that there are no parentheses following its call. `Length` is a property of `string`, and C# syntax allows access to a property as though it were a member variable (known in C# as a **field**). In other words, a property has the behavior of special methods called setters and getters, but the syntax for accessing that behavior is that of a field.

Examining the underlying CIL implementation of a property reveals that it compiles into two methods: `set_<PropertyName>` and `get_<PropertyName>`. Neither of these, however, is directly accessible from C# code, except through the C# property constructs. See Chapter 6 for more details on properties.

String Length

To determine the length of a string, you use a string member called `Length`. This particular member is called a **read-only property**. As such, it cannot be set, nor does calling it require any parameters. Listing 2.22 demonstrates how to use the `Length` property, and Output 2.12 shows the results.

LISTING 2.22: Using `string`'s `Length` Member

```
public class PalindromeLength
{
    public static void Main()
    {
        string palindrome;

        Console.Write("Enter a palindrome: ");
        palindrome = Console.ReadLine();

        Console.WriteLine(
            $"The palindrome \"{palindrome}\" is"
            + $" {palindrome.Length} characters.");
    }
}
```

OUTPUT 2.12

```
Enter a palindrome: Never odd or even
The palindrome "Never odd or even" is 17 characters.
```

The length for a string cannot be set directly; it is calculated from the number of characters in the string. Furthermore, the length of a string cannot change because a string is **immutable**.

Strings Are Immutable

A key characteristic of the `string` type is that it is immutable. A string variable can be assigned an entirely new value, but there is no facility for modifying the contents of a `string`. It is not possible, therefore, to convert a `string` to all uppercase letters. It is trivial to create a new string that is composed of an uppercase version of the old string, but the old string is not modified in the process. Consider Listing 2.23 as an example.

LISTING 2.23: Error; `string` Is Immutable

```
Console.Write("Enter text: ");
string text = Console.ReadLine();

// UNEXPECTED: Does not convert text to uppercase
text.ToUpper();

Console.WriteLine(text);
```

Output 2.13 shows the results of Listing 2.23.

OUTPUT 2.13

```
Enter text: This is a test of the emergency broadcast system.
This is a test of the emergency broadcast system.
```

At a glance, it would appear that `text.ToUpper()` should convert the characters within `text` to uppercase. However, strings are immutable and, therefore, `text.ToUpper()` will make no such modification. Instead, `text.ToUpper()` returns a new string that needs to be saved into a variable or passed to `Console.WriteLine()` directly. The corrected code is shown in Listing 2.24, and its output is shown in Output 2.14.

LISTING 2.24: Working with Strings

```
public class Uppercase
{
    public static void Main()
    {
        string text, uppercase;

        Console.Write("Enter text: ");
        text = Console.ReadLine();
```

```
        // Return a new string in uppercase
        uppercase = text.ToUpper();

        Console.WriteLine(uppercase);
    }
}
```

Output 2.14

```
Enter text: This is a test of the emergency broadcast system.
THIS IS A TEST OF THE EMERGENCY BROADCAST SYSTEM.
```

If the immutability of a string is ignored, mistakes like those shown in Listing 2.17 can occur with other string methods as well.

To actually change the value of `text`, assign the value from `ToUpper()` back into `text`, as in the following code:

```
text = text.ToUpper();
```

System.Text.StringBuilder

If considerable string modification is needed, such as when constructing a long string in multiple steps, you should use the data type `System.Text.StringBuilder` rather than `string`. The `StringBuilder` type includes methods such as `Append()`, `AppendFormat()`, `Insert()`, `Remove()`, and `Replace()`, some of which are also available with `string`. The key difference, however, is that with `StringBuilder` these methods will modify the data in the `StringBuilder` itself and will not simply return a new string.

`null` and `void`

Two additional keywords relating to types are `null` and `void`. The `null` value, identified with the `null` keyword, indicates that the variable does not refer to any valid object. `void` is used to indicate the absence of a type or the absence of any value altogether.

null

null can also be used as a type of "literal." The value null indicates that a variable is set to nothing. Code that sets a variable to null explicitly assigns a "nothing" value. In fact, it is even possible to check whether a variable refers to a null value.

Assigning the value null is not equivalent to not assigning it at all. In other words, a variable that has been assigned null has still been set, whereas a variable with no assignment has not been set and, therefore, will often cause a compile error if used prior to assignment.

Note that assigning the value null to a string variable is distinctly different from assigning an empty string, "". Use of null indicates that the variable has no value, whereas "" indicates that there is a value—an empty string. This type of distinction can be quite useful. For example, the programming logic could interpret a string variable named homePhone of null to mean that the home phone number is unknown, while a homePhone value of "" could indicate that there is no home phone number.

Begin 8.0

ADVANCED TOPIC

Nullable Modifier

Listing 2.25 demonstrates assigning null to an integer variable by adding nullable modifier—a question mark (?)—to the type declaration.

LISTING 2.25: Assigning null to a String

```
public static void Main()
{
    int? age;
    //...

    // Clear the value of age
    age = null;

    // ...
}
```

Prior to the nullable modifier,[6] there was no way to assign `null` to a variable of any of the types we have introduced so far (value types) except `string` (which is a reference type). (See Chapter 3 for more information on value types and reference types.)

Furthermore, prior to C# 8.0, reference types (like `string`) supported `null` assignment by default, and as such, you couldn't decorate a reference type with a nullable modifier. Since `null` could implicitly be assigned anyway, decorating it with a nullable modifier was redundant.

ADVANCED TOPIC

Nullable Reference Types

Prior to C# 8.0, since all reference types were nullable by default, there was no concept of a nullable reference type—all reference types just were nullable. In C# 8.0, however, the behavior became configurable such that reference types could be declared as nullable with the nullable modifier or default to not `null` otherwise. In so doing, C# 8.0 introduced the concept of nullable reference types. Reference type variables with the nullable modifier are nullable reference types. And, when nullable reference types are enabled, a warning will appear when assigning `null` to a variable of reference type without the nullable modifier.

The only reference type covered so far in this book is `string`. If configured to support the nullable modifier on reference types, you could, for example, declare a string variable such as

```
string? homeNumber = null;
```

To support nullability, be sure that the `Nullable` element in the `.csproj` file is set to `enable`.

End 8.0

6. Support for the nullable modifier was added in C# 2.0.

The `void` "Type"

Sometimes the C# syntax requires a data type to be specified, but no data is passed. For example, if no return from a method is needed, C# allows you to specify `void` as the data type instead. The declaration of `Main` within the `HelloWorld` program (Listing 1.1) is an example. The use of `void` as the return type indicates that the method is not returning any data and tells the compiler not to expect a value. `void` is not a data type per se but rather an indication that there is no data being returned.

Language Contrast: C++

In both C++ and C#, `void` has two meanings: as a marker that a method does not return any data and to represent a pointer to a storage location of unknown type. In C++ programs, it is quite common to see pointer types such as `void**`. C# can also represent pointers to storage locations of unknown type using the same syntax, but this usage is comparatively rare in C# and typically encountered only when writing programs that interoperate with unmanaged code libraries.

Conversions between Data Types

Given the thousands of types predefined in .NET and the unlimited number of types that code can define, it is important that types support conversion from one type to another where it makes sense. The most common operation that results in a conversion is **casting**.

Consider the conversion between two numeric types: converting from a variable of type `long` to a variable of type `int`. A `long` type can contain values as large as 9,223,372,036,854,775,808; however, the maximum size of an `int` is 2,147,483,647. As such, that conversion could result in a loss of data—for example, if the variable of type `long` contains a value greater than the maximum size of an `int`. Any conversion that could result in a loss of data (such as magnitude and/or precision) or an exception because the conversion failed requires an **explicit cast**. Conversely, a numeric conversion that will not lose magnitude and will not throw an exception regardless of the operand types is an **implicit conversion**.

Explicit Cast

In C#, you cast using the **cast operator**. By specifying the type, you would like the variable converted to within parentheses, you acknowledge that if an explicit cast is occurring, there may be a loss of precision and data, or an exception may result. The code in Listing 2.26 converts a `long` to an `int` and explicitly tells the system to attempt the operation.

Listing 2.26: Explicit Cast Example

```
long longNumber = 50918309109;
int intNumber = (int)longNumber; // (int) is a cast operator.
```

With the cast operator, the programmer essentially says to the compiler, "Trust me, I know what I am doing. I know that the value will fit into the target type." Making such a choice will cause the compiler to allow the conversion. However, with an explicit conversion, there is still a chance that either a data loss or an error, in the form of an exception, might occur during execution. It is therefore the programmer's responsibility to ensure the data is successfully converted, or else to provide the necessary error-handling code when the conversion fails.

ADVANCED TOPIC

Checked and Unchecked Conversions

C# provides special keywords for marking a code block to indicate what should happen if the target data type is too small to contain the assigned data. By default, if the target data type cannot contain the assigned data, the data will be truncated during assignment. For an example, see Listing 2.27 and Output 2.15.

Listing 2.27: Overflowing an Integer Value

```
// int.MaxValue equals 2147483647
int n = int.MaxValue;
n = n + 1;
Console.WriteLine(n);
```

OUTPUT 2.15

```
-2147483648
```

Listing 2.27 writes the value `-2147483648` to the console. However, placing the code within a checked block, or using the `checked` option when running the compiler, will cause the runtime to throw an exception of type `System.OverflowException`. The syntax for a checked block uses the `checked` keyword, as shown in Listing 2.28 with Output 2.16.

LISTING 2.28: A Checked Block Example

```
checked
{
    // int.MaxValue equals 2147483647
    int n = int.MaxValue;
    n = n + 1;
    Console.WriteLine(n);
}
```

OUTPUT 2.16

```
Unhandled Exception: System.OverflowException: Arithmetic operation
resulted in an overflow at Program.Main() in ...Program.cs:line 12
```

The result is that an exception is thrown if, within the checked block, an overflow assignment occurs at runtime.

To change the default checked behavior from unchecked to checked, add the `<CheckForOverflowUnderflow>true</CheckForOverflowUnderflow>` element to the `.csproj` file. C# also supports an unchecked block that overflows the data instead of throwing an exception for assignments within the block (see Listing 2.29 and Output 2.17).

LISTING 2.29: An Unchecked Block Example

```
unchecked
{
    // int.MaxValue equals 2147483647
    int n = int.MaxValue;
    n = n + 1;
```

```
        Console.WriteLine(n);
    }
```

Output 2.17

```
-2147483648
```

Even if the checked option is on during compilation, the unchecked keyword in the preceding code will prevent the runtime from throwing an exception during execution.

Readers might wonder why, when adding 1 to int.MaxValue unchecked, the result yields −2147483648. The behavior is caused by wraparound semantics. The binary representation of int.MaxValue is 01111111111111111111111111111111, where the first digit (0) indicates a positive value. Incrementing this value yields the next value of 10000000000000000000000000000000, the smallest integer (int.MinValue), where the first digit (1) signifies the number is negative. Adding 1 to int.MinValue would result in 10000000000000000000000000000001 (−2147483647) and so on.

You cannot convert any type to any other type simply because you designate the conversion explicitly using the cast operator. The compiler will still check that the operation is valid. For example, you cannot convert a long to a bool. No such conversion is defined and, therefore, the compiler does not allow such a cast.

Language Contrast: Converting Numbers to Booleans

It may be surprising to learn that there is no valid cast from a numeric type to a Boolean type, since this is common in many other languages. The reason no such conversion exists in C# is to avoid any ambiguity, such as whether −1 corresponds to true or false. More important, as you will see in the next chapter, this constraint reduces the chance of using the assignment operator in place of the equality operator (e.g., avoiding if(x=42){...} when if(x==42){...} was intended).

Implicit Conversion

In other instances, such as when going from an `int` type to a `long` type, there is no loss of precision, and no fundamental change in the value of the type occurs. In these cases, the code needs to specify only the assignment operator; the conversion is **implicit**. In other words, the compiler can determine that such a conversion will work correctly. The code in Listing 2.30 converts from an `int` to a `long` by simply using the assignment operator.

Listing 2.30: Not Using the Cast Operator for an Implicit Conversion

```
int intNumber = 31416;
long longNumber = intNumber;
```

Even when no explicit cast operator is required (because an implicit conversion is allowed), it is still possible to include the cast operator (see Listing 2.31).

Listing 2.31: Using the Cast Operator for an Implicit Cast

```
int intNumber = 31416;
long longNumber = (long)intNumber;
```

Type Conversion without Casting

No conversion is defined from a string to a numeric type, so methods such as `Parse()` are required. Each numeric data type includes a `Parse()` function that enables conversion from a string to the corresponding numeric type. Listing 2.32 demonstrates this call.

Listing 2.32: Using `float.Parse()` to Convert a `string` to a Numeric Data Type

```
string text = $"{9.11E-31}";
float kgElectronMass = float.Parse(text);
```

Another special type is available for converting one type to the next. This type is `System.Convert`, and an example of its use appears in Listing 2.33.

LISTING 2.33: Type Conversion Using `System.Convert`

```
string middleCText = $"{261.626}";
double middleC = Convert.ToDouble(middleCText);
bool boolean = Convert.ToBoolean(middleC);
```

`System.Convert` supports only a small number of types and is not extensible. It allows conversion from any of the types `bool`, `char`, `sbyte`, `short`, `int`, `long`, `ushort`, `uint`, `ulong`, `float`, `double`, `decimal`, `DateTime`, and `string` to any other of those types.

All types support a `ToString()` method that can be used to provide a string representation of a type. Listing 2.34 demonstrates how to use this method. The resultant output is shown in Output 2.18.

LISTING 2.34: Using `ToString()` to `Convert` to a `string`

```
bool boolean = true;
string text = boolean.ToString();
// Display "True"
Console.WriteLine(text);
```

OUTPUT 2.18

```
True
```

For the majority of types, the `ToString()` method returns the name of the data type rather than a string representation of the data. The string representation is returned only if the type has an explicit implementation of `ToString()`. One last point to make is that it is possible to code custom conversion methods, and many such methods are available for classes in the runtime.

ADVANCED TOPIC

TryParse()

All the numeric primitive types include a static `TryParse()` method.[7] This method is similar to the `Parse()` method, except that instead of throwing an exception if the conversion fails, the `TryParse()` method returns `false`, as demonstrated in Listing 2.35 and Output 2.19.

Listing 2.35: Using `TryParse()` in Place of an Invalid Cast Exception

```
double number;
string input;

Console.Write("Enter a number: ");
input = Console.ReadLine();
if (double.TryParse(input, out number))
{
    // Converted correctly, now use number
    // ...
}
else
{
    Console.WriteLine(
        "The text entered was not a valid number.");
}
```

Output 2.19

```
Enter a number: forty-two
The text entered was not a valid number.
```

The resultant value that the code parses from the input `string` is returned via an `out` parameter (see "Output Parameters (out)" in Chapter 5 (https://essentialcsharp.com/output-parameters-out))—in this case, `number`.

In addition to the various number types, the `TryParse()` method is available for enums.

7. Starting with C# 2.0.

Starting with C# 7.0, it is no longer necessary to declare a variable before using it as an `out` argument. Using this feature, the declaration for number is shown in Listing 2.36.

Listing 2.36: Using `TryParse()` with Inline `out` Declaration in C# 7.0

```
// double number;
string input;

Console.Write("Enter a number: ");
input = Console.ReadLine();
if (double.TryParse(input, out double number))
{
    Console.WriteLine(
        $"input was parsed successfully to {number}.");
}
else
{
    // Note: number scope is here too (although not assigned)
    Console.WriteLine(
        "The text entered was not a valid number.");
}

Console.WriteLine(
    $"'number' currently has the value: {number}");
```

Notice that the data type of `number` is specified following the `out` modifier and before the variable that it declares. The result is that the `number` variable is available from both the true and false consequences of the `if` statement and even outside the `if` statement.

The key difference between `Parse()` and `TryParse()` is that `TryParse()` won't throw an exception if it fails. Frequently, the conversion from a `string` to a numeric type depends on a user entering the text. It is expected, in such scenarios, that the user will enter invalid data that will not parse successfully. By using `TryParse()` rather than `Parse()`, you can avoid throwing exceptions in expected situations. (The expected situation in this case is that the user will enter invalid data, and we try to avoid throwing exceptions for expected scenarios.)

Summary

Even for experienced programmers, C# introduces several new programming constructs. For example, as part of the section on data types, this chapter covered the type `decimal`, which can be used to perform financial calculations without floating-point anomalies. In addition, the chapter introduced the fact that the Boolean type, `bool`, does not convert implicitly to or from the integer type, thereby preventing the mistaken use of the assignment operator in a conditional expression. Other characteristics of C# that distinguish it from many of its predecessors are the `@` verbatim string qualifier and raw string literals (both force a string to ignore the escape character); string interpolation, which makes code easier to read by embedding it into the string; and the immutable nature of the `string` data type.

In Chapter 3, we continue the topic of data types by elaborating more on the two types of data types: value types and reference types. In addition, we look at combining data elements together into tuples and arrays.

3

More with Data Types

In Chapter 2, we covered all the C# predefined types and briefly touched on the topic of reference types versus value types. In this chapter, we continue the discussion of data types with further explanation of the categories of types.

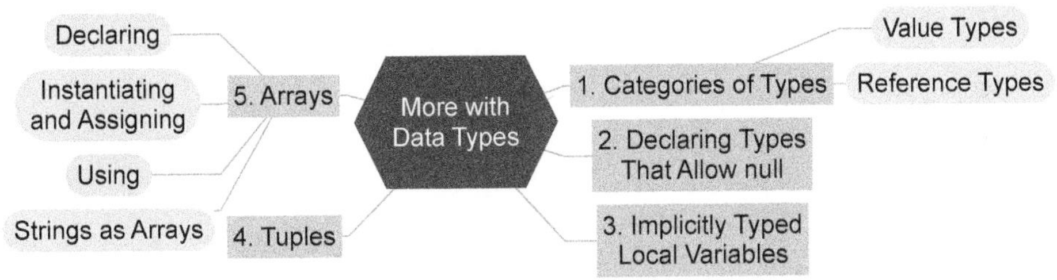

In addition, we delve into the details of combining data elements together into tuples—a feature introduced in C# 7.0—followed by grouping data into sets called **arrays**. To begin, let's delve further into understanding value types and reference types.

Categories of Types

All types fall into one of two categories: **value types** and **reference types**. The differences between the types in each category stem from how they are copied: Value type data is always copied by value, whereas reference type data is always copied by reference.

Value Types

Except for `string`, all the predefined types in the book so far have been value types. Variables of value types contain the value directly. In other words, the variable refers to the same location in memory where the value is stored. Because of this, when a different variable is assigned the same value, a copy of the original variable's value is made to the location of the new variable. A second variable of the same value type cannot refer to the same location in memory as the first variable. Consequently, changing the value of the first variable will not affect the value in the second variable, as Figure 3.1 demonstrates. In the figure, `number1` refers to a location in memory that contains the value `42`. After assigning `number1` to `number2`, both variables will contain the value `42`. However, modifying either variable's value will not affect the other.

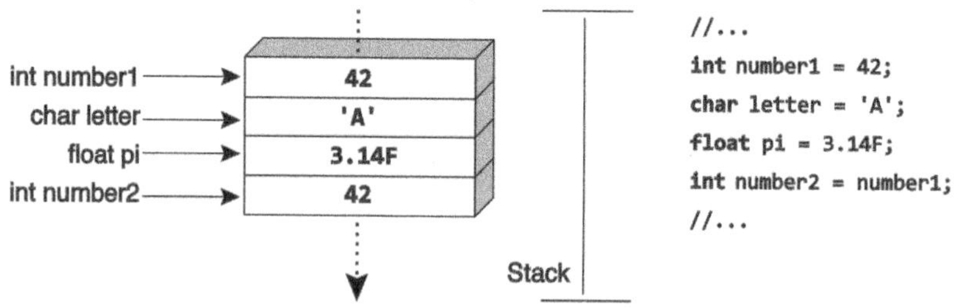

FIGURE 3.1: Value types contain the data directly

Similarly, passing a value type to a method such as `Console.WriteLine()` will result in a memory copy, and any changes to the parameter inside the method will not affect the original value within the calling function. Since value types require a memory copy, they generally should be defined to consume a small amount of memory; value types should almost always be less than 16 bytes in size.

Reference Types

By contrast, the value of a variable of reference type is a reference to a storage location that contains data. Reference types store the reference where the data is located instead of storing the data directly, as value types do. Therefore, to access the data, the runtime reads the memory location out of the variable and then "jumps" to the location in memory that contains the data, an operation known as **dereferencing**. The memory area of the data a reference type points to is called the **heap** (see Figure 3.2).

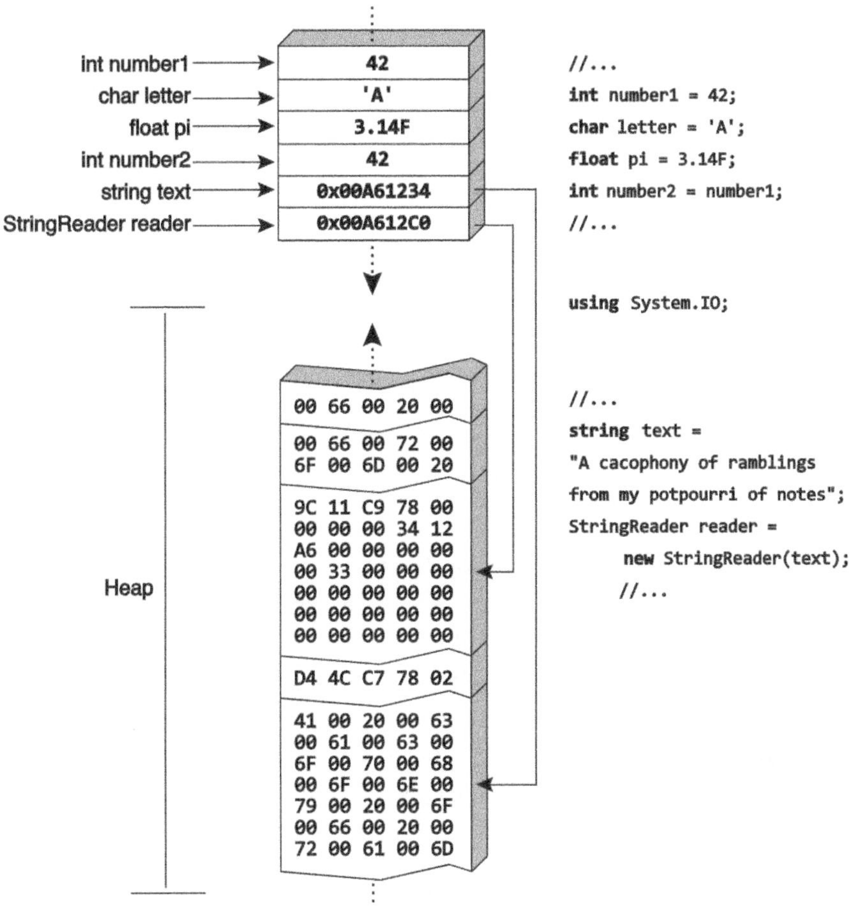

FIGURE 3.2: Reference types point to the heap

A reference type does not require the same memory copy of the data that a value type does, which makes copying reference types far more efficient than copying large value types. When assigning the value of one reference type variable to another reference type variable, only the reference is copied, not the data referred to. In practice, a reference is always the same size as the "native size" of the processor—a

32-bit processor will copy a 32-bit reference, a 64-bit processor will copy a 64-bit reference, and so on. Obviously, copying the small reference to a large block of data is faster than copying the entire block, as a value type would.

Since reference types copy a reference to data, two different variables can refer to the same data. If two variables refer to the same object, changing data in the object via one variable causes the effect to be seen when accessing the same data via another variable. This happens both for assignment and for method calls. Therefore, a method can affect the data of a reference type, and that change can be observed when control returns to the caller. For this reason, a key factor when choosing between defining a reference type or a value type is whether the object is logically like an immutable value of fixed size (and therefore possibly a value type), or logically a mutable thing that can be referred to (and therefore likely to be a reference type).

Besides `string` and any custom classes such as `Program`, all types discussed so far are value types. However, most types are reference types. Although it is possible to define custom value types, it is relatively rare to do so in comparison to the number of custom reference types.

Begin 8.0

Declaring Types That Allow `null`

Often it is desirable to represent values that are "missing." When specifying a `count`, for example, what do you store if the `count` is unknown or unassigned? One possible solution is to designate a "magic" value, such as `-1` or `int.MaxValue`. However, these are valid integers, so it can be ambiguous as to when the magic value is a normal `int` or when it implies a missing value. A preferable approach is to assign `null` to indicate that the value is invalid or that the value has not been assigned. Assigning `null` is especially useful in database programming. Frequently, columns in database tables allow `null` values. Retrieving such columns and assigning them to corresponding variables within C# code is problematic, unless the data type in C# can contain `null` as well.

You can declare a type as either nullable or not nullable, meaning you can declare a type to allow a `null` value or not, with the **nullable modifier**.[1] To enable nullability, simply follow the type declaration with a nullable modifier—a question mark immediately following the type name. For example, `int? number = null` will declare a variable of type `int` that is nullable and assign it the value `null`. Unfortunately, nullability includes some pitfalls, requiring the use of special handling when nullability is enabled.

Dereferencing a `null` Reference

While support for assigning `null` to a variable is invaluable (pun intended), it is not without its drawbacks. While copying or passing a `null` value to other variables and methods is inconsequential, dereferencing (invoking a member on) an instance of `null` will throw a `System.NullReferenceException`—for example, invoking `text.GetType()` when `text` has the value `null`. Anytime production code throws a `System.NullReferenceException`, it is always a bug. This exception indicates that the developer who wrote the code did not remember to check for `null` before the invocation. Further exacerbating the problem, checking for `null` requires an awareness on the developer's part that a `null` value is possible and, therefore, an explicit action is necessary. It is for this reason that declaring of a nullable variable requires explicit use of the nullable modifier—rather than the opposite approach where `null` is allowed by default (see "Nullable Reference Types" later in the section). In other words, when the programmer opts to allow a variable to be `null`, they takes on the additional responsibility of being sure to avoid dereferencing a variable whose value is `null`.

Since checking for `null` requires the use of statements and/or operators that we haven't discussed yet, the details on how to check for `null` appear in "Advanced Topic: Checking for `null`." Full explanations, however, are in Chapter 4.

---

1. Technically, C# includes support for the nullable modifier only with value types in C# 2.0 and reference types in C# 8.0.

ADVANCED TOPIC

Checking for `null`

There are numerous statements and operators that developers can use to check for `null`. Listing 3.1 provides a few examples. The clearest way to check for `null` is with an `if` statement and the `is` operator, as demonstrated in Listing 3.1.

Listing 3.1: Checking for `null`

```
public static void Main(string[] args)
{
    int? number = null;
    // ...
    if (number is null)
    {
        Console.WriteLine(
            "'number' requires a value and cannot be null");
    }
    else
    {
        Console.WriteLine(
            $"'number' doubled is { number * 2 }.");
    }
}
```

The `if` statement checks whether `number` is `null` and then takes different actions depending on the condition. Although you can also use the equality operator (==), it is possible to change the way the equality operator behaves (with overriding); thus, using the `is` keyword is preferable.

Another useful operator[2] when working with `null` is the `null`-conditional operator. It first checks for `null` before dereferencing a nullable value. For example, `int? length = text?.Length;` automatically returns `null` if `text` has the value `null` and the length of the string stored in `text` otherwise. Notice that because the value returned from `text?.Length` could be `null` (if `text` is `null`), the variable `length` must be declared as nullable.

2. Added in C# 6.0.

Both the `if` statement and the `null`-conditional operator are described in more detail in Chapter 4. While the `is` keyword also appears in Chapter 4 briefly, the full explanation isn't provided until Chapter 7, which discusses the concept of pattern matching.

Nullable Value Types

Since a value type refers directly to the actual value, value types cannot innately contain a `null` because, by definition, they cannot contain references, including references to nothing. Nonetheless, we still use the term "dereferencing a value type" when invoking members on the value type. In other words, while not technically correct, using the term "dereferencing" when invoking a member, regardless of whether it is a value type, is common.[3]

ADVANCED TOPIC

Dereferencing `null` on Value Types

Technically, value types declared with the nullable modifier are still value types, so even though they have `null` behavior, under the covers they are not actually `null`. Thus, for the most part, dereferencing a nullable value type that represents `null` will not throw a nullable exception. Members like `HasValue`, `ToString()`, and even the equality-related members (`GetHashCode()` and `Equals()`) are all implemented on `Nullable<T>`, so they won't throw exceptions when the value is representing `null`. (Instead, dereferencing a `null` value type throws an `InvalidOperationException`—not a `NullReferenceException`—to remind programmers that they should check for a value before dereferencing.) However, invoking `GetType()` when the value represents `null` does throw a `NullReferenceException`. The inconsistency occurs because `GetType()` is not a virtual method, so `Nullable<T>` can't

3. Nullable value types were introduced with C# 2.0.

overload the behavior. That leaves the default—throwing a NullReferenceException.

Nullable Reference Types

Prior to C# 8.0, all reference type variables allowed null. Unfortunately, this resulted in numerous bugs because avoiding a null reference exception required the developer to realize the need to check for null and defensively program to avoid dereferencing the null value. Further exacerbating the problem, reference type variables are nullable by default. If no value is assigned to a variable of reference type, the value will default to null. Moreover, if you dereferenced a reference-type local variable whose value was unassigned, the compiler would (appropriately) issue an error, "Use of unassigned local variable 'text'", for which the easiest correction was to simply assign null during declaration, rather than to ensure a more appropriate value was assigned regardless of the path that execution might follow (see Listing 3.2). In other words, developers would easily fall into the trap of declaring a variable and assigning a null value as the simplest resolution to the error, (perhaps mistakenly) expecting the code would reassign the variable before it was dereferenced.

Listing 3.2: Dereferencing an Unassigned Variable

```
#nullable enable
public static void Main()
{
    string? text;
    // ...
    // Compile Error: Use of unassigned local variable 'text'
    System.Console.WriteLine(text.Length);
}
```

In summary, the nullability of reference types by default was a frequent source of defects in the form of System.NullReferenceExceptions, and the behavior of the complier led developers astray unless they took explicit actions to avoid the pitfall.

To improve this scenario significantly, the C# team introduced the concept of nullability to reference types in C# 8.0—a feature known as **nullable reference types** (implying, of course, that reference types could be non-nullable as well). Nullable reference types bring reference types on par with value types, in that reference type declarations can occur with or without a nullable modifier. In C# 8.0, declaring a variable without the nullable modifier implies it is not nullable.

Unfortunately, supporting the declaration of a reference type with a nullable modifier and defaulting the reference type declaration with no `null` modifier to non-nullable has major implications for code that is upgraded from earlier versions of C#. Given that C# 7.0 and earlier supported the assignment of `null` to all reference type declarations (i.e., `string text = null`), does all the code fail compilation in C# 8.0?

Fortunately, backward compatibility is extremely important to the C# team, so support for reference type nullability is not enabled by default on existing projects. In contrast, on new projects like the `HelloWorld` program in Chapter 1, nullability is enabled at the start.

There are several mechanisms to configure nullability: the `#nullable` directive, project properties, and even the command line. First, the null reference type feature is activated in this example with the `#nullable` directive:

```
#nullable enable
```

The directive supports values of `enable`, `disable`, and `restore`—the last of which restores the nullable context to the project-wide setting. Listing 3.2 provides an example that sets `nullable` to `enable` with a `nullable` directive. In so doing, the declaration of `text` as `string?` is enabled and no longer causes a compiler warning.

Alternatively, programmers can use project properties to enable reference type nullability. If not specified, a project file's (`*.csproj`) project-wide setting has `nullable` disabled. To enable it, include a `Nullable` project property whose value is `enable` (see Chapter 1, Listing 1.2 for the full listing).

```
<Nullable>enable</Nullable>
```

All sample code for this book has `nullable` enabled at the project level.

One last way to enable nullability is to set the project properties on the dotnet command line with the `/p` argument:

```
dotnet build /p:Nullable=enable
```

End 8.0

Specifying the value for `Nullable` on the command line will override any value set in the project file.

Implicitly Typed Local Variables

The contextual keyword `var` is used for declaring an **implicitly typed local variable.**[4] If the code initializes a variable at declaration time with an expression of unambiguous type, C# allows for the variable data type to be implied rather than stated, as shown in Listing 3.3.

LISTING 3.3: Working with Strings

```
Console.Write("Enter text: ");
var text = Console.ReadLine();

// Return a new string in uppercase
var uppercase = text.ToUpper();

Console.WriteLine(uppercase);
```

This listing differs from Listing 2.18 in two ways. First, rather than using the explicit data type `string` for the declaration, Listing 3.3 uses `var`. The resultant CIL code is identical to using `string` explicitly. However, `var` indicates to the compiler that it should infer the data type from the value assigned within the declaration—in this case, the value returned by `Console.ReadLine()`.

Second, the variables `text` and `uppercase` are initialized by their declarations. Not doing so would result in an error at compile time. As mentioned earlier, the compiler determines the data type of the initializing expression and declares the

4. Introduced in C# 3.0.

variable accordingly, just as it would if the programmer had specified the type explicitly.

Although using `var` rather than the explicit data type is allowed, consider avoiding such use when the data type is not obvious—for example, use `string` for the declaration of `text` and `uppercase`. Not only does this make the code more understandable, but it also allows the compiler to verify your intent, that the data type returned by the right-hand side expression is the type expected. When using a `var` -declared variable, the right-hand side data type should be obvious; if it isn't, use of the `var` declaration should be avoided.

Guidelines

AVOID using implicitly typed local variables (var) unless the data type of the assigned value is obvious.

Language Contrast: C++/Visual Basic/JavaScript—`void*`, `Variant`, and `var`

An implicitly typed variable is not the equivalent of `void*` in C++, `Variant` in Visual Basic, or `var` in JavaScript. In each of these cases, the variable declaration is restrictive because the variable may be assigned a value of any type, just as can be done in C# with a variable declaration of type `object`. In contrast, `var` is definitively typed by the compiler; once established at declaration, the type may not change, and type checks and member calls are verified at compile time.

Tuples

On occasion, you will find it useful to combine data elements together. Consider, for example, information about a country such as the poorest country in the world in 2022: Burundi, whose capital is Bujumbura, with a GDP per capita of $263.67. Given the constructs we have established so far, we could store each data element in individual variables, but the result would be no association of the data elements together. That is, $263.67 would have no association with Burundi, except perhaps by a common suffix or prefix in the variable names. Another option would be to combine all the data into a single string, albeit with the disadvantage that to work with each data element individually would require parsing it out.

C# 7.0 provides a third option, a tuple. Tuples allow you to combine the assignment to each variable in a single statement, as shown here for the country data:

```
(string country, string capital, double gdpPerCapita) =

("Burundi", "Bujumbura", 263.67);
```

Tuples have several additional syntax possibilities, as shown in Table 3.1.

TABLE 3.1: Sample Code for Tuple Declaration and Assignment

Description	Example Code

Ex. 1
Assign a tuple to individually declared variables.
	`(string country, string capital, double gdpPerCapita) =`
	`("Burundi", "Bujumbura", 263.67);`
	`Console.WriteLine(`
	`$@"The poorest country in the world in 2017 was {`
	`country}, {capital}: {gdpPerCapita}");`

Ex. 2
Assign a tuple to individually declared variables that are pre-declared.
	`string country;`
	`string capital;`
	`double gdpPerCapita;`
	`(country, capital, gdpPerCapita) =`
	`("Burundi", "Bujumbura", 263.67);`
	`Console.WriteLine(`
	`$@"The poorest country in the world in 2017 was {`
	`country}, {capital}: {gdpPerCapita}");`

Ex. 3
Assign a tuple to individually declared and implicitly typed variables.
	`(var country, var capital, var gdpPerCapita) =`
	`("Burundi", "Bujumbura", 263.67);`
	`Console.WriteLine(`
	`$@"The poorest country in the world in 2017 was {`
	`country}, {capital}: {gdpPerCapita}");`

Table 3.1: Sample Code for Tuple Declaration and Assignment (continued)

Description	Example Code

Ex. 4
Assign a tuple to individually declared variables that are implicitly typed with a distributive syntax.
	`var (country, capital, gdpPerCapita) =`
	`("Burundi", "Bujumbura", 263.67);`
	`Console.WriteLine(`
	`$@"The poorest country in the world in 2017 was {`
	`country}, {capital}: {gdpPerCapita}");`

Ex. 5
Declare a named item tuple and assign it tuple values, and then access the tuple items by name.
	`(string Name, string Capital, double GdpPerCapita) countryInfo =`
	`("Burundi", "Bujumbura", 263.67);`
	`Console.WriteLine(`
	`$@"The poorest country in the world in 2017 was {`
	`countryInfo.Name}, {countryInfo.Capital}: {`
	`countryInfo.GdpPerCapita}");`

Ex. 6
Assign a named item tuple to a single implicitly typed variable that is implicitly typed, and then access the tuple items by name.
	`var countryInfo =`
	`(Name: "Burundi", Capital: "Bujumbura", GdpPerCapita: 263.67);`
	`Console.WriteLine(`
	`$@"The poorest country in the world in 2017 was {`
	`countryInfo.Name}, {countryInfo.Capital}: {`
	`countryInfo.GdpPerCapita}");`

Ex. 7
Assign an unnamed tuple to a single implicitly typed variable, and then access the tuple elements by their item-number property.
	`Var countryInfo =`
	`("Burundi", "Bujumbura", 263.67);`
	`Console.WriteLine(`
	`$@"The poorest country in the world in 2017 was {`
	`countryInfo.Item1}, {countryInfo.Item2}: {`
	`countryInfo.Item3}");`

TABLE 3.1: Sample Code for Tuple Declaration and Assignment (continued)

Description	Example Code

Ex. 8
Assign a named item tuple to a single implicitly typed variable, and then access the tuple items by their item-number property.
	`var countryInfo =`
	`(Name: "Burundi", Capital: "Bujumbura", GdpPerCapita: 263.67);`
	`Console.WriteLine(`
	`$@"The poorest country in the world in 2017 was {`
	`countryInfo.Item1}, {countryInfo.Item2}: {`
	`countryInfo.Item3}");`

Ex. 9 Discard portions of the tuple with underscores.	`(string name, _, double gdpPerCapita) =` `("Burundi", "Bujumbura", 263.67);`

Ex. 10
Tuple element names can be inferred from variable and property names (starting in C# 7.1).
	`string country = "Burundi";`
	`string capital = "Bujumbura";`
	`double gdpPerCapita = 263.67;`
	`var countryInfo =`
	`(country, capital, gdpPerCapita);`
	`Console.WriteLine(`
	`$@"The poorest country in the world in 2017 was {`
	`countryInfo.country}, {countryInfo.capital}: {`
	`countryInfo.gdpPerCapita}");`

In the first four examples, although the right-hand side represents a tuple, the left-hand side still represents individual variables that are assigned together using **tuple syntax**, a syntax involving two or more elements separated by commas and associated together with parentheses. (The term *tuple syntax* is used here because the underlying data type that the compiler generates on the left-hand side isn't technically a tuple.) The result is that although we start with values combined as a tuple on the right, the assignment to the left deconstructs the tuple into its constituent parts. In Example 2, the left-hand side assignment is to pre-declared variables. However, in Examples 1, 3, and 4, the variables are declared within the tuple syntax. Given that we are only declaring variables, the naming and casing convention follows the guidelines we discussed in Chapter 1—"DO use camelCase for local variable names," for example.

Note that although implicit typing (`var`) can be distributed across each variable declaration within the tuple syntax, as shown in Example 4, you cannot do the same with an explicit type (such as `string`). Since tuples allow each item to be a different data type, distributing the explicit type name across all elements wouldn't necessarily work unless all the item data types were identical (and even then, the compiler doesn't allow it).

In Example 5, we declare a tuple on the left-hand side and then assign the tuple on the right. Note that the tuple has named items—names that we can then reference to retrieve the item values from the tuple. This is what enables the `countryInfo.Name`, `countryInfo.Capital`, and `countryInfo.GdpPerCapita` syntax in the `Console.WriteLine` statement. The result of the tuple declaration on the left is a grouping of the variables into a single variable (`countryInfo`) from which you can then access the constituent parts. This is useful because, as discussed in Chapter 4, you can then pass this single variable around to other methods, and those methods will also be able to access the individual items within the tuple.

As already mentioned, variables defined using tuple syntax use camelCase. However, the convention for tuple item names is not well defined. Suggestions include using parameter naming conventions when the tuple behaves like a parameter—such as when returning multiple values that before tuple syntax would have used `out` parameters. The alternative is to use PascalCase, following the naming convention for members of a type (properties, functions, and public fields, as discussed in Chapters 5 and 6). We strongly favor the latter approach of PascalCase, consistent with the casing convention of all member identifiers in C# and .NET. Even so, since the convention isn't broadly agreed upon, we use the word CONSIDER rather than DO in the guideline, "CONSIDER using PascalCasing for all tuple item names."

Guidelines

DO use camelCasing for variable declarations using tuple syntax.

CONSIDER using PascalCasing for all tuple item names.

Example 6 provides the same functionality as Example 5, although it uses named tuple items on the right-hand side tuple value and an implicit type declaration on the left. The items' names are persisted to the implicitly typed variable, however, so they are still available for the `WriteLine` statement. Of course, this opens up the possibility that you could name the items on the left-hand side with different names than what you use on the right. While the C# compiler allows this, it will issue a warning that the item names on the right will be ignored, as those on the left will take precedence.

If no item names are specified, the individual elements are still available from the assigned tuple variable. However, the names are `Item1`, `Item2`, `...`, as shown in Example 7. In fact, the `ItemX` names are always available on the tuple even when custom names are provided (see Example 8). However, when using integrated development environment (IDE) tools such as one of the flavors of Visual Studio (one that supports C# 7.0 or higher), the `ItemX` property will not appear within the IntelliSense dropdown—a good thing, since presumably the provided name is preferable. As shown in Example 9, portions of a tuple assignment can be discarded using an underscore—referred to as a **discard**.

The ability to infer the tuple item names as shown in Example 10 wasn't introduced until C# 7.1. As the example demonstrates, the item name within the tuple can be inferred from a variable name or even a property name.

Tuples are a lightweight solution for encapsulating data into a single object in the same way that a bag might capture miscellaneous items you pick up from the store. Unlike arrays (which we discuss next), tuples contain item data types that can vary without constraint,[5] except that they are identified by the code and cannot be changed at runtime. Also, unlike with arrays, the number of items within the tuple is hardcoded at compile time. Lastly, you cannot add custom behavior to a tuple (extension methods notwithstanding). If you need behavior associated with the encapsulated data, then leveraging object-oriented programming and defining a class is the preferred approach—a concept we begin exploring in depth in Chapter 6.

5. Technically, they can't be pointers—a topic we introduce in Chapter 23.

ADVANCED TOPIC

The System.ValueTuple<...> Type

The C# compiler generates code that relies on a set of generic value types (structs), such as System.ValueTuple<T1, T2, T3>, as the underlying implementation for the tuple syntax for all tuple instances on the right-hand side of the examples in Table 3.1. Similarly, the same set of System.ValueTuple<...> generic value types is used for the left-hand side data type starting with Example 5. As we would expect with a tuple type, the only methods included are those related to comparison and equality.

Given that the custom item names and their types are not included in the System.ValueTuple<...> definition, how is it possible that each custom item name is seemingly a member of the System.ValueTuple<...> type and accessible as a member of that type? What is surprising (particularly for those familiar with the anonymous type implementation) is that the compiler does not generate underlying CIL code for the members corresponding to the custom names. However, even without an underlying member with the custom name, there is (seemingly), from the C# perspective, such a member.

For all the named tuple examples in Table 3.1, it is clearly possible that the names could be known by the compiler for the remainder of the scope of the tuple, since said scope is bounded within the member in which it is declared. And, in fact, the compiler (and IDE) quite simply rely on this scope to allow accessing each item by name. In other words, the compiler looks at the item names within the tuple declaration and leverages them to allow code that uses those names within the scope. It is for this reason as well that the ItemX names are not shown in the IDE IntelliSense as available members on the tuple.

Determining the item names from those scoped within a member is reasonable for the compiler, but what happens when a tuple is exposed outside the member, such as a parameter or return from a method that is in a different assembly (for which there is possibly no source code available)? For all tuples that are part of the API (whether a public or private API), the compiler adds item names to the metadata of the member in the form of attributes. For example, the C# equivalent of what the compiler generates for

```
public (string First, string Second) ParseNames(string fullName)
```

is shown in Listing 3.4.

LISTING 3.4: The C# Equivalent of Compiler-Generated CIL Code for a `ValueTuple` Return

```
[return: System.Runtime.CompilerServices.TupleElementNames(
    new { "First", "Second" })]
public System.ValueTuple<string, string> ParseNames(
    string fullName)
{
    // ...
}
```

On a related note, C# 7.0 does not enable the use of custom item names when using the explicit `System.ValueTuple<...>` data type. Therefore, if you replace `var` in Example 8 of Table 3.1, you end up with warnings that each item name will be ignored.

Here are a few additional miscellaneous facts to keep in mind about `System.ValueTuple<...>`.

- There are eight generic `System.ValueTuple<...>`s corresponding to the possibility of supporting tuples with up to seven items. For the eighth tuple, `System.ValueTuple<T1, T2, T3, T4, T5, T6, T7, TRest>`, the last type parameter allows specifying an additional `ValueTuple`, thus enabling support for *n* items. If, for example, you specify a tuple with eight parameters, the compiler automatically generates a `System.ValueTuple<T1, T2, T3, T4, T5, T6, T7, System.ValueTuple<TSub1>>` as the underlying implementing type. (For completeness, the `System.Value<T1>` exists but will rarely be used, since the C# tuple syntax requires a minimum of two items.)
- There is a non-generic `System.ValueTuple` that serves as a tuple factory with `Create()` methods corresponding to each `ValueTuple` arity. The ease of using a tuple literal `var t1 = ("Inigo Montoya", 42)` supersedes the `Create()` method at least for C# 7.0 (or later) programmers.
- For all practical purposes, C# developers can essentially ignore `System.ValueTuple` and `System.ValueTuple<T>`.

There is another tuple type that was first included with the Microsoft .NET Framework 4.5: `System.Tuple<...>`. At the time it was included, it was expected to be the core tuple implementation going forward. However, once C# supported tuple syntax, it was realized that a value type was generally more performant. In turn, `System.ValueTuple<...>` was introduced—effectively replacing `System.Tuple<...>` in all cases except backward compatibility with existing APIs that depend on `System.Tuple<...>`.

ADVANCED TOPIC

Anonymous Types

Support for `var` was added to the language in C# 3.0 to permit the use of anonymous types. Anonymous types are data types that are declared "on the fly" within a method rather than through explicit class definitions, as shown in Listing 3.5 with Output 3.1. (See Chapter 15 for more details on anonymous types.)

Listing 3.5: Implicit Local Variables with Anonymous Types

```
var patent1 =
    new { Title = "Bifocals",
        YearOfPublication = "1784" };
var patent2 =
    new { Title = "Phonograph",
        YearOfPublication = "1877" };

Console.WriteLine(
    $"{patent1.Title} ({patent1.YearOfPublication})");
Console.WriteLine(
    $"{patent2.Title} ({patent2.YearOfPublication})");
```

Output 3.1

```
Bifocals (1784)
Phonograph (1877)
```

Listing 3.5 demonstrates the anonymous type assignment to an implicitly typed (`var`) local variable. This type of operation provided critical functionality in tandem with C#'s support for joining (associating) data types or reducing the size of a particular type down to fewer data elements. However, C# 7.0 introduces syntax for tuples, which all but replaces the need for anonymous types.

Begin 8.0

Arrays

One particular aspect of variable declaration that Chapter 1 didn't cover is array declaration. With array declaration, you can store multiple items of the same type using a single variable and still access them individually using the index when required. In C#, the array index starts at zero. Therefore, arrays in C# are zero based.

BEGINNER TOPIC

Arrays

Arrays provide a means of declaring a collection of data items that are of the same type using a single variable. Each item within the array is uniquely designated using an integer value called the **index**. The first item in a C# array is accessed using index 0. Programmers should be careful to specify an index value that is less than the array size. Since C# arrays are zero based, the index for the last element in an array is one less than the total number of items in the array. In C# 8.0, there is an "index from end" operator. For example, an index value of `^1` would access the last element in the array.

For beginners, it is helpful sometimes to think of the index as an offset. The first item is zero away from the start of the array. The second item is one away from the start of the array—and so on.

Arrays are a fundamental part of nearly every programming language, so they are required learning for virtually all developers. Although arrays are frequently used in C# programming, and necessary for the beginner to understand, most C# programs now use generic collection types rather than arrays when storing collections of data. Therefore, readers should skim over the following section, "Declaring an Array," simply to become familiar with their instantiation and assignment. Table 3.2 provides the highlights of what to note. Generic collections are covered in detail in Chapter 15.

TABLE 3.2: Array Highlights

Description	Example

Declaration
Note that the brackets appear with the data type.
Multidimensional arrays are declared using commas, where the comma+1 specifies the number of dimensions.
	`// 1.`
	`string[] languages; // one-dimensional`
	`int[,] cells; // two-dimensional`

Assignment
The `new` keyword is optional but only at declaration time.
If not assigned during declarations, the `new` keyword is required when instantiating an array.
Specifying the data type is optional.[6] However, without the data type, the size cannot be specified.
Both the size and the values do not have to be literals; they can be determined at runtime.
If both values and size are specified, the quantities must be consistent.
Arrays can be assigned without values. As a result, the value of each item in the array is initialized to its default.
The data type and the size are required if no values are specified.
	`// 2.`
	`string[] languages = {`
	`"C#", "COBOL", "Java",`
	`"C++", "TypeScript", "Pascal",`
	`"Python", "Lisp", "JavaScript"};`
	`languages = new string[]{`
	`"C#", "COBOL", "Java",`
	`"C++", "TypeScript", "Pascal",`
	`"Python", "Lisp", "JavaScript" };`
	`// Multidimensional array assignment`
	`// and initialization`
	`int[,] cells = new [,]`
	`{`
	`{1, 0, 2},`
	`{1, 2, 0},`
	`{1, 2, 1}`
	`};`
	`languages = new string[9];`

6. Starting with C# 3.0.

Table 3.2: Array Highlights (continued)

Description	Example

Forward Accessing an Array
Arrays are zero based, so the first element in an array is at index 0. The square brackets are used to store and retrieve data from an array.
	// 3.
	string[] languages = **new** []{
	"C#", "COBOL", "Java",
	"C++", "TypeScript", "Visual Basic",
	"Python", "Lisp", "JavaScript"};
	// Retrieve fifth item in languages array (TypeScript)
	string language = languages[4];
	// Write “TypeScript”
	Console.WriteLine(language);
	// Retrieve second item from the end (Python)
	language = languages[^3];
	// Write “Python”
	Console.WriteLine(language);

Reverse Accessing an Array Starting in C# 8.0, you can also index an array from the end. For example, item ^1 corresponds to indexing the last element of the array and ^3 corresponds to indexing the third-from-the-last element.	

Ranges
C# 8.0 allows you to identify and extract an array of elements using the range operator, which identifies the starting item up to but excluding the end item.
	Console.WriteLine($@"^3..^0: {
	// Python, Lisp, JavaScript
	string.Join(", ", languages[^3..^0])
	}");
	Console.WriteLine($@"^3..: {
	// Python, Lisp, JavaScript
	string.Join(", ", languages[^3..])
	}");
	Console.WriteLine($@" 3..^3: {
	// C++, TypeScript, Visual Basic
	string.Join(", ", languages[3..^3])
	}");
	Console.WriteLine($@" ..^6: {
	// C#, COBOL, Java
	string.Join(", ", languages[..^6])
	}");

End 8.0

In addition, the final section of this chapter, “Common Array Errors,” provides a review of some of the array idiosyncrasies.

Declaring an Array

In C#, you declare arrays using square brackets. First, you specify the element type of the array, followed by open and closed square brackets; then you enter the name of the variable. Listing 3.6 declares a variable called `languages` to be an array of strings.

Listing 3.6: Declaring an Array

```
string[] languages;
```

Obviously, the first part of the array identifies the data type of the elements within the array. The square brackets that are part of the declaration identify the **rank**, or the number of dimensions, for the array; in this case, it is an array of rank 1. These two pieces form the data type for the variable `languages`.

> **Language Contrast: C++ and Java—Array Declaration**
>
> The square brackets for an array in C# appear immediately following the data type instead of after the variable declaration. This practice keeps all the type information together instead of splitting it up both before and after the identifier, as occurs in C++ and Java—with the latter also allowing the square brackets to appear after either the data type or the variable name.

Listing 3.6 defines an array with a rank of 1. Commas within the square brackets define additional dimensions. Listing 3.7, for example, defines a two-dimensional array of cells for a game of chess or tic-tac-toe.

Listing 3.7: Declaring a Two-Dimensional Array

```
//    |   |
// ---+---+---
//    |   |
// ---+---+---
//    |   |
int[,] cells;
```

In Listing 3.7, the array has a rank of 2. The first dimension could correspond to cells going across and the second dimension to cells going down. Additional dimensions are added, with additional commas, and the total rank is one more than the number of commas. Note that the number of items that occur for a particular dimension is not part of the variable declaration. This is specified when creating (instantiating) the array and allocating space for each element.

Instantiating and Assigning Arrays

Once an array is declared, you can immediately fill its values using a comma-delimited list of items enclosed within a pair of curly braces. Listing 3.8 declares an array of strings and then assigns the names of nine languages within curly braces.

LISTING 3.8: Array Declaration with Assignment

```
string[] languages = { "C#", "COBOL", "Java",
    "C++", "TypeScript", "Visual Basic",
    "Python", "Lisp", "JavaScript" };
```

The first item in the comma-delimited list becomes the first item in the array, the second item in the list becomes the second item in the array, and so on. The curly brackets are the notation for defining an array literal.

The assignment syntax shown in Listing 3.8 is available only if you declare and assign the value within one statement. To assign the value after declaration requires the use of the keyword `new`, as shown in Listing 3.9.

LISTING 3.9: Array Assignment Following Declaration

```
string[] languages;
languages = new string[]{ "C#", "COBOL", "Java",
    "C++", "TypeScript", "Visual Basic",
    "Python", "Lisp", "JavaScript" };
```

Specifying the data type of the array (`string`) following `new` is optional[7] as long as the compiler is able to deduce the element type of the array from the types of the elements in the array initializer. The square brackets are still required.

7. Starting with C# 3.0.

C# also allows use of the `new` keyword as part of the declaration statement, so it allows the assignment and the declaration shown in Listing 3.10.

LISTING 3.10: Array Assignment with `new` during Declaration

```
string[] languages = new string[]{
    "C#", "COBOL", "Java",
    "C++", "TypeScript", "Visual Basic",
    "Python", "Lisp", "JavaScript" };
```

The use of the `new` keyword tells the runtime to allocate memory for the data type. It instructs the runtime to instantiate the data type—in this case, an array.

Whenever you use the `new` keyword as part of an array assignment, you may also specify the size of the array within the square brackets. Listing 3.11 demonstrates this syntax.

LISTING 3.11: Declaration and Assignment with the `new` Keyword

```
string[] languages = new string[9]{
    "C#", "COBOL", "Java",
    "C++", "TypeScript", "Visual Basic",
    "Python", "Lisp", "JavaScript" };
```

The array size in the initialization statement and the number of elements contained within the curly braces must match. Furthermore, it is possible to assign an array but not specify the initial values of the array, as demonstrated in Listing 3.12.

LISTING 3.12: Assigning without Literal Values

```
string[] languages = new string[9];
```

Assigning an array but not initializing the initial values still initializes each element. The runtime initializes array elements to their default values, as follows:

- Reference types—whether nullable or not (such as `string` and `string?`)—are initialized to `null`.
- Nullable value types are all initialized to `null`.
- Non-nullable numeric types are initialized to `0`.
- `bool` is initialized to `false`.

- `char` is initialized to `\0`.

Nonprimitive value types are recursively initialized by initializing each of their fields to their default values. As a result, it is not necessary to individually assign each element of an array before using it.

Because the array size is not included as part of the variable declaration, it is possible to specify the size at runtime. For example, Listing 3.13 creates an array based on the size specified in the `Console.ReadLine()` call.

Listing 3.13: Defining the Array Size at Runtime

```
string[] groceryList;
Console.Write("How many items on the list? ");
int size = int.Parse(Console.ReadLine());
groceryList = new string[size];
// ...
```

C# initializes multidimensional arrays similarly. A comma separates the size of each rank. Listing 3.14 initializes a tic-tac-toe board with no moves.

Listing 3.14: Declaring a Two-Dimensional Array

```
int[,] cells = new int[3,3];
```

Initializing a tic-tac-toe board with a specific position could be done as shown in Listing 3.15.

Listing 3.15: Initializing a Two-Dimensional Array of Integers

```
int[,] cells = {
    {1, 0, 2},
    {1, 2, 0},
    {1, 2, 1}
};
```

The initialization follows the pattern in which there is an array of three elements of type `int[]`, and each element has the same size; in this example, the size is 3. Note that the sizes of each `int[]` element must all be identical. The declaration shown in Listing 3.16, therefore, is not valid.

LISTING 3.16: A Multidimensional Array with Inconsistent Size, Causing an Error

```
// ERROR: Each dimension must be consistently sized
// ...
```

Representing tic-tac-toe does not require an integer in each position. One alternative is to construct a separate virtual board for each player, with each board containing a `bool` that indicates which positions the players selected. Listing 3.17 corresponds to a three-dimensional board.

LISTING 3.17: Initializing a Three-Dimensional Array

```
bool[, ,] cells;
cells = new bool[2, 3, 3]
{
    // Player 1 moves
    //  X |   |
    // ---+---+---
    //  X |   |
    // ---+---+---
    //  X |   | X
    {
        {true, false, false},
        {true, false, false},
        {true, false, true}
    },
    // Player 2 moves
    //    |   | O
    // ---+---+---
    //    | O |
    // ---+---+---
    //    | O |
    {
        {false, false, true},
        {false, true, false},
        {false, true, true}
    }
};
```

In this example, the board is initialized and the size of each rank is explicitly identified. In addition to identifying the size as part of the new expression, the literal values for the array are provided. The literal values of type `bool[,,]` are broken into two arrays of type `bool[,]`, size 3 × 3. Each two-dimensional array is composed of three `bool` arrays, size 3.

As already mentioned, each dimension in a multidimensional array must be consistently sized. However, it is also possible to define a **jagged array**, which is an array of arrays. Jagged array syntax is slightly different from that of a multidimensional array; furthermore, jagged arrays do not need to be consistently sized. Therefore, it is possible to initialize a jagged array as shown in Listing 3.18.

LISTING 3.18: Initializing a Jagged Array

```
int[][] cells = {
    new [] {1, 0, 2, 0},
    new [] {1, 2, 0},
    new [] {1, 2},
    new [] {1}
};
```

A jagged array doesn't use a comma to identify a new dimension. Rather, it defines an array of arrays. In Listing 3.18, `[]` is placed after the data type `int[]`, thereby declaring an array of type `int[]`.

Notice that a jagged array requires an array instance (or `null`) for each internal array. In the preceding example, you use `new` to instantiate the internal element of the jagged arrays. Leaving out the instantiation would cause a compile error. (As noted, specifying the data type is optional when values are provided.)

Begin 8.0

Using an Array

You access a specific item in an array using the square bracket notation, known as the **array accessor**. To retrieve the first item from an array, you specify zero as the index. In Listing 3.19, the value of the fifth item (using the index 4 because the first item is index 0) in the `languages` variable is stored in the variable `language`.

LISTING 3.19: Declaring and Accessing an Array

```
string[] languages = new []{
    "C#", "COBOL", "Java",
    "C++", "TypeScript", "Visual Basic",
    "Python", "Lisp", "JavaScript"};
    // Retrieve fifth item in languages array (TypeScript)
    string language = languages[4];
```

```
// Write "TypeScript"
Console.WriteLine(language);
    // Retrieve second item from the end (Python)
    language = languages[^3];
// Write "Python"
Console.WriteLine(language);
```

Starting with C# 8.0, you can also access items relative to the end of the array using the **index from end operator**, also known as the ^ (hat) operator. Indexing with `^1`, for example, retrieves the last item in the array, whereas the first element using the index from end operator would be `^9` (where 9 is the number of items in the array). In Listing 3.19, `^3` specifies that the value stored in the third item from the end (`"Python"`) in the `languages` variable is assigned to `language`.

Since item `^1` is the last element, item `^0` corresponds to one past the end of the list. Of course, there is no such element, so you can't successfully index the array using `^0`. Similarly, using the length of the array, 9 in this case, refers to an element off the end of the array. In addition, you can't use negative values when indexing into an array.

There is seemingly a discrepancy between indexing from the beginning of the array with a positive integer and indexing from the end of the array using a ^ integer value (or an expression that returns an integer value). The first begins counting at 0 to access the first element, while the second starts at `^1` to access the last element. The C# design team chose to index from the beginning using 0 for consistency with other languages on which C# is based (C, C++, and Java, for example). When indexing from the end, C# followed Python's precedence (since the C-based languages didn't support an index from end operator) and started counting from the end with 1 as well. Unlike in Python, however, the C# team selected the ^ operator (rather than negative integers) to ensure there was no backward incompatibility when using the index operator on collection types (not arrays) that allow negative values. (The ^ operator has additional advantages when supporting ranges, as discussed later in the chapter.)

Language Contrast: C++/Java/JavaScript/Python—Array Indexing

Like its heritage (C++/Java/JavaScript/Python), C# indexes arrays from 0. While most of these same predecessors don't index from the end, Python does so. Like Python, C#'s indexing from the end starts with 1; albeit, the indexing from the end operator is ^ rather than -.

One way to remember how the index from end operator works is to notice that when indexing from the end with a positive integer, the value begins with length –1 for the last element, length –2 for the second-to-last element, and so on. The integer subtracted from the length corresponds to the "last from end" index value—`^1`, `^2`, and so on. Furthermore, with this approach the value of the index from the beginning of the array plus the value of the index from the end of the array always totals the length of the array.

Note that the index from end operator is not limited to a literal integer value. You can also use expressions such as

```
languages[^languages.Length]
```

which will return the first item.

NOTE

In C#, an index begins counting at 0 to access the first element, while the index from the end index starts at `^1` to access the last element. When indexing from the end, using the ^ operator, the value begins with length—1. The integer subtracted from the length corresponds to the "last from end" index value. Thus, the value of the index from the beginning of the array plus the value of the index from the end of the array always totals the length of the array.

The square bracket (array accessor) notation is also used to store data into an array. Listing 3.20 switches the order of `"C++"` and `"Java"`.

LISTING 3.20: Swapping Data between Positions in an Array

```
string[] languages = new [] {
    "C#", "COBOL", "Java",
    "C++", "TypeScript", "Visual Basic",
    "Python", "Lisp", "JavaScript" };
// Save "C++" to variable called language
string language = languages[3];
// Assign "Java" to the C++ position
languages[3] = languages[2];
// Assign language to location of "Java"
languages[2] = language;
```

For multidimensional arrays, an element is identified with an index for each dimension, as shown in Listing 3.21.

LISTING 3.21: Initializing a Two-Dimensional Array of Integers

```
int[,] cells = {
    {1, 0, 2},
    {0, 2, 0},
    {1, 2, 1}
};
// Set the winning tic-tac-toe move to be player 1
cells[1, 0] = 1;
```

Jagged array element assignment is slightly different because it is consistent with the jagged array declaration. The first element is an array within the array of arrays; the second index specifies the item within the selected array element (see Listing 3.22).

LISTING 3.22: Declaring a Jagged Array

```
int[][] cells = {
    new []{1, 0, 2},
    new []{0, 2, 0},
    new []{1, 2, 1}
};

cells[1][0] = 1;
// ...
```

You can obtain the length of an array, as shown in Listing 3.23.

LISTING 3.23: Retrieving the Length of an Array

```
Console.WriteLine(
    $"There are {languages.Length} languages in the array.");
```

Arrays have a fixed length; they are bound such that the length cannot be changed without re-creating the array. Furthermore, overstepping the **bounds** (or length) of the array will cause the runtime to report an error. This can occur when you attempt to access (either retrieve or assign) the array with an index for which no element exists in the array. Such an error frequently occurs when you use the array length as an index into the array, as shown in Listing 3.24.

LISTING 3.24: Accessing Outside the Bounds of an Array, Throwing an Exception

```
string[] languages = new string[9];
// ...
// RUNTIME ERROR: index out of bounds - should
// be 8 for the last element
languages[4] = languages[9];
```

NOTE

The `Length` member returns the number of items in the array, not the highest index. The `Length` member for the `languages` variable is `9`, but the highest runtime allowable index for the `languages` variable is `8`, because that is how far it is from the start.

Language Contrast: C++—Buffer Overflow Bugs

Unmanaged C++ does not always check whether you overstep the bounds on an array. Not only can this be difficult to debug, but making this mistake can also result in a potential security vulnerability called a **buffer overrun**. In contrast, the Common Language Runtime protects all C# (and Managed C++) code from overstepping array bounds, virtually eliminating the possibility of a buffer overrun issue in managed code.

With C# 8.0, the same problem occurs when accessing the `^0` item: Since `^1` is the last item, `^0` is one past the end of the array—and there is no such item.

To avoid overstepping the bounds on an array when accessing the last element, use a length check to verify that the array has a length greater than 0, and use `^1` (starting with C# 8.0) or `Length - 1` in place of a hardcoded value when accessing the last item in the array. To use `Length` as an index, it is necessary to subtract 1 to avoid an out-of-bounds error (see Listing 3.25).

Listing 3.25: Using `Length - 1` in the Array Index

```
string[] languages = new string[9];
// ...
languages[4] = languages[languages.Length - 1];
```

(Of course, first check for `null` before accessing the array if there is a chance there is no array instance in the first place.)

Guidelines

CONSIDER checking the array length before indexing into an array rather than assuming the length.

CONSIDER using the index from end operator (^) rather than `Length - 1` with C# 8.0 or higher.

`Length` returns the total number of elements in an array. Therefore, if you had a multidimensional array such as `bool cells[,,]` of size 2 × 3 × 3, `Length` would return the total number of elements, 18.

For a jagged array, `Length` returns the number of elements in the first array. Because a jagged array is an array of arrays, `Length` evaluates only the outside containing array and returns its element count, regardless of what is inside the internal arrays.

Ranges

Another indexing-related feature added to C# 8.0 is support for array slicing—that is, extracting a slice of an array into a new array. The syntax for specifying a range is `..`, the range operator, which may optionally be placed between indices (including the indices from the end). Listing 3.26 provides examples.

Listing 3.26: Examples of the Range Operator

```
string[] languages = new [] {
    "C#", "COBOL", "Java",
    "C++", "TypeScript", "Swift",
    "Python", "Lisp", "JavaScript"};

Console.WriteLine($@"  0..3: {
    string.Join(", ", languages[0..3])  // C#, COBOL, Java
}");
Console.WriteLine($@"^3..^0: {
    string.Join(", ", languages[^3..^0]) // Python, Lisp, JavaScript
}");
Console.WriteLine($@" 3..^3: {
    string.Join(", ", languages[3..^3]) // C++, TypeScript, Swift
}");
Console.WriteLine($@"  ..^6: {
    string.Join(", ", languages[..^6])  // C#, COBOL, Java
}");
Console.WriteLine($@"   6..: {
    string.Join(", ", languages[6..])  // Python, Lisp, JavaScript
}");
Console.WriteLine($@"    ..: {
    // C#, COBOL, Java, C++, TypeScript, Swift, Python, Lisp, JavaScript
    string.Join(", ", languages[..])  // Python, Lisp, JavaScript
}");
Console.WriteLine($@"    ..: {
    // C#, COBOL, Java, C++, TypeScript, Swift, Python, Lisp, JavaScript
    string.Join(", ", languages[0..^0])  // Python, Lisp, JavaScript
}");
```

The important thing to note about the range operator is that it identifies the items by specifying the first (inclusive) up to the end (exclusive). Therefore, in the `0..3` example of Listing 3.26, `0` specifies the slice to include everything from the first item up to, *but not including*, the fourth item (3 is used to identify the fourth item because the forward index starts counting at 0). In Example 2, therefore, specifying

`^3..^0` retrieves the last three items. The `^0` does not cause an error by attempting to access the item past the end of the array because the index at the end of the range does not include the identified item.

Specifying either the beginning index or "up to" (the end) index is optional, as shown in Examples 4–6 of Listing 3.26. As such, if indices are missing entirely, it is equivalent to specifying `0..^0`.

Finally, note that indices and ranges are first-class types in .NET/C# (as described in the `System.Index` and `System.Range` advanced block). Their behavior is not limited to use in an array accessor.

> **NOTE**
>
> The range operator identifies items by specifying the first item – inclusive to the end item – exclusive.

ADVANCED TOPIC

`System.Index` and `System.Range`

Using the index from end operator is a literal way of specifying a `System.Index` value. Therefore, you can use indexes outside the context of the square brackets. For example, you could declare an index and assign it a literal value: `System.Index index = ^42`. Regular integers can also be assigned to a `System.Index`. The `System.Index` type has two properties, a `Value` of type `int`, and an `IsFromEnd` property of type bool. The latter is obviously used to indicate whether the index counts from the beginning of the array or the end.

In addition, the data type used to specify a range is a `System.Range`. As such, you can declare and assign a range value: `System.Range range = ..^0` or even `System.Range range = ..`, for example. `System.Range` has two properties, `Start` and `End`.

By making these types available, C# enables you to write custom collections that support ranges and the "from the end" indices. (We discuss how to write custom collections in Chapter 17.)

More Array Methods

Arrays include additional methods for manipulating the elements within the array—for example, `Sort()`, `BinarySearch()`, `Reverse()`, and `Clear()` (see Listing 3.27 with Output 3.2).

LISTING 3.27: Additional Array Methods

```
string[] languages = new string[]{
    "C#", "COBOL", "Java",
    "C++", "TypeScript", "Swift",
    "Python", "Lisp", "JavaScript"};

Array.Sort(languages);

string searchString = "COBOL";
int index = Array.BinarySearch(
    languages, searchString);
Console.WriteLine(
    "The wave of the future, "
    + $"{ searchString }, is at index { index }.");

Console.WriteLine();
Console.WriteLine(
    $"{ "First Element",-20 }\t{ "Last Element",-20 }");
Console.WriteLine(
    $"{ "-------------",-20 }\t{ "------------",-20 }");
Console.WriteLine(
        $"{ languages[0],-20 }\t{ languages[^1],-20 }");
Array.Reverse(languages);
Console.WriteLine(
        $"{ languages[0],-20 }\t{ languages[^1],-20 }");
// Note this does not remove all items from the array
// Rather it sets each item to the type's default value
Array.Clear(languages, 0, languages.Length);
Console.WriteLine(
        $"{ languages[0],-20 }\t{ languages[^1],-20 }");
```

```
Console.WriteLine(
    $"After clearing, the array size is: { languages.Length }");
```

Output 3.2

```
The wave of the future, COBOL, is at index 2.

First Element        Last Element
-------------        ------------
C#                   TypeScript
TypeScript           C#

After clearing, the array size is: 9
```

Access to these methods is obtained through the `System.Array` class. For the most part, using these methods is self-explanatory, except for two noteworthy items:

- Before using the `BinarySearch()` method, it is important to sort the array. If values are not sorted in increasing order, the incorrect index may be returned. If the search element does not exist, the value returned is negative. (Using the complement operator, `~index`, returns the first index, if any, that is larger than the searched value.)
- The `Clear()` method does not remove elements of the array and does not set the length to zero. The array size is fixed and cannot be modified. Therefore, the `Clear()` method sets each element in the array to its default value (`null`, `0`, or `false`). This explains why `Console.WriteLine()` creates a blank line when writing out the array after `Clear()` is called.

End 8.0

Array Instance Members

Like strings, arrays have instance members that are accessed not from the data type but directly from the variable. `Length` is an example of an instance member because access to `Length` occurs through the array variable, not the class. Other significant instance members are `GetLength()`, `Rank`, and `Clone()`.

Retrieving the length of a particular dimension does not utilize the `Length` property. To retrieve the size of a particular rank, an array includes a `GetLength()` instance method. When calling this method, it is necessary to specify the rank whose length will be returned (see Listing 3.28 with Output 3.3).

Listing 3.28: Retrieving a Particular Dimension's Size

```
bool[, ,] cells;
cells = new bool[2, 3, 3];
Console.WriteLine(cells.GetLength(0)); // Displays 2
Console.WriteLine(cells.Rank); // Displays 3
```

Output 3.3

```
2
```

Listing 3.28 displays 2 because that is the number of elements in the first dimension.

It is also possible to retrieve the entire array's rank by accessing the array's `Rank` member, `cells.` `cells.Rank`, for example, returns 3 (see Listing 3.28).

By default, assigning one array variable to another copies only the array reference, not the individual elements of the array. To make an entirely new copy of the array, use the array's `Clone()` method. The `Clone()` method returns a copy of the array; changing any of the members of this new array does not affect the members of the original array.

Strings as Arrays

Variables of type `string` are accessible like an array of characters. For example, to retrieve the fourth character of a string called `palindrome`, you can call `palindrome[3]`. Note, however, that because strings are immutable, it is not possible to assign particular characters within a string. C#, therefore, would not allow `palindrome[3]='a'`, where `palindrome` is declared as a string. Listing 3.29 uses the array accessor to determine whether an argument on the command line is an option, where an option is identified by a dash as the first character.

Listing 3.29: Looking for Command-Line Options

```
public static void Main(string[] args)
{
    // ...
    if(args[0][0] == '-')
    {
        // This parameter is an option
```

```
    }
}
```

This snippet uses the `if` statement, which is covered in Chapter 4. In addition, it presents an interesting example because you use the array accessor to retrieve the first element in the array of strings, `args`. Following the first array accessor is a second one, which retrieves the first character of the string. The code, therefore, is equivalent to that shown in Listing 3.30.

LISTING 3.30: Looking for Command-Line Options (Simplified)

```
public static void Main(string[] args)
{
    // ...
    string arg = args[0];
    if(arg[0] == '-')
    {
        // This parameter is an option
    }
}
```

Not only can string characters be accessed individually using the array accessor, but it is also possible to retrieve the entire string as an array of characters using the string's `ToCharArray()` method. Using this approach, you could reverse the string with the `System.Array.Reverse()` method, as demonstrated in Listing 3.31 with Output 3.4, which determines whether a string is a palindrome.

LISTING 3.31: Reversing a String

```
string reverse, palindrome;
char[] temp;

Console.Write("Enter a palindrome: ");
palindrome = Console.ReadLine();

// Remove spaces and convert to lowercase
reverse = palindrome.Replace(" ", "");
reverse = reverse.ToLower();

// Convert to an array
temp = reverse.ToCharArray();
```

```
// Reverse the array
Array.Reverse(temp);

// Convert the array back to a string and
// check if reverse string is the same
if (reverse == new string(temp))
{
    Console.WriteLine(
        $"\"{palindrome}\" is a palindrome.");
}
else
{
    Console.WriteLine(
        $"\"{palindrome}\" is NOT a palindrome.");
}
```

Output 3.4

```
Enter a palindrome: NeverOddOrEven
"NeverOddOrEven" is a palindrome.
```

This example uses the `new` keyword; this time, it creates a new string from the reversed array of characters.

Common Array Errors

This section introduced the three types of arrays: single-dimensional, multidimensional, and jagged. Several rules and idiosyncrasies govern array declaration and use. Table 3.3 points out some of the most common errors and helps solidify the rules. Try reviewing the code in the Common Mistake column first (without looking at the Error Description and Corrected Code columns) as a way of verifying your understanding of arrays and their syntax.

Table 3.3: Common Array Coding Errors

Common Mistake	Error Description	Corrected Code
`// 1.` `int numbers[];`	The square brackets for declaring an array appear after the data type, not after the variable identifier.	`int[] numbers;`

TABLE 3.3: Common Array Coding Errors (continued)

Common Mistake	Error Description	Corrected Code

`// 2.`
`int[] numbers;`
`numbers = {42, 84, 168 };`
	When assigning an array after declaration, it is necessary to use the `new` keyword and then specify the data type.	`int[] numbers;`
		`numbers = new int[]{`
		`42, 84, 168 }`

`// 3.`
`int[3] numbers =`
`{ 42, 84, 168 };`
	It is not possible to specify the array size as part of the variable declaration.	`int[] numbers =`
		`{ 42, 84, 168 };`

`// 4.`
`int[] numbers =`
`new int[];`
	The array size is required at initialization time unless an array literal is provided.	`int[] numbers =`
		`new int[3];`

`// 5.`
`int[] numbers =`
`new int[3]{};`
	The array size is specified as 3, but there are no elements in the array literal. The array size must match the number of elements in the array literal.	`int[] numbers =`
		`new int[3]`
		`{ 42, 84, 168 };`

`// 6.`
`int[] numbers =`
`new int[3];`
`Console.WriteLine(`
`numbers[3]);`
	Array indices start at zero. Therefore, the last item is one less than the array size. (Note that this is a runtime error, not a compile-time error.)	`int[] numbers =`
		`new int[3];`
		`Console.WriteLine(`
		`numbers[2]);`

TABLE 3.3: Common Array Coding Errors (continued)

Common Mistake	Error Description	Corrected Code

`// 7.`
`int[] numbers =`
`new int[3];`
`numbers[^0] = 42;`
	Same as previous error. The index from end operator uses `^1` to identify the last item in the array. `^0` is one item past the end, which doesn't exist. (Note that this is a runtime error, not a compile-time error.)	`int[] numbers =`
		`new int[3];`
		`numbers[^1] =`
		`42;`

`// 8.`
`int[] numbers =`
`new int[3];`
`numbers[numbers.Length]`
`= 42;`
	Same as previous error: 1 needs to be subtracted from the `Length` to access the last element. (Note that this is a runtime error, not a compile-time error.)	`int[] numbers =`
		`new int[3];`
		`numbers[numbers.Length-1]`
		`= 42;`

`// 9.`
`int[,] numbers =`
`{ {42}, {84, 42} };`
	Multidimensional arrays must be structured consistently.	`int[,] numbers =`
		`{ {42, 168},`
		`{84, 42} };`

`// 10.`
`int[][] numbers =`
`{ {42, 84}, {84, 42} };`
	Jagged arrays require instantiated arrays to be specified for the arrays within the array.	`int[][] numbers =`
		`{ new int[]{42, 84},`
		`new int[]{84, 42} };`

Summary

We began the chapter with a discussion of two different categories of types: value types and reference types. These fundamental concepts are important for C# programmers to understand because they change the underlying way a type behaves, even though that might not be obvious when reading through the code.

Before discussing arrays, we looked at two language constructs that were not initially part of C#. First, we introduced the nullable modifier (?). The nullable modifier enables the declaration of nullability. (Technically, it enables value types to store `null` and reference types to specify explicitly the intent to store `null` or not.) Second, we introduced tuples and a new syntax introduced with C# 7.0 that provides language support for working with tuples without having to work explicitly with the underlying data type.

This chapter closed with coverage of C# syntax for arrays, along with the various means of manipulating arrays. For many developers, the syntax can seem rather daunting at first, so this section included a list of the common errors associated with coding arrays.

The next chapter looks at expressions and control flow statements. The `if` statement, which appeared a few times toward the end of this chapter, is discussed as well.

4

Operators and Control Flow

In this chapter, you learn about operators, control flow statements, and the C# preprocessor. **Operators** provide syntax for performing different calculations or actions appropriate for the operands within the calculation. **Control flow statements** provide the means for conditional logic within a program or looping over a section of code multiple times. After introducing the `if` control flow statement, the chapter looks at the concept of Boolean expressions, which are embedded within many control flow statements. Included is mention of how integers cannot be converted (even explicitly) to `bool` and the advantages of this restriction. The chapter ends with a discussion of the C# preprocessor directives.

Operators

Now that you have been introduced to the predefined data types (refer to Chapter 2), you can begin to learn how to use these data types in combination with operators to perform calculations. For example, you can make calculations on variables that you have declared.

BEGINNER TOPIC

Operators

Operators are used to perform mathematical or logical operations on values (or variables) called **operands** to produce a new value, called the **result**. For example, in

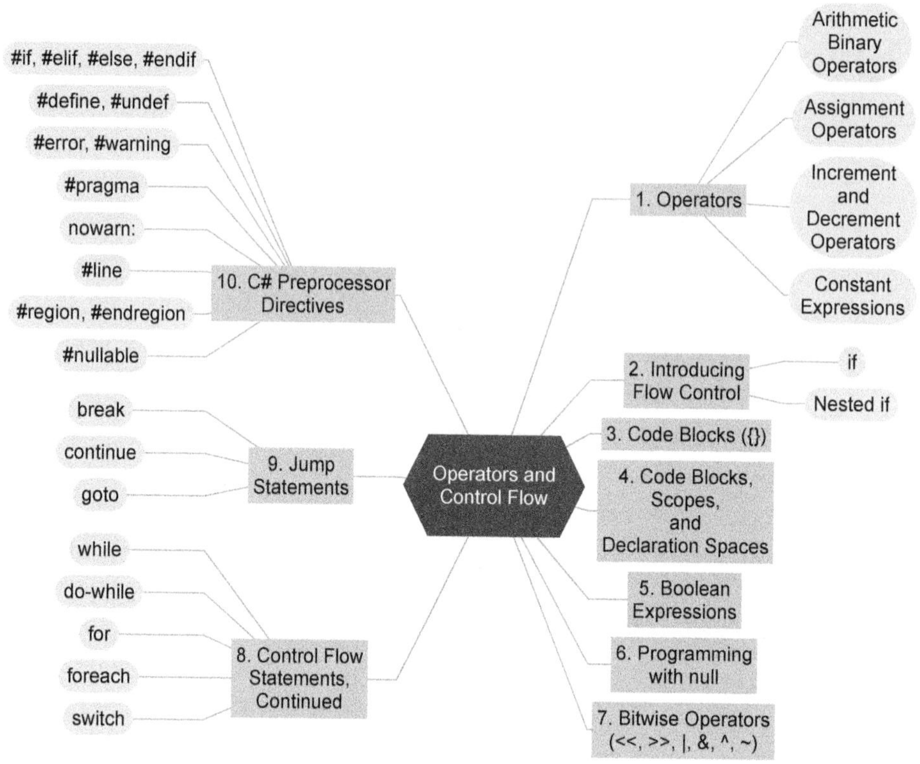

Listing 4.1 the subtraction operator, `-`, is used to subtract two operands, the numbers `4` and `2`. The result of the subtraction is stored in the variable `difference`.

LISTING 4.1: A Simple Operator Example

```
int difference = 4 - 2;
```

There are three operator categories—unary, binary, and ternary—corresponding to the number of operands (one, two, and three, respectively). Furthermore, while some operators are represented with symbols like `+`, `-`, `?.`, and `??`, other operators take the form of keywords, like `default` and `is`. This section covers some of the most basic unary and binary operators. The ternary operators appear later in the chapter.

Plus and Minus Unary Operators (+, -)

Sometimes you may want to change the sign of a numeric value. In these cases, the unary minus operator (-) comes in handy. For example, Listing 4.2 changes the total current U.S. debt to a negative value to indicate that it is an amount owed.

Listing 4.2: Specifying Negative Values

```
// World Debt on 2022-11-06
// see https://worlddebtclocks.com/
decimal debt = -72748555131730M;
```

Using the minus operator *is equivalent to subtracting the operand from zero.*

The unary plus operator (+) rarely[1] has any effect on a value. It is a superfluous addition to the C# language and was included for the sake of symmetry.

Arithmetic Binary Operators (+, -, *, /, %)

Binary operators require two operands. C# uses infix notation for binary operators: The operator appears between the left and right operands. The result of every binary operator other than assignment must be used somehow—for example, by using it as an operand in another expression such as an assignment.

Language Contrast: C++—Operator-Only Statements

In contrast to the rule mentioned previously, C++ allows a single binary expression to form the entirety of a statement, such as `4+5;`, and compile. In C#, only assignment, call, increment, decrement, await, and object creation expressions are allowed to be the entirety of a statement.

The subtraction example in Listing 4.3 with Output 4.1 illustrates the use of a binary operator—more specifically, an arithmetic binary operator. The operands appear on each side of the arithmetic operator, and then the calculated value is

---

1. The unary + operator is defined to take operands of type `int`, `uint`, `nint`, `nuint`, `long`, `ulong`, `float`, `double`, and `decimal` (and nullable versions of those types). Using it on other numeric types such as `short` converts its operand to one of these types as appropriate.

assigned. The other arithmetic binary operators are addition (+), division (/), multiplication (*), and remainder (% [sometimes called the mod operator]).

Listing 4.3: Using Binary Operators

```
int numerator;
int denominator;
int quotient;
int remainder;

Console.Write("Enter the numerator: ");
numerator = int.Parse(Console.ReadLine());

Console.Write("Enter the denominator: ");
denominator = int.Parse(Console.ReadLine());

quotient = numerator / denominator;
remainder = numerator % denominator;

Console.WriteLine(
    $"{numerator} / {denominator} = {
        quotient} with remainder {remainder}");
```

Output 4.1

```
Enter the numerator: 23
Enter the denominator: 3
23 / 3 = 7 with remainder 2
```

In the highlighted assignment statements, the division and remainder operations are executed before the assignments. The order in which operators are executed is determined by their **precedence** and **associativity**. The precedence for the operators used so far is as follows:

1. *, /, and % have the highest precedence.
2. + and - have lower precedence.
3. = has the lowest precedence of these six operators.

Therefore, you can assume that the statement behaves as expected, with the division and remainder operators executing before the assignment.

If you forget to assign the result of one of these binary operators, you will receive the compile error shown in Output 4.2.

OUTPUT 4.2

```
... error CS0201: Only assignment, call, increment, decrement,
await, and new object expressions can be used as a statement
```

BEGINNER TOPIC

Parentheses, Associativity, Precedence, and Evaluation

When an expression contains multiple operators, it can be unclear precisely what the operands of each operator are. For example, in the expression `x+y*z`, clearly the expression `x` is an operand of the addition, and `z` is an operand of the multiplication. But is `y` an operand of the addition or the multiplication?

Parentheses allow you to unambiguously associate an operand with its operator. If you wish `y` to be a summand, you can write the expression as `(x+y)*z`; if you want it to be a multiplicand, you can write `x+(y*z)`.

However, C# does not require you to parenthesize every expression containing more than one operator; instead, the compiler can use associativity and precedence to figure out from the context which parentheses you have omitted. **Associativity** determines how similar operators are parenthesized; **precedence** determines how dissimilar operators are parenthesized.

A binary operator may be *left-associative* or *right-associative*, depending on whether the expression "in the middle" belongs to the operator on the left or the right. For example, `a-b-c` is assumed to mean `(a-b)-c`, and not `a-(b-c)`; subtraction is therefore said to be left-associative. Most operators in C# are left-associative; the assignment operators are right-associative.

When the operators are dissimilar, the **precedence** for those operators is used to determine the side to which the operand in the middle belongs. For example, multiplication has higher precedence than addition, so the expression `x+y*z` is evaluated as `x+(y*z)` rather than `(x+y)*z`.

It is often good practice to use parentheses to make the code more readable, even when the use of parentheses does not change the meaning of the expression. For example, when performing a Celsius-to-Fahrenheit temperature conversion, `(c*9.0/5.0)+32.0` is easier to read than `c*9.0/5.0+32.0`, even though the parentheses are completely unnecessary.

Guidelines

DO use parentheses to make code more readable, particularly if the operator precedence is not clear to the casual reader.

Clearly, operators of higher precedence must execute before adjoining operators of lower precedence: in `x+y*z`, the multiplication must be executed before the addition because the result of the multiplication is the right-hand operand of the addition. However, it is important to realize that precedence and associativity affect only the order in which the *operators* themselves are executed; they do not in any way affect the order in which the *operands* are evaluated.

Operands are always evaluated from left to right in C#. In an expression with three method calls, such as `A()+B()*C()`, first `A()` is evaluated, then `B()`, then `C()`; then the multiplication operator determines the product; and finally the addition operator determines the sum. Just because `C()` is involved in a multiplication and `A()` is involved in a lower-precedence addition, that does not imply that method invocation `C()` happens before method invocation `A()`.

Language Contrast: C++: Evaluation Order of Operands

In contrast to the rule mentioned here, the C++ specification allows an implementation broad latitude to decide the evaluation order of operands. When given an expression such as `A()+B()*C()`, a C++ compiler can choose to evaluate the function calls in any order, as long as the product is one of the summands. For example, a legal compiler could evaluate `B()`, then `A()`, then `C()`; then the product; and finally the sum.

Using the Addition Operator with Strings

Operators can also work with non-numeric operands. For example, it is possible to use the addition operator to concatenate two or more strings, as shown in Listing 4.4 with Output 4.3.

Listing 4.4: Using Binary Operators with Non-numeric Types

```
public class FortyTwo
{
    public static void Main()
    {
        short windSpeed = 42;
        Console.WriteLine(
            $"The original Tacoma Bridge in Washington" +
            $"{Environment.NewLine}was "
            + "brought down by a "
            + windSpeed + " mile/hour wind.");
    }
}
```

Output 4.3

```
The original Tacoma Bridge in Washington
was brought down by a 42 mile/hour wind.
```

Because sentence structure varies among languages in different cultures, developers should be careful not to use the addition operator with strings that possibly will require localization. Similarly, although we can embed expressions within a string using string interpolation, localization to other languages still requires moving the string to a resource file, neutralizing the string interpolation. For this reason, you should use the addition operator sparingly, favoring composite formatting when localization is a possibility.

Guidelines

DO favor composite formatting over use of the addition operator for concatenating strings when localization is a possibility.

Using Characters in Arithmetic Operations

When introducing the `char` type in Chapter 2, we mentioned that even though it stores characters and not numbers, the `char` type is an **integral** type (*integral* means it is based on an integer). It can participate in arithmetic operations with other integer types. However, interpretation of the value of the `char` type is not based on the character stored within it but rather on its underlying value. The digit `3`, for example, is represented by the Unicode value `0x33` (hexadecimal), which in base 10 is `51`. The digit `4` is represented by the Unicode value `0x34`, or `52` in base 10. Adding `3` and `4` in Listing 4.5 results in a hexadecimal value of `0x67`, or `103` in base 10, which is the Unicode value for the letter g, as shown in Output 4.4.

Listing 4.5: Using the Plus Operator with the `char` Data Type

```
int n = '3' + '4';
char c = (char)n;
Console.WriteLine(c);  // Writes out g
```

Output 4.4

```
g
```

You can use this trait of character types to determine how far two characters are from each other. For example, the letter `f` is three characters away from the letter `c`. You can determine this value by subtracting the letter `c` from the letter `f`, as Listing 4.6 with Output 4.5 demonstrates.

Listing 4.6: Determining the Character Difference between Two Characters

```
int distance = 'f' - 'c';
Console.WriteLine(distance);
```

Output 4.5

```
3
```

Special Floating-Point Characteristics

The binary floating-point types, `float` and `double`, have some special characteristics, such as the way they manage precision. This section looks at some specific examples, as well as some unique floating-point type characteristics.

A `float`, with seven decimal digits of precision, can hold the value 1,234,567 and the value 0.1234567. However, if you add these two `floats` together, the result will be rounded to 1,234,567, because the exact result requires more precision than the seven significant digits that a `float` can hold. The error introduced by rounding off to seven digits can become large compared to the value computed, especially with repeated calculations. (See also "Advanced Topic: Unexpected Inequality with Floating-Point Types" later in this section.)

Internally, the binary floating-point types store a binary fraction, not a decimal fraction. Consequently, "representation error" inaccuracies can occur with a simple assignment, such as `double number = 140.6F`. The exact value of 140.6 is the fraction 703/5, but the denominator of that fraction is not a power of 2, so a binary floating-point number cannot represent it exactly. Instead, the value represented is the closest fraction with a power of 2 in the denominator that fits into the 32 bits of a `float`.

Since the `double` can hold a more accurate value than the `float` can store, the C# compiler actually evaluates this expression to `double number = 140.600006103516` because `140.600006103516` is the closest binary fraction to 140.6 as a `float`. This fraction is slightly larger than 140.6 when represented as a `double`.

Guidelines

AVOID binary floating-point types when exact decimal arithmetic is required; use the `decimal` floating-point type instead.

ADVANCED TOPIC

Unexpected Inequality with Floating-Point Types

Because floating-point numbers can be unexpectedly rounded off to non-decimal fractions, comparing floating-point values for equality can be quite confusing. Consider Listing 4.7 with Output 4.6.

Listing 4.7: Unexpected Inequality Due to Floating-Point Inaccuracies

```
decimal decimalNumber = 4.2M;
double doubleNumber1 = 0.1F * 42F;
double doubleNumber2 = 0.1D * 42D;
float floatNumber = 0.1F * 42F;

// 1. Displays: 4.2 != 4.2000002861023
Console.WriteLine(
    $"{decimalNumber} != {(decimal)doubleNumber1}");

// 2. Displays: 4.2 != 4.200000286102295
Console.WriteLine(
    $"{(double)decimalNumber} != {doubleNumber1}");

// 3. Displays: (float)4.2M != 4.2000003F
Console.WriteLine(
    $"(float){(float)decimalNumber}M != {floatNumber}F");

// 4. Displays: 4.200000286102295 != 4.2
Console.WriteLine(
    $"{doubleNumber1} != {doubleNumber2}");

// 5. Displays: 4.2000003F != 4.2D
Console.WriteLine(
    $"{floatNumber}F != {doubleNumber2}D");

// 6. Displays: 4.199999809265137 != 4.2
Console.WriteLine(
    $"{(double)4.2F} != {4.2D}");

// 7. Displays: 4.2F != 4.2D
Console.WriteLine(
    $"{4.2F}F != {4.2D}D");
```

OUTPUT 4.6

```
4.2 != 4.20000006258488
4.2 != 4.20000006258488
(float)4.2M != 4.2F
4.20000006258488 != 4.20000028610229
4.20000006258488 != 4.2
4.2F != 4.2D
4.19999980926514 != 4.2
4.2F != 4.2D
```

The `Assert()` methods alert the developer whenever arguments evaluate to `false`. However, of all the `Assert()` calls in this code listing, only half have arguments that evaluate to `true`. Despite the apparent equality of the values in the code listing, they are not actually equivalent due to the inaccuracies associated with `float` values.

Guidelines

AVOID using equality conditionals with binary floating-point types. Either subtract the two values and see if their difference is less than a tolerance or use the `decimal` type.

You should be aware of some additional unique floating-point characteristics as well. For instance, you would expect that dividing an integer by zero would result in an error—and it does with data types such as `int` and `decimal`. The `float` and `double` types, however, allow for certain special values. Consider Listing 4.8, and its resultant output, Output 4.7.

LISTING 4.8: Dividing a Float by Zero, Displaying NaN

```
float n = 0f;
// Displays: NaN
Console.WriteLine(n / 0);
```

OUTPUT 4.7

```
NaN
```

In mathematics, certain mathematical operations are undefined, including dividing zero by itself. In C#, the result of dividing the `float` zero by zero results in a special **Not a Number** (NaN) value; all attempts to print the output of such a number will result in `NaN`. Similarly, taking the square root of a negative number with `System.Math.Sqrt(-1)` will result in `NaN`.

A floating-point number could overflow its bounds as well. For example, the upper bound of the `float` type is approximately 3.4×10^{38}. Should the number overflow that bound, the result would be stored as **positive infinity**, and the output of printing the number would be `Infinity`. Similarly, the lower bound of a `float` type is -3.4×10^{38}, and computing a value below that bound would result in **negative infinity**, which would be represented by the string `-Infinity`. Listing 4.9 produces negative and positive infinity, respectively, and Output 4.8 shows the results.

Listing 4.9: Overflowing the Bounds of a `float`

```
// Displays: -Infinity
Console.WriteLine(-1f / 0);
// Displays: Infinity
Console.WriteLine(3.402823E+38f * 2f);
```

Output 4.8

```
-Infinity
Infinity
```

Further examination of the floating-point number reveals that it can contain a value very close to zero without actually containing zero. If the value exceeds the lower threshold for the `float` or `double` type, the value of the number can be represented as **negative zero** or **positive zero**, depending on whether the number is negative or positive, and is represented in output as `-0` or `0`.

Compound Mathematical Assignment Operators (+=, -=, *=, /=, %=)

Chapter 1 discussed the simple assignment operator, which places the value of the right-hand side of the operator into the variable on the left-hand side. **Compound mathematical assignment operators** combine common binary operator calculations with the assignment operator. For example, consider Listing 4.10.

LISTING 4.10: Common Increment Calculation

```
int x = 123;
x = x + 2;
```

In this assignment, first you calculate the value of `x + 2`, and then you assign the calculated value back to `x`. Since this type of operation is performed relatively frequently, an assignment operator exists to handle both the calculation and the assignment with one operator. The `+=` operator increments the variable on the left-hand side of the operator with the value on the right-hand side of the operator, as shown in Listing 4.11.

LISTING 4.11: Using the `+=` Operator

```
int x = 123;
x += 2;
```

This code, therefore, is equivalent to Listing 4.10.

Numerous other compound assignment operators exist to provide similar functionality. You can also use the assignment operator with subtraction, multiplication, division, and remainder operators (as demonstrated in Listing 4.12).

LISTING 4.12: Other Assignment Operator Examples

```
x -= 2;
x /= 2;
x *= 2;
x %- 2;
```

Increment and Decrement Operators (++, --)

C# includes special unary operators for incrementing and decrementing counters. The **increment operator**, `++`, increments a variable by one each time it is used. In other words, all of the code lines shown in Listing 4.13 are equivalent.

LISTING 4.13: Increment Operator

```
spaceCount = spaceCount + 1;
spaceCount += 1;
spaceCount++;
```

Similarly, you can decrement a variable by 1 using the **decrement operator**, `--`. Therefore, all the code lines shown in Listing 4.14 are also equivalent.

LISTING 4.14: Decrement Operator

```
lines = lines - 1;
lines -= 1;
lines--;
```

BEGINNER TOPIC

A Decrement Example in a Loop

The increment and decrement operators are especially prevalent in loops, such as the `while` loop described later in the chapter. For example, Listing 4.15 with Output 4.9 uses the decrement operator to iterate backward through each letter in the alphabet.

LISTING 4.15: Displaying Each Character's Unicode Value in Descending Order

```
char current;
int unicodeValue;

// Set the initial value of current
current = 'z';

do
{
    // Retrieve the Unicode value of current
```

```
        unicodeValue = current;
        Console.Write($"{current}={unicodeValue}\t");

        // Proceed to the previous letter in the alphabet
        current--;
    }
    while(current >= 'a');
```

Output 4.9

```
z=122   y=121   x=120   w=119   v=118   u=117   t=116   s=115   r=114
q=113   p=112   o=111   n=110   m=109   l=108   k=107   j=106   i=105
h=104   g=103   f=102   e=101   d=100   c=99    b=98    a=97
```

Listing 4.15 uses the increment and decrement operators to control how many times a particular operation is performed. In this example, notice that the decrement operator acts on a character (`char`) data type. You can use increment and decrement operators on various data types given some meaning is programmed to the concept of the "next" or "previous" value for that data type. See the section "Operator Overloading" (https://essentialcsharp.com/operator-overloading) in Chapter 10.

We saw that the assignment operator first computes the value and then performs the assignment. The result of the assignment operator is the value that was assigned. The increment and decrement operators are similar: They compute the value, perform the assignment, and return a value. It is therefore possible to use the assignment operator with the increment or decrement operator, though doing so carelessly can be extremely confusing. See Listing 4.16 and Output 4.10 for an example.

Listing 4.16: Using the Post-increment Operator

```
int count = 123;
int result;
result = count++;
Console.WriteLine(
    $"result = {result} and count = {count}");
```

You might be surprised that `result` was assigned the value that was `count` *before* `count` was incremented. Where you place the increment or decrement

OUTPUT 4.10

```
result = 123 and count = 124
```

operator determines whether the assigned value should be the value of the operand before or after the calculation. If you want the value of `result` to be the value assigned to `count`, you need to place the operator before the variable being incremented, as shown in Listing 4.17 with Output 4.11.

LISTING 4.17: Using the Pre-increment Operator

```
int count = 123;
int result;
result = ++count;
Console.WriteLine(
    $"result = {result} and count = {count}");
```

OUTPUT 4.11

```
result = 124 and count = 124
```

In this example, the increment operator appears before the operand, so the result of the expression is the value assigned to the variable after the increment. If `count` is `123`, `++count` assigns `124` to `count` and produces the result `124`. By contrast, the postfix increment operator `count++` assigns `124` to `count` and produces the value that `count` held before the increment: `123`. Regardless of whether the operator is postfix or prefix, the variable `count` is incremented before the value is produced; the only difference is which value is produced. The difference between prefix and postfix behavior is illustrated in Listing 4.18. The resultant output is shown in Output 4.12.

LISTING 4.18: Comparing the Prefix and Postfix Increment Operators

```
public class IncrementExample
{
    public static void Main()
    {
        int x = 123;
        // Displays 123, 124, 125
        Console.WriteLine($"{x++}, {x++}, {x}");
        // x now contains the value 125
```

```
        // Displays 126, 127, 127
        Console.WriteLine($"{++x}, {++x}, {x}");
        // x now contains the value 127
    }
}
```

OUTPUT 4.12

```
123, 124, 125
126, 127, 127
```

As Listing 4.18 demonstrates, where the increment and decrement operators appear relative to the operand can affect the result produced by the expression. The result of the prefix operators is the value that the variable had before incrementing or decrementing. The result of the postfix operators is the value that the variable had after incrementing or decrementing. Use caution when embedding these operators in the middle of a statement. When in doubt as to what will happen, use these operators independently, placing them within their own statements. This way, the code is also more readable and there is no mistaking the intention.

Language Contrast: C++—Implementation-Defined Behavior

Earlier we discussed how the operands in an expression can be evaluated in any order in C++, whereas they are always evaluated from left to right in C#. Similarly, in C++ an implementation may legally perform the side effects of increments and decrements in any order. For example, in C++ a call of the form `M(x++, x++)`, where `x` begins as `1`, can legally call either `M(1,2)` or `M(2,1)` at the whim of the compiler. In contrast, C# always calls `M(1,2)` because C# makes two guarantees: (1) The arguments to a call are always computed from left to right, and (2) the assignment of the incremented value to the variable always happens before the value of the expression is used. C++ makes neither guarantee.

Guidelines

AVOID confusing usage of the increment and decrement operators.

DO be cautious when porting code between C, C++, and C# that uses increment and decrement operators; C and C++ implementations need not follow the same rules as C#.

ADVANCED TOPIC

Thread-Safe Incrementing and Decrementing

Despite the brevity of the increment and decrement operators, these operators are not atomic. A thread context switch can occur during the execution of the operator and can cause a race condition. You could use a `lock` statement to prevent the race condition. However, for simple increments and decrements, a less expensive alternative is to use the thread-safe `Increment()` and `Decrement()` methods from the `System.Threading.Interlocked` class. These methods rely on processor functions for performing fast, thread-safe increments and decrements. See Chapter 19 for more details.

Constant Expressions and Constant Locals

Chapter 3 discussed literal values, or values embedded directly into the code. It is possible to combine multiple literal values in a **constant expression** using operators. By definition, a constant expression is one that the C# compiler can evaluate at compile time (instead of evaluating it when the program runs) because it is composed entirely of constant operands. Constant expressions can then be used to initialize constant locals, which allow you to give a name to a constant value (similar to the way local variables allow you to give a name to a storage location). For example, the computation of the number of seconds in a day can be a constant expression that is then used in other expressions by name.

The `const` keyword in Listing 4.19 declares two constant locals: `secondsPerDay` and `secondsPerWeek`. Since a constant local is, by definition, the opposite of a **variable**—*constant* means "not able to vary"—any attempt to modify the value later in the code would result in a compile-time error.

Listing 4.19: Declaring a Constant

```
const int secondsPerDay = 60 * 60 * 24;
const int secondsPerWeek = secondsPerDay * 7;
```

> ### Guidelines
>
> **DO NOT** use a constant for any value that can possibly change over time. The value of pi and the number of protons in an atom of gold are constants; the price of gold, the name of your company, and the version number of your program can change.

In Listing 4.19, `60 * 60 * 34` and `secondsPerDay * 7` are both constant expressions. Note that the expression assigned to `secondsPerWeek` is a constant expression because all the operands in the expression are also constants.

C# 10 added support for constant interpolated strings whereby you can define a constant string with interpolation if it is comprised solely of other constant strings and, as such, it can be evaluated at compile time (see Listing 4.20).

Listing 4.20: Using Binary Operators with Non-numeric Types

```
const string windSpeed = "42";
const string announcement = $"""
        The original Tacoma Bridge in Washington
        was brought down by a { windSpeed } mile/hour wind.
        """;
Console.WriteLine(announcement);
```

Even though `announcement` in Listing 4.20 is an interpolated string, the values within the code portions of the string are also constants, enabling the compiler to evaluate them at compile time rather than waiting until execution time. Also note, however, that `windspeed` is a string, not an integer. Constant string interpolation works when formed solely of other constant strings, not of other data types even if those types are constant. The restriction is to allow conversion to a string to account for culture variation at execution time. For example, converting the golden ratio to a string could be 1.6180339887 or 1,6180339887 depending on the culture.

Introducing Flow Control

Later in this chapter is a code listing (Listing 4.46) that shows a simple way to view a number in its binary form. Even such a simple program, however, cannot be written without using control flow statements. Such statements control the execution path of the program. This section discusses how to change the order of statement execution based on conditional checks. Later, you will learn how to execute statement groups repeatedly through loop constructs.

A summary of the control flow statements appears in Table 4.1. Note that the General Syntax Structure column indicates common statement use, not the complete lexical structure. An `embedded-statement` in Table 4.1 may be any statement other than a labeled statement or a declaration but is frequently multiple statements combined into a code block as defined later in this section.

TABLE 4.1: Control Flow Statements

Statement	General Syntax Structure	Example

`if` statement	`if(`*`boolean-expression`*`)`
	`embedded-statement`
		`if (input == "quit")`
		`{`
		`Console.WriteLine(`
		`"Game end");`
		`return;`
		`}`

	`if(`*`boolean-expression`*`)`
	`embedded-statement`
	`else`
	`embedded-statement`
		`if (input == "quit")`
		`{`
		`Console.WriteLine(`
		`"Game end");`
		`return;`
		`}`
		`else`
		`GetNextMove();`

`while` statement	`while(`*`boolean-expression`*`)`
	`embedded-statement`
		`while(`*`count < total`*`)`
		`{`
		`Console.WriteLine(`
		`$"count = {count}");`
		`count++;`
		`}`

`do while` statement	`do`
	`embedded-statement`
	`while(`*`boolean-expression`*`);`
		`do`
		`{`
		`Console.WriteLine(`
		`"Enter name:");`
		`input =`
		`Console.ReadLine();`
		`}`
		`while(`*`input != "exit"`*`);`

TABLE 4.1: Control Flow Statements (continued)

Statement	General Syntax Structure	Example

for statement	for(for-initializer;
	boolean-expression;
	for-iterator)
	embedded-statement
		for (int count = 1;
		count <= 10;
		count++)
		{
		Console.WriteLine(
		$"count = {count}");
		}

foreach statement	foreach(type
	identifier in
	expression)
	embedded-statement
		foreach (char letter in email)
		{
		if(!insideDomain)
		{
		if (letter == '@')
		{
		insideDomain = true;
		}
		continue;
		}
		Console.Write(
		letter);
		}

continue statement	continue;	

switch statement	switch(governing-
	type-expression)
	{
	...
	case const-
	expression:
	statement-list
	jump-statement
	default:
	statement-list
	jump-statement
	}
		switch(input)
		{
		case "exit":
		case "quit":
		Console.WriteLine(
		"Exiting app....");
		break;
		case "restart":
		Reset();
		goto case "start";
		case "start":
		GetMove();
		break;
		default:
		Console.WriteLine(
		input);
		break;
		}

break statement	break;	
goto statement	goto identifier;	
	goto case const- expression;	

TABLE 4.1: Control Flow Statements (continued)

Statement	General Syntax Structure	Example
	`goto default;`	

Each C# control flow statement in Table 4.1 appears in the tic-tac-toe[2] program and is available in Chapter 4's source code in the file TicTacToe.cs (https://github.com/IntelliTect/EssentialCSharp/blob/v9.0/src/Chapter04/TicTacToe.cs). The program displays the tic-tac-toe board, prompts each player, and updates with each move.

The rest of this chapter looks at each statement in more detail. After covering the `if` statement, it introduces code blocks, scope, Boolean expressions, and bitwise operators before continuing with the remaining control flow statements. Readers who find Table 4.1 familiar because of C#'s similarities to other languages can jump ahead to the section titled "C# Preprocessor Directives" or skip to the Summary at the end of the chapter.

`if` Statement

The `if` statement is one of the most common statements in C#. It evaluates a **Boolean expression** (an expression that results in either `true` or `false`) called the **condition**. If the condition is `true`, the **consequence statement** executes. An `if` statement may optionally have an `else` clause that contains an **alternative statement** to be executed if the condition is `false`. The general form is as follows:

```
if (condition)
  consequence-statement
else
  alternative-statement
```

In Listing 4.21, if the user enters `1`, the program displays `Play against computer selected.` Otherwise, it displays `Play against another player.`

2. Known as noughts and crosses to readers outside the United States.

LISTING 4.21: `if/else` **Statement Example**

```
string input;

// Prompt the user to select a 1- or 2- player game
Console.Write($"""
        1 - Play against the computer
        2 - Play against another player.
        Choose:
        """
);
input = Console.ReadLine();

if (input == "1")
    // The user selected to play the computer
    Console.WriteLine(
        "Play against computer selected.");
else
    // Default to 2 players (even if user didn't enter 2)
    Console.WriteLine(
        "Play against another player.");
```

Nested `if`

Sometimes code requires multiple `if` statements. The code in Listing 4.22 first determines whether the user has chosen to exit by entering a number less than or equal to `0`; if the user has not chosen to exit, it checks whether the user knows the maximum number of turns in tic-tac-toe (see accompanying Output 4.13).

LISTING 4.22: Nested `if` **Statements**

```
int input;    // Declare a variable to store the input

Console.Write(
    "What is the maximum number " +
    "of turns in tic-tac-toe?" +
    " (Enter 0 to exit.): ");

// int.Parse() converts the ReadLine()
// return to an int data type
input = int.Parse(Console.ReadLine());

// Condition 1.
if (input <= 0) // line 16
```

```
        // Input is less than or equal to 0
        Console.WriteLine("Exiting...");
    else
        // Condition 2.
        if (input < 9) // line 20
            // Input is less than 9
            Console.WriteLine(
                $"Tic-tac-toe has more than {input}" +
                " maximum turns.");
        else
            // Condition 3.
            if (input > 9) // line 26
                // Input is greater than 9
                Console.WriteLine(
                    $"Tic-tac-toe has fewer than {input}" +
                    " maximum turns.");
            // Condition 4.
            else
                // Input equals 9
                Console.WriteLine(  // line 33
                    "Correct, tic-tac-toe " +
                    "has a maximum of 9 turns.");
```

OUTPUT 4.13

```
What is the maximum number of turns in tic-tac-toe? (Enter 0 to exit.):
 9
Correct, tic-tac-toe has a maximum of 9 turns.
```

Assume the user enters 9 when prompted at line 14. Here is the execution path:

1. *Condition 1:* Check if input is less than 0. Since it is not, jump to Condition 2.
2. *Condition 2:* Check if input is less than 9. Since it is not, jump to Condition 3.
3. *Condition 3:* Check if input is greater than 9. Since it is not, jump to Condition 4.
4. *Condition 4:* Display that the answer was correct.

Listing 4.22 contains nested `if` statements. To clarify the nesting, the lines are indented. However, as you learned in Chapter 1, whitespace does not affect the execution path. If this code was written without the indenting and without the newlines, the execution would be the same. The code that appears in the nested `if` statement in Listing 4.23 is equivalent to Listing 4.22.

LISTING 4.23: `if`/`else` **Formatted Sequentially**

```
if (input < 0)
    Console.WriteLine("Exiting...");
else if(input < 9)
    Console.WriteLine(
        $"Tic-tac-toe has more than {input}" +
        " maximum turns.");
else if (input > 9)
    Console.WriteLine(
        $"Tic-tac-toe has less than {input}" +
        " maximum turns.");
else
    Console.WriteLine(
        "Correct, tic-tac-toe has a maximum" +
        " of 9 turns.");
```

Although the latter format is more common, in each situation you should use the format that results in the clearest code.

Both of the `if` statement listings omit the braces. However, as discussed next, this is not in accordance with the guidelines, which advocate the use of code blocks except, perhaps, in the simplest of single-line scenarios.

Code Blocks ({})

In the previous `if` statement examples, only one statement follows `if` and `else`: a single `System.Console.WriteLine()`, similar to Listing 4.24.

LISTING 4.24: `if` **Statement with No Code Block**

```
if (input < 9)
    Console.WriteLine("Exiting");
```

With curly braces, however, we can combine statements into a single statement called a **block statement** or **code block**, allowing the grouping of multiple statements into a single statement that is the consequence. Take, for example, the highlighted code block in the radius calculation in Listing 4.25 with Output 4.14.

Listing 4.25: `if` Statement Followed by a Code Block

```
double radius;  // Declare a variable to store the radius
double area;    // Declare a variable to store the area

Console.Write("Enter the radius of the circle: ");

// double.Parse converts the ReadLine()
// return to a double
string temp = Console.ReadLine();
radius = double.Parse(temp);
if(radius >= 0)
{
    // Calculate the area of the circle
    area = Math.PI * radius * radius;
    Console.WriteLine(
        $"The area of the circle is: {area:0.00}");
}
else
{
    Console.WriteLine(
        $"{radius} is not a valid radius.");
}
```

Output 4.14

```
Enter the radius of the circle: 3
The area of the circle is: 28.27
```

In this example, the `if` statement checks whether the `radius` is positive. If so, the area of the circle is calculated and displayed; otherwise, an invalid radius message is displayed.

Notice that in this example, two statements follow the first `if`. However, these two statements appear within curly braces. The curly braces combine the statements into a code block, which is itself a single statement.

If you omit the curly braces that create a code block in Listing 4.25, only the statement immediately following the Boolean expression executes conditionally. Subsequent statements execute regardless of the `if` statement's Boolean expression. The invalid code is shown in Listing 4.26.

LISTING 4.26: Relying on Indentation, Resulting in Invalid Code

```
if (radius >= 0)
    area = Math.PI * radius * radius;
    Console.WriteLine(
        $"The area of the circle is: {area:0.00}");
```

In C#, indentation is used solely to enhance the code readability. The compiler ignores it, so Listing 4.26 is semantically equivalent to Listing 4.27.

LISTING 4.27: `if` Statement with Curly Braces

```
if (radius >= 0)
{
    area = Math.PI * radius * radius;
}
Console.WriteLine(
    $"The area of the circle is: {area:0.00}");
```

Programmers should take great care to avoid subtle bugs such as this, perhaps even going so far as to always include a code block after a control flow statement, even if there is only one statement. A widely accepted coding guideline is to avoid omitting braces, except possibly for the simplest of single-line `if` statements.

Although unusual, it is possible to have a code block that is not lexically a direct part of a control flow statement. In other words, placing curly braces on their own (e.g., without a conditional or loop) is legal syntax.

In Listing 4.26 and Listing 4.27, the value of pi was represented by the `PI` constant in the `System.Math` class. Instead of hardcoding values for π and e (the base of natural logarithms), code should use `System.Math.PI` and `System.Math.E`.

Guidelines

AVOID omitting braces, except for the simplest of single-line `if` statements.

Code Blocks, Scopes, and Declaration Spaces

Code blocks are often referred to as *scopes*, but the two terms are not exactly interchangeable. The **scope** of a named thing is the region of source code in which it is legal to refer to the thing by its unqualified name. The scope of a local variable, for example, is exactly the text of the code block that encloses it, which explains why it is common to refer to code blocks as scopes.

Scopes are often confused with declaration spaces. A **declaration space** is a logical container of named things in which two things may not have the same name. A code block defines not only a scope but also a local variable declaration space. It is illegal for two local variable declarations with the same name to appear in the same declaration space. Similarly, it is not possible to declare two methods with the signature of `Main()` within the same class. (This rule is relaxed somewhat for methods: Two methods may have the same name in a declaration space provided that they have different signatures. The signature of a method includes its name and the number and types of its parameters.) Within a block, a local variable can be mentioned by name and must be the unique thing that is declared with that name in the block. Outside the declaring block, there is no way to refer to a local variable by its name; the local variable is said to be "out of scope" outside the block.

In summary, C# uses a scope to determine what thing a name refers to; a declaration space determines when two things declared with the same name conflict with each other. In Listing 4.28 (with Output 4.15), declaring the local variable `message` inside the block statement embedded in the `if` statement restricts its scope to the block statement only; the local variable is out of scope when its name is used later in the method. To avoid an error, you must declare the variable outside the block.

LISTING 4.28: Variables Inaccessible outside Their Scope

```
string playerCount;
Console.Write(
    "Enter the number of players (1 or 2):");
playerCount = Console.ReadLine();
if (playerCount != "1" && playerCount != "2")
{
    string message =
        "You entered an invalid number of players.";
}
else
{
    // ...
}
// ERROR: message is not in scope:
Console.WriteLine(message);
```

OUTPUT 4.15

```
...
...\Program.cs(18,26): error CS0103: The name 'message' does not exist
in the current context
```

The declaration space in which a local variable's name must be unique encompasses all the child code blocks textually enclosed within the block that originally declared the local. The C# compiler prevents the name of a local variable declared immediately within a method code block (or as a parameter) from being reused within a child code block. In Listing 4.28, because `args` and `playerCount` are declared within the method code block, they cannot be declared again anywhere within the method.

The name `message` refers to this local variable throughout the scope of the local variable—that is, the block immediately enclosing the declaration. Similarly, `playerCount` refers to the same variable throughout the block containing the declaration, including within both of the child blocks that are the consequence and the alternative of the `if` statement.

Language Contrast: C++—Local Variable Scope

In C++, a local variable declared in a block is in scope from the point of the declaration statement through the end of the block. Thus, an attempt to refer to the local variable before its declaration will fail to find the local variable because that variable is not in scope. If there is another thing with that name "in scope," the C++ language will resolve the name to that thing, which might not be what you intended. In C#, the rule is subtly different: A local variable is in scope throughout the entire block in which it is declared, but it is illegal to refer to the local variable before its declaration. That is, an attempt to find the local variable will succeed, and the usage will then be treated as an error. This is just one of C#'s many rules intended to prevent errors common in C++ programs.

Boolean Expressions

The parenthesized condition of the `if` statement is a **Boolean expression**. In Listing 4.29, the condition is highlighted.

Listing 4.29: Boolean Expression

```
if (input < 9)
{
    // Input is less than 9
    Console.WriteLine(
        $"Tic-tac-toe has more than {input}" +
         " maximum turns.");
}
// ...
```

Boolean expressions appear within many control flow statements. Their key characteristic is that they always evaluate to `true` or `false`. For `input < 9` to be allowed as a Boolean expression, it must result in a `bool`. The compiler disallows `x = 42`, for example, because this expression assigns `x` and results in the value that was assigned instead of checking whether the value of the variable is `42`.

Language Contrast: C++—Mistakenly Using = in Place of ==

C# eliminates a coding error commonly found in C and C++. In C++, Listing 4.30 is allowed.

LISTING 4.30: C++, but Not C#, Allows Assignment as a Condition

```
if (input = 9) // Allowed in C++, not in C#
  System.Console.WriteLine(
    "Correct, tic-tac-toe has a maximum of 9 turns.");
```

Although at first glance this code appears to check whether `input` equals `9`, Chapter 1 showed that `=` represents the assignment operator, not a check for equality. The return from the assignment operator is the value assigned to the variable—in this case, `9`. However, `9` is an `int`, so it does not qualify as a Boolean expression and is not allowed by the C# compiler. The C and C++ languages treat integers that are nonzero as `true` and integers that are zero as `false`. C#, by contrast, requires that the condition actually be of a Boolean type; integers are not allowed.

Relational and Equality Operators

Relational and **equality operators** determine whether a value is greater than, less than, or equal to another value. Table 4.2 lists all the relational and equality operators. All are binary operators.

TABLE 4.2: Relational and Equality Operators

Operator	Description	Example
<	Less than	`input < 9;`
>	Greater than	`input > 9;`
<=	Less than or equal to	`input <= 9;`
>=	Greater than or equal to	`input >= 9;`
==	Equality operator	`input == 9;`

Table 4.2: Relational and Equality Operators (continued)

Operator	Description	Example
`!=`	Inequality operator	`input != 9;`

The C# syntax for equality uses `==`, just as many other programming languages do. For example, to determine whether `input` equals 9, you use `input == 9`. The equality operator uses two equal signs to distinguish it from the assignment operator, `=`. The exclamation point signifies NOT in C#, so to test for inequality you use the inequality operator, `!=`.

Relational and equality operators always produce a `bool` value, as shown in Listing 4.31.

Listing 4.31: Assigning the Result of a Relational Operator to a `bool` Variable

```
bool result = 70 > 7;
```

In the full tic-tac-toe program listing, you use the equality operator to determine whether a user has quit. The Boolean expression in Listing 4.32 includes an OR (`||`) logical operator, which the next section discusses in detail.

Listing 4.32: Using the Equality Operator in a Boolean Expression

```
if (input.Length == 0 || input == "quit")
{
    Console.WriteLine($"Player {currentPlayer} quit!!");
}
```

Logical Boolean Operators

The **logical operators** have Boolean operands and produce a Boolean result. Logical operators allow you to combine multiple Boolean expressions to form more complex Boolean expressions. The logical operators are `|`, `||`, `&`, `&&`, and `^`, corresponding to OR, AND, and exclusive OR. The `|` and `&` versions of OR and AND are rarely used for Boolean logic, for reasons which we discuss in this section.

OR Operator (||)

In Listing 4.32, if the user enters `quit` or presses the Enter key without typing in a value, it is assumed that they want to exit the program. To enable two ways for the user to resign, you can use the logical OR operator, `||`. The `||` operator evaluates Boolean expressions and results in a `true` value if *either* operand is `true` (see Listing 4.33).

LISTING 4.33: Using the OR Operator

```
if ((hourOfTheDay > 23) || (hourOfTheDay < 0))
    Console.WriteLine("The time you entered is invalid.");
```

It is not necessary to evaluate both sides of an OR expression, because if one operand is `true`, the result is known to be `true` regardless of the value of the other operand. Like all operators in C#, the left operand is evaluated before the right one, so if the left portion of the expression evaluates to `true`, the right portion is ignored. In the example in Listing 4.33, if `hourOfTheDay` has the value `33`, then `(hourOfTheDay > 23)` evaluates to `true` and the OR operator ignores the second half of the expression, **short-circuiting** it. Short-circuiting an expression also occurs with the Boolean AND operator. (Note that the parentheses are not necessary here; the logical operators are of lower precedence than the relational operators. However, it is clearer to the novice reader when the subexpressions are parenthesized for clarity.)

AND Operator (&&)

The Boolean AND operator, `&&`, evaluates to `true` only if both operands evaluate to `true`. If either operand is `false`, the result will be `false`. Listing 4.34 writes a message if the given variable is both greater than 10 and less than 24.[3] Similarly to the OR operator, the AND operator will not always evaluate the right side of the expression. If the left operand is determined to be `false`, the overall result will be `false` regardless of the value of the right operand, so the runtime skips evaluating the right operand.

3. The typical hours that programmers work each day.

LISTING 4.34: Using the AND Operator

```
if ((10 < hourOfTheDay) && (hourOfTheDay < 24))
    Console.WriteLine(
        "Hi-Ho, Hi-Ho, it's off to work we go.");
```

Exclusive OR Operator (^)

The caret symbol, ^, is the exclusive OR (XOR) operator. When applied to two Boolean operands, the XOR operator returns `true` only if exactly one of the operands is true, as shown in Table 4.3.

TABLE 4.3: Conditional Values for the XOR Operator

Left Operand	Right Operand	Result
True	True	False
True	False	True
False	True	True
False	False	False

Unlike the Boolean AND and Boolean OR operators, the Boolean XOR operator does not short-circuit: It always checks both operands, because the result cannot be determined unless the values of both operands are known. Note that the XOR operator is exactly the same as the Boolean inequality operator.

Logical Negation Operator (`!`)

The **logical negation operator**, or **NOT operator**, `!`, inverts a `bool` value. This operator is a unary operator, meaning it requires only one operand. Listing 4.35 demonstrates how it works, and Output 4.16 shows the result.

LISTING 4.35: Using the Logical Negation Operator

```
bool valid = false;
bool result = !valid;
```

```
// Displays "result = True"
Console.WriteLine($"result = { result }");
```

OUTPUT 4.16

```
result = True
```

At the beginning of Listing 4.35, `valid` is set to `false`. You then use the negation operator on `valid` and assign the value to `result`.

Conditional Operator (?:)

As an alternative to using an `if-else` statement to select one of two values, you can use the **conditional operator**. The conditional operator uses both a question mark and a colon; the general format is as follows:

```
condition ? consequent : alternative
```

The conditional operator is a ternary operator because it has three operands: `condition`, `consequent`, and `alternative`. (As it is the only ternary operator in C#, it is often called the *ternary operator*, but it is clearer to refer to it by its name than by the number of operands it takes.) Like the logical operators, the conditional operator uses a form of short-circuiting. If the condition operator evaluates to `true`, the conditional operator evaluates only `consequent`. If the conditional evaluates to `false`, it evaluates only `alternative`. The result of the operator is the evaluated expression.

Listing 4.36 illustrates the use of the conditional operator. The full listing of this program appears in of the source code.

LISTING 4.36: Conditional Operator

```
public class TicTacToe
{
    public static void Main()
    {
        // Initially set the currentPlayer to Player 1
        int currentPlayer = 1;

        // ...
```

```
            for(int turn = 1; turn <= 10; turn++)
            {
                // ...

                // Switch players
                currentPlayer = (currentPlayer == 2) ? 1 : 2;
            }
        }
    }
```

The program swaps the current player. To do so, it checks whether the current value is 2. This is the *conditional* portion of the conditional expression. If the result of the condition is `true`, the conditional operator results in the *consequent* value, 1. Otherwise, it results in the *alternative* value, 2. Unlike in an `if` statement, the result of the conditional operator must be assigned (or passed as a parameter); it cannot appear as an entire statement on its own.

Guidelines

CONSIDER using an `if-else` statement instead of an overly complicated conditional expression.

Begin 9.0

Prior to C# 9.0, the language required that the output (the consequent and alternative) expressions in a conditional operator be consistently typed and that the consistent type be determined without examination of the surrounding context of the expression, including the resulting type assigned. However, C# 9.0 added support for target-typed conditional expressions so that even if the consequent and alternative expressions are of different types (such as `string` and `int`) and neither is convertible to the other, the statement is still allowed if both types will implicitly cast to the targeted type. For example, even if you have `object result = condition ? "abc" : 123;`, the C# compiler will allow it because both the potential conditional output types will implicitly cast to `object`.

End 9.0

Programming with `null`

As described in Chapter 3, while `null` can be a useful value, it also comes with a few challenges—namely, the need to check a value isn't null before invoking the object's member or changing the value from `null` to something more appropriate to the circumstance.

Although you can check for `null` using the equality operators and even the relational equality operators, there are several other ways to do so, including C# 7.0's support for `is null` and C# 10.0's support for `is not null`. In addition, several operators are designed exclusively for working with the potential of a `null` value. These include the null-coalescing operator (and C# 8.0's null-coalescing assignment) and the null-conditional operator. There is even an operator to tell the compiler when you believe a value isn't `null` even if it isn't obvious to the compiler—the null-forgiving operator. Let's start by simply checking whether a value is `null` or not.

Checking for null and Not null

It turns out there are multiple ways to check for `null`, as shown in Table 4.4. For each listing, assume a declaration of `string? uriString` precedes it:

```
string? uriString = null;
```

Begin 8.0

TABLE 4.4: Checking for `null`

Description	Example

`is null` **Operator Pattern Matching**
The `is` operator provides multiple approaches to check for null. Starting with C# 7.0, you can check whether a value is null using the `is null` expression. This is a succinct and clear approach to checking if a value is null.
	`// 1.`
	`if (uriString is null)`
	`{`
	`Console.WriteLine(`
	`"Uri is null");`
	`}`

`is not null` **Operator Pattern Matching**
Similarly, in C# 9.0, `is not null` support was added. And, when checking for not null, this is the preferred approach.
	`// 2.`
	`if (uriString is not null)`
	`{`
	`Console.WriteLine(`
	`"Uri is not null");`
	`}`

TABLE 4.4: Checking for `null` (continued)

Description	Example

Equality/Inequality
Using the equality and inequality operators works with all versions of C#.
In addition, checking for `null` this way is readable.
The only disadvantage of this approach is that it is possible to override the equality/inequality operator, potentially introducing minor performance impacts.
	`// 3.`
	`if(uriString == null)`
	`{`
	`Console.WriteLine(`
	`"Uri is null");`
	`}`
	`if(uriString != null)`
	`{`
	`Console.WriteLine(`
	`$"Uri is: { uriString }");`
	`}`

`is object`
Since C# 1.0, `is object` checks whether the operand is null, although this syntax isn't as clear as `is not null`.
`is object` is preferable over the `is {}` expression described in the next row because it issues a warning when the operand is a non-nullable value type. What is the point in checking for null if the operand can't be null?
	`// 4.`
	`int number = 0;`
	`if( (uriString is object )`
	`    // Warning CS0183: The given`
	`    // expression is always not`
	`    // null.`
	`&& (number is object)`
	`)`
	`{`
	`Console.WriteLine(`
	`$"Uri is: { uriString }");`
	`}`

`is { }` **Operator Pattern Matching**
The property pattern matching expression, `<operand>` is { }, (which was added in C# 8.0) provides virtually the same functionality as `is object`. Besides being less readable, the only noticeable disadvantage is that `is {}` with a value type expression doesn't issue a warning, while `is object` does. And, since a value type cannot be null, the warning is preferable because there is no point in checking a non-nullable value for null. Therefore, favor using `is object` over `is { }`,
	`// 5.`
	`if (uriString is {})`
	`{`
	`Console.WriteLine(`
	`$"Uri is: { uriString }");`
	`}`

`ReferenceEquals()`
While `object.ReferenceEquals()` is a somewhat long syntax for such a simple operation, like equality/inequality it works with all versions of C# and has the advantage of not allowing overriding; thus, it always executes what the name states.
	`// 6.`
	`if(ReferenceEquals(`
	`uriString, null))`
	`{`
	`Console.WriteLine(`
	`"Uri is null");`
	`}`

Of course, having multiple ways to check whether a value is null raises the question as to which one to use. C# 7.0's enhanced `is null` and C# 9.0's `is not null` syntax are preferable if you are using a modern version of C#.

Obviously, if you are programming with C# 6.0 or earlier, the equality/inequality operators are the only option aside from using `is object` to check for not `null`. The latter has a slight advantage since it is not possible to change the definition of the `is object` expression and (albeit unlikely) introduce a minor performance hit. This renders `is {}` effectively obsolete. Using `ReferenceEquals()` is rare, but it does allow comparison of values that are of unknown data types, which is helpful when implementing a custom version of the equality operator (see "Operator Overloading" (https://essentialcsharp.com/operator-overloading) in Chapter 10).

Several of the rows in Table 4.4 leverage pattern matching, a concept covered in more detail in the "Pattern Matching" (https://essentialcsharp.com/pattern-matching) section of Chapter 7.

Null-Coalescing and Null-Coalescing Assignment Operators (??, ??=)

The **null-coalescing operator** is a concise way to express "If this value is `null`, then use this other value." It has the following form:

```
expression1 ?? expression2
```

The null-coalescing operator also uses a form of short-circuiting. If `expression1` is not `null`, its value is the result of the operation and the other expression is not evaluated. If `expression1` does evaluate to `null`, the value of `expression2` is the result of the operator. Unlike the conditional operator, the null-coalescing operator is a binary operator.

Listing 4.37 illustrates the use of the null-coalescing operator.

Listing 4.37: Null-Coalescing Operator

```
string? fullName = GetSaveFilePath();
// ...

// Null-coalescing operator
string fileName = GetFileName() ?? "config.json";
```

```
string directory = GetConfigurationDirectory() ??
    GetApplicationDirectory() ??
    Environment.CurrentDirectory;

// Null-coalescing assignment operator
fullName ??= $"{ directory }/{ fileName }";

// ...
```

In this listing, we use the null-coalescing operator to set `fileName` to `"config.json"` if `GetFileName()` is `null`. If `GetFileName()` is not `null`, `fileName` is simply assigned the value of `GetFileName()`.

The null-coalescing operator "chains" nicely. For example, an expression of the form `x ?? y ?? z` results in `x` if `x` is not `null`; otherwise, it results in `y` if `y` is not `null`; otherwise, it results in `z`. That is, it goes from left to right and picks out the first non-`null` expression, or uses the last expression if all the previous expressions were `null`. The assignment of `directory` in Listing 4.37 provides an example.

C# 8.0 provides a combination of the null-coalescing operator and the assignment operator with the addition of the **null-coalescing assignment operator**. With this operator, you can evaluate if the left-hand side is `null` and assign the value on the righthand side if it is. Listing 4.37 uses this operator when assigning `fullName`.

Null-Conditional Operator (`?.`, `?[]`)

In recognition of the frequency of the pattern of checking for `null` before invoking a member, you can use the `?.` operator, known as the **null-conditional operator**,[4] as shown in Listing 4.38.[5]

LISTING 4.38: Null-Conditional Operator

```
string[]? segments = null;
string? uri = null;

// ...
```

4. Introduced in C# 6.0.

5. This code could be improved with a `using` statement—a construct that we have avoided because it has not yet been introduced.

```
int? length = segments?.Length;
// ...
if (length is not null && length != 0)
{
    uri = string.Join('/', segments!);
}

if (uri is null || length is 0)
{
    Console.WriteLine(
        "There were no segments to combine.");
}
else
{
    Console.WriteLine(
        $"Uri: { uri }");
}
```

The null-conditional operator example (`int? length = segments?.Length`) checks whether the operand (the `segments` in Listing 4.38) is `null` prior to invoking the method or property (in this case, `Length`). The logically equivalent explicit code would be the following (although in the original syntax, the value of `segments` is evaluated only once):

```
int? length =

(segments != null) ? (int?)segments.Length : null
```

An important thing to note about the null-conditional operator is that it always produces a nullable value. In this example, even though the `string.Length` member produces a non-nullable `int`, invoking `Length` with the null-conditional operator produces a nullable `int` (`int?`).

You can also use the null-conditional operator with the array accessor. For example, `uriString = segments?[0]` produces the first element of the `segments` array if the `segments` array was not `null`. Using the array accessor version of the null-conditional operator is relatively rare, however, as it is only useful when you don't know whether the operand is null, but you do know the number of elements, or at least whether a particular element exists.

What makes the null-conditional operator especially convenient is that it can be chained (with and without more null-coalescing operators). For example, in the following code, both ToLower() and StartWith() will be invoked only if both segments and segments[0] are not null:

```
segments?[0]?.ToLower().StartsWith("file:");
```

In this example, of course, we assume that the elements in segments could potentially be null, so the declaration (assuming C# 8.0) would more accurately have been

```
string?[]? segments;
```

The segments array is nullable, in other words, and each of its elements is a nullable string.

When null-conditional expressions are chained, if the first operand is null, the expression evaluation is short-circuited, and no further invocation within the expression call chain will occur. You can also chain a null-coalescing operator at the end of the expression so that if the operand is null, you can specify which default value to use:

```
string uriString = segments?[0]?.ToLower().StartsWith(
"file:")??"intellitect.com";
```

Notice that the data type resulting from the null-coalescing operator is not nullable (assuming the right-hand side of the operator ["intellitect.com" in this example] is not null—which would make little sense).

Be careful, however, that you don't unintentionally neglect additional null values. Consider, for example, what would happen if ToLower() (hypothetically, in this case) returned null. In this scenario, a NullReferenceException would occur upon invocation of StartsWith(). This doesn't mean you must use a chain of null-conditional operators, but rather that you should be intentional about the logic. In this example, because ToLower() can never be null, no additional null-conditional operator is necessary.

Although perhaps a little peculiar (in comparison to other operator behavior), the return of a nullable value type is produced only at the end of the call chain. Consequently, calling the dot (`.`) operator on `Length` allows invocation of only `int` (not `int?`) members. However, encapsulating `segments?.Length` in parentheses—thereby forcing the `int?` result via parentheses operator precedence—will invoke the `int?` return and make the `Nullable<T>` specific members (`HasValue` and `Value`) available. In other words, `segments?.Length.Value` won't compile because `int` (the data type returned by `Length`) doesn't have a member called `Value`. However, changing the order of precedence using `(segments?.Length).Value` will resolve the compiler error because the return of `(segments?.Length)` is `int?`, so the `Value` property is available.

Null-Forgiving Operator (!)

Notice that the `Join()` invocation of Listing 4.38 includes an exclamation point after `segments`:

```
uriString = string.Join('/', segments!);
```

At this point in the code, `segments?.Length` is assigned to the `length` variable, and since the `if` statement verifies that `length` is not `null`, we know that `segments` can't be null either.

```
int? length = segments?.Length;
if (length is not null && length != 0){ }
```

However, the compiler doesn't have the capability to make the same determination. And, since `Join()` requires a non-nullable string array, it issues a warning when passing an unmodified `segments` variable whose declaration was nullable. To avoid the warning, we can add the **null-forgiving operator** (`!`), starting in C# 8.0. It declares to the compiler that we, as the programmer, know better, and that the `segments` variable is not `null`. Then, at compile time, the compiler assumes we know better and dismisses the warning (although the runtime still checks that our assertion is not `null` at execution time).

Note that while the null-conditional operator checks that `segments` isn't null, it doesn't check how many elements there are or check that each element isn't null.

In Chapter 1 we encountered warning CS8600, "Converting null literal or possible null value to non-nullable type," when assigning `Console.ReadLine()` to a `string`. The occurs because `Console.ReadLine()` returns a `string?` rather than a non-nullable `string`. In reality, `Console.ReadLine()` returns `null` only if the input is redirected, which isn't a use case we are expecting in these intro programs, but the compiler doesn't know that. To avoid the warning, we could use the null-forgiving operator on the `Console.ReadLine()` return—stating we know better that the value returned won't be null (and if it is, we are comfortable throwing a null-reference exception).

End 8.0

```
string text = Console.ReadLine()!;
```

ADVANCED TOPIC

Leveraging the Null-Conditional Operator with Delegates

The null-conditional operator is a great feature on its own. However, using it in combination with a delegate invocation resolves a C# pain point that has existed since C# 1.0. Notice in Listing 4.39 how the `PropertyChanged` event handler is assigned to a local copy (`propertyChanged`) before we check the value for `null` and finally fire the event. This is the easiest thread-safe way to invoke events without running the risk that an event unsubscribe will occur between the time when the check for `null` occurs and the time when the event is fired. Unfortunately, this approach is nonintuitive, and frequently developers neglect to follow this pattern—with the result of throwing inconsistent `NullReferenceExceptions`. Fortunately, with the introduction of the null-conditional operator, this issue has been resolved.

LISTING 4.39: Null-Conditional Operator with Event Handlers

```
System.EventHandler propertyChanged =
    PropertyChanged;
if (propertyChanged != null)
{
    propertyChanged(this,
        new System.EventArgs());
}
```

The check for a delegate value changes from what is shown in Listing 4.39 to simply

```
PropertyChanged?.Invoke(propertyChanged(
this, new PropertyChangedEventArgs(nameof(Name)));
```

Because an event is just a delegate, the same pattern of invoking a delegate via the null-conditional operator and an `Invoke()` is always possible.

Bitwise Operators (<<, >>, |, &, ^, ~)

An additional set of operators that is common to virtually all programming languages is the set of operators for manipulating values in their binary formats: the bit operators.

BEGINNER TOPIC

Bits and Bytes

All values within a computer are represented in a binary format of 1s and 0s, called **binary digits** (**bits**). Bits are grouped together in sets of eight, called **bytes**. In a byte, each successive bit corresponds to a value of 2 raised to a power, starting from 2^0 on the right and moving to 2^7 on the left, as shown in Figure 4.1.

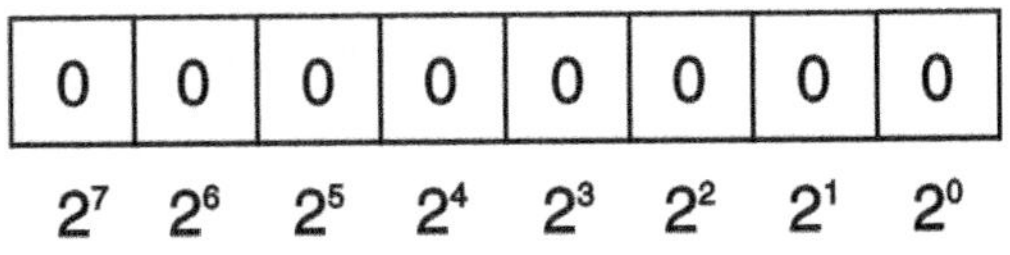

FIGURE 4.1: Corresponding placeholder values

In many scenarios, particularly when dealing with low-level or system services, information is retrieved as binary data. To manipulate these devices and services, you need to perform manipulations of binary data.

In Figure 4.2, each box corresponds to a value of 2 raised to the power shown. The value of the byte (8-bit number) is the sum of the powers of 2 of all of the eight bits that are set to 1.

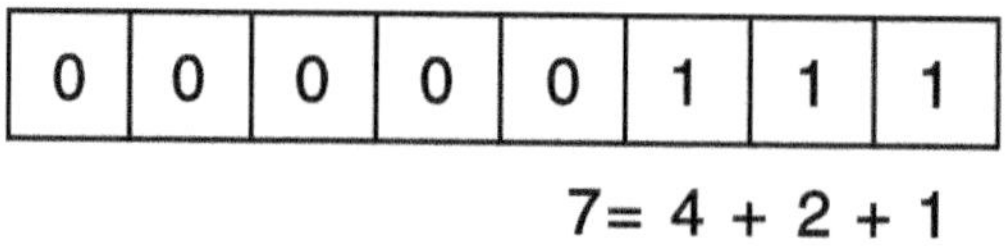

FIGURE 4.2: Calculating the value of an unsigned byte

The binary translation just described is significantly different for signed numbers. Signed numbers (`long`, `short`, `int`) are represented using a *two's complement* notation. This practice ensures that addition continues to work when adding a negative number to a positive number, as though both were positive operands. With this notation, negative numbers behave differently from positive numbers. Negative numbers are identified by a 1 in the leftmost location. If the leftmost location contains a 1, you add the locations with 0s rather than the locations with 1s. Each location corresponds to the negative power of 2 value. Furthermore, from the result, it is also necessary to subtract 1. This is demonstrated in Figure 4.3.

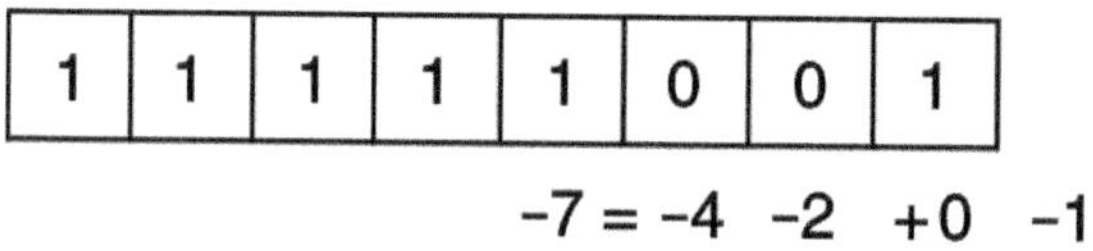

FIGURE 4.3: Calculating the value of a signed byte

Therefore, `1111 1111 1111 1111` corresponds to –1, and `1111 1111 1111 1001` holds the value –7. The binary representation `1000 0000 0000 0000` corresponds to the lowest negative value that a 16-bit integer can hold.

Shift Operators (<<, >>, <<=, >>=)

Sometimes you want to shift the binary value of a number to the right or left. In executing a left shift, all bits in a number's binary representation are shifted to the left by the number of locations specified by the operand on the right of the shift operator. Zeroes then backfill the locations on the right side of the binary number. A right-shift operator does almost the same thing in the opposite direction. However, if the number is a negative value of a signed type, the values used to backfill the left side of the binary number are 1s, rather than 0s. The shift operators are `>>` and `<<`, known as the right-shift and left-shift operators, respectively. In addition, C# includes combination shift and assignment operators, `<<=` and `>>=`.

Consider the following example. Suppose you had the `int` value `-7`, which would have a binary representation of `1111 1111 1111 1111 1111 1111 1111 1001`. In Listing 4.40 (with Output 4.17), you right-shift the binary representation of the number –7 by two locations.

Listing 4.40: Using the Right-Shift Operator

```
int x;
x = (-7 >> 2); // 11111111111111111111111111111001 becomes
               // 11111111111111111111111111111110
// Write out "x is -2."
Console.WriteLine($"x = {x}.");
```

Output 4.17

```
x = -2.
```

Because of the right shift, the value of the bit in the rightmost location has "dropped off" the edge, and the negative bit indicator on the left shifts by two locations to be replaced with 1s. The result is `-2`.

Although legend has it that `x << 2` is faster than `x * 4`, you should not use bit-shift operators for multiplication or division. This difference might have held true for certain C compilers in the 1970s, but modern compilers and modern microprocessors are perfectly capable of optimizing arithmetic. Using shifting for multiplication or division is confusing and frequently leads to errors when code maintainers forget that the shift operators are lower precedence than the arithmetic operators.

Bitwise Operators (&, |, ^)

In some instances, you might need to perform logical operations, such as AND, OR, and XOR, on a bit-by-bit basis for two operands. You do this via the `&`, `|`, and `^` operators, respectively.

BEGINNER TOPIC

Logical Operators Explained

If you have two numbers, as shown in Figure 4.4, the bitwise operations will compare the values of the locations beginning at the leftmost significant value and continuing right until the end. The value of "1" in a location is treated as "true," and the value of "0" in a location is treated as "false."

12:	0	0	0	0	1	1	0	0
7:	0	0	0	0	0	1	1	1

FIGURE 4.4: The numbers 12 and 7 represented in binary

The bitwise AND of the two values in Figure 4.4 would entail the bit-by-bit comparison of bits in the first operand (12) with the bits in the second operand (7), resulting in the binary value `000000100`, which is 4. Alternatively, a bitwise OR of the two values would produce `00001111`, the binary equivalent of 15. The XOR result would be `00001011`, or decimal 11.

Listing 4.41 demonstrates the use of these bitwise operators. The results of Listing 4.41 appear in Output 4.18.

LISTING 4.41: Using Bitwise Operators

```
byte and, or, xor;
and = 12 & 7;   // and = 4
or = 12 | 7;    // or = 15
xor = 12 ^ 7;   // xor = 11
```

```
Console.WriteLine( $"""
        and = { and }
        or = { or }
        xor = { xor }
        """);
```

OUTPUT 4.18

```
and = 4
or = 15
xor = 11
```

In Listing 4.41, the value 7 is the **mask**; it is used to expose or eliminate specific bits within the first operand using the specified operator expression. Note that, unlike the AND (`&&`) operator, the `&` operator always evaluates *both* sides even if the left portion is false. Similarly, the `|` version of the OR operator is *not* "short-circuiting": It always evaluates both operands, even if the left operand is true. The bit versions of the AND and OR operators, therefore, are not short-circuiting.

To convert a number to its binary representation, you need to iterate across each bit in a number. Listing 4.42 is an example of a program that converts an integer to a string of its binary representation. The results of Listing 4.42 appear in Output 4.19.

LISTING 4.42: Getting a String Representation of a Binary Display

```
public class BinaryConverter
{
    public static void Main()
    {
        const int size = 64;
        ulong value;
        char bit;

        Console.Write("Enter an integer: ");
        // Use long.Parse() to support negative numbers
        // Assumes unchecked assignment to ulong
        // If ReadLine returns null, use "42" as default input
        value = (ulong)long.Parse(Console.ReadLine() ?? "42");

        // Set initial mask to 100....
        ulong mask = 1UL << size - 1;
        for(int count = 0; count < size; count++)
        {
            bit = ((mask & value) != 0) ? '1' : '0';
```

```
                Console.Write(bit);
                // Shift mask one location over to the right
                mask >>= 1;
            }
            Console.WriteLine();
        }
    }
```

OUTPUT 4.19

```
Enter an integer: 42
0000000000000000000000000000000000000000000000000000000000101010
```

Within each iteration of the `for` loop in Listing 4.42 (as discussed later in this chapter), we use the right-shift assignment operator to create a mask corresponding to each bit position in `value`. By using the `&` bit operator to mask a particular bit, we can determine whether the bit is set. If the mask test produces a nonzero result, we write `1` to the console; otherwise, we write `0`. In this way, we create output describing the binary value of an unsigned `long`.

Note also that the parentheses in `(mask & value) != 0` are necessary because inequality is higher precedence than the AND operator. Without the explicit parentheses, this expression would be equivalent to `mask & (value != 0)`, which does not make any sense; the left side of the `&` is a `ulong` and the right side is a `bool`.

This example is provided for learning purposes only. There is actually a built-in CLR method, `System.Convert.ToString(value, 2)`, that does such a conversion. In fact, the second argument specifies the base (e.g., 2 for binary, 10 for decimal, or 16 for hexadecimal), allowing for more than just conversion to binary.

Bitwise Compound Assignment Operators (`&=`, `|=`, `^=`)

Not surprisingly, you can combine these bitwise operators with assignment operators as follows: `&=`, `|=`, and `^=`. As a result, you could take a variable, OR it with a number, and assign the result back to the original variable, which Listing 4.43 with Output 4.20 demonstrates.

Listing 4.43: Using Logical Assignment Operators

```
byte and = 12, or = 12, xor = 12;
and &= 7;    // and = 4
or |= 7;    // or = 15
xor ^= 7;    // xor = 11
Console.WriteLine( $"""
        and = {and}
        or = {or}
        xor = {xor}
        """);
```

Output 4.20

```
and = 4
or = 15
xor = 11
```

Combining a bitmap with a mask using something like `fields &= mask` clears the bits in `fields` that are not set in the `mask`. The opposite, `fields &= ~mask`, clears the bits in `fields` that are set in `mask`.

Bitwise Complement Operator (~)

The **bitwise complement operator** takes the complement of each bit in the operand, where the operand can be an `int`, `uint`, `long`, or `ulong`. The expression `~1`, therefore, returns the value with binary notation `1111 1111 1111 1111 1111 1111 1111 1110`, and `~(1<<31)` returns the number with binary notation `0111 1111 1111 1111 1111 1111 1111 1111`.

Control Flow Statements, Continued

Now that we've described Boolean expressions in more detail, we can more clearly describe the control flow statements supported by C#. Many of these statements will be familiar to experienced programmers, so you can skim this section looking for details specific to C#. Note in particular the `foreach` loop, as it may be new to many programmers.

The `while` and `do/while` Loops

Thus far you have learned how to write programs that do something only once. However, computers can easily perform similar operations multiple times. To do so, you need to create an instruction loop. The first instruction loop we discuss is the `while` loop, because it is the simplest conditional loop. The general form of the `while` statement is as follows:

```
while (condition)
  statement
```

The computer repeatedly executes the statement that is the "body" of the loop as long as the condition (which must be a Boolean expression) evaluates to `true`. If the condition evaluates to `false`, code execution skips the body and executes the code following the loop statement. Note that `statement` continues to execute even if it causes the condition to become `false`. The loop exits only when the condition is reevaluated "at the top of the loop." The Fibonacci calculator shown in Listing 4.44 demonstrates the `while` loop.

Listing 4.44: `while` **Loop Example**

```
decimal current;
decimal previous;
decimal temp;
decimal input;

Console.Write("Enter a positive integer:");

// decimal.Parse convert the ReadLine to a decimal
// If ReadLine returns null, use "42" as default input
input = decimal.Parse(Console.ReadLine() ?? "42");

// Initialize current and previous to 1, the first
// two numbers in the Fibonacci series
current = previous = 1;

// While the current Fibonacci number in the series is
// less than the value input by the user
while (current <= input)
{
    temp = current;
    current = previous + current;
    previous = temp; // Executes even if previous
```

```
    // statement caused current to exceed input
}

Console.WriteLine(
        $"The Fibonacci number following this is { current }");
```

A **Fibonacci number** is a member of the **Fibonacci series**, which includes all numbers that are the sum of the previous two numbers in the series, beginning with 1 and 1. In Listing 4.44, you prompt the user for an integer. Then you use a `while` loop to find the first Fibonacci number that is greater than the number the user entered.

BEGINNER TOPIC

When to Use a `while` Loop

The remainder of this chapter considers other statements that cause a block of code to execute repeatedly. The term *loop body* refers to the statement (frequently a code block) that is to be executed within the `while` statement, since the code is executed in a "loop" until the exit condition is achieved. It is important to understand which loop construct to select. You use a `while` construct to iterate while the condition evaluates to `true`. You use a `for` loop whenever the number of repetitions is known, such as when counting from 0 to *n*. A `do/while` loop is similar to a `while` loop, except that it always executes the loop body at least once.

The `do/while` loop is very similar to the `while` loop except that a `do/while` loop is preferred when the number of repetitions is from 1 to *n* and *n* is not known when iterating begins. This pattern frequently occurs when prompting a user for input. Listing 4.45 is taken from the tic-tac-toe program.

LISTING 4.45: `do/while` **Loop Example**

```
// Repeatedly request player to move until he
// enters a valid position on the board
bool valid;
do
{
    valid = false;
```

```
        // Request a move from the current player
        Console.Write(
            $"Player {currentPlayer}: Enter move:");
        string? input = Console.ReadLine();

        // Check the current player's input
        // ...

} while(!valid);
```

In Listing 4.45, you initialize `valid` to `false` at the beginning of each **iteration**, or loop repetition. Next, you prompt and retrieve the number the user input. Although not shown here, you then check whether the input was correct, and if it was, you assign `valid` equal to `true`. Since the code uses a `do/while` statement rather than a `while` statement, the user is prompted for input at least once.

The general form of the `do/while` loop is as follows:

```
do
  statement
while (condition);
```

As with all the control flow statements, a code block is generally used for the statement in the general form. This of course allows multiple statements to be executed as the loop body. However, C# also allows any single statement except for a labeled statement (see the `switch` statement later in the chapter) or a local variable declaration.

The `for` Loop

The `for` loop iterates a code block until reaching a specified condition. In that way, it is like the `while` loop. The difference is that the `for` loop has built-in syntax for initializing, incrementing, and evaluating the value of a counter, known as the **loop variable**. Because there is a specific location in the loop syntax for an increment operation, the increment and decrement operators are frequently used as part of a `for` loop.

Listing 4.46 shows the `for` loop used to display an integer in binary form. The results of this listing appear in Output 4.21.

LISTING 4.46: Using the `for` Loop

```
const int size = 64; // Also available from sizeof(ulong)
ulong value;
char bit;

Console.Write("Enter an integer: ");
// Use long.Parse() to support negative numbers
// Assumes unchecked assignment to ulong
// If ReadLine returns null, use "42" as default input
value = (ulong)long.Parse(Console.ReadLine() ?? "42");

// Set initial mask to 100....
ulong mask = 1UL << size - 1;
for(int count = 0; count < size; count++)
{
    bit = ((mask & value) > 0) ? '1' : '0';
    Console.Write(bit);
    // Shift mask one location over to the right
    mask >>= 1;
}
```

OUTPUT 4.21

```
Enter an integer: -42
1111111111111111111111111111111111111111111111111111111111010110
```

Listing 4.46 performs a bit mask 64 times—once for each bit in the number. The three parts of the `for` loop header first declare and initialize the variable `count`, then describe the condition that must be met for the loop body to be executed, and finally describe the operation that updates the loop variable. The general form of the `for` loop is as follows:

```
for (initial ; condition ; loop)
  statement
```

Here is a breakdown of the `for` loop:

- The `initial` section performs operations that precede the first iteration. In Listing 4.46, it declares and initializes the variable `count`. The `initial` expression does not have to be a declaration of a new variable (though it frequently is). It is possible, for example, to declare the variable beforehand and simply initialize it in the `for` loop, or to skip the initialization section entirely by leaving it blank. Variables declared here are in scope throughout the header and body of the `for` statement.

- The `condition` portion of the `for` loop specifies an end condition. The loop exits when this condition is `false`, exactly like the `while` loop does. The `for` loop executes the body only as long as the condition evaluates to `true`. In Listing 4.46, the loop exits when `count` is greater than or equal to 64.
- The `loop` expression executes after each iteration. In Listing 4.46, `count++` executes after the right shift of the mask (`mask >>= 1`) but before the condition is evaluated. During the 64th iteration, `count` is incremented to 64, causing the condition to become `false` and therefore terminating the loop.
- The `statement` portion of the `for` loop is the "loop body" code that executes while the conditional expression remains `true`.

If you wrote out each `for` loop execution step in pseudocode without using a `for` loop expression, it would look like this:

1. Declare and initialize `count` to 0.
2. If `count` is less than 64, continue to step 3; otherwise, go to step 7.
3. Calculate `bit` and display it.
4. Shift the mask.
5. Increment `count` by 1.
6. Jump back to line 2.
7. Continue the execution of the program after the loop.

The `for` statement doesn't require any of the elements in its header. The expression `for(;;){ ... }` is perfectly valid, although there still needs to be a means to escape from the loop so that it will not continue to execute indefinitely. (If the condition is missing, it is assumed to be the constant `true`.)

The initial and loop expressions have an unusual syntax to support loops that require multiple loop variables, as shown in Listing 4.47 (with Output 4.22).

LISTING 4.47: `for` Loop Using Multiple Expressions

```
for (int x = 0, y = 5; ((x <= 5) && (y >= 0)); y--, x++)
{
    Console.Write(
        $"{ x }{ ((x > y) ? '>' : '<')}{ y }\t");
}
```

OUTPUT 4.22

```
0<5    1<4    2<3    3>2    4>1    5>0
```

Here the initialization clause contains a complex declaration that declares and initializes two loop variables, but this is at least similar to a declaration statement that declares multiple local variables. The loop clause is quite unusual because it can consist of a comma-separated list of expressions, not just a single expression.

Guidelines

CONSIDER refactoring the method to make the control flow easier to understand if you find yourself writing `for` loops with complex conditionals and multiple loop variables.

The `for` loop is little more than a more convenient way to write a `while` loop; you can always rewrite a `for` loop like this:

```
{
  initial;
  while (condition)
  {
    statement;
    loop;
  }
}
```

Guidelines

DO use the `for` loop when the number of loop iterations is known in advance and the "counter" that gives the number of iterations executed is needed in the loop.

DO use the `while` loop when the number of loop iterations is not known in advance and a counter is not needed.

The `foreach` Loop

The last loop statement in the C# language is `foreach`. The `foreach` loop iterates through a collection of items, setting a loop variable to represent each item in turn. In the body of the loop, operations may be performed on the item. A nice property of the `foreach` loop is that every item is iterated over exactly once; it is not possible to accidentally miscount and iterate past the end of the collection, as can happen with other loops.

The general form of the `foreach` statement is as follows:

```
foreach(type variable in collection)
  statement
```

Here is a breakdown of the `foreach` statement:

- `type` is used to declare the data type of the variable for each item within the collection. It may be `var`, in which case the compiler infers the type of the item from the type of the collection.
- `variable` is a read-only variable into which the `foreach` loop automatically assigns the next item within the collection. The scope of the variable is limited to the body of the loop.
- `collection` is an expression, such as an array, representing any number of items.
- `statement` is the loop body that executes for each iteration of the loop.

Consider the `foreach` loop in the context of the simple example shown in Listing 4.48 with Output 4.23.

LISTING 4.48: Determining Remaining Moves Using the `foreach` Loop

```
// Hardcode initial board as follows
// ---+---+---
//  1 | 2 | 3
// ---+---+---
//  4 | 5 | 6
```

```
// ---+---+---
//  7 | 8 | 9
// ---+---+---
char[] cells = {
    '1', '2', '3', '4', '5', '6', '7', '8', '9'
};

Console.Write(
    "The available moves are as follows: ");

// Write out the initial available moves
foreach(char cell in cells)
{
    if(cell != 'O' && cell != 'X')
    {
        Console.Write($"{ cell } ");
    }
}
```

OUTPUT 4.23

```
The available moves are as follows: 1 2 3 4 5 6 7 8 9
```

When the execution engine reaches the `foreach` statement, it assigns to the variable `cell` the first item in the `cells` array—in this case, the value `'1'`. It then executes the code within the block that makes up the `foreach` loop body. The `if` statement determines whether the value of `cell` is `'O'` or `'X'`. If it is neither, the value of `cell` is written out to the console. The next iteration then assigns the next array value to `cell`, and so on.

Note that the compiler prevents modification of the variable (`cell`) during the execution of a `foreach` loop.

BEGINNER TOPIC

Where the `switch` Statement Is More Appropriate

Sometimes you might compare the same value in several continuous `if` statements, as shown with the `input` variable in Listing 4.49.

LISTING 4.49: Checking the Player's Input with an `if` Statement

```
// ...

// Check the current player's input
if ((input == "1") ||
    (input == "2") ||
    (input == "3") ||
    (input == "4") ||
    (input == "5") ||
    (input == "6") ||
    (input == "7") ||
    (input == "8") ||
    (input == "9"))
{
    // Save/move as the player directed
    // ...

}
else if((input.Length == 0) || (input == "quit"))
{
    // Retry or quite
    // ...

}
else
{
    Console.WriteLine( $"""
            ERROR:  Enter a value from 1-9.
            Push ENTER to quit
            """);
}

// ...
```

This code validates the text entered to ensure that it is a valid tic-tac-toe move. If the value of `input` were `9`, for example, the program would have to perform nine different evaluations. It would be preferable to jump to the correct code after only one evaluation. To enable this, you use a `switch` statement.

The Basic `switch` Statement

A basic `switch` statement is simpler to understand than a complex `if` statement when you have a value that must be compared against different constant values. The `switch` statement looks like this:

```
switch (expression)
{
    case constant:
      statements
    default:
      statements
}
```

Here is a breakdown of the `switch` statement:

> **Guidelines**
>
> **DO NOT** use `continue` as the jump statement that exits a switch section. This is legal when the `switch` is inside a loop, but it is easy to become confused about the meaning of `break` in a later switch section.

- `expression` is the value that is being compared against the different constants. The type of this expression determines the "governing type" of the switch. Allowable governing data types are `bool`, `sbyte`, `byte`, `short`, `ushort`, `int`, `uint`, `long`, `ulong`, `char`, any `enum` type (covered in Chapter 9), the corresponding nullable types of each of those value types, and `string`.
- `constant` is any constant expression compatible with the governing type.
- A group of one or more case labels (or the default label) followed by a group of one or more statements is called a **switch section**. The pattern given previously has two switch sections; Listing 4.50 shows a `switch` statement with three switch sections.
- `statements` is one or more statements to be executed when the expression equals one of the constant values mentioned in a label in the switch section. The end point of the group of statements must not be reachable. Typically, the last statement is a jump statement such as a `break`, `return`, or `goto` statement.

A `switch` statement should have at least one switch section; `switch(x){}` is legal but will generate a warning. Also, the guideline provided earlier was to avoid omitting braces in general. One exception to this rule of thumb is to omit braces for `case` and `break` statements because they serve to indicate the beginning and end of a block.

Listing 4.50, with a `switch` statement, is semantically equivalent to the series of `if` statements in Listing 4.49.

LISTING 4.50: Replacing the `if` Statement with a `switch` Statement

```
public static bool ValidateAndMove(
    int[] playerPositions, int currentPlayer, string input)
{
    bool valid = false;

    // Check the current player's input
    switch(input)
    {
        case "1":
        case "2":
        case "3":
        case "4":
        case "5":
        case "6":
        case "7":
        case "8":
        case "9":
            // Save/move as the player directed
            // ...
            valid = true;
            break;
        case "":
        case "quit":
            valid = true;
            break;
        default:
            // If none of the other case statements
            // is encountered then the text is invalid
            Console.WriteLine(
            "ERROR:  Enter a value from 1-9. "
            + "Push ENTER to quit");
            break;
    }
```

```
    return valid;
}
```

In Listing 4.50, `input` is the test expression. Since `input` is a string, the governing type is `string`. If the value of `input` is one of the strings `1`, `2`, `3`, `4`, `5`, `6`, `7`, `8`, or `9`, the move is valid and you change the appropriate cell to match that of the current user's token (X or O). Once execution encounters a `break` statement, control leaves the `switch` statement.

The next switch section describes how to handle the empty string or the string `quit`; it sets `valid` to `true` if `input` equals either value. The `default` switch section is executed if no other switch section had a case label that matched the test expression.

Language Contrast: C++—`switch` Statement Fall-Through

In C++, if a switch section does not end with a jump statement, control "falls through" to the next switch section, executing its code. Because unintended fall-through is a common error in C++, C# does not allow control to accidentally fall through from one switch section to the next. The C# designers believed it was better to prevent this common source of bugs and encourage better code readability than to match the potentially confusing C++ behavior. If you do want one switch section to execute the statements of another switch section, you may do so explicitly with a `goto` statement, as demonstrated later in this chapter.

There are several things to note about the `switch` statement:

- A `switch` statement with no switch sections will generate a compiler warning, but the statement will still compile.
- Switch sections can appear in any order; the `default` section does not have to appear last. In fact, the `default` switch section does not have to appear at all—it is optional.
- The C# language requires that every switch section, including the last section, ends with a jump statement (see the next section). This means that switch sections usually end with a `break`, `return`, `throw`, or `goto`.

C# 7.0 introduced an improvement to the `switch` statement that enables pattern matching so that any data type—not just the limited few identified earlier—can be used for the `switch` expression. Pattern matching enables the use of `switch` statements based on the type of the `switch` expression and the use of case labels that also declare variables. Lastly, pattern matching `switch` statements support conditional expressions so that not only the type but also a Boolean expression at the end of the case label can identify which case label should execute. For more information on pattern matching with `switch` statements and expressions, see Chapter 7.

Jump Statements

It is possible to alter the execution path of a loop. In fact, with jump statements, it is possible to escape out of the loop or to skip the remaining portion of an iteration and begin with the next iteration, even when the loop condition remains `true`. This section considers some of the ways to jump the execution path from one location to another.

The `break` Statement

To escape out of a loop or a `switch` statement, C# uses a `break` statement. Whenever the `break` statement is encountered, control immediately leaves the loop or switch. Listing 4.51 examines the `foreach` loop from the tic-tac-toe program, and Output 4.24 shows the output.

LISTING 4.51: Using `break` to Escape Once a Winner Is Found

```
int winner = 0;
// Stores locations each player has moved
int[] playerPositions = { 0, 0 };

// Hardcoded board position
//  X | 2 | O
// ---+---+---
//  O | O | 6
// ---+---+---
//  X | X | X
playerPositions[0] = 449;
```

```
playerPositions[1] = 28;

// Determine if there is a winner
int[] winningMasks = {
    7, 56, 448, 73, 146, 292, 84, 273 };

// Iterate through each winning mask to determine
// if there is a winner
foreach (int mask in winningMasks)
{
    if ((mask & playerPositions[0]) == mask)
    {
        winner = 1;
        break;
    }
    else if((mask & playerPositions[1]) == mask)
    {
        winner = 2;
        break;
    }
}

Console.WriteLine(
    $"Player { winner } was the winner");
```

Output 4.24

```
Player 1 was the winner
```

Listing 4.51 uses a `break` statement when a player holds a winning position. The `break` statement forces its enclosing loop (or a `switch` statement) to cease execution, and control moves to the next line outside the loop. For this listing, if the bit comparison returns `true` (if the board holds a winning position), the `break` statement causes control to jump and display the winner.

BEGINNER TOPIC

Bitwise Operators for Positions

The full tic-tac-toe listing uses the bitwise operators to determine which player wins the game. First, the code saves the positions of each player into a bitmap called `playerPositions`. (It uses an array with two items so that the positions for both players can be saved.)

To begin, both `playerPositions` are `0`. As each player moves, the bit corresponding to the move is set. If, for example, the player selects cell 3, `shifter` is set to `3 - 1`. The code subtracts 1 because C# is zero based and you need to adjust for 0 as the first position instead of 1. Next, the code sets `position`, the bit corresponding to cell 3, using the shift operator `000000000000001 << shifter`, where `shifter` now has a value of 2. Lastly, it sets `playerPositions` for the current player (subtracting 1 again to shift to zero based) to `0000000000000100`. Listing 4.52 uses `|=` so that previous moves are combined with the current move.

LISTING 4.52: Setting the Bit That Corresponds to Each Player's Move

```
int shifter;  // The number of places to shift
              // over to set a bit
int position; // The bit that is to be set

// int.Parse() converts "input" to an integer.
// "int.Parse(input) - 1" because arrays
// are zero based.
shifter = int.Parse(input) - 1;

// Shift mask of 00000000000000000000000000000001
// over by cellLocations.
position = 1 << shifter;

// Take the current player cells and OR them to set the
// new position as well.
// Since currentPlayer is either 1 or 2,
// subtract 1 to use currentPlayer as an
// index in a zero based array.
playerPositions[currentPlayer - 1] |= position;
```

Later in the program, you can iterate over each mask corresponding to winning positions on the board to determine whether the current player has a winning position, as shown in Listing 4.51.

The `continue` Statement

You might have a block containing a series of statements within a loop. If you determine that some conditions warrant executing only a portion of these statements for some iterations, you can use the `continue` statement to jump to the end of the current iteration and begin the next iteration. The `continue` statement exits the current iteration (regardless of whether additional statements remain) and jumps to the loop condition. At that point, if the loop conditional is still `true`, the loop continues execution.

Listing 4.53 uses the `continue` statement so that only the letters of the domain portion of an email are displayed. Output 4.25 shows the results of Listing 4.53.

LISTING 4.53: Determining the Domain of an Email Address

```
string email;
bool insideDomain = false;

Console.Write("Enter an email address: ");
email = Console.ReadLine() ?? string.Empty;

Console.Write("The email domain is: ");

// Iterate through each letter in the email address
foreach(char letter in email)
{
    if(!insideDomain)
    {
        if(letter == '@')
        {
            insideDomain = true;
        }
        continue;
    }
```

```
    Console.Write(letter);
}
```

Output 4.25

```
Enter an email address: mark@IntelliTect.com
The email domain is: IntelliTect.com
```

In Listing 4.53, if you are not yet inside the domain portion of the email address, you can use a `continue` statement to move control to the end of the loop and process the next character in the email address.

You can almost always use an `if` statement in place of a `continue` statement, and this format is usually more readable. The problem with the `continue` statement is that it provides multiple flows of control within a single iteration, which compromises readability. In Listing 4.54, the example in Listing 4.53 has been rewritten by replacing the `continue` statement with the `if/else` construct to demonstrate a more readable version that does not use the `continue` statement.

Listing 4.54: Replacing a `continue` Statement with an `if` Statement

```
// Iterate through each letter in the email address
foreach (char letter in email)
{
    if(insideDomain)
    {
        Console.Write(letter);
    }
    else
    {
        if(letter == '@')
        {
            insideDomain = true;
        }
    }
}
```

The `goto` Statement

Early programming languages lacked the sophisticated "structured" control flows that modern languages such as C# have as a matter of course. Instead, they relied on simple conditional branching (`if`) and unconditional branching (`goto`) statements for most of their control flow needs. The resultant programs were often hard to understand. The continued existence of a `goto` statement within C# seems like an anachronism to many experienced programmers. However, C# supports `goto`, and it is the only method for supporting fall-through within a `switch` statement. In Listing 4.55, if the `/out` option is set, code execution jumps to the `default` case using the `goto` statement, and similarly for `/f`. Output 4.26 provides an example of the program executing.

LISTING 4.55: Demonstrating a `switch` with `goto` Statements

```
// ...
public static void Main(string[] args)
{
    bool isOutputSet = false;
    bool isFiltered = false;
    bool isRecursive = false;

    foreach(string option in args)
    {
        switch(option)
        {
            case "/out":
                isOutputSet = true;
                isFiltered = false;
                // ...
                goto default;
            case "/f":
                isFiltered = true;
                isRecursive = false;
                // ...
                goto default;
            default:
                if(isRecursive)
                {
                    // Recurse down the hierarchy
                    Console.WriteLine("Recursing...");
                    // ...
                }
                else if(isFiltered)
                {
                    // Add option to list of filters
                    Console.WriteLine("Filtering...");
                    // ...
```

```
                }
                break;
        }
    }

    // ...
}
```

Output 4.26

```
C:\SAMPLES>Generate /r /f "*.xml,*.wsdl"
```

To branch to a switch section label other than the default label, you can use the syntax `goto case constant;`, where `constant` is the constant associated with the case label you wish to branch to. To branch to a statement that is not associated with a switch section, precede the target statement with any identifier followed by a colon; you can then use that identifier with the `goto` statement. For example, you could have a labeled statement `myLabel : Console.WriteLine();`. The statement `goto myLabel;` would then branch to the labeled statement. Fortunately, C# prevents you from using `goto` to branch outside of the `goto` statements scope; instead, `goto` may be used only to branch within the immediate code block or to an enclosing code block. By enforcing these restrictions, C# avoids most of the serious `goto` abuses possible in other languages.

In spite of the improvements, use of `goto` is generally considered to be inelegant, difficult to understand, and symptomatic of poorly structured code. If you need to execute a section of code multiple times or under different circumstances, either use a loop or extract code to a method of its own.

Guidelines

AVOID using `goto`.

C# Preprocessor Directives

Control flow statements evaluate expressions at execution time. In contrast, the C# preprocessor is invoked during compilation. The preprocessor commands are directives to the C# compiler, specifying the sections of code to compile or identifying how to handle specific errors and warnings within the code. C# preprocessor commands can also provide directives to C# editors regarding the organization of code.

Language Contrast: C++—Preprocessing

Languages such as C and C++ use a **preprocessor** to perform actions on the code based on special tokens. Preprocessor directives generally tell the compiler how to compile the code in a file and do not participate in the compilation process itself. In contrast, the C# compiler handles "preprocessor" directives as part of the regular lexical analysis of the source code. As a result, C# does not support preprocessor macros beyond defining a constant. In fact, the term *preprocessor* is generally a misnomer in C#.

Each preprocessor directive begins with a hash symbol (#), and all preprocessor directives must appear on one line. A newline rather than a semicolon indicates the end of the directive.

A list of each preprocessor directive appears in Table 4.5.

Begin 8.0

TABLE 4.5: Preprocessor Directives

Statement or Expression	General Syntax Structure	Example

`#if` directive	`#if preprocessor-expression`
	`code`
	`#endif`
		`#if CSHARP2PLUS`
		`Console.Clear();`
		`#endif`

`#elif` directive	`#if preprocessor-expression1`
	`code`
	`#elif preprocessor-expression2`
	`code`
	`#endif`
		`#if LINUX`
		`...`
		`#elif WINDOWS`
		`...`
		`#endif`

`#else` directive	`#if`
	`code`
	`#else`
	`code`
	`#endif`
		`#if CSHARP1`
		`...`
		`#else`
		`...`
		`#endif`

`#define` directive	`#define conditional-symbol`	`#define CSHARP2PLUS`
`#undef` directive	`#undef conditional-symbol`	`#undef CSHARP2PLUS`

TABLE 4.5: Preprocessor Directives (continued)

Statement or Expression	General Syntax Structure	Example
`#error` directive	`#error preproc-message`	`#error Buggy implementation`
`#warning` directive	`#warning preproc-message`	`#warning Needs code review`
`#pragma` directive	`#pragma warning`	`#pragma warning disable 1030`

`#line` directive	`#line org-line new-line`	`#line 467 "TicTacToe.cs"`
		`...`
		`#line default`

	`#line default`	

`#region` directive	`#region pre-proc-message`
	`code`
	`#endregion`
		`#region Methods`
		`...`
		`#endregion`

`#nullable` directive	`#nullable enable | disable | restore`	`#nullable enable`
		`..string? text = null;`
		`#nullable restore`

End 8.0

Excluding and Including Code (#if, #elif, #else, #endif)

Perhaps the most common use of preprocessor directives is in controlling when and how code is included. For example, to write code that could be compiled by both C# 2.0 and later compilers and the prior version 1.0 compilers, you would use a preprocessor directive to exclude C# 2.0–specific code when compiling with a version 1.0 compiler. You can see this in the tic-tac-toe example and in Listing 4.56.

LISTING 4.56: Excluding C# 2.0 Code from a C# 1.x Compiler

```
#if CSHARP2PLUS
System.Console.Clear();
#endif
```

In this case, you call the `System.Console.Clear()` method. Using the `#if` and `#endif` preprocessor directives, this line of code is compiled only if the preprocessor symbol `CSHARP2PLUS` is defined.

Another use of preprocessor directives would be to handle differences among platforms, such as surrounding Windows- and Linux-specific APIs with `WINDOWS` and `LINUX` `#if` directives. Developers often use these directives in place of multiline comments (`/*...*/`) because they are easier to remove by defining the appropriate symbol or via a search and replace.

A final common use of the directives is for debugging. If you surround code with an `#if DEBUG`, you will remove the code from a release build on most IDEs. The IDEs define the `DEBUG` symbol by default in a debug compile and `RELEASE` by default for release builds.

To handle an `else-if` condition, you can use the `#elif` directive within the `#if` directive instead of creating two entirely separate `#if` blocks, as shown in Listing 4.57.

Listing 4.57: Using `#if`, `#elif`, and `#endif` Directives

```
#if LINUX
// ...
#elif WINDOWS
// ...
#endif
```

Defining Preprocessor Symbols (#define, #undef)

You can define a preprocessor symbol in two ways. The first is with the `#define` directive, as shown in Listing 4.58.

Listing 4.58: A `#define` Example

```
#define CSHARP2PLUS
```

The second method uses the `define` command line. Output 4.27 demonstrates this with Dotnet command-line interface.

Output 4.27

```
>dotnet.exe -define:CSHARP2PLUS TicTacToe.cs
```

To add multiple definitions, separate them with a semicolon. The advantage of the `define` compiler option is that no source code changes are required, so you may use the same source files to produce two different binaries.

To undefine a symbol, you use the `#undef` directive in the same way you use `#define`.

Emitting Errors and Warnings (`#error`, `#warning`)

Sometimes you may want to flag a potential problem with your code. You do this by inserting `#error` and `#warning` directives to emit an error or a warning, respectively. Listing 4.59 uses the tic-tac-toe example to warn that the code does not yet prevent players from entering the same move multiple times. The results of Listing 4.59 appear in Output 4.28.

Listing 4.59: Defining a Warning with `#warning`

```
#warning "Same move allowed multiple times."
```

Output 4.28

```
Performing main compilation...
...\tictactoe.cs(471,16): warning CS1030: #warning: '"Same move allowed
multiple times."'

Build complete -- 0 errors, 1 warnings
```

By including the `#warning` directive, you ensure that the compiler will report a warning, as shown in Output 4.28. This particular warning is a way of flagging the fact that there is a potential enhancement or bug within the code. It could be a simple way of reminding the developer of a pending task.

Turning Off Warning Messages (#pragma)

Warnings are helpful because they point to code that could potentially be troublesome. However, sometimes it is preferred to turn off specific warnings explicitly because they can be ignored legitimately. C# provides the preprocessor #pragma directive for just this purpose (see Listing 4.60).[6]

Listing 4.60: Using the Preprocessor #pragma Directive to Disable the #warning Directive

```
#pragma warning disable CS1030
```

To reenable the warning, #pragma supports the restore option following the warning, as shown in Listing 4.61.

Listing 4.61: Using the Preprocessor #pragma Directive to Restore a Warning

```
#pragma warning restore CS1030
```

In combination, these two directives can surround a particular block of code where the warning is explicitly determined to be irrelevant.

Perhaps one of the most common warnings to disable is CS1591. This warning appears when you elect to generate XML documentation using the /doc compiler option, but you neglect to document all of the public items within your program.

Code warnings occur frequently throughout this book because listings often are incomplete—that is, we are showing initial code snippets that aren't fully developed. To suppress the warnings, since they are not relevant in an example code scenario, we add #pragma directives to the file. Table 4.6 provides an example of some of the warnings that are disabled within various code snippets in Chapter 4.

Table 4.6: Sample Warnings

Category	Warning
CS0168	Variable is declared but never used

6. Introduced in C# 2.0.

TABLE 4.6: Sample Warnings (continued)

Category	Warning
CS0219	Variable is assigned but its value is never used
IDE0059	Unnecessary assignment of a value

Such `#pragma` disable-warning directives are often embedded within the book's source code to address warnings that crop up because the example code is not fully developed but rather intended for the purpose of elucidation.

Note that C# warning numbers are prefixed with the letters *CS* in the compiler output, a prefix that is optional in the `#pragma` directive. Such a number corresponds to the warning error number emitted by the compiler when there is no preprocessor command. However, there are other prefixes like "IDE" that are part of the identity. The IDE0059 message is an example. Code analyzers generate IDE-prefixed warnings to suggest code improvements, and removing the prefix will no longer refer to the same warning.

`nowarn:<warn list>` Option

In addition to the `#pragma` directive, C# compilers generally support the `nowarn=<warn list>` option. This achieves the same result as `#pragma`, except that instead of adding it to the source code, you can insert the command as a compiler option. The `nowarn` option affects the entire compilation, whereas the `#pragma` option affects only the file in which it appears. To turn off the CS0219 warning, for example, you would use the command line as shown in Output 4.29.

OUTPUT 4.29

```
> dotnet build /p:NoWarn="0219"
```

Specifying Line Numbers (`#line`)

The `#line` directive controls on which line number the C# compiler reports an error or warning. It is used predominantly by utilities and designers that emit C# code. In Listing 4.62, the actual line numbers within the file appear on the left.

LISTING 4.62: The `#line` Preprocessor Directive

```
#line 113 "TicTacToe.cs"
#warning "Same move allowed multiple times."
#line default
```

Including the `#line` directive causes the compiler to report the warning found on line 125 as though it were on line 113, as shown in the compiler error message in Output 4.30.

OUTPUT 4.30

```
Performing main compilation...
...\tictactoe.cs(113,18): warning CS1030: #warning: '"Same move allowed
multiple times."'

Build complete -- 0 errors, 1 warnings
```

Following the `#line` directive with `default` reverses the effect of all prior `#line` directives and instructs the compiler to report true line numbers rather than the ones designated by previous uses of the `#line` directive.

Hints for Visual Editors (`#region`, `#endregion`)

C# contains two preprocessor directives, `#region` and `#endregion`, that are useful only within the context of visual code editors. Code editors, such as Microsoft Visual Studio, can search through source code and find these directives to provide editor features when writing code. C# allows you to declare a region of code using the `#region` directive. You must pair the `#region` directive with a matching `#endregion` directive, both of which may optionally include a descriptive string following the directive. In addition, you may nest regions within one another.

Listing 4.63 shows the tic-tac-toe program as an example.

LISTING 4.63: `#region` and `#endregion` Preprocessor Directives

```
// ...
#region Display Tic-tac-toe Board

#if CSHARP2PLUS
    System.Console.Clear();
#endif
```

```
// Display the current board
border = 0;    //  set the first border (border[0] = "|")

// Display the top line of dashes
// ("\n---+---+---\n")
Console.Write(borders[2]);
foreach(char cell in cells)
{
    // Write out a cell value and the border that comes after it
    Console.Write($" { cell } { borders[border] }");

    // Increment to the next border
    border++;

    // Reset border to 0 if it is 3
    if(border == 3)
    {
        border = 0;
    }
}

#endregion Display Tic-tac-toe Board

// ...
```

These preprocessor directives are used, for example, with Microsoft Visual Studio. Visual Studio examines the code and provides a tree control to open and collapse the code (on the left-hand side of the code editor window) that matches the region demarcated by the `#region` directives (see Figure 4.5).

Begin 8.0

Activating Nullable Reference Types (`#nullable`)

As described in Chapter 3, the `#nullable` preprocessor directive activates (or deactivates) support for nullable reference types. `#nullable enable` turns on the nullable reference type feature, and `#nullable disable` turns it off. In addition, `#nullable restore` returns the nullable reference type feature back to the default value identified in the project file's `Nullable` element.

End 8.0

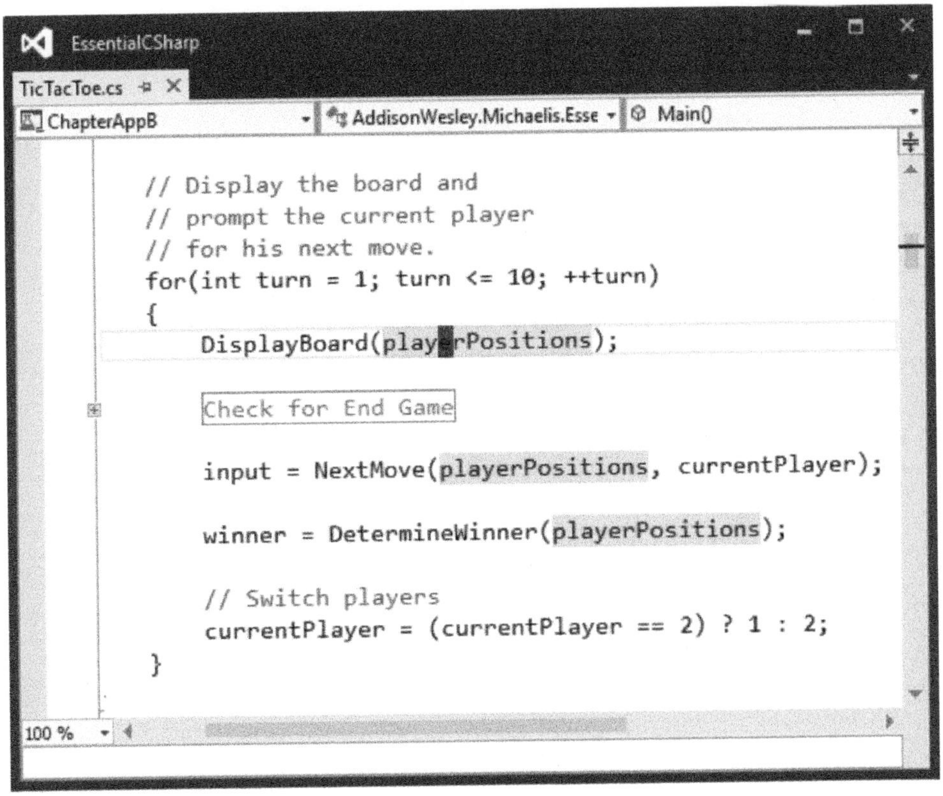

FIGURE 4.5: Collapsed region in Microsoft Visual Studio .NET

Summary

This chapter began by introducing the C# operators related to assignment and arithmetic. Next, we used the operators along with the `const` keyword to declare constants. Coverage of all the C# operators was not sequential, however. Before discussing the relational and logical comparison operators, the chapter introduced the `if` statement and the important concepts of code blocks and scope. To close out the coverage of operators, we discussed the bitwise operators, especially regarding masks. We also discussed other control flow statements such as loops, `switch`, and `goto`, and ended the chapter with a discussion of the C# preprocessor directives.

Operator precedence was discussed earlier in the chapter; Table 4.7 summarizes the order of precedence across all operators, including several that have not yet been covered.

TABLE 4.7: Operator Order of Precedence*

<table>
<tr><th>Category</th><th>Operators</th></tr>
<tr><td>Primary</td><td>x.y f(x) a[x] x++ x-- new
typeof(T) checked(x) unchecked(x) default(T)
nameof(x) delegate{} ()</td></tr>
<tr><td>Unary</td><td>+ - ! ~ ++x --x (T)x await x</td></tr>
<tr><td>Multiplicative</td><td>* / %</td></tr>
<tr><td>Additive</td><td>+ -</td></tr>
<tr><td>Shift</td><td><< >></td></tr>
<tr><td>Relational and type testing</td><td>< > <= >= is as</td></tr>
<tr><td>Equality</td><td>== !=</td></tr>
<tr><td>Logical AND</td><td>&</td></tr>
<tr><td>Logical XOR</td><td>^</td></tr>
<tr><td>Logical OR</td><td>|</td></tr>
<tr><td>Conditional AND</td><td>&&</td></tr>
<tr><td>Conditional OR</td><td>||</td></tr>
<tr><td>Null-coalescing</td><td>??</td></tr>
<tr><td>Conditional</td><td>?:</td></tr>
<tr><td>Assignment and lambda</td><td>= *= /= %= += -= <<= >>= &= ^= |= =></td></tr>
</table>

* Rows appear in order of precedence from highest to lowest.

Perhaps one of the best ways to review all of the content covered in Chapters 1, 2, and 3 is to look at the tic-tac-toe program found in Chapter04\TicTacToe.cs (http://itl.tc/esc/TicTacToe). By reviewing this program, you can see one way in which you can combine all that you have learned into a complete program.

5

Parameters and Methods

From what you have learned about C# programming so far, you should be able to write straightforward programs consisting of a list of statements, similar to the way programs were created in the 1970s. Programming has come a long way since the 1970s, however; as programs have become more complex, new paradigms have emerged to manage that complexity. Procedural or structured programming provides constructs by which statements are grouped together to form units. Furthermore, with structured programming, it is possible to pass data to a group of statements and then have data returned once the statements have executed.

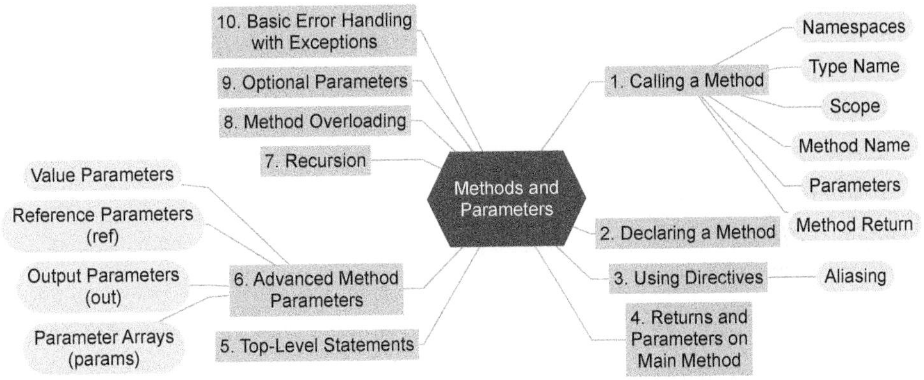

Besides the basics of calling and defining methods, this chapter covers some slightly more advanced concepts—namely, recursion, method overloading, optional parameters, and named arguments. All method calls discussed so far and through the end of this chapter are static (a concept that Chapter 6 explores in detail).

Even as early as the `HelloWorld` program in Chapter 1, you learned how to define a method. In that example, you defined the `Main()` method. In this chapter, you will learn about method creation in more detail, including the special C# syntaxes (`ref` and `out`) for parameters that pass variables rather than values to methods. Lastly, we will touch on some rudimentary error handling.

Calling a Method

BEGINNER TOPIC

What Is a Method?

Up to this point, almost all of the statements in the programs you have written have appeared together in a list without any grouping outside of what the statement or code block provided. When programs become any more complex, this approach quickly becomes difficult to maintain and complicated to read through and understand.

A **method** is a means of grouping together sequence a of statements to perform a particular action or compute a particular result. This provides greater structure and organization for the statements that compose a program. Consider, for example, a `Main()` method that counts the lines of source code in a directory. Instead of having one large `Main()` method, you can provide a shorter version that allows you to hone in on the details of each method implementation as necessary. Listing 5.1 shows an example.

LISTING 5.1: Grouping Statements into Methods

```
public class Program
{
    public static void Main()
    {
        int lineCount;
```

```
            string files;

            DisplayHelpText();
            files = GetFiles();
            lineCount = CountLines(files);
            DisplayLineCount(lineCount);
        }

        // ...
        // ...
    }
```

Instead of placing all of the statements into `Main()`, the listing breaks them into groups called methods. The `System.Console.WriteLine()` statements that display the help text have been moved to the `DisplayHelpText()` method. All of the statements used to determine which files to count appear in the `GetFiles()` method. To actually count the lines, the code calls the `CountLines()` method before displaying the results using the `DisplayLineCount()` method. With a quick glance, it is easy to review the code and gain an overview, because the method name describes the purpose of the method.

BEGINNER TOPIC

What Is a Function?

Functions are virtually identical to methods, used for grouping together a sequence of statements to perform a particular action or compute a particular result. In fact, frequently, *method* and *function* are used interchangably. Technically, however, methods are always associated with a type—such as `Program` in Listing 5.1. In contrast, functions have no such association. A function doesn't necessarily have an owning type.

Guidelines

DO give methods names that are verbs or verb phrases.

A method provides a means of grouping related code together. Methods can receive data via **arguments** that are passed to the method **parameters**. Parameters are variables used for passing data from the **caller** (the code containing the method call or **invocation**) to the called or **invoked** method (`Write()`, `WriteLine()`, `GetFiles()`, `CountLines()`, and so on). In Listing 5.1, `files` and `lineCount` are examples of arguments passed to the `CountLines()` and `DisplayLineCount()` methods via their parameters. Methods can also return data to the caller via a **return value** (in Listing 5.1, the `GetFiles()` method call has a return value that is assigned to `files`).

To begin, we reexamine `System.Console.Write()`, `System.Console.WriteLine()`, and `System.Console.ReadLine()` from Chapter 1. This time we look at them as examples of method calls in general instead of looking at the specifics of printing and retrieving data from the console. Listing 5.2 shows each of the three methods in use.

Listing 5.2: A Simple Method Call

```
public static void Main()
{
    string? firstName;
    string? lastName;

    Console.WriteLine("Hey you!");

    Console.Write("Enter your first name: ");
    firstName = Console.ReadLine();

    Console.Write("Enter your last name: ");
    lastName = Console.ReadLine();

    Console.WriteLine(
        $"Your full name is { firstName } { lastName }.");
}
```

The parts of the method call include the method name, argument list, and returned value. A fully qualified method name includes a namespace, type name, and method name; a period separates each part of a fully qualified method name. As we saw in type names (https://essentialcsharp.com/type-name-forms) in Chapter 2, methods may also be called with only the last part of their fully qualified name.

Namespaces

Namespaces are a categorization mechanism for grouping all types related to a particular area of functionality. Namespaces are hierarchical and can have arbitrarily many levels in the hierarchy, though namespaces with more than half a dozen levels are rare. Typically, the hierarchy begins with a company name, and then a product name, and then the functional area. For example, in `Microsoft.Win32.Networking`, the outermost namespace is `Microsoft`, which contains an inner namespace `Win32`, which in turn contains an even more deeply nested `Networking` namespace.

Namespaces are primarily used to organize types by area of functionality so that they can be more easily found and understood. However, they can also be used to avoid type name collisions. For example, the compiler can distinguish between two types with the name `Button` as long as each type has a different namespace. Thus you can disambiguate types `System.Web.UI.WebControls.Button` and `System.Windows.Controls.Button`.

In Listing 5.2, the `Console` type is found within the `System` namespace. The `System` namespace contains the types that enable the programmer to perform many fundamental programming activities. Almost all C# programs use types within the `System` namespace. Table 5.1 provides a listing of other common namespaces.

TABLE 5.1: Common Namespaces

Namespace	Description
`System`	Contains the fundamental types and types for conversion between types, mathematics, program invocation, and environment management.
`System.Collections.Generics`	Contains strongly typed collections that use generics.
`System.Data.Entity`	A framework designed to store and retrieve data from a relational database through code generation that maps entities into tables.
`System.Drawing`	Contains types for drawing to the display device and working with images. Note, however, it is mostly Windows specific.

Table 5.1: Common Namespaces (continued)

Namespace	Description
`System.IO`	Contains types for working with directories and manipulating, loading, and saving files.
`System.Linq`	Contains classes and interfaces for querying data in collections using a Language Integrated Query.
`System.Text`	Contains types for working with strings and various text encodings and for converting between those encodings.
`System.Text.RegularExpressions`	Contains types for working with regular expressions.
`System.Threading`	Contains types for multithreaded programming.
`System.Threading.Tasks`	Contains types for task-based asynchrony.
`System.Windows`	Contains types for creating rich user interfaces when working with UI technologies such as Windows Presentation Foundation (WPF), or Windows UI Library (WinUI), leveraging Extensible Application Markup Language (XAML) for declarative design of the UI.
`System.Xml.Linq`	Contains standards-based support for XML processing using an object query language called LINQ (See Chapter 15).

It is not always necessary to provide the namespace when calling a method. For example, if the call expression appears in a type in the same namespace as the called method, the compiler can infer the namespace to be the namespace that contains the type. Later in this chapter, you will see how the using directive eliminates the need for a namespace qualifier as well.

Guidelines

DO use PascalCasing for namespace names.

CONSIDER organizing the directory hierarchy for source code files to match the namespace hierarchy.

Type Name

Calls to static methods require the type name qualifier as long as the target method is not within the same type.[1] (As discussed later in the chapter, a using static directive allows you to omit the type name.) For example, a call expression of `Console.WriteLine()` found in the method `HelloWorld.Main()` requires the type, `Console`, to be specified. However, just as with the namespace, C# allows the omission of the type name from a method call whenever the method is a member of the type containing the call expression. (Examples of method calls such as this appear in Listing 5.4.) The type name is unnecessary in such cases because the compiler infers the type from the location of the call. If the compiler can make no such inference, the name must be provided as part of the method call.

At their core, types are a means of grouping together methods and their associated data. For example, `Console` is the type that contains the `Write()`, `WriteLine()`, and `ReadLine()` methods (among others). All of these methods are in the same *group* because they belong to the `Console` type.

Scope

In Chapter 4, you learned that the *scope* of a program element is the region of text in which it can be referred to by its unqualified name. A call that appears inside a type declaration to a method declared in that type does not require the type qualifier because the method is in scope throughout its containing type. Similarly, a type is in scope throughout the namespace that declares it; therefore, a method call that appears in a type in a particular namespace need not specify that namespace in the method call name.

Method Name

Every method call contains a method name, which might or might not be qualified with a namespace and type name, as we have discussed. After the method name comes the argument list, which is a parenthesized, comma-separated list of the values that correspond to the parameters of the method.

1. Or base class.

Parameters and Arguments

A method can take any number of parameters, and each parameter is of a specific data type. The values that the caller supplies for parameters are called the **arguments**; every argument must correspond to a particular parameter. For example, the following method call has three arguments:

```
System.IO.File.Copy(
oldFileName, newFileName, false)
```

The method is found on the class `File`, which is in the namespace `System.IO`. It is declared to have three parameters, with the first and second being of type `string` and the third being of type `bool`. In this example, we use variables (`oldFileName` and `newFileName`) of type `string` for the old and new filenames, and then specify `false` to indicate that the copy should fail if the new filename already exists.

Method Return Values

In contrast to `Console.WriteLine()`, the method call `Console.ReadLine()` in Listing 5.2 does not have any arguments because the method is declared to take no parameters. However, this method happens to have a **method return value**. The method return value is a means of transferring results from a called method back to the caller. Because `Console.ReadLine()` has a return value, it is possible to assign the return value to the variable `firstName`. In addition, it is possible to pass this method return value itself as an argument to another method call, as shown in Listing 5.3.

Listing 5.3: Passing a Method Return Value as an Argument to Another Method Call

```
public static void Main()
{
    Console.Write("Enter your first name: ");
    Console.WriteLine($"Hello { Console.ReadLine() }!");
}
```

Instead of assigning the returned value to a variable and then using that variable as an argument to the call to `Console.WriteLine()`, Listing 5.3 calls the `Console.ReadLine()` method within the call to `Console.WriteLine()`. At execution time, the `Console.ReadLine()` method executes first, and its return value is passed directly into the `Console.WriteLine()` method, rather than into a variable.

Not all methods return data. Both versions of `Console.Write()` and `Console.WriteLine()` are examples of such methods. As you will see shortly, these methods specify a return type of `void`, just as the `HelloWorld` declaration of `Main` returned `void`.

Statement versus Method Call

Listing 5.3 provides a demonstration of the difference between a statement and a method call. Although `Console.WriteLine($"Hello { System.Console.ReadLine()}!");` is a single statement, it contains two method calls. A statement often contains one or more expressions, and in this example, two of those expressions are method calls. Therefore, method calls form parts of statements.

Although coding multiple method calls in a single statement often reduces the amount of code, it does not necessarily increase the readability and seldom offers a significant performance advantage. Developers should favor readability over brevity.

> **NOTE**
>
> In general, developers should favor readability over brevity. Readability is critical to writing code that is self-documenting and therefore more maintainable over time.

Declaring a Method

This section expands on the explanation of declaring a method to include parameters or a return type. Listing 5.4 contains examples of these concepts, and Output 5.1 shows the results.

Listing 5.4: Declaring a Method

```
public class IntroducingMethods
{
    public static void Main()
```

```
    {
        string firstName;
        string lastName;
        string fullName;
        string initials;

        Console.WriteLine("Hey you!");

        firstName = GetUserInput("Enter your first name: ");
        lastName = GetUserInput("Enter your last name: ");

        fullName = GetFullName(firstName, lastName);
        initials = GetInitials(firstName, lastName);
        DisplayGreeting(fullName, initials);
    }

    static string GetUserInput(string prompt)
    {
        Console.Write(prompt);
        return Console.ReadLine() ?? string.Empty;
    }

    static string GetFullName(
          string firstName, string lastName) =>
              $"{ firstName } { lastName }";


    static void DisplayGreeting(string fullName, string initials)
    {
        Console.WriteLine(
            $"Hello { fullName }! Your initials are { initials }");
        return;
    }

    static string GetInitials(string firstName, string lastName)
    {
        return $"{ firstName[0] }. { lastName[0] }.";
    }
}
```

Output 5.1

```
Hey you!
Enter your first name: Inigo
```

```
Enter your last name: Montoya
Hello Inigo Montoya! Your initials are I. M.
```

Listing 5.4 declares five methods. From `Main()` the code calls `GetUserInput()`, followed by a call to `GetFullName()` and `GetInitials()`. All of the last three methods return a value and take arguments. In addition, the listing calls `DisplayGreeting()`, which doesn't return any data.

Language Contrast: C++/Visual Basic—Global Methods

C# provides no global method support; everything must appear within a type declaration. This is why the `Main()` method was marked as `static`—the C# equivalent of a C++ global and Visual Basic "shared" method. The statements that appear independent from a method and the methods that appear independent from a class are even conforming to this rule because the C# complier generates the surrounding method and class for these seemingly independent constructs. For more information, see "Top-Level Statements" later in this chapter.

BEGINNER TOPIC

Refactoring into Methods

Moving a set of statements into a method instead of leaving them inline within a larger method is a form of **refactoring**. Refactoring reduces code duplication, because you can call the method from multiple places instead of duplicating the code. Refactoring also increases code readability. As part of the coding process, it is a best practice to continually review your code and look for opportunities to refactor. This involves looking for blocks of code that are difficult to understand at a glance and moving them into a method with a name that clearly defines the code's behavior. This practice is often preferred over adding comments to a block of code, because the method name serves to describe what the implementation does. Listing 5.4 is easy to grasp at a glance by just viewing the `Main()` method and not worrying about the details of each called method's implementation.

Visual Studio allows you to right-click on a block of code within a method and click **Quick Actions and Refactorings...** (Ctrl+.) to extract the block into its own method, automatically inserting code to call the new method from the original location.

Formal Parameter Declaration

Consider the declarations of the `DisplayGreeting()`, `GetFullName()`, and the `GetInitials()` methods. The text that appears between the parentheses of a method declaration is the **formal parameter list**. (As we will see when we discuss generics, methods may also have a **type parameter list**. When it is clear from the context which kind of parameters we are discussing, we simply refer to them as *parameters* in a *parameter list*.) Each parameter in the parameter list includes the type of the parameter along with the parameter name. A comma separates each parameter in the list.

Behaviorally, most parameters are virtually identical to local variables, and the naming convention of parameters follows accordingly. Therefore, parameter names use camelCase. Also, it is not possible to declare a local variable (a variable declared inside a method) with the same name as a parameter of the containing method, because this would create two local variables of the same name.

Guidelines

DO use camelCasing for parameter names.

Method Return Type Declaration

In addition to `GetUserInput()`, `GetFullName()`, and the `GetInitials()` methods requiring parameters to be specified, each of these methods includes a **method return type**. You can tell that a method returns a value because a data type appears immediately before the method name in the method declaration. Each of these method examples specifies a `string` return type. Unlike parameters, of which there can be any number, only one method return type is allowable.

As with `GetUserInput()` and `GetInitials()`, methods with a return type almost always[2] contain one or more `return` statements that return control to the caller. A `return` statement consists of the `return` keyword followed by an expression that computes the value the method is returning. For example, the `GetInitials()` method's `return` statement is `return $"{ firstName[0] }. { lastName[0] }.";`. The expression (an interpolated string in this case) following the `return` keyword must be compatible with the stated return type of the method.

If a method has a return type, the block of statements that makes up the body of the method must not have an *unreachable end point*. That is, there must be no way for control to "fall off the end" of a method without returning a value. Often the easiest way to ensure that this condition is met is to make the last statement of the method a `return` statement. However, `return` statements can appear in locations other than at the end of a method implementation. For example, an `if` or `switch` statement in a method implementation could include a `return` statement within it; see Listing 5.5 for an example.

LISTING 5.5: A `return` Statement before the End of a Method

```
public class Program
{
    // ...

    public static bool MyMethod()
    {
        string command = ObtainCommand();
        switch(command)
        {
            case "quit":
                return false;
            // ... omitted, other cases
            default:
                return true;
        }
    }
```

2. For example, you could throw an exception instead.

```
    // ...
}
```

(Note that a `return` statement transfers control out of the `switch`, so no `break` statement is required to prevent illegal fall-through in a switch section that ends with a `return` statement.)

In Listing 5.5, the last statement in the method is not a `return` statement; it is a `switch` statement. However, the compiler can deduce that every possible code path through the method results in a `return`, so that the end point of the method is not reachable. Thus, this method is legal even though it does not end with a `return` statement.

If particular code paths include unreachable statements following the `return`, the compiler will issue a warning that indicates the additional statements will never execute.

Though C# allows a method to have multiple `return` statements, code is generally more readable and easier to maintain if there is a single exit location rather than having multiple returns sprinkled through various code paths of the method.

Specifying `void` as a return type indicates that there is no return value from the method. As a result, a call to the method may not be assigned to a variable or used as a parameter type at the call site. A `void` method call may be used only as a statement. Furthermore, within the body of the method the `return` statement becomes optional, and when it is specified, there must be no value following the `return` keyword. For example, the return of `Main()` in Listing 5.4 is `void`, and there is no `return` statement within the method. However, `DisplayGreeting()` includes an (optional) `return` statement that is not followed by any returned result.

Although, technically, a method can have only one return type, the return type could be a tuple. As a result, starting with C# 7.0, it is possible to return multiple values packaged as a tuple using C# tuple syntax. For example, you could declare a `GetName()` method, as shown in Listing 5.6.

Listing 5.6: Returning Multiple Values Using a Tuple

```
public class Program
{
    static string GetUserInput(string prompt)
    {
```

```
        Console.Write(prompt);
        return Console.ReadLine() ?? string.Empty;
    }
    static (string First, string Last) GetName()
    {
        string firstName, lastName;
        firstName = GetUserInput("Enter your first name: ");
        lastName = GetUserInput("Enter your last name: ");
        return (firstName, lastName);
    }
    static public void Main()
    {
        (string First, string Last) name = GetName();
        Console.WriteLine($"Hello { name.First } { name.Last }!");
    }
}
```

Technically, we are still returning only one data type, a `ValueTuple<string, string>`. However, effectively, you can return any (preferably reasonable) number you like using each item within the tuple.

Expression Bodied Methods

To support the simplest of method declarations without the formality of a method body, C# 6.0 introduced **expression bodied methods**, which are declared using an expression rather than a full method body. Listing 5.4's `GetFullName()` method provides an example of the expression bodied method:

```
static string GetFullName( string firstName, string lastName) =>
```

In place of the curly brackets typical of a method body, an expression bodied method uses the "goes to" operator (fully introduced in Chapter 13), for which the resulting data type must match the return type of the method. In other words, even though there is no explicit `return` statement in the expression bodied method implementation, it is still necessary that the return type from the expression match the method declaration's return type.

Expression bodied methods are syntactic shortcuts to the fuller method body declaration. As such, their use should be limited to the simplest of method implementations—generally expressible on a single line.

Language Contrast: C++—Header Files

Unlike in C++, C# classes never separate the implementation from the declaration. In C#, there is no header (.h) file or implementation (.cpp) file. Instead, declaration and implementation appear together in the same file. (C# does support an advanced feature called *partial methods*, in which the method's defining declaration is separate from its implementation, but for the purposes of this chapter, we consider only nonpartial methods.) The lack of a separate declaration and implementation in C# removes the requirement to maintain redundant declaration information in two places found in languages that have separate header and implementation files, such as C++.

Local Functions

C# 7.0 introduced the ability to declare functions within methods. In other words, rather than always declaring a method within a class, the method (technically a function) could be declared within another method (see Listing 5.7).

LISTING 5.7: Declaring a Local Function

```
public static void Main()
{
    string GetUserInput(string prompt)
    {
        string? input;
        do
        {
            Console.Write(prompt + ": ");
            input = Console.ReadLine();
        }
        while(string.IsNullOrWhiteSpace(input));
        return input!;
    };

    string firstName = GetUserInput("First Name");
    string lastName = GetUserInput("Last Name");
    string email = GetUserInput("Email Address");

    Console.WriteLine($"{firstName} {lastName} <{email}>");
    //...
```

This language construct is called a **local function**. The reason to declare it like this is that the function's scope is limited to invocation from within the method where it is declared. Outside of the method's scope, it is not possible to call the local function. In addition, the local function can access local variables in the method that are declared before the local function. Alternatively, this can explicitly be prevented by adding the `static` to the beginning of the local function declaration (see "Static Anonymous Functions" (https://essentialcsharp.com/outer-variables) in Chapter 13).

Using Directives

Fully qualified namespace names can become quite long and unwieldy. It is possible, however, to import all the types from one or more namespaces so that they can be used without full qualification.

Using Directive Overview

Rather than a declarative that applies to the entire project, C# includes a using directive that applies only to the current file. For example, Listing 5.8 (with Output 5.2) doesn't prefix `RegEx` with `System.Text.RegularExpressions`. The namespace may be omitted because of the `using System.Text.RegularExpressions` directive that appears at the top of the listing.

Listing 5.8: Using Directive Example

```
// The using directive imports all types from the
// specified namespace into the entire file
using System.Text.RegularExpressions;

public class Program
{
    public static void Main()
    {
        const string firstName = "FirstName";
        const string initial = "Initial";
        const string lastName = "LastName";

        // Explaining regular expressions is beyond the
        // scope of this book.
```

```
            // See https://www.regular-expressions.info/ for
            // more information.
            const string pattern = $"""
                (?<{firstName}>\w+)\s+((?<{
                initial}>\w)\.\s+)?(?<{
                lastName}>\w+)\s*
                """;

            Console.WriteLine(
                "Enter your full name (e.g. Inigo T. Montoya): ");
            string name = Console.ReadLine()!;

            // No need to qualify RegEx type with
            // System.Text.RegularExpressions because
            // of the using directive above
            Match match = Regex.Match(name, pattern);

            if (match.Success)
            {
                Console.WriteLine(
                    $"{firstName}: {match.Groups[firstName]}");
                Console.WriteLine(
                    $"{initial}: {match.Groups[initial]}");
                Console.WriteLine(
                    $"{lastName}: {match.Groups[lastName]}");
            }
        }
    }
```

Output 5.2

```
Hello, my name is Inigo Montoya
```

A using directive such as `using System.Text` does not enable you to omit `System.Text` from a type declared within a **nested namespace** such as `System.Text.RegularExpressions`. For example, if your code accessed the `RegEx` type from the `System.Text.RegularExpressions` namespace, you would have to either include an additional `using System.Text.RegularExpressions` directive or fully qualify the type as `System.Text.RegularExpressions.RegEx`, not just `RegularExpressions.RegEx`. In short, a using directive does not import types from any nested namespaces. Nested namespaces, which are identified by the period in the namespace, always need to be imported explicitly.

Language Contrast: Java—Wildcards in the `import` Directive

Java enables importing namespaces using a wildcard such as the following:

```
import javax.swing.*;
```

In contrast, C# does not support a wildcard using directive but instead requires each namespace to be imported explicitly.

Frequent use of types within a particular namespace implies that the addition of a using directive for that namespace is a good idea, instead of fully qualifying all types within the namespace. Accordingly, almost all C# files include the `using System` directive at the top. Throughout the remainder of this book, code listings often omit the `using System` directive from the manuscript. Other namespace directives are generally included explicitly, however.

One interesting effect of the `using System` directive is that the string data type can be identified with varying case: `String` or `string`. The former version relies on the `using System` directive, and the latter uses the `string` keyword. Both are valid C# references to the `System.String` data type, and the resultant Common Intermediate Language (CIL) code is unaffected by which version is chosen.

BEGINNER TOPIC

Namespaces

As described earlier, **namespaces** are an organizational mechanism for categorizing and grouping together related types. Developers can discover related types by examining other types within the same namespace as a familiar type. Additionally, through namespaces, two or more types may have the same name as long as they are disambiguated by different namespaces.

Begin 10.0

Implicit Using Directives

Readers will recall from Chapter 1 there was an `ImplicitUsings` element within the `.csproj` file for C# 10.0 and later:

```
<ImplicitUsings>enable</ImplicitUsings>
```

In addition, the source code consistently refers to things like `Console`, even though the fully qualified name is `System.Console`. The ability to abbreviate is afforded by the `ImplicitUsings` element, which tells the compiler to infer the namespace automatically rather than require the programmer to provide it. Using directives, therefore, allows the use of type identifiers without specifying their fully qualified name. To accomplish this, the complier generates global using directives whenever the `ImplicitUsings` element is set to `enable`.

Global Using Directives

If you search the subdirectory of a C# 10.0 (or higher) project, you will notice there is a file with the extension `.GlobalUsing.g.cs`, generally found in an `obj` folder subdirectory, and it contains multiple global using directives such as those found in Listing 5.9.

Listing 5.9: Implicit Usings Generated Global Using Declaratives[3]

```
// <auto-generated/>
global using global::System;
global using global::System.Collections.Generic;
global using global::System.IO;
global using global::System.Linq;
global using global::System.Net.Http;
global using global::System.Threading;
global using global::System.Threading.Tasks;
```

3. Although removed from this listing for elucidation purposes, the generated global using statements prefix the namespace with "global::" as in `global using global::System`. Discussion of namespace alias qualifiers appears later in the section.

Each of these lines[4] is a global using directive that tells the compiler to imply the namespace qualifier for any type that appears within the namespace specified. For example, `global using global::System` allows implicit using directives like `Console.WriteLine("Hello! My name is Inigo Montoya!")` rather than the fully qualified name `System.Console.WriteLine(...)` because `Console` is defined in the `System` namespace.

Of course, you can provide your own global using declaratives. Say, for example, you frequently are using the `System.Text.StringBuilder` class (initially introduced in Chapter 2). Instead of always referring to it by the fully qualified name, you can provide a global using directive for the `System.Text` namespace and then just refer to the type using the abbreviation `StringBuilder` (see Listing 5.10), also still relying on implicit usings for `System.Console`.

Listing 5.10: Implicit Using Directives with `StringBuilder`

```
// The global using directive imports all types from
// the specified namespace into the project
global using System.Text;
// ...
public class Program
{
    public static void Main()
    {
        // See Chapter 6 for explanation of new();
        StringBuilder name = new();

        Console.WriteLine("Enter your first name: ");
        name.Append(Console.ReadLine()!.Trim());

        Console.WriteLine("Enter your middle initial: ");
        name.Append( $" { Console.ReadLine()!.Trim('.').Trim() }." );

        Console.WriteLine("Enter your last name: ");
        name.Append($" { Console.ReadLine()!.Trim() }");

        Console.WriteLine($"Hello {name}!");
    }
}
```

4. Ignoring the comment that shows the code was generated by the compiler.

The global using directives applies to the entire project regardless of in which file it appears. And, although C# allows the same global using declarative multiple times, doing so is redundant. For this reason, it is preferable to place all the global using directives into a single file named `Usings.cs` by convention. Collocating them here also provides a well-known location to place them or remove such declaratives.

While global using directives apply to the entire project, C# also supports using directives that apply only to the current file. The global using declarative, however, must appear before any other (non-global) using directives, which we cover after the `.csproj` using element.

csproj Using Element

It is also possible to specify global using declaratives within your project (`.csproj`) file with a `Using` element, as shown in Listing 5.11

Listing 5.11: Sample .NET Console Project File with Using Element

```
<Project Sdk="Microsoft.NET.Sdk">
  <PropertyGroup>
    <OutputType>Exe</OutputType>
    <TargetFramework>net7.0</TargetFramework>
    <ImplicitUsings>enable</ImplicitUsings>
    <Nullable>enable</Nullable>
  </PropertyGroup>
  <ItemGroup>
    <Using Include="System.Net" />
    <Using Static="true" Include="System.Console"/>
  </ItemGroup>
</Project>
```

The important thing to note is that unlike the `ImplicitUsings` element, the `Using` element is a subelement to the `ItemGroup` element rather than the `PropertyGroup` element. And, given the `Using` element for `System.Net` specified, it is no longer necessary to fully qualify `HttpClient`, which is part of the `System.Net` namespace. Instead, the compiler will generate a global using `System.Net` directive when building the project. There is also another `Using` statement that includes a `Static` attribute on it, which we will explain further in the next section.

ADVANCED TOPIC

Nested Using Directives

Not only can you have using directives at the top of a file, but you can also include them at the top of a namespace declaration. For example, if a new namespace, `EssentialCSharp`, were declared, it would be possible to add a using declarative at the top of the namespace declaration (see Listing 5.12).

LISTING 5.12: Specifying the `using` Directive inside a Namespace Declaration

```
// The using directive imports all types from the
// specified namespace into the entire file
using System.Text.RegularExpressions;

public class Program
{
    public static void Main()
    {
        // ...
        // No need to qualify RegEx type with
        // System.Text.RegularExpressions because
        // of the using directive above
        Match match = Regex.Match(name, pattern);
        // ...
    }
}
```

The difference between placing the using directive at the top of a file and placing it at the top of a namespace declaration is that the directive is active only within the namespace declaration. If the code includes a new namespace declaration above or below the `EssentialCSharp` declaration, the `using System` directive within a different namespace would not be active. Code seldom is written this way, especially given the standard practice of providing a single type declaration per file.

End 10.0

Using Static Directive

The using directive allows you to abbreviate a type name by omitting the namespace portion of the name—such that just the type name can be specified for any type within the stated namespace. In contrast, the using static directive allows you to omit both the namespace and the type name from any static member of the stated type. A `using static System.Console` directive, for example, allows you to specify `WriteLine()` rather than the fully qualified method name of `System.Console.WriteLine()`. Continuing with this example, we can update Listing 5.2 to leverage the `using static System.Console` directive to create Listing 5.13.

Listing 5.13: Using Static Directive

```
using static System.Console;

public class HeyYou
{
    public static void Main()
    {
        string firstName;
        string lastName;

        WriteLine("Hey you!");

        Write("Enter your first name: ");
        firstName = ReadLine() ?? string.Empty;

        Write("Enter your last name: ");
        lastName = ReadLine() ?? string.Empty;

        WriteLine(
            $"Your full name is { firstName } { lastName }.");
    }
}
```

In this case, there is no loss of readability of the code: `WriteLine()`, `Write()`, and `ReadLine()` all clearly relate to a console directive. In fact, one could argue that the resulting code is simpler and therefore clearer than before.

However, sometimes this is not the case. For example, if your code uses classes that have overlapping behavior names, such as an `Exists()` method on a file and an `Exists()` method on a directory, then a using static directive would reduce clarity when you invoke `Exists()`. Similarly, if the class you were writing had its own members with overlapping behavior names—for example, `Display()` and `Write()`—then clarity would be lost to the reader.

This ambiguity would not be allowed by the compiler. If two members with the same signature were available (through either using static directives or separately declared members), any invocation of them that was ambiguous would result in a compile error.

Begin 10.0

Note that C# 10 or later also support global static using directives such as:

```
global using static System.Console;
```

Similarly, a global using static directive can be configured in the csproj file:

```
<Using Static="true" Include="System.Console"/>
```

This is also shown in Listing 5.11.

End 10.0

Begin 12.0

Aliasing

Starting in C# 12.0, the using directive also allows **aliasing** a namespace or any type including tuples, pointers (Chapter 23), array types, and generic types (Chapter 12). An alias is an alternative name that you can use within the text to which the using directive applies. The two most common reasons for aliasing are to disambiguate two types that have the same name and to abbreviate a long name. In Listing 5.14, for example, the `CountDownTimer` alias is declared as a means of referring to the type `System.Timers.Timer`. Simply adding a `using System.Timers` directive will not sufficiently enable the code to avoid fully qualifying the `Timer` type. The reason is that `System.Threading` also includes a type called `Timer`; therefore, using just `Timer` within the code will be ambiguous.

Listing 5.14: Declaring a Type Alias

```
using CountDownTimer = System.Timers.Timer;
using StartStop = (DateTime Start, DateTime Stop);

public class HelloWorld
{
    public static void Main()
    {
        CountDownTimer timer;
        StartStop startStop;
```

```
        // ...
    }
}
```

Listing 5.14 uses an entirely new name, `CountDownTimer`, as the alias. It is possible, however, to specify the alias as `Timer`, as shown in Listing 5.15.

LISTING 5.15: Declaring a Type Alias with the Same Name

```
// Declare alias Timer to refer to System.Timers.Timer to
// avoid code ambiguity with System.Threading.Timer
using Timer = System.Timers.Timer;

public class HelloWorld
{
    public static void Main()
    {
        Timer timer;

        // ...
    }
}
```

Because of the alias directive, "Timer" is not an ambiguous reference. Furthermore, to refer to the `System.Threading.Timer` type, you will have to either qualify the type or define a different alias.

End 12.0

Begin 10.0

Of course, C# 10 and later also support global aliasing using directives such as:

```
global using Timer = Timers.Timer;
```

And like with all other global using directives, a global using alias directive can be configured in the csproj file:

```
<Using Include=" System.Timers.Timer" Alias="Timer"/>
```

End 10.0

Returns and Parameters on Main Method

So far, declaration of an executable's Main method has been the simplest declaration possible. You have not included any parameters or non-`void` return type in your

Main method declarations. However, C# supports the ability to retrieve the command-line arguments when executing a program, and it is possible to return a status indicator from the Main method.

The runtime passes the command-line arguments to `Main()` using a single `string` array parameter—named `args` by convention. All you need to do to retrieve the parameters is to access the array, as demonstrated in Listing 5.16 with Output 5.3. The output shows a run with no parameters and a second run with two parameters. The purpose of this program is to download a file whose location is specified by a URL. The first command-line argument identifies the URL, and the second argument is the filename to which to save the file. The listing begins with a `switch` statement that evaluates the number of parameters (`args.Length`) as follows:

1. If there are not two parameters, display an error indicating that it is necessary to provide the URL and filename.

2. The presence of two arguments indicates the user has provided both the URL of the resource and the download target filename.

LISTING 5.16: Passing Command-Line Arguments to a Main Method

```
public class Program
{
    public static int Main(string[] args)
    {
        int result;
        if(args?.Length != 2 )
        {
            // Exactly two arguments must be specified; give an error
            Console.WriteLine(
                "ERROR:  You must specify the "
                + "URL and the file name");
            Console.WriteLine(
                "Usage: Downloader.exe <URL> <TargetFileName>");
            result = 1;
        }
        else
        {
            string urlString = args[0];
            string fileName = args[1];
```

```
            HttpClient client = new();
            byte[] response =
                client.GetByteArrayAsync(urlString).Result;
            client.Dispose();
            File.WriteAllBytes(fileName, response);
            Console.WriteLine($"Downloaded '{ fileName }' from '{
↪urlString }'.");
            result = 0;
        }
        return result;
    }
}
```

Output 5.3

```
>Downloader
ERROR:  You must specify the URL and the file name
Usage: Downloader.exe <URL> <TargetFileName>
>Downloader https://IntelliTect.com Index.html
Downloaded 'Index.html' from 'https://IntelliTect.com'.
```

If you were successful in calculating the target filename, you would use it to save the downloaded file. Otherwise, you would display the help text. The `Main()` method also returns an `int` rather than a `void`. This is optional for a Main method declarations, but if it is used, the program can return an exit code to a caller (such as a script or a batch file). By convention, a return other than zero indicates an error.

Although all command-line arguments can be passed to `Main()` via an array of strings, sometimes it is convenient to access the arguments from inside a method other than `Main()`. The `System.Environment.GetCommandLineArgs()` method returns the command-line arguments array in the same form that `Main(string[] args)` passes the arguments into the Main method except that the first item in the array is the executable filename.

To download the file, Listing 5.16 uses a `System.Net.Http.HttpClient` object but only specified `HttpClient`—its namespace is imported by the `ImplicitUsings` element in the `.csproj` file.

ADVANCED TOPIC

Disambiguate Multiple Main Methods

If a program includes two classes with Main methods, it is possible to specify which one to use as the entry point. In Visual Studio, right-clicking on the project from Solution Explorer and selecting **Properties** provides a user interface on top of the project file. By selecting the **Application** tab on the left, you can edit the Startup Object and select which type's Main method will start the program. The result will be an additional element in the `PropertyGroup`:

```
<StartupObject>AddisonWesley.Michaelis.EssentialCSharp.
Shared.Program
</StartupObject>
```

On the command line, you can specify the same value, setting the `StartupObject` property when running a build. For example:

```
dotnet build /p:StartupObject=AddisonWesley.Program2
```

where `AddisonWesley.Program2` is the namespace and class that contains the selected Main method. (In fact, any item in the `PropertyGroup` section of a csproj file can be specified on the command line this way.)

BEGINNER TOPIC

Call Stack and Call Site

As code executes, methods call more methods, which in turn call additional methods, and so on. In the simple case of Listing 5.4, `Main()` calls `GetUserInput()`, which in turn calls `System.Console.ReadLine()`, which in turn calls even more methods internally. Every time a new method is invoked, the runtime creates an *activation frame* that contains information about the arguments passed to the new call, the local variables of the new call, and information about where control should resume when the new method returns. The set of calls within calls within calls, and so on, produces a series of activation frames that is termed the **call stack**.[5] As

5. Except for async or iterator methods, which move their activator records onto the heap.

program complexity increases, the call stack generally gets larger and larger as each method calls another method. As calls complete, however, the call stack shrinks until another method is invoked. The process of removing activation frames from the call stack is termed **stack unwinding**. Stack unwinding always occurs in the reverse order of the method calls. When the method completes, execution returns to the **call site**—that is, the location from which the method was invoked.

Begin 9.0

Top-Level Statements

Until C# 9.0, all executable code in C# was required to appear within a type definition and a member such as a method within a type. As we saw in Listing 1.1, this is no longer required. Instead, it is possible for a single file to have **top-level statements**, statements that appear independent of any type definition and even without a Main method. Such statements are allowed in only one file, and they will be the first statements to execute within the program—the equivalent of the many statements that appear in the Main method. In fact, given top-level statements, the compiler generates a class called `Program` that wraps the top-level statements and places them into a Main method. Furthermore, the method has a contextual keyword —`args`—that is the equivalent of the `string[] args` parameter of a Main method.

With top-level statements, C# syntax allows the statements outside a method as a simplification—especially for new C# developers familiar with other languages that are less structured—but then moves these statements into the Main method at compiler time. The end result, therefore, is that there are never any statements in the underlying CIL that are not placed within a type definition and within a type member.

Since the C# compiler moves top-level methods into its own generated main method that is defined within a class named `Program`, the compiler issues an error if you try to define an additional class called `Program`.[6] One additional restriction

6. As the compiler warning indicates, you could define a `Program` class as partial, indicating that the two definitions will be merged into the same `Program` class. For more information, see "Partial Classes" in Chapter 6.

on top-level statements is that any type definition within the same file as the top-level statements must appear after such statements.

The file with top-level statements can also contain methods, which we will call **top-level methods**, and such methods can optionally appear independent of a type definition as well.

When running some of the New Project wizards in Visual Studio, there is frequently an option called "Do not use top-level statements" that allows you to choose whether to go with the simpler version or to generate the structure explicitly, resulting in code that looks more like Listing 1.1 (without a class or Main method). Similarly, on the dotnet command line, some of the project templates (i.e., the Console argument when running the `dotnet new Console` command) frequently have a `--use-program-main` option. However, top-level statements are available to only those projects that have entry points, in other words, Main methods. The compiler doesn't allow top-level statements on programs that do not have Main methods (such as class libraries).

Top-level statements were mainly introduced to remove unnecessary ceremony when writing simple programs, reducing the complexity for beginners especially. Prior to top-level statements, a program with a single statement would require both a type definition and a Main method just to code the single statement. With top-level statements, this structure is optionally eliminated. In addition, top-level statements allow for easier embedding of seemingly complete C# snippets within text like Polyglot notebooks (https://github.com/dotnet/interactive) or the online version of this book (https://essentialcsharp.com).

End 9.0

Advanced Method Parameters

So far this chapter's examples have returned data via the method return value. This section demonstrates how methods can return data via their method parameters and how a method may take a variable number of arguments.

Value Parameters

Arguments to method calls are usually **passed by value**, which means the value of the argument expression is copied into the target parameter. For example, in Listing

5.17, the value of each variable that Main() uses when calling Combine() will be copied into the parameters of the Combine() method. Output 5.4 shows the results of this listing.

Listing 5.17: Passing Variables by Value

```
public class Program
{
    public static void Main()
    {
        // ...
        string fullName;
        string driveLetter = "C:";
        string folderPath = "Data";
        string fileName = "index.html";

        fullName = Combine(driveLetter, folderPath, fileName);

        Console.WriteLine(fullName);
        // ...
    }

    static string Combine(
        string driveLetter, string folderPath, string fileName)
    {
        string path;
        path = string.Format("{1}{0}{2}{0}{3}",
            Path.DirectorySeparatorChar,
            driveLetter, folderPath, fileName);
        return path;
    }
}
```

Output 5.4

```
C:\Users\Inigo\Data\index.html
```

Even if the Combine() method assigned null to driveLetter, folderPath, and fileName before returning, the corresponding variables within Main() will maintain their original values because the variables are copied when calling a method. When the call stack unwinds at the end of a call, the copied data is thrown away.

BEGINNER TOPIC

Matching Caller Variables with Parameter Names

In Listing 5.17, the variable names in the caller exactly matched the parameter names in the called method. This matching is provided simply for readability purposes, whether names match is irrelevant to the behavior of the method call. The parameters of the called method and the local variables of the calling method are found in different declaration spaces and have nothing to do with each other.

ADVANCED TOPIC

Reference Types versus Value Types

For the purposes of this section, it is inconsequential whether the parameter passed is a value type or a reference type. Rather, the important issue is whether the called method can write a value into the caller's original variable. Since a copy of the caller variable's value is made, the caller's variable cannot be reassigned. Nevertheless, it is helpful to understand the difference between a variable that contains a value type and a variable that contains a reference type.

The value of a reference type variable is, as the name implies, a reference to the location where the data associated with the object is stored. How the runtime chooses to represent the value of a reference type variable is an implementation detail of the runtime; typically, it is represented as the address of the memory location in which the object's data is stored, but it need not be.

If a reference type variable is passed by value, the reference itself is copied from the caller to the method parameter. As a result, the target method cannot update the caller variable's value, but it may update the data referred to by the reference.

Alternatively, if the method parameter is a value type, the value itself is copied into the parameter, and changing the parameter in the called method will not affect the original caller's variable.

Reference Parameters (ref)

Consider Listing 5.18, which calls a function to swap two values, and Output 5.5, which shows the results.

Listing 5.18: Passing Variables by Reference

```
public class Program
{
    public static void Main()
    {
        // ...
        string first = "hello";
        string second = "goodbye";
        Swap(ref first, ref second);

        Console.WriteLine(
            $@"first = ""{ first }"", second = ""{ second }""");
        // ...
    }

    static void Swap(ref string x, ref string y)
    {
        string temp = x;
        x = y;
        y = temp;
    }
}
```

Output 5.5

```
first = "goodbye", second = "hello"
```

The values assigned to `first` and `second` are successfully switched. To do this, the variables are **passed by reference**. The obvious difference between the call to `Swap()` and Listing 5.17's call to `Combine()` is the inclusion of the keyword `ref` in front of the parameter's data type. This keyword changes the call such that the variables used as arguments are passed by reference, so the called method can update the original caller's variables with new values.

When the called method specifies a parameter as `ref`, the caller is required to supply a variable, not a value, as an argument and to place `ref` in front of the variables passed. In so doing, the caller explicitly recognizes that the target method could reassign the values of the variables associated with any `ref` parameters it receives. Furthermore, it is necessary to initialize any local variables passed as `ref` because target methods could read data from `ref` parameters without first assigning them. In Listing 5.18, for example, `temp` is assigned the value of `first`, assuming that the variable passed in `first` was initialized by the caller. Effectively, a `ref` parameter is an alias for the variable passed. In other words, it is essentially giving a parameter name to an existing variable, rather than creating a new variable and copying the value of the argument into it.

> **NOTE**
>
> The `ref` modifier assigns a parameter to refer to an existing variable on the stack rather than creating a new variable and copying the argument value into the parameters.

Output Parameters (`out`)

As mentioned earlier, a variable used as a `ref` parameter must be assigned before it is passed to the called method, because the called method might read from the variable. The "swap" example given previously must read and write from both variables passed to it. However, it is often the case that a method that takes a reference to a variable intends to write to the variable but not to read from it. In such cases, clearly it could be safe to pass an uninitialized local variable by reference.

To achieve this, code needs to decorate parameter types with the keyword `out`. This is demonstrated in the `TryGetPhoneButton()` method in Listing 5.19, which returns the phone button corresponding to a character.

Listing 5.19: Passing Variables Out Only

```
public static int Main(string[] args)
{
    if(args.Length == 0)
    {
        Console.WriteLine(
            "ConvertToPhoneNumber.exe <phrase>");
        Console.WriteLine(
```

```
                "'_' indicates no standard phone button");
            return 1;
        }
        foreach(string word in args)
        {
            foreach(char character in word)
            {
                if (TryGetPhoneButton(character, out char button))
                {
                    Console.Write(button);
                }
                else
                {
                    Console.Write('_');
                }
            }
        }
        Console.WriteLine();
        return 0;
    }

    static bool TryGetPhoneButton(char character, out char button)
    {
        bool success = true;
        switch(char.ToLower(character))
        {
            case '1':
                button = '1';
                break;
            case '2':
            case 'a':
            case 'b':
            case 'c':
                button = '2';
                break;

            // ...

            case '-':
                button = '-';
                break;
            default:
                // Set the button to indicate an invalid value
                button = '_';
                success = false;
                break;
        }
```

```
    return success;
}
```

Output 5.6 shows the results of Listing 5.19.

OUTPUT 5.6

```
>ConvertToPhoneNumber.exe CSharpIsGood
274277474663
```

In this example, the `TryGetPhoneButton()` method returns `true` if it can successfully determine the `character`'s corresponding phone button. The function also returns the corresponding button by using the `button` parameter, which is decorated with `out`.

An `out` parameter is functionally identical to a `ref` parameter; the only difference is which requirements the language enforces regarding how the aliased variable is read from and written to. Whenever a parameter is marked with `out`, the compiler checks that the parameter is set for all code paths within the method that return normally (i.e., the code paths that do not throw an exception). If, for example, the code does not assign `button` a value in some code path, the compiler will issue an error indicating that the code didn't initialize `button`. Listing 5.19 assigns `button` to the underscore character because even though it cannot determine the correct phone button, it is still necessary to assign a value.

A common coding mistake when working with `out` parameters is to forget to declare the `out` variable before you use it. Starting with C# 7.0, it is possible to declare the `out` variable inline when invoking the function. Listing 5.19 uses this feature with the statement `TryGetPhoneButton(character, out char button)` without ever declaring the `button` variable beforehand. Prior to C# 7.0, it would be necessary to first declare the `button` variable and then invoke the function with `TryGetPhoneButton(character, out button)`.

Another C# 7.0 feature is the ability to discard an `out` parameter entirely. If, for example, you simply wanted to know whether a character was a valid phone button but not actually return the numeric value, you could discard the `button` parameter using an underscore: `TryGetPhoneButton(character, out _)`.

Prior to C# 7.0's tuple syntax, a developer of a method might declare one or more `out` parameters to get around the restriction that a method may have only one return type; a method that needs to return two values can do so by returning one value normally, as the return value of the method, and a second value by writing it into an aliased variable passed as an `out` parameter. Although this pattern is both common and legal, there are usually better ways to achieve that aim. For example, if you are considering returning two or more values from a method and C# 7.0 is available, it is likely preferable to use C# 7.0 tuple syntax. Prior to that, consider writing two methods, one for each value, or still using the `System.ValueTuple` type but without C# 7.0 syntax.

NOTE

Each and every normal code path must result in the assignment of all `out` parameters.

Read-Only Pass by Reference (`in`)

In C# 7.2, support was added for passing a value type by reference that was read only. Rather than passing the value type to a function so that it could be changed, read-only pass by reference was added: It allows the value type to be passed by reference so that not only copy of the value type occurs but, in addition, the invoked method cannot change the value. In other words, the purpose of the feature is to reduce the memory copied when passing a value while still identifying it as read only, thus improving the performance. This syntax is to add an `in` modifier to the parameter. For example:

```
int Method(in int number) { ... }
```

With the `in` modifier, any attempts to reassign `number` (`number++`, for example) results in a compile error indicating that `number` is read only.

Return by Reference

Another C# 7.0 addition is support for returning a reference to a variable. Consider, for example, a function that returns the first pixel in an image that is associated with red-eye, as shown in Listing 5.20.

LISTING 5.20: `ref` Return and `ref` Local Declaration

```
// Returning a reference
public static ref byte FindFirstRedEyePixel(byte[] image)
{
    // Do fancy image detection perhaps with machine learning
    for (int counter = 0; counter < image.Length; counter++)
    {
        if (image[counter] == (byte)ConsoleColor.Red)
        {
            return ref image[counter];
        }
    }
    throw new InvalidOperationException("No pixels are red.");
}
public static void Main()
{
    byte[] image = new byte[254];
    // Load image
    int index = new Random().Next(0, image.Length - 1);
    image[index] =
        (byte)ConsoleColor.Red;
    Console.WriteLine(
        $"image[{index}]={(ConsoleColor)image[index]}");
    // ...

    // Obtain a reference to the first red pixel
    ref byte redPixel = ref FindFirstRedEyePixel(image);
    // Update it to be Black
    redPixel = (byte)ConsoleColor.Black;
    Console.WriteLine(
        $"image[{index}]={(ConsoleColor)image[redPixel]}");
}
```

By returning a reference to the variable, the caller is then able to update the pixel to a different color, as shown in the highlighted lines of Listing 5.20. Checking for the update via the array shows that the value is now black.

There are two important restrictions on return by reference, both due to object lifetime: (1) Object references shouldn't be garbage collected while they're still referenced, and (2) they shouldn't consume memory when they no longer have any references. To enforce these restrictions, you can only return the following from a reference-returning function:

- References to fields or array elements
- Other reference-returning properties or functions
- References that were passed in as parameters to the by-reference-returning function

For example, `FindFirstRedEyePixel()` returns a reference to an item in the image array, which was a parameter to the function. Similarly, if the image was stored as a field within the class, you could return the field by reference:

```
byte[] _Image;
public ref byte[] Image { get { return ref _Image; } }
```

In addition, `ref` locals are initialized to refer to a particular variable and can't be modified to refer to a different variable.

There are several return-by-reference characteristics of which to be cognizant:

- If you're returning a reference, you obviously must return it. This means, therefore, that in the example in Listing 5.20, even if no red-eye pixel exists, you still need to return a reference byte. The only workaround would be to throw an exception. In contrast, the by-reference parameter approach allows you to leave the parameter unchanged and return a `bool` indicating success. In many cases, this might be preferable.
- When declaring a reference local variable, initialization is required. This involves assigning it a `ref` return from a function or a reference to a variable:

```
ref string text; // Error
```

- Although it's possible in C# 7.0 to declare a reference local variable, declaring a field of type `ref` isn't allowed (see "Instance Fields" (https://essentialcsharp.com/instance-fields) in Chapter 6 for more information on declaring fields):

```
class Thing { ref string _Text; /* Error */ }
```

- You can't declare a by-reference type for an auto-implemented property (see "Properties" (https://essentialcsharp.com/properties) in Chapter 6 for more information on declaring auto-properties):

```
class Thing { ref string Text { get;set; } /* Error */ }
```

- Properties that return a reference are allowed (see "Properties" (https://essentialcsharp.com/properties) in Chapter 6 for more information on declaring properties):

```
class Thing { string _Text = "Inigo Montoya";
ref string Text { get { return ref _Text; } } }
```

- A reference local variable can't be initialized with a value (such as `null` or a constant). It must be assigned from a by-reference-returning member or a local variable, field, or array element:

```
ref int number = 42; // ERROR
```

Parameter Arrays (`params`)

In the examples so far, the number of arguments that must be passed has been fixed by the number of parameters declared in the target method declaration. However, sometimes it is convenient if the number of arguments may vary. Consider the `Combine()` method from Listing 5.17. In that method, you passed the drive letter, folder path, and filename. What if the path had more than one folder, and the caller wanted the method to join additional folders to form the full path? Perhaps the best option would be to pass an array of strings for the folders. However, this would make the calling code a little more complex, because it would be necessary to construct an array to pass as an argument.

To make it easier on the callers of such a method, C# provides a keyword that enables the number of arguments to vary in the calling code instead of being set by the target method. Before we discuss the method declaration, observe the calling code declared within `Main()`, as shown in Listing 5.21 with Output 5.7.

Listing 5.21: Passing a Variable Parameter List

```
using System;
using System.IO;

public class Program
{
    public static void Main()
    {
        string fullName;

        // ...

        // Call Combine() with four parameters
        fullName = Combine(
            Directory.GetCurrentDirectory(),
            "bin", "config", "index.html");
        Console.WriteLine(fullName);

        // ...

        // Call Combine() with only three parameters
        fullName = Combine(
            Environment.SystemDirectory,
            "Temp", "index.html");
        Console.WriteLine(fullName);

        // ...

        // Call Combine() with an array
        fullName = Combine(
            new string[] {
                $"{Environment.GetFolderPath(Environment.SpecialFolder.
↪UserProfile)}", "Documents",
                "Web", "index.html" });
        Console.WriteLine(fullName);
        // ...
    }
```

```
    static string Combine(params string[] paths)
    {
        string result = string.Empty;
        foreach(string path in paths)
        {
            result = Path.Combine(result, path);
        }
        return result;
    }
}
```

Output 5.7

```
C:\Users\Inigo\src\Chapter05.Tests\bin\Debug\net7.0\index.html
C:\WINDOWS\system32\Temp\index.html
C:\Users\Inigo\index.html
```

In the first call to `Combine()`, four arguments are specified. The second call contains only three arguments. In the final call, a single argument is passed using an array. In other words, the `Combine()` method takes a variable number of arguments—presented either as any number of string arguments separated by commas or as a single array of strings. The former syntax is called the *expanded* form of the method call, and the latter form is called the *normal* form.

To allow invocation using either form, the `Combine()` method does the following:

1. Places `params` immediately before the last parameter in the method declaration
2. Declares the last parameter as an array

With a **parameter array** declaration, it is possible to access each corresponding argument as a member of the `params` array. In the `Combine()` method implementation, you iterate over the elements of the `paths` array and call `System.IO.Path.Combine()`. This method automatically combines the parts of the path, appropriately using the platform-specific directory separator character. Note that `PathEx.Combine()` is for demonstration only as it provides a rough implementation of what `System.IO.Path.Combine()` does already.

There are a few notable characteristics of the parameter array:

- The parameter array is not necessarily the only parameter on a method.
- The parameter array must be the last parameter in the method declaration. Since only the last parameter may be a parameter array, a method cannot have more than one parameter array.
- The caller can specify zero arguments that correspond to the parameter array parameter, which will result in an array of zero items being passed as the parameter array.
- Parameter arrays are type-safe: The arguments given must be compatible with the element type of the parameter array.
- The caller can use an explicit array rather than a comma-separated list of arguments.
- If the target method implementation requires a minimum number of parameters, those parameters should appear explicitly within the method declaration, forcing a compile error instead of relying on runtime error handling if required parameters are missing. For example, if you have a method that requires one or more integer arguments, declare the method as `int Max(int first, params int[] operands)` rather than as `int Max(params int[] operands)` so that at least one value is passed to `Max()`.

Using a parameter array, you can pass a variable number of arguments of the same type into a method. The section "Method Overloading," which appears later in this chapter, discusses a means of supporting a variable number of arguments that are not necessarily of the same type.

Guidelines

DO use parameter arrays when a method can handle any number—including zero—of additional arguments.

By the way, a path `Combine()` function is a contrived example since, in fact, `System.IO.Path.Combine()` is an existing function that is overloaded to support parameter arrays.

Recursion

Calling a method **recursively** or implementing the method using **recursion** refers to use of a method that calls itself. Recursion is sometimes the simplest way to implement a particular algorithm. Listing 5.22 counts the lines of all the C# source files (`*.cs`) in a directory and its subdirectory.

Listing 5.22: Counting the Lines within `*.cs` Files, Given a Directory

```
using System.IO;

public static class LineCounter
{
    // Use the first argument as the directory
    // to search, or default to the current directory
    public static void Main(string[] args)
    {
        int totalLineCount = 0;
        string directory;
        if(args.Length > 0)
        {
            directory = args[0];
        }
        else
        {
            directory = Directory.GetCurrentDirectory();
        }
        totalLineCount = DirectoryCountLines(directory);
        Console.WriteLine(totalLineCount);
    }

    static int DirectoryCountLines(string directory)
    {
        int lineCount = 0;
        foreach(string file in
            Directory.GetFiles(directory, "*.cs"))
        {
            lineCount += CountLines(file);
        }

        foreach(string subdirectory in
            Directory.GetDirectories(directory))
        {
            lineCount += DirectoryCountLines(subdirectory);
        }
```

```
        return lineCount;
    }

    private static int CountLines(string file)
    {
        string? line;
        int lineCount = 0;
        // This can be improved with a using statement
        // which is not yet described.
        FileStream stream = new(file, FileMode.Open);
        StreamReader reader = new(stream);
        line = reader.ReadLine();

        while(line != null)
        {
            if(line.Trim() != "")
            {
                lineCount++;
            }
            line = reader.ReadLine();
        }

        reader.Dispose();  // Automatically closes the stream
        return lineCount;
    }
}
```

Output 5.8 shows the results of Listing 5.22.

Output 5.8

```
104
```

The program begins by passing the first command-line argument to `DirectoryCountLines()` or by using the current directory if no argument is provided. This method first iterates through all the files in the current directory and totals the source code lines for each file. After processing each file in the directory, the code processes each subdirectory by passing the subdirectory back into the `DirectoryCountLines()` method, rerunning the method using the subdirectory. The same process is repeated recursively through each subdirectory until no more directories remain to process.

Readers unfamiliar with recursion may find it confusing at first. Regardless, it is often the simplest pattern to code, especially with hierarchical type data such as the filesystem. However, although it may be the most readable approach, it is generally not the fastest implementation. If performance becomes an issue, developers should seek an alternative solution to a recursive implementation. The choice generally hinges on balancing readability with performance.

BEGINNER TOPIC

Infinite Recursion Error

A common programming error in recursive method implementations appears in the form of a stack overflow during program execution. This usually happens because of **infinite recursion**, in which the method continually calls back on itself, never reaching a point that triggers the end of the recursion. It is a good practice for programmers to review any method that uses recursion and to verify that the recursion calls are finite.

A common pattern for recursion using pseudocode is as follows:

```
M(x)
{
if x is trivial
return the result
else
a. Do some work to make the problem smaller
b. Recursively call M to solve the smaller problem
c. Compute the result based on a and b
return the result
}
```

Things go wrong when this pattern is not followed. For example, if you don't make the problem smaller or if you don't handle all possible "smallest" cases, the recursion never terminates.

Method Overloading

Listing 5.22 called `DirectoryCountLines()`, which counted the lines of `*.cs` files. However, if you want to count code in `*.h`/`*.cpp` files or in `*.vb` files, `DirectoryCountLines()` will not work. Instead, you need a method that takes the file extension but still keeps the existing method definition so that it handles `*.cs` files by default.

All methods within a class must have a unique signature, and C# defines uniqueness by variation in the method name, parameter data types, or number of parameters. This does not include method return data types; defining two methods that differ only in their return data types will cause a compile error. This is true even if the return type is two different tuples. **Method overloading** occurs when a class has two or more methods with the same name and the parameter count and/or data types vary between the overloaded methods.

> **NOTE**
>
> A method is considered unique as long as there is variation in the method name, parameter data types, or number of parameters.

Method overloading is a type of **operational polymorphism**. Polymorphism occurs when the same logical operation takes on many ("poly") forms ("morphs") because the data varies. For example, calling `WriteLine()` and passing a format string along with some parameters is implemented differently than calling `WriteLine()` and specifying an integer. However, logically, to the caller, the method takes care of writing the data, and it is somewhat irrelevant how the internal implementation occurs. Listing 5.23 provides an example, and Output 5.9 shows the results.

Listing 5.23: Counting the Lines within `*.cs` Files Using Overloading

```
public static class LineCounter
{
    public static void Main(string[] args)
    {
        int totalLineCount;
```

```
        if(args.Length > 1)
        {
            totalLineCount = DirectoryCountLines(args[0], args[1]);
        }
        else if(args.Length > 0)
        {
            totalLineCount = DirectoryCountLines(args[0]);
        }
        else
        {
            totalLineCount = DirectoryCountLines();
        }

        Console.WriteLine(totalLineCount);
    }

    static int DirectoryCountLines()
    {
        return DirectoryCountLines(
            Directory.GetCurrentDirectory());
    }

    static int DirectoryCountLines(string directory)
    {
        return DirectoryCountLines(directory, "*.cs");
    }

    static int DirectoryCountLines(
        string directory, string extension)
    {
        int lineCount = 0;
        foreach(string file in
            Directory.GetFiles(directory, extension))
        {
            lineCount += CountLines(file);
        }

        foreach(string subdirectory in
            Directory.GetDirectories(directory))
        {
            lineCount += DirectoryCountLines(subdirectory);
        }

        return lineCount;
    }
```

```
    private static int CountLines(string file)
    {
        int lineCount = 0;
        string? line;
        // This can be improved with a using statement
        // which is not yet described.
        FileStream stream = new(file, FileMode.Open);
        StreamReader reader = new(stream);
        line = reader.ReadLine();
        while(line is not null)
        {
            if(line.Trim() != "")
            {
                lineCount++;
            }
            line = reader.ReadLine();
        }

        reader.Dispose();  // Automatically closes the stream
        return lineCount;
    }
}
```

Output 5.9

```
>LineCounter.exe .\ *.cs
28
```

The effect of method overloading is to provide optional ways to call the method. As demonstrated inside `Main()`, you can call the `DirectoryCountLines()` method with or without passing the directory to search and the file extension.

Notice that the parameterless implementation of `DirectoryCountLines()` was changed to call the single-parameter version, `int DirectoryCountLines (string directory)`. This is a common pattern when implementing overloaded methods. The idea is that developers implement only the core logic in one method, and all the other overloaded methods will call that single method. If the core implementation changes, it needs to be modified in only one location rather than within each implementation. This pattern is especially prevalent when using method overloading to enable optional parameters that do not have values determined at compile time, so they cannot be specified using optional parameters.

> **NOTE**
>
> Placing the core functionality into a single method that all other overloading methods invoke means that you can make changes in implementation in just the core method, which the other methods will automatically take advantage of.

Optional Parameters

The C# language designers also added support for **optional parameters**.[7] By allowing the association of a parameter with a constant value as part of the method declaration, it is possible to call a method without passing an argument for every parameter of the method (see Listing 5.24).

LISTING 5.24: Methods with Optional Parameters

```
public static class LineCounter
{
    public static void Main(string[] args)
    {
        int totalLineCount;

        if(args.Length > 1)
        {
            totalLineCount =
                DirectoryCountLines(args[0], args[1]);
        }
        else if(args.Length > 0)
        {
            totalLineCount = DirectoryCountLines(args[0]);
        }
        else
        {
            totalLineCount = DirectoryCountLines();
        }

        Console.WriteLine(totalLineCount);
    }
```

7. Introduced in C# 4.0.

```
    static int DirectoryCountLines()
    {
        // ...
    }

    /*
      static int DirectoryCountLines(string directory)
      { ... }
    */

    static int DirectoryCountLines(
        string directory, string extension = "*.cs")
    {
        int lineCount = 0;
        foreach(string file in
            Directory.GetFiles(directory, extension))
        {
            lineCount += CountLines(file);
        }

        foreach(string subdirectory in
            Directory.GetDirectories(directory))
        {
            lineCount += DirectoryCountLines(subdirectory);
        }

        return lineCount;
    }

    private static int CountLines(string file)
    {
        // ...
    }
}
```

In Listing 5.24, the `DirectoryCountLines()` method declaration with a single parameter has been removed (commented out), but the call from `Main()` (specifying one parameter) remains. When no `extension` parameter is specified in the call, the value assigned to `extension` within the declaration (`*.cs` in this case) is used. This allows the calling code to not specify a value if desired, and it eliminates the additional overload that would otherwise be required. Note that optional parameters must appear after all required parameters (those that don't have default values). Also, the fact that the default value needs to be a constant, compile-time–resolved value is fairly restrictive. You cannot, for example, declare a method like

```
DirectoryCountLines(
string directory = Environment.CurrentDirectory,
string extension = "*.cs")
```

because `Environment.CurrentDirectory` is not a constant. In contrast, because `"*.cs"` is a constant, C# does allow it for the default value of an optional parameter.

Guidelines

DO provide good defaults for all parameters where possible.

DO provide simple method overloads that have a small number of required parameters.

CONSIDER organizing overloads from the simplest to the most complex.

A second method call feature is the use of **named arguments**.[8] With named arguments, it is possible for the caller to explicitly identify the name of the parameter to be assigned a value, rather than relying solely on parameter and argument order to correlate them (see Listing 5.25).

Listing 5.25: Specifying Parameters by Name

```
public static void Main()
{
    DisplayGreeting(
        firstName: "Inigo", lastName: "Montoya");
}

public static void DisplayGreeting(
    string firstName,
    string? middleName = null,
    string? lastName = null
    )
```

8. Introduced in C# 4.0.

```
{
    // ...
}
```

In Listing 5.25, the call to `DisplayGreeting()` from within `Main()` assigns a value to a parameter by name. Of the two optional parameters (`middleName` and `lastName`), only `lastName` is given as an argument. For cases where a method has lots of parameters and many of them are optional,[9] using the named argument syntax is certainly a convenience. However, along with the convenience comes an impact on the flexibility of the method interface. In the past, parameter names could be changed without causing C# code that invokes the method to no longer compile. With the addition of named parameters, the parameter name becomes part of the interface because changing the name would cause code that uses the named parameter to no longer compile.

Guidelines

DO treat parameter names as part of the API, and avoid changing the names if version compatibility between APIs is important.

For many experienced C# developers, this is a surprising restriction. However, the restriction has been imposed as part of the Common Language Specification ever since .NET 1.0. Moreover, Visual Basic has always supported calling methods with named arguments. Therefore, library developers should already be following the practice of not changing parameter names to successfully interoperate with other .NET languages from version to version. In essence, named arguments now impose the same restriction on changing parameter names that many other .NET languages already require.

Given the combination of method overloading, optional parameters, and named parameters, resolving which method to call becomes less obvious. A call is **applicable** (compatible) with a method if all parameters have exactly one

9. A common occurrence when accessing Microsoft COM libraries such as Microsoft Word or Microsoft Excel.

corresponding argument (either by name or by position) that is type-compatible, unless the parameter is optional (or is a parameter array). Although this restricts the possible number of methods that will be called, it doesn't identify a unique method. To further distinguish which specific method will be called, the compiler uses only explicitly identified parameters in the caller, ignoring all optional parameters that were not specified at the caller. Therefore, if two methods are applicable because one of them has an optional parameter, the compiler will resolve to the method without the optional parameter.

ADVANCED TOPIC

Method Resolution

When the compiler must choose which of several applicable methods is the best one for a particular call, the one with the *most specific* parameter types is chosen. Assuming there are two applicable methods, each requiring an implicit conversion from an argument to a parameter type, the method whose parameter type is the more derived type will be used.

For example, a method that takes a `double` parameter is chosen over a method that takes an `object` parameter if the caller passes an argument of type `int`. This is because `double` is more specific than `object`. There are `objects` that are not `doubles`, but there are no `doubles` that are not `objects`, so `double` must be more specific.

If more than one method is applicable and no unique best method can be determined, the compiler issues an error indicating that the call is ambiguous.

For example, given the following methods

```
static void Method(object thing){}
static void Method(double thing){}
static void Method(long thing){}
static void Method(int thing){}
```

a call of the form `Method(42)` resolves as `Method(int thing)` because that is an exact match from the argument type to the parameter type. Were that method to be removed, overload resolution would choose the `long` version, because `long` is more specific than either `double` or `object`.

The C# specification includes additional rules governing implicit conversion between byte, ushort, uint, ulong, and the other numeric types. In general, though, it is better to use a cast to make the intended target method more recognizable.

Basic Error Handling with Exceptions

This section examines how to handle error reporting via a mechanism known as **exception handling**. With exception handling, a method can pass information about an error to a calling method without using a return value or explicitly providing any parameters to do so. Listing 5.26 with Output 5.10 contains a slight modification to Listing 1.16—the HeyYou program from Chapter 1. Instead of requesting the last name of the user, it prompts for the user's age.

Listing 5.26: Converting a string to an int

```
public static void Main()
{
    string? firstName;
    string ageText;
    int age;

    Console.WriteLine("Hey you!");

    Console.Write("Enter your first name: ");
    firstName = Console.ReadLine();

    Console.Write("Enter your age: ");
    // Assume not null for clarity
    ageText = Console.ReadLine()!;
    age = int.Parse(ageText);

    Console.WriteLine(
        $"Hi { firstName }!  You are { age * 12 } months old.");
}
```

Output 5.10

```
Hey you!
Enter your first name: Inigo
```

```
Enter your age: 42
Hi Inigo!  You are 504 months old.
```

The return value from `System.Console.ReadLine()` is stored in a variable called `ageText` and is then passed to a method with the `int` data type, called `Parse()`. This method is responsible for taking a string value that represents a number and converting it to an `int` type.

BEGINNER TOPIC

42 as a String versus 42 as an Integer

C# requires that every non-`null` value have a well-defined type associated with it. Therefore, not only the data value but also the type associated with the data is important. A string value of `"42"`, therefore, is distinctly different from an integer value of `42`. The string is composed of the two characters `4` and `2`, whereas the `int` is the number 42.

Given the converted string, the final `System.Console.WriteLine()` statement will print the age in months by multiplying the age value by 12.

But what happens if the user does not enter a valid integer string? For example, what happens if the user enters "forty-two"? The `Parse()` method cannot handle such a conversion. It expects the user to enter a string that contains only numerical digits. If the `Parse()` method is sent an invalid value, it needs some way to report this fact back to the caller.

Trapping Errors

To indicate to the calling method that the parameter is invalid, `int.Parse()` will **throw an exception**. Throwing an exception halts further execution in the current control flow and jumps into the first code block within the call stack that handles the exception.

Since you have not yet provided any such handling, the program reports the exception to the user as an **unhandled exception**. Assuming there is no registered debugger on the system, console applications will display the error on the console with a message such as that shown in Output 5.11.

Output 5.11

```
Hey you!
Enter your first name: Inigo
Enter your age: forty-two

Unhandled Exception: System.FormatException: Input string was
        not in a correct format.
    at System.Number.ThrowOverflowOrFormatException(...)
    at System.Number.ParseInt32(String s)
    at ...ExceptionHandling.Main()
```

Obviously, such an error is not particularly helpful. To fix this, it is necessary to provide a mechanism that handles the error, perhaps reporting a more meaningful error message back to the user.

This process is known as **catching an exception**. The syntax is demonstrated in Listing 5.27, and the output appears in Output 5.12.

Listing 5.27: Catching an Exception

```
public class ExceptionHandling
{
    public static int Main(string[] args)
    {
        string? firstName;
        string ageText;
        int age;
        int result = 0;

        Console.Write("Enter your first name: ");
        firstName = Console.ReadLine();

        Console.Write("Enter your age: ");
        // Assume not null for clarity
        ageText = Console.ReadLine()!;

        try
        {
            age = int.Parse(ageText);
            Console.WriteLine(
```

```
                $"Hi { firstName }! You are { age * 12 } months old.");
        }
        catch(FormatException)
        {
            Console.WriteLine(
                $"The age entered, { ageText }, is not valid.");
            result = 1;
        }
        catch(Exception exception)
        {
            Console.WriteLine(
                $"Unexpected error: { exception.Message }");
            result = 1;
        }
        finally
        {
            Console.WriteLine($"Goodbye { firstName }");
        }

        return result;
    }
}
```

Output 5.12

```
Enter your first name: Inigo
Enter your age: forty-two
The age entered, forty-two, is not valid.
Goodbye Inigo
```

To begin, surround the code that could potentially throw an exception (`age = int.Parse()`) with a **try block**. This block begins with the `try` keyword. It indicates to the compiler that the developer is aware of the possibility that the code within the block might throw an exception, and if it does, one of the **catch blocks** will attempt to handle the exception.

One or more catch blocks (or the finally block) must appear immediately following a try block. The catch block header (see "Advanced Topic: General Catch" later in this chapter) optionally allows you to specify the data type of the exception. As long as the data type matches the exception type, the catch block will execute. If, however, there is no appropriate catch block, the exception will fall through and go unhandled as though there were no exception handling. The resultant control flow appears in Figure 5.1.

For example, assume the user enters “forty-two” for the age in the previous example. In this case, `int.Parse()` will throw an exception of type `System.FormatException`, and control will jump to the set of catch blocks. (`System.FormatException` indicates that the string was not of the correct format to be parsed appropriately.) Since the first catch block matches the type of exception that `int.Parse()` threw, the code inside this block will execute. If a statement within the try block threw a different exception, the second catch block would execute because all exceptions are of type `System.Exception`.

If there were no `System.FormatException` catch block, the `System.Exception` catch block would execute even though `int.Parse` throws a `System.FormatException`. This is because a `System.FormatException` is also of type `System.Exception`. (`System.FormatException` is a more specific implementation of the generic exception, `System.Exception`.)

The order in which you handle exceptions is significant. Catch blocks must appear from most specific to least specific. The `System.Exception` data type is least specific, so it appears last. `System.FormatException` appears first because it is the most specific exception that Listing 5.27 handles.

Regardless of whether control leaves the try block normally or because the code in the try block throws an exception, the **finally block** of code executes after control leaves the try-protected region. The purpose of the finally block is to provide a location to place code that will execute regardless of how the try/catch blocks exit —with or without an exception. Finally blocks are useful for cleaning up resources, regardless of whether an exception is thrown. In fact, it is possible to have a try block with a finally block and no catch block. The finally block executes regardless of whether the try block throws an exception or whether a catch block is even written to handle the exception. Listing 5.28 demonstrates the try/finally block, and Output 5.13 shows the results.

Listing 5.28: Finally Block without a Catch Block

```
using System;

public class ExceptionHandling
```

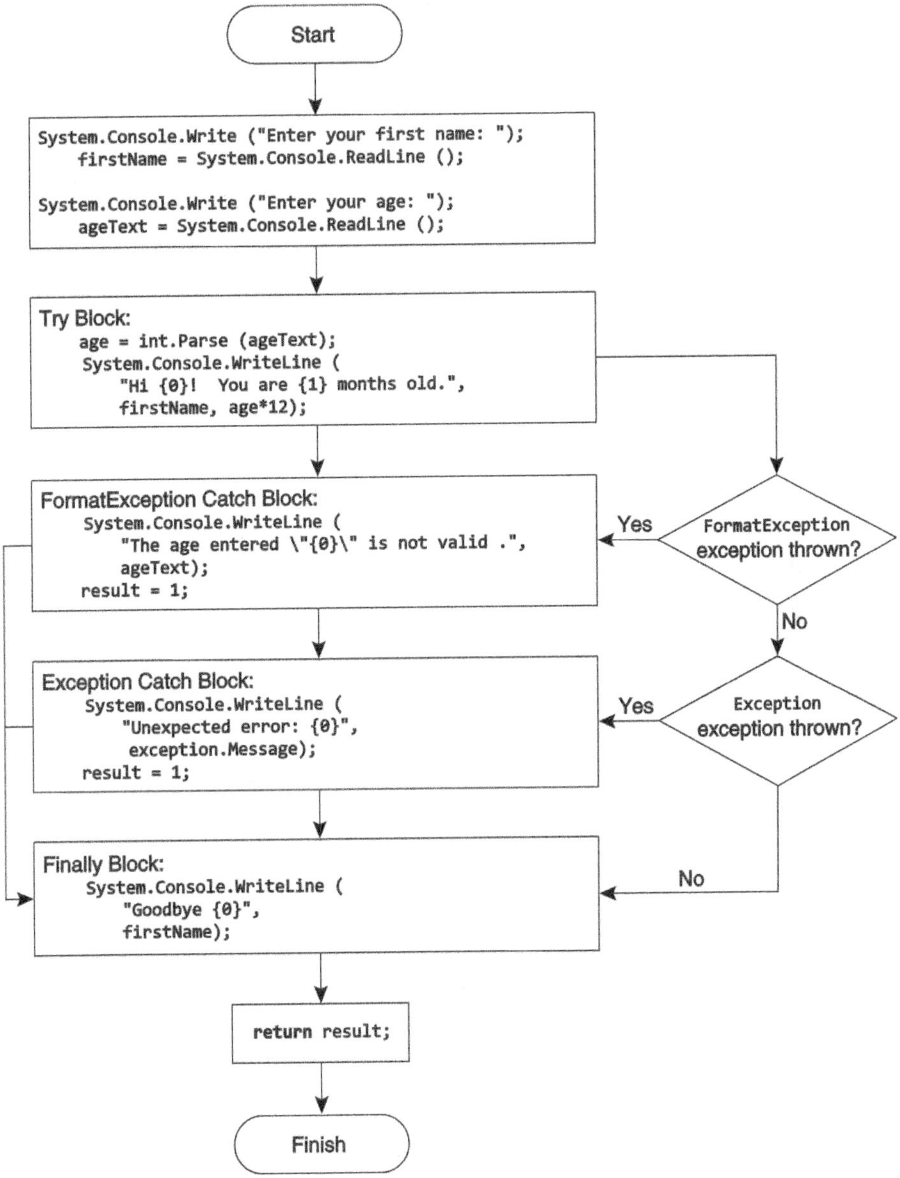

FIGURE 5.1: Exception-handling control flow

```
{
    public static int Main()
    {
```

```
        string? firstName;
        string ageText;
        int age;
        int result = 0;

        Console.Write("Enter your first name: ");
        firstName = Console.ReadLine();

        Console.Write("Enter your age: ");
        // Assume not null for clarity
        ageText = Console.ReadLine()!;

        try
        {
            age = int.Parse(ageText);
            Console.WriteLine(
                $"Hi { firstName }! You are { age * 12 } months old.");
        }
        finally
        {
            Console.WriteLine($"Goodbye { firstName }");
        }

        return result;
    }
}
```

OUTPUT 5.13

```
Enter your first name: Inigo
Enter your age: forty-two

Unhandled Exception: System.FormatException: Input string was
        not in a correct format.
    at System.Number.ThrowOverflowOrFormatException(...)
    at System.Number.ParseInt32(String s)
    at ...ExceptionHandling.Main()
Goodbye Inigo
```

The attentive reader will have noticed something interesting here: The runtime first reported the unhandled exception and then ran the finally block. What explains this unusual behavior?

First, the behavior is legal because when an exception is unhandled, the behavior of the runtime is implementation defined—any behavior is legal! The runtime chooses this particular behavior because it knows before it chooses to run the finally block that the exception will be unhandled; the runtime has already examined all of the activation frames on the call stack and determined that none of them is associated with a catch block that matches the thrown exception.

As soon as the runtime determines that the exception will be unhandled, it checks whether a debugger is installed on the machine, because you might be the software developer who is analyzing this failure. If a debugger is present, it offers the user the chance to attach the debugger to the process *before* the finally block runs. If there is no debugger installed or if the user declines to debug the problem, the default behavior is to print the unhandled exception to the console and then see if there are any finally blocks that could run. Due to the "implementation-defined" nature of the situation, the runtime is not required to run finally blocks in this situation; an implementation may choose to do so or not.

NOTE

If an exception goes unhandled before the process exits, the order of execution of the finally block, and whether it even executes, is implementation defined.

Guidelines

AVOID explicitly throwing exceptions from finally blocks. (Implicitly thrown exceptions resulting from method calls are acceptable.)

DO favor try/finally and avoid using try/catch for cleanup code.

DO throw exceptions that describe which exceptional circumstance occurred and, if possible, how to prevent it.

ADVANCED TOPIC

Exception Class Inheritance

All objects thrown as exceptions derive from `System.Exception`. (Objects thrown from other languages that do not derive from `System.Exception` are automatically "wrapped" by an object that does.) Therefore, they can be handled by the `catch(System.Exception exception)` block. It is preferable, however, to include a catch block that is specific to the most derived type (e.g., `System.FormatException`), because then it is possible to get the most information about an exception and handle it less generically. In so doing, the `catch` statement that uses the most derived type can handle the exception type specifically, accessing data related to the exception thrown and avoiding conditional logic to determine what type of exception occurred.

Therefore, C# enforces the rule that catch blocks appear from most derived to least derived. For example, a `catch` statement that catches `System.Exception` cannot appear before a statement that catches `System.FormatException` because `System.FormatException` derives from `System.Exception`.

A method could throw many exception types. Table 5.2 lists some of the more common ones within the framework.

TABLE 5.2: Common Exception Types

Exception Type	Description
`System.Exception`	The "base" exception from which all other exceptions derive.
`System.ArgumentException`	Indicates that one of the arguments passed into the method is invalid.
`System.ArgumentNullException`	Indicates that a particular argument is `null` and that this is not a valid value for that parameter.
`System.ApplicationException`	To be avoided. The original idea was that you might want to have one kind of handling for system exceptions and another for application exceptions, which, although plausible, doesn't actually work well in the real world.

TABLE 5.2: Common Exception Types (continued)

Exception Type	Description
`System.FormatException`	Indicates that the string format is not valid for conversion.
`System.IndexOutOfRangeException`	Indicates that an attempt was made to access an array or other collection element that does not exist.
`System.InvalidCastException`	Indicates that an attempt to convert from one data type to another was not a valid conversion.
`System.InvalidOperationException`	Indicates that an unexpected scenario has occurred such that the application is no longer in a valid state of operation.
`System.NotImplementedException`	Indicates that although the method signature exists, it has not been fully implemented.
`System.NullReferenceException`	Thrown when code tries to find the object referred to by a reference that is `null`.
`System.ArithmeticException`	Indicates an invalid math operation, not including divide by zero.
`System.ArrayTypeMismatchException`	Occurs when attempting to store an element of the wrong type into an array.
`System.StackOverflowException`	Indicates an unexpectedly deep recursion.

ADVANCED TOPIC

General Catch

It is possible to specify a catch block that takes no parameters, as shown in Listing 5.29.

LISTING 5.29: General Catch Blocks

```
// A previous catch clause already catches all exceptions
#pragma warning disable CS1058
// ...
        try
```

```
        {
            age = int.Parse(ageText);
            Console.WriteLine(
                $"Hi { firstName }! You are { age * 12 } months old.");
        }
        catch(FormatException exception)
        {
            Console.WriteLine(
                $"The age entered ,{ageText}, is not valid.");
            result = 1;
        }
        catch(Exception exception)
        {
            Console.WriteLine(
                $"Unexpected error: { exception.Message }");
            result = 1;
        }
        catch
        {
            Console.WriteLine("Unexpected error!");
            result = 1;
        }
        finally
        {
            Console.WriteLine($"Goodbye { firstName }");
        }
```

A catch block with no data type, called a **general catch block**, is equivalent to specifying a catch block that takes an `object` data type—for instance, `catch(object exception){...}`. For this reason, a warning is triggered stating that the catch block already exists; hence the `#pragma warning disable` directive.

Because all classes ultimately derive from `object`, a catch block with no data type must appear last.

General catch blocks are rarely used because there is no way to capture any information about the exception. In addition, C# doesn't support the ability to throw an exception of type `object`. (Only libraries written in languages such as C++ allow exceptions of any type.)

Guidelines

AVOID general catch blocks and replace them with a catch of `System.Exception`.

AVOID catching exceptions for which the appropriate action is unknown. It is better to let an exception go unhandled than to handle it incorrectly.

Reporting Errors Using a `throw` Statement

C# allows developers to throw exceptions from their code, as demonstrated in Listing 5.30 and Output 5.14.

Listing 5.30: Throwing an Exception

```
public static void Main()
{
    try
    {
        Console.WriteLine("Begin executing");
        Console.WriteLine("Throw exception");
        throw new Exception("Arbitrary exception");
        // Catch 1
        Console.WriteLine("End executing");
    }
    catch(FormatException exception)
    {
        Console.WriteLine(
            "A FormatException was thrown");
    }
    // Catch 1
    catch(Exception exception)
    {
        Console.WriteLine(
            $"Unexpected error: { exception.Message }");
        // Jump to Post Catch
    }

    // Post Catch
    Console.WriteLine(
        "Shutting down...");
}
```

OUTPUT 5.14

```
Begin executing
Throw exception...
Unexpected error:  Arbitrary exception
Shutting down...
```

As the comments in Listing 5.30 depict, throwing an exception causes execution to jump from where the exception is thrown into the first compatible catch block (`Catch 1`).[10] In this case, the second catch block handles the exception and writes out an error message. In Listing 5.30, there is no finally block, so following the `WriteLine()` method of `Catch 1`, execution falls through to the `Console.WriteLine()` statement following the try/catch block (after the `Post Catch` comment).

To throw an exception, it is necessary to have an instance of an exception. Listing 5.30 creates an instance using the keyword `new` followed by the type of the exception. Most exception types allow a message to be specified for the exception's construction parameter, so that when the exception occurs, the message can be retrieved.

Sometimes a catch block will trap an exception but be unable to handle it appropriately or fully. In these circumstances, a catch block can rethrow the exception using the `throw` statement without specifying any exception, as shown in Listing 5.31.

LISTING 5.31: Rethrowing an Exception

```
// ...
catch (Exception exception)
{
    Console.WriteLine(
        "Rethrowing unexpected error:  "
        + $"{ exception.Message }");

    throw;
}
// ...
```

10. Technically, it could be caught by a compatible exception filter as well.

In Listing 5.31, the `throw` statement is "empty" rather than specifying that the exception referred to by the `exception` variable is to be thrown. This illustrates a subtle difference: `throw;` preserves the *call stack* information in the exception, whereas `throw exception;` replaces that information with the current call stack information. For debugging purposes, it is usually better to know the original call stack. Of course, this is allowed only in a catch statement where the caught exception can be determined.

Guidelines

DO prefer using an empty throw when catching and rethrowing an exception, to preserve the call stack.

DO report execution failures by throwing exceptions rather than returning error codes.

DO NOT have public members that return exceptions as return values or an `out` parameter. Throw exceptions to indicate errors; do not use them as return values to indicate errors.

AVOID catching and logging an exception before rethrowing it. Instead, allow the exception to escape until it can be handled appropriately.

Reporting Null Argument Exceptions

When nullability reference types are enabled, the compiler will make a best effort to identify when there is the possibility of a nullable argument passed as a non-nullable argument. If you assign a possible null value to a non-nullable argument, the compiler will issue a warning stating that you are attempting to convert a possible null value to a non-nullable argument. Assuming you address all such warnings appropriately, the compiler will catch most of the cases. However, if the caller is outside of your control (such as from a library you didn't write), doesn't turn on nullable reference types, ignores the warnings, or invokes the method from C# 7.0 or earlier, there is nothing preventing a null argument even though the parameter is declared as non-nullable. For this reason, the best practice is to check that any public non-nullable reference types are not null. With .NET 6.0 you can use a conditional `if (is null)` check:

```
if (is null) throw new ArgumentNullException(...)
```

You can accomplish this in a single statement using the null coalescing assignment operator with a `throw ArgumentNullException` expression if the parameter value is null (see Listing 5.32).

Listing 5.32: Parameter Validation by Throwing `ArgumentNullException`

```
httpsUrl = httpsUrl ??
    throw new ArgumentNullException(nameof(httpsUrl));
fileName = fileName??
    throw new ArgumentNullException(nameof(fileName));


// ...
```

With .NET 7.0, you can use the `ArgumentNullException.ThrowIfNull()` method (see Listing 5.33).

Listing 5.33: Parameter Validation with `ArgumentException.ThrowIfNull()`

```
ArgumentNullException.ThrowIfNull(httpsUrl);
ArgumentNullException.ThrowIfNull(fileName);

// ...
```

Internally, the `ArgumentNullException.ThrowIfNull()` method also throws the `ArgumentNullException`.

Guidelines

DO verify that non-null reference types parameters are not null and throw an `ArgumentNullException` when they are.

DO use `ArgumentException.ThrowIfNull()` to verify values are null in .NET 7.0 or later.

Additional Parameter Validation

There are obviously a myriad of other type constraints that a method may have on its parameters. Perhaps a string argument should not be an empty string, should not be comprised only of whitespace, or must have "HTTPS" as a prefix. Listing 5.34 displays the full `DownloadSSSL()` method, demonstrating this validation.

Listing 5.34: Custom Parameter Validation

```
public class Program
{
    public static int Main(string[] args)
    {
        int result = 0;
        if(args.Length != 2 )
        {
            // Exactly two arguments must be specified; give an error
            Console.WriteLine(
                "ERROR:  You must specify the "
                + "URL and the file name");
            Console.WriteLine(
                "Usage: Downloader.exe <URL> <TargetFileName>");
            result = 1;
        }
        else
        {
            DownloadSSL(args[0], args[1]);
        }
        return result;
    }

private static void DownloadSSL(string httpsUrl, string fileName)
{
#if !NET7_0_OR_GREATER
    httpsUrl = httpsUrl?.Trim() ??
        throw new ArgumentNullException(nameof(httpsUrl));
    fileName = fileName ??
        throw new ArgumentNullException(nameof(fileName));
    if (fileName.Trim().Length == 0)
    {
        throw new ArgumentException(
            $"{nameof(fileName)} cannot be empty or only whitespace");
    }
#else
    ArgumentException.ThrowIfNullOrEmpty(httpsUrl = httpsUrl?.Trim()!);
    ArgumentException.ThrowIfNullOrEmpty(fileName = fileName?.Trim()!);
```

```
#endif

        if (!httpsUrl.ToUpper().StartsWith("HTTPS"))
        {
            throw new ArgumentException("URL must start with 'HTTPS'.");
        }

        HttpClient client = new();
        byte[] response =
            client.GetByteArrayAsync(httpsUrl).Result;
        client.Dispose();
        File.WriteAllBytes(fileName!, response);
        Console.WriteLine($"Downloaded '{fileName}' from '{httpsUrl}'.");
    }
}
```

When using .NET 7.0 or higher, you can rely on the `ArgumentException.ThrowIfNullOrEmpty()` method to check for both null and an empty string. And, if you invoke the `string.Trim()` method when invoking `ThrowIfNullOrEmpty()`, you can throw an exception if the argument content is only whitespace. (Admittedly, the exception message will not indicate whitespace only is invalid.) The equivalent code for .NET 6.0 or earlier is shown in the else directive.

If the null, empty, and whitespace validation pass, Listing 5.34 has an if statement that checks for the "HTTPS" prefix. If the validation fails, the resulting code throws an `ArgumentException`, with a custom message describing the problem.

Introducing the `nameof` Operator

When the parameter fails validation, it is necessary to throw an exception—generally of type `ArgumentException()` or `ArgumentNullException()`. Both exceptions take an argument of type `string` called `paramName` that identifies the name of the parameter that is invalid. In Listing 5.33, we use the `nameof` operator[11] for this argument. The `nameof` operator takes an identifier, like the `httpsUrl` variable, and returns a string representation of that name—in this case, `"httpsUrl"`.

11. Introduced in C# 6.0.

The advantage of using the `nameof` operator is that if the identifier name changes, then refactoring tools will automatically change the argument to `nameof` as well. If no refactoring tool is used, the code will no longer compile, forcing the developer to change the argument manually, which is preferable because the former value would presumably be invalid. The result is that `nameof` will even check for spelling errors. The resulting guideline is: DO use `nameof` for the `paramName` argument passed into exceptions such as `ArgumentException` and `ArgumentNullException` that take such a parameter. For more information, see Chapter 18.

> **Guidelines**
>
> **DO** use `nameof(value)` (which resolves to `"value"`) for the `paramName` argument when creating `ArgumentException()` or `ArgumentNullException()` type exceptions. (`value` is the implicit name of the parameter on property setters.)

Avoid Using Exception Handling to Deal with Expected Situations

Developers should avoid throwing exceptions for expected conditions or normal control flow. For example, developers should not expect users to enter valid text when specifying their age.[12] Therefore, instead of relying on an exception to validate data entered by the user, developers should provide a means of checking the data before attempting the conversion. (Better yet, they should prevent the user from entering invalid data in the first place.) Exceptions are designed specifically for tracking exceptional, unexpected, and potentially fatal situations. Using them for an unintended purpose such as expected situations will cause your code to be hard to read, understand, and maintain.

Consider, for example, the `int.Parse()` method we used in Chapter 2 to convert a string to an integer. In this scenario, the code converted user input that was expected to not always be a number. One of the problems with the `Parse()` method

12. In general, developers should expect their users to perform unexpected actions; in turn, they should code defensively to handle "stupid user tricks."

is that the only way to determine whether the conversion will be successful is to attempt the cast and then catch the exception if it doesn't work. Because throwing an exception is a relatively expensive operation, it is better to attempt the conversion without exception handling. Toward this effort, it is preferable to use one of the `TryParse()` methods, such as `int.TryParse()`. It requires the use of the `out` keyword because the return from the `TryParse()` function is a `bool` rather than the converted value. Listing 5.35 is a code snippet that demonstrates the conversion using `int.TryParse()`.

LISTING 5.35: Conversion Using `int.TryParse()`

```
if (int.TryParse(ageText, out int age))
{
    Console.WriteLine(
        $"Hi { firstName }! " +
        $"You are { age * 12 } months old.");
}
else
{
    Console.WriteLine(
        $"The age entered, { ageText }, is not valid.");
}
```

With the `TryParse()` method, it is no longer necessary to include a try/catch block simply for the purpose of handling the string-to-numeric conversion.

Another factor in favor of avoiding exceptions for expected scenarios is performance. Like most languages, C# incurs a slight performance hit when throwing an exception—taking microseconds compared to the nanoseconds most operations take. This delay is generally not noticeable in human time—except when the exception goes unhandled. For example, when Listing 5.26 is executed and the user enters an invalid age, the exception is unhandled and there is a noticeable delay while the runtime searches the environment to see whether there is a debugger to load. Fortunately, slow performance when a program is shutting down isn't generally a factor to be concerned with.

> **Guidelines**
>
> **DO NOT** use exceptions for handling normal, expected conditions; use them for exceptional, unexpected conditions.

Summary

This chapter discussed the details of declaring and calling methods, including the use of the keywords `out` and `ref` to pass and return variables rather than via return values. In addition to method declaration, this chapter introduced exception handling.

A method is a fundamental construct that is a key to writing readable code. Instead of writing large methods with lots of statements, you should use methods to create "paragraphs" of roughly 10 or fewer statements within your code. The process of breaking large functions into smaller pieces is one of the ways you can refactor your code to make it more readable and maintainable.

The next chapter considers the class construct and describes how it encapsulates methods (behavior) and fields (data) into a single unit.

6
Classes

You briefly saw in Chapter 1 how to declare a new class called `HelloWorld`. In Chapters 2 and 3, you learned about the built-in primitive types included with C#. Since you have now also learned about control flow and how to declare methods, it is time to discuss defining your own types. Type definition is a core construct of any C# program; this support for classes and the objects created from them is what makes C# an object-oriented language.

This chapter introduces the basics of object-oriented programming using C#. A key focus is on how to define **classes**, which are the templates for objects themselves.

All the constructs of structured, control-flow-based programming from the previous chapters still apply within object-oriented programming. However, by wrapping those constructs within classes, you can create much larger, more organized programs, significantly increasing maintainability.

One of the key advantages of object-oriented programming is that instead of creating new programs entirely from scratch, you can assemble a collection of existing objects from prior work, extending the classes with new features, adding more classes, and thereby providing new functionality.

Readers unfamiliar with object-oriented programming should read the Beginner Topic blocks for an introduction. The general text outside the Beginner Topics focuses on using C# for object-oriented programming, under the assumption that readers are already familiar with object-oriented concepts.

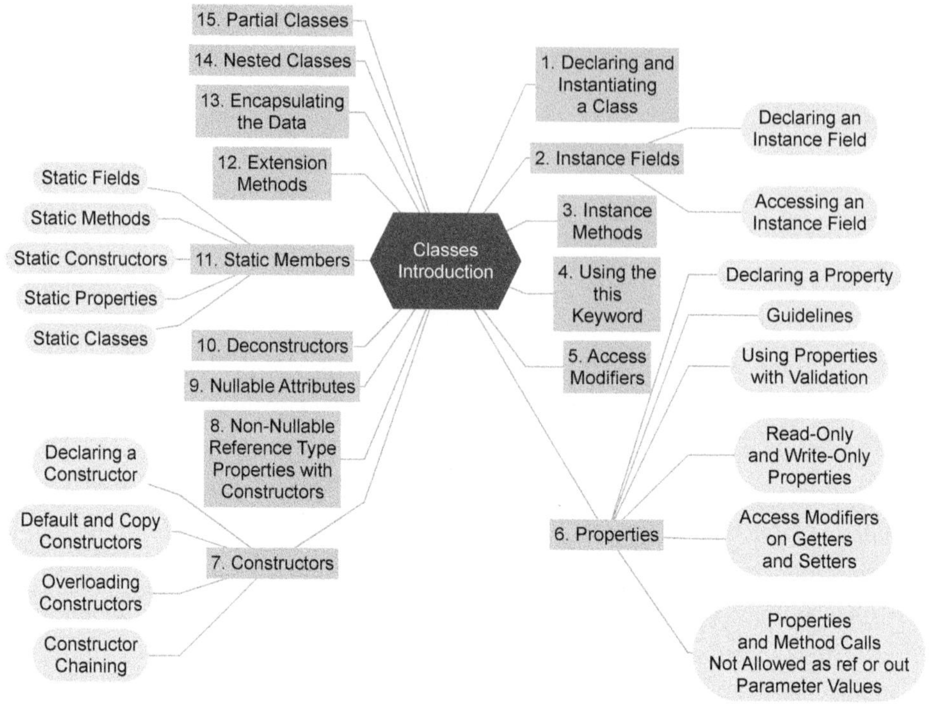

This chapter delves into how C# supports encapsulation through constructs such as classes, properties, and access modifiers; we covered methods in Chapter 5. Chapter 7 builds on this foundation by introducing inheritance and the polymorphism that object-oriented programming enables.

BEGINNER TOPIC

Object-Oriented Programming

The key to successful programming today lies in the ability to organize and structure the implementation of complex requirements in large applications. Object-oriented programming provides one of the key methodologies in accomplishing this goal, to the point that it is difficult for object-oriented programmers to envision transitioning back to structured programming, except for the most trivial programs.

The most fundamental construct in object-oriented programming is the class. A group of classes form a programming abstraction, model, or template of what is often a real-world concept. The class `OpticalStorageMedia`, for example, may have an `Eject()` method on it that causes a disk to eject from the player. The `OpticalStorageMedia` class is the programming abstraction of the real-world object of a CD or DVD player.

Classes exhibit the three principal characteristics of object-oriented programming: encapsulation, inheritance, and polymorphism.

Encapsulation

Encapsulation allows you to hide details. The details can still be accessed when necessary, but by intelligently encapsulating the details, large programs are made easier to understand, data is protected from inadvertent modification, and code becomes easier to maintain because the effects of a code change are limited to the scope of the encapsulation. Methods are examples of encapsulation. Although it is possible to take the code from a method and embed it directly inline with the caller's code, refactoring of code into a method provides encapsulation benefits.

Inheritance

Consider the following example: A DVD drive is a type of optical media device. It has a specific storage capacity along with the ability to hold a digital movie. A CD drive is also a type of optical media device, but it has different characteristics. The copy protection on CDs is different from DVD copy protection, and the storage capacity is different as well. Both CD drives and DVD drives are different from hard drives, memory cards, and floppy drives (remember those?). All fit into the category of storage devices, but each has special characteristics, even for fundamental functions such as the supported filesystems and whether instances of the media are read-only or read/write.

Inheritance in object-oriented programming allows you to form "is a kind of" relationships between these similar but different items. It is reasonable to say that a DVD drive "is a kind of" storage media and that a CD drive "is a kind of" storage media, and as such, that each has storage capacity. We could also reasonably say that both have an "is a kind of" relationship with "optical storage media," which in turn "is a kind of" storage media.

If you define classes corresponding to each type of storage device mentioned, you will have defined a **class hierarchy**, which is a series of "is a kind of" relationships. The base class, from which all storage devices derive, could be the class `StorageMedia`. As such, classes that represent CD drives, DVD drives, hard drives, USB drives, and floppy drives are derived from the class `StorageMedia`. However, the classes for CD and DVD drives don't need to derive from `StorageMedia` directly. Instead, they can derive from an intermediate class, `OpticalStorageMedia`. You can view the class hierarchy graphically using a Unified Modeling Language (UML)–like class diagram, as shown in Figure 6.1.

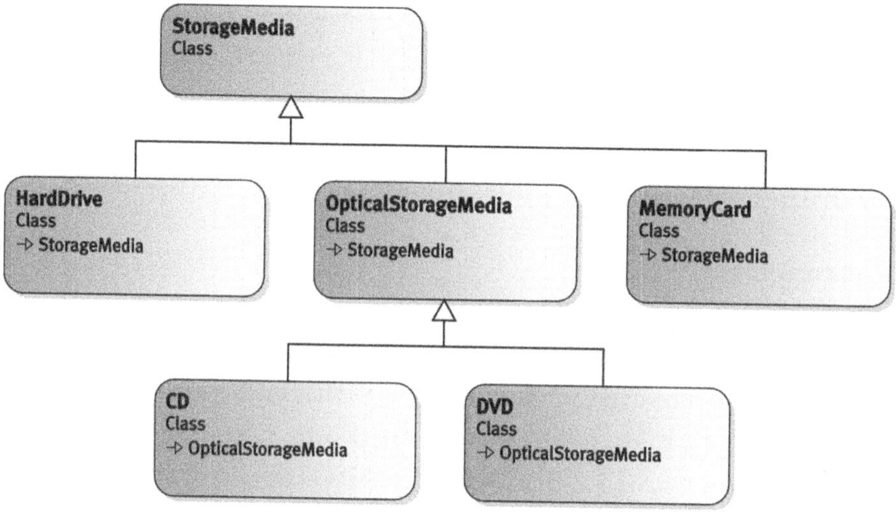

FIGURE 6.1: Class hierarchy

The inheritance relationship involves a minimum of two classes, such that one class is a more specific kind of the other; in Figure 6.1, `HardDrive` is a more specific kind of `StorageMedia`. Although the more specialized type, `HardDrive`, is a kind of `StorageMedia`, the reverse is not true—that is, an instance of `StorageMedia` is not necessarily a `HardDrive`. As Figure 6.1 shows, inheritance can involve more than two classes.

The more specialized type is called the **derived type** or the **subtype**. The more general type is called the **base type** or the **super type**. The base type is also often called the *parent* type, and its derived types are often called its *child* types. Though this usage is common, it can be confusing: After all, a child is not a kind of parent! In this book, we stick to *derived type* and *base type*.

To **derive** or **inherit** from another type is to **specialize** that type, which means to customize the base type so that it is more suitable for a specific purpose. The base type may contain those implementation details that are common to all the derived types.

The key feature of inheritance is that all derived types inherit the members of the base type. Often, the implementation of the base members can be modified, but regardless, the derived type contains the base type's members in addition to any other members that the derived type contains explicitly.

Derived types allow you to organize your classes into a coherent hierarchy where the derived types have greater specificity than their base types.

Polymorphism

Polymorphism is formed from the roots *poly*, meaning "many," and *morph*, meaning "form." In the context of objects, polymorphism means that a single method or type can have many forms of implementation.

Suppose you have a media player that can play both music CDs and DVDs containing MP3s. However, the exact implementation of the `Play()` method will vary depending on the media type. Calling `Play()` on an object representing a music CD or on an object representing a music DVD will play music in both cases, because each object's type understands the intricacies of playing. All that the media player knows about is the common base type, `OpticalStorageMedia`, and the fact that it defines the `Play()` method. Polymorphism is the principle that a type can take care of the exact details of a method's implementation because the method appears on multiple derived types, each of which shares a common base type (or interface) that also contains the same method signature.

Declaring and Instantiating a Class

Defining a class involves first specifying the keyword `class`, followed by an identifier, as shown in Listing 6.1.

LISTING 6.1: Defining a Class

```
public class Employee
{
}
```

All code that belongs to the class will appear between the curly braces following the class declaration. Although not a requirement, generally you place each class into its own file. This makes it easier to find the code that defines a particular class, because the convention is to name the file using the class name.

Guidelines

AVOID placing more than one class in a single source file.

DO name the source file with the name of the public type it contains.

Once you have defined a new class, you can use that class as though it were built into the framework. In other words, you can declare a variable of that type or define a method that takes a parameter of the new class type. Listing 6.2 demonstrates such declarations.

LISTING 6.2: Declaring Variables of the Class Type

```
public class Program
{
    public static void Main()
    {
        Employee employee1, employee2;
        // ...
    }

    public static void IncreaseSalary(Employee employee)
    {
        // ...
```

```
    }
}
```

BEGINNER TOPIC

Objects and Classes Defined

In casual conversation, the terms *class* and *object* appear interchangeably. However, they actually have distinct meanings. A **class** is a template for what an object will look like at instantiation time. An **object**, therefore, is an instance of a class. Classes are like the mold for what a widget will look like; objects correspond to widgets created by the mold. The process of creating an object from a class is called **instantiation** because an object is an instance of a class.

Now that you have defined a new class type, it is time to instantiate an object of that type. Mimicking its predecessors, C# uses the `new` keyword to instantiate an object (see Listing 6.3).

Listing 6.3: Instantiating a Class

```
public class Program
{
    public static void Main()
    {
        Employee employee1 = new Employee();
        Employee employee2;
        employee2 = new();

        IncreaseSalary(employee1);
        IncreaseSalary(employee2);
    }
    // ...
}
```

Not surprisingly, the assignment can occur either in the same statement as the declaration or in a separate statement.

Unlike the primitive types you have worked with so far, there is no literal way to specify an `Employee`. Instead, the `new` operator provides an instruction to the runtime to allocate memory for an `Employee` object, initialize the object, and return a reference to the instance. While you can specify the data type (`Employee`), it is optional if the compiler can infer the type from the left-hand side of the assignment starting in C# 9.0. In this case, the compiler can determine the targeted type is `Employee` and, therefore, infer that the new expression is for an `Employee` and allow a target-typed new expression for the instantiation—where no type is specified when invoking the constructor. That said, developers should use caution if the targeted type is not obvious from the line of code. For example, assigning `text = new()` gives no indication what the data type could be. And, while `string` could be inferred, `System.Text.StringBuilder` is also an obvious choice. For this reason, avoid target-typed expressions when the data type is not obvious.

Guidelines

AVOID target-typed new expressions when the data type of the constructor is not obvious.

CONSIDER use target-typed new expressions when the data type of the constructor is obvious.

Although an explicit operator for allocating memory exists, there is no such operator for de-allocating the memory. Instead, the runtime automatically reclaims the memory sometime after the object becomes inaccessible. The **garbage collector** is responsible for the automatic de-allocation. It determines which objects are no longer referenced by other active objects and then de-allocates the memory for those objects. As a result, there is no compile-time–determined program location where the memory will be collected and restored to the system.

In this trivial example, no explicit data or methods are associated with an `Employee`, which renders the object essentially useless. The next section focuses on adding data to an object.

BEGINNER TOPIC

Encapsulation Part 1: Objects Group Data with Methods

If you received a stack of index cards with employees' first names, a stack of index cards with their last names, and a stack of index cards with their salaries, the cards would be of little value unless you knew that the cards were in the same order in each stack. Even so, the data would be difficult to work with because determining a person's full name would require searching through two stacks. Worse, if you dropped one of the stacks, there would be no way to reassociate the first name with the last name and the salary. Instead, you would need one stack of employee cards in which the data for each employee is grouped on one card. With this approach, first names, last names, and salaries will be encapsulated together.

Outside the object-oriented programming context, to **encapsulate** a set of items is to enclose those items within a capsule. Similarly, object-oriented programming encapsulates methods and data together into an object. This provides a grouping of all the class **members** (the data and methods within a class) so that they no longer need to be handled individually. Instead of passing a first name, a last name, and a salary as three separate parameters to a method, objects enable a call to pass a reference to an employee object. Once the called method receives the object reference, it can send a message (e.g., it can call a method such as `AdjustSalary()`) to the object to perform a particular operation.

Language Contrast: C++—The `delete` Operator

C# programmers should view the `new` operator as a call to instantiate an object, not as a call to allocate memory. Both objects allocated on the heap and objects allocated on the stack support the `new` operator, emphasizing the point that `new` is not about how memory allocation should take place and whether de-allocation is necessary.

Thus, C# does not need the `delete` operator found in C++. Memory allocation and de-allocation are details that the runtime manages, allowing the developer to focus more on domain logic. However, although memory is managed by the runtime, the runtime does not manage other resources such as database connections, network ports, and so on. Unlike C++, C# does not support **implicit deterministic resource cleanup** (the occurrence of implicit object destruction at a compile-time–defined location in the code). Fortunately, C# does support **explicit deterministic resource cleanup** via a `using` statement and **implicit nondeterministic resource cleanup** using finalizers.

Instance Fields

One of the key aspects of object-oriented design is the grouping of data to provide structure. This section discusses how to add data to the `Employee` class. The general object-oriented term for a variable that stores data within a class is **member variable.** This term is well understood in C#, but the more standard term—and the one used in the specification—is **field**, which is a named unit of storage associated with the containing type. **Instance fields** are variables declared at the class level to store data associated with an object. Hence, **association** is the relationship between the field data type and the containing field.

Declaring an Instance Field

In Listing 6.4, the class `Employee` has been modified to include three fields: `FirstName`, `LastName`, and `Salary`.

LISTING 6.4: Declaring Fields

```
public class Employee
{
    public string FirstName;
    public string LastName;
```

```
    public string? Salary;
}
```

With these fields added, it is possible to store some fundamental data with every `Employee` instance. In this case, you prefix the fields with an access modifier of `public`. The use of `public` on a field indicates that the data within the field is accessible from classes other than `Employee` (see the "Access Modifiers" (https://essentialcsharp.com/access-modifiers) section later in this chapter).

Like a local variable declaration, a field declaration includes the data type to which the field refers. Furthermore, it is possible to assign fields an initial value at declaration time, as demonstrated with the `Salary` field in Listing 6.5.

Listing 6.5: Setting Initial Values of Fields at Declaration Time

```
// Non-nullable field uninitialized warning disabled while code is
↪incomplete
#pragma warning disable CS8618
public class Employee
{
    public string FirstName;
    public string LastName;
    public string? Salary = "Not enough";
}
```

We delay the guidelines of naming and coding fields until later in the chapter, after C# properties (https://essentialcsharp.com/properties) and constructors (https://essentialcsharp.com/constructors) have been introduced. Suffice it to say, until then the listings frequently do *not* follow the standard coding guidelines. In fact, there is a preponderance of the following warnings:

- "CS0649: Field is never assigned to, and will always have its default value null."
- "CS8618: Non-nullable field is uninitialized. Consider declaring as nullable."

In this case, since `FirstName` and `LastName` are not initialized, they trigger the CS8618 warning.

For purposes of elucidation, these warnings are ignored and, in fact, disabled with `#pragma` directives in the accompanying source code until the concepts are fully developed later in the chapter.

Accessing an Instance Field

You can set and retrieve the data within fields. However, the fact that a field does not include a `static` modifier indicates that it is an instance field. You can access an instance field only from an instance of the containing class (an object). You cannot access it from the class directly (without first creating an instance, in other words).

Listing 6.6 shows an updated look at the `Program` class and its utilization of the `Employee` class, and Output 6.1 shows the results.

LISTING 6.6: Accessing Fields

```
public class Program
{
    public static void Main()
    {
        Employee employee1 = new();
        Employee employee2;
        employee2 = new Employee();

        employee1.FirstName = "Inigo";
        employee1.LastName = "Montoya";
        employee1.Salary = "Too Little";
        IncreaseSalary(employee1);
        Console.WriteLine(
           $"{
            employee1.FirstName } {
            employee1.LastName }: {
            employee1.Salary }");
        // ...
    }

    public static void IncreaseSalary(Employee employee)
    {
        employee.Salary = "Enough to survive on";
    }
}
```

OUTPUT 6.1

```
Inigo Montoya: Enough to survive on
```

Listing 6.6 instantiates two `Employee` objects, as you saw earlier. It then sets each field, calls `IncreaseSalary()` to change the salary, and displays each field associated with the object referenced by `employee1`.

Notice that you first have to specify which `Employee` instance you are working with. Therefore, the `employee1` variable appears as a prefix to the field name when assigning and accessing the field.

Instance Methods

One alternative to formatting the names in the `WriteLine()` method call within `Main()` is to provide a method in the `Employee` class that takes care of the formatting. Changing the functionality to be within the `Employee` class rather than a member of `Program` is consistent with the encapsulation of a class. Why not group the methods relating to the employee's full name with the class that contains the data that forms the name? Listing 6.7 demonstrates the creation of such a method.

LISTING 6.7: Accessing Fields from within the Containing Class

```
public class Employee
{
    public string FirstName;
    public string LastName;
    public string? Salary;

    public string GetName()
    {
        return $"{ FirstName }  { LastName }";
    }
}
```

There is nothing particularly special about this method compared to what you learned in Chapter 5, except that now the `GetName()` method accesses fields on the object instead of just local variables. In addition, the method declaration is not marked with `static`. As you will see later in this chapter, static methods cannot directly access instance fields within a class. Instead, it is necessary to obtain an instance of the class to call any instance member, whether a method or a field.

Given the addition of the `GetName()` method, you can update `Program.Main()` to use the method, as shown in Listing 6.8 and Output 6.2.

Listing 6.8: Accessing Fields from outside the Containing Class

```
public class Program
{
    public static void Main()
    {
        Employee employee1 = new();
        Employee employee2;
        employee2 = new();

        employee1.FirstName = "Inigo";
        employee1.LastName = "Montoya";
        employee1.Salary = "Too Little";
        IncreaseSalary(employee1);
        Console.WriteLine(
            $"{ employee1.GetName() }: { employee1.Salary }");
        // ...
    }
    // ...
}
```

Output 6.2

```
Inigo Montoya: Enough to survive on
```

Using the `this` Keyword

You can obtain the reference to a class from within instance members that belong to the class. To indicate explicitly that the field or method accessed is an instance member of the containing class in C#, you use the keyword `this`. Use of `this` is implicit when calling any instance member, and it returns an instance of the object itself.

For example, consider the `SetName()` method shown in Listing 6.9.

LISTING 6.9: Using `this` to Identify the Field's Owner Explicitly

```
public class Employee
{
    public string FirstName;
    public string LastName;
    public string? Salary;

    public string GetName()
    {
        return $"{ FirstName }  { LastName }";
    }

    public void SetName(
        string newFirstName, string newLastName)
    {
        this.FirstName = newFirstName;
        this.LastName = newLastName;
    }
}
```

This example uses the keyword `this` to indicate that the fields `FirstName` and `LastName` are instance members of the class.

Although the `this` keyword can prefix any and all references to local class members, the general guideline is not to clutter code when there is no additional value. Therefore, you should avoid using the `this` keyword unless it is required. Listing 6.12 (later in this chapter) is an example of one of the few circumstances when such a requirement exists. Listing 6.9 and Listing 6.10, however, are not good examples. In Listing 6.9, `this` can be dropped entirely without changing the meaning of the code. And in Listing 6.10 (presented next), by changing the naming convention for fields and following the naming convention for parameters, we can avoid any ambiguity between local variables and fields.

BEGINNER TOPIC

Relying on Coding Style to Avoid Ambiguity

In the `SetName()` method, you did not have to use the `this` keyword because `FirstName` is obviously different from `newFirstName`. But suppose that, instead of calling the parameter "newFirstName," you called it "FirstName" (using PascalCase), as shown in Listing 6.10.

LISTING 6.10: Using `this` to Avoid Ambiguity

```
public class Employee
{
    public string FirstName;
    public string LastName;
    public string? Salary;

    public string GetName()
    {
        return $"{ FirstName }  { LastName }";
    }

    // Caution:  Parameter names use PascalCase
    public void SetName(string FirstName, string LastName)
    {
        this.FirstName = FirstName;
        this.LastName = LastName;
    }
}
```

In this example, it is not possible to refer to the `FirstName` field without explicitly indicating that the `Employee` object owns the variable. `this` acts just like the `employee1` variable prefix used in the `Program.Main()` method (see Listing 6.8); it identifies the object as the one on which `SetName()` was called.

Listing 6.10 does not follow the C# naming convention in which parameters are declared like local variables, using camelCase. This can lead to subtle bugs, because assigning `FirstName` (intending to refer to the field) to `FirstName` (the parameter) will lead to code that still compiles and even runs. To avoid this problem, it is a good practice to have a different naming convention for parameters and local variables than the naming convention for fields and properties. We demonstrate one such convention later in this chapter.

In Listing 6.9 and Listing 6.10, the `this` keyword is not used in the `GetName()` method—it is optional. However, if local variables or parameters exist with the same name as the field (see the `SetName()` method in Listing 6.10), omitting `this` would result in accessing the local variable/parameter when the intention was to access the field; given this scenario, use of `this` is required.

You also can use the keyword `this` to access a class's methods explicitly. For example, `this.GetName()` is allowed within the `SetName()` method, permitting you to print out the newly assigned name (see Listing 6.11 and Output 6.3).

Listing 6.11: Using `this` with a Method

```
public class Employee
{
    // ...

    public string GetName()
    {
        return $"{ FirstName } { LastName }";
    }

    public void SetName(string newFirstName, string newLastName)
    {
        this.FirstName = newFirstName;
        this.LastName = newLastName;
        Console.WriteLine(
            $"Name changed to '{ this.GetName() }'");
    }
}

public class Program
{
    public static void Main()
    {
        Employee employee = new();

        employee.SetName("Inigo", "Montoya");
        // ...
    }
```

```
    // ...
}
```

Output 6.3

```
Name changed to 'Inigo Montoya'
```

Sometimes it may be necessary to use `this` to pass a reference to the currently executing object. Consider the `Save()` method in Listing 6.12.

Listing 6.12: Passing `this` in a Method Call

```
public class Employee
{
    public string FirstName;
    public string LastName;
    public string? Salary;

    public void Save()
    {
        DataStorage.Store(this);
    }
}

public class DataStorage
{
    // Save an employee object to a file
    // named with the Employee name
    public static void Store(Employee employee)
    {
        // ...
    }
}
```

The `Save()` method in Listing 6.12 calls a method on the `DataStorage` class, called `Store()`. The `Store()` method, however, needs to be passed the `Employee` object, which needs to be persisted. This is done using the keyword `this`, which passes the instance of the `Employee` object on which `Save()` was called.

Storing and Loading with Files

The actual implementation of the `Store()` method inside `DataStorage` involves classes within the `System.IO` namespace, as shown in Listing 6.13. Inside `Store()`, you begin by instantiating a `FileStream` object that you associate with a file corresponding to the employee's full name. The `FileMode.Create` parameter indicates that you want a new file to be created if there isn't already one with the `<firstname><lastname>.dat` name; if the file exists already, it will be overwritten. Next, you create a `StreamWriter` class, which is responsible for writing text into the `FileStream`. You write the data using `WriteLine()` methods, just as though writing to the console.

LISTING 6.13: Data Persistence to a File

```
public class DataStorage
{
    // Save an employee object to a file
    // named with the Employee name
    // Error handling not shown
    public static void Store(Employee employee)
    {
        // Instantiate a FileStream using FirstNameLastName.dat
        // for the filename. FileMode.Create will force
        // a new file to be created or override an
        // existing file
        // Note: This code could be improved with a using
        // statement - a construct that we have avoided because
        // it has not yet been introduced.
        FileStream stream = new(
            employee.FirstName + employee.LastName + ".dat",
            FileMode.Create);

        // Create a StreamWriter object for writing text
        // into the FileStream
        StreamWriter writer = new(stream);

        // Write all the data associated with the employee
        writer.WriteLine(employee.FirstName);
        writer.WriteLine(employee.LastName);
        writer.WriteLine(employee.Salary);

        // Dispose the StreamWriter and its stream
        writer.Dispose();  // Automatically closes the stream
    }
```

```
    // ...
}
```

Once the write operations are completed, both the `FileStream` and the `StreamWriter` need to be closed so that they are not left open indefinitely while waiting for the garbage collector to run. Listing 6.13 does not include any error handling, so if an exception is thrown, neither `Close()` method will be called.

The load process is similar (see Listing 6.14 with Output 6.4).

Listing 6.14: Data Retrieval from a File

```
using System;
// IO namespace
using System.IO;

public class Employee
{
    // ...
}

public class DataStorage
{
    // ...

    public static Employee Load(string firstName, string lastName)
    {
        Employee employee = new();

        // Instantiate a FileStream using FirstNameLastName.dat
        // for the filename. FileMode.Open will open
        // an existing file or else report an error
        FileStream stream = new(
            firstName + lastName + ".dat", FileMode.Open);

        // Create a StreamReader for reading text from the file
        StreamReader reader = new(stream);

        // Read each line from the file and place it into
        // the associated property.
        employee.FirstName = reader.ReadLine()??
            throw new InvalidOperationException(
                "FirstName cannot be null");
        employee.LastName = reader.ReadLine()??
            throw new InvalidOperationException(
                "LastName cannot be null");
```

```
        employee.Salary = reader.ReadLine();

        // Dispose the StreamReader and its Stream
        reader.Dispose();  // Automatically closes the stream

        return employee;
    }
}

public class Program
{
    public static void Main()
    {
        Employee employee1;

        Employee employee2 = new();
        employee2.SetName("Inigo", "Montoya");
        employee2.Save();

        // Modify employee2 after saving
        IncreaseSalary(employee2);

        // Load employee1 from the saved version of employee2
        employee1 = DataStorage.Load("Inigo", "Montoya");

        Console.WriteLine(
            $"{ employee1.GetName() }: { employee1.Salary }");
    }
    // ...
}
```

Output 6.4

```
Name changed to 'Inigo Montoya'
Inigo Montoya:
```

The reverse of the save process appears in Listing 6.14, which uses a `StreamReader` rather than a `StreamWriter`. Again, `Close()` needs to be called on both `FileStream` and `StreamReader` once the data has been read.

Output 6.4 does not show any salary after `Inigo Montoya:` because `Salary` was not set to `Enough to survive on` by a call to `IncreaseSalary()` until after the call to `Save()`.

Notice in `Main()` that we can call `Save()` from an instance of an employee, but to load a new employee we call `DataStorage.Load()`. To load an employee, we generally don't already have an employee instance to load into, so an instance method on `Employee` would be less than ideal. An alternative to calling `Load` on `DataStorage` would be to add a static `Load()` method (see the section "Static Members" later in this chapter) to `Employee` so that it would be possible to call `Employee.Load()` (using the `Employee` class, not an instance of `Employee`).

Access Modifiers

When declaring a field earlier in the chapter, you prefixed the field declaration with the keyword `public`. `public` is an **access modifier** that identifies the level of encapsulation associated with the member it decorates. Seven access modifiers are available: `public`, `private`, `protected`, `internal`, `protected internal`, `private protected`, and `file`. This section considers the first two.

BEGINNER TOPIC

Encapsulation Part 2: Information Hiding

Besides wrapping data and methods together into a single unit, encapsulation deals with hiding the internal details of an object's data and behavior. To some degree, methods do this; from outside a method, all that is visible to a caller is the method declaration. None of the internal implementation is visible. Object-oriented programming enables this further, however, by providing facilities for controlling the extent to which members are visible from outside the class. Members that are not visible outside the class are **private members**.

In object-oriented programming, *encapsulation* is a term meaning not only grouping data and behavior, but also hiding data and behavior implementation details within a class (the capsule) so that the inner workings of a class are not exposed. This reduces the chance that callers will modify the data inappropriately or program according to the implementation, only to have it change in the future.

The purpose of an access modifier is to provide encapsulation. By using `public`, you explicitly indicate that it is acceptable that the modified fields are accessible from outside the `Employee` class—that they are accessible from the `Program` class, for example.

But consider an `Employee` class that includes a `Password` field. It should be possible to call an `Employee` object and verify the password using a `Logon()` method. Conversely, it should not be possible to access the `Password` field on an `Employee` object from outside the class.

To define a `Password` field as hidden and inaccessible from outside the containing class, you use the keyword `private` for the access modifier, in place of `public` (see Listing 6.15). As a result, the `Password` field is only accessible from inside the `Employee` class, for example.

Listing 6.15: Using the `private` Access Modifier

```
public class Employee
{
    public string FirstName;
    public string LastName;
    public string? Salary;
    // Working de-crypted passwords for elucidation only
    // this is not recommended.
    // Uninitialized; pending explanation of constructors
    private string Password;
    private bool IsAuthenticated;

    public bool Logon(string password)
    {
        if(Password == password)
        {
            IsAuthenticated = true;
        }
        return IsAuthenticated;
    }

    public bool GetIsAuthenticated()
    {
        return IsAuthenticated;
```

```
    }
    // ...
}

public class Program
{
    public static void Main()
    {
        Employee employee = new();

        employee.FirstName = "Inigo";
        employee.LastName = "Montoya";

        // ...


        // ERROR: Password is private, so it cannot be
        // accessed from outside the class
        Console.WriteLine(
           "Password = {0}", employee.Password);
    }
    // ...
}
```

Although this option is not shown in Listing 6.15, it is possible to decorate a method with an access modifier of `private` as well.

If no access modifier is placed on a class member, the declaration defaults to `private`. In other words, members are private by default and programmers need to specify explicitly that a member is to be public.

Properties

The preceding section, "Access Modifiers," demonstrated how you can use the `private` keyword to encapsulate a password, preventing access from outside the class. This type of encapsulation is often too strict, however. For example, sometimes you might need to define fields that external classes can only read but whose values you can change internally. Alternatively, perhaps you want to allow access to write some data in a class, but you need to be able to validate changes made to the data. In yet another scenario, perhaps you need to construct the data on the fly. Traditionally, languages enabled the features found in these examples by marking fields as private and then providing getter and setter methods for accessing and modifying the data. The code in Listing 6.16 changes both `FirstName` and `LastName` to private fields. Public getter and setter methods for each field allow their values to be accessed and changed.

LISTING 6.16: Declaring Getter and Setter Methods

```
public class Employee
{
    private string FirstName;
    // FirstName getter
    public string GetFirstName()
    {
        return FirstName;
    }
    // FirstName setter
    public void SetFirstName(string newFirstName)
    {
        if(newFirstName != null && newFirstName != "")
        {
            FirstName = newFirstName;
        }
    }

    private string LastName;
    // LastName getter
    public string GetLastName()
    {
        return LastName;
    }
    // LastName setter
    public void SetLastName(string newLastName)
    {
        if(newLastName != null && newLastName != "")
        {
            LastName = newLastName;
        }
    }
    // ...
}
```

Unfortunately, this change affects the programmability of the `Employee` class. You can no longer use the assignment operator to set data within the class, nor can you access the data without calling a method.

Declaring a Property

Recognizing the frequency of this pattern, the C# designers provided explicit syntax for it. This syntax is called a **property** (see Listing 6.17 and Output 6.5).

Listing 6.17: Defining Properties

```
public class Program
{
    public static void Main()
    {
        Employee employee = new();

        // Call the FirstName property's setter
        employee.FirstName = "Inigo";

        // Call the FirstName property's getter
        System.Console.WriteLine(employee.FirstName);
    }
}

public class Employee
{
    // FirstName property
    public string FirstName
    {
        get
        {
            return _FirstName;
        }
        set
        {
            _FirstName = value;
        }
    }
    private string _FirstName;

    // ...
}
```

Output 6.5

```
Inigo
```

The first thing to notice in Listing 6.17 is not the property code itself, but rather the code within the `Program` class. Although you no longer have the fields with the `FirstName` and `LastName` identifiers, you cannot see this by looking at the `Program` class. The syntax for accessing an employee's first and last names has not changed at all. It is still possible to assign the parts of the name using a simple assignment operator—for example, `employee.FirstName = "Inigo"`.

The key feature is that properties provide a syntax that looks programmatically like a field. In actuality, no such fields exist. A property declaration looks exactly like a field declaration, but following it are curly braces in which to place the property implementation. Two optional parts make up the property implementation. The `get` part defines the getter portion of the property. It corresponds directly to the `GetFirstName()` and `GetLastName()` functions defined in Listing 6.16. To access the `FirstName` property, you call `employee.FirstName`. Similarly, setters (the `set` portion of the implementation) enable the calling syntax of the field assignment:

```
employee.FirstName = "Inigo";
```

Property definition syntax uses three contextual keywords. You use the `get` and `set` keywords to identify either the retrieval or the assignment portion of the property, respectively. In addition, the setter uses the `value` keyword to refer to the right side of the assignment operation. When `Program.Main()` calls `employee.FirstName = "Inigo"`, therefore, `value` is set to `"Inigo"` inside the setter and can be used to assign `_FirstName`. Listing 6.17's property implementations are the most commonly used. When the getter is called (such as in `Console.WriteLine(employee.FirstName)`), the value from the field (`_FirstName`) is obtained and written to the console.

It is also possible to declare property getters and setters using expression bodied members,[1] as shown in Listing 6.18.

Listing 6.18 uses two different syntaxes for an identical property implementation. In real-world code, you should try to be consistent in your choice of syntax.

1. Starting with C# 7.0.

Automatically Implemented Properties

Listing 6.18: Defining Properties with Expression Bodied Members

```
public class Employee
{
    // FirstName property
    public string FirstName
    {
        get
        {
            return _FirstName;
        }
        set
        {
            _FirstName = value;
        }
    }
    private string _FirstName;
    // LastName property
    public string LastName
    {
        get => _LastName;
        set => _LastName = value;
    }
    private string _LastName;
    // ...
}
```

Since a property with a single backing field that is assigned and retrieved by the get and set accessors is so trivial and common (see the implementations of `FirstName` and `LastName`), the compiler allows the declaration of a property without any accessor implementation or backing field declaration.[2] Listing 6.19 demonstrates the syntax with the `Title` and `Manager` properties, and Output 6.6 shows the results.

Listing 6.19: Automatically Implemented Properties

```
public class Program
{
    public static void Main()
```

2. Introduced in C# 3.0.

```
    {
        Employee employee1 =
            new();
        Employee employee2 =
            new();

        // Call the FirstName property's setter
        employee1.FirstName = "Inigo";

        // Call the FirstName property's getter
        System.Console.WriteLine(employee1.FirstName);

        // Assign an auto-implemented property
        employee2.Title = "Computer Nerd";
        employee1.Manager = employee2;

        // Print employee1's manager's title
        System.Console.WriteLine(employee1.Manager.Title);
    }
}

public class Employee
{
    // FirstName property
    public string FirstName
    {
        get
        {
            return _FirstName;
        }
        set
        {
            _FirstName = value;
        }
    }
    private string _FirstName;

    // LastName property
    public string LastName
    {
        get => _LastName;
        set => _LastName = value;
    }
    private string _LastName;

    // Title property
    public string? Title { get; set; }
```

```
    // Manager property
    public Employee? Manager { get; set; }

    public string? Salary { get; set; } = "Not Enough";
    // ...
}
```

OUTPUT 6.6

```
Inigo
Computer Nerd
```

Auto-implemented properties provide for a simpler way of writing properties in addition to reading them. Furthermore, when it comes time to add something such as validation to the setter, any existing code that calls the property will not have to change, even though the property declaration will have changed to include an implementation.

One final thing to note about automatically declared properties is that it is possible to initialize them[3] as Listing 6.19 does for `Salary`:

```
public string? Salary { get; set; } = "Not Enough";
```

Automatically implemented property initialization (auto-property initialization) using declaration syntax is much like that used for field initialization.

Property and Field Guidelines

Given that it is possible to write explicit setter and getter methods rather than properties, on occasion a question may arise as to whether it is better to use a property or a method. The general guideline is that methods should represent actions and properties should represent data. Properties are intended to provide simple access to simple data with a simple computation. The expectation is that invoking a property will not be significantly more expensive than accessing a field.

With regard to naming, notice that in Listing 6.19 the property name is `FirstName`, and the field name changed from earlier listings to `_FirstName`—

3. Starting in C# 6.0.

that is, PascalCase with an underscore prefix. Other common naming conventions for the private field that backs a property are `_firstName` and, on occasion, the camelCase convention, just like with local variables.[4] The camelCase convention should be avoided, however. The camelCase used for property names is the same as the naming convention used for local variables and parameters, meaning that overlaps in names become highly probable. Also, to respect the principles of encapsulation, fields should not be declared as public.

Regardless of which naming pattern you use for private fields, the coding standard for properties is PascalCase. Therefore, properties should use the `LastName` and `FirstName` pattern with names that represent nouns, noun phrases, or adjectives. It is not uncommon, in fact, for the property name to be the same as the type name. Consider an `Address` property of type `Address` on a `Person` object, for example.

Guidelines

DO use properties for simple access to simple data with simple computations.

AVOID throwing exceptions from property getters.

DO preserve the original property value if the property throws an exception.

CONSIDER using the same casing on a property's backing field as that used in the property, distinguishing the backing field with an "_" prefix.

DO name properties using a noun, noun phrase, or adjective.

CONSIDER giving a property the same name as its type.

AVOID naming fields with camelCase.

DO favor prefixing Boolean properties with "Is," "Can," or "Has," when that practice adds value.

---

4. We prefer `_FirstName` because the `m` in front of the name is unnecessary when compared with an underscore (_). Also, by using the same casing as the property, it is possible to have only one string within the Visual Studio code template expansion tools instead of having one for both the property name and the field name.

DO declare all instance fields as private (and expose them via a property).

DO name properties with PascalCase.

DO favor automatically implemented properties over fields.

DO favor automatically implemented properties over using fully expanded ones if there is no additional implementation logic.

Using Properties with Validation

Notice in Listing 6.20 that the `Initialize()` method of `Employee` uses the property rather than the field for assignment as well. Although this is not required, the result is that any validation within the property setter will be invoked both inside and outside the class. Consider, for example, what would happen if you changed the `LastName` property so that it checked `value` for `null` or an empty string before assigning it to `_LastName`. (Recall checking for null is necessary because even though the data type is a non-nullable string, the caller may have nullable reference types disabled, or the method may be invoked from C# 7.0 or earlier—before nullable reference types existed.)

LISTING 6.20: Providing Property Validation

```
public class Employee
{
    // ...
    public void Initialize(
        string newFirstName, string newLastName)
    {
        // Use property inside the Employee
        // class as well
        FirstName = newFirstName;
        LastName = newLastName;
    }

    // LastName property
    public string LastName
    {
        get => _LastName;
        set
        {
            // ...
```

```
            // Validate LastName assignment

            ArgumentException.ThrowIfNullOrEmpty(value = value?.Trim()!);
            // ...
            _LastName = value;
        }
    }
    private string _LastName;
// ...
}
```

With this new implementation, the code throws an exception if `LastName` is assigned an invalid value, either from another member of the same class or via a direct assignment to `LastName` from inside `Program.Main()`. The ability to intercept an assignment and validate the parameters by providing a field-like API is one of the advantages of properties.

It is a good practice to access a property-backing field only from inside the property implementation. In other words, you should always use the property rather than calling the field directly. In many cases, this principle holds even from code within the same class as the property. If you follow this practice, when you add code such as validation code, the entire class immediately takes advantage of it.[5]

Although rare, it is possible to assign `value` inside the setter, as Listing 6.20 does. In this case, the call to `value.Trim()` removes any whitespace surrounding the new last name value.

Guidelines

AVOID accessing the backing field of a property outside the property, even from within the containing class.

5. As described later in the chapter, one exception to this occurs when the field is marked as read-only, because then the value can be set only in the constructor. In C# 6.0, you can directly assign the value of a read-only property, completely eliminating the need for the read-only field.

Read-Only and Write-Only Properties

By removing either the getter or the setter portion of a property, you can change a property's accessibility. Properties with only a setter are write-only, which is a relatively rare occurrence. Similarly, providing only a getter will cause the property to be read-only; any attempts to assign a value will cause a compile error. To make `Id` read-only, for example, you would use the code shown in Listing 6.21.

Listing 6.21: Defining a Read-Only Property Prior to C# 6.0

```
public class Program
{
    public static void Main()
    {
        Employee employee1 = new();
        employee1.Initialize(42);

        // ERROR:  Property or indexer 'Employee.Id'
        // cannot be assigned to; it is read-only
        employee1.Id = "490";
    }
}

public class Employee
{
    public void Initialize(int id)
    {
        // Use field because Id property has no setter;
        // it is read-only
        _Id = id.ToString();
    }

    // ...
    // Id property declaration
    public string Id
    {
        get => _Id;
        // No setter provided
    }
    private string _Id;
}
```

Listing 6.21 assigns the field from within the `Employee` `Initialize()` method rather than the property (`_Id = id`). Assigning via the property causes a compile error, as it does in `Program.Main()`.

There is also support for read-only, **automatically implemented properties,**[6] as follows:

```
public bool[] Cells { get; } = new bool[9];
```

One important note about a read-only automatically implemented property is that, like read-only fields, the compiler requires that such a property be initialized via an auto-property initializer (or in the constructor). In the preceding snippet we use an initializer, but the assignment of `Cells` from within the constructor is also permitted, as we shall see shortly.

Given the guideline that fields should not be accessed from outside their wrapping property, the programmer should instead use a read-only, automatically implemented property. The only exception might be when the data type of the read-only modified field does not match the data type of the property—for example, if the field was of type `int` and the read-only property was of type `double`.

> **Guidelines**
>
> **DO create read-only properties if the property value should not be changed.**
>
> **DO create read-only automatically implemented properties, rather than read-only properties with a backing field if the property value should not be changed.**

Calculated Properties

In some instances, you do not need a backing field at all. Instead, the property getter returns a calculated value, while the setter parses the value and persists it to some other member fields (if it even exists). Consider, for example, the `Name` property implementation shown in Listing 6.22. Output 6.7 shows the results.

---

6. Starting in C# 6.0.

Listing 6.22: Defining Calculated Properties

```
public class Program
{
    public static void Main()
    {
        Employee employee1 = new();

        employee1.Name = "Inigo Montoya";
        System.Console.WriteLine(employee1.Name);

        // ...
    }
}

public class Employee
{
    // ...

    // FirstName property
    public string FirstName
    {
        get
        {
            return _FirstName;
        }
        set
        {
            _FirstName = value;
        }
    }
    private string _FirstName;

    // LastName property
    public string LastName
    {
        get => _LastName;
        set => _LastName = value;
    }
    private string _LastName;
    // ...

    // Name property
    public string Name
    {
        get
        {
```

```
            return $"{ FirstName } { LastName }";
        }
        set
        {
            // ...
            ArgumentException.ThrowIfNullOrEmpty(value = value?.Trim()!);
            // ...
            // Split the assigned value into
            // first and last names
            string[] names;
            names = value.Split(new char[] { ' ' });
            if(names.Length == 2)
            {
                FirstName = names[0];
                LastName = names[1];
            }
            else
            {
                // Throw an exception if the full
                // name was not assigned
                throw new System.ArgumentException(
                    $"Assigned value '{ value }' is invalid",
                    nameof(value));
            }
        }
    }

    public string Initials => $"{ FirstName[0] } { LastName[0] }";
    // ...
}
```

Output 6.7

```
Inigo Montoya
```

The getter for the `Name` property concatenates the values returned from the `FirstName` and `LastName` properties. In fact, the name value assigned is not actually stored. When the `Name` property is assigned, the value on the right side is parsed into its first and last name parts.

Access Modifiers on Getters and Setters

As previously mentioned, it is a good practice not to access fields from outside their properties because doing so circumvents any validation or additional logic that may be inserted.

An access modifier can appear on either the get or the set portion of the property implementation[7] (not on both), thereby overriding the access modifier specified on the property declaration. Listing 6.23 demonstrates how to do this.

Listing 6.23: Placing Access Modifiers on the Setter

```
public class Program
{
    public static void Main()
    {
        Employee employee1 = new();
        employee1.Initialize(42);
        // ERROR: The property or indexer 'Employee.Id'
        // cannot be used in this context because the set
        // accessor is inaccessible
        employee1.Id = "490";
    }
}

public class Employee
{
    public void Initialize(int id)
    {
        // Set Id property
        Id = id.ToString();
    }

    // ...
    // Id property declaration
    public string Id
    {
        get => _Id;
        private set => _Id = value;
```

7. Introduced in C# 2.0. C# 1.0 did not allow different levels of encapsulation between the getter and setter portions of a property. It was not possible, therefore, to create a public getter and a private setter so that external classes would have read-only access to the property while code within the class could write to the property.

```
    }
    private string _Id;
}
```

By using `private` on the setter, the property appears as read-only to classes other than `Employee`. From within `Employee`, the property appears as read/write, so you can assign the property within the class itself. When specifying an access modifier on the getter or setter, take care that the access modifier is more restrictive than the access modifier on the property as a whole. It is a compile error, for example, to declare the property as `private` and the setter as `public`.

Guidelines

DO apply appropriate accessibility modifiers on implementations of getters and setters on all properties.

DO NOT provide set-only properties or properties with the setter having broader accessibility than the getter.

Properties and Method Calls Not Allowed as `ref` or `out` Parameter Values

C# allows properties to be used identically to fields, except when they are passed as `ref` or `out` parameter values. `ref` and `out` parameter values are internally implemented by passing the memory address to the target method. However, because properties may not have a backing field or can be read-only or write-only, it is not possible to pass the address for the underlying storage. As a result, you cannot pass properties as `ref` or `out` parameter values. The same is true for method calls. Instead, when code needs to pass a property or method call as a `ref` or `out` parameter value, the code must first copy the value into a variable and then pass the variable. Once the method call has completed, the code must assign the variable back into the property.

ADVANCED TOPIC

Property Internals

Listing 6.24 shows that getters and setters are exposed as `get_FirstName()` and `set_FirstName()` in the Common Intermediate Language (CIL).

Listing 6.24: CIL Code Resulting from Properties

```
// ...

.field private string _FirstName
.method public hidebysig specialname instance string
        get_FirstName() cil managed
    {
        // Code size       12 (0xc)
        .maxstack  1
        .locals init (string V_0)
        IL_0000:  nop
        IL_0001:  ldarg.0
        IL_0002:  ldfld      string Employee::_FirstName
        IL_0007:  stloc.0
        IL_0008:  br.s IL_000a

        IL_000a:  ldloc.0
        IL_000b:  ret
    } // End of method Employee::get_FirstName

    .method public hidebysig specialname instance void
            set_FirstName(string 'value') cil managed
    {
      // Code size       9 (0x9)
      .maxstack  8
      IL_0000:  nop
      IL_0001:  ldarg.0
      IL_0002:  ldarg.1
      IL_0003:  stfld      string Employee::_FirstName
      IL_0008:  ret
    } // End of method Employee::set_FirstName

    .property instance string FirstName()
    {
      .get instance string Employee::get_FirstName()
      .set instance void Employee::set_FirstName(string)
    } // End of property Employee::FirstName
```

```
    // ...
```

Just as important to their appearance as regular methods is the fact that properties are an explicit construct within the CIL, too. As Listing 6.25 shows, the getters and setters are called by CIL properties, which are an explicit construct within the CIL code. Because of this, languages and compilers are not restricted to always interpreting properties based on a naming convention. Instead, CIL properties provide a means for compilers and code editors to provide special syntax.

Listing 6.25: Properties Are an Explicit Construct in CIL

```
.property instance string FirstName()
{
  .get instance string Program::get_FirstName()
  .set instance void Program::set_FirstName(string)
} // End of property Program::FirstName
```

Notice in Listing 6.24 that the getters and setters that are part of the property include the `specialname` metadata. This modifier is what IDEs, such as Visual Studio, use as a flag to hide the members from IntelliSense.

An automatically implemented property is almost identical to one for which you define the backing field explicitly. In place of the manually defined backing field, the C# compiler generates a field with the name `<PropertyName>k_BackingField` in CIL. This generated field includes an attribute (see Chapter 18) called `System.Runtime.CompilerServices.CompilerGeneratedAttribute`. Both the getters and the setters are decorated with the same attribute because they, too, are generated—with the same implementation as in Listings 5.23 and 5.24.

Begin 8.0

Constructors

Now that you have added fields to a class and can store data, you need to consider the validity of that data. As you saw in Listing 6.6, it is possible to instantiate an object using the `new` operator. The result, however, is the ability to create an employee with invalid data. Immediately following the assignment of `employee`, you have an `Employee` object whose name and salary are not initialized. In Listing 6.6, you assigned the uninitialized fields immediately following the instantiation of an employee—but if you failed to do the initialization, you would not receive a warning from the compiler. As a result, you could end up with an `Employee` object with an invalid name. (Technically, in C# 8.0, non-nullable reference types will trigger a warning suggesting that the data type be switched to nullable to avoid a default of `null`. Regardless, initialization is required to avoid instantiating objects whose fields contain invalid data.)

End 8.0

Begin 12.0

Declaring a Primary Constructor

To correct this problem, you need to provide a means of specifying the required data when the object is created. You do this using a constructor, as demonstrated in Listing 6.26.

LISTING 6.26: Defining a Primary Constructor

```
// Employee constructor
public class Employee(string firstName, string lastName)
{
    public string FirstName { get; set; } = firstName;
    public string LastName { get; set; } = lastName;
    public string? Salary { get; set; } = "Not Enough";

    // ...
}
```

For the primary constructor, notice how the type declaration has a method signature following it. This provides variables (called **positional parameters**) that are scoped to the class and, as shown in Listing 6.26, can be assigned as property initializers. The primary constructor variables are available to any instance member of the class, thus allowing the assignment of `firstName` and `lastName` to `FirstName` and `LastName` properties respectively.

The constructor is the method that the runtime calls to initialize an instance of the object. In this case, the constructor takes the first name and the last name as parameters, allowing the programmer to specify these names when instantiating the `Employee` object. Listing 6.27 is an example of how to call a constructor.

Listing 6.27: Calling a Constructor

```
public class Program
{
    public static void Main()
    {
        Employee employee;
        employee = new("Inigo", "Montoya");
        employee.Salary = "Too Little";

        System.Console.WriteLine(
            "{0} {1}: {2}",
            employee.FirstName,
            employee.LastName,
            employee.Salary);
    }
    // ...
}
```

Notice that the `new` operator returns the type of the object being instantiated. In addition, the initialization for the first and last names occurs via the property initializers that execute during construction. In this example, you don't initialize `Salary` within the constructor, so the code assigning the salary still appears.

End 12.0

ADVANCED TOPIC

Implementation Details of the new Operator

Internally, the interaction between the `new` operator and the constructor is as follows. The `new` operator retrieves "empty" memory from the memory manager and then calls the specified constructor, passing a reference to the empty memory to the constructor as the implicit `this` parameter. Next, the remainder of the constructor chain executes, passing around the reference between constructors. None of the constructors have a return type; behaviorally they all return `void`. When execution of the constructor chain is complete, the `new` operator returns the memory reference, now referring to the memory in its initialized form.

Defining a Constructor

It is also possible to define constructors separately from the type declaration. As shown in Listing 6.28, to define a (non-primary) constructor, you create a method with no return type, whose method name is identical to the type name. Even though no return type or return statement was specified in the constructor's declaration or implementation, invoking the constructor (via the new operator), still returns an instance of the type.

Listing 6.28: Defining a Constructor

```
public class Employee
{
    // Employee constructor
    public Employee(string firstName, string lastName)
    {
        FirstName = firstName;
        LastName = lastName;
    }

    public string FirstName { get; set; }
    public string LastName { get; set; }
    public string? Salary { get; set; } = "Not Enough";

    // ...
}
```

Developers should take care when using both assignment at declaration time and assignment within constructors. Assignments within the constructor will occur after any assignments are made when a property or field is declared (such as `string Salary { get; set; } = "Not enough"` in Listing 6.26). Therefore, assignment within a constructor will override any value assigned at declaration time. This subtlety can lead to a misinterpretation of the code by a casual reader who assumes the value after instantiation is the one assigned in the property or field declaration. Therefore, it is worth considering a coding style that does not mix both declaration assignment and constructor assignment for the same field or property

Default and Copy Constructors

When you add a constructor explicitly, you can no longer instantiate an `Employee` from within `Main()` without specifying the first and last names. The code shown in Listing 6.29, therefore, will not compile.

LISTING 6.29: Default Constructor No Longer Available

```
public class Program
{
    public static void Main()
    {
        Employee employee;

        // ERROR: No overload because method 'Employee'
        // takes '0' arguments
        employee = new Employee();

        // ...
    }
}
```

If a class has no explicitly defined constructor, the C# compiler adds one during compilation. This constructor takes no parameters so, by definition, it is the **default constructor**. As soon as you add an explicit constructor to a class, the C# compiler no longer provides a default constructor. Therefore, with `Employee(string firstName, string lastName)` defined, the default constructor, `Employee()`, is not added by the compiler. You could manually add such a constructor, but then you would again be allowing construction of an `Employee` without specifying the employee's name.

It is not necessary to rely on the default constructor defined by the compiler. That is, programmers can define a default constructor explicitly—perhaps one that initializes some fields to particular values. Defining the default constructor simply involves declaring a constructor that takes no parameters.

A **copy constructor** is a constructor that takes a single parameter of the containing type. For example:

```
public Employee(Employee original)
{
// Copy properties between employees here.
}
```

Constructors like this are useful for cloning an instance of an object into a new duplicate instance.

Object Initializers

To initialize an object's accessible fields and properties, you can use the concept of an **object initializer**—a set of member initializers enclosed in curly braces following the constructor call to create the object. Each member initializer is the assignment of an accessible field or property name with a value (see Listing 6.30).

LISTING 6.30: Calling an Object Initializer with Explicit Member Assignment

```
public class Program
{
    public static void Main()
    {
        Employee employee = new("Inigo", "Montoya")
            { Title = "Computer Nerd", Salary = "Not enough" };
        // ...
    }
}
```

Notice that the same constructor rules apply even when using an object initializer. The order of member initializers in C# provides the sequence for property and field assignment in the statements following the constructor call within CIL.

In general, all properties should be initialized to reasonable default values by the time the constructor exits. Moreover, by using validation logic on the setter, it is possible to restrict the assignment of invalid data to a property. On occasion, the values on one or more properties may cause other properties on the same object to contain invalid values. When this occurs, exceptions from the invalid state should be postponed until the invalid interrelated property values become relevant.

Guidelines

DO provide sensible defaults for all properties, ensuring that defaults do not result in a security hole or significantly inefficient code.

DO allow properties to be set in any order, even if this results in a temporarily invalid object state.

ADVANCED TOPIC

Collection Initializers

Using a similar syntax to that of object initializers, **collection initializers**[8] support a similar feature set as object initializers, only with collections. Specifically, a collection initializer allows the assignment of items within the collection at the time of the collection's instantiation. Borrowing the same syntax used for arrays, the collection initializer initializes each item within the collection as part of collection creation. Initializing a list of `Employee` objects, for example, involves specifying each item within curly braces following the constructor call, as shown in Listing 6.31.

LISTING 6.31: Calling an Object Initializer

```
public class Program
{
    public static void Main()
    {
        List<Employee> employees = new()
            {
                new("Inigo", "Montoya"),
                new("Kevin", "Bost")
            };
        // ...
    }
}
```

After the assignment of a new collection instance, the compiler-generated code instantiates each object in sequence and adds them to the collection via the `Add()` method.

8. Added in C# 3.0.

Begin 9.0

Init Only Setters

Object initializers allow for specifying member values during object initialization. Any read-only properties cannot be set this way, however, because properties with only getters may only be set during object construction and object initializers runs after this. To address the problem, C# 9.0 added support for init only setters, which can be set from within object initializers but not afterward. Listing 6.32 demonstrates the use of `init` only setter for the `Salary` property.

Listing 6.32: Init Only Setter

```
public class Employee
{
    public Employee(int id, string name)
    {
        Id = id;
        Name = name;
        Salary = null;
    }

    // ...

    public int Id { get; }
    public string Name { get; }

    public string? Salary
    {
        get => _Salary;
        init => _Salary = value;
    }
    private string? _Salary;
}

public class Program
{
    public static void Main()
    {
        Employee employee = new(42, "Inigo Montoya")
        {
            Salary = "Sufficient"
        };

        // ERROR:  Property or indexer 'Employee.Salary'
        // cannot be assigned after initialization completes.
```

```
        employee.Salary = "Enough";
    }
}
```

Notice that while you can set the value of `Salary` from the object initializer, you can't change the value once the initializer is complete. After that, the value is read-only.

End 9.0

ADVANCED TOPIC

Finalizers

Constructors define what happens during the instantiation process of a class. To define what happens when an object is destroyed, C# provides the finalizer construct. Unlike destructors in C++, finalizers do not run immediately after an object goes out of scope. Rather, the finalizer executes at some unspecified time after an object is determined to be "unreachable." Specifically, the garbage collector identifies objects with finalizers during a garbage collection cycle, and instead of immediately de-allocating those objects, it adds them to a finalization queue. A separate thread runs through each object in the finalization queue and calls the object's finalizer before removing it from the queue and making it available for the garbage collector again. Chapter 10 discusses this process, along with resource cleanup, in depth.

Overloading Constructors

Constructors can be overloaded—you can have more than one constructor if the number or types of the parameters vary. For example, as Listing 6.33 shows, you could provide a constructor that has an employee ID with first and last names, or even just the employee ID.

LISTING 6.33: Overloading a Constructor

```
public class Employee
{
    public Employee(string firstName, string lastName)
    {
        FirstName = firstName;
```

```
        LastName = lastName;
    }

    public Employee(
        int id, string firstName, string lastName)
    {
        Id = id;
        FirstName = firstName;
        LastName = lastName;
    }

    // FirstName & LastName set inside Id property setter.
    #pragma warning disable CS8618
    public Employee(int id) => Id = id;
    #pragma warning restore CS8618

    private int _Id;
    public int Id
    {
        get => _Id;
        private set
        {
            // Look up employee name...
            // ...
        }
    }
    // ...
    public string FirstName { get; set; }
    // ...
    public string LastName { get; set; }
    public string? Salary { get; set; } = "Not Enough";

    // ...
}
```

This approach enables `Program.Main()` to instantiate an employee from the first and last names either by passing in the employee ID only or by passing both the names and the IDs. You would use the constructor with both the names and the IDs when creating a new employee in the system. You would use the constructor with only the ID to load the employee data from a file or a database.

As is the case with method overloading, multiple constructors are used to both support simple scenarios using a small number of parameters and complex scenarios with additional parameters. Consider using optional parameters in favor of overloading so that the default values for "defaulted" properties are visible in the API. For example, a constructor signature of `Person(string firstName, string lastName, int? age = null)` provides signature documentation that if the `Age` of a `Person` is not specified, it will default to `null`.

Begin 8.0

Notice also that it is possible to have expression bodied member implementations of constructors,[9] as in

```
// FirstName&LastName set inside Id property setter.
#pragma warning disable CS8618
public Employee(int id) => Id = id;
```

In this case, we invoke the `Id` property to assign `FirstName` and `LastName`. Unfortunately, the compiler doesn't detect the assignment and, starting with C# 8.0, issues a warning to consider marking those properties as nullable. Since we are, in fact, setting them, the warning is disabled.

End 8.0

Guidelines

DO use the same name for constructor parameters (camelCase) and properties (PascalCase) if the constructor parameters are used to simply set the property.

DO provide constructor optional parameters or constructor overloads that initialize properties with good defaults.

Constructor Chaining: Calling Another Constructor Using `this`

Notice in Listing 6.33 that the initialization code for the `Employee` object is now duplicated in multiple places, so it also must be maintained in multiple places. The amount of code is small, but there are ways to eliminate the duplication by calling one constructor from another—a practice known as **constructor chaining**—using **constructor initializers**. Constructor initializers determine which constructor to call before executing the implementation of the current constructor (see Listing 6.34).

---

9. Starting with C# 7.0.

LISTING 6.34: Calling One Constructor from Another

```
public class Employee
{
    public Employee(string firstName, string lastName)
    {
        FirstName = firstName;
        LastName = lastName;
    }

    public Employee(
        int id, string firstName, string lastName)
        : this(firstName, lastName)
    {
        Id = id;
    }

    // FirstName&LastName set inside Id property setter.
    #pragma warning disable CS8618
    public Employee(int id)
    {
        Id = id;

        // Look up employee name...
        // ...

        // NOTE: Member constructors cannot be
        // called explicitly inline
        // this(id, firstName, lastName);
    }
    #pragma warning restore CS8618

    public int Id { get; private set; }
    public string FirstName { get; set; }
    public string LastName { get; set; }
    public string? Salary { get; set; } = "Not Enough";

    // ...
}
```

To call one constructor from another within the same class (for the same object instance), C# uses a colon followed by the `this` keyword, followed by the parameter list on the called constructor's declaration. In this case, the constructor that takes all three parameters calls the constructor that takes two parameters. Often, this calling pattern is reversed—that is, the constructor with the fewest parameters calls the constructor with the most parameters, passing defaults for the parameters that are not known.

BEGINNER TOPIC

Centralizing Initialization

Notice that in the `Employee(int id)` constructor implementation in Listing 6.34, you cannot call `this(firstName, lastName)` because no such parameters exist on this constructor. To enable such a pattern, in which all initialization code happens through one method, you must create a separate method, as shown in Listing 6.35.

LISTING 6.35: Providing an Initialization Method

```
public class Employee
{
    // FirstName&LastName set inside Initialize() method.
    #pragma warning disable CS8618
    public Employee(string firstName, string lastName)
    {
        int id;
        // Generate an employee ID...
        // ...
        Initialize(id, firstName, lastName);
    }

    public Employee(int id, string firstName, string lastName)
    {
        Initialize(id, firstName, lastName);
    }

    public Employee(int id)
    {
        string firstName;
        string lastName;
        Id = id;

        // Look up employee data
        // ...

        Initialize(id, firstName, lastName);
    }
```

```
    #pragma warning restore CS8618

    private void Initialize(
        int id, string firstName, string lastName)
    {
        Id = id;
        FirstName = firstName;
        LastName = lastName;
    }
    // ...
}
```

In this case, the method is called `Initialize()`, and it takes both the names and the employee IDs. Note that you can continue to call one constructor from another, as shown in Listing 6.34.

In the same way that setting the `LastName` and `FirstName` via the `Id` property wasn't detected by the compiler, assignment via the `Initialize` method goes undetected, so the warning is disabled.

Begin 8.0

Non-Nullable Reference Type Properties with Constructors

Throughout this chapter, we have consistently disabled the C# nullable warning:

```
CS8618: Non-nullable field/property is uninitialized. Consider
declaring as nullable.
```

When you declare reference type (1) non-nullable fields or (2) non-nullable automatically implemented properties, it is obvious that these fields and properties need to be initialized before the containing object is fully instantiated. Not doing so would leave those fields and properties with a default `null` value—so they shouldn't be declared as non-nullable.

The problem is that frequently the non-nullable fields and properties are initialized indirectly, outside the immediate scope of the constructor and therefore beyond the scope of the compiler's code analysis, even if they are still, in fact, initialized, perhaps via a method or property that the constructor invokes.[10] Following are some examples of this practice:

- A simple property with validation that checks the value to be assigned to a field is not `null` before assigning it to the backing field that the compiler reports is uninitialized (see Listing 6.20).
- The calculated `Name` property (such as Listing 6.22) sets other non-nullable properties or fields within the class.
- The centralized initialization occurs in the manner shown in Listing 6.34 and Listing 6.35.
- Public properties are initialized by external agents that trigger the instantiation and then initialize the properties.[11]

In most cases, the reference type non-nullable field or non-nullable automatically implemented property (referred to as a non-nullable field/property in this section—"reference type" is implied) is assigned indirectly via properties or methods that the constructor invokes. Unfortunately, the C# compiler doesn't recognize an indirect assignment of a non-nullable field/property.

Furthermore, all non-nullable fields/properties need to ensure that they are not assigned a value of `null`. In the case of fields, they need to be wrapped in properties with the setter validation ensuring that a `null` value will not be assigned. (Remember that field validation relies on the guideline that we do not access fields outside of the property that wraps them.) The result is that non-nullable read-write fully implemented reference type properties should have validation preventing `null` assignment.

Non-nullable automatically implemented properties need to be limited to read-only encapsulation, with any values assigned during instantiation and validated as not `null` prior to assignment. Read-write non-nullable reference type automatically implemented properties should be avoided, especially with public setters, since preventing `null` assignment is problematic. Although the uninitialized non-`null` property compiler warning can be avoided by assigning the property

10. Or potentially via an external agent like reflection; see Chapter 18.

11. Examples include the `TestContext` property in MSTest or objects initialized through dependency injection.

from the constructor, this is not enough: The property is read-write, so it could be assigned `null` after instantiation, thereby voiding your intent for it to be non-nullable.

Read/Write Non-Nullable Reference Type Properties

Listing 6.36 demonstrates how to inform the compiler and avoid the false warning that a non-nullable field/property is uninitialized. The end goal is to allow the programmer to inform the compiler that the properties/fields are non-nullable so that the compiler can inform callers about the (non-)nullability of those properties/fields.

Listing 6.36: Providing Validation on Non-Nullable Property

```
public class Employee
{
    public Employee(string name)
    {
        Name = name;
    }

    public string Name
    {
        get => _Name!;
        set => _Name = value ?? throw new ArgumentNullException(
            nameof(value));
    }
    private string? _Name;
    // ...
}
```

The code snippet to handle non-nullable properties/fields that are not directly initialized by the constructor has several important qualities (listed in no particular order here):

- The property setter includes a check for `null` that occurs before setting the value of the non-nullable field. In Listing 6.36, this is done by using the null-coalescing operator and throwing an `ArgumentNullException` if the new value is `null`.
- The constructor invokes a method or property that indirectly assigns the non-nullable field but fails to recognize that the field is initialized to a value other than `null`.

- The backing field is declared as nullable to avoid the compiler warning that the field is uninitialized.
- The getter returns the field with a null-forgiveness operator—declaring that it is not `null` thanks to the setter validation.

For a non-nullable property, it is seemingly nonsensical to declare the backing field as nullable. This is necessary, however, since the compiler is oblivious to non-nullable field/property assignments outside from the constructor. Fortunately, this is a case where you, as the programmer, are justified in using the null-forgiveness operator when returning the field because of the not-`null` check in the setter that ensures the field is never `null`.

Read-Only Automatically Implemented Reference Type Properties

As pointed out earlier in this section, non-nullable automatically implemented reference-type properties need to be read-only to avoid invalid `null` assignments. However, you still need to validate any parameters that may be assigned during instantiation, as shown in Listing 6.37.

Listing 6.37: Validation of Non-Null Reference Type Automatically Implemented Properties

```
public class Employee
{
    public Employee(string name)
    {
        Name = name ?? throw new ArgumentNullException(nameof(name));
    }

    public string Name { get; }
}
```

One could debate whether a private setter should be allowed on non-nullable automatically implemented reference-type properties. While possible, the more appropriate question to ask is whether your class could mistakenly assign `null` to the property. If you don't encapsulate the field with validation in a setter, can you be sure you won't mistakenly assign a `null` value? While the compiler will verify your intent during instantiation, it is questionable that the developer will always remember to check for `null` in values coming into your class that should be non-nullable—as occurs in the constructor shown in Listing 6.37.

> **Guidelines**
>
> **DO** implement non-nullable read/write reference fully implemented properties with a nullable backing field, a null-forgiveness operator when returning the field from the getter, and non-`null` validation in the property setter.
>
> **DO** assign non-nullable reference type properties before instantiation completes.
>
> **DO** implement non-nullable reference type automatically implemented properties as read-only.
>
> **DO** use a nullable check for all reference type properties and fields that are not initialized before instantiation completes.

Begin 11.0

`required` Modifier

In C# 11, the designers add the ability to mark either a field or a property as required. This designates them as "required" such that they must be assigned inside the object initializer during construction (see Listing 6.38).

Listing 6.38: Using the Required Modifier

```
public class Book
{
    string? _Title;
    public required string Title
    {
        get
        {
            return _Title!;
        }
        set
        {
            _Title = value ?? throw new
↪ArgumentNullException(nameof(value));
        }
    }

    string? _Isbn;
```

```
    public required string Isbn
    {
        get
        {
            return _Isbn!;
        }
        set
        {
            _Isbn = value ?? throw new
↪ArgumentNullException(nameof(value));
        }
    }

    public string? Subtitle { get; set; }

    // ...
}

public class Program
{
    public static void Main()
    {
        // ...
        Book book = new()
        {
            Isbn = "978-0135972267",
            Title = "Harold and the Purple Crayon"
        };
        // ...
    }
}
```

By adding the `required` modifier, we can no longer instantiate a book without supplying an object initializer that provides value for both the `Isbn` number and the `Title` (see Listing 6.39).

Listing 6.39: Specifying Required Members within the Object Initializer

```
// Error CS9035:
// Required member 'Book.Isbn' must be set in the object
// initializer or attribute constructor
Book book = new() { Title= "Essential C#" };

// ...
```

Notice that since we don't include an explicit constructor for Book, we rely on the automatically generated default constructor to instantiate the book. This is ideal since the required members define how to construct the object in place of any constructor. Providing a constructor with parameters for the required members will result in having to specify the values both as constructor arguments and, redundantly, in the object initializer. A constructor with a Title parameter, for example, will result in an instantiation like this:

```
Book book = new("A People's History of the United States")
{
Title= "A People's History of the United States",
Isbn="978-0062397348"
};
```

To avoid this redundancy, you can decorate a constructor with the SetRequireParameters attribute, instructing the compiler to disable all the object initializer requirements when invoking the associated constructor. (Effectively, the SetRequireParameters attribute instructs the compiler that the developer will take care of setting all the required members so the compiler can ignore checking for initialization assignment. Unfortunately, however, there is little to no verification that such initialization did occur—the compiler doesn't check. See Listing 6.40 for an example of how to use the SetsRequiredMembers attribute.

LISTING 6.40: Disabling `required` Object Initialization

```
[SetsRequiredMembers]
public Book(int id)
{
    Id = id;

    // Look up book data
    // ...
    // ...
}
```

And, given such a constructor, we can instantiate a book without setting any required members:

```
Book book = new(42) {
Subtitle = "The Comprehensive, Expert Guide " +
```

```
"to C# for Programmers at All Levels" };
```

The disadvantage, of course, it this assumes that the constructor has valid values to assign the required members. There is no point in telling the compiler to ignore the required members if in fact there are no available ways to determine the valid required member values. Doing so will allow the constructor invocation to not set the required members while leaving invalid values. Furthermore, is there enough of an advantage in using a constructor to set non-required rather than just allowing them to be set via an object initializer. On the flip side, obviously don't mark a value as required when the default value of the data type is valid.

As you would expect, you cannot have a required public type with a private setter. Rather, the setter on a required member must match the visibility of the type that contains the member. Since `Book` is `public`, its `Isbn` property setter must also be public.

One last important point to note. Adding a required member after your class is already published to production will cause existing code that instantiates the type to no longer compile because the added required members will need to be specified in the object initializer. This makes the new version incompatible with existing code; therefore, you should avoid it.

Guidelines

DO NOT use constructor parameters to initialize required properties; instead, rely on object initializer–specified values.

DO NOT use the `SetRequiredParameters` attribute unless all required parameters are assigned valid values during construction.

CONSIDER having a default constructor only on types with required parameters, relying on the object initializer to set both required and non-required members.

AVOID adding required members to released types to avoid breaking the compilo on existing code.

AVOID required members where the default value of the type is valid.

End 11.0

Nullable Attributes

Rather than disable nullable reference types or nullable warnings, occasionally it is helpful to provide the compiler with hints about your nullable intent. This is possible using metadata that you can place directly into your code with a construct called an attribute (see Chapter 18). There are seven different nullable attributes, each defined in the `System.Diagnostics.CodeAnalysis` namespace and identified as either pre-conditions or post-conditions (Table 6.1).

TABLE 6.1: Nullable Attributes

Attribute	Category	Description
`AllowNull`	Precondition	Non-nullable input argument may be `null`.
`DisallowNull`	Precondition	Nullable input argument should never be `null`.
`MaybeNull`	Postcondition	Non-nullable return value may be `null`.
`NotNull`	Postcondition	Nullable return value will never be `null`.
`MaybeNullWhen`	Postcondition	A non-nullable input argument may be `null` when the method returns the specified `bool` value.
`NotNullWhen`	Postcondition	Nullable input argument will not be `null` when the method returns the specified `bool` value.
`NotNullIfNotNull`	Postcondition	Return value isn't `null` if the argument for the specified parameter isn't `null`.

It is helpful to have such attributes because occasionally, the nullability of the data type is insufficient. You can overcome this insufficiency with an attribute that decorates either incoming (a pre-condition nullable attribute) or outgoing (a post-condition nullable attribute) data on a method. The pre-condition communicates to the caller whether the value specified is intended to be `null`, whereas the post-condition communicates to the caller about the nullability of the outgoing data. Consider, for example, the methods that follow the try-get pattern shown in Listing 6.41.

Listing 6.41: Using `NotNullWhen` and `NotNullIfNotNull` Attributes

```
using System.Diagnostics.CodeAnalysis;
// ...
    static public bool TryGetDigitAsText(
        char number, [NotNullWhen(true)]out string? text) =>
            (text = number switch
            {
                '1' => "one",
                '2' => "two",
                '3' => "three",
                '4' => "four",
                // ...
                '9' => "nine",
                _ => null
            }) is not null;

    // nameof() on parameters is not supported prior to C# 11/.NET 7.0
    [return: NotNullIfNotNull(nameof(text))]
    static public string? TryGetDigitsAsText(string? text)
    {
        if (text == null) return null;

        string result = "";
        foreach (char character in text)
        {
            if (TryGetDigitAsText(character, out string? digitText))
            {
                if (result != "") result += '-';
                result += digitText.ToLower();
            }
        }
        return result;
    }
```

Notice that the call to `digitText.ToLower()` from `TryGetDigitAsText()` has no coalescing operator and does not issue a warning even though `text` is declared as nullable. This is possible because the `text` parameter in `TryGetDigitAsText()` is decorated with the `NotNullWhen(true)` attribute, which informs the compiler that, if the method returns true (the value specified with the `NotNullWhen` attribute), then your intent is that `digitText` will not be `null`. The `NotNullWhen` attribute is a post-condition declaration, informing the caller that output (`text`) is not `null` if the method returns `true`.

Similarly, for `TryGetDigitsAsText()`, if the value specified for the `text` parameter is not `null`, then the return value will not be `null`. This is possible because the pre-condition nullable attribute, `NotNullIfNotNull`, uses whether the input value of the `text` parameter is `null` to determine whether the return value may potentially be `null`.

ADVANCED TOPIC

Decorating Generic Type Parameters with the Null Modifier

When declaring a generic member or type, you will occasionally want to decorate the type parameter with a nullable modifier. The problem is that a nullable value type (a `Nullable<T>`) is a different data type than a nullable reference type. As a result, type parameters decorated with nullability will require a constraint that restricts the type parameter to be either a value type or a reference type. Without this constraint, you will receive the following error:

```
Error CS8627 A nullable type parameter must be known to be a value
type or non-nullable reference type. Consider adding a 'class',
'struct', or type constraint.
```

However, if the logic is identical for both value types and reference types, it can be frustrating to implement two different methods—especially since different constraints do not result in different signatures to allow overloading. Consider the code in Listing 6.42.

Listing 6.42: Potential Null Return With `MaybeNull` Attribute

```
// ...
[return: MaybeNull]
static public T GetObject<T>(
  IEnumerable<T> sequence, Func<T, bool> match)
=>
// ...
```

Imagine that the behavior is to return an item from the collection if one satisfies the match predicate. However, if no such item exists, the intent would be to return `default(T)`, which is `null` for a reference type. Unfortunately, the compiler won't allow `T?` without a constraint. To avoid the warning while still declaring to callers that the return could be `null`, we use the post-condition `MaybeNull` attribute and leave the return type as `T` (with no nullable modifier).

End 8.0

Deconstructors

Constructors allow you to take multiple parameters and encapsulate them all into a single object. Until now, we haven't introduced any constructs for implementing the reverse—unwrapping the encapsulated item into its constituent parts. Sure, you could manually assign each property to a variable; however, if there were a significant number of such variables, it would require many separate statements. With tuples, however, this becomes significantly easier. You could, for example, declare a method like the `Deconstruct()` method shown in Listing 6.43.

Listing 6.43: Defining and Using a Deconstructor

```
public class Employee
{
    // ...
    public void Deconstruct(
        out int id, out string firstName,
        out string lastName, out string? salary)
    {
       (id, firstName, lastName, salary) =
           (Id, FirstName, LastName, Salary);
    }
    // ...
}

public class Program
{
    public static void Main()
    {
        Employee employee;
        employee = new ("Inigo", "Montoya")
        {
            // Leveraging object initializer syntax
            Salary = "Too Little"
        };
        // ...

        employee.Deconstruct(out _, out string firstName,
```

```
        out string lastName, out string? salary);

        System.Console.WriteLine(
            "{0} {1}: {2}",
            firstName, lastName, salary);
    }
}
```

Such a method could be invoked directly, as one would expect from Chapter 5, by declaring the `out` parameters inline. However, you can invoke the `Deconstruct()` method—the **deconstructor**[12]—implicitly by assigning the object instance to a tuple directly as shown in Listing 6.44.

LISTING 6.44: Implicitly Invoking Deconstructors

```
public class Program
{
    public static void Main()
    {
        Employee employee;
        employee = new ("Inigo", "Montoya")
        {
            // Leveraging object initializer syntax
            Salary = "Too Little"
        };

        // ...

        (_, string firstName, string lastName, string? salary) =
↪employee;

        System.Console.WriteLine(
            "{0} {1}: {2}",
            firstName, lastName, salary);
    }
}
```

The syntax results in the identical CIL code as that highlighted in Listing 6.43—it is just a simpler syntax (and a little less indicative that the `Deconstruct()` method is invoked). Note that the syntax allows for variables matching the `out` parameter

12. Introduced in C# 7.0.

assignments using tuple syntax. It does not allow for the assignment of a tuple type, either

```
(int, string, string, string) tuple = employee;
```

or with named items as in

```
(int id, string firstName, string lastName, string salary) tuple =

employee
```

To declare a deconstructor, the method name must be `Deconstruct` and have a signature that returns `void` and exclusively accepts two or more `out` parameters. And, given such a signature, it is possible to assign an object instance directly to a tuple without the explicit method invocation.

Begin 10.0

Note that prior to C# 10, all the assigned values needed to be newly declared or pre-declared—you couldn't mix newly declared with existing variables. With C# 10, this restriction was removed.

End 10.0

Static Members

The `HelloWorld` example in Chapter 1 briefly touched on the keyword `static`. This section defines the `static` keyword more fully.

First, let's consider an example. Assume that the employee `Id` value needs to be unique for each employee. One way to accomplish this is to store a counter to track each employee ID. If the value is stored as an instance field, however, every time you instantiate an object, a new `NextId` field will be created such that every instance of the `Employee` object will consume memory for that field. The biggest problem is that each time an `Employee` object is instantiated, the `NextId` value on all of the previously instantiated `Employee` objects needs to be updated with the next ID value. In this case, what you need is a single field that all `Employee` object instances share.

Language Contrast: C++—Global Variables and Functions

Unlike many of the languages that came before it, C# does not have global variables or global functions. All fields and methods in C# appear within the context of a class. The equivalent of a global field or function within the realm of C# is a static field or function. There is no functional difference between global variables/functions and C# static fields/methods, except that static fields/methods can include access modifiers, such as `private`, that can limit the access and provide better encapsulation.

Static Fields

To define data that is available across multiple instances, you use the `static` keyword, as demonstrated in Listing 6.45.

LISTING 6.45: Declaring a Static Field

```
public class Employee
{
    public Employee(string firstName, string lastName)
    {
        FirstName = firstName;
        LastName = lastName;
        Id = NextId;
        NextId++;
    }

    // ...

    public static int NextId;
    public int Id { get; private set; }
    public string FirstName { get; set; }
    public string LastName { get; set; }
    public string? Salary { get; set; } = "Not Enough";

    // ...
}
```

In this example, the `NextId` field declaration includes the `static` modifier and therefore is called a **static field**. Unlike `Id`, a single storage location for `NextId` is shared across all instances of `Employee`. Inside the `Employee` constructor, you assign the new `Employee` object's `Id` the value of `NextId` immediately before incrementing the `Id`. When another instance of the `Employee` class is created, `NextId` will be incremented, and the new `Employee` object's `Id` field will hold a different value.

Just as **instance fields** (non-static fields) can be initialized at declaration time, so can static fields, as demonstrated in Listing 6.46.

LISTING 6.46: Assigning a Static Field at Declaration

```
public class Employee
{
    // ...
    public static int NextId = 42;
    // ...
}
```

Unlike with instance fields, if no initialization for a static field is provided, the static field will automatically be assigned its default value (`0`, `null`, `false`, and so on)—the equivalent of `default(T)`, where `T` is the name of the type. As a result, it will be possible to access the static field even if it has never been explicitly assigned in the C# code.

Non-static fields, or instance fields, provide a new storage location for each object to which they belong. In contrast, static fields don't belong to the instance, but rather to the class itself. As a result, you access a static field from outside a class via the class name. Consider the new `Program` class shown in Listing 6.47 (using the `Employee` class from Listing 6.45 along with Output 6.8).

LISTING 6.47: Accessing a Static Field

```
using System;

public class Program
{
    public static void Main()
    {
        Employee.NextId = 1000000;

        Employee employee1 = new(
            "Inigo", "Montoya");
        Employee employee2 = new(
```

```
                "Princess", "Buttercup");

            Console.WriteLine(
                "{0} {1} ({2})",
                employee1.FirstName,
                employee1.LastName,
                employee1.Id);
            Console.WriteLine(
                "{0} {1} ({2})",
                employee2.FirstName,
                employee2.LastName,
                employee2.Id);

            Console.WriteLine(
                $"NextId = {Employee.NextId}");
        }
        // ...
    }
```

OUTPUT 6.8

```
Inigo Montoya (1000000)
Princess Buttercup (1000001)
NextId = 1000002
```

To set and retrieve the initial value of the `NextId` static field, you use the class name, `Employee`, rather than a reference to an instance of the type. The only place you can omit the class name is within the class itself (or a derived class). In other words, the `Employee(...)` constructor did not need to use `Employee.NextId` because the code appeared within the context of the `Employee` class itself, and therefore, the context was implied. The scope of a variable is the program context in which the variable can be referred to by its unqualified name; the scope of a static field is the context of the class (and any derived classes).

Even though you refer to static fields slightly differently than you refer to instance fields, it is not possible to define a static field and an instance field with the same name in the same class. The possibility of mistakenly referring to the wrong field is high, so the C# designers decided to prevent such code. Overlap in names, therefore, introduces conflict within the declaration space.

BEGINNER TOPIC

Data Can Be Associated with Both a Class and an Object

Both classes and objects can have associated data, just as can the molds and the widgets created from them.

For example, a mold could have data corresponding to the number of widgets it created, the serial number of the next widget, the current color of the plastic injected into the mold, and the number of widgets it produces per hour. Similarly, a widget has its own serial number, its own color, and perhaps the date and time when the widget was created. Although the color of the widget corresponds to the color of the plastic within the mold at the time the widget was created, it obviously does not contain data corresponding to the color of the plastic currently in the mold, or the serial number of the next widget to be produced.

In designing objects, programmers should take care to declare fields, properties, and methods appropriately, as static or instance based. In general, you should declare methods that don't access any instance data as static methods. Static fields store data corresponding to the class, such as defaults for new instances or the number of instances that have been created. Instance fields store data associated with the object.

Static Methods

Just as with static fields, you access static methods directly off the class name—for example, as `Console.ReadLine()`. Furthermore, it is not necessary to have an instance to access the method.

Listing 6.48 provides another example of both declaring and calling a static method.

LISTING 6.48: Defining a Static Method on `DirectoryInfoExtension`

```
public static class DirectoryInfoExtension
{
    public static void CopyTo(
        DirectoryInfo sourceDirectory, string target,
        SearchOption option, string searchPattern)
    {
        if (target[^1] !=
            Path.DirectorySeparatorChar)
```

```
            {
                target += Path.DirectorySeparatorChar;
            }
            Directory.CreateDirectory(target);

            for (int i = 0; i < searchPattern.Length; i++)
            {
                foreach (string file in
                    Directory.EnumerateFiles(
                        sourceDirectory.FullName, searchPattern))
                {
                    File.Copy(file,
                        target + Path.GetFileName(file), true);
                }
            }

            // Copy subdirectories (recursively)
            if (option == SearchOption.AllDirectories)
            {
                foreach (string element in
                    Directory.EnumerateDirectories(
                        sourceDirectory.FullName))
                {
                    Copy(element,
                        target + Path.GetFileName(element),
                        searchPattern);
                }
            }
        }
        // ...
    }

    public class Program
    {
        public static void Main(params string[] args)
        {
            DirectoryInfo source = new(args[0]);
            string target = args[1];

            DirectoryInfoExtension.CopyTo(
                source, target,
                SearchOption.AllDirectories, "*");
        }
    }
```

In Listing 6.48, the `DirectoryInfoExtension.CopyTo()` method takes a `DirectoryInfo` object and copies the underlying directory structure to a new location.

Because static methods are not referenced through a particular instance, the `this` keyword is invalid inside a static method. In addition, it is not possible to access either an instance field or an instance method directly from within a static method without a reference to the instance to which the field or method belongs. (Note that `Main()` is another example of a static method.)

One might have expected this method on the `System.IO.Directory` class or as an instance method on `System.IO.DirectoryInfo`. Since neither exists, Listing 6.48 defines such a method on an entirely new class. In the section "Extension Methods" later in this chapter, we show how to make it appear like an instance method on `DirectoryInfo`.

Static Constructors

In addition to static fields and methods, C# supports **static constructors**. Static constructors are provided as a means to initialize the class itself rather than the instances of a class. Such constructors are not called explicitly; instead, the runtime calls static constructors automatically upon first access to the class, whether by calling a regular constructor or by accessing a static method or field on the class. Because the static constructor cannot be called explicitly, no parameters are allowed on static constructors.

You use static constructors to initialize the static data within the class to a particular value, primarily when the initial value involves more complexity than a simple assignment at declaration time. Consider Listing 6.49.

LISTING 6.49: Declaring a Static Constructor

```
public class Employee
{
    static Employee()
    {
        Random randomGenerator = new();
        NextId = randomGenerator.Next(101, 999);
    }

    // ...
```

```
    public static int NextId = 42;
    // ...
}
```

Listing 6.49 assigns the initial value of `NextId` to be a random integer between 100 and 1,000. Because the initial value involves a method call, the `NextId` initialization code appears within a static constructor and not as part of the declaration.

If assignment of `NextId` occurs within both the static constructor and the declaration, it is not obvious what the value will be when initialization concludes. The C# compiler generates CIL in which the declaration assignment is moved to be the first statement within the static constructor. Therefore, `NextId` will contain the value returned by `randomGenerator.Next(101, 999)` instead of a value assigned during `NextId`'s declaration. Assignments within the static constructor, therefore, will take precedence over assignments that occur as part of the field declaration, as was the case with instance fields. Note that there is no support for defining a static finalizer.

Be careful not to throw an exception from a static constructor, as this will render the type unusable for the remainder of the application's lifetime.[13]

ADVANCED TOPIC

Favor Static Initialization during Declaration

Static constructors execute before the first access to any member of a class, whether it is a static field, another static member, or an instance constructor. To support this practice, the runtime checks that all static members and constructors to ensure that the static constructor runs first.

Without the static constructor, the compiler initializes all static members to their default values and avoids adding the static constructor check. The result is that static assignment initialization is called before any static fields are accessed but not necessarily before all static methods or any instance constructor is invoked. This

13. Technically the application domain's lifetime—the Common Language Runtime's virtual equivalent of an operating system process.

might provide a performance improvement if initialization of static members is expensive and is not needed before accessing a static field. For this reason, you should consider either initializing static fields inline rather than using a static constructor or initializing them at declaration time.

Guidelines

CONSIDER initializing static fields inline rather than explicitly using static constructors or declaration assigned values.

Static Properties

You also can declare properties as static. For example, Listing 6.50 wraps the data for the next ID into a property.

Listing 6.50: Declaring a Static Property

```
public class Employee
{
    // ...
    public static int NextId
    {
        get
        {
            return _NextId;
        }
        private set
        {
            _NextId = value;
        }
    }
    public static int _NextId = 42;
    // ...
}
```

It is almost always better to use a static property rather than a public static field, because public static fields are callable from anywhere, whereas a static property offers at least some level of encapsulation.

The entire NextId implementation—including an inaccessible backing field—can be simplified to an automatically implemented property with an initializer:[14]

```
public static int NextId { get; private set; } = 42;
```

Static Classes

Some classes do not contain any instance fields. Consider, for example, a SimpleMath class that has functions corresponding to the mathematical operations Max( ) and Min( ), as shown in Listing 6.51.

Listing 6.51: Declaring a Static Class

```
public static class SimpleMath
{
    // params allows the number of parameters to vary
    public static int Max(params int[] numbers)
    {
        // Check that there is at least one item in numbers
        if(numbers.Length == 0)
        {
            throw new ArgumentException(
                "numbers cannot be empty", nameof(numbers));
        }

        int result;
        result = numbers[0];
        foreach(int number in numbers)
        {
            if(number > result)
            {
                result = number;
            }
        }
        return result;
    }

    // params allows the number of parameters to vary
    public static int Min(params int[] numbers)
    {
        // Check that there is at least one item in numbers
```

14. Starting in C# 6.0.

```
        if(numbers.Length == 0)
        {
            throw new ArgumentException(
                "numbers cannot be empty", nameof(numbers));
        }

        int result;
        result = numbers[0];
        foreach(int number in numbers)
        {
            if(number < result)
            {
                result = number;
            }
        }
        return result;
    }
}

public class Program
{
    public static void Main(string[] args)
    {
        int[] numbers = new int[args.Length];
        for (int index = 0; index < args.Length; index++)
        {
            numbers[index] = args[index].Length;
        }

        Console.WriteLine(
            $@"Longest argument length = {
                Max(numbers) }");

        Console.WriteLine(
            $@"Shortest argument length = {
                Min(numbers) }");
    }
}
```

This class does not have any instance fields (or methods), so the creation of such a class would be pointless. Consequently, the class is decorated with the `static` keyword. The `static` keyword on a class provides two benefits. First, it prevents a programmer from writing code that instantiates the `SimpleMath` class. Second, it prevents the declaration of any instance fields or methods within the class. Because the class cannot be instantiated, instance members would be pointless. The `Program` class in prior listings is another good candidate for a static class because it, too, contains only static members.

Another distinguishing characteristic of the static class is that the C# compiler automatically marks it as `abstract` and `sealed` within the CIL. This designates the class as **inextensible**; in other words, no class can be derived from this class or even instantiate it. (The sealed and abstract keywords are covered in more detail in Chapter 7.)

In Chapter 5, we saw that the `using static` directive can be used with static classes such as `SimpleMath`. For example, adding a `using static SimpleMath;` declarative at the top of Listing 6.51 would allow you to invoke `Max` without the `SimpleMath` prefix:

```
Console.WriteLine(
$@"Longest argument length = { Max(numbers) }");
```

Extension Methods

Consider the `System.IO.DirectoryInfo` class, which is used to manipulate filesystem directories. This class supports functionality to list the files and subdirectories (`DirectoryInfo.GetFiles()`), as well as the capability to move the directory (`DirectoryInfo.Move()`). One feature it doesn't support directly is the copy feature. If you needed such a method, you would have to implement it, as shown earlier in Listing 6.48.

The `DirectoryInfoExtension.CopyTo()` method is a standard static method declaration. However, notice that calling this `CopyTo()` method is different from calling the `DirectoryInfo.Move()` method. This is unfortunate. Ideally, we want to add a method to `DirectoryInfo` so that, given an instance, we could call `CopyTo()` as an instance method: `directory.CopyTo()`.

You can simulate the creation of an instance method on a different class via **extension methods** To do this, we simply change the signature of our static method so that the first parameter—that is, the data type we are extending—is prefixed with the `this` keyword (see Listing 6.52).

LISTING 6.52: Static Copy Method for `DirectoryInfoExtension`

```
public static class DirectoryInfoExtension
{
    public static void CopyTo(
        this DirectoryInfo sourceDirectory, string target,
        SearchOption option, string searchPattern)
    {
        // ...
    }
}

// ...
        DirectoryInfo directory = new(".\\Source");
        directory.CopyTo(".\\Target",
            SearchOption.TopDirectoryOnly, "*");
        // ...
    }
}
```

With extension methods, it is now possible to add "instance methods" to any class, including classes outside of your assembly. The resultant CIL code, however, is virtually identical to what the compiler creates when calling the extension method as a normal static method.

Extension method requirements are as follows:

- The first parameter corresponds to the type that the method extends or on which it operates.
- To designate the extension method, prefix the first parameter with the `this` modifier.
- To access the method as an extension method, import the extending type's namespace via a `using` directive (or place the extending class in the same namespace as the calling code).

If the extension method signature matches a signature already found on the extended type (i.e., if `CopyTo()` already existed on `DirectoryInfo`), the extension method will never be called except as a normal static method.

Note that specializing a type via inheritance (covered in detail in Chapter 7) is generally preferable to using an extension method. Extension methods do not provide a clean versioning mechanism, because the addition of a matching signature to the extended type will take precedence over the extension method without warning of the change. The subtlety of this behavior is more pronounced for extended classes whose source code you don't control. Another minor point is that although development IDEs support IntelliSense for extension methods, simply reading through the calling code does not make it obvious that a method is an extension method.

In general, you should use extension methods sparingly. Do not, for example, define them on type `object`. Chapter 8 discusses how to use extension methods in association with an interface. Without such an association, defining extension methods is rare.

> **Guidelines**
>
> **AVOID** frivolously defining extension methods, especially on types you don't own.

Encapsulating the Data

In addition to properties and the access modifiers we examined earlier in the chapter, there are several other specialized ways to encapsulate the data within a class. For instance, there are two more field modifiers. The first is the `const` modifier, which you encountered when declaring local variables. The second is the ability to define fields as read-only.

const

Just as with `const` values, a `const` field contains a compile-time–determined value that cannot be changed at runtime. Values such as pi make good candidates for constant field declarations. Listing 6.53 shows an example of declaring a `const` field.

Listing 6.53: Declaring a Constant Field

```
public class ConvertUnits
{
    public const float CentimetersPerInch = 2.54F;
    public const int CupsPerGallon = 16;
```

```
    // ...
}
```

Constant fields are static, since no new field instance is required for each object instance. Declaring a constant field as `static` explicitly will cause a compile error. Also, constant fields are usually declared only for types that have literal values (e.g., `string`, `int`, and `double`). Types such as `Program` or `System.Guid` cannot be used for constant fields.

It is important that the types of values used in `public` constant expressions are permanent in time (see the Public Constants Should Be Permanent Values Advanced Block). Values such as pi, Avogadro's number, and Earth's circumference are good examples. However, values that could potentially change over time are not. For example, population counts, the poorest country, and exchange rates would be poor choices for constants.

Guidelines

DO use constant fields for values that will never change.

AVOID constant fields for values that will change over time.

ADVANCED TOPIC

Public Constants Should Be Permanent Values

Publicly accessible constants should be permanent, because changing the value of a constant will not necessarily take effect in the assemblies that use it. If an assembly references a constant from a different assembly, the value of the constant is compiled directly into the referencing assembly. Therefore, if the value in the referenced assembly is changed but the referencing assembly is not recompiled, the referencing assembly will still use the original value, not the new value. Values that could potentially change in the future should be specified as `readonly` instead.

readonly

Unlike const, the readonly modifier is available only for fields (not for local variables). It declares that the field value is modifiable only from inside the constructor or via an initializer. Listing 6.54 demonstrates how to declare a read-only field.

Listing 6.54: Declaring a Field as readonly

```
public class Employee
{
    public Employee(int id)
    {
      _Id = id;
    }

    // ...

    private readonly int _Id;
    public int Id
    {
      get { return _Id; }
    }

    // Error: A readonly field cannot be assigned to (except
    // in a constructor or a variable initializer)
    public void SetId(int id) =>
        _Id = id;

    // ...
}
```

Unlike constant fields, readonly-decorated fields can vary from one instance to the next. In fact, a read-only field's value can change within the constructor. Furthermore, read-only fields occur as either instance or static fields. Another key distinction is that you can assign the value of a read-only field at execution time rather than just at compile time. Given that readonly fields must be set in the constructor or initializer, such fields are the one case where the compiler requires the fields to be accessed from code outside their corresponding property. Besides this one exception, you should avoid accessing a backing field from anywhere other than its wrapping property.

Another important feature of `readonly`-decorated fields over `const` fields is that `readonly` fields are not limited to types with literal values. It is possible, for example, to declare a `readonly System.Guid` instance field:

```
public static readonly Guid ComIUnknownGuid =
new Guid("00000000-0000-0000-C000-000000000046");
```

In contrast, this is not possible using a constant, because there is no C# literal representation of a GUID.

Given the guideline that fields should not be accessed from outside their wrapping property, those programming will discover that that there is almost never a need to use the `readonly` modifier.[15] Instead, it is preferable to use a read-only automatically implemented property, as discussed earlier in the chapter.

Listing 6.55 shows one more read-only example.

LISTING 6.55: Declaring a Read-Only Automatically Implemented Property

```
class TicTacToeBoard
{
    // Set both player's initial board to all false (blank)
    //    |   |          |   |
    // ---+---+---    ---+---+---
    //    |   |          |   |
    // ---+---+---    ---+---+---
    //    |   |          |   |
    // Player 1 - X    Player 2 - O
    public bool[,,] Cells { get; } = new bool[2, 3, 3];
    // Error: The property Cells cannot
    // be assigned to because it is read-only
    // public void SetCells(bool[,,] value) =>
    //           _Cells = new bool[2, 3, 3];

    // ...
}
```

Whether read-only automatically implemented properties or the `readonly` modifier on a field, ensuring immutability of the array reference is a useful defensive coding technique. It ensures that the array instance remains the same, while allowing

15. In C# 6.0 or later.

the elements within the array to change. Without the read-only constraint, it would be all too easy to mistakenly assign a new array to the member, thereby discarding the existing array rather than updating individual array elements. In other words, using a read-only approach with an array does not freeze the contents of the array. Rather, it freezes the array instance (and therefore the number of elements in the array) because it is not possible to reassign the value to a new instance. The elements of the array are still writeable.

Guidelines

DO favor read-only automatically implemented properties over read-only fields.

Nested Classes

In addition to defining methods and fields within a class, it is possible to define a class within a class. Such classes are called **nested classes**. You use a nested class when the class makes little sense outside the context of its containing class.

Consider a class that handles the command-line options of a program. Such a class is generally unique to each program, so there is no reason to make a `CommandLine` class accessible from outside the class that contains `Main()`. Listing 6.56 demonstrates such a nested class.

Listing 6.56: Defining a Nested Class

```
// CommandLine is nested within program
public class Program
{
    // Define a nested class for processing the command line
    private class CommandLine
    {
        public CommandLine(string[] arguments)
        {
            for (int argumentCounter = 0;
                argumentCounter < arguments.Length;
                argumentCounter++)
            {
                _ = argumentCounter switch
```

```
            {
                0 => Action = arguments[0].ToLower(),
                1 => Id = arguments[1],
                2 => FirstName = arguments[2],
                3 => LastName = arguments[3],
                _ => throw new ArgumentException(
                    $"Unexpected argument " +
                    $"'{arguments[argumentCounter]}'")
            };
        }
    }
    public string? Action { get; }
    public string? Id { get; }
    public string? FirstName { get; }
    public string? LastName { get; }
}

public static void Main(string[] args)
{
    CommandLine commandLine = new(args);

    // Error handling intentionally missing for elucidation.

    switch (commandLine.Action)
    {
        case "new":
            // Create a new employee
            // ...
            break;
        case "update":
            // Update an existing employee's data
            // ...
            break;
        case "delete":
            // Remove an existing employee's file
            // ...
            break;
        default:
            Console.WriteLine(
                "Employee.exe " +
                "new|update|delete " +
                "<id> [firstname] [lastname]");
            break;
    }
}
}
```

The nested class in this example is `Program.CommandLine`. As with all class members, no containing class identifier is needed from inside the containing class, so you can simply refer to it as `CommandLine`.

One unique characteristic of nested classes is the ability to specify `private` as an access modifier for the class itself. Because the purpose of this class is to parse the command line and place each argument into a separate field, `Program.CommandLine` is relevant only to the `Program` class in this application. The use of the `private` access modifier defines the intended accessibility of the class and prevents access from outside the class. You can do this only if the class is nested.

The `this` member within a nested class refers to an instance of the nested class, not the containing class. One way for a nested class to access an instance of the containing class is if the containing class instance is explicitly passed, such as via a constructor or a method parameter.

Another interesting characteristic of nested classes is that they can access any member on the containing class, including private members. The converse is not true, however: It is not possible for the containing class to access a private member of the nested class.

Nested classes are rare. They should not be defined if they are likely to be referenced outside the containing type. Furthermore, treat `public` nested classes with suspicion; they may be confusing and hard to discover.

Guidelines

AVOID publicly exposed nested types. The only exception is if the declaration of such a type is unlikely or pertains to an advanced customization scenario.

Language Contrast: Java—Inner Classes

Java includes not only the concept of a nested class but also the concept of an inner class. Inner classes correspond to objects that are associated with the containing class instance, rather than having just a syntactic relationship. In C#, you can achieve the same structure by including an instance field of a nested type within the outer class. A factory method or constructor can ensure a reference to the corresponding instance of the outer class is set within the inner class instance as well.

Partial Classes

Partial classes[16] are portions of a class that the compiler can combine to form a complete class. Although you could define two or more partial classes within the same file, the general purpose of a partial class is to allow the splitting of a class definition across multiple files. Primarily this is useful for tools that are generating or modifying code. With partial classes, the tools can work on a file separate from the one the developer is manually coding.

Defining a Partial Class

C# allows declaration of a partial class by prepending a contextual keyword, `partial`, immediately before `class`,[17] as Listing 6.57 shows.

LISTING 6.57: Defining a Partial Class

```
// File: Program1.cs
partial class Program
{
}
// File: Program2.cs
partial class Program
{
}
```

16. Introduced with C# 2.0.
17. Interfaces (Chapter 8) structs (Chapter 9) can also be partial.

In this case, each portion of `Program` is placed into a separate file, as identified by the comment.

Besides their use with code generators, another common use of partial classes is to place any nested classes into their own files. This is in accordance with the coding convention that places each class definition within its own file. For example, Listing 6.58 places the `Program.CommandLine` class into a file separate from the core `Program` members.

Listing 6.58: Defining a Nested Class in a Separate Partial Class

```
// File: Program.cs
partial class Program
{
    static void Main(string[] args)
    {
        CommandLine commandLine = new(args);

        switch(commandLine.Action)
        {
            // ...
        }
    }
}

// File: Program+CommandLine.cs
partial class Program
{
    // Define a nested class for processing the command line
    private class CommandLine
    {
        // ...
    }
}
```

Partial classes do not allow for extending compiled classes or classes in other assemblies. They are simply a means of splitting a class implementation across multiple files within the same assembly.

Partial Methods

Extending the concept of partial classes is the concept of partial methods,[18] which are allowed only within partial types. Like partial classes, their primary purpose is to accommodate code generation.

Consider a code generation tool that generates the `Person.Designer.cs` file for the `Person` class based on a `Person` table within a database. This tool examines the table and creates properties for each column in the table. The problem, however, is that frequently the tool cannot generate any validation logic that may be required because this logic is based on business rules that are not embedded into the database table definition. To overcome this difficulty, the developer of the `Person` class needs to add the validation logic. It is undesirable to modify `Person.Designer.cs` directly, because if the file is regenerated (e.g., to accommodate an additional column in the database), the changes would be lost. Instead, the structure of the code for `Person` needs to be separated out so that the generated code appears in one file, and the custom code (with business rules) is placed into a separate file, unaffected by any regeneration. As we saw in the preceding section, partial classes are well suited for the task of splitting a class across multiple files, but they are not always sufficient. In many cases, we also need **partial methods**.

Partial methods allow for a declaration of a method without requiring an implementation. However, when the optional implementation is included, it can be located in one of the sister partial class definitions—likely in a separate file. Listing 6.59 shows the partial method declaration and the implementation for the `Person` class.

LISTING 6.59: Defining a Partial Method to Access Its Implementation

```
// File: Person.Designer.cs
public partial class Person
{
    #region Extensibility Method Definitions
    static partial void OnLastNameChanging(string value);
    static partial void OnFirstNameChanging(string value);
    #endregion Extensibility Method Definitions
```

18. Introduced with C# 3.0.

```
    // ...
    public string LastName
    {
        get
        {
            return _LastName;
        }
        set
        {
            if (_LastName != value)
            {
                OnLastNameChanging(value);
                _LastName = value;
            }
        }
    }
    private string _LastName;

    // ...
    public string FirstName
    {
        get
        {
            return _FirstName;
        }
        set
        {
            if (_FirstName != value)
            {
                OnFirstNameChanging(value);
                _FirstName = value;
            }
        }
    }
    private string _FirstName;

    public partial string GetName();
}

// File: Person.cs
partial class Person
{
    static partial void OnLastNameChanging(string value)
    {
        value = value ??
            throw new ArgumentNullException(nameof(value));
```

```
            if (value.Trim().Length == 0)
            {
                throw new ArgumentException(
                    $"{nameof(LastName)} cannot be empty.",
                    nameof(value));
            }
        }

        // ...

        public partial string GetName() => $"{FirstName} {LastName}";
    }
```

In the listing of `Person.Designer.cs` are declarations for the `OnLastNameChanging()` and `OnFirstNameChanging()` methods. Furthermore, the properties for the last and first names make calls to their corresponding changing methods. Even though the declarations of the changing methods contain no implementation, this code will successfully compile. The key is that the method declarations are prefixed with the contextual keyword `partial`, in addition to the class that contains such methods.

In Listing 6.59, only the `OnLastNameChanging()` method is implemented. In this case, the implementation checks the suggested new `LastName` value and throws an exception if it is not valid. Notice that the signatures for `OnLastNameChanging()` between the two locations match.

Begin 9.0

Prior to C# 9.0, partial methods must return `void`. If the method didn't return `void` and the implementation was not provided, what would the expected return be from a call to a non-implemented method? To avoid any invalid assumptions about the return, the C# designers decided to prohibit methods with returns other than `void`. Similarly, `out` parameters are not allowed on partial methods. If a return value is required, `ref` parameters may be used. Lastly, partial members cannot be decorated with an accessibility modifier (e.g., `private` or `public`). Rather, partial methods are implicitly `private`.

Starting with C# 9.0, these restrictions were all removed. Partial methods could return values, have out parameters, and even have access modifiers. In fact, distinguishing this unrestricted version of a partial method, C# required the access modifier, even for methods that were intended to be private. To remove the restrictions, C# 9.0 required that all partial methods with access modifiers also had an accompanying method pair with the implementation. As demonstrated by Listing 6.59, if you declared a partial member as `public string GetName()` with no implementation, you were also required to have a second partial method declaration with the same signature and with the implementation, such as `public partial string GetName() => $"{FirstName} {LastName}"`. In this way, the C# compiler ensured that any return values (including returns via out parameters) were successful because, in fact, the method had an implementation.

End 9.0

In summary, partial methods allow generated code to call methods that have not necessarily been implemented. Furthermore, if no implementation is provided for a partial method, no trace of the partial method appears in the CIL. This helps keep code size small while keeping flexibility high.

Summary

This chapter explained C# constructs for classes and object orientation in C#. Its coverage included a discussion of declaring fields and how to access them on a class instance.

This chapter also discussed the key decision of whether to store data on a per-instance basis or across all instances of a type. Static data is associated with the class, whereas instance data is stored on each object.

In addition, the chapter explored encapsulation in the context of access modifiers for methods and data. The C# construct of properties was introduced, and you saw how to use it to encapsulate private fields.

The next chapter focuses on how to associate classes with each other via inheritance and explores the benefits derived from this object-oriented construct.

7

Inheritance

Chapter 6 discussed how one class can reference other classes via fields and properties. This chapter discusses how to use the inheritance relationship between classes to build class hierarchies that form an "is a" relationship.

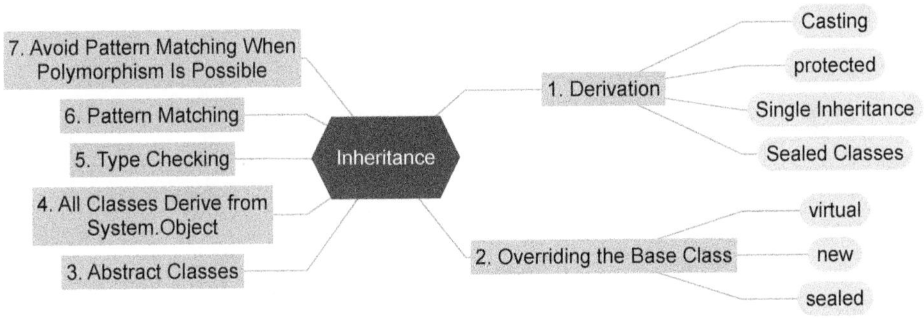

BEGINNER TOPIC

Inheritance Definitions

Chapter 6 provided an overview of inheritance. Here's a review of the defined terms:

- *Derive/inherit:* Specialize a base class to include additional members or customization of the base class members.

- *Derived/sub/child type:* The specialized type that inherits the members of the more general type.
- *Base/super/parent type:* The general type whose members a derived type inherits.

Inheritance forms an "is a kind of" relationship. The derived type is always implicitly also of the base type. Just as a hard drive is a kind of storage device, so any other type derived from the storage device type is a kind of storage device. Notice that the converse is not necessarily true: A storage device is not necessarily a hard drive.

NOTE

Inheritance within code is used to define an "is a kind of" relationship between two classes where the derived class is a specialization of the base class.

Derivation

It is common to want to extend a given type to add features, such as behavior and data. The purpose of inheritance is to do exactly that. Given a `Person` class, you create an `Employee` class that additionally contains `EmployeeId` and `Department` properties. The reverse approach may also be applied. Given, for example, a `Contact` class within a personal digital assistant (PDA), you may decide to add calendaring support. Toward this effort, you create an `Appointment` class. However, instead of redefining the methods and properties that are common to both classes, you might choose to **refactor** the `Contact` class. Specifically, you could move the common methods and properties for `Contact` into a base class called `PdaItem` from which both `Contact` and `Appointment` derive, as shown in Figure 7.1.

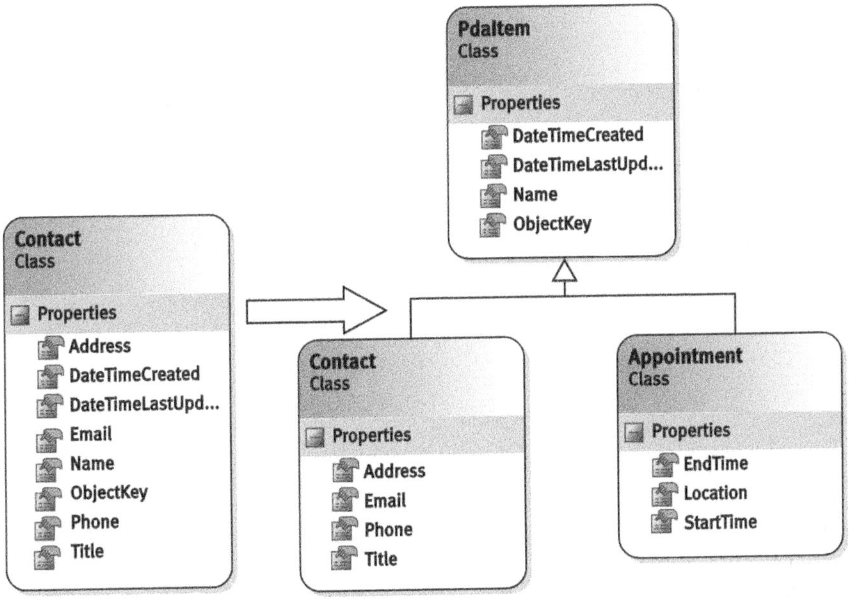

FIGURE 7.1: Refactoring into a base class

The common items in this case are `Created`, `LastUpdated`, `Name`, `ObjectKey`, and the like. Through derivation, the methods defined on the base class, `PdaItem`, are accessible from all classes derived from `PdaItem`.

When declaring a derived class, follow the class identifier with a colon and then the base class, as Listing 7.1 demonstrates.

LISTING 7.1: Deriving One Class from Another

```
public class PdaItem
{
    [DisallowNull]
    public string? Name { get; set; }
    public DateTime LastUpdated { get; set; }
}
// Define the Contact class as inheriting the PdaItem class
public class Contact : PdaItem
{
    public string? Address { get; set; }
    public string? Phone { get; set; }
```

```
    // ...
}
```

Listing 7.2 shows how to access the properties defined in `Contact`.

Listing 7.2: Using Inherited Methods

```
public class Program
{
    public static void Main()
    {
        Contact contact = new();
        contact.Name = "Inigo Montoya";

        // ...
    }
}
```

Even though `Contact` does not directly have a property called `Name`, all instances of `Contact` can still access the `Name` property from `PdaItem` and use it as though it was part of `Contact`. Furthermore, any additional classes that derive from `Contact` will also inherit the members of `PdaItem` or any class from which `PdaItem` was derived. The inheritance chain has no practical limit, and each derived class will have all the members of its base class inheritance chain combined (see Listing 7.3). In other words, although `Customer` doesn't derive from `PdaItem` directly, it still inherits the members of `PdaItem`.

> **NOTE**
>
> Via inheritance, each member of a base class will also appear within the chain of derived classes.

Listing 7.3: Classes Deriving from One Another to Form an Inheritance Chain

```
public class PdaItem : object
{
    // ...
}
public class Appointment : PdaItem
```

```
{
    // ...
}
public class Contact : PdaItem
{
    // ...
}
public class Customer : Contact
{
    // ...
}
```

In Listing 7.3, `PdaItem` is shown explicitly to derive from `object`. Although C# allows such syntax, it is unnecessary because all classes that don't have some other derivation will derive from `object`, regardless of whether it is specified.

> **NOTE**
>
> Unless an alternative base class is specified, all classes will derive from `object` by default.

Casting between Base and Derived Types

As Listing 7.4 shows, because derivation forms an "is a" relationship, a derived type value can always be directly assigned to a base type variable.

Listing 7.4: Implicit Base Type Casting

```
public class Program
{
    public static void Main()
    {
        // Derived types can be implicitly converted to
        // base types
        Contact contact = new();
        PdaItem item = contact;
        // ...

        // Base types must be cast explicitly to derived types
        contact = (Contact)item;
        // ...
```

```
    }
}
```

The derived type, `Contact`, is a `PdaItem` and can be assigned directly to a variable of type `PdaItem`. This is known as an **implicit conversion** because no cast operator is required and the conversion will, in principle, always succeed; that is, it will not throw an exception.

The reverse, however, is not true. A `PdaItem` is not necessarily a `Contact`; it could be an `Appointment` or some other derived type. Therefore, casting from the base type to the derived type requires an **explicit cast**, which could fail at runtime. To perform an explicit cast, you identify the target type within parentheses prior to the original reference, as Listing 7.4 demonstrates.

With the explicit cast, the programmer essentially communicates to the compiler to trust her—she knows what she is doing—and the C# compiler allows the conversion to proceed if the target type is derived from the originating type. Although the C# compiler allows an explicit conversion at compile time between potentially compatible types, the Common Language Runtime (CLR) will still verify the explicit cast at execution time, throwing an exception if the object instance is not actually of the targeted type.

The C# compiler allows use of the cast operator even when the type hierarchy allows an implicit conversion. For example, the assignment from `contact` to `item` could use a cast operator as follows:

```
item = (PdaItem)contact;
```

or even when no conversion is necessary:

```
contact = (Contact)contact;
```

> **NOTE**
>
> A derived object can be implicitly converted to its base class. In contrast, converting from the base class to the derived class requires an explicit cast operator, as the conversion could fail. Although the compiler will allow an explicit cast if it is potentially valid, the runtime will still prevent an invalid cast at execution time by throwing an exception.

BEGINNER TOPIC

Casting within the Inheritance Chain

An implicit conversion to a base class does not instantiate a new instance. Instead, the same instance is simply referred to as the base type, and the capabilities (the accessible members) are those of the base type. It is just like referring to a CD-ROM drive as a "storage device." Since not all storage devices support an eject operation, a CD-ROM drive that is viewed as a storage device cannot be ejected either, and a call to `storageDevice.Eject()` would not compile, even though the instantiated object may have been a `CDROM` object that supported the `Eject()` method.

Similarly, casting down from the base class to the derived class simply begins referring to the type more specifically, expanding the available operations. The restriction is that the actual instantiated type must be an instance of the targeted type (or something derived from it).

ADVANCED TOPIC

Defining Custom Conversions

Conversion between types is not limited to types within a single inheritance chain. It is possible to convert between unrelated types as well, such as converting from an `Address` to a `string` and vice versa. The key is the provision of a conversion operator between the two types. C# allows types to include either explicit or implicit conversion operators. If the operation could possibly fail, such as in a cast from `long` to `int`, developers should choose to define an explicit conversion operator. This warns developers performing the conversion to do so only when they are certain the conversion will succeed, or else to be prepared to catch the exception if it doesn't. They should also use an explicit conversion over an implicit conversion when the conversion is lossy. Converting from a `float` to an `int`, for example, truncates the decimal, which a return cast (from `int` back to `float`) would not recover.

Listing 7.5 shows an example of an implicit conversion operator signature.

LISTING 7.5: Defining Cast Operators

```
class GpsCoordinates
{
    // ...

    public static implicit operator UtmCoordinates(
        GpsCoordinates coordinates)
    {
        // ...
    }
}
```

In this case, you have an implicit conversion from `GpsCoordinates` to `UtmCoordinates`. A similar conversion could be written to reverse the process. Note that an explicit conversion could also be written by replacing `implicit` with `explicit`.

`private` Access Modifier

All members of a base class, except for constructors and destructors, are inherited by the derived class. However, just because a member is inherited, that does not mean it is accessible. For example, in Listing 7.6, the `private` field, `_Name`, is not available in `Contact` because private members are accessible only inside the type that declares them.

LISTING 7.6: Private Members Are Inherited but Not Accessible

```
public class PdaItem
{
```

```
    // ...
    private string _Name;

    public string Name
    {
        get { return _Name; }
        set { _Name = value; }
    }
    // ...
}

public class Contact : PdaItem
{
    // ...
}

public class Program
{
    public static void Main()
    {
        Contact contact = new();
        // ERROR:  'PdaItem._Name' is inaccessible
        // due to its protection level
        contact._Name = "Inigo Montoya";
    }
}
```

As part of respecting the principle of encapsulation, derived classes cannot access members declared as `private`.[1] This forces the base class developer to make an explicit choice as to whether a derived class gains access to a member. In this case, the base class is defining an API in which `_Name` can be changed only via the `Name` property. That way, if validation is added, the derived class will gain the validation benefit automatically because it was unable to access `_Name` directly from the start. Regardless of the access modifier, all members can be accessed from the class that defines them.

1. Except for the corner case, when the derived class is also a nested class of the base class.

> **NOTE**
>
> Derived classes cannot access members declared as private in a base class.

`protected` Access Modifier

Encapsulation is finer grained than just `public` or `private`, however. It is possible to define members in base classes that only derived classes can access. (Any member can also always access other members within the same type.) As an example, consider the `ObjectKey` property shown in Listing 7.7.

LISTING 7.7: `protected` **Members Are Accessible Only from Derived Classes**

```
using System.IO;

public class PdaItem
{
    public PdaItem(Guid objectKey) => ObjectKey = objectKey;
    protected Guid ObjectKey { get; }
}

public class Contact : PdaItem
{
    public Contact(Guid objectKey)
        : base(objectKey) { }

    public void Save()
    {
        // Instantiate a FileStream using <ObjectKey>.dat
        // for the filename
        using FileStream stream = File.OpenWrite(
            ObjectKey + ".dat");
        // ...
        stream.Dispose();
    }
    static public Contact Copy(Contact contact)
        => new(contact.ObjectKey);

    static public Contact Copy(PdaItem pdaItem) =>
    // ERROR: Cannot access protected member PdaItem.ObjectKey.
    // Use ((Contact)pdaItem).ObjectKey instead.
        new(pdaItem.ObjectKey);
```

```
}

public class Program
{
    public static void Main()
    {
        Contact contact = new(Guid.NewGuid());

        // ERROR:  'PdaItem.ObjectKey' is inaccessible
        Console.WriteLine(contact.ObjectKey);
    }
}
```

ObjectKey is defined using the protected access modifier. The result is that it is accessible only outside of PdaItem from members in classes that derive from PdaItem. Because Contact derives from PdaItem, all members of Contact (i.e., Save()) have access to ObjectKey. In contrast, Program does not derive from PdaItem, so using the ObjectKey property within Program results in a compile-time error.

> **NOTE**
>
> Protected members in the base class are accessible only from the base class and other classes within the derivation chain.

An important subtlety shown in the static Contact.Copy(PdaItem pdaItem) method is worth noting. Developers are often surprised that it is not possible to access the protected ObjectKey of a PdaItem from code within Contact, even though Contact derives from PdaItem. The reason is that a PdaItem could potentially be an Address, and Contact should not be able to access protected members of Address. Therefore, encapsulation prevents Contact from potentially modifying the ObjectKey of an Address. A successful cast of PdaItem to Contact will bypass this restriction (i.e., ((Contact)pdaItem).ObjectKey), as does accessing contact.ObjectKey. The governing rule is that accessing a protected member from a derived class requires a compile-time determination that the protected member is an instance of the derived class.

Extension Methods

Extension methods are technically not members of the type they extend and, therefore, are not inherited. Nevertheless, because every derived class may be used as an instance of any of its base classes, an extension method for one type also extends every derived type. In other words, if we extend a base class such as `PdaItem`, all the extension methods will also be available in the derived classes. However, as with all extension methods, priority is given to instance methods. If a compatible signature appears anywhere within the inheritance chain, it will take precedence over an extension method.

Requiring extension methods for base types is rare. As with extension methods in general, if the base type's code is available, it is preferable to modify the base type directly. Even in cases where the base type's code is unavailable, programmers should consider whether to add extension methods to an interface that the base type or the individual derived types implement. We cover interfaces and their use with extension methods in Chapter 8.

Single Inheritance

In theory, you can place an unlimited number of classes in an inheritance tree. For example, `Customer` derives from `Contact`, which derives from `PdaItem`, which derives from `object`. However, C# is a **single-inheritance** programming language (as is the Common Intermediate Language [CIL] to which C# compiles). Consequently, a class cannot derive from two classes directly. It is not possible, for example, to have `Contact` derive from both `PdaItem` and `Person`.

Language Contrast: C++—Multiple Inheritance

C#'s single inheritance is one of its major object-oriented differences from C++.

For the rare cases that require a multiple-inheritance class structure, one solution is to use **aggregation**; instead of one class inheriting from another, one class contains an instance of the other. C# 8.0 provides additional constructs for achieving this, so we defer the details of implementing aggregation until Chapter 8.

Sealed Classes

Designing a class correctly so that others can extend it via derivation can be a tricky task that requires testing with examples to verify the derivation will work successfully. Listing 7.8 shows how to avoid unexpected derivation scenarios and problems by marking classes as **sealed**.

Listing 7.8: Preventing Derivation with Sealed Classes

```
public sealed class CommandLineParser
{
    // ...
}

// ERROR:  Sealed classes cannot be derived from
public sealed class DerivedCommandLineParser
    : CommandLineParser
{
    // ...
}
```

Sealed classes include the `sealed` modifier, so they cannot be derived from. The `string` type is an example of a type that uses the `sealed` modifier to prevent derivation.

Overriding the Base Class

All members of a base class are inherited in the derived class, except for constructors and destructors. However, sometimes the base class does not have the optimal implementation of a particular member. Consider the `Name` property on `PdaItem`, for example. The implementation is probably acceptable when inherited by the `Appointment` class. For the `Contact` class, however, the `Name` property should return the `FirstName` and `LastName` properties combined. Similarly, when `Name` is assigned, it should be split across `FirstName` and `LastName`. In other words, the base class property declaration is appropriate for the derived class, but the implementation is not always valid. A mechanism is needed for **overriding** the base class implementation with a custom implementation in the derived class.

`virtual` Modifier

C# supports overriding on instance methods and properties but not on fields or on any static members. It requires an explicit action within both the base class and the derived class. The base class must mark each member for which it allows overriding as `virtual`. If `public` or `protected` members do not include the `virtual` modifier, subclasses will not be able to override those members.

> **Language Contrast: Java—Virtual Methods by Default**
>
> By default, methods in Java are virtual, and they must be explicitly sealed if nonvirtual behavior is preferred. In contrast, C# defaults to nonvirtual.

Listing 7.9 shows an example of property overriding.

Listing 7.9: Overriding a Property

```
public class PdaItem
{
    public virtual string Name { get; set; }
    // ...
}

public class Contact : PdaItem
{
    public override string Name
    {
        get
        {
            return $"{ FirstName } { LastName }";
        }

        set
        {
            string[] names = value.Split(' ');
            // Error handling not shown
            FirstName = names[0];
            LastName = names[1];
        }
    }

    public string FirstName { get; set; }
    public string LastName { get; set; }
```

```
    // ...
}
```

Not only does `PdaItem` include the `virtual` modifier on the `Name` property, but `Contact`'s `Name` property is also decorated with the keyword `override`. Eliminating `virtual` would result in an error and omitting `override` would cause a warning to be generated, as you will see shortly. C# requires the overriding methods to use the `override` keyword explicitly. In other words, `virtual` identifies a method or property as available for replacement (overriding) in the derived type.

Language Contrast: Java and C++—Implicit Overriding

Unlike in Java and C++, the `override` keyword is required on the derived class in C#. C# does not allow implicit overriding. To override a method, both the base class and the derived class members must match and have corresponding `virtual` and `override` keywords. Furthermore, when the `override` keyword is specified, the derived implementation is assumed to replace the base class implementation.

Overriding a member causes the runtime to call the most derived implementation (see Listing 7.10 with Output 7.1).

LISTING 7.10: Runtime Calling the Most Derived Implementation of a Virtual Method

```
public class Program
{
    public static void Main()
    {
        Contact contact;
        PdaItem item;

        contact = new Contact();
        item = contact;

        // Set the name via PdaItem variable
        item.Name = "Inigo Montoya";

        // Display that FirstName & LastName
```

```
        // properties were set
        Console.WriteLine(
            $"{ contact.FirstName } { contact.LastName}");
    }
}
```

Output 7.1

```
Inigo Montoya
```

In Listing 7.10, when `item.Name`, which is declared on the `PdaItem`, is assigned, the `contact`'s `FirstName` and `LastName` are still set. The rule is that whenever the runtime encounters a virtual method, it calls the most derived and overriding implementation of the virtual member. In this case, the code instantiates a `Contact` and calls `Contact.Name` because `Contact` contains the most derived implementation of `Name`.

Virtual methods provide default implementations only—that is, implementations that derived classes could override entirely. However, because of the complexities of inheritance design, it is important to consider (and preferably to implement) a specific scenario that requires the virtual method definition rather than to declare members as `virtual` by default.

This step is also important because converting a method from a virtual method to a nonvirtual method could break derived classes that override the method. Once a virtual member is published, it should remain virtual if you want to avoid introducing a breaking change. So be careful when introducing a virtual member—perhaps making it `private protected`, for example.

Language Contrast: C++—Dispatch Method Calls during Construction

In C++, methods called during construction will not dispatch the virtual method. Instead, during construction, the type is associated with the base type rather than the derived type, and virtual methods call the base implementation. In contrast, C# dispatches virtual method calls to the most derived type. This is consistent with the principle of calling the most derived virtual member, even if the derived constructor has not completely executed. Regardless, in C#, the situation should be avoided.

Finally, only instance members can be `virtual`. The CLR uses the concrete type, specified at instantiation time, to determine where to dispatch a `virtual` method call; thus `static virtual` methods are meaningless and the compiler prohibits them.

Begin 9.0

Covariant Return Types

Generally, the signature of the overriding method must match the signature of the base method being overridden. However, starting in C# 9.0, an improvement was made that allowed the overriding method to specify a return type different from the base method if the return type was compatible with the base method's return type. The feature is called **covariant return types**. Listing 7.11 provides an example.

LISTING 7.11: Covariant Return Types

```
public class Base
{
    public virtual Base Create() => new();
}

public class Derived : Base
{
    public override Derived Create() => new();
}
```

Notice how the `Base` class's `Create()` method returns `Base` while the `Derived` class's returns `Derived`. Even though the latter's signature overrides the former, the return types may be different if the latter is a derived type of the former's return type. Covariance will be discussed more in Chapter 12.

End 9.0

`new` Modifier

When an overriding method does not use `override`, the compiler issues a warning similar to that shown in Output 7.2 or Output 7.3.

OUTPUT 7.2

```
warning CS0114: '<derived method name>' hides inherited member
'<base method name>'. To make the current member override that
implementation, add the override keyword. Otherwise add the new
keyword.
```

OUTPUT 7.3

```
warning CS0108: The keyword new is required on '<derived property
name>' because it hides inherited member '<base property name>'
```

The obvious solution is to add the `override` modifier (assuming the base member is virtual). However, as the warnings point out, the `new` modifier is also an option. Consider the scenario shown in Table 7.1—a specific example of the more general case known as the **brittle** or **fragile base class** problem.

TABLE 7.1: Why the New Modifier?

Activity	Code

Programmer A defines class `Person` that includes properties `FirstName` and `LastName`	`public class Person`
	`{`
	`public string FirstName { get; set; }`
	`public string LastName { get; set; }`
	`}`

TABLE 7.1: Why the New Modifier? (continued)

Activity	Code

Programmer B derives from `Person` and defines `Contact` with the additional property `Name`. In addition, he defines the `Program` class whose `Main()` method instantiates `Contact`, assigns `Name`, and then prints out the name.	`public class Contact : Person`
	`{`
	`public string Name`
	`{`
	`get`
	`{`
	`return FirstName + " " + LastName;`
	`}`
	`set`
	`{`
	`string[] names = value.Split(' ');`
	`// Error handling not shown`
	`FirstName = names[0];`
	`LastName = names[1];`
	`}`
	`}`
	`}`

Because `Person.Name` is not `virtual`, Programmer A expects `Display()` to use the `Person` implementation, even if a `Person`-derived data type, `Contact`, is passed in. However, Programmer B expects `Contact.Name` to be used in all cases where the variable data type is a `Contact`. (Programmer B has no code where `Person.Name` was used, since no `Person.Name` property existed initially.) To allow the addition of `Person.Name` without breaking either programmer's expected behavior, you cannot assume `virtual` was intended. Furthermore, because C# requires an override member to explicitly use the `override` modifier, some other semantic must be assumed instead of allowing the addition of a member in the base class to cause the derived class to no longer compile.

This semantic is the `new` modifier, which hides a redeclared member of the derived class from the base class. Instead of calling the most derived member, a member of the base class calls the most derived member in the inheritance chain prior to the member with the `new` modifier. If the inheritance chain contains only two classes, a member in the base class will behave as though no method was declared on the derived class (if the derived implementation overrides the base class member). Although the compiler will report the warning shown in either Output 7.2 or Output 7.3, if neither `override` nor `new` is specified, `new` will be assumed, thereby maintaining the desired version safety.

Consider Listing 7.12 as an example. Its output appears in Output 7.4.

Listing 7.12: `override` **versus** `new` **Modifier**

```
public class Program
{
    public class BaseClass
    {
        public static void DisplayName()
        {
            Console.WriteLine("BaseClass");
        }
    }

    public class DerivedClass : BaseClass
    {
        // Compiler WARNING: DisplayName() hides inherited
        // member. Use the new keyword if hiding was intended
        public virtual void DisplayName()
        {
            Console.WriteLine("DerivedClass");
        }
    }

    public class SubDerivedClass : DerivedClass
    {
        public override void DisplayName()
        {
            Console.WriteLine("SubDerivedClass");
        }
    }

    public class SuperSubDerivedClass : SubDerivedClass
    {
        public new static void DisplayName()
        {
            Console.WriteLine("SuperSubDerivedClass");
        }
    }

    public static void Main()
    {
        SuperSubDerivedClass superSubDerivedClass = new();

        SubDerivedClass subDerivedClass = superSubDerivedClass;
        DerivedClass derivedClass = superSubDerivedClass;
        BaseClass baseClass = superSubDerivedClass;
```

```
            SuperSubDerivedClass.DisplayName();
            subDerivedClass.DisplayName();
            derivedClass.DisplayName();
            BaseClass.DisplayName();
        }
}
```

OUTPUT 7.4

```
SuperSubDerivedClass
SubDerivedClass
SubDerivedClass
BaseClass
```

These results occur for the following reasons:

- `SuperSubDerivedClass`: `SuperSubDerivedClass.DisplayName()` displays `SuperSubDerivedClass` because there is no derived class and therefore no override.
- `SubDerivedClass`: `SubDerivedClass.DisplayName()` is the most derived member to override a base class's virtual member. `SuperSubDerivedClass.DisplayName()` is hidden because of its `new` modifier.
- `SubDerivedClass`: `DerivedClass.DisplayName()` is virtual and `SubDerivedClass.DisplayName()` is the most derived member to override it. As before, `SuperSubDerivedClass.DisplayName()` is hidden because of the `new` modifier.
- `BaseClass`: `BaseClass.DisplayName()` does not redeclare any base class member and it is not virtual; therefore, it is called directly.

When it comes to the CIL, the `new` modifier has no effect on which statements the compiler generates. However, a "new" method results in the generation of the `newslot` metadata attribute on the method. From the C# perspective, its only effect is to remove the compiler warning that would appear otherwise.

`sealed` Modifier

Just as you can prevent inheritance using the `sealed` modifier on a class, so virtual members may be `sealed` as well (see Listing 7.13). This approach prevents a subclass from overriding a base class member that was originally declared as `virtual` higher in the inheritance chain. Such a situation arises when a subclass `B` overrides a base class `A`'s member and then needs to prevent any further overriding below subclass `B`.

LISTING 7.13: Sealing Members

```
class A
{
    public virtual void Method()
    {
    }
}

class B : A
{
    public override sealed void Method()
    {
    }
}

class C : B
{
    // ERROR:  Cannot override sealed members
    //public override void Method()
    //{
    //}
}
```

In this example, the use of the `sealed` modifier on class `B`'s `Method()` declaration prevents class `C` from overriding `Method()`.

In general, marking a class as `sealed` is rarely done and should be reserved only for those situations in which there are strong reasons favoring such a restriction. In fact, leaving types unsealed has become increasingly desirable as unit testing has assumed greater prominence, because of the need to support mock (test double) object creation in place of real implementations. One possible scenario in which sealing a class might be warranted is when the cost of sealing individual virtual members outweighs the benefits of leaving the class unsealed. However, a more targeted sealing of individual members—perhaps because of dependencies in the base implementation that are necessary for correct behavior—is likely to be preferable.

base Member

In choosing to override a member, developers often want to invoke the member on the base class (see Listing 7.14).

Listing 7.14: Accessing a Base Member

```
using static System.Environment;

public class Address
{
    public string StreetAddress;
    public string City;
    public string State;
    public string Zip;

    public override string ToString()
    {
        return $"{ StreetAddress + NewLine }"
            + $"{ City }, { State }  { Zip }";
    }
}

public class InternationalAddress : Address
{
    public string Country;

    public override string ToString()
    {
        return base.ToString() +
            NewLine + Country;
    }
}
```

In Listing 7.14, `InternationalAddress` inherits from `Address` and implements `ToString()`. To call the parent class's implementation, you use the `base` keyword. The syntax is virtually identical to the use of the `this` keyword, including support for using `base` as part of the constructor (discussed shortly).

Parenthetically, in the `Address.ToString()` implementation, you are required to `override` because `ToString()` is also a member of `object`. Any members that are decorated with `override` are automatically designated as virtual, so additional child classes may further specialize the implementation.

> **NOTE**
>
> Any methods decorated with `override` are automatically virtual. A base class method can be overridden only if it is virtual, and the overriding method is therefore virtual as well.

Invoking Base Class Constructors

When instantiating a derived class, the runtime first invokes the base class's constructor so that the base class initialization is not circumvented. However, if there is no accessible (non-private) default constructor on the base class, it is not clear how to construct the base class; in turn, the C# compiler reports an error.

To avoid the error caused by the lack of an accessible default constructor, programmers need to designate explicitly, in the derived class constructor header, which base constructor to run (see Listing 7.15).

Listing 7.15: Specifying Which Base Constructor to Invoke

```
public class PdaItem
{
    public PdaItem(string name)
    {
        Name = name;
    }
    public virtual string Name { get; set; }
    // ...
}
public class Contact : PdaItem
{
    // Disable warning since FirstName&LastName set via Name property
    // Non-nullable field is uninitialized.
    #pragma warning disable CS8618
    public Contact(string name) :
        base(name)
```

```
    {
    }
    #pragma warning restore CS8618

    public override string Name
    {
        get
        {
            return $"{ FirstName } { LastName }";
        }

        set
        {
            string[] names = value.Split(' ');
            // Error handling not shown
            FirstName = names[0];
            LastName = names[1];
        }
    }

    [NotNull] [DisallowNull]
    public string FirstName { get; set; }
    [NotNull] [DisallowNull]
    public string LastName { get; set; }

    // ...
}

public class Appointment : PdaItem
{
    public Appointment(string name, string location,
        DateTime startDateTime, DateTime endDateTime) :
        base(name)
    {
        Location = location;
        StartDateTime = startDateTime;
        EndDateTime = endDateTime;
    }

    public DateTime StartDateTime { get; set; }
    public DateTime EndDateTime { get; set; }
    public string Location { get; set; }

    // ...
}
```

By identifying the base constructor in the code, you let the runtime know which base constructor to invoke before invoking the derived class constructor.

Abstract Classes

Many of the inheritance examples so far have defined a class called `PdaItem` that defines the methods and properties common to `Contact`, `Appointment`, and so on, which are type objects that derive from `PdaItem`. `PdaItem` is not intended to be instantiated itself, however. A `PdaItem` instance has no meaning by itself; instead, it has meaning only when it is used as a base class—to share default method implementations across the set of data types that derive from it. These characteristics are indicative of the need for `PdaItem` to be an **abstract** class rather than a **concrete** class. Abstract classes are designed for derivation only. It is not possible to instantiate an abstract class, except in the context of instantiating a class that derives from it. Classes that are not abstract and can instead be instantiated directly are concrete classes.

Begin 8.0

Abstract classes are a fundamental object-oriented principle, so we describe them here accordingly. However, starting with C# 8.0, interfaces almost (specifically, no instance fields can be declared) support a superset of the functionality previously limited to abstract classes. While the details of the new interface capabilities are available in Chapter 8, understanding the concepts regarding abstract members is a prerequisite, so we will provide the details of abstract classes here.

End 8.0

BEGINNER TOPIC

Abstract Classes

Abstract classes represent abstract entities. Their **abstract members** define what an object derived from an abstract entity should contain, but they don't include the implementation. Often, much of the functionality within an abstract class is unimplemented. Before a class can successfully derive from an abstract class, however, it needs to provide the implementation for the abstract methods in its abstract base class.

To define an abstract class, C# requires the abstract modifier to the class definition, as shown in Listing 7.16.

LISTING 7.16: Defining an Abstract Class

```
// Define an abstract class
public abstract class PdaItem
{
    public PdaItem(string name)
    {
        Name = name;
    }

    public virtual string Name { get; set; }
}

public class Program
{
    public static void Main()
    {

        // ERROR:  Cannot create an instance of the abstract class
        PdaItem item = new("Inigo Montoya");
    }
}
```

Although abstract classes cannot be instantiated, this restriction is a minor characteristic of an abstract class. Their primary significance is achieved when abstract classes include **abstract members**. An abstract member is a method or property that has no implementation. Its purpose is to force all derived classes to provide the implementation.

Consider Listing 7.17 as an example.

LISTING 7.17: Defining Abstract Members

```
using static System.Environment;

// Define an abstract class
public abstract class PdaItem
{
    public PdaItem(string name)
    {
        Name = name;
    }
```

```
    public virtual string Name { get; set; }
    public abstract string GetSummary();
}

public class Contact : PdaItem
{
    // ...
    public override string Name
    {
        get
        {
            return $"{ FirstName } { LastName }";
        }
        set
        {
            string[] names = value.Split(' ');
            // Error handling not shown
            FirstName = names[0];
            LastName = names[1];
        }
    }

    public string FirstName
    {
        get
        {
            return _FirstName!;
        }
        set
        {
            _FirstName = value ??
                throw new ArgumentNullException(nameof(value)); ;
        }
    }
    private string? _FirstName;

    public string LastName
    {
        get
        {
            return _LastName!;
        }
        set
        {
            _LastName = value ?? throw new
↪ArgumentNullException(nameof(value));
```

```
        }
    }
    private string? _LastName;
    public string? Address { get; set; }

    public override string GetSummary()
    {
        return $"FirstName: { FirstName + NewLine }"
        + $"LastName: { LastName + NewLine }"
        + $"Address: { Address + NewLine }";
    }

    // ...
}

public class Appointment : PdaItem
{
    public Appointment(string name, string location,
        DateTime startDateTime, DateTime endDateTime) :
        base(name)
    {
        Location = location;
        StartDateTime = startDateTime;
        EndDateTime = endDateTime;
    }

    public DateTime StartDateTime { get; set; }
    public DateTime EndDateTime { get; set; }
    public string Location { get; set; }

    // ...
    public override string GetSummary()
    {
        return $"Subject: { Name + NewLine }"
            + $"Start: { StartDateTime + NewLine }"
            + $"End: { EndDateTime + NewLine }"
            + $"Location: { Location }";
    }
}
```

Listing 7.17 defines the `GetSummary()` member as `abstract`, so it doesn't include any implementation. The code then overrides this member within `Contact` and provides the implementation. Because abstract members are supposed to be overridden, such members are automatically virtual and cannot be declared so explicitly. In addition, abstract members cannot be private because derived classes would not be able to see them.

It is surprisingly difficult to develop a well-designed object hierarchy. For this reason, when programming abstract types, you should be sure to implement at least one (and preferably more) concrete type that derives from the abstract type to validate the design.

If you don't provide a `GetSummary()` implementation in `Contact`, the compiler will report an error.

NOTE

Abstract members must be overridden, so they are automatically virtual and cannot be declared so explicitly.

Language Contrast: C++—Pure Virtual Functions

C++ allows for the definition of abstract functions using the cryptic notation `=0`. These functions are called pure virtual functions in C++. In contrast to C#, however, C++ does not require the class itself to have any special declaration. Unlike C#'s `abstract` class modifier, C++ has no class declaration change when the class includes pure virtual functions.

NOTE

By declaring an abstract member, the abstract class programmer states that to form an "is a" relationship between a concrete class and an abstract base class (that is, a `PdaItem`), it is necessary to implement the abstract members, the members for which the abstract class could not provide an appropriate default implementation.

BEGINNER TOPIC

Polymorphism

When the implementation for the same member signature varies between two or more classes, the scenario demonstrates a key object-oriented principle: **polymorphism**. *Poly* means "many" and *morph* means "form," so polymorphism refers to the existence of multiple implementations of the same signature. Also, because the same signature cannot be used multiple times within a single class, each implementation of the member signature occurs on a different class.

The idea behind polymorphism is that the object itself knows best how to perform a particular operation. Moreover, by enforcing common ways to invoke those operations, polymorphism encourages code reuse when taking advantage of the commonalities. Given multiple types of documents, each document type class knows best how to perform a `Print()` method for its corresponding document type. Therefore, instead of defining a single print method that includes a `switch` statement with the special logic to print each document type, with polymorphism you call the `Print()` method corresponding to the specific type of document you wish to print. For example, calling `Print()` on a word processing document class behaves according to word processing specifics, whereas calling the same method on a graphics document class will result in print behavior specific to the graphic. Given the document types, however, all you have to do to print a document is call `Print()`, regardless of the type.

Moving the custom print implementation out of a `switch` statement offers a number of maintenance advantages. First, the implementation appears in the context of each document type's class rather than in a location far removed from it; this is in keeping with encapsulation. Second, adding a new document type doesn't require a change to the `switch` statement. Instead, all that is necessary is for the new document type class to implement the `Print()` signature.

Abstract members are intended to be a way to enable polymorphism. The base class specifies the signature of the method, and the derived class provides the implementation (see Listing 7.18 with Output 7.5).

Listing 7.18: Using Polymorphism to List the `PdaItems`

```
public class Program
{
    public static void Main()
    {
        PdaItem[] pda = new PdaItem[3];

        Contact contact = new("Sherlock Holmes")
        {
            Address = "221B Baker Street, London, England"
        };
        pda[0] = contact;

        Appointment appointment = new(
                "Soccer tournament", "Estádio da Machava",
                new DateTime(2008, 7, 18), new DateTime(2008, 7, 19));
        pda[1] = appointment;

        contact = new Contact("Anne Frank")
        {
            Address = "Apt 56B, Whitehaven Mansions, Sandhurst Sq,
↪London"
        };
        pda[2] = contact;

        List(pda);
    }

    public static void List(PdaItem[] items)
    {
        // Implemented using polymorphism. The derived
        // type knows the specifics of implementing
        // GetSummary().
        foreach(PdaItem item in items)
        {
            Console.WriteLine("________");
            Console.WriteLine(item.GetSummary());
        }
    }
}
```

Output 7.5

```
________
FirstName: Sherlock
LastName: Holmes
```

```
Address: 221B Baker Street, London, England
---------
Subject: Soccer tournament
Start: 7/18/2008 12:00:00 AM
End: 7/19/2008 12:00:00 AM
Location: Estádio da Machava
---------
FirstName: Hercule
LastName: Poirot
Address: Apt 56B, Whitehaven Mansions, Sandhurst Sq, London
```

In this way, you can call the method on the base class, but the implementation is specific to the derived class. Output 7.5 shows that the `List()` method from Listing 7.18 is able to successfully display both `Contacts` and `Addresses`, and display them in a way tailored to each. The invocation of the abstract `GetSummary()` method actually invokes the overriding method specific to the instance.

All Classes Derive from `System.Object`

Given any class, whether a custom class or one built into the system, the methods shown in Table 7.2 will be defined.

TABLE 7.2: Members of `System.Object`

Method Name	Description
`public virtual bool Equals(object o)`	Returns `true` if the object supplied as a parameter is equal in value, not necessarily in reference, to the instance.
`public virtual int GetHashCode()`	Returns an integer corresponding to an evenly spread hash code. This is useful for collections such as `HashTable` collections.
`public Type GetType()`	Returns an object of type `System.Type` corresponding to the type of the object instance.
`public static bool ReferenceEquals( object a, object b)`	Returns `true` if the two supplied parameters refer to the same object.
`public virtual string ToString()`	Returns a string representation of the object instance.

TABLE 7.2: Members of `System.Object` (continued)

Method Name	Description
`public virtual void Finalize()`	An alias for the destructor; informs the object to prepare for termination. C# prevents you from calling this method directly.
`protected object MemberwiseClone()`	Clones the object in question by performing a shallow copy; references are copied, but not the data within a referenced type.

All of the methods listed in Table 7.2 appear on all objects through inheritance; all classes derive (either directly or via an inheritance chain) from `object`. Even literals include these methods, enabling somewhat peculiar-looking code such as this:

```
Console.WriteLine( 42.ToString() );
```

Even class definitions that don't have any explicit derivation from `object` derive from `object` anyway. The two declarations for `PdaItem` in Listing 7.19, therefore, result in identical CIL.

LISTING 7.19: `System.Object` Derivation Implied When No Derivation Is Specified Explicitly

```
public class PdaItem
{
    // ...
}
public class PdaItem : object
{
    // ...
}
```

When the `object`'s default implementation isn't sufficient, programmers can override one or more of the three virtual methods. Chapter 10 describes the details involved in doing so.

Type Checking

Begin 8.0

Since C# 1.0, there have been multiple ways to check an object's type including the `is` operator and the `switch` statement. In C# 8.0, the `switch` expression was introduced to enable a value return from the expression.

End 8.0

Type Checking with the `is` Operator

Since C# allows casting down the inheritance chain, it is sometimes desirable to determine what the underlying type is before attempting a conversion. Also, checking the type may be necessary for type-specific actions where polymorphism was not implemented. To determine the type, C# has included an `is` operator since C# 1.0 (see Listing 7.20).

LISTING 7.20: `is` Operator Determining the Underlying Type

```
public class Person
{
    // ...
}

public class Employee : Person
{
    // ...
}

public class Program
{
    private static object? GetObjectById(string id)
    {
        // ...
    }

    public static void Main(params string[] args)
    {
        string id = args[0];
        object? entity = GetObjectById(id);

        if (entity is Person)
        {
            Person person = (Person) entity;
            Console.WriteLine(
```

```
                $"Id corresponds to a {
                    nameof(Person) } object: {
                    person.FirstName} {
                    person.LastName}."
                );

            if (entity is Employee employee)
            {
                Console.WriteLine(
                    $"Id ({ employee.Id }) is also an {
                        nameof(Employee)} object.");
            }
        }
        else if(entity is null)
        {
            Console.WriteLine(
                $"Id was unknown so null was returned.");
        }
        else
        {
            Console.WriteLine(
                $"Id '{id}' not an {
                    nameof(Employee)} or a {nameof(Person)} object.");
        }
    }
}
```

After invoking `GetObjectById()`, which returns a nullable object based on the `id` specified, Listing 7.20 invokes the `is` operator on the returned instance. Initially, it checks that the value isn't `null`. Next it determines if the return is a `Person` and then an `Employee`. If `GetObjectById()` returns a `Person`, then the output will be, "Id corresponds to a Person object…." When `GetObjectById()` returns, an `Employee` output will show both a `Person` and an `Employee` message; since `Employee` derives from `Person`, all `Employee` objects are also `Person` objects.

Type Checking with Declaration

With an explicit cast, it is the programmer's responsibility to understand the code logic sufficiently to avoid an invalid cast exception. If an invalid cast might occur, it would be preferable to leverage a type check and avoid the exception entirely. Listing

7.20 demonstrates this by first checking whether `entity` is a `Person` and then casting `Entity` to a `Person`:

```
// ...
if (entity is Person)
{
Person person = (Person) entity;
// ...
```

The advantage is that the `is` operator enables a code path for when the explicit cast might fail without the expense of exception handling. With the addition of declaration in C# 7.0 and later, the `is` operator (and `switch` syntax shown next) will make the type check and the assignment in the same step. Listing 7.20 demonstrates this with the `is Employee` code snippet:

```
if (entity is Employee employee)
{
// ...
}
```

Here, in checking whether the input operand is an employee, it also declares a new variable of type `Employee`. The result from `GetObjectById(id)`, therefore, is checked against the `Employee` type—**type pattern matching**—and assigned to the variable `employee` in the same expression. If the result of `GetObjectById(id)` is `null` or not an `Employee`, then `false` is produced, and the `else` clause executes.

Note that the `employee` variable is available within and after the `if` statement; however, it would need to be assigned a value before accessing it inside or after the `else` clause. Also, you can implicitly specify the data type with `var`, as expected, but as with local variable declaration in general, use caution when the data type isn't obvious.

Type Checking with `switch` Statements

The `switch` statement also allows for type checking, but it can check for multiple types in addition to `null` checking—all within the same statement. In Listing 7.21, we demonstrate this with a method that returns the time (using .NET 6.0's `TimeOnly`), from a variety of types.

Listing 7.21: Type Checking with a `switch` Statement

```
public static TimeOnly GetTime(object input)
{
    switch (input)
    {
        case DateTime datetime:
            return TimeOnly.FromDateTime(datetime);
        case DateTimeOffset datetimeOffset:
            return TimeOnly.FromDateTime(datetimeOffset.DateTime);
        case string dateText:
            return TimeOnly.Parse(dateText);
        case null:
           throw new ArgumentNullException(nameof(input));
        default:
            throw new ArgumentException(
                $"Invalid type - {input.GetType().FullName}");
    };
}
```

Begin 8.0

Listing 7.21 includes a case for `null`, but if none of the cases matches, then default provides a catchall and throws an exception. Also, like with the `is` operator, you can declare a variable simultaneously, providing access to an instance of the object that matches the case.

Starting in C# 8.0, the `switch` statement includes a more succinct expression form that returns a value.

Type Checking with `switch` Expressions

Like the `switch` statement, the `switch` expression (C# 8.0) provides multiple paths for each case—generically a match expression (for both `switch` expressions and statements). Unlike the `switch` statement, there are no labels, no `break` statements, and, in fact, no enclosed statements at all. Most importantly, the `switch` expression returns a value (except when it throws an exception). This makes it a preferable option to the `switch` statement in Listing 7.21, which allows for a return only because the function of the embedded return statements. You couldn't, for example, assign the `switch` statement result to a variable. Listing 7.22 provides an example.

From Listing 7.22 you will notice that unlike a `switch` statement, the input operand for the `switch` statement appears before the `switch` keyword. Each match expression is simply identified by the type, optionally followed by a variable

Listing 7.22: Using `switch` Expressions to Return a Value

```
public static TimeOnly GetTime(object input) =>
    input switch
    {
        DateTime datetime
            => TimeOnly.FromDateTime(datetime),
        DateTimeOffset datetimeOffset
                => TimeOnly.FromDateTime(datetimeOffset.DateTime),
        string dateText => TimeOnly.Parse(
            dateText),
        null => throw new ArgumentNullException(nameof(input)),
        _ => throw new ArgumentException(
            $"Invalid type - {input.GetType().FullName}"),
    };
```

declaration. Also, instead of the colon designating a label, the `switch` expression uses a **lambda operator** `=>`. Lastly, instead of the `default` keyword, the `switch` expression uses the discard symbol: _.

Functionally, Listing 7.21 and Listing 7.22 are equivalent. They both check the type, allow for variable declaration, allow `null` checking, and have a default. One noteworthy `switch` expression characteristic, however, is that the `_` (`default`) catchall must appear at the end or it will obscure later match expressions. In contrast, `default` on a `switch` statement provides the same functionality regardless of where it appears.

Begin 9.0

Begin 10.0

Begin 11.0

Pattern Matching

The `is` operator and `switch` statement remained relatively static until C# 7.0 where declaration and significant pattern matching capabilities were added. Pattern matching provides a syntax through which criteria can be evaluated and the code execution branched accordingly. The C# team continued pattern matching enhancements all the way to C# 11.

In this section we will review all the pattern matching functionality: type patterns constant patterns (C# 7.0), relational patterns (C# 9.0), logical patterns (C# 9.0), tuple patterns (C# 8.0), positional patterns (C# 9.0), extended (C# 10) property

End 9.0

End 10.0

End 11.0

patterns (C# 7.0), and list patterns (C# 11.0). All of these features leverage the recursive pattern capability that allows for multiple checks on a type to be made.

Constant Patterns (C# 7.0)

In Chapter 4, we demonstrated constant patterns when using the `is` operator to check for `null` (i.e., `data is null`) and `not null` and in explaining the basic `switch` statement (https://essentialcsharp.com/the-basic-switch-statement). The principle is that you can compare the input operand against any constant. You could, for example, compare `data.Day` against with the value `21`. Listing 7.23 provides both `is` and `switch` expression examples.

Listing 7.23: Constant Pattern Matching with `is` Operator

```
using System.Diagnostics.CodeAnalysis;

public static class SolsticeHelper
{
    public static bool IsSolstice(
        DateTime date)
    {
        if (date.Day is 21)
        {
            if (date.Month is 12)
            {
                return true;
            }
            if (date.Month is 6)
            {
                return true;
            }
        }
        return false;
    }

    public static bool TryGetSolstice(DateTime date,
        [NotNullWhen(true)] out string? solstice
    )
    {
        if (date.Day is 21)
        {
            if ((solstice = date.Month switch
            {
                12 => "Winter Solstice",
```

```
                6 => "Summer Solstice",
                _ => null
            }) is not null) return true;
        }
        solstice = null;
        return false;
    }
}
```

Constants can be any literal including strings, defined constants, and, of course, `null`. Note that the comparison of a string to the literal empty string `""` will work, but comparing it to `string.Empty` will fail because `string.Empty` is not declared as a constant.

Begin 9.0

Relational Patterns (C# 9.0)

With relational patterns you can compare to a constant relatively using the operators `<`, `>`, `<=`, and `>=`. Listing 7.24 provides both `is` operator and `switch` expression versions of relational patterns. (Note that == is not one of the operators since this functionality is already available in the constant pattern matching.)

Listing 7.24: Relational Pattern Matching Examples

```
public static bool IsDeveloperWorkHours(
    int hourOfTheDay) =>
        hourOfTheDay is > 10 &&
            hourOfTheDay is < 24;


public static string GetPeriodOfDay(int hourOfTheDay) =>
    hourOfTheDay switch
    {
        < 6 => "Dawn",
        < 12 => "Morning",
        < 18 => "Afternoon",
        < 24 => "Evening",
        int hour => throw new ArgumentOutOfRangeException(
            $"The hour of the day specified is invalid
↪.", nameof(hourOfTheDay))
    };
```

It is important to note that starting in C# 7.0, match expressions are no longer necessarily mutually exclusive. For example, we could have a match expression of > 0 and another with < 24 and both would be true regardless of the hour. Order will make the final determination of which path the code execution follows. For this reason, use caution when ordering the match expressions in `switch` statements and expressions (in the same way you would be careful about ordering a series of `if` statements).

Logical Patterns (C# 9.0)

With logical patterns we can combine relational match expressions with a single variable and the operators `not`, `and`, and `or`, providing negated, conjunctive, and disjunctive patterns respectively. Therefore, rather than using the logical operators like `&&` or `||` (see the `IsDeveloperWorkHours()` method in Listing 7.24 for example) you can specify the input operand once and then have multiple match expressions as shown in Listing 7.25.

Listing 7.25: Logical Pattern Matching Examples

```
public bool IsStandardWorkHours(
    TimeOnly time) =>
        time.Hour is > 8
            and < 17
            and not 12; // lunch

static bool TryGetPhoneButton(
    char character,
    [NotNullWhen(true)] out char? button)
{
    return (button = char.ToLower(character) switch
    {
        '1' => '1',
        '2' or >= 'a' and <= 'c' => '2',
        // not operator and parenthesis example (C# 10)
        '3' or not (< 'd' or > 'f') => '3',
        '4' or >= 'g' and <= 'i' => '4',
        '5' or >= 'j' and <= 'l' => '5',
        '6' or >= 'm' and <= 'o' => '6',
        '7' or >= 'p' and <= 's' => '7',
        '8' or >= 't' and <= 'v' => '8',
        '9' or >= 'w' and <= 'z' => '9',
        '0' or '+' => '0',
```

```
        _ => null,// Set the button to indicate an invalid value
    }) is not null;
}
```

The order of precedence is not, and, or; thus the first two examples don't need parentheses. Parentheses, however, are allowed to change the default order of precedence as demonstrated (arbitrarily) by match expressions in the switch expression of Listing 7.24.

Be aware that when using the or and not operators, you cannot also declare a variable. For instance:

```
if (input is "data" or string text) { }
```

will result in an error: "CS8780: A variable may not be declared within a 'not' or 'or' pattern." Doing so would result in ambiguity about whether initialization of text occurred.

Parenthesized Patterns (C# 9.0)

To override the order of precedence of logical pattern operators you can group them together using parentheses (see Listing 7.26).

LISTING 7.26: Parenthesized Patterns

```
public bool IsOutsideOfStandardWorkHours(
    TimeOnly time) =>
        time.Hour is not
            (> 8 and < 17 and not 12); // Parenthesis Pattern - C# 10.
```

End 9.0

Parenthesizing is available with both is operators and switch syntax.

Tuple Patterns (C# 8.0)

With tuple pattern matching, you can check for constant values within the tuple or assign tuple items to a variable (see Listing 7.27).

LISTING 7.27: Tuple Pattern Matching with the is Operator

```
public static void Main(params string[] args)
{
```

```
    const int command = 0;
    const int fileName = 1;
    const string dataFile = "data.dat";

    // ...
    if ((args.Length, args[command].ToLower()) is (1, "cat"))
    {
        Console.WriteLine(File.ReadAllText(dataFile));
    }
    else if ((args.Length, args[command].ToLower())
        is (2, "encrypt"))
    {
        string data = File.ReadAllText(dataFile);
        File.WriteAllText(
            args[fileName], Encrypt(data).ToString());
    }
}
```

As expected, the same is possible with the `switch` expression or statement syntax (see Listing 7.28)

Listing 7.28: Tuple Pattern Matching with the `switch` Statement

```
public static void Main(params string[] args)
{
    const int action = 0;
    const int fileName = 1;
    const string dataFile = "data.dat";

    // ...
    switch ((args.Length, args[action].ToLower()))
    {
        case (1, "cat"):
            Console.WriteLine(File.ReadAllText(dataFile));
            break;
        case (2, "encrypt"):
            {
                string data = File.ReadAllText(dataFile);
                File.WriteAllText(
                    args[fileName], Encrypt(data).ToString());
            }
            break;
        default:
            Console.WriteLine("Arguments are invalid.");
            break;
```

```
    }
}
```

In both Listing 7.27 and Listing 7.28, we pattern match against a tuple that is populated with the length and the elements of `args`. In the first match expression, we check for one argument and the action `"cat"`. In the second match expression, we evaluate whether the first item in the array is equal to `"encrypt"`. In addition, Listing 7.27 assigns the third element in the tuple to the variable `fileName` if the initial match expression evaluates to true. The `switch` statement in Listing 7.28 doesn't make the variable assignment since the input operand of the `switch` statement is the same for all match expressions.

Each element match can be a constant or a variable. Since the tuple is instantiated before the `is` operator executes, we can't use the `"encrypt"` scenario first because `args[FileName]` would not be a valid index if the `"cat"` action was requested.

Positional Patterns (C# 8.0)

Building on the deconstructor construct introduced in C# 7.0 (see Chapter 6), C# 8.0 enables positional pattern matching with a syntax that closely matches tuple pattern matching (see Listing 7.29).

Listing 7.29: Positional Pattern Matching with the `is` Operator

```
using System.Drawing;

public static class PointHelper
{
    public static void Deconstruct(
        this Point point, out int x, out int y) =>
            (x, y) = (point.X, point.Y);

    public static bool IsVisibleOnVGAScreen(Point point) =>
        point is (>=0 and <=1920, >=0 and <=1080);

    public static string GetQuadrant(Point point) => point switch
    {
        (>=0, >=0) => "Quadrant I",    //  II | I
        (<=0, >=0) => "Quadrant II",   // ____|____
        (<=0, <=0) => "Quadrant III",  //     |
        (>=0, <=0) => "Quadrant IV"    // III | IV
```

```
    };
}
```

The `System.Drawing.Point` type doesn't have a deconstructor. However, we are able to add one as an extension method, which satisfies the criteria for converting the `Point` to a tuple of `X` and `Y`. The deconstructor is then used to match the order of each comma-separated match expression in the pattern. In the example of `IsVisibleOnVGAScreen()`, `X` is matched with `>=0 and <=1920` and `Y` with `>=0 and <=1080`. Similar range expressions are used with the `switch` expression in `GetQuadrant()`.

Begin 9.0

Property Patterns (C# 8.0 & 10.0)

With property patterns, the match expression is based on property names and values of the data type identified in the `switch` expression, as shown in Listing 7.30.

Listing 7.30: Property Pattern Matching with the `is` Operator

```
public record class Employee
{
    public int Id { get; set; }
    public string Name { get; set; }
    public string Role { get; set; }

    public Employee(int id, string name, string role) =>
        (Id, Name, Role) = (id, name, role);
}


public class ExpenseItem
{
    public int Id { get; set; }
    public string ItemName { get; set; }
    public decimal CostAmount { get; set; }
    public DateTime ExpenseDate { get; set; }
    public Employee Employee { get; set; }

    public ExpenseItem(
        int id, string name, decimal amount, DateTime date,
            Employee employee) =>
                (Id, Employee, ItemName, CostAmount, ExpenseDate) =
                (id, employee, name, amount, date);
```

```
    public static bool ValidateExpenseItem(ExpenseItem expenseItem) =>
        expenseItem switch
        {
            // Note: A property pattern checks that the input value is
↪not null
            // Expanded Property Pattern
            { ItemName.Length: > 0, Employee.Role: "Admin" } => true,
            #pragma warning disable IDE0170 // Property pattern can be
↪simplified
            // Property Pattern
            { ItemName: { Length: > 0 }, Employee: {Role: "Manager" },
                ExpenseDate: DateTime date }
            #pragma warning restore IDE0170 // Property pattern can be
↪simplified
                when date >= DateTime.Now.AddDays(-30) => true,
            { ItemName.Length: > 0,  Employee.Name.Length: > 0,
                CostAmount: <= 1000, ExpenseDate: DateTime date }
                when date >= DateTime.Now.AddDays(-30) => true,
            { } => false, // This not null check can be eliminated.
            _ => false
        };
}
```

The first important thing to note about all property match expressions is that they will match only when the input operand is not `null`. This is why, for example, a match expression of `{ }`, an empty property match expression, matches whenever the input operand is not `null`. (In Listing 7.30, the `{ }` match expression is redundant as the default match expression at the end of the `switch` will catch both `null` and remaining non-`null` input operands that fall through anyway.) While `{ }` works as a not `null` check, simply specifying not `null` (C# 9.0) is preferred as the syntax is clearer.

In Listing 7.30, the first match expressions within the `switch` expression starts with `ItemName.Length: > 0`, requiring that `ItemName.Length` be greater than 0. Implied in the expression is that `ItemName` is also not `null`. In fact, since the initial `null` check is implicit, the compiler disallows using the `null` conditional in the property expression (`ItemName?.Length`).

In Listing 7.30, the first match expression also requires that `Employee.Role` is set to `"Admin"`. And, if these first two match expressions match, the `switch` expression returns true, indicating `ExpenseItem` is valid. The complete match expression uses an expanded property pattern match syntax introduced in C# 10 and identified by the dot notation that accesses subproperties (`Length` and `Role`).

The second match expression for Listing 7.30, `{ ItemName: { Length: > 0 }, Employee: {Role: "Manager" }, ExpenseDate: DateTime date }`, is also a property match expression (rather than an expanded property match expression) but with a slightly different syntax. The property match expression was introduced in C# 7.0 and is still supported, albeit with a warning, because the expanded syntax is simpler and preferred in all cases.

This second match expression includes a property match for `ExpenseDate` for which it declares a variable, `date`. While `date` is still used as part of the `switch` filter, it appears in a **when clause** rather than the match expression.

When Clause

For all forms of constant and relational match expressions, it is necessary to use a constant. This, however, can be restrictive given that frequently the comparative operand is not known at compiler time. To avoid the restriction, C# 7.0 includes a `when` clause into which you can add any conditional expression (an expression that returns a Boolean).

The code in Listing 7.30 declares a DateTime date variable to check that the `ExpenseItem.ExpenseDate` is no older than 30 days. However, because `age` is dependent on the current date and time, the value isn't constant, and we can't use a match expression. Instead, the code uses a `when` clause following the match expression where the `date` value is compared to `DateTime.Now.AddDays(-30)`. The `when` clause provides a catchall location for (optionally) more complex conditionals without the restriction of only using constants.

The addition of `when` clauses is the core reason why C# 7.0 allowed match expressions to no longer be mutually exclusive. With a `when` clause, it is no longer possible to determine at compile time to evaluate the full case logic and check for exclusivity. As a reminder, be careful of the order that each case appears within a `switch` expression to avoid having earlier cases catch conditions meant for later cases.

End 9.0

Pattern Matching with Unrelated Types

An interesting capability of pattern matching is that it becomes possible to extract data from unrelated types and morph the data into a common format. Listing 7.31 provides an example.

LISTING 7.31: Pattern Matching within a `switch` Expression

```
public static string? CompositeFormatDate(
        object input, string compositeFormatString) =>
    input switch
    {
        DateTime
            { Year: int year, Month: int month, Day: int day }
            => (year, month, day),
        DateTimeOffset
            { Year: int year, Month: int month, Day: int day }
                => (year, month, day),
        DateOnly
            { Year: int year, Month: int month, Day: int day }
                => (year, month, day),
        string dateText => DateTime.TryParse(
            dateText, out DateTime dateTime) ?
                (dateTime.Year, dateTime.Month, dateTime.Day) :
                // default ((int Year, int Month, int Day)?)
                // preferable but not covered until Chapter 12.
                ((int Year, int Month, int Day)?) null,
        _ => null
    } is (int, int, int) date ? string.Format(
        compositeFormatString, date.Year, date.Month, date.Day) : null;
```

The first match expression of the `switch` expression in Listing 7.32 uses type pattern matching (C# 7.0) to check whether the input is of type `DateTime`. If the result is `true`, it passes the result to the property pattern matching to declare and assign the values `year`, `month`, and `day`; it then uses those variables in a tuple expression that returns the tuple `(year, month, day)`. The `DateTimeOffset` and `DateOnly` match expressions work the same way.

Given a match on the `string` match expression, if `TryParse()` is unsuccessful, we return a `default((int Year, int Month, int Day)?)`,[2]

2. See Chapter 12 for more information.

which evaluates to `null`. It is not possible to simply return `null` because there is no implicit conversion from `(int Year, int Month, int Day)` (the ValueTuple type returned by the other match expressions) and `null`. Rather, a nullable tuple data type needs to be specified to accurately determine the `switch` expression's type. (The alternative to using the default operator would be to cast `((int Year, int Month, int Day)?) null`..

In Listing 7.31, we have four data types that, while conceptually similar, have no inheritance relationship between them other than their derivation from `object`. As such, the only data type available for the input operand is `object`. Yet, from each we can extract properties for year, month, and day (even if the names don't exist or they vary between the data types). In this case, we extract `(int Year, int Month, int Day)?`, a nullable tuple. And, as long as the tuple is not `null`, we are able to use the extracted value for year, month, and day into the `compositeFormatString` value.

Recursive Pattern Matching (C# 7.0)

As mentioned earlier, much of the power of pattern matching doesn't really emerge until it is leveraged within a `switch` statement or expression. The one exception, however, might be when pattern matching is used recursively. Listing 7.32 provides an (admittedly contrived) example of the potential complexity when applying patterns recursively.

Listing 7.32: Recursive Pattern Matching with the `is` Operator

```
// ...
Person inigo = new("Inigo", "Montoya");
var buttercup =
    (FirstName: "Princess", LastName: "Buttercup");

(Person inigo, (string FirstName, string LastName) buttercup) couple =
    (inigo, buttercup);

if (couple is
    ( // Tuple: Retrieved from deconstructor of Person
        ( // Positional: Select left side or tuple
            { // Property of firstName
                Length: int inigoFirstNameLength
            },
```

```
            _ // Discard last name portion of tuple
          ),
        { // Property of Princess Buttercup tuple
            FirstName: string buttercupFirstName }))
{
    Console.WriteLine(
        $"({ inigoFirstNameLength }, { buttercupFirstName })");
}
else
{
    // ...
}
// ...
```

In this example, `couple` is of the following type:

```
(Person, (string FirstName, string LastName))
```

As such, the first match occurs on the outer tuple, `(inigo, buttercup)`. Next, positional pattern matching is used against `inigo`, leveraging the `Person` deconstructor. This selects a `(FirstName, LastName)` tuple, from which property pattern matching is used to extract the `Length` of the `inigo.FirstName` value. The `LastName` portion of the positional pattern matching is discarded with an underscore. Finally, property pattern matching is used to select `buttercup.FirstName`.

While pattern matching is a powerful means to select data, it is not without a caution: Be mindful of readability. Even with the comments of Listing 7.32, it is likely challenging to understand the code. Without them, it would be even harder:

```
if (couple is ( ( { Length: int inigoFirstNameLength }, _ ),
{ FirstName: string buttercupFirstName })) { ...}
```

Even so, where pattern matching really proves useful is in `switch` statements and expressions.

Begin 11.0

List Patterns (C# 11.0)

One important new feature in C# 11 was the introduction of list patterns. These enable pattern matching over a list of items such as an array. As such, you can use any type of pattern matching on the elements within the list. Listing 7.33 demonstrates the feature to parse the `args` parameter of the Main method.

LISTING 7.33: Pattern Matching within a `switch` Expression

```
public static void Main(string[] args)
{
    // For simplicity, options are assumed
    // to all be lower case.

    // The first argument is the option and is
    // identified by a '/', '-', or '--' prefix.

    switch (args)
    {
        case ["--help" or ['/' or '-', 'h' or '?']]:
            // e.g. --help, /h, -h, /?, -?
            DisplayHelp();
            break;
        case [ ['/' or '-', char option], ..]:
            // Option begins with '/', '-' and has 0 or more arguments.
            if(!EvaluateOption($"{option}", args[1..]))
            {
                DisplayHelp();
            }
            break;
        case [ ['-', '-', ..] option, ..]:
            // Option begins with "--" and has 0 or more arguments.
            if(!EvaluateOption(option[2..], args[1..]))
            {
                DisplayHelp();
            }
            break;

        // The following cases are redundant with default
        // but provided for demonstration purposes.
        case []:
            // No command line arguments

        default:
            DisplayHelp();
```

```
            break;
    }
}

private static bool EvaluateOption(string option, string[] args) =>
    (option, args) switch
    {
        ("cat" or "c", [string fileName]) =>
            CatalogFile(fileName),
        ("copy", [string sourceFile, string targetFile]) =>
            CopyFile(sourceFile, targetFile),
        _ => false
    };

private static bool CopyFile(object sourceFile, string targetFile)
{
    Console.WriteLine($"Copy '{sourceFile}' '{targetFile}'...");
    return true;
}
```

The first case in Listing 7.33 looks for the text `"—help"` as the first and only element of the `args` array. If there is no match, then the remainder of the list match expression matches on a first element that starts with `/` or `-` followed by `?` or `h`. The latter part of the list pattern looks for exactly two characters (because a string is an array of characters) as identified by the comma (,) within the expression, separating the prefix from the single character expression:

```
['/' or '-', 'h' or '?']
```

The next two cases evaluate the first element of `args` as well, determining whether the first character is a `/` or a `-` or, in the third case, whether the first element of `args` starts with `--`. In both cases, if there is a match, `args[0]` is assigned to the `option` variable. Unfortunately, there is no way to capture the remaining elements of the list into a variable. List pattern matching always looks for an exact number of elements or allows for `..` to mean no further evaluation of the remaining elements is required. For this reason, when invoking `EvaluateOptions()`, we use the range `args[1..]` to pass all the elements in `args` except the first one (see Chapter 3 (https://essentialcsharp.com/arrays) for examples on ranges).

The fourth case uses `[ ]` to identify a list with 0 elements. In this example, it is redundant because the default case would also capture the case when `args` has zero elements.

Within the `EvaluateOptions()` method of Listing 7.33, we use a tuple to first evaluate the command portion. The second element in the tuple evaluates the remaining arguments. For the `"cat"` match expression, it looks for a list with one item, whereas for the `"copy"` match expression, it looks for a list of exactly two elements. In both cases, it captures the array elements into variables and uses them to invoke the corresponding command method.

There is a lot of power in the list pattern matching capability, and because it works with the characters of strings, it enables a host of simple scenarios for string parsing without resorting to regular expressions.

End 11.0

Avoid Pattern Matching When Polymorphism Is Possible

Although the pattern matching capability is important, you should consider issues related to polymorphism prior to using pattern matching. Polymorphism supports the expansion of a behavior to other data types without requiring any modification of the implementation that defines the behavior. For example, placing a member like `Name` in the base class `PdaItem` and then working with values derived from `PdaItem` is preferable to using pattern matching with match expressions for each type. The former allows adding an additional type that derives from `PdaItem` (potentially even in a different assembly) without recompiling. In contrast, the latter requires additionally modifying the pattern matching code to address a newly introduced type. Regardless, polymorphism is not always possible, and when it isn't, pattern matching, specifically something like property pattern matching, provides a good alternative.

One scenario where polymorphism fails is when no object hierarchy matches your goals—if you are working with classes that are part of unrelated systems, for example. Furthermore, it is assumed the code requiring polymorphism is out of your control and can't be modified. Working with the dates in Listing 7.33 is one such example. A second scenario is when functionality you're adding isn't part of the core abstraction for these classes. For example, the toll paid by drivers changes for different types of vehicles traveling on a toll road, but the toll isn't a core function of the vehicle.

End 8.0

ADVANCED TOPIC

Conversion Using the `as` Operator

In addition to the `is` operator, C# has an `as` operator. Originally, the `as` operator offered an advantage over the `is` operator: It not only checks whether the operand is of a specific type but also attempts a conversion to the particular data type and assigns `null` if the source type is not inherently (within the inheritance chain) of the target type. Furthermore, it provides an advantage over casting because it won't throw an exception. Listing 7.34 demonstrates the use of the `as` operator.

LISTING 7.34: Data Conversion Using the `as` Operator

```
public class PdaItem
{
    protected Guid ObjectKey { get; }
    // ...
}

public class Contact : PdaItem
{
    // ...
    public Contact(string name) => Name = name;

    static public Contact Load(PdaItem pdaItem)
    {
        #pragma warning disable IDE0019 // Use pattern matching
        Contact? contact = pdaItem as Contact;
        #pragma warning restore IDE0019 // Use pattern matching
        if (contact != null)
        {
            System.Diagnostics.Trace.WriteLine(
                $"ObjectKey: {contact.ObjectKey}");
            return (Contact)pdaItem;
        }
        else
        {
            throw new ArgumentException(
```

```
                $"{nameof(pdaItem)} was not of type {nameof(Contact)}");
        }
    }
    // ...
}
```

By using the `as` operator, you can avoid additional try/catch handling code if the conversion is invalid, because the `as` operator provides a way to attempt a cast without throwing an exception if the cast fails.

One advantage of the `is` operator over the `as` operator is that the latter cannot successfully determine the underlying type. The `as` operator may implicitly cast up or down an inheritance chain. Unlike the `as` operator, the `is` operator can determine the underlying type. Also, the `as` operator works mainly with reference types, whereas the `is` operator works with all types.

More important, the `as` operator generally requires the additional step of checking the assigned variable for `null`. Since the pattern matching `is` operator includes this conditional check automatically, it effectively eliminates the need for the `as` operator—assuming C# 7.0 or later is available.

Summary

This chapter discussed how to specialize a class by deriving from it and adding additional methods and properties. This coverage included a discussion of the `private` and `protected` access modifiers that control the level of encapsulation.

The chapter also investigated the details of overriding the base class implementation and, alternatively, hiding it using the `new` modifier. To control overriding, C# provides the `virtual` modifier, which identifies to the deriving class developer which members they intend for derivation. To prevent any derivation, the `sealed` modifier may be used on the class. Similarly, placing the `sealed` modifier on a member prevents further overriding from subclasses.

This chapter briefly discussed how all types derive from `object`. Chapter 10 discusses this derivation in more depth, looking at how `object` includes three virtual methods with specific rules and guidelines that govern overloading. Before you get there, however, you need to consider another programming paradigm that builds on object-oriented programming: interfaces. This is the subject of Chapter 8.

The chapter ended with an examination of pattern matching with the `is` operator and both the `switch` statement and C# 8.0's `switch` expression/statement. While C# 7.0 provided the initial pattern matching support, all versions through C# 11 have expanded these capabilities.

8

Interfaces

Polymorphism is available in C# not only via inheritance (as discussed in Chapter 7) but also via interfaces. Unlike abstract classes, interfaces could not include any implementation—until C# 8.0. (But even in C# 8.0, it is questionable whether you should use this capability except for "versioning" the interfaces.) Like abstract classes, however, interfaces define a set of members that callers can rely on being implemented.

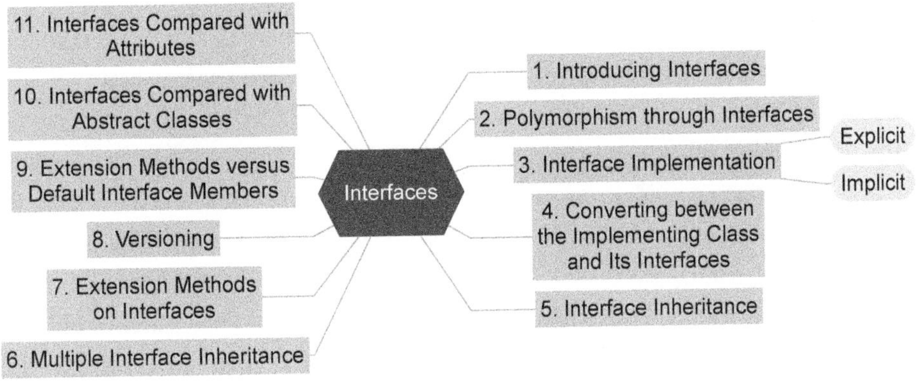

By implementing an interface, a type defines its capabilities. **The interface implementation relationship is a "can do" relationship.** The type can do what the interface requires an implementing type to do. The interface defines the contract between the types that implement the interface and the code that uses the interface.

Types that implement interfaces must declare methods with the same signatures as the methods declared by the implemented interfaces. This chapter discusses implementing and using interfaces. It concludes with default implemented members on interfaces and the host of paradigms (and complexities) that this new feature introduces.

Introducing Interfaces

BEGINNER TOPIC

Why Interfaces?

Interfaces are useful because—unlike abstract classes—they enable the complete separation of implementation details from services provided. For a real-world example, consider the "interface" that is an electrical wall socket. How the electrical power gets to the socket is an implementation detail: It might be generated by chemical, nuclear, or solar energy; the generator might be in the next room or far away; and so on. The socket provides a "contract": It agrees to supply a particular voltage at a specific frequency, and in return it requires that the appliance using that interface provide a compatible plug. The appliance need not care about the implementation details that get power to the socket; all it needs to worry about is providing a compatible plug.

Consider the following example: A huge number of file compression formats are available (`.zip`, `.7-zip`, `.cab`, `.lha`, `.tar`, `.tar.gz`, `.tar.bz2`, `.bh`, `.rar`, `.arj`, `.arc`, `.ace`, `.zoo`, `.gz`, `.bzip2`, `.xxe`, `.mime`, `.uue`, and `.yenc`, just to name a few). If you created classes for each compression format, you could end up with different method signatures for each compression implementation and no ability to apply a standard calling convention across them. Alternatively, the desired method could be declared as abstract in the base class. However, deriving from a common base class uses up a class's one and only opportunity for inheritance. It is unlikely that there is any code common to the various compression implementations that can be put in the base class, thereby ruling out the potential benefits of having a base class implementation. The key point is that base classes let you share implementation along with the member signatures, whereas interfaces allow you to share the member signatures without necessarily sharing the implementation.

Instead of sharing a common base class, each compression class needs to implement a common interface. Interfaces define the contract that a class supports to interact with the other classes that expect the interface. If all the classes implemented the `IFileCompression` interface and its `Compress()` and `Uncompress()` methods, the code for calling the algorithm on any particular compression class would simply involve a conversion to the `IFileCompression` interface and a call to the members. The result is polymorphism because each compression class has the same method signature but individual implementations of that signature.

The `IFileCompression` interface shown in Listing 8.1 is an example of an interface implementation. By convention—a convention so strong it is universal—the interface name is PascalCase with a capital "I" prefix.

LISTING 8.1: Defining an Interface

```
interface IFileCompression
{
    void Compress(string targetFileName, string[] fileList);
    void Uncompress(
        string compressedFileName, string expandDirectoryName);
}
```

`IFileCompression` defines the methods a type must implement to be used in the same manner as other compression-related classes. The power of interfaces is that they grant the ability to callers to switch among implementations without modifying the calling code.

Begin 8.0

Prior to C# 8.0, one of the key characteristics of an interface was that it had no implementation and no data (fields). Method declarations in an interface always had a single semicolon in place of curly braces after the declaration. Properties, while looking like automatically implemented properties, had no backing fields. In fact, fields (data) could not appear in an interface declaration either.

Many of these rules were relaxed in C# 8.0 for the purposes of allowing interfaces to have some level of restricted changes after publishing. However, until the section "Interface Versioning in C# 8.0 or Later" in this chapter, we will ignore the new capabilities and discuss interfaces for the purposes of establishing polymorphism. This is where the real power of interfaces lies, and it is easier to discuss them in that context before opening up the new capabilities and describing the scenario for making an exception. So let's stick with the simplification that interfaces cannot have any implementation (without mentioning C# 8.0) and postpone the removal of that restriction until we explore the C# 8.0 capabilities.

The declared members of an interface describe the members that must be accessible on an implementing type. The purpose of non-public members is to make those members inaccessible to other code. Therefore, C# does not allow access modifiers on interface members; instead, it automatically defines them as public.[1]

Guidelines

DO use PascalCasing and an "I" prefix for interface names.

End 8.0

Polymorphism through Interfaces

Consider another example, as shown in Listing 8.2 with Output 8.1: `IListable` defines the members that a class needs to support if the `ConsoleListControl` class is to display it. As such, any class that implements `IListable` can use the `ConsoleListControl` to display itself. The `IListable` interface requires a read-only property, `CellValues`.

Listing 8.2: Implementing and Using Interfaces

```
public interface IListable
{
    // Return the value of each cell in the row
    string?[] CellValues { get; }
}

public abstract class PdaItem
{
```

1. Before C# 8.0.

```
    public PdaItem(string name)
    {
        Name = name;
    }

    public virtual string Name { get; set; }
}

public class Contact : PdaItem, IListable
{
    public Contact(string firstName, string lastName,
        string address, string phone)
        : base(GetName(firstName, lastName))
    {
        FirstName = firstName;
        LastName = lastName;
        Address = address;
        Phone = phone;
    }

    public string FirstName { get; }
    public string LastName { get; }
    public string Address { get; }
    public string Phone { get; }
    static public string GetName(string firstName, string lastName)
        => $"{ firstName } { lastName }";

    public string[] CellValues
    {
        get
        {
            return new string[]
            {
                FirstName,
                LastName,
                Phone,
                Address
            };
        }
    }

    public static string[] Headers
    {
        get
        {
            return new string[] {
                "First Name", "Last Name    ",
```

```
                "Phone       ",
                "Address                       " };
        }
    }
    // ...
}

public class Publication : IListable
{
    public Publication(string title, string author, int year)
    {
        Title = title;
        Author = author;
        Year = year;
    }

    public string Title { get; }
    public string Author { get; }
    public int Year { get; }

    public string?[] CellValues
    {
        get
        {
            return new string?[]
            {
                Title,
                Author,
                Year.ToString()
            };
        }
    }

    public static string[] Headers
    {
        get
        {
            return new string[] {
                "Title
↪   ",
                "Author              ",
                "Year" };
        }
    }

    // ...
}
```

```
public class Program
{
    public static void Main()
    {
        Contact[] contacts = new Contact[]
        {
          new Contact(
              "Dick", "Traci",
              "123 Main St., Spokane, WA  99037",
              "123-123-1234"),
          new Contact(
              "Andrew", "Littman",
              "1417 Palmary St., Dallas, TX 55555",
              "555-123-4567"),
          new Contact(
              "Mary", "Hartfelt",
              "1520 Thunder Way, Elizabethton, PA 44444",
              "444-123-4567"),
          new Contact(
              "John", "Lindherst",
              "1 Aerial Way Dr., Monteray, NH 88888",
              "222-987-6543"),
          new Contact(
              "Pat", "Wilson",
              "565 Irving Dr., Parksdale, FL 22222",
              "123-456-7890"),
          new Contact(
              "Jane", "Doe",
              "123 Main St., Aurora, IL 66666",
              "333-345-6789")
        };

        // Classes are cast implicitly convertible to
        // their supported interfaces
        ConsoleListControl.List(Contact.Headers, contacts);

        Console.WriteLine();

        Publication[] publications = new Publication[3] {
            new Publication(
                "The End of Poverty: Economic Possibilities for Our
↪Time",
                "Jeffrey Sachs", 2006),
            new Publication("Orthodoxy",
                "G.K. Chesterton", 1908),
            new Publication(
```

```
                "The Hitchhiker's Guide to the Galaxy",
                "Douglas Adams", 1979)
            };
        ConsoleListControl.List(
            Publication.Headers, publications);
    }
}

public class ConsoleListControl
{
    public static void List(string[] headers, IListable[] items)
    {
        int[] columnWidths = DisplayHeaders(headers);

        for(int count = 0; count < items.Length; count++)
        {
            string?[] values = items[count].CellValues;
            DisplayItemRow(columnWidths, values);
        }
    }

    /// <summary>Displays the column headers</summary>
    /// <returns>Returns an array of column widths</returns>
    private static int[] DisplayHeaders(string[] headers)
    {
        // ...
    }

    private static void DisplayItemRow(
        int[] columnWidths, string?[] values)
    {
        // ...
    }
}
```

Output 8.1

```
First Name  Last Name     Phone         Address
Dick        Traci         123-123-1234  123 Main St., Spokane, WA
99037
Andrew      Littman       555-123-4567  1417 Palmary St., Dallas, TX
55555
Mary        Hartfelt      444-123-4567  1520 Thunder Way,
Elizabethton, PA 44444
John        Lindherst     222-987-6543  1 Aerial Way Dr., Monteray, NH
```

```
88888
Pat          Wilson          123-456-7890  565 Irving Dr., Parksdale, FL
22222
Jane         Doe             333-345-6789  123 Main St., Aurora, IL 66666

Title                                                        Author
    Year
The End of Poverty: Economic Possibilities for Our Time  Jeffrey Sachs
    2006
Orthodoxy                                                    G.K.
Chesterton    1908
The Hitchhiker's Guide to the Galaxy                         Douglas Adams
    1979
```

In Listing 8.2, the `ConsoleListControl` can display seemingly unrelated classes (`Contact` and `Publication`). Any class can be displayed provided that it implements the required interface. As a result, the `ConsoleListControl.List()` method relies on polymorphism to appropriately display whichever set of objects it is passed. Each class has its own implementation of `CellValues`, and converting a class to `IListable` still allows the particular class's implementation to be invoked.

Interface Implementation

Declaring a class to implement an interface is similar to deriving from a base class: The implemented interfaces appear in a comma-separated list along with the base class. The base class specifier (if there is one) must come first, but otherwise order is not significant. Classes can implement multiple interfaces but may derive directly from only one base class. An example appears in Listing 8.3.

LISTING 8.3: Implementing an Interface

```
public class Contact : PdaItem, IListable, IComparable
{
    // ...
```

```
    #region IComparable Members
    /// <summary>
    ///
    /// </summary>
    /// <param name="obj"></param>
    /// <returns>
    /// Less than zero:      This instance is less than obj
    /// Zero                 This instance is equal to obj
    /// Greater than zero    This instance is greater than obj
    /// </returns>
    public int CompareTo(object? obj) => obj switch
    {
        null => 1,
        Contact contact when ReferenceEquals(this, obj) => 0,
        Contact { LastName: string lastName }
            when LastName.CompareTo(lastName) != 0 =>
                LastName.CompareTo(lastName),
        Contact { FirstName: string firstName }
            when FirstName.CompareTo(firstName) != 0 =>
                FirstName.CompareTo(firstName),
        Contact _ => 0,
        _ => throw new ArgumentException(
            $"The parameter is not a value of type { nameof(Contact) }",
            nameof(obj))
    };
    #endregion

    #region IListable Members
    string?[] IListable.CellValues
    {
        get
        {
            return new string?[]
            {
                FirstName,
                LastName,
                Phone,
                Address
            };
        }
    }
    #endregion

    // ...
}
```

Once a class declares that it implements an interface, all (abstract[2]) members of the interface must be implemented. An abstract class is permitted to supply an abstract implementation of an interface member. A non-abstract implementation may throw a `NotImplementedException` type exception in the method body, but an implementation of the member must always be supplied.

One important characteristic of interfaces is that they can never be instantiated; you cannot use `new` to create an interface, so interfaces do not have instance constructors or finalizers. Interface instances are available only by instantiating a type that implements the interface. Furthermore, interfaces cannot include static members.[3] One key interface purpose is polymorphism, and polymorphism without an instance of the implementing type has little value.

Each (non-implemented[4]) interface member is abstract, forcing the derived class to implement it. Therefore, it is not possible to use the abstract modifier on interface members explicitly.[5]

When implementing an interface member in a type, there are two ways to do so: **explicitly** or **implicitly**. So far, we've seen only implicit implementations, where the type member that implements the interface member is a public member of the implementing type.

Explicit Member Implementation

Explicitly implemented methods are available only by calling them through the interface itself; this is typically achieved by casting an object to the interface. For example, to call `IListable.CellValues` in Listing 8.4, you must first cast the contact to `IListable` because of `CellValues`' explicit implementation.

Listing 8.4: Calling Explicit Interface Member Implementations

```
string?[] values;
Contact contact = new("Inigo Montoya");
```

2. The capability of adding non-abstract members to an interface was added in C# 8.0 but is essentially ignored until the end of the chapter.

3. Before C# 8.0.

4. Implemented members were only became available in C# 8.0 or later.

5. Before C# 8.0.

```
// ...

// ERROR:  Unable to call .CellValues directly
//         on a contact
values = contact.CellValues;

// First cast to IListable
values = ((IListable)contact).CellValues;

// ...
```

The cast and the call to `CellValues` occur within the same statement in this case. Alternatively, you could assign `contact` to an `IListable` variable before calling `CellValues`.

To declare an explicit interface member implementation, prefix the member name with the interface name (see Listing 8.5).

Listing 8.5: Explicit Interface Implementation

```
public class Contact : PdaItem, IListable, IComparable
{
    // ...

    #region IListable Members
    string?[] IListable.CellValues
    {
        get
        {
            return new string?[]
            {
                FirstName,
                LastName,
                Phone,
                Address
            };
        }
    }
    #endregion

    // ...
}
```

Listing 8.5 implements `CellValues` explicitly by prefixing the property name with `IListable`. Furthermore, since explicit interface implementations are directly associated with the interface, there is no need to modify them with `virtual`, `override`, or `public`. In fact, these modifiers are not allowed. The method is not treated as a public member of the class, so marking it as `public` would be misleading.

Note that even though the `override` keyword is not allowed on an interface, we will still use the term "override" when referring to members that implement the interface-defined signature.

Implicit Member Implementation

Notice that `CompareTo()` in Listing 8.5 does not include the `IComparable` prefix; it is implemented implicitly. With implicit member implementation, it is necessary only for the member to be public and for the member's signature to match the interface member's signature. Interface member implementation does not require use of the `override` keyword or any indication that this member is tied to the interface. Furthermore, since the member is declared just like any other class member, code that calls implicitly implemented members can do so directly, just as it would any other class member:

```
result = contact1.CompareTo(contact2);
```

In other words, implicit member implementation does not require a cast because the member is not hidden from direct invocation on the implementing class.

Many of the modifiers disallowed on an explicit member implementation are required or are optional on an implicit implementation. For example, implicit member implementations must be `public`. Furthermore, `virtual` is optional, depending on whether derived classes may override the implementation. Eliminating `virtual` will cause the member to behave as though it is `sealed`.

Explicit versus Implicit Interface Implementation

The key difference between implicit and explicit member interface implementation lies not in the syntax of the method declaration but rather in the ability to access the method by name through an instance of the type rather than via the interface.

When building a class hierarchy, it's desirable to model real-world "is a" relationships—a giraffe is a mammal, for example. These are *semantic* relationships. Interfaces are often used to model *mechanism* relationships. A `PdaItem` "is not a comparable," but it might well be `IComparable`. This interface has nothing to do with the semantic model; instead, it's a detail of the implementation mechanism. Explicit interface implementation is a technique for enabling the separation of mechanism concerns from model concerns. Forcing the caller to cast the object to an interface such as `IComparable` before treating the object as comparable explicitly separates in the code the concepts of talking to the model and dealing with its implementation mechanisms.

In general, it is preferable to limit the public surface area of a class to be "all model" with as little extraneous mechanism as possible. (Unfortunately, some mechanisms are unavoidable in .NET. In the real world, for example, you cannot get a giraffe's hash code or convert a giraffe to a string. However, you can get a `Giraffe`'s hash code [`GetHashCode()`] and convert it to a `string` [`ToString()`] in .NET. By using `object` as a common base class, .NET mixes model code with mechanism code, even if only to a limited extent.) Here are several guidelines that will help you choose between an explicit implementation and an implicit implementation.

- Is the member a core part of the class functionality?

  Consider the `CellValues` property implementation on the `Contact` class. This member is not an integral part of a `Contact` type, but rather a peripheral member probably accessed only by the `ConsoleListControl` class. As such, it doesn't make sense for the member to be immediately visible on a `Contact` object, cluttering up what could potentially already be a large list of members.

  Alternatively, consider the `IFileCompression.Compress()` member. Including an implicit `Compress()` implementation on a `ZipCompression` class is a perfectly reasonable choice: `Compress()` is a core part of the `ZipCompression` class's behavior, so it should be directly accessible from the `ZipCompression` class.

- Is the interface member name appropriate as a class member?

  Consider an `ITrace` interface with a member called `Dump()` that writes out a class's data to a trace log. Implementing `Dump()` implicitly on a `Person` or

`Truck` class would result in confusion as to which operation the method performs. Instead, it is preferable to implement the member explicitly so that the `Dump()` method can be called only from a data type of `ITrace`, where the meaning is clearer. Consider using an explicit implementation if a member's purpose is unclear on the implementing class.

- Does a class member with the same signature already exist? Explicit interface member implementation does not add a named element to the type's declaration space. Therefore, if there is already a potentially conflicting member of a type, a second one can be provided with the same name or signature as long as it is an explicit interface member.

Much of the decision-making regarding implicit versus explicit interface member implementation comes down to intuition. However, these questions provide suggestions about which issues to consider when making your choice. Since changing an implementation from implicit to explicit results in a version-breaking change, it is better to err on the side of defining interfaces explicitly, allowing them to be changed to implicit implementations later. Furthermore, since the decision between implicit and explicit does not have to be consistent across all interface members, defining some methods as explicit and others as implicit is fully supported.

Converting between the Implementing Class and Its Interfaces

Just as with a derived type and a base class, a conversion from an implementing type to its implemented interface is an implicit conversion. No cast operator is required because an instance of the implementing type will always provide all the members in the interface; therefore, the object can always be converted successfully to the interface type.

Although the conversion will always be successful from the implementing type to the implemented interface, many different types could implement a particular interface. Consequently, you can never be certain that a "downward" cast from an interface to one of its implementing types will be successful. Therefore, converting from an interface to one of its implementing types requires an explicit cast.

Interface Inheritance

Interfaces can derive from each other, resulting in an interface that inherits all the members[6] in its base interfaces. As shown in Listing 8.6, the interfaces directly derived from `IReadableSettingsProvider` are the explicit base interfaces.

LISTING 8.6: Deriving One Interface from Another

```
interface IReadableSettingsProvider
{
    string GetSetting(string name, string defaultValue);
}

interface ISettingsProvider : IReadableSettingsProvider
{
    void SetSetting(string name, string value);
}

public class FileSettingsProvider : ISettingsProvider
{
    #region ISettingsProvider Members
    public void SetSetting(string name, string value)
    {
        // ...
    }
    #endregion

    #region IReadableSettingsProvider Members
    public string GetSetting(string name, string defaultValue)
    {
        // ...
    }
    #endregion
}
```

In this case, `ISettingsProvider` is derived from `IReadableSettingsProvider` and therefore inherits its members. If `IReadableSettingsProvider` also had an explicit base interface, `ISettingsProvider` would inherit those members as well, and the full set of

6. Except C# 8.0's introduced non-private members.

interfaces in the derivation hierarchy would simply be the accumulation of base interfaces.

Note that if `GetSetting()` is implemented explicitly, it must be done using `IReadableSettingsProvider`. The declaration with `ISettingsProvider` in Listing 8.7 (with Output 8.2) will not compile.

LISTING 8.7: Explicit Member Declaration without the Containing Interface (Failure)

```
// ERROR:  GetSetting() not available on ISettingsProvider
string ISettingsProvider.GetSetting(
    string name, string defaultValue)
{
    // ...
}
```

OUTPUT 8.2

```
'ISettingsProvider.GetSetting' in explicit interface declaration
is not a member of interface.
```

This output appears in addition to an error indicating that `IReadableSettingsProvider.GetSetting()` is not implemented. The fully qualified interface member name used for explicit interface member implementation must reference the interface name in which it was originally declared.

Even though a class implements an interface (`ISettingsProvider`) that is derived from a base interface (`IReadableSettingsProvider`), the class can still declare an implementation of both interfaces overtly, as Listing 8.8 demonstrates.

LISTING 8.8: Using a Base Interface in the Class Declaration

```
public class FileSettingsProvider : ISettingsProvider,
    IReadableSettingsProvider
{
    #region ISettingsProvider Members
    public void SetSetting(string name, string value)
    {
        // ...
    }
    #endregion
```

```
    #region IReadableSettingsProvider Members
    public string GetSetting(string name, string defaultValue)
    {
        // ...
    }
    #endregion
}
```

In this listing, there is no change to the interface's implementations on the class. Although the additional interface implementation declaration on the class header is superfluous, it provides for better readability.

The decision to provide multiple interfaces rather than just one combined interface depends largely on what the interface designer wants to require of the implementing class. By providing an `IReadableSettingsProvider` interface, the designer communicates that implementers are required only to implement a settings provider that retrieves settings; they do not have to be able to write to those settings. This reduces the implementation burden by not imposing the complexities of writing settings as well.

In contrast, implementing `ISettingsProvider` assumes that there is never a reason to have a class that can write settings without reading them. The inheritance relationship between `ISettingsProvider` and `IReadableSettingsProvider`, therefore, forces the combined total of both interfaces on the `ISettingsProvider` class.

One final but important note: Although *inheritance* is the correct term, conceptually it is more accurate to say that an interface represents a contract, and one contract can specify that the provisions of another contract must also be followed. So, the code `ISettingsProvider : IReadableSettingsProvider` conceptually states that the `ISettingsProvider` contract requires also respecting the `IReadableSettingsProvider` contract, rather than that the `ISettingsProvider` "is a kind of" `IReadableSettingsProvider`. That being said, the remainder of the chapter will continue using the inheritance relationship terminology in accordance with the standard C# terminology.

Multiple Interface Inheritance

Just as classes can implement multiple interfaces, so interfaces can inherit from multiple interfaces. The syntax used for this purpose is consistent with class derivation and implementation, as shown in Listing 8.9.

LISTING 8.9: Multiple Interface Inheritance

```
interface IReadableSettingsProvider
{
    string GetSetting(string name, string defaultValue);
}

interface IWriteableSettingsProvider
{
    void SetSetting(string name, string value);
}

interface ISettingsProvider : IReadableSettingsProvider,
    IWriteableSettingsProvider
{
}
```

It is unusual to have an interface with no members, but it is a reasonable choice when implementing both interfaces together. The difference between Listing 8.9 and Listing 8.6 is that it is now possible to implement `IWriteableSettingsProvider` without supplying any read capability. Listing 8.6's `FileSettingsProvider` is unaffected. If it used explicit member implementation, however, specifying the interface to which a member belongs changes slightly.

Extension Methods on Interfaces

Perhaps one of the most important features of extension methods is the fact that they work with interfaces in addition to classes. The syntax used is identical to that used for extension methods for classes. The extended type (the first parameter and the parameter prefixed with `this`) is the interface that we extend. Listing 8.10 shows an extension method for `IListable()` that is declared on the `Listable` class.

In this example, the extension method is not for an `IListable` parameter (although it could have been), but rather for an `IListable[]` parameter. This demonstrates that C# allows extension methods not only on an instance of a

Listing 8.10: Interface Extension Methods

```
public class Program
{
    public static void Main()
    {
        Contact[] contacts = new Contact[] {
            new Contact(
                "Dick", "Traci",
                "123 Main St., Spokane, WA  99037",
                "123-123-1234")
            // ...
        };

        // Classes are implicitly converted to
        // their supported interfaces
        contacts.List(Contact.Headers);

        Console.WriteLine();

        Publication[] publications = new Publication[3] {
            new Publication("The End of Poverty: Economic Possibilities
↪for Our Time",
                "Jeffrey Sachs", 2006),
            new Publication("Orthodoxy",
                "G.K. Chesterton", 1908),
            new Publication(
                "The Hitchhiker's Guide to the Galaxy",
                "Douglas Adams", 1979)
            };
        publications.List(Publication.Headers);
    }
}

public static class Listable
{
    public static void List(
        this IListable[] items, string[] headers)
    {
        int[] columnWidths = DisplayHeaders(headers);

        for(int itemCount = 0; itemCount < items.Length; itemCount++)
        {
            if (items[itemCount] != null)
            {
```

```
                string?[] values = items[itemCount].CellValues;

                DisplayItemRow(columnWidths, values);
            }
        }
    }
    // ...
}
```

particular type but also on a collection of those objects. Support for extension methods is the foundation on which the Language Integrated Query (LINQ) capability is implemented. `IEnumerable` is the fundamental interface that all collections implement. By defining extension methods for `IEnumerable`, LINQ support was added to all collections. This radically changed programming with collections. We explore this topic in detail in Chapter 15.

BEGINNER TOPIC

Interface Diagramming

Interfaces in a UML-like[7] figure take two possible forms. First, you can show the interface as though it is an inheritance relationship similar to a class inheritance, as demonstrated in Figure 8.1 between `IPerson` and `IContact`. Alternatively, you can show the interface using a small circle, often referred to as a *lollipop*, exemplified by `IPerson` and `IContact` in Figure 8.1.

In Figure 8.1, `Contact` derives from `PdaItem` and implements `IContact`. In addition, it aggregates the `Person` class, which implements `IPerson`. Although the Visual Studio Class Designer does not support this practice, interfaces are sometimes shown as using a derivation-type arrow to a class. For example, `Person` could have an arrow to `IPerson` instead of a lollipop.

7. Unified Modeling Language (UML), a standard specification for modeling object design using graphical notation.

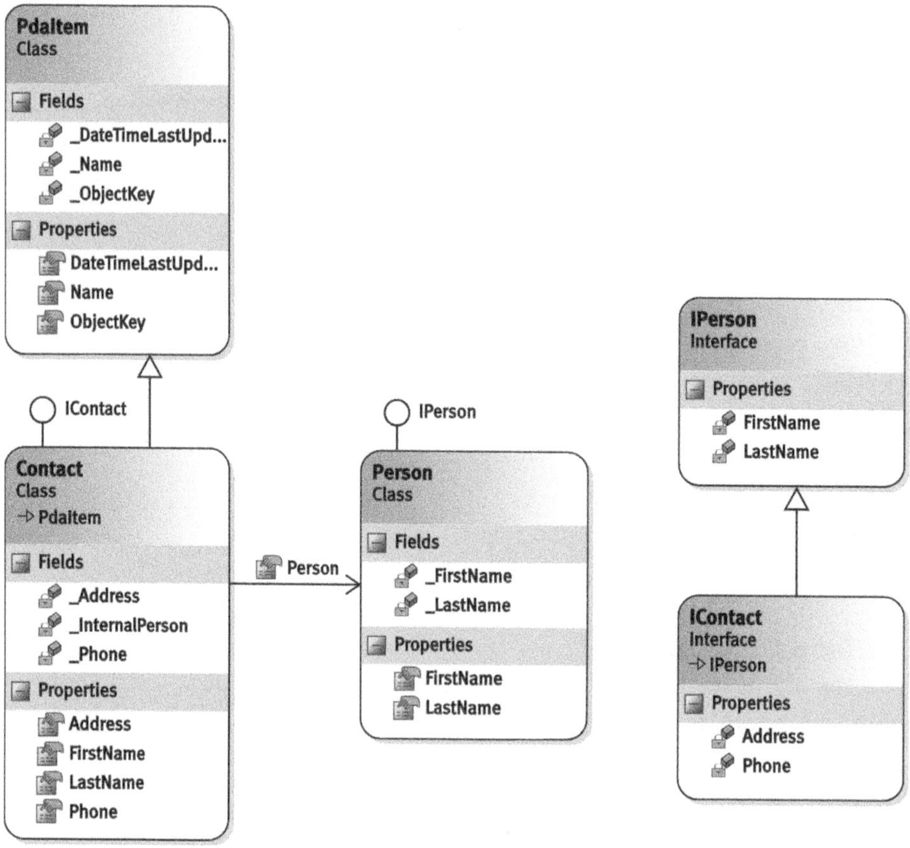

FIGURE 8.1: Working around single inheritance with aggregation and interfaces.

Begin 8.0

Versioning

Prior to C# 8.0, when creating a new version of a component or application that other developers have programmed against, you should not change interfaces. Because interfaces define a contract between the implementing class and the class using the interface, changing the interface is equivalent to changing the contract, which will possibly break any code written against the interface.

Changing or removing an interface member signature is obviously a code-breaking change, as any call to that member will no longer compile without modification. The same is true when you change public or protected member signatures on a class. However, unlike with classes, adding members to an interface could also prevent code from compiling without additional changes. The problem is that any class implementing the interface must do so entirely, and implementations for all members must be provided. With new interface members, the compiler will require that developers add new interface members to the class implementing the interface.

With C# 8.0, the "don't change interfaces" rule changes slightly. C# 8.0 added a mechanism for enabling a default implementation for an interface member, such that adding a member (you still can't remove or modify an existing member in a version-compatible way) will not trigger compiler errors on all implementations. Prior to C# 8.0, there is a way to achieve a similar result to changing an interface by adding an additional interface. In this section, we discuss both approaches.

Guidelines

DO NOT add members without a default implementation to a published interface.

Interface Versioning Prior to C# 8.0

The creation of `IDistributedSettingsProvider` in Listing 8.11 serves as a good example of extending an interface in a version-compatible way. Imagine that initially only the `ISettingsProvider` interface is defined (as it was in Listing 8.6). In the next version, however, it is determined that settings could be distributed to multiple resources (URIs[8]) (perhaps on a per-machine basis). To enable this constraint, the `IDistributedSettingsProvider` interface is created; it derives from `ISettingsProvider`.

8. Universal resource identifiers.

Listing 8.11: Deriving One Interface from Another

```
interface IDistributedSettingsProvider : ISettingsProvider
{
    /// <summary>
    /// Get the settings for a particular URI
    /// </summary>
    /// <param name="uri">
    /// The URI name the setting is related to</param>
    /// <param name="name">The name of the setting</param>
    /// <param name="defaultValue">
    /// The value returned if the setting is not found</param>
    /// <returns>The specified setting</returns>
    string GetSetting(
        string uri, string name, string defaultValue);

    /// <summary>
    /// Set the settings for a particular URI
    /// </summary>
    /// <param name="uri">
    /// The URI name the setting is related to</param>
    /// <param name="name">The name of the setting</param>
    /// <param name="value">The value to be persisted</param>
    /// <returns>The specified setting</returns>
    void SetSetting(
        string uri, string name, string value);
}
```

The important issue is that programmers with classes that implement `ISettingsProvider` can choose to upgrade the implementation to include `IDistributedSettingsProvider`, or they can ignore it.

If, instead of creating a new interface, the URI-related methods are added to `ISettingsProvider`, classes implementing this interface will potentially throw an exception at runtime and certainly will not successfully compile with the new interface definition. In other words, changing `ISettingsProvider` is a version-breaking change, both at the binary level and at the source code level.

Changing interfaces during the development phase is obviously acceptable, although perhaps laborious if implemented extensively. However, once an interface is published, it should not be changed. Instead, a second interface should be created, possibly deriving from the original interface. (Listing 8.11 includes XML comments describing the interface members, as discussed further in Chapter 10.)

Interface Versioning in C# 8.0 or Later

Until now, we have ignored the new C# 8.0 interface features except to mention that they exist. In this section, we abandon that restriction and describe the C# 8.0 feature set known as **default interface members**. As described earlier, changing a published interface in any way prior to C# 8.0 will break any code that implements the interface; therefore, published interfaces should not be changed. However, starting with C# 8.0, Microsoft introduced a new C# language feature that allows interfaces to have members with implementation—that is, concrete members, not just declarations. Consider, for example, the `CellColors` property included in Listing 8.12.

LISTING 8.12: Versioning Interfaces with Default Interface Members

```
public interface IListable
{
    // Return the value of each cell in the row
    string?[] CellValues
    {
        get;
    }

    ConsoleColor[] CellColors
    {
        get
        {
            var result = new ConsoleColor[CellValues.Length];
            // Using generic Array method to populate array
            // (see Chapter 12)
            Array.Fill(result, DefaultColumnColor);
            return result;
        }
    }
    static public ConsoleColor DefaultColumnColor { get; set; }
}

// ...

public class Contact : PdaItem, IListable
{
    // ...

    #region IListable
    string[] IListable.CellValues
```

```
    {
        get
        {
            return new string[]
            {
                FirstName,
                LastName,
                Phone,
                Address
            };
        }
    }
    // *** No CellColors implementation *** //
    #endregion IListable

    // ...
}

public class Publication : IListable
{
    // ...

    #region IListable
    string?[] IListable.CellValues
    {
        get
        {
            return new string[]
            {
                Title,
                Author,
                Year.ToString()
            };
        }
    }

    ConsoleColor[] IListable.CellColors
    {
        get
        {
            string?[] columns = ((IListable)this).CellValues;
            ConsoleColor[] result = ((IListable)this).CellColors;
            if (columns[YearIndex]?.Length != 4)
            {
                result[YearIndex] = ConsoleColor.Red;
            }
            return result;
```

```
        }
    }
    #endregion IListable
    // ...
}
```

In this listing, notice the addition of the `CellColors` property getter. As you can see, it includes an implementation even though it is the member of an interface. The feature is called a *default* interface member because it provides a default implementation of the method so that any class that implements the interface will already have a default implementation—so that code will continue to compile without any changes even though the interface has additional members. The `Contact` class, for example, has no implementation for the `CellColors` property getter, so it relies on the default implementation provided by the `IListable` interface.

Not surprisingly, you can override a default implementation of the method in the implementing class to provide a different behavior that makes more sense to the class. This behavior is all consistent with the purpose of enabling polymorphism as outlined at the beginning of the chapter.

However, the default interface member feature includes additional features. The primary purpose of these features is to support refactoring of default interface members (though some would debate this interpretation). To use them for any other purpose likely indicates a flaw in the code structure, because it implies the interface is used for more than polymorphism. Table 8.1 lists the additional language constructs along with some of their important limitations.

TABLE 8.1: Default Interface Refactoring Features

<table>
<tr><th>C# 8.0–Introduced Interface Construct</th><th>Sample Code</th></tr>
<tr><td>Static Members
The ability to define static members on the interface including fields, constructors, and methods. (This includes support for defining a static <code>Main</code> method—an entry point into your program.) The default accessibility for static members on interfaces is public.</td><td><pre>public interface ISampleInterface
{
private static string? _Field;
public static string? Field
{
get => _Field;
private set => _Field = value; }
static IsampleInterface() =>
Field = "Nelson Mandela";
public static string? GetField() => Field;
}</pre></td></tr>
<tr><td>Implemented Instance Properties and Methods
You can define implemented properties and members on interfaces. Since instance fields are not supported, properties cannot work against backing fields. Also, without instance fields support, there is no automatically implemented property support.
Note that to access a default implemented property, it is necessary to cast to the interface containing the member. The class (<code>Person</code>) does not have the default interface member available unless it is implemented.</td><td><pre>public interface IPerson
{
// Standard abstract property definitions
string FirstName { get; set; }
string LastName { get; set; }
string MiddleName { get; set; }
// Implemented instance properties and methods
public string Name => GetName();
public string GetName() =>
$"{FirstName} {LastName}";
}
public class Person
{
// ...
}
public class Program
{
public static void Main()
{
Person inigo = new Person("Inigo", "Montoya");
Console.Write(
((IPerson)inigo).Name);
}
}</pre></td></tr>
<tr><td><code>public</code> Access Modifier
The default for all instance interface members. Use this keyword to help clarify the accessibility of the code. Note, however, that the compiler-generated CIL code is identical with or without the <code>public</code> access modifier.</td><td><pre>public interface IPerson
{
// All members are public by default
string FirstName { get; set; }
public string LastName { get; set; }
string Initials =>
$"{FirstName[0]}{LastName[0]}";
public string Name => GetName();
public string GetName() =>
$"{FirstName} {LastName}";
}</pre></td></tr>
</table>

TABLE 8.1: Default Interface Refactoring Features (continued)

C# 8.0–Introduced Interface Construct	Sample Code

`protected` Access Modifier
Accessible only from members in classes that derive from `the defining class.`.
	`public interface IPerson`
	`{`
	`// ...`
	`protected void Initialize() =>`
	`{ /* ... */ };`
	`}`

`private` Access Modifier
The `private` access modifier restricts a member to be available for invocation only from the interface that declares it. It is designed to support refactoring of default interface members. All `private` members must include an implementation.
	`public interface IPerson`
	`{`
	`string FirstName { get; set; }`
	`string LastName { get; set; }`
	`string Name => GetName();`
	`private string GetName() =>`
	`$"{FirstName} {LastName}";`
	`}`

`internal` Access Modifier
`internal` members are only visible from within the same assembly in which they are declared.
	`public interface IPerson`
	`{`
	`string FirstName { get; set; }`
	`string LastName { get; set; }`
	`string Name => GetName();`
	`internal string GetName() =>`
	`$"{FirstName} {LastName}";`
	`}`

`private protected` Access Modifier
A super set of `private` and `protected`; `private protected` members are visible from within the same assembly and from within other interfaces that derive from the containing interface. Like `protected` members, classes external to the assembly cannot see `protected` internal members.
	`public interface IPerson`
	`{`
	`string FirstName { get; set; }`
	`string LastName { get; set; }`
	`string Name => GetName();`
	`protected internal string GetName() =>`
	`$"{FirstName} {LastName}";`
	`}`

Table 8.1: Default Interface Refactoring Features (continued)

C# 8.0–Introduced Interface Construct	Sample Code

`private protected` Access Modifier
Accessing a `private protected` member is only possible from the containing interface or interfaces that derive from the implementing interface. Even classes implanting the interface cannot access a `private protected` member, as demonstrated by the `PersonTitle` property in `Person`.
	`class Program`
	`{`
	`static void Main()`
	`{`
	`IPerson? person = null;`
	`// Non-deriving classes cannot call`
	`// private protected member.`
	`// _ = person?.GetName();`
	`Console.WriteLine(person);`
	`}`
	`}`
	`public interface IPerson`
	`{`
	`string FirstName { get; }`
	`string LastName { get; }`
	`string Name => GetName();`
	`private protected string GetName() =>`
	`$"{FirstName} {LastName}";`
	`}`
	`public interface IEmployee: IPerson`
	`{`
	`int EmpoyeeId => GetName().GetHashCode();`
	`}`
	`public class Person : IPerson`
	`{`
	`public Person(`
	`string firstName, string lastName)`
	`{`
	`FirstName = firstName ??`
	`throw new ArgumentNullException(nameof(firstName));`
	`LastName = lastName ??`
	`throw new ArgumentNullException(nameof(lastName));`
	`}`
	`public string FirstName { get; }`
	`public string LastName { get; }`
	`// private protected interface members`
	`// are not accessible in derived classes.`
	`// public int PersonTitle =>`
	`// GetName().ToUpper();`
	`}`

TABLE 8.1: Default Interface Refactoring Features (continued)

<table>
<tr><th>C# 8.0–Introduced Interface Construct</th><th>Sample Code</th></tr>
<tr><td><code>virtual</code> Modifier
By default, an implemented interface member is <code>virtual</code>, meaning that derived implementations of the method with the same signature will be invoked when the interface member is invoked. As with the <code>public</code> access modifier, however, you can decorate a member as <code>virtual</code> explicitly to provide clarity. For non-implemented interface members, <code>virtual</code> is not allowed. Similarly, <code>virtual</code> is incompatible with <code>private</code>, <code>static</code>, and <code>sealed</code> modifiers.</td><td><code>public interface IPerson
{
// virtual is not allowed on members
// without implementation
/* virtual */ string FirstName { get; set; }
string LastName { get; set; }
virtual string Name => GetName();
private string GetName() =>
$"{FirstName} {LastName}";
}</code></td></tr>
<tr><td><code>sealed</code> Modifier
To prevent a derived class from overriding a method, mark it as <code>sealed</code>, thus ensuring that the method implementation cannot be modified by derived classes.
See Listing 8.13 for more information.</td><td><code>public interface IWorkflowActivity
{
// Private and, therefore, not virtual
private void Start() =>
Console.WriteLine(
"IWorkflowActivity.Start()...");
// Sealed to prevent overriding
sealed void Run()
{
try
{
Start();
InternalRun();
}
finally
{
Stop();
}
}
protected void InternalRun();
// Private and, therefore, not virtual
private void Stop() =>
Console.WriteLine(
"IWorkflowActivity.Stop()..");
}</code></td></tr>
</table>

TABLE 8.1: Default Interface Refactoring Features (continued)

<table>
<tr><th>C# 8.0–Introduced Interface Construct</th><th>Sample Code</th></tr>
<tr><td><code>abstract</code> Modifier
The <code>abstract</code> modifier is only allowable on members without an implementation, but the keyword has no effect as such members are abstract by default.
All abstract members are automatically <code>virtual</code> and explicitly declaring abstract members as <code>virtual</code> triggers a compile error.</td><td><pre>
public interface IPerson
{
// virtual is not allowed on members
// without implementation
/* virtual */ abstract string FirstName
{ get; set; }
string LastName { get; set; }
// abstract is not allowed on members
// with implementation
/* abstract */ string Name => GetName();
private string GetName() =>
$"{FirstName} {LastName}";
}
</pre></td></tr>
<tr><td>Partial Interfaces and Partial Methods
It is now possible to provide partial implementations of a method with no outgoing data (returns or <code>ref</code>/<code>out</code> data) and optionally the fully implemented method in a second declaration of the same interface.
Partial methods are always <code>private</code>—they do not support access modifiers</td><td><pre>
public partial interface IThing
{
string Value { get; protected set; }
void SetValue(string value)
{
AssertValueIsValid(value);
Value = value;
}
partial void AssertValueIsValid(string value);
}
public partial interface IThing
{
partial void AssertValueIsValid(string value)
{
// Throw if value is invalid.
switch(value)
{
case null:
throw new ArgumentNullException(
nameof(value));
case "":
throw new ArgumentException(
"Empty string is invalid",
nameof(value));
case string _ when
string.IsNullOrWhiteSpace(value):
throw new ArgumentException(
"Can't be whitespace",
nameof(value));
};
}
}
</pre></td></tr>
</table>

There are a couple of points to highlight in Table 8.1. First, it is important to note that automatically implemented property support is not available because instance fields (which back an automatically implemented property) are not supported. This is a significant difference from abstract classes, which do support instance fields and automatically implemented properties.

Second, notice static members on interfaces are also `public` by default. While static members always have an implementation and map closely to class static members in this regard, in contrast, the purpose of interface instance members is to support polymorphism, so they default to `public`.

Additional Encapsulation and Polymorphism with Protected Interface Members

When creating a class, programmers should be careful about choosing to allow overriding of a method, since they cannot control the derived implementation. Virtual methods should not include critical code because such methods may never be called if the derived class overrides them.

Listing 8.13 includes a virtual `Run()` method. If the `WorkflowActivity` programmer calls `Run()` with the expectation that the critical `Start()` and `Stop()` methods will be called, then the `Run()` method may fail.

LISTING 8.13: Carelessly Relying on a Virtual Method Implementation

```
public class WorkflowActivity
{
    private static void Start()
    {
        // Critical code
    }
    public virtual void Run()
    {
        Start();
        // Do something...
        Stop();
    }
    private static void Stop()
    {
        // Critical code
    }
}
```

In overriding `Run()`, a developer could perhaps not call the critical `Start()` and `Stop()` methods.

Now consider a fully implemented version of this scenario with the following encapsulation requirements:

- It should not be possible to override `Run()`.
- It should not be possible to invoke `Start()` or `Stop()`, as the order in which they execute is entirely under the control of the containing type (which we will name `IWorkflowActivity`).
- It should be possible to replace whatever executes in the "Do something ..." code block.
- If it were reasonable to override `Start()` and `Stop()`, then the class implementing them should not necessarily be able to invoke them—they are part of the base implementation.
- The deriving types should be allowed to provide a `Run()` method, but it should not be invoked when the `Run()` method is invoked on `IWorkflowActivity`.

To meet all these requirements and more, C# 8.0 provides support for a protected interface member, which has some significant differences from a protected member on a class. Listing 8.14 demonstrates the differences, and Output 8.3 shows the results.

Listing 8.14: Forcing the Desirable `Run()` Encapsulation

```
public interface IWorkflowActivity
{
    // Private and, therefore, not virtual
    private static void Start() =>
        Console.WriteLine(
            "IWorkflowActivity.Start()...");

    // Sealed to prevent overriding.
    sealed void Run()
    {
        try
        {
            Start();
            InternalRun();
        }
        finally
        {
            Stop();
```

```
        }
    }

    protected void InternalRun();

    // Private and, therefore, not virtual
    private static void Stop() =>
        Console.WriteLine(
            "IWorkflowActivity.Stop()...");
}

public interface IExecuteProcessActivity : IWorkflowActivity
{
    protected void RedirectStandardInOut() =>
        Console.WriteLine(
            "IExecuteProcessActivity.RedirectStandardInOut()...");

    // Sealed not allowed when overriding.
    /* sealed */
    void IWorkflowActivity.InternalRun()
    {
        RedirectStandardInOut();
        ExecuteProcess();
        RestoreStandardInOut();
    }
    protected void ExecuteProcess();
    protected void RestoreStandardInOut() =>
        Console.WriteLine(
            "IExecuteProcessActivity.RestoreStandardInOut()...");
}

public class ExecuteProcessActivity : IExecuteProcessActivity
{
    public ExecuteProcessActivity(string executablePath) =>
        ExecutableName = executablePath
            ?? throw new ArgumentNullException(nameof(executablePath));

    public string ExecutableName { get; }

    void IExecuteProcessActivity.RedirectStandardInOut() =>
        Console.WriteLine(
            "ExecuteProcessActivity.RedirectStandardInOut()...");

    void IExecuteProcessActivity.ExecuteProcess() =>
        Console.WriteLine(
            $"ExecuteProcessActivity.IExecuteProcessActivity.
↪ExecuteProcess()...");
```

```
    public static void Run()
    {
        ExecuteProcessActivity activity = new("dotnet");
        // Protected members cannot be invoked
        // by the implementing class even when
        //  implemented in the class.
        // ((IWorkflowActivity)this).InternalRun();
        //  activity.RedirectStandardInOut();
        //  activity.ExecuteProcess();
        Console.WriteLine(
            @$"Executing non-polymorphic Run() with process '{
                activity.ExecutableName}'.");
    }
}

public class Program
{
    static public void Main()
    {
        ExecuteProcessActivity activity = new("dotnet");

        Console.WriteLine(
            "Invoking ((IExecuteProcessActivity)activity).Run()...");
        // Output:
        // Invoking ((IExecuteProcessActivity)activity).Run()...
        // IWorkflowActivity.Start()...
        // ExecuteProcessActivity.RedirectStandardInOut()...
        // ExecuteProcessActivity.IExecuteProcessActivity.
        // ExecuteProcess()...
        // IExecuteProcessActivity.RestoreStandardInOut()...
        // IWorkflowActivity.Stop()..
        ((IExecuteProcessActivity)activity).Run();

        // Output:
        // Invoking activity.Run()...
        // Executing non-polymorphic Run() with process 'dotnet'.
        Console.WriteLine();
        Console.WriteLine(
            "Invoking activity.Run()...");
        ExecuteProcessActivity.Run();
    }
}
```

Let's consider how Listing 8.14 meets the requirements outlined earlier.

OUTPUT 8.3

```
Invoking ((IExecuteProcessActivity)activity).Run()...
IWorkflowActivity.Start()...
ExecuteProcessActivity.RedirectStandardInOut()...
ExecuteProcessActivity.IExecuteProcessActivity.ExecutProcess()...
IExecuteProcessActivity.RestoreStandardInOut()...
IWorkflowActivity.Stop()..

Invoking activity.Run()...
Executing non-polymorphic Run() with process 'dotnet'.
```

Notice that `IWorkflowActivity.Run()` is sealed and, therefore, not virtual. This prevents any derived types from changing its implementation. Any invocation of `Run()`, given a `IWorkflowActivity` type, will always execute the `IWorkflowActivity` implementation.

`IWorkflowActivity`'s `Start()` and `Stop()` methods are private, so they are invisible to all other types. Even though `IExecutProcessActivity` seemingly has start/stop-type activities, `IWorkflowActivity` doesn't allow for replacing its implementations.

`IWorkflowActivity` defines a protected `InternalRun()` method that allows `IExecuteProcessActivity` (and `ExecuteProcessActivity`, if desirable) to overload it. However, notice that no member of `ExecuteProcessActivity` can invoke `InternalRun()`. Perhaps that method should never be run out of sequence from `Start()` and `Stop()`, so only an interface (`IWorkflowActivity` or `IExecuteProcessActivity`) in the hierarchy is allowed to invoke the protected member.

All interface members that are protected can override any default interface member if they do so explicitly. For example, both the `RedirectStandardInOut()` and `RestoreStandardInOut()` implementations on `ExecuteProcessActivity` are prefixed with `IExecuteProcessActivity`. And, like with the protected `InternalRun()` method, the type implementing the interface cannot invoke the protected members; for example, `ExecuteProcessActivity` can't invoke `RedirectStandardInOut()` and `RestoreStandardInOut()`, even though they are implemented on the same type.

Even though only one of them is explicitly declared as virtual, both `RedirectStandardInOut()` and `RestoreStandardInOut()` are virtual

(virtual is the default unless a member is sealed). As such, the most derived implementation will be invoked. Therefore, when `IExecuteProcessActivity.InternalRun()` invokes `RedirectStandardInOut()`, the implementation on `ExecuteProcessActivity()` will execute instead of the implementation from `IExecuteProcessActivity`.

A derived type's implementation can potentially provide a method that matches a sealed signature in the parent. For example, if `ExecuteProcessActivity` provides a `Run()` method that matches the signature of `Run()` in `IWorkflowActivity`, the implementation associated with the type will execute, rather than the most derived implementation. In other words, `Program.Main()`'s invocation of `((IExecuteProcessActivity)activity).Run()` calls `IExecuteProcessActivity.Run()`, while `activity.Run()` calls `ExecuteProessActivity.Run()`—where `activity` is of type `ExecuteProcessActivity`.

In summary, the encapsulation available with protected interface members, along with the other member modifiers, provides a comprehensive mechanism for encapsulation—albeit an admittedly complicated one.

Extension Methods versus Default Interface Members

When it comes to extending a published interface with additional functionality, when is a default interface member preferable to creating an extension method or creating a second interface that derives from the first and adds additional members? The following factors should be considered when making this decision:

- Both conceptually support overriding by implementing a method of the same signature on an instance of the interface.
- Extension methods can be added from outside the assembly that contains the interface definition.
- While default interface properties are allowed, there is no instance storage location available (fields are not allowed) for the property value, limiting the applicability to calculated properties.

- While there is no support for extension properties, calculations can be provided with "getter" extension methods (e.g., `GetData()`), without limiting them to .NET Core 3.0 or later frameworks.
- Providing a second derived interface supports defining both properties and methods without introducing a version incompatibility or a framework limitation.
- The derived interface approach requires implementing types to add the new interface and take advantage of the new capability.
- Default interface members can be invoked only from the interface type. Even implementing objects don't have access to the default interface members without casting to the interface. In other words, default interface members behave like explicitly implemented interface members unless the base class provides an implementation.
- Protected virtual members can be defined on interfaces, but they are only available as such to deriving interfaces—not to classes implementing the interface.
- A default interface member may be overridden by the implementing classes, thereby allowing each class to define the behavior if desired. With extension methods, the binding is resolved based on the extension method being accessible at compile time. As a result, the implementation is determined at compile time instead of at runtime. With extension methods, therefore, the implementing class author can't provide a different implementation for the method when it's called from libraries. For example, `System.Linq.Enumerable.Count()` provides a special implementation index-based collection by casting to the list implementation to retrieve the count. As a result, the only way to take advantage of the improved efficiency is to implement a list-based interface. In contrast, with a default interface implementation, any implementing class could override this method to provide a better version.

In summary, adding property polymorphic behavior is only possible with a second interface or default interface members. When only methods, and not properties, are part of the updated interface, extension methods are preferred.

Guidelines

CONSIDER using extension methods or an additional interface in place of default interface members when adding methods to a published interface.

DO use extension methods when the interface providing the polymorphic behavior is not under your control.

Interfaces Compared with Abstract Classes

Interfaces introduce another category of data types. (They are one of the few categories of types that don't extend `System.Object`.[9]) Unlike classes, however, interfaces can never be instantiated. An interface instance is accessible only via a reference to an object that implements the interface. It is not possible to use the `new` operator with an interface; therefore, interfaces cannot contain any instance constructors or finalizers. Prior to C# 8.0, static members are not allowed on interfaces.

Interfaces are similar to abstract classes, sharing such features as the lack of instantiation capability. Table 8.2 lists additional comparisons. Given that abstract classes and interfaces have their own sets of advantages and disadvantages, you must make a cost–benefit decision based on the comparisons in Table 8.2 and the guidelines that follow to make the right choice.

Begin 11.0

TABLE 8.2: Comparing Abstract Classes and Interfaces

Abstract Classes	Interfaces
Cannot be instantiated directly, but only by instantiating a non-abstract derived class.	Cannot be instantiated directly, but only by instantiating an implementing type.

9. The others are pointer types and type parameter types. However, every interface type is convertible to `System.Object`, and it is permissible to call the methods of `System.Object` on any instance of an interface, so perhaps this is a hairsplitting distinction.

TABLE 8.2: Comparing Abstract Classes and Interfaces (continued)

Abstract Classes	Interfaces
Derived classes either must be abstract themselves or must implement all abstract members.	Implementing types must implement all abstract interface members.
Can add additional non-abstract members that all derived classes can inherit without breaking cross-version compatibility.	Can add additional default interface members in C# 8.0/.NET Core 3.0 that all derived classes can inherit without breaking cross-version compatibility.
Can declare methods, properties, and fields (along with all other member types, including constructors and finalizers).	Instance members are limited to methods and properties, not fields, constructors, or finalizers. All static members are possible, including static constructors, static events, and static fields.
Members may be instance or static, and optionally abstract, and may provide implementations for non-abstract members that can be used by derived classes.	Starting with C# 8.0/.NET Core 3.0, members may be instance, abstract, or static, and may provide implementations for non-abstract members that can be used by derived classes.
Members may be declared as virtual or not. Members that should not be overridden (see Listing 8.13) would not be declared as virtual.	All (non-sealed) members are virtual, whether explicitly designated as such or not; therefore, there is no way for an interface to prevent overriding the behavior.
A derived class may derive from only a single base class.	An implementing type may arbitrarily implement many interfaces.
Static abstract members are not supported.	C# 11 introduced static abstract members.

Guidelines

CONSIDER defining an interface if you need to support its functionality on types that already inherit from some other type.

In summary, assuming a .NET Core 3.0 framework is acceptable, C# 8.0 (or later) defined interfaces have all the capabilities of abstract classes except the ability to declare an instance field. Given that an implementing type can override an interface's property to provide storage, which the interface then leverages, interfaces virtually provide a superset of what an abstract class provides. Furthermore, interfaces support a more encapsulated version of protected access in addition to multiple inheritance. Regardless, default interface members are intended for versioning not polymorphism so use caution when leveraging them for the latter.

C# 11 added support for static abstract members that would be included in the contract that implementing interfaces would need to implement. Since these don't become fully functional without generics, we postpone a discussion on this topic until Chapter 12.

End 11.0

End 8.0

Interfaces Compared with Attributes

Interfaces with no members at all, inherited or otherwise, are sometimes used to represent information about a type. For example, you might create a marker `IObsolete` interface to indicate that a type has been replaced by another type. This is generally considered to be an abuse of the interface mechanism: Interfaces should be used to represent which functions a type can perform, not to indicate facts about particular types. Instead of marker interfaces, use attributes for this purpose. See Chapter 18 for more details.

Guidelines

AVOID using "marker" interfaces with no members; use attributes instead.

Summary

Interfaces are a key element of object-oriented programming in C#. They provide polymorphic capabilities like abstract classes without using up the single-inheritance option, because classes can implement multiple interfaces. Starting with C# 8.0/.NET Core 3.0, interfaces can include implementation via the use of default interface members, almost giving them a superset of the capabilities of abstract classes if backward compatibility is not required.

In C#, the implementation of interfaces can be either explicit or implicit, depending on whether the implementing class is used to expose an interface member directly or only via a conversion to the interface. Furthermore, the granularity of whether the implementation is explicit or implicit is determined at the member level: One member may be implicitly implemented, while another member of the same interface is explicitly implemented.

9

Introducing Structs and Records

You have used value types throughout this book; for example, `int` is a value type. This chapter discusses not only using value types but also defining custom value types. One of the key concepts for a value type is the ability to compare instances for the same value, a concept also possible on reference types. However, rather than coding this feature from scratch, C# 9.0 and 10.0 provide shortcuts via the record construct using a record struct and a record class, respectively. This chapter explores structs, records, and a specific value type called an enum.

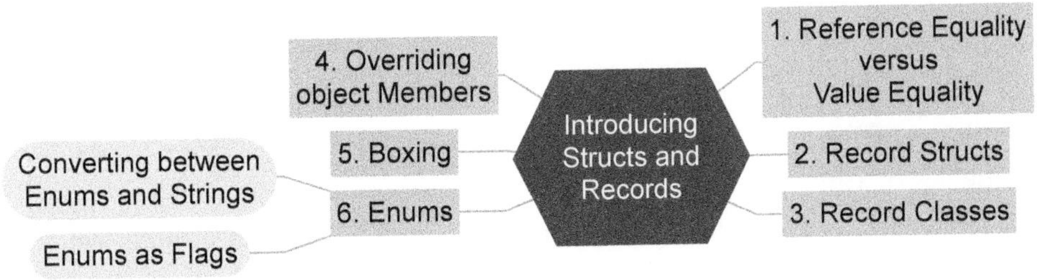

While there are noticeable complications to correctly implementing custom-built structs, they are relatively rare. They obviously play an important role within C# development, but the number of custom-built structs declared by typical developers is usually tiny compared to the number of custom-built classes. Heavy use of custom-built structs is most common in code intended to interoperate with unmanaged code. Furthermore, they should not be defined unless a single value consumes 16 bytes or less of storage, is immutable, and is infrequently boxed. These are concepts we flush out within this chapter.

Guidelines

DO NOT define a struct unless it logically represents a single value, consumes 16 bytes or less of storage, is immutable, and is infrequently boxed.

BEGINNER TOPIC

Categories of Types

All types discussed so far have fallen into one of two categories: reference types and value types. The differences between the types in each category stem from differences in copying strategies, which in turn result in each type being stored differently in memory. As a review, this Beginner Topic reintroduces the value type/reference type discussion for those readers who are unfamiliar with these issues.

Value Types

Variables of **value types** directly contain their values, as shown in Figure 9.1. The variable name is associated directly with the storage location in memory where the value is stored. Because of this, when a second variable is assigned the value of an original variable, a copy of the original variable's value is made to the storage location associated with the second variable. Two variables never refer to the same storage location (unless one or both are `out` or `ref` parameters, which are, by definition, aliases for another variable). Changing the value of the original variable will not affect the value in the second variable, because each variable is associated with a different storage location. Consequently, changing the value of one value type variable cannot affect the value of any other value type variable.

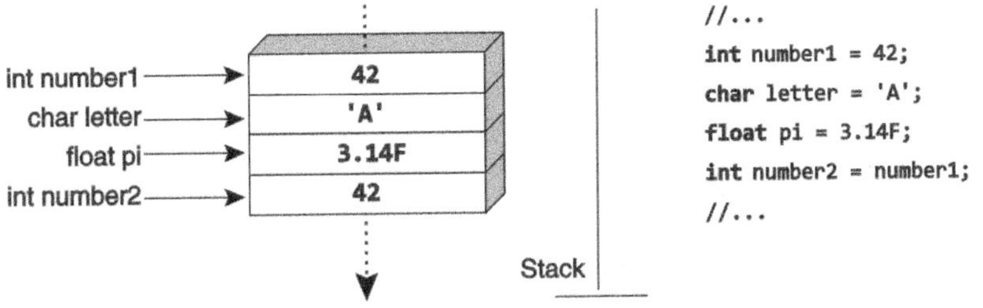

FIGURE 9.1: Value types contain the data directly

A value type variable is like a piece of paper that has a number written on it. If you want to change the number, you can erase it and replace it with a different number. If you have a second piece of paper, you can copy the number from the first piece of paper, but the two pieces of paper are then independent; erasing and replacing the number on one of them does not change the other.

Similarly, passing an instance of a value type to a method such as `Console.WriteLine()` will also result in a memory copy from the storage location associated with the argument to the storage location associated with the parameter, and any changes to the parameter variable inside the method will not affect the original value within the caller. Since value types require a memory copy, they generally should be defined to consume a small amount of memory (typically 16 bytes or less).

Guidelines

AVOID creating value types that consume more than 16 bytes of memory.

Values of value types are often short-lived; in many situations, a value is needed only for a portion of an expression or for the activation of a method. In these cases, variables and temporary values of value types can often be stored in the **temporary storage pool**, called the *stack*. (This term is actually a misnomer: There is no requirement that the temporary pool allocates its storage off the stack. In fact, as an implementation detail, it frequently chooses to allocate storage out of available registers instead.)

The temporary pool is less costly to clean up than the garbage-collected heap. However, value types tend to be copied more than reference types, and that copying can impose a performance cost of its own. Do not fall into the trap of believing that value types are faster because they can be allocated on the stack.

Reference Types

In contrast, the value of a reference type variable is a reference to an instance of an object (see Figure 9.2). Variables of reference types store the reference (typically implemented as the memory address) where the data for the object instance is located instead of storing the data directly, as a variable of a value type does. Therefore, to access the data, the runtime reads the reference out of the variable and then dereferences it to reach the location in memory that actually contains the data for the instance.

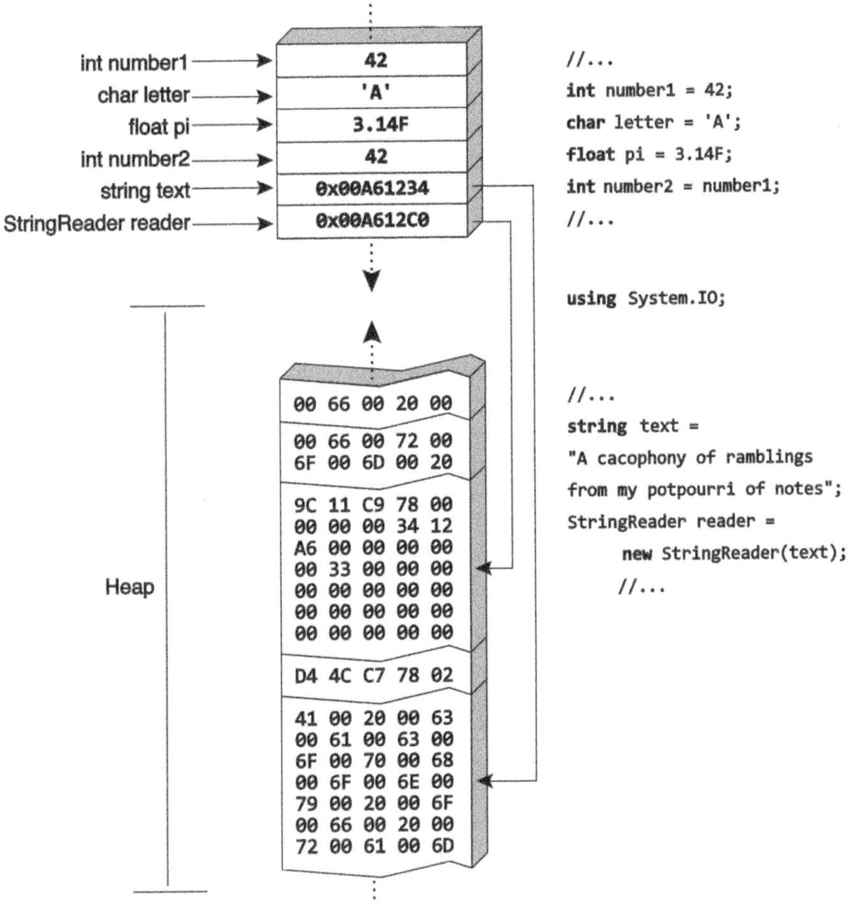

FIGURE 9.2: Reference types point to the heap

A reference type variable, therefore, has two storage locations associated with it: the storage location directly associated with the variable and the storage location referred to by the reference that is the value stored in the variable.

A reference type variable is, again, like a piece of paper that always has something written on it. Imagine a piece of paper that has a house address written on it—for example, "123 Sesame Street, New York City." The piece of paper is a variable; the address is a reference to a building. Neither the paper nor the address written on it is the building, and the location of the paper need not have anything whatsoever to do with the location of the building to which its contents refer. If you make a copy of that reference on another piece of paper, the contents of both pieces of paper refer to the same building. If you then paint that building green, the building referred to by both pieces of paper can be observed to be green, because the references refer to the same thing.

The storage location directly associated with the variable (or temporary value) is treated no differently than the storage location associated with a value type variable: If the variable is known to be short-lived, it is allocated on the short-term storage pool. The value of a reference type variable is always either a reference to a storage location in the garbage-collected heap or `null`.

Compared to a variable of a value type, which stores the data of the instance directly, accessing the data associated with a reference involves an extra hop: First, the reference must be dereferenced to find the storage location of the actual data, and then the data can be read or written. Copying a reference type value copies only the reference, which is small. (A reference is guaranteed to be no larger than the bit size of the processor: A 32-bit machine has 4-byte references, a 64-bit machine has 8-byte references, and so on.) Copying the value of a value type copies all the data, which could be large. Therefore, in some circumstances, reference types are more efficient to copy. This is why the guideline for value types is to ensure that they are never more than 16 bytes or thereabouts; if a value type is more than four times as expensive to copy as a reference, it probably should simply be a reference type.

Since reference types copy only a reference to the data, two different variables can refer to the same data. In such a case, changing the data through one variable will be observed to change the data for the other variable as well. This happens both for assignments and for method calls.

To continue our previous analogy, if you pass the address of a building to a method, you make a copy of the paper containing the reference and hand the copy to the method. The method cannot change the contents of the original paper to refer to a different building. Suppose the method paints the referred-to building. Then, when the method returns, the caller can observe that the building to which the caller is still referring is now a different color.

Reference Equality versus Value Equality

Before we consider examples, however, let's consider why we need to implement **value-based equality** (or **value equality** for short) in the first place. Two references are identical (**reference equal**) if both refer to the same instance of an object. On the other hand, objects that have the same values are **value equal**. And, to support value equal, a type needs to implement **value-based equality**. Two objects that are reference equal obviously are also value equal—the comparison is between two references to the same object. However, two objects can be of equal value if the (relevant) data between them is also equal. Only reference types can be reference equal, thereby supporting the concept of **identity**—the two references refer to the same instance.

In contrast, value types can never be reference equal. If you compare whether 42 is reference equal to 42, the answer is always false. Each value type is stored in a different location (reference) in memory, and even the simple act of passing value types to method for comparison will create additional copies of the value types.

> **NOTE**
>
> Calling `ReferenceEquals()` on value types will always return `false`.

While value types can never be reference equal, a reference type can support value equals. `object` includes a static method called `ReferenceEquals()` that checks whether the two arguments are identical—reference equal. In addition, `object` defines a virtual `Equals()` method that, by default, relies on `ReferenceEquals()` for reference types. However, this `Equals()` method can be customized (on both reference types and value types) so that they implement value equality rather than reference.

In fact, you should always override `Equals()` on value types because otherwise you would be left with the default implementation that compares only the first field for value equality. This, however, is insufficient. If a value type had three properties, for example, then checking for value equality by comparing only the first one would likely be inadequate. For example, given an `Angle` object, a comparison of the first property (`Degrees`) is not adequate. Two `Angles` are equal only if `Degrees`,

`Minutes`, and `Seconds` are equal (and potentially any other properties that the `Angle` includes). Therefore, it is almost always necessary to provide a custom implementation of value equality on a value type.

Value equality is not limited to value types, however. Value type equality might also make sense on a reference type. `string` is a great example. Although `string` is a reference type, the comparison of two strings should be equal if all the letters in the string are identical, even if the two strings are different instances.

In addition, a correct override of `Equals()` requires a host of additional members to exist and potentially be overridden, as described later in the section "Implementing Value Equality" (https://essentialcsharp.com/implementing-value-equality). These include `GetHashCode()` and the `==` and `!=` operators. Before then, however, let's delve into how to define a value type.

> **NOTE**
>
> The implementation of `object.Equals()`, the default implementation on all objects before overriding, relies on `ReferenceEquals()` alone. All value types override the default implementation to instead compare one or more values within the value type. Reference types can optionally also override `Equals()` to support value equality. It is always necessary to implement equality on custom value types.

Begin 9.0

Structs

All the C# built-in types, such as `bool` and `int`, are value types, except for `string` and `object`, which are reference types. Numerous additional value types are provided within the framework. Developers can also define their own value types.

To define a custom value type, you use a syntax similar to the syntax you would use to define class and interface types. The key difference in the syntax is that value types use the keyword `struct` (Listing 9.1).

Unfortunately, the commented-out ellipses represent a host of complexity as we will come to see later in the chapter.

Listing 9.1: Example `struct`

```
public struct Angle
{
    // ...
}
```

Declaring a Record Struct

Fortunately, starting with C# 9.0, a lot of the complexity associated with creating a struct is eliminated with a new contextual keyword—`record`—that triggers the compiler into generating much of the important and complex code related to value type behavior. Listing 9.2 provides an example. With this simple syntax, we have a value type that describes a high-precision angle in terms of its degrees, minutes, and seconds. (A *minute* is one-sixtieth of a degree, and a *second* is one-sixtieth of a minute.) This system is used in navigation because it has the nice property that an arc of one minute over the surface of the ocean at the equator is exactly one nautical mile.

Listing 9.2: Declaring a `struct`

```
// Use the record struct construct to declare a value type
public readonly record struct Angle(
    int Degrees, int Minutes, int Seconds, string? Name = null);
```

The syntax, which uses a primary constructor, is all that is needed to define the entire type. Unlike regular primary constructors explained in Chapter 6 (and not available until C# 12.0), however, a record's primary constructor also generates an initial set of properties from the (optional[1]) positional parameters. As a result, this simple code construct, called a **record struct**, has all the requisites of what you need to build a value type including value type declaration, data storage with properties, immutability, constructor initialization, deconstruction, equivalence behavior, and

1. Both the positional parameters and the parentheses surrounding them (when there are no positional parameters) are optional. Although it would be peculiar to declare with only parenthesis, as doing so would be similar to declaring an empty struct or class.

even ToString() diagnostic capabilities. Listing 9.3 demonstrates working with the Angle type.

LISTING 9.3: Working with the Record Struct

```
using System.Diagnostics;

public class Program
{
    public static void Main()
    {
        (int degrees, int minutes, int seconds) = (90, 0, 0);

        // The constructor is generated using positional parameters
        Angle angle = new(degrees, minutes, seconds);

        // Records include a ToString() implementation
        // that returns:
        //   "Angle { Degrees = 90, Minutes = 0, Seconds = 0, Name =  }"
        Console.WriteLine(angle.ToString());

        // Records have a deconstructor using the
        // positional parameters.
        if (angle is (int, int, int, string) angleData)
        {
            Trace.Assert(angle.Degrees == angleData.Degrees);
            Trace.Assert(angle.Minutes == angleData.Minutes);
            Trace.Assert(angle.Seconds == angleData.Seconds);
        }

        Angle copy = new(degrees, minutes, seconds);
        // Records provide a custom equality operator.
        Trace.Assert(angle == copy);

        // The with operator is the equivalent of
        // Angle copy = new(degrees, minutes, seconds);
        copy = angle with { };
        Trace.Assert(angle == copy);

        // The with operator has object initializer type
        // syntax for instantiating a modified copy.
        Angle modifiedCopy = angle with { Degrees = 180 };
        Trace.Assert(angle != modifiedCopy);
    }
}
```

You will notice from the Listing 9.2 that there is both a generated constructor and a deconstructor based solely on the positional parameters. This is in addition to the properties (not shown) defined for the same. Also, two instances of the `Angle` are evaluated as equal if the properties are equivalent, an equivalence implemented according to the guidelines for overriding the equality operator.

Record Struct Code Generation

All the functionality of a record struct is generated by the C# compiler at compile time. The C# equivalent of the generated code appears in Listing 9.4.

LISTING 9.4: Equivalent Record Struct Generated C# Code

```
using System.Runtime.CompilerServices;
using System.Text;

[CompilerGenerated]
public readonly struct Angle : IEquatable<Angle>
{
    public int Degrees { get; init; }
    public int Minutes { get; init; }
    public int Seconds { get; init; }
    public string? Name { get; init; }
    public Angle(int Degrees, int Minutes, int Seconds, string? Name)
    {
        this.Degrees = Degrees;
        this.Minutes = Minutes;
        this.Seconds = Seconds;
        this.Name = Name;
    }

    public override string ToString()
    {
        StringBuilder stringBuilder = new();
        stringBuilder.Append("Angle");
        stringBuilder.Append(" { ");
        if (PrintMembers(stringBuilder))
        {
            stringBuilder.Append(' ');
        }
        stringBuilder.Append('}');
        return stringBuilder.ToString();
    }
```

```
    private bool PrintMembers(StringBuilder builder)
    {
        builder.Append("Degrees = ");
        builder.Append(Degrees);
        builder.Append(", Minutes = ");
        builder.Append(Minutes);
        builder.Append(", Seconds = ");
        builder.Append(Seconds);
        builder.Append(", Name = ");
        builder.Append(Name);
        return true;
    }

    public static bool operator !=(Angle left, Angle right) =>
        !(left == right);

    public static bool operator ==(Angle left, Angle right) =>
        left.Equals(right);

    public override int GetHashCode()
    {
        static int GetHashCode(int integer) =>
            EqualityComparer<int>.Default.GetHashCode(integer);

        return GetHashCode(Degrees) * -1521134295
            + GetHashCode(Minutes) * -1521134295
            + GetHashCode(Seconds) * -1521134295
            + EqualityComparer<string>.Default.GetHashCode(Name!);
    }

    public override bool Equals(object? obj) =>
        obj is Angle angle && Equals(angle);

    public bool Equals(Angle other) =>
        EqualityComparer<int>.Default.Equals(Degrees, other.Degrees)
        && EqualityComparer<int>.Default.Equals(Minutes, other.Minutes)
        && EqualityComparer<int>.Default.Equals(Seconds, other.Seconds)
        && EqualityComparer<string>.Default.Equals(Name, other.Name);

    public void Deconstruct(out int Degrees, out int Minutes,
        out int Seconds, out string? Name)
            => (Degrees, Minutes, Seconds, Name) =
                (this.Degrees, this.Minutes, this.Seconds, this.Name);
}
```

From the one line of code in Listing 9.1, Listing 9.3 shows a significant amount of code is generated. To start, the `Angle` is not a class but a struct, and the `record` contextual keyword dropped. In C#, to define a custom value type it must be a struct. And, while C# allows you to write the entire struct from scratch as demonstrated by Listing 9.3, C# 9.0's `record` keyword jumpstarts much of the boilerplate code such that there is no longer any reason not to use the `record` keyword to start, especially since you can define custom versions of all the generated code, thus overriding the default generated implementations as needed.

Begin 10.0

Note that in C# 9.0, the record keyword without the struct keyword was all that the compiler allowed. However, in C# 10.0 (with the introduction of records for structs), the explicit declaration of `record class` was added. For clarity, we recommend using `record class` always, rather than the abbreviated `record` -only syntax.

Guidelines

DO use `record struct` when declaring a struct (C# 10.0).

DO use `record class` (C# 10.0) for clarity, rather than the abbreviated `record`-only syntax.

All value types are implicitly sealed (you can't derive from them). In addition, all non-enum value types (enums are discussed later in the chapter) derive from `System.ValueType`. Consequently, the inheritance chain for structs is always from `object` to `System.ValueType` to the custom struct.

`System.ValueType` brings with it the behavior of value types by overriding all the virtual methods of `object`: `Equals()`, `ToString()`, and `GetHashCode()`. However, this implantation is generally not sufficient, leaving the developer with the responsibility of further specializing each of these methods—of course, that is until C# 10.0 and the introduction of the `record` modifier, where now the C# compiler generates custom overrides that are much more suited for production code. Much of the same record functionality is also available on classes.

Record Classes

Importantly, the record modifier is not limited to creating value types. Starting in C# 9.0, support was added for **record classes**, as demonstrated by Listing 9.5.

Listing 9.5: Declaring a Record Class

```
// Use the record class construct to declare a reference type
public record class Coordinate(
    Angle Longitude, Angle Latitude)
```

In this record class, we have used the `Angle` type as positional parameters into the `Coordinate` to represent longitude and latitude.

To distinguish record structs and classes from their non-record versions, we will refer to them as **standard structs** and **standard classes** within this chapter. One of the most critical questions that the record class feature introduces is, when should you use a record class rather than a standard class, and vice versa? The key, and perhaps the only reason to define a record class, is if the type needs to have value equality behavior. In fact, whenever a custom type needs to implement value equality (always the case for a value type), the record construct should be used if possible. An example of when it might not be possible is working with a C# version prior to C# 9.0 (for a reference type) or C# 10.0 (for a value type).

Another time when the record construct cannot be used on a class is when the base class is not a record. A record class can inherit only from another record class, while a standard class can inherit only from another standard class. The inheritance chain cannot mix and match between standard classes and records.

> **NOTE**
>
> Reference types should be implemented as standard classes by default and record classes only when requiring a value equality implementation.

Many of the features associated with record struct are also used in record classes, including succinct declaration, data storage with properties, constructor initialization, deconstruction, `ToString()` diagnostic capabilities, and, perhaps most importantly because of the complexities, value equivalence, not just reference equivalence. The equivalent record class generated C# code is shown in Listing 9.6.

LISTING 9.6: Equivalent Record Class–Generated C# Code

```
using System.Runtime.CompilerServices;
using System.Text;

[CompilerGenerated]
public class Coordinate : IEquatable<Coordinate>
{

    public Angle Longitude { get; init; }
    public Angle Latitude { get; init; }

    public Coordinate(Angle Longitude, Angle Latitude) : base()
    {
        this.Longitude = Longitude;
        this.Latitude = Latitude;
    }

    public override string ToString()
    {
        StringBuilder stringBuilder = new ();
        stringBuilder.Append("Coordinate");
        stringBuilder.Append(" { ");
        if (PrintMembers(stringBuilder))
        {
            stringBuilder.Append(' ');
        }
        stringBuilder.Append('}');
        return stringBuilder.ToString();
    }

    protected virtual bool PrintMembers(StringBuilder builder)
    {
        RuntimeHelpers.EnsureSufficientExecutionStack();
        builder.Append("Longitude = ");
        builder.Append(Longitude.ToString());
        builder.Append(", Latitude = ");
        builder.Append(Latitude.ToString());
        return true;
    }

    public static bool operator !=(
        Coordinate? left, Coordinate? right) =>
```

```
            !(left == right);

    public static bool operator ==(
        Coordinate? left, Coordinate? right) =>
            ReferenceEquals(left, right) ||
                (left?.Equals(right) ?? false);

    public override int GetHashCode()
    {
        static int GetHashCode(Angle angle) =>
            EqualityComparer<Angle>.Default.GetHashCode(angle);

        return (EqualityComparer<Type>.Default.GetHashCode(
            EqualityContract()) * -1521134295
            + GetHashCode(Longitude)) * -1521134295
            + GetHashCode(Latitude);
    }

    public override bool Equals(object? obj) =>
        Equals(obj as Coordinate);

    public virtual bool Equals(Coordinate? other) =>
        (object)this == other || (other is not null
            && EqualityContract() == other!.EqualityContract()
            && EqualityComparer<Angle>.Default.Equals(
                Longitude, other!.Longitude)
            && EqualityComparer<Angle>.Default.Equals(
                Latitude, other!.Latitude));

    public void Deconstruct(
        out Angle Longitude, out Angle Latitude)
    {
        Longitude = this.Longitude;
        Latitude = this.Latitude;
    }

    protected virtual Type EqualityContract() => typeof(Coordinate);

    public Type ExternalEqualityContract => EqualityContract();

    // Actual name in IL is "<Clone>$". However,
    // you can't add a Clone method to a record.
    public Coordinate Clone() => new(this);

    protected Coordinate(Coordinate original)
    {
        Longitude = original.Longitude;
```

```
        Latitude = original.Latitude;
    }
}
```

There are several expected differences in the records struct versus record class–generated code.

First, several members are decorated with virtual modifiers (`PrintMembers(StringBuilder builder)`, `Equals(Coordinate? Other)`, and `EqualityContract()`). `virtual` was never used in the record struct since all structs are sealed, making `virtual` nonsensical in the record struct case.

Second, a record class needs to account for `the` possibility of a null value. Thus, `Equals()`, the `== operator`, and both of the `Equals()` methods need to check for a null parameter value.

In the next two sections, we will explore records in detail; we'll discuss each feature, its implementation where noteworthy, and the unique differences between the record struct and record class implementations.

> **Guidelines**
>
> **DO use records, where possible, if you want equality based on data rather than identity.**

Record Class Inheritance

While there is no inheritance on record structs since they are sealed, record classes do support inheritance. The main restriction is that record classes can inherit only from other record classes, not even from standard classes. Listing 9.7 provides an example.

LISTING 9.7: Record Class Inheritance

```
public record class NamedCoordinate(
    Angle Longitude, Angle Latitude, string Name)
```

```
    : Coordinate(Longitude, Latitude);
```

Notice that in defining the inheritance relationship, you can also identify how the base constructor will be invoked with arguments following the base class name. In this case, we pass `Longitude` and `Latitude` into the positional parameter–generated constructor for `Coordinate`.

End 9.0

Records

In this section, we delve into the details of the code behind records, highlight the differences between record classes and record structs, and, most importantly, dig into the details of implementing value equivalence. We begin the discussion with a record's data storage.

Data Storage with Properties

Notice how the positional parameters `Degree`, `Minutes`, and `Seconds` map into autogenerated properties on the `Angle` struct. It's similar with `Longitude` and `Latitude` on `Coordinate`. Properties are read-only (init-only setters) once initialization is complete. The fact that they are read-only is the default for record classes or caused by the `readonly` modifier on the `record struct` declaration—the modifier that causes the value type to be immutable once initialization is complete.

The one minor peculiarity with the record is that the positional parameters are, by convention, PascalCase, and, therefore, so are the parameters for the constructor. While not required by the compiler, using PascalCase for positional parameters ensures that that the corresponding properties will also have PascalCase—the latter being a more visible part of the type's API.

To customize the default implementation, you can define your own version of each property using the same name—perhaps using a backing field and custom validation. You could even replace the property with a field with the same name. Furthermore, you can code additional properties and fields, even if they were not included as positional parameters. The only restriction is that with the struct's `readonly` modifier, all properties and fields must also be read-only.

Note that there is no validation associated with the generated properties. Therefore, a non-nullable reference type positional parameter will not include a check for null. For this reason, consider always defining reference type positional parameters as nullable unless you provide a custom implementation that checks for null.

Guidelines

DO use PascalCase for the positional parameters of the record (C# 9.0).

DO define all reference type positional parameters as nullable if not providing a custom property implementation that checks for null.

DO implement custom non-nullable properties for all non-nullable positional parameters.

Immutable Value Types

An important guideline is for all value types and record classes to be immutable: Once you have instantiated either of these, you should not be able to modify the same instance. There are three good reasons for this guideline.

First, with structs, value types should represent values. One does not think of adding two integers together as mutating either of them; rather, the two addends are immutable, and a third value is produced as the result. Second, because value types are copied by value, not by reference, it is easy to get confused and incorrectly believe that a mutation in one value type variable can be observed to cause a mutation in another, as it would with a reference type.

Third, for both structs and record classes, is the fact that hash codes are calculated from the data stored within the type, and hash codes should never change. (See "Advanced Topic: Overriding `GetHashCode()`" later in the chapter.) If the data within these types changed and a new hash code value is calculated, searches for the new hash code value in collections where the old hash code was present could result in values never getting found and the resulting incorrect behavior.

Note that the Angle struct in Listing 9.3 is immutable because all properties are automatically implemented read-only properties[2] declared using init-only setters rather than set. To verify conformance to the immutable guideline, you can use the readonly modifier with a struct definition[3] (for both record structs and standard structs). See Listing 9.8:

LISTING 9.8: Using Read-Only Modifier on Structs

```
readonly struct Angle { }
```

Like with a record, now the compiler will verify that the entire struct is immutable, reporting an error if there is a field that is not read-only or a property that has a setter. However, using the readonly modifier on a record class or a standard class is not supported.

Begin 8.0

In the irregular case where you need finer-grained control than declaring the entire struct as read-only, C# 8.0 allows you to define any struct (not class) member as read-only (including methods and even getters—which potentially may modify an object's state even though they shouldn't). For example, a Move() method can include a readonly modifier (see Listing 9.9):

LISTING 9.9: Defining a struct Member as Read-Only

```
public readonly Angle Move(int degrees, int minutes, int seconds)
{
    return new Angle(
        Degrees + degrees,
        Minutes + minutes,
        Seconds + seconds);
}
```

Note that in members where modifying a struct is seemingly desirable, you should instead create a new instance as the Move() method demonstrates by returning a new Angle.

Any readonly modified members that modify a struct's data (properties or fields), or invoke a non-read-only member, will report a compile-time error. By

2. Automatically implemented read-only properties became available in C# 6.0.
3. Starting in C# 7.2.

supporting the concept of read-only access to members, developers declare the behavioral intent of whether a member can modify the object instance. Note that properties that are not automatically implemented can use the `readonly` modifier on either the getter or the setter (although the latter would be strange). To decorate both, the `readonly` modifier would be placed on the property itself, rather than on the getter and setter individually.

While allowable, using the `readonly` modifier on struct members is redundant when the struct is read-only. However, favor read-only (`{get;}`) or `init`-only setter (`{get;init;}`) automatically implemented properties over fields within structs.

End 8.0

Guidelines

DO use the `readonly` **modifier on a struct definition, making value types immutable.**

DO use read-only or init-only setter automatically implemented properties rather than fields within structs.

Remarkably, the tuple (`System.ValueTuple`) is one example that breaks the immutable guideline. To understand why it is an exception, see https://intellitect.com/WhyTupleBreaksTheImmutableRuleshttps://IntelliTect.com/WhyTupleBreaksTheImmutableRules.

Cloning Records Using the `with` Operator

Since most records, especially record structs, are immutable, in place of changing them you will create new instances with the modified data. The easiest way to achieve this is using the C# 9.0–introduced **with operator**. As demonstrated at the end of Listing 9.3, the `with` operator clones the existing instance into a new copy. However, you are not restricted to an exact replica. Rather, you can use an object initializer type syntax to create the new instance with modified data (see Listing 9.10).

The source (left) operand for the `with` operator is the source instance. And while you could create an exact clone, using the object initializer syntax allows you to modify any accessible member and assign it a different value during instantiation.

LISTING 9.10: Cloning Records via the `With` Operator

```
Angle angle = new(90, 0, 0, null);

 // The with operator is the equivalent of
// Angle copy = new(degrees, minutes, seconds);
Angle copy = angle with { };
Trace.Assert(angle == copy);

// The with operator has object initializer type
// syntax for instantiating a modified copy.
Angle modifiedCopy = angle with { Degrees = 180 };
Trace.Assert(angle != modifiedCopy);
```

Cloning a record struct is a memory copy, the same as when creating a copy to invoke a method with pass by value. For this reason, you can't change the implementation for cloning a record struct.

For record classes, the process is slightly different. The C# compiler generates a hidden `Clone()` method (shown in Listing 9.5) that in turn invokes the copy constructor with a parameter for the source instance. You can also view that same code in Listing 9.11:

LISTING 9.11: Cloning Record Classes via the `Clone` Method

```
// Actual name in IL is "<Clone>$". However,
// you can't add a Clone method to a record.
public Coordinate Clone() => new(this);

protected Coordinate(Coordinate original)
{
    Longitude = original.Longitude;
    Latitude = original.Latitude;
}
```

The clone method in turn calls the copy constructor.[4] Note that in the case where the object initializer syntax is used, the assigned property cannot be read-only (either a setter or an init-only setter is required). Also, the `Clone()` method uses a special non-C#–compliant name, making it accessible only via the with operator. If you want

4. A constructor that takes single parameter or the containing type. See Chapter 6.

to customize the clone behavior, however, you can provide your own implementation of the copy constructor.

Record Constructors

Note that the record declaration of Listing 9.1 looks virtually identical to the constructor signature in Listing 9.3. Similarly, with the record class associated code in Listing 9.4 and its equivalent C#-generated equivalent in Listing 9.5, a record declaration and its positional parameters provide the structure for the C# compiler to generate a constructor with an equivalent-looking signature.

As with the properties themselves, one minor peculiarity with the record is that the positional parameters are, by convention, PascalCase, and, therefore, so are the parameters for the constructor. (Consequently, when initializing the properties, the generated constructor code uses the `this` qualifier to distinguish the parameters from the properties.)

You can add additional constructors to the record's definition. For example, you could provide a constructor that has strings rather than integers as parameters, as shown in Listing 9.12:

Listing 9.12: Adding Additional Record Constructors

```
public Angle(
    string degrees, string minutes, string seconds)
    : this(int.Parse(degrees),
           int.Parse(minutes),
           int.Parse(seconds))
{ }
```

The implementation of an additional constructor uses the same syntax as any other constructor. The only additional constraint is that it must invoke the `this` constructor initializer—it must call the record-generated constructor or another constructor that calls the record-generated constructor. This ensures that the initialization of the positional parameter–generated properties are all initialized.

Record Struct Initialization

Prior to C# 10.0, no default constructor could be defined. Regardless, if not explicitly instantiating a struct via the `new` operator's call to the constructor, all data contained within the struct is implicitly initialized to that data's default value. The default value is `null` for a field of reference type data, a zero value for a field of numeric type, and `false` for a field of Boolean type, including fields backing an automatically implemented property. Similarly, since field and property initialization during declaration[5] (such as `string Description { get; init; } = ""`) is injected into the constructor by the compiler, it also will not execute without the `new` operator invocation.

It is important to be aware of this because, unlike with reference types, it is common for value types to be instantiated without the new operator. Assigning a value type to `default` or not initializing a value type field on a class, for example, will not execute any constructor, and neither will an uninitialized array item such as the one displayed in Listing 9.13:

Listing 9.13: Uninitialized Array Item

```
Angle[] angles = new[42];
```

In both cases, regardless of what the default constructor initializes data members to, they will end up with default values. For this reason, do not rely on either default constructors or member initialization at declaration time.

Begin 11.0

Prior to C# 11.0, every constructor in a struct must initialize all fields (and read-only, automatically implemented properties[6]) within the struct. Failure to initialize all data within the struct causes a compile-time error in C# 10.0 and earlier:

```
CS0171: Field must be fully assigned before control is returned to
the caller. Consider updating to language version '11.0'
to auto-default the field.
```

Because of the struct's field initialization requirement, the succinctness of read-only field declaration, automatically implemented property support, and the guideline to avoid accessing fields from outside of their wrapping property, you

5. Enabled starting in C# 10.0

6. Initialization via a read-only, automatically implemented property is sufficient starting in C# 6.0, because the backing field is unknown and its initialization would not be possible otherwise.

should favor read-only, automatically implemented properties over fields within structs.

Guidelines

DO ensure that the default value of a struct is valid; encapsulation cannot prevent obtaining the default "all zero" value of a struct.

DO NOT rely on either default constructors or member initialization at declaration to run on a value type.

End 11.0

End 10.0

ADVANCED TOPIC

Using `new` with Value Types

Invoking the `new` operator with a reference type causes the runtime to create a new instance of the object on the garbage-collected heap, initialize all of its fields to their default values, and call the constructor, passing a reference to the instance as `this`. The result is the reference to the instance, which can then be copied to its final destination. In contrast, invoking the `new` operator with a value type causes the runtime to create a new instance of the object on the temporary storage pool, initialize all of its fields to their default values, and call the constructor (passing the temporary storage location as a `ref` variable through `this`), resulting in the value being stored in the temporary storage location, which can then be copied to its final destination.

Unlike classes, structs do not support finalizers. Structs are copied by value; they do not have referential identity, as reference types do. Therefore, it is hard to know when it would be safe to execute the finalizer and free an unmanaged resource owned by the struct. The garbage collector knows when there are no "live" references to an instance of reference type and can choose to run the finalizer for an instance of reference type at any time after there are no more live references. Nevertheless, no part of the runtime tracks how many copies of a given value type exist at any moment.

Language Contrast: C++—`struct` Defines Type with Public Members

In C++, the difference between a type declared with `struct` and one declared with `class` is whether the default accessibility is public or private. The contrast is far greater in C#, where the difference is whether instances of the type are copied by value or by reference.

Record Deconstructors

In addition to the properties and constructor, the C# compiler also generates a positional parameter–corresponding deconstructor, as seen in Listing 9.14:

Listing 9.14: Record Deconstructor

```
public void Deconstruct(
    out int Degrees, out int Minutes, out int Seconds)
{
    Degrees = this.Degrees;
    Minutes = this.Minutes;
    Seconds = this.Seconds;
}
```

This enables pattern matching like that used in Listing 9.2 (displayed again in Listing 9.15):

Listing 9.15: Pattern Matching

```
if (angle is (int, int, int, string) angleData)
{
    // ...
}
```

Overriding `object` Members

Chapter 6 discussed how all classes and structs ultimately derive from `object`. In addition, it reviewed each method available on `object` and discussed how some of them are virtual. This section discusses the details concerning overriding these virtual methods. Doing so is automatic for records, but the generated code also provides an example of what is required if you choose to customize the generated code or implement an override on a non-record type implementation.

Overriding `ToString()`

By default, calling `ToString()` on any object will return the fully qualified name of the object type. Calling `ToString()` on a `System.IO.FileStream` object will return the string `System.IO.FileStream`, for example. For some classes, however, `ToString()` can be more meaningful. On `string`, for example, `ToString()` returns the string value itself. Similarly, when invoking `ToString()` on an `Angle` (Listing 9.1), the result returns:

```
Angle { Degrees = 90, Minutes = 0, Seconds = 0, Name = }
```

(This also happens to be the output of Listing 9.2.)

Write methods such as `System.Console.WriteLine()` and `System.Diagnostics.Trace.Write()` call an object's `ToString()` method,[7] so overriding the method often outputs more meaningful information than the default implementation.

Overriding `ToString()` requires nothing more than declaring the `ToString()` method as `override` and returning a `string`. Take Listing 9.16 for example:

Listing 9.16: Overriding the `ToString` Method

```
public override string ToString()
{
    string prefix =
        string.IsNullOrWhiteSpace(Name) ? string.Empty : Name + ": ";
```

7. Unless there is an implicit cast operator, as described in "Advanced Topic: Cast Operator".

```
        return $"{prefix}{Degrees}° {Minutes}' {Seconds}\"";
    }
```

Regardless, do not return an empty string or `null`, as the lack of output will be very confusing. `ToString()` is useful for debugging from within a developer IDE or writing to a log file. Be mindful of implementing localization overload methods and other advanced formatting features to ensure suitability for general end-user text display. Also, keep the strings relatively short so that they are not truncated off the end of the screen – especially in during debugging in an IDE.

Begin 10.0

Consider overriding the `ToString()` method whenever relevant diagnostic information can be provided from the output—specifically, when the target audience is developers, since the default `object.ToString()` output is a type name and is not end-user friendly. Alternatively, starting in C# 10.0, you can seal a record's `ToString()` implementation, preventing its override by derived-type—including a code generated implementation.

End 10.0

Guidelines

DO override `ToString()` whenever useful developer-oriented diagnostic strings can be returned.

CONSIDER trying to keep the string returned from `ToString()` short.

DO NOT return an empty string or `null` from `ToString()`.

DO NOT throw exceptions or make observable side effects (change the object state) from `ToString()`.

DO provide an overloaded `ToString(string format)` or implement `IFormattable` if the return value requires formatting or is culture-sensitive (e.g., `DateTime`).

CONSIDER returning a unique string from `ToString()` so as to identify the object instance.

Implementing Value Equality

Frequently, developers expect implementing value equivalence to be trivial. How hard could it be to compare two objects? However, it includes a surprising number of subtleties and complexities that require careful thought and testing. Fortunately, there are two approaches that significantly simplify the code. Firstly, if you use a record construct, then the C# compiler takes care of generating the `Equals()` method and all its associated members for you, comparing all automatically implemented properties and fields of the record—whether they are included as positional parameters or not. Secondly, you can group the identifying data elements (automatically implemented properties and fields) into a tuple and then compare the tuples. In the case of reference type, you also need to pay attention to any potential null values.

Listing 9.3 shows the implementation of `Equals()` that was generated for a record and enables value equality. And one of the big advantages of C# records is that they generate a value equality implementation for you, relieving you of the exercise of manually implementing what could be a surprisingly complex method considering inheritance, null, varying data types, and value/reference type in addition to comparing the contained values themselves. That said, if the record-generated implementation doesn't suit your needs, then you will need to write your own. One reason to do that is that you may not want some of the properties to be included as part of the value equals determination. For example, perhaps you don't want the `Name` property on `Angle` to be part of an `Angle`'s value identity, instead relying solely on `Degrees`, `Minutes`, and `Seconds`. Listing 9.24 provides such a full customized record struct with the following snippet of a custom equality implementation in Listing 9.17:

Listing 9.17: Custom Equality Implementation

```
public bool Equals(Angle other) =>
    (Degrees, Minutes, Seconds).Equals(
        (other.Degrees, other.Minutes, other.Seconds));
```

Notice that the value-identifying properties are combined into tuples and compared with the same values of `other`. In addition, be aware that the equals implementation is overloaded. The previous snippet shows the implementation with an `Angle` parameter. That is because the C# compiler generates all the additional value equality functionality for you. However, this is not the case on types that are not records—you must provide all such customization yourself. Also, whenever you update the `Equals()` method, you should update `GetHashCode()`, so use the same data elements. A failure to override `GetHashCode()` when overriding `Equals()`, and vice -versa, will generate a warning:

```
CS8851 '<ClassName>' defines 'Equals' but not 'GetHashCode'
```

While this snippet looks different from the record-generated version of `Equals()` shown in Listing 9.3, internally the tuple (`System.ValueTuple<...>`) uses `EqualityComparer<T>` as well. In turn, `EqualityComparer<T>` relies on the type parameters implementation of `IEquatable<T>` (which contains only a single `Equals<T>(T other)` member). Therefore, to correctly override `Equals`, you need to implement `IEquatable<T>`.

Once `Equals()` is overridden, there is a possible inconsistency. That is, two objects could return true for `Equals()` but false for the `==` operator because `==` performs a reference equality check by default. To correct this flaw, it is important to override the equals (`==`) and not equals (`!=`) operators as well. Of course, this code is generated for you as part of the record implementation as you can see in Listing 9.18:

Listing 9.18: Overriding the == and != Operators

```
public static bool operator ==(Coordinate? left, Coordinate? right) =>
    ReferenceEquals(left, right) || (left?.Equals(right) ?? false);
// ...
public static bool operator !=(Angle left, Angle right) =>
    !(left == right);
```

For the most part, the implementation for these operators can delegate the logic to `Equals()`, or vice versa. Take care, however, not to invoke an infinite recursive loop with the `==` operator calling back on itself. In this case, such a recursion is avoided because we use `ReferenceEquals()` initially, which will return true if both values are null. For value types, there is, of course, no need to check for null. See Chapter 10 (https://essentialcsharp.com/operator-overloading) for more information on operator overloading.

Lastly, consider implementing `IComparable<T>` if the custom type can be sorted along with the `IFormattable` interface if localization is needed. For the full implementation of value equality without using a record construct, see "Advanced Topic: Overriding GetHashCode()." There are two more important topics related to value types that we still need to cover. The first is boxing, and the second is enums, and both are discussed in the following sections.

ADVANCED TOPIC

Value Equality Principles

Notice that the signature of Equals() in Listing 9.24 does not match the signature object in Listing 9.19.

LISTING 9.19: Nonmatching Signature

```
public override bool Equals(object? obj)
```

(If it did, we would need to use the override modifier.) When implementing Equals() on a class or struct (that are not records), there are several other considerations to be aware of. All are available in Listing 9.3 for a struct and Listing 9.5 for a class (because the record modifier generates them).

The steps for implementing value equality on a custom type are as follows:

1. Implement the IEquatable<T>[8] interface.
2. Implement the Equals(object? obj) method, checking that obj is the same type as the custom type and invoking the strongly typed Equals() helper method that can treat the operand as the custom type rather than an object (Listing 9.20).

LISTING 9.20: Implementing Value Equality on a Custom Type

```
public override bool Equals(object? obj)
{
    return Equals(obj as Foo);
}
```

8. Generics are discussed in Chapter 12.

3. Implement the strongly typed `Equals()` helper method, as shown in Listing 9.21, and check if `obj` is `null` (reference types only).

LISTING 9.21: Implementing Strongly Typed `Equals`

```
public bool Equals(Foo? other)
{
    if (other is null) return false;
    // Step 5
    // return (this.Number, this.Name) == (other.Number, other.Name);
    return true;
}
```

4. For reference types that don't derive from `System.Object`, check `base.Equals()`, thus enabling refactoring.

5. Compare each identifying data members for equality, preferably using a tuple.

6. Override `GetHashCode()`.

7. Override the `==` and `!=` operators (see Chapter 10 – Operator Overloading).

Steps 3 to 4 occur in an overload of `Equals()` that takes the custom data type specifically (such as `Coordinate`). This way, a comparison of two `Coordinate`s will avoid `Equals(object? obj)` and its type check altogether.

`Equals()` should never throw any exceptions. It is a valid choice to compare any object with any other object, and doing so should never result in an exception.

Guidelines

DO implement `GetHashCode()`, `Equals()`, the `==` operator, and the `!=` operator together—not one of these without the other three.

DO use the same algorithm when implementing `Equals()`, `==`, and `!=`.

DO NOT throw exceptions from implementations of `GetHashCode()`, `Equals()`, `==`, and `!=`.

AVOID including mutable data when overriding the equality-related members on mutable reference types or if the implementation would be significantly slower with such overriding.

DO implement all the equality-related methods when implementing `IEquatable`.

Begin 10.0

ADVANCED TOPIC

Overriding `GetHashCode()`

If you rely on a record construct, `GetHashCode()` is automatically implemented for you as part of the value equality implementation (see Listing 9.3 and Listing 9.5). Without the record implementation, you have to implement `GetHashCode()` on your own, however, if you are providing an equality implementation. Even with a record, if you customize the `Equals()` implementation, you will likely want to override `GetHashCode()` to use a similar set of values as the new `Equals()` implementation. And, if you override only `Equals()` and not `GetHashCode()`, you will have a warning that:

```
CS0659: '<Class Name>' overrides Object.Equals(object o) but
does not override Object.GetHashCode(),
```

In other words, when not leveraging the record construct, overriding equals requires that you also override `GetHashCode()`.

The purpose of the hash code is to *efficiently balance a hash table* by generating a number that corresponds to the value of an object. And, while there are numerous guidelines (see https://bit.ly/39yP8lm for a discussion), the easiest approach is as follows:

1. Rely on the record generated implementation (see Listing 9.2). If you need to override `GetHashCode()`, you are probably overriding `Equals()`and using a record is the best approach by default.

2. Call `System.HashCode`'s `Combine()` method, specifying each of the identifying fields (see Listing 9.22):

LISTING 9.22: Overriding `GetHashCode` with `Combine` Method

```
public override int GetHashCode() =>
    HashCode.Combine(Degrees, Minutes, Seconds);
```

3. Invoke `ValueTuple`'s `GetHashCode()` method using the fields that produce your object's uniqueness as the tuple elements, as demonstrated in Listing 9.23. (If the identifying fields are numbers, be wary of mistakenly using the fields themselves rather than their hash code values.)

LISTING 9.23: Overriding `GetHashCode` with `Combine` Method

```
public override int GetHashCode() =>
    (Degrees, Minutes, Seconds).GetHashCode();
```

4. `ValueTuple` invokes `HashCode.Combine()`; thus, it may be easier to remember that you can adequately create a `ValueTuple` with the same identifying fields and invoke the resulting tuple's `GetHashCode()` member

In summary, use a record if overriding `GetHashCode()` and `Equals()` unless there is a strong reason not to (such as an older version of C# in which records are not available).

Fortunately, once you have determined that you need `GetHashCode()`, you can follow some well-established `GetHashCode()` implementation principles:

- *Required:* Equal objects must have equal hash codes (if `a.Equals(b)`, then `a.GetHashCode() == b.GetHashCode()`).
- *Required:* `GetHashCode()`'s returns should be constant (the same value), even if the object's data changes. In many cases, you should cache the method return to enforce this constraint. However, when caching the value, be sure not to use the hash code when checking equality; if you do, two identical objects —one with a cached hash code of changed identity properties—will not return the correct result.

- *Required:* `GetHashCode()` should not throw any exceptions; `GetHashCode()` must always successfully return a value.
- *Performance:* Hash codes should be unique whenever possible. However, since hash codes return only an `int`, there inevitably will be an overlap in hash codes for objects that have potentially more values than an `int` can hold, which is virtually all types. (An obvious example is `long`, since there are more possible `long` values than an `int` could uniquely identify.)
- *Performance:* The possible hash code values should be distributed evenly over the range of an `int`. For example, creating a hash that doesn't consider the distribution of a string in Latin-based languages primarily centered on the initial 128 ASCII characters would result in a very uneven distribution of string values and would not be a strong `GetHashCode()` algorithm.
- *Performance:* `GetHashCode()` should be optimized for performance. `GetHashCode()` is generally used in `Equals()` implementations to short-circuit a full equals comparison if the hash codes are different. As a result, it is frequently called when the type is used as a key type in dictionary collections.
- *Performance:* Small differences between two objects should result in large differences between hash code values—ideally, a 1-bit difference in the object should result in approximately 16 bits of the hash code changing, on average. This helps ensure that the hash table remains balanced no matter how it is "bucketing" the hash values.

These guidelines and rules are, of course, contradictory: It is very difficult to come up with a hash algorithm that is fast and meets all of these guidelines. As with any design problem, you'll need to use a combination of good judgment and realistic performance measurements to come up with a good solution. The easiest approach, of course, is to rely on one of the previously identified algorithms

End 10.0

Customizing Record Behavior

Clearly, the C# compiler generates a significant amount of code for the record struct and record class constructs. However, all the behavior is customizable. As mentioned earlier in the chapter, for example, you can add any additional members, including properties, fields, constructors, and methods. More importantly, you can provide your own versions of the generated members. Coding any record member with a matching signature to the otherwise synthesized member, you can replace the default behavior with your own. If you prefer a read-only property rather than an `init`-only setter property, you simply declare the property (or field) to match the positional property name. Or, by providing your own copy constructor, you can inject custom behavior into how a record class handles cloning (via the `with` operator). Similarly, if you want to change the semantics of equality, perhaps to simplify it to a subset of the record's properties/fields, you can define your own `Equals()` method, likely only the method that takes a single parameter of the containing type. Listing 9.24 provides several examples of possible customizations on a record.

Listing 9.24: Customizing a Record

```
public readonly record struct Angle(
    int Degrees, int Minutes, int Seconds, string? Name = null)
{

    public int Degrees { get; } = Degrees;

    public Angle(
        string degrees, string minutes, string seconds)
        : this(int.Parse(degrees),
              int.Parse(minutes), int.Parse(seconds))
    {
    }

    public override readonly string ToString()
    {
        string prefix =
            string.IsNullOrWhiteSpace(Name)?string.Empty : Name+": ";
        return $"{prefix}{Degrees}° {Minutes}' {Seconds}\"";
    }

    // Changing Equals() to ignore Name
    public bool Equals(Angle other) =>
        (Degrees, Minutes, Seconds).Equals(
            (other.Degrees, other.Minutes, other.Seconds));

    public override int GetHashCode() =>
        HashCode.Combine(Degrees.GetHashCode(),
            Minutes.GetHashCode(), Seconds.GetHashCode);

    #if UsingTupleToGenerateHashCode
```

```
    public override int GetHashCode() =>
        (Degrees, Minutes, Seconds).GetHashCode();
    #endif // UsingTupleToGenerateHashCode
}
```

Boxing

We know that variables of value types directly contain their data, whereas variables of reference types contain a reference to another storage location. But what happens when a value type is converted to one of its implemented interfaces or to its root base class, `object`? The result of the conversion must be a reference to a storage location that contains something that looks like an instance of a reference type, but the variable contains a value of value type. Such a conversion, which is known as **boxing**, has special behavior. Converting a variable of a value type that directly refers to its data to a reference type that refers to a location on the garbage-collected heap involves several steps.

1. Memory is allocated on the heap that will contain the value type's data and the other overhead necessary to make the object look like every other instance of a managed object of the reference type (namely, a `SyncBlockIndex` and method table pointer).

2. The value of the value type is copied from its current storage location into the newly allocated location on the heap.

3. The result of the conversion is a reference to the new storage location on the heap.

The reverse operation is called **unboxing**. The unboxing conversion first checks whether the type of the boxed value is the same as the type to which the value is being unboxed, and then results in a copy of the value stored in the heap location.

Boxing and unboxing are important to consider because boxing has some performance and behavioral implications. Besides learning how to recognize these conversions within C# code, a developer can count the box/unbox instructions in a particular snippet of code by looking through the Common Intermediate Language (CIL). Each operation has specific instructions, as shown in Table 9.1.

Table 9.1: Boxing Code in CIL

<table>
<tr><th>C# Code</th><th>CIL Code</th></tr>
<tr><td><pre>static void Main()
{
int number;
object thing;
number = 42;
// Boxing
thing = number;
// Unboxing
number = (int)thing;
return;
}</pre></td><td><pre>.method private hidebysig
static void Main() cil managed
{
.entrypoint
// Code size 21 (0x15)
.maxstack 1
.locals init ([0] int32 number,
[1] object thing)
IL_0000: nop
IL_0001: ldc.i4.s 42
IL_0003: stloc.0
IL_0004: ldloc.0
IL_0005: box [mscorlib]System.Int32
IL_000a: stloc.1
IL_000b: ldloc.1
IL_000c: unbox.any [mscorlib]System.Int32
IL_0011: stloc.0
IL_0012: br.s IL_0014
IL_0014: ret
} // end of method Program::Main</pre></td></tr>
</table>

When boxing and unboxing occur infrequently, their implications for performance are irrelevant. However, boxing can occur in some unexpected situations, and frequent occurrences can have a significant impact on performance. Consider Listing 9.25 and Output 9.1. The `ArrayList` type maintains a list of references to objects, so adding an integer or floating-point number to the list will box the value so that a reference can be obtained.

Listing 9.25: Subtle Box and Unbox Instructions

```
public class DisplayFibonacci
{
    public static void Main()
    {
        // Intentionally using ArrayList to demonstrate boxing
        System.Collections.ArrayList list = new();

        Console.Write("Enter an integer between 2 and 1000: ");
        string? inputText = Console.ReadLine();
        if (!int.TryParse(inputText, out int totalCount))
        {
```

```
            Console.WriteLine($"'{inputText}' is not a valid integer.");
            return;
        }

        if (totalCount == 7)  // Magic number used for testing
        {
            // Triggers exception when retrieving  value as double.
            list.Add(0);  // Cast to double or 'D' suffix required.
                          // Whether cast or using 'D' suffix,
                          // CIL is identical.


        }
        else
        {
            list.Add((double)0);
        }

        list.Add((double)1);

        for(int count = 2; count < totalCount; count++)
        {
            list.Add(
                (double)list[count - 1]! +
                (double)list[count - 2]!);
        }

        // Using a foreach to clarify the box operation rather than
        // Console.WriteLine(string.Join(", ", list.ToArray()));
        foreach (double? count in list)
        {
            Console.Write("{0}, ", count);
        }
    }
}
```

Output 9.1

```
Enter a number between 2 and 1000: 42
0, 1, 1, 2, 3, 5, 8, 13, 21, 34, 55, 89, 144, 233, 377, 610, 987, 1597,
2584, 4181, 6765, 10946, 17711, 28657, 46368, 75025, 121393, 196418,
```

```
317811, 514229, 832040, 1346269, 2178309, 3524578, 5702887, 9227465,
14930352, 24157817, 39088169, 63245986, 102334155, 165580141,
```

The code shown in Listing 9.9, when compiled, produces five box instructions and three unbox instructions in the resultant CIL.

1. The first two box instructions occur in the initial calls to `list.Add()`. The signature for the `ArrayList`[9] method is `int Add(object value)`. As such, any value type passed to this method is boxed.

2. Next are two unbox instructions in the call to `Add()` within the `for` loop. The return from an `ArrayList`'s index operator is always `object` because that is what `ArrayList` contains. To add the two values, you need to cast them back to `double`s. This cast from a reference to an object to a value type is implemented as an unbox call.

3. Now you take the result of the addition and place it into the `ArrayList` instance, which again results in a box operation. Note that the first two unbox instructions and this box instruction occur within a loop.

4. In the `foreach` loop, you iterate through each item in `ArrayList` and assign the items to `count`. As you saw earlier, the items within `ArrayList` are references to `object`s, so assigning them to a `double` is, in effect, unboxing each of them.

5. The signature for `Console.WriteLine()`, which is called within the `foreach` loop, is `void Console.Write(string format, object arg)`. As a result, each call to it boxes the `double` to `object`.

Every boxing operation involves both an allocation and a copy; every unboxing operation involves a type check and a copy. Doing the equivalent work using the

9. It is important that we use a collection of type object, not a strongly typed collection like a generic collection, as discussed in Chapter 12.

unboxed type would eliminate the allocation and type check. Obviously, you can easily improve this code's performance by eliminating many of the boxing operations. Using an `object` rather than `double` in the last `foreach` loop is one such improvement. Another would be to change the `ArrayList` data type to a generic collection (see Chapter 12). The point being made here is that boxing can be rather subtle, so developers need to pay special attention and notice situations where it could potentially occur repeatedly and affect performance.

Another unfortunate boxing-related problem also occurs at runtime: When calling `Add()` without first casting to a `double` (or using a `double` literal), you could insert integers into the array list. Since `int`s will implicitly be converted to `double`s, this would appear to be an innocuous modification. However, the casts to `double` when retrieving the value from within the `foreach` loop would fail. The problem is that the unbox operation is immediately followed by an attempt to perform a memory copy of the value of the boxed `int` into a `double`. You cannot do this without first casting to an `int`, because the code will throw an `InvalidCastException` at execution time. Listing 9.26 shows a similar error commented out and followed by the correct cast.

Listing 9.26: Unboxing Must Be to the Underlying Type

```
// ...

int number;
object thing;
double bigNumber;

number = 42;
thing = number;
// ERROR: InvalidCastException
// bigNumber = (double)thing;
bigNumber = (double)(int)thing;
// ...
```

ADVANCED TOPIC

Value Types in the `lock` Statement

C# supports a `lock` statement for synchronizing code. This statement compiles down to `System.Threading.Monitor`'s `Enter()` and `Exit()` methods, which must be called in pairs. `Enter()` records the unique reference argument passed so that when `Exit()` is called with the same reference, the lock can be released. The trouble with using value types is the boxing. Each time `Enter()` or `Exit()` is called in such a case, a new value is created on the heap. Comparing the reference of one copy to the reference of a different copy will always return `false`, so you cannot hook up `Enter()` with the corresponding `Exit()`. Therefore, value types in the `lock()` statement are not allowed.

Listing 9.27 points out a few more runtime boxing idiosyncrasies, and Output 9.2 shows the results.

LISTING 9.27: Subtle Boxing Idiosyncrasies

```
interface IAngle
{
    void MoveTo(int degrees, int minutes, int seconds);
}

struct Angle : IAngle
{
    // ...

    // NOTE:  This makes Angle mutable, against the general
    //        guideline
    public void MoveTo(int degrees, int minutes, int seconds)
    {
        _Degrees = degrees;
        _Minutes = minutes;
        _Seconds = seconds;
    }
    // ...
}
public class Program
{
    public static void Main()
    {
        // ...
```

```
        Angle angle = new(25, 58, 23);
        // Example 1: Simple box operation
        object objectAngle = angle;  // Box
        Console.Write(((Angle)objectAngle).Degrees);

        // Example 2: Unbox, modify unboxed value,
        //            and discard value
        ((Angle)objectAngle).MoveTo
            (26, 58, 23);
        Console.Write(", " + ((Angle)objectAngle).Degrees);

        // Example 3: Box, modify boxed value,
        //            and discard reference to box
        ((IAngle)angle).MoveTo(26, 58, 23);
        Console.Write(", " + ((Angle)angle).Degrees);

        // Example 4: Modify boxed value directly
        ((IAngle)objectAngle).MoveTo(26, 58, 23);
        Console.WriteLine(", " + ((Angle)objectAngle).Degrees);

        // ...
    }
}
```

Output 9.2

```
25, 25, 25, 26
```

Listing 9.11 uses the `Angle` struct and `IAngle` interface. Note also that the `IAngle.MoveTo()` interface changes `Angle` to be mutable. This change brings out some of the idiosyncrasies of mutable value types and, in so doing, demonstrates the importance of the guideline that advocates making structs immutable.

In Example 1 of Listing 9.11, after you initialize `angle`, you then box it into a variable called `objectAngle`. Next, Example 2 calls `MoveTo()` to change `_Degrees` to `26`. However, as the output demonstrates, no change actually occurs the first time. The problem is that to call `MoveTo()`, the compiler unboxes `objectAngle` and (by definition) makes a copy of the value. Value types are copied by value—that is why they are called value types. Although the resultant value is successfully modified at execution time, this copy of the value is discarded and no change occurs on the heap location referenced by `objectAngle`.

Recall our analogy that suggested variables of value types are like pieces of paper with the value written on them. When you box a value, you make a photocopy of the paper and put the copy in a box. When you unbox the value, you make a photocopy of the paper in the box. Making an edit to this second copy does not change the copy that is in the box.

In Example 3, a similar problem occurs, but in reverse. Instead of calling `MoveTo()` directly, the value is cast to `IAngle`. The conversion to an interface type boxes the value, so the runtime copies the data in `angle` to the heap and provides a reference to that box. Next, the method call modifies the value in the referenced box. The value stored in variable `angle` remains unmodified.

In the last case, the cast to `IAngle` is a reference conversion, not a boxing conversion. The value has already been boxed by the conversion to `object` in this case, so no copy of the value occurs on this conversion. The call to `MoveTo()` updates the `_Degrees` value stored in the box, and the code behaves as desired.

As you can see from this example, mutable value types are quite confusing because it is often unclear when you are mutating a copy of the value rather than the storage location you actually intend to change. By avoiding mutable value types in the first place, you can eliminate this sort of confusion.

Guidelines

AVOID mutable value types.

ADVANCED TOPIC

How Boxing Can Be Avoided during Method Calls

Anytime a method is called on a value type, the value type receiving the call (represented by `this` in the body of the method) must be a variable, not a value, because the method might be trying to mutate the receiver. Clearly, it must be mutating the receiver's storage location, rather than mutating a copy of the receiver's value and then discarding it. Examples 2 and 4 of Listing 9.11 illustrate how this fact affects the performance of a method invocation on a boxed value type.

In Example 2, the unboxing conversion logically produces the boxed value, not a reference to the storage location on the heap that contains the boxed copy. Which storage location, then, is passed via `this` to the mutating method call? It cannot be the storage location from the box on the heap, because the unboxing conversion produces a copy of that value, not a reference to that storage location.

When this situation arises—a variable of a value type is required but only a value is available—one of two things happens: either the C# compiler generates code that makes a new, temporary storage location and copies the value from the box into the new location, resulting in the temporary storage location becoming the needed variable, or the compiler produces an error and disallows the operation. In this case, the former strategy is used. The new temporary storage location is then the receiver of the call; after it is mutated, the temporary storage location is discarded.

This process—performing a type check of the boxed value, unboxing to produce the storage location of the boxed value, allocating a temporary variable, copying the value from the box to the temporary variable, and then calling the method with the location of the temporary storage—happens every time you use the unbox-and-then-call pattern, regardless of whether the method actually mutates the variable. Clearly, if it does not mutate the variable, some of this work could be avoided. Because the C# compiler does not know whether any particular method you call will try to mutate the receiver, it must err on the side of caution.

These expenses are all eliminated when calling an interface method on a boxed value type. In such a case, the expectation is that the receiver will be the storage location in the box; if the interface method mutates the storage location, it is the boxed location that should be mutated. Therefore, the expense of performing a type check, allocating new temporary storage, and making a copy is avoided. Instead, the runtime simply uses the storage location in the box as the receiver of the call to the struct's method.

In Listing 9.28, we call the two-argument version of `ToString()` that is found on the `IFormattable` interface, which is implemented by the `int` value type. In this example, the receiver of the call is a boxed value type, but it is not unboxed to make the call to the interface method.

Listing 9.28: Avoiding Unboxing and Copying

```
int number;
object thing;
number = 42;
// Boxing
thing = number;
// No unboxing conversion
string text = ((IFormattable)thing).ToString(
    "X", null);
Console.WriteLine(text);
```

Now suppose that we had instead called the virtual `ToString()` method declared by `object` with an instance of a value type as the receiver. What happens then? Is the instance boxed, unboxed, or something else? A number of different scenarios are possible depending on the details:

- If the receiver is unboxed and the struct overrides `ToString()`, the overridden method is called directly. There is no need for a virtual call because the method cannot be overridden further by a more derived class; all value types are automatically sealed.
- If the receiver is unboxed and the struct does not override `ToString()`, the base class implementation must be called, and it expects a reference to an object as its receiver. Therefore, the receiver is boxed.
- If the receiver is boxed and the struct overrides `ToString()`, the storage location in the box is passed to the overriding method without unboxing it.
- If the receiver is boxed and the struct does not override `ToString()`, the reference to the box is passed to the base class's implementation of the method, which is expecting a reference.

Enums

Compare the two code snippets shown in Listing 9.29.

Obviously, the difference in terms of readability is tremendous—in the second snippet, the cases are self-documenting. However, the performance at runtime is identical. To achieve this outcome, the second snippet uses **enum values**.

Listing 9.29: Comparing an Integer Switch to an Enum Switch

```
int connectionState;
// ...
switch (connectionState)
{
    case 0:
        // ...
        break;
    case 1:
        // ...
        break;
    case 2:
        // ...
        break;
    case 3:
        // ...
        break;
}
// ...
ConnectionState connectionState;
// ...
switch (connectionState)
{
    case ConnectionState.Connected:
        // ...
        break;
    case ConnectionState.Connecting:
        // ...
        break;
    case ConnectionState.Disconnected:
        // ...
        break;
    case ConnectionState.Disconnecting:
        // ...
        break;
}
```

An enum is a value type that the developer can declare. The key characteristic of an enum is that it declares, at compile time, a set of possible constant values that can be referred to by name, thereby making the code easier to read. The syntax for a typical enum declaration is shown in Listing 9.30.

LISTING 9.30: Defining an Enum

```
enum ConnectionState
{
    Disconnected,
    Connecting,
    Connected,
    Disconnecting
}
```

> **NOTE**
>
> An enum can be used as a more readable replacement for Boolean values as well. For example, a method call such as `SetState(true)` is less readable than `SetState(DeviceState.On)`.

You use an enum value by prefixing it with the enum's name. To use the `Connected` value, for example, you would use the syntax `ConnectionState.Connected`. Do not make the enum type name a part of the value's name to avoid the redundancy of `ConnectionState.ConnectionStateConnected` and similar references. By convention, the enum name itself should be singular (unless the enum values are bit flags, as discussed shortly). That is, the nomenclature should be `ConnectionState`, not `ConnectionStates`.

> **Guidelines**
>
> **DO NOT** use the enum type name as part of the values name.
>
> **DO** use an enum type name that is singular unless the enum is a flag.

Enum values are actually implemented as nothing more than integer constants. By default, the first enum value is given the value `0`, and each subsequent entry increases by 1. Alternatively, you can assign explicit values to enum members, as shown in Listing 9.31.

In this code, `Disconnected` has a default value of `0` and `Connecting` has been explicitly assigned `10`; consequently, `Connected` will be assigned `11`. `Joined` is assigned `11`, the value assigned to `Connected`. (In this case, you do not need to

Listing 9.31: Defining an Enum Type

```
enum ConnectionState : short
{
    Disconnected,
    Connecting = 10,
    Connected,
    Joined = Connected,
    Disconnecting
}
```

prefix `Connected` with the enum name, since it appears within its scope.) `Disconnecting` is 12.

An enum always has an underlying type, which may be any integral type other than `char`. In fact, the enum type's performance is identical to that of the underlying type. By default, the underlying value type is `int`, but you can specify a different type using inheritance type syntax. Instead of `int`, for example, Listing 9.15 uses a `short`. For consistency, the syntax for enums emulates the syntax of inheritance, but it doesn't actually create an inheritance relationship. The base class for all enums is `System.Enum`, which in turn is derived from `System.ValueType`. Furthermore, these enums are sealed; you can't derive from an existing enum type to add more members.

Guidelines

CONSIDER using the default 32-bit integer type as the underlying type of an enum. Use a smaller type only if you must do so for interoperability; use a larger type only if you are creating a flags enum[10] with more than 32 flags.

An enum is really nothing more than a set of names thinly layered on top of the underlying type; there is no mechanism that restricts the value of an enumerated type variable to just the values named in the declaration. For example, because it is possible to cast the integer `42` to `short`, it is also possible to cast the integer `42` to

10. See the discussion in the section "Enums as Flags" later in this chapter.

the `ConnectionState` type, even though there is no corresponding `ConnectionState` enum value. If the value can be converted to the underlying type, the conversion to the enum type will also be successful.

The advantage of this odd feature is that enums can have new values added in later API releases, without breaking earlier versions. Additionally, the enum values provide names for the known values while still allowing unknown values to be assigned at runtime. The burden is that developers must code defensively for the possibility of unnamed values. It would be unwise, for example, to replace `case ConnectionState.Disconnecting` with `default` and expect that the only possible value for the `default` case was `ConnectionState.Disconnecting`. Instead, you should handle the `Disconnecting` case explicitly, and the `default` case should report an error or behave innocuously. As indicated earlier, however, conversion between the enum and the underlying type, and vice versa, requires an explicit cast; it is not an implicit conversion. For example, code cannot call `ReportState(10)` if the method's signature is `void ReportState(ConnectionState state)`. The only exception occurs when passing `0`, because there is an implicit conversion from `0` to any enum.

Although you can add more values to an enum in a later version of your code, you should do so with care. Inserting an enum value in the middle of an enum will bump the values of all later enum values (adding `Flooded` or `Locked` before `Connected` will change the `Connected` value, for example). This will affect the versions of all code that is recompiled against the new version. However, any code compiled against the old version will continue to use the old values, making the intended values entirely different. Besides inserting an enum value at the end of the list, one way to avoid changing enum values is to assign values explicitly.

Guidelines

CONSIDER adding new members to existing enums, but keep in mind the compatibility risk.

AVOID creating enums that represent an "incomplete" set of values, such as product version numbers.

AVOID creating "reserved for future use" values in an enum.

AVOID enums that contain a single value.

DO provide a value of `0` (none) for simple enums, knowing that `0` will be the default value when no explicit initialization is provided.

ADVANCED TOPIC

Type Compatibility between Enums

C# also does not support a direct cast between arrays of two different enums. However, the CLR does, provided that both enums share the same underlying type. To work around this restriction of C#, the trick is to cast first to `System.Array`, as shown at the end of Listing 9.32.

LISTING 9.32: Casting between Arrays of Enums

```
enum ConnectionState1
{
    Disconnected,
    Connecting,
    Connected,
    Disconnecting
}

enum ConnectionState2
{
    Disconnected,
    Connecting,
    Connected,
    Disconnecting
}
public class Program
{
    public static void Main()
    {
        ConnectionState1[] states =
            (ConnectionState1[])(Array)new ConnectionState2[42];
    }
}
```

This example exploits the fact that the CLR's notion of assignment compatibility is more lenient than C#'s concept. (The same trick is possible for other illegal conversions, such as from int[] to uint[].) However, you should use this approach cautiously, because no C# specification requires that this behavior work across different CLR implementations.

Converting between Enums and Strings

One of the conveniences associated with enums is that the ToString() method, which is called by methods such as System.Console.WriteLine(), writes out the enum value identifier as shown in Listing 9.33:

LISTING 9.33: Writing Enum Value Identifier to the Trace Buffer

```
System.Diagnostics.Trace.WriteLine(
    $"The connection is currently {ConnectionState.Disconnecting}");
```

The preceding code will write the text in Output 9.3 to the trace buffer.

OUTPUT 9.3

```
The connection is currently Disconnecting.
```

Conversion from a string to an enum is a little less obvious because it involves a static method on the System.Enum base class. Listing 9.34 provides an example of how to do it without generics (see Chapter 12). "Idle" appears as the output.

LISTING 9.34: Converting a String to an Enum Using Enum.TryParse()

```
System.Diagnostics.ThreadPriorityLevel priority;
if(Enum.TryParse("Idle", out priority))
{
    Console.WriteLine(priority);
}
```

This example depicts a compile-time way of identifying the type, like a literal for the type value (see Chapter 18). The TryParse()[11] method (technically TryParse<T>()) uses generics, but the type parameters can be inferred, resulting in the to-enum conversion syntax shown in Listing 9.17. There is also an equivalent

11. Available starting in Microsoft .NET Framework 4.

Parse() method that throws an exception if it fails, making it suboptimal unless success is certain.

Regardless of whether the code uses the "Parse" or "TryParse" approach, the key caution about converting from a string to an enum is that such a cast is not localizable. Therefore, developers should use this type of cast only for messages that are not exposed to users (assuming localization is a requirement).

Guidelines

AVOID direct enum/string conversions where the string must be localized into the user's language.

Enums as Flags

Many times, developers not only want enum values to be unique but also want to be able to represent a combination of values. For example, consider System.IO .FileAttributes. This enum, shown in Listing 9.35, indicates various attributes of a file: read-only, hidden, archive, and so on. Unlike with the ConnectionState attribute, where each enum's values were mutually exclusive, the FileAttributes enum values can be, and are, intended for combination: A file can be both read-only and hidden. To support this behavior, each enum member's value is a unique bit.

LISTING 9.35: Using Enums as Flags

```
[Flags]
public enum FileAttributes
{
    None = 0,                       // 000000000000000
    ReadOnly = 1 << 0,              // 000000000000001
    Hidden = 1 << 1,                // 000000000000010
    System = 1 << 2,                // 000000000000100
    Directory = 1 << 4,             // 000000000010000
    Archive = 1 << 5,               // 000000000100000
    Device = 1 << 6,                // 000000001000000
    Normal = 1 << 7,                // 000000010000000
    Temporary = 1 << 8,             // 000000100000000
    SparseFile = 1 << 9,            // 000001000000000
    ReparsePoint = 1 << 10,         // 000010000000000
    Compressed = 1 << 11,           // 000100000000000
    Offline = 1 << 12,              // 001000000000000
```

```
        NotContentIndexed = 1 << 13,     // 010000000000000
        Encrypted = 1 << 14,             // 100000000000000
    }
```

> **NOTE**
>
> Note that the name of a bit flags enum is usually pluralized, indicating that a value of the type represents a set of flags.

To join enum values, you use a bitwise OR operator. To test for the existence of a particular flag, use the `Enum.HasFlags()` method or use the bitwise AND operator. Both cases are illustrated in Listing 9.36 with Output 9.4.

Listing 9.36: Using Bitwise OR and AND with Flag Enums[12]

```
using System;
using System.IO;

public class Program
{
    public static void Main()
    {
        // ...

        string fileName = @"enumtest.txt";

        // ...
            System.IO.FileInfo file = new(fileName);

            file.Attributes = FileAttributes.Hidden |
                FileAttributes.ReadOnly;

            Console.WriteLine($"{file.Attributes} = {(int)file.
↪Attributes}");

            // Only the ReadOnly attribute works on Linux
            // (The Hidden attribute does not work on Linux)
            if (!System.Runtime.InteropServices.RuntimeInformation.
↪IsOSPlatform(System.Runtime.InteropServices.OSPlatform.Linux))
```

12. Note that the `FileAttributes.Hidden` value does not work on Linux.

```
            {
                // Added in C# 4.0/Microsoft .NET Framework  4.0
                if (!file.Attributes.HasFlag(FileAttributes.Hidden))
                {
                    throw new Exception("File is not hidden.");
                }
            }

            if ((file.Attributes & FileAttributes.ReadOnly) !=
            FileAttributes.ReadOnly)
            {
                throw new Exception("File is not read-only.");
            }
        // ...
    }
}
```

Output 9.4

```
Hidden | ReadOnly = 3
```

Using the bitwise OR operator allows you to set the file attributes to both read-only and hidden.

Each value within the enum does not need to correspond to only one flag. It is perfectly reasonable to define additional flags that correspond to frequent combinations of values. Listing 9.37 shows an example.

Listing 9.37: Defining Enum Values for Frequent Combinations

```
[Flags]
enum DistributedChannel
{
    None = 0,
    Transacted = 1,
    Queued = 2,
    Encrypted = 4,
    Persisted = 16,
    FaultTolerant =
        Transacted | Queued | Persisted
}
```

It is a good practice to have a zero `None` member in a flags enum because the initial default value of a field of enum type or an element of an array of enum type is

0. Avoid enum values corresponding to items such as `Maximum` as the last enum, because `Maximum` could be interpreted as a valid enum value. To check whether a value is included within an enum, use the `System.Enum.IsDefined()` method.

Guidelines

DO use the `FlagsAttribute` to mark enums that contain flag values.

DO provide a `None` value equal to `0` for all enums.

AVOID creating flag enums where the zero value has a meaning other than "no flags are set."

CONSIDER providing special values for commonly used combinations of flags.

DO NOT include "sentinel" values (such as a value called `Maximum`); such values can be confusing to the user.

DO use powers of 2 to ensure that all flag combinations are represented uniquely.

ADVANCED TOPIC

FlagsAttribute

If you decide to use bit flag enums, you should mark the declaration of the enum with `FlagsAttribute`. In such a case, the attribute appears in square brackets (see Chapter 18) just prior to the enum declaration, as shown in Listing 9.38 with Output 9.5.

LISTING 9.38: Using `FlagsAttribute`

```
//FileAttributes are defined in System.IO

using System;
using System.IO;

public class Program
{
    public static void Main()
    {
```

```
            string fileName = @"enumtest.txt";
            // ...
            FileInfo file = new(fileName);
            file.Open(FileMode.OpenOrCreate).Dispose();

            FileAttributes startingAttributes =
                file.Attributes;

            file.Attributes = FileAttributes.Hidden |
                FileAttributes.ReadOnly;

            Console.WriteLine("\"{0}\" outputs as \"{1}\"",
                file.Attributes.ToString().Replace(",", " |"),
                file.Attributes);

            FileAttributes attributes =
                (FileAttributes)Enum.Parse(typeof(FileAttributes),
                file.Attributes.ToString());

            Console.WriteLine(attributes);

            File.SetAttributes(fileName,
                startingAttributes);
            file.Delete();
        }
    }
```

OUTPUT 9.5

```
"ReadOnly | Hidden" outputs as "ReadOnly, Hidden"
ReadOnly, Hidden
```

The attribute documents that the enum values can be combined. Furthermore, it changes the behavior of the `ToString()` and `Parse()` methods. For example, calling `ToString()` on an enum that is decorated with `FlagsAttribute` writes out the strings for each enum flag that is set. In Listing 9.21, `file.Attributes.ToString()` returns `ReadOnly, Hidden` rather than the 3 it would have returned without the `FileAttributes` flag. If two enum values are the same, the `ToString()` call would return the first value. As mentioned earlier, you should use caution when relying on this behavior because it is not localizable.

Parsing a value from a string to the enum also works. Each enum value identifier is separated from the others by a comma.

Note that `FlagsAttribute` does not automatically assign unique flag values or check that they have unique values. Doing this wouldn't make sense, given that duplicates and combinations are often desirable. Instead, you must assign the values of each enum item explicitly.

Summary

This chapter began with a discussion comparing reference equality with value equality and how, by default, reference types use reference equality when checking for equality, where value types check the values themselves or, for custom value types, the data within the custom value type. Recall, however, that custom-built value types, structs, are relatively rare compared to the number of custom-built classes and are generally limited to code intended to interoperate with unmanaged code.

We then introduced record structs and record classes, identifying that while the code generation is mostly the same, there are some important differences. Most importantly, both record structs and record classes override equality to use value type equality. This provides a significant feature if value equivalence is needed on a type because implementing such is complex and error prone. Another similarity is that they both use the positional parameters to generate properties, a constructor, `ToString()` implementations, and a deconstructor. Where they differ, however, is that by default record structs are read/write, while record classes use init-only setters by default for all positional parameters. That said, because it is easy to write confusing or buggy code when mutating value types and because value types are typically used to model immutable values, the best practice is to declare record structs with the readonly modifier. Also, only record classes support inheritance—although only from other record classes. In fact, all structs (record or standard) don't support inheritance.

Value types are boxed when they must be treated polymorphically as reference types. The idiosyncrasies introduced by boxing are subtle, and the vast majority of them lead to problematic issues at execution time rather than at compile time. Although it is important to know about these quirks to try to avoid them, in many ways paying too much attention to the potential pitfalls overshadows the usefulness and performance advantages of value types. Programmers should not be overly concerned about using value types. Value types permeate virtually every chapter of this book, yet the idiosyncrasies associated with them come into play infrequently. We have staged the code surrounding each issue to demonstrate the concern, but in reality, these types of patterns rarely occur. The key to avoiding most of them is to follow the guideline of not creating mutable value types—and following this constraint explains why you don't encounter them within the built-in value types.

Perhaps the only issue to occur with some frequency is repetitive boxing operations within loops. However, generics greatly reduce boxing, and even without them, performance is rarely affected enough to warrant their avoidance until a particular algorithm with boxing is identified as a bottleneck.

This chapter also introduced enums. Enumerated types are a standard construct available in many programming languages. They help improve both API usability and code readability.

Chapter 10 presents more guidelines for creating well-formed types—both value types and reference types. It begins by defining operator-overloading methods. These two topics apply to both structs and classes, but they are somewhat more important when completing a struct definition and making it well formed.

10

Well-Formed Types

The previous chapters covered most of the constructs for defining records and value types (structs and enums). However, several details remain to round out the type definition with fit-and-finish-type functionality. This chapter explains how to put the final touches on a type declaration, which includes such concepts as operator overloading, referencing other libraries, additional access modifiers, namespaces, inline documentation with XML comments, and resource management.

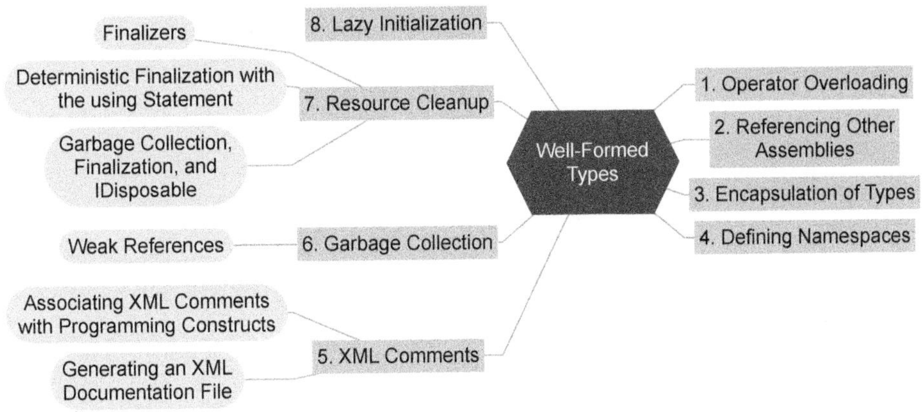

Operator Overloading

The preceding chapter looked at implementing value equality behavior and provided the guideline that the class should also implement `==` and `!=`. Implementing any operator is called operator overloading. This section describes how to perform such overloading not only for `==` and `!=`, but also for other supported operators.

For example, `string` provides a `+` operator that concatenates two strings. This is perhaps not surprising, because `string` is a predefined type, so it could possibly have special compiler support. However, C# provides for adding `+` operator support to a class or struct. In fact, all operators are supported except `x.y`, `f(x)`, `new`, `typeof`, `default`, `checked`, `unchecked`, `delegate`, `is`, `as`, `=`, and `=>`. One particularly noteworthy operator that cannot be implemented is the assignment operator; there is no way to change the behavior of the `=` operator.

Before going through the exercise of implementing an operator overload, consider the fact that such operators are not discoverable through IntelliSense. Unless the intent is for a type to act like a primitive type (e.g., a numeric type), you should avoid overloading an operator as the only means of accessing the behavior.

Comparison Operators (==, !=, <, >, <=, >=)

In Chapter 9 (https://essentialcsharp.com/implementing-value-equality) we reviewed the code generated for a record's implementation of the `==` and `!=` operators. In addition, you can override the greater and less than operators, including when combined with equality checks (see Listing 10.1).

Listing 10.1: Implementing the `==` and `!=` Operators

```
public sealed class ProductSerialNumber
{
    // ...

    public static bool operator ==(
        ProductSerialNumber leftHandSide,
        ProductSerialNumber rightHandSide)
    {

        // Check if leftHandSide is null
        // (operator == would be recursive)
        if(leftHandSide is null)
```

```
        {
            // Return true if rightHandSide is also null
            // and false otherwise
            return rightHandSide is null;
        }

        return (leftHandSide.Equals(rightHandSide));
    }

    public static bool operator !=(
        ProductSerialNumber leftHandSide,
        ProductSerialNumber rightHandSide)
    {
        return !(leftHandSide == rightHandSide);
    }
}
```

Note that the compiler enforces implementing these comparison operators in pairs (`==`, `!=`), (`<`, `>`), (`<=`, `>=`). The implementation in Listing 10.1 relies on one pair element calling the other. Also, for reference types, be sure to handle null appropriately—before invoking any of the members. You should never throw an exception from within an operator overloading implementation.

> **Guidelines**
>
> **DO NOT** throw exceptions from within the implementation of operator overloading.

Binary Operators (+, -, *, /, %, &, |, ^, <<, >>)

You can add an `Arc` to a `Coordinate`. However, the code so far provides no support for the addition operator. Instead, you need to define such a method, as Listing 10.2 demonstrates.

Listing 10.2: Adding an Operator

```
public readonly struct Arc
{
    public Arc(
        Longitude longitudeDifference,
        Latitude latitudeDifference)
```

```
    {
        LongitudeDifference = longitudeDifference;
        LatitudeDifference = latitudeDifference;
    }

    public Longitude LongitudeDifference { get; }
    public Latitude LatitudeDifference { get; }

}

public readonly struct Coordinate
{
    // ...
    public static Coordinate operator +(
        Coordinate source, Arc arc)
    {
        Coordinate result = new(
            new Longitude(
                source.Longitude + arc.LongitudeDifference),
            new Latitude(
                source.Latitude + arc.LatitudeDifference));
        return result;
    }
    // ...
}
```

The +, -, *, /, %, &, |, ^, <<, and >> operators are implemented as binary static methods, where at least one parameter is of the containing type. The method name is the operator symbol prefixed by the keyword `operator`. As shown in Listing 10.3 with Output 10.1, given the definition of the - and + binary operators, you can add and subtract an `Arc` to and from the coordinate. Note that `Longitude` and `Latitude` will also require implementations of the + operator because they are called by `source.Longitude + arc.LongitudeDifference` and `source.Latitude + arc.LatitudeDifference`.

Listing 10.3: Calling the – and + Binary Operators

```
// Use compound assignment suppressed for demonstration purposes
#pragma warning disable IDE0054
public class Program
{
    public static void Main()
```

```
    {
        Coordinate coordinate1, coordinate2;
        coordinate1 = new Coordinate(
            new Longitude(48, 52), new Latitude(-2, -20));
        Arc arc = new(new Longitude(3), new Latitude(1));

        coordinate2 = coordinate1 + arc;
        Console.WriteLine(coordinate2);

        coordinate2 = coordinate2 - arc;
        Console.WriteLine(coordinate2);

        coordinate2 += arc;
        Console.WriteLine(coordinate2);
    }
}
```

OUTPUT 10.1

```
51° 52' 0 E  -1° -20' 0 N
48° 52' 0 E  -2° -20' 0 N
51° 52' 0 E  -1° -20' 0 N
```

For `Coordinate`, you implement the – and + operators to return coordinate locations after adding/subtracting `Arc`. This allows you to string multiple operators and operands together, as in `result = ((coordinate1 + arc1) + arc2) + arc3`. Moreover, by supporting the same operators (+/-) on `Arc` (see Listing 10.4 later in this chapter), you could eliminate the parentheses. This approach works because the result of the first operand (`arc1 + arc2`) is another `Arc`, which you can then add to the next operand of type `Arc` or `Coordinate`.

In contrast, consider what would happen if you provided a – operator that had two `Coordinates` as parameters and returned a `double` corresponding to the distance between the two `coordinates`. Adding a `double` to a `Coordinate` is undefined, so you could not string together operators and operands. Caution is in order when defining operators that return a different type, because doing so is counterintuitive.

Combining Assignment with Binary Operators (+=, -=, *=, /=, %=, &=, ...)

As previously mentioned, there is no support for overloading the assignment operator. However, assignment operators in combination with binary operators (+=, -=, *=, /=, %=, &=, |=, ^=, <<=, and >>=) are effectively overloaded when overloading the binary operator. Given the definition of a binary operator without the assignment, C# automatically allows for assignment in combination with the operator. Using the definition of `Coordinate` in Listing 10.2, therefore, you can have code such as

```
coordinate += arc;
```

which is equivalent to the following:

```
coordinate = coordinate + arc;
```

Conditional Logical Operators (&&, ||)

Like assignment operators, conditional logical operators cannot be overloaded explicitly. However, because the logical operators & and | can be overloaded, and the conditional operators comprise the logical operators, effectively it is possible to overload conditional operators. `x && y` is processed as `x & y`, where `y` must evaluate to `true`. Similarly, `x || y` is processed as `x | y` only if `x` is `false`. To enable support for evaluating a type to `true` or `false`—in an `if` statement, for example—it is necessary to override the `true`/`false` unary operators.

Unary Operators (+, -, !, ~, ++, --, true, false)

Overloading unary operators is very similar to overloading binary operators, except that they take only one parameter, also of the containing type. Listing 10.4 overloads the + and – operators for `Longitude` and `Latitude` and then uses these operators when overloading the same operators in `Arc`.

Just as with numeric types, the + operator in this listing doesn't have any effect and is provided for symmetry.

Listing 10.4: Overloading the – and + Unary Operators

```
public struct Latitude
{
    // ...
    public static Latitude operator -(Latitude latitude)
    {
        return new Latitude(-latitude.Degrees);
    }

    public static Latitude operator +(Latitude latitude)
    {
        return latitude;
    }

    // ...
}

public struct Longitude
{
    // ...
    public static Longitude operator -(Longitude longitude)
    {
        return new Longitude(-longitude.Degrees);
    }

    public static Longitude operator +(Longitude longitude)
    {
        return longitude;
    }
    // ...
}
public readonly struct Arc
{
    // ...
    public static Arc operator -(Arc arc)
    {
        // Uses unary - operator defined on
        // Longitude and Latitude
        return new Arc(-arc.LongitudeDifference,
            -arc.LatitudeDifference);
    }

    public static Arc operator +(Arc arc)
    {
        return arc;
```

```
    }
}
```

Overloading the `true` and `false` operators is subject to the additional requirement that *both* must be overloaded—not just one of the two. The signatures are the same as with other operator overloads; however, the return must be a `bool`, as demonstrated in Listing 10.5.

LISTING 10.5: Overloading the `true` and `false` Operators

```
public static bool operator false(object item)
{
    // ...
}
public static bool operator true(object item)
{
    // ...
}
```

You can use types with overloaded `true` and `false` operators in `if`, `do`, `while`, and `for` controlling expressions.

Conversion Operators

Currently, there is no support in `Longitude`, `Latitude`, and `Coordinate` for casting to an alternative type. For example, there is no way to cast a `double` into a `Longitude` or `Latitude` instance. Similarly, there is no support for assigning a `Coordinate` using a `string`. Fortunately, C# provides for the definition of methods specifically intended to handle the converting of one type to another. Furthermore, the method declaration allows for specifying whether the conversion is implicit or explicit.

ADVANCED TOPIC

Cast Operator (())

Implementing the explicit and implicit conversion operators is not technically overloading the cast operator (()). However, this action is effectively what takes place, so *defining a cast operator* is common terminology for implementing explicit or implicit conversion.

Defining a conversion operator is similar in style to defining any other operator, except that the "operator" is the resultant type of the conversion. Additionally, the `operator` keyword follows a keyword that indicates whether the conversion is implicit or explicit (see Listing 10.6).

LISTING 10.6: Providing an Implicit Conversion between `Latitude` and `double`

```
public readonly struct Latitude
{
    // ...

    public Latitude(double decimalDegrees)
    {
        DecimalDegrees = Normalize(decimalDegrees);
    }

    public double DecimalDegrees { get; }

    // ...

    public static implicit operator double(Latitude latitude)
    {
        return latitude.DecimalDegrees;
    }
    public static implicit operator Latitude(double degrees)
    {
        return new Latitude(degrees);
    }

    // ...
}
```

With these conversion operators, you now can convert `doubles` implicitly to and from `Latitude` objects. Assuming similar conversions exist for `Longitude`, you can simplify the creation of a `Coordinate` object by specifying the decimal degrees portion of each coordinate portion (e.g., `coordinate = new Coordinate(43, 172);`).

> **NOTE**
>
> When implementing a conversion operator, either the return or the parameter must be of the enclosing type—in support of encapsulation. C# does not allow you to specify conversions outside the scope of the converted type.

Guidelines for Conversion Operators

The difference between defining an implicit and an explicit conversion operator centers on preventing an unintentional implicit conversion that results in undesirable behavior. You should be aware of two possible consequences of using the explicit conversion operator. First, conversion operators that throw exceptions should always be explicit. For example, it is highly likely that a string will not conform to the format that a conversion from `string` to `Coordinate` requires. Given the chance of a failed conversion, you should define the particular conversion operator as explicit, thereby requiring that you be intentional about the conversion and ensure that the format is correct or, alternatively, that you provide code to handle the possible exception. Frequently, the pattern for conversion is that one direction (`string` to `Coordinate`) is explicit and the reverse (`Coordinate` to `string`) is implicit.

A second consideration is that some conversions will be lossy. Converting from a `float` (`4.2`) to an `int` is entirely valid, assuming an awareness of the fact that the decimal portion of the `float` will be lost. Any conversions that will lose data and will not successfully convert back to the original type should be defined as explicit. If an explicit cast is unexpectedly lossy or invalid, consider throwing a `System.InvalidCastException`.

Guidelines

DO NOT provide an implicit conversion operator if the conversion is lossy.

DO NOT throw exceptions from implicit conversions.

Referencing Other Assemblies

Instead of placing all code into one monolithic binary file, C# and the underlying CLI framework allow you to spread code across multiple assemblies. This approach enables you to reuse assemblies across multiple executables.

BEGINNER TOPIC

Class Libraries

The `HelloWorld` program is one of the most trivial programs you can write. Real-world programs are more complex, and as complexity increases, it helps to organize the complexity by breaking programs into multiple parts. To do this, developers move portions of a program into separate compiled units called **class libraries** or, simply, **libraries**. Programs then reference and rely on class libraries to provide parts of their functionality. The power of this concept is that two programs can rely on the same class library, thereby sharing the functionality of that class library across both programs and reducing the total amount of code needed.

With this approach, it is possible to write features once, place them into a class library, and allow multiple programs to include those features by referencing the same class library. Later in the development cycle, when developers fix a bug or add functionality to the class library, all the programs will have access to the increased functionality, just because they continue to reference the now improved class library.

Frequently, the code we write could be useful to more than one program. Imagine, for example, using the `Longitude`, `Latitude`, and `Coordinate` classes from a mapping program and a digital photo geocoding program or writing a command-line parser class. Classes and sets of classes like these can be written once and then reused from many different programs. As such, they need to be grouped together into an assembly called a *library* or *class library* and written for the purposes of reuse rather than only within a single program.

To create a library rather than a console project, follow the same directions as provided in Chapter 1, with one exception: For Dotnet CLI, use Class Library or classlib for the template.

Similarly, with Visual Studio 2022, from the **File->New Project...** menu item (Ctrl+Shift+N), use the **Search** text box to find all Class Library templates, and then select **Class Library**—the Visual C# version, of course. Use GeoCoordinates for the project name.

Next, place the source code from Listing 10.4 into separate files for each struct and name the file after the struct name and build the project. Building the project will compile the C# code into an assembly—a `GeoCoordinates.dll` file—and place it into a subdirectory of `.\bin\`.

Referencing a Library

Given the library, we need to **reference** it from a program. For example, for a new console program using the `Program` class from Listing 10.3, we need to add a reference to the `GeoCoordinates.dll` assembly, identifying where the library is located and embedding metadata that uniquely identifies the library into the program. There are several ways to do this. First, you can reference the library project file (`*.csproj`), thus identifying which project contains the library source code and forming a dependency between the two projects. You can't compile the program referencing the library until the library is compiled. This dependency causes the library to compile (if it isn't compiled already) when the program compiles.

The second approach is to reference the assembly file itself. In other words, reference the compiled library (`*.dll`) rather than the project. This makes sense when the library is compiled separately from the program, such as by another team within your organization.

Third, you can reference a NuGet package, as described in the next section.

Note that it isn't only console programs that can reference libraries and packages. In fact, any assembly can reference any other assembly. Frequently, one library will reference another library, creating a chain of dependencies.

Referencing a Project or Library with Dotnet CLI

In Chapter 1, we discussed creating a console program. Doing so created a program that included a `Main` method—the entry point at which the program will begin executing. To add a reference to the newly created assembly, we continue where we left off with an additional command for adding a reference:

```
dotnet add .\HelloWorld\HelloWord.csproj package
.\GeoCordinates\bin\Debug\netcoreapp2.0\GeoCoordinates.dll
```

Following the `add` argument is a file path for the compiled assembly referenced by the project.

Rather than referencing the assembly, you can reference the project file. As already mentioned, this chains the projects together so that building the program will trigger the class library to compile first if it hasn't compiled already. The advantage is that as the program compiles, it will automatically locate the compiled class library assembly—whether it be in the debug or release directory, for example. The command for referencing a project file is as follows:

```
dotnet add .\HelloWorld\HelloWord.csproj reference
.\GeoCoordinates\GeoCoordinates.csproj
```

If you have the source code for a class library and that source code changes frequently, consider referencing the class library using the class library project file rather than the compiled assembly.

Upon completion of either the project or the compiled assembly reference, your project can compile with the `Program` class source code found in Listing 10.3.

Referencing a Project or Library with Visual Studio 2022

In Chapter 1, we also discussed creating a console program with Visual Studio. This created a program that included a `Main` method. To add a reference to the `GeoCoordinates` assembly, click the **Project->Add Reference...** menu item.

Next, from the **Projects\Solution** tab, select the **GeoCoordinates** project and **OK** to confirm the reference.

Similarly, to add an assembly reference, follow the same process as before, clicking the **Project->Add Reference...** menu item. However, this time click the **Browse...** button and navigate to and select the `GeoCordinates.dll` assembly.

As with Dotnet CLI, you can compile the program project with the `Program` class source code found in Listing 10.3.

NuGet Packaging

Starting with Visual Studio 2010, Microsoft introduced a library packaging system called NuGet. This system is intended to provide a means to easily share libraries across projects and between companies. Frequently, a library assembly is more than just a single compiled file. It might have configuration files, additional resources, and metadata associated with it. Unfortunately, before NuGet, there was no manifest that identified all the dependencies. Furthermore, there was no standard provider or package library for where the referenced assemblies could be found.

NuGet addresses both issues. Not only does NuGet include a manifest that identifies the author(s), companies, dependencies, and more, it also comes with a default package provider at NuGet.org where packages can be uploaded, updated, indexed, and then downloaded by projects that are looking to leverage them. With NuGet, you can reference a **NuGet package** (`*.nupkg`) and have it automatically installed from one of your preconfigured NuGet provider URLs.

The NuGet package is accompanied by a manifest (a `*.nuspec` file) that contains all the additional metadata included in the package. Additionally, it provides all the additional resources you may want—localization files, config files, content files, and so on. In the end, the NuGet package is an archive of all the individual resources combined into a single ZIP file—albeit with the `.nupkg` extension. If you rename the file with a `*.zip` extension, you can open and examine the file using any common compression utility.

NuGet References with Dotnet CLI

To add a NuGet package to your project using Dotnet CLI requires executing a single command:

```
>dotnet add .\HelloWorld\HelloWorld.csproj package Microsoft
.Extensions.Logging.Console
```

This command checks each of the registered NuGet package providers for the specified package and downloads it. (You can also trigger the download explicitly using the command `dotnet restore`.)

To create a local NuGet package, use the `dotnet pack` command. This command generates a `GeoCoordinates.1.0.0.nupkg` file, which you can reference using the `add ... package` command.

The digits following the assembly name correspond to the package version number. To specify the version number explicitly, edit the project file (`*.csproj`) and add a `<Version>...</Version>` child element to the `PropertyGroup` element.

NuGet References with Visual Studio 2022

If you followed the instructions laid out in Chapter 1, you already have a `HelloWorld` project. Starting with that project, you can add a NuGet package using Visual Studio 2022 as follows:

1. Click the **Project->Manage NuGet Packages...** menu item (see Figure 10.1).
2. Select the **Browse** filter (generally the Installed filter is selected, so be sure to switch to **Browse** to add new package references), and then enter *Microsoft.Extensions.Logging.Console* into the **Search** (Ctrl+E) text box. Note that a partial name such as *Logging.Console* will also filter the list (see Figure 10.2).
3. Click the **Install** button to install the package into the project.

Upon completion of these steps, it is possible to begin using the `Microsoft.Extensions.Logging.Console` library, along with any dependencies that it may have (which are automatically added in the process).

As with Dotnet CLI, you can use Visual Studio to build your own NuGet package using the **Build->Pack <Project Name>** menu item. Similarly, you can specify the package version number from the **Package** tab of the **Project Properties**.

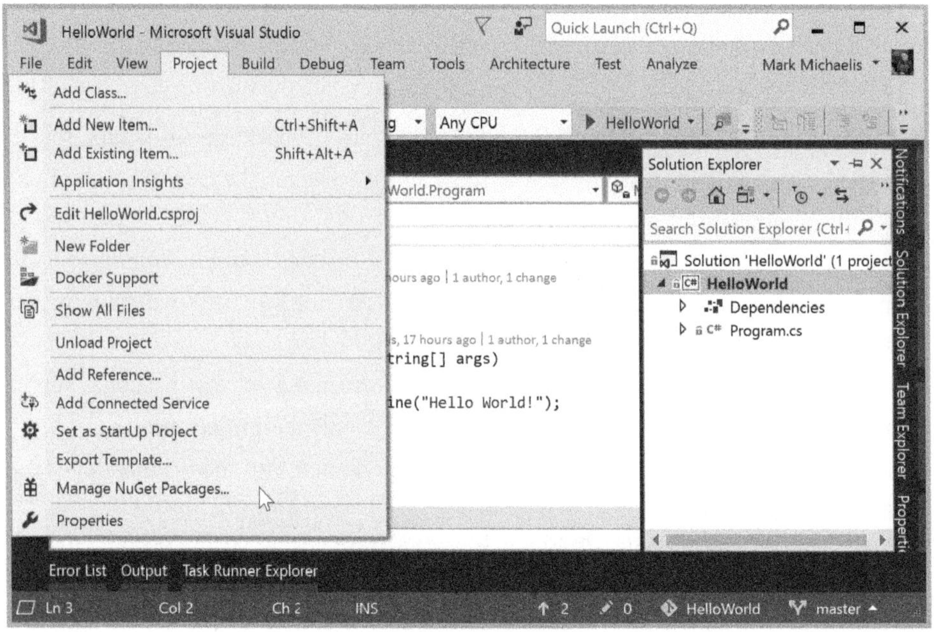

FIGURE 10.1: The Project menu

Invoking a Referenced Package or Project

Once the package or project is referenced, you can begin using it as though all the source code was included in the project. Listing 10.7 shows, for example, how to use the `Microsoft.Extensions.Logging` library, and Output 10.2 shows the sample output.

LISTING 10.7: Invoking a NuGet Package Reference

```
public sealed class Program
{
    public static void Main(string[] args)
    {
        using ILoggerFactory loggerFactory =
            LoggerFactory.Create(builder =>
            builder.AddConsole().AddDebug());

        ILogger logger = loggerFactory.CreateLogger<Program>();
```

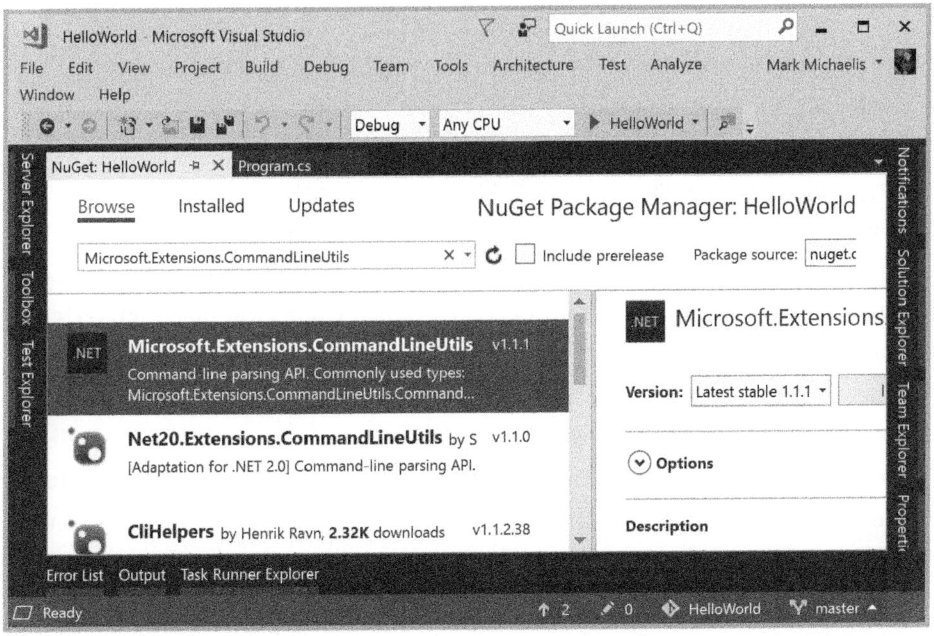

FIGURE 10.2: The Browse filter

```
        logger.LogInformation($@"Hospital Emergency Codes: = '{
            string.Join("', '", args)}'");
        // ...

        logger.LogWarning("This is a test of the emergency...");
        // ...
    }
}
```

OUTPUT 10.2

```
>dotnet run -- black blue brown CBR orange purple red yellow
info: Console[0]
      Hospital Emergency Codes: = 'black', 'blue', 'brown', 'CBR',
'orange', 'purple', 'red', 'yellow'
warn: Console[0]
      This is a test of the emergency...
```

This library `Microsoft.Extensions.Logging.Console` NuGet package is used to log data to the console. In this case, we log both an information message and a warning and the messages appear in the console.

If you also referenced the `Microsoft.Extensions.Logging.Debug` library, you could add an `.AddDebug()` invocation after or before the `AddConsole()` invocation. The result would be that output similar to Output 10.2 would also appear in the debug output window of Visual Studio (select the **Debug->Windows->Output** menu) or Visual Studio Code (with the **View->Debug Console** menu).

The Microsoft.Extensions.Logging.Console NuGet package has three dependencies, including Microsoft.Extensions.Logging. Each of these is listed under the **Dependencies\Packages** node of the project in the **Visual Studio Explorer** window of Visual Studio. By adding a NuGet package, all dependencies are automatically added.

Encapsulation of Types

Just as classes serve as an encapsulation boundary for behavior and data, so assemblies provide for similar boundaries among groups of types. Developers can break a system into assemblies and then share those assemblies with multiple applications or integrate them with assemblies provided by third parties.

`public` or `internal` Access Modifiers on Type Declarations

By default, a class or struct without any access modifier is defined as `internal`.[1] The result is that the class is inaccessible from outside the assembly. Even if another assembly references the assembly containing the class, all internal classes within the referenced assemblies will be inaccessible.

Just as `private` and `protected` provide levels of encapsulation to members within a class, so C# supports the use of access modifiers at the class level for control over the encapsulation of the classes within an assembly. The access modifiers available are `public` and `internal`. To expose a class outside the assembly, the

1. Excluding nested types, which are `private` by default.

assembly must be marked as `public`. Therefore, before compiling the `Coordinates.dll` assembly, it is necessary to ensure the type declaration is `public` (see Listing 10.8).

Listing 10.8: Making Types Available outside an Assembly

```
public struct Coordinate
{
    // ...
}

public struct Latitude
{
    // ...
}

public struct Longitude
{
    // ...
}

public struct Arc
{
    // ...
}
```

Similarly, declarations such as `class` and `enum` can be either `public` or `internal`.[2] The internal access modifier is not limited to type declarations; that is, it is also available on type members. Consequently, you can designate a type as `public` but mark specific methods within the type as `internal` so that the members are available only from within the assembly. It is not possible for the members to have a greater accessibility than the type. If the class is declared as `internal`, public members on the type will be accessible only from within the assembly.

2. . You can decorate nested classes with any access modifier available to other class members (e.g., `private`). However, outside the class scope, the only access modifiers that are available are `public` and `internal`.

The `protected internal` Type Modifier

Another type member access modifier is `protected internal`. Members with an accessibility modifier of `protected internal` will be accessible from all locations within the containing assembly *and* from classes that derive from the type, even if the derived class is not in the same assembly. The default member access modifier is `private`, so when you add an access modifier (other than `public`), the member becomes slightly more visible.

> **NOTE**
>
> Members with an accessibility modifier of `protected internal` will be accessible from all locations within the containing assembly *and* from classes that derive from the type, even if the derived class is not in the same assembly.

Begin 11.0

The `file` Type Modifier

C# 11 introduced a new access modifier, the `file` modifier. Decorating a type with the file modifier restricts its visibility to within the file only. A `file class Thing{ }` defined in one file would not be visible outside the file. In fact, you could have multiple files with the same project all defined as `file class Thing{}` and there would be no conflict since they would not be visible to each other. The `file` modifier is mostly used in code generation so that and types generated specifically for internal purposes would not affect existing code, and, in fact, the same code generation in multiple files would be encapsulated locally to the file.[3]

3. `file` cannot be used for nested type definitions—only top-level definitions.

BEGINNER TOPIC

Type Member Accessibility Modifiers

The full list of access modifiers appears in Table 10.1.

TABLE 10.1: Accessibility Modifiers

Modifier	Description
`public`	The member is accessible anywhere the type is accessible.
`internal`	The member is accessible from within the assembly only.
`private`	The member is accessible from within the containing type but inaccessible otherwise.
`protected`	The member is accessible within the containing type and any subtypes derived from it, regardless of the assembly.
`protected internal`	The member is accessible from anywhere within the containing assembly *and* from any types derived from the containing type, even if the derived types are within a different assembly.
`private protected`	The member is accessible from any types derived from the containing type that are also in the same assembly.[4]
`file`	The member is accessible only from the same file.

End 11.0

Begin 10.0

Defining Namespaces

As mentioned in Chapter 2, all data types are identified by the combination of their namespace and their name. However, in the CLR, there is no such thing as a "namespace." The type's name actually is the fully qualified type name, including the namespace. For the classes you defined earlier, there was no explicit namespace

4. Added in C# 7.2.

declaration. Classes such as these are automatically declared as members of the default global namespace. It is likely that such classes will experience a name collision, however, which occurs when you attempt to define two classes with the same name. Once you begin referencing other assemblies from third parties, the likelihood of a name collision increases even further.

More important, there are thousands of types in the CLI framework and multiple orders of magnitude more outside the framework. Finding the right type for a particular problem, therefore, could potentially be a significant challenge.

The resolution to both of these problems is to organize all the types, grouping them into logical related categories called namespaces. For example, classes outside the `System` namespace are generally placed into a namespace corresponding with the company, product name, or both. Classes from Addison-Wesley, for example, are placed into an `Awl` or `AddisonWesley` namespace, and classes from Microsoft (not `System` classes) are in the `Microsoft` namespace. Namespaces may include a period in the name, and doing so provides for a hierarchical organization of classes. All the `System` classes relating to network APIs are in the namespace `System.Net`, for example, and those relating to the Web are in `System.Web`. The second level of a namespace should be a stable product name that will not vary between versions. Stability, in fact, is key at all levels. Changing a namespace name is a version-incompatible change that should be avoided. For this reason, you should avoid using volatile names (organization hierarchy, fleeting brands, and so on) within a namespace name. While generally namespaces should be labeled using PascalCase, if your brand uses nontraditional casing, it is acceptable to use the brand casing. (Consistency is key, so if that will be problematic—with PascalCase or brand-based casing—favor the use of whichever convention will produce the greater consistency.)

You use the `namespace` keyword to create a namespace and to assign a class to it, as shown in Listing 10.9.

Listing 10.9: Defining a File-Scoped Namespace

```
// Define the namespace AddisonWesley.Michaelis.EssentialCSharp
namespace AddisonWesley.Michaelis.EssentialCSharp;
class Program
{
```

```
    // ...
}
```

A **file-scoped namespace declaration** (added in C# 10.0) has a statement like syntax with the ending semicolon. The file-scoped namespace declaration must precede all other member definitions in the file and there can be only one such declaration. And, given the declaration, all members within the file will be assigned to that namespace. In Listing 10.9, for example, `Program` is placed into the namespace `AddisonWesley.Michaelis.EssentialCSharp`, making its full name `AddisonWesley.Michaelis.EssentialCSharp.Program`. If you are programming in C# 10.0 or later, I recommend using this form. It cuts down on unnecessary indentation and handles all standard cases of namespace declaration. Additionally, except for HelloWorld scenarios, you should specify a namespace for all your types.

> **NOTE**
>
> In the CLR, there is no such thing as a "namespace." Rather, the type's name is the fully qualified type name.

Prior to C# 10, namespace declarations used curly braces to identify the scope as demonstrated in Listing 10.10.

Listing 10.10: Defining a Namespace

```
// Define the namespace AddisonWesley
namespace AddisonWesley.Michaelis.EssentialCSharp
{
    class Program
    {
        // ...
    }
}
// End of AddisonWesley namespace declaration
```

All content between the namespace declaration's curly braces will then belong within the specified namespace. Declaring a namespace using curly braces allows multiple namespace declarations it to occur in a single file. However, given the guideline of one-to-one correlation between files and type definitions (i.e., one class per file), it would be unusual to have multiple namespaces in the same file.

ADVANCED TOPIC

Nesting Namespaces

Like classes, namespaces declared using curly braces support nesting. In the examples so far, the hierarchy of namespaces is defined simply using a period in the namespace name. However, it is also possible to define the hierarchy using nesting within the curly braces (similar to classes), as demonstrated in Listing 10.11.

Listing 10.11: Nesting Namespaces within One Another

```
// Define the namespace AddisonWesley.Michaelis
namespace AddisonWesley.Michaelis
{
        // Define the namespace
        // AddisonWesley.Michaelis.EssentialCSharp
        namespace EssentialCSharp
        {
            // Declare the class
            // AddisonWesley.Michaelis.EssentialCSharp.Program
            class Program
            {
                // ...
            }
    }
}
// End of AddisonWesley namespace declaration
```

All three namespace related listings (Listing 10.9 - Listing 10.11) will assign the `Program` class to the `AddisonWesley.Michaelis.EssentialCSharp` namespace.

Given that namespaces are key for organizing types, it is frequently helpful to use the namespace for organizing all the class files. For this reason, it is a good idea to create a folder for each namespace, placing a class such as `AddisonWesley.Fezzik.Services.RegistrationService` into a folder hierarchy corresponding to the name. For example, if the project name is `AddisonWesley.Fezzik`, you should create one subfolder called `Services` into which `RegistrationService.cs` is placed. You would then create another subfolder (`Data`, for example) into which you place classes relating to entities within the program (`RealestateProperty`, `Buyer`, and `Seller`, for example).

Guidelines

DO use file-scoped namespaces (C# 10.0 or later).

DO prefix namespace names with a company name to prevent namespaces from different companies having the same name.

DO use a stable, version-independent product name at the second level of a namespace name.

DO NOT define types without placing them into a namespace.

CONSIDER creating a folder structure that matches the namespace hierarchy.

End 10.0

XML Comments

Chapter 1 introduced comments. However, you can use XML comments for more than just notes to other developers reviewing the source code. XML-based comments follow a practice popularized with Java. Although the C# compiler ignores all comments as far as the resultant executable goes, the developer can use command-line options to instruct the compiler[5] to extract the XML comments into a separate XML file. By taking advantage of the XML file generation, the developer can generate documentation of the API from the XML comments. In addition, C# editors can parse the XML comments in the code and display them to developers as distinct regions (e.g., as a different color from the rest of the code) or parse the XML comment data elements and display them to the developer.

5. The C# standard does not specify whether the C# compiler or a separate utility should take care of extracting the XML data. However, all mainstream C# compilers include the necessary functionality via a compile switch instead of within an additional utility.

Figure 10.3 demonstrates how an IDE can take advantage of XML comments to assist the developer with a tip about the code he is trying to write. Such coding tips offer significant assistance in large programs, especially when multiple developers share code. For this to work, however, the developer obviously must take the time to enter the XML comments within the code and then direct the compiler to create the XML file. The next section explains how to accomplish this.

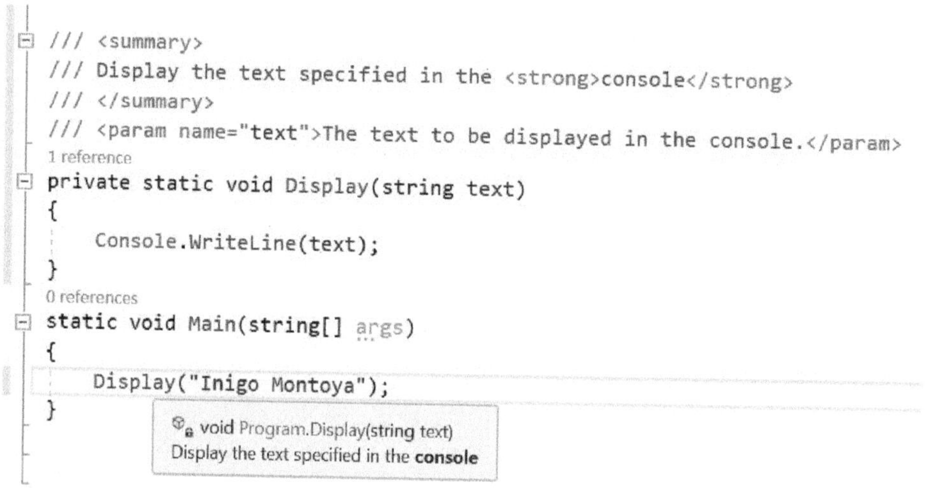

FIGURE 10.3: XML comments as tips in Visual Studio IDE

Starting with Visual Studio 2019, you can also embed simple HTML into a comment, and it will be reflected in the tips. For example, surrounding `console` with `<strong>` and `</strong>` will cause the word "console" to display in bold in Figure 10.3.

Associating XML Comments with Programming Constructs

Consider the listing of the `DataStorage` class, as shown in Listing 10.12.

LISTING 10.12: Commenting Code with XML Comments

```
/// <summary>
/// DataStorage is used to persist and retrieve
/// employee data from the files.
```

```
/// </summary>
class DataStorage
{
    /// <summary>
    /// Save an employee object to a file
    /// named with the Employee name.
    /// </summary>
    /// <remarks>
    /// This method uses <seealso cref="System.IO.FileStream"/>
    /// in addition to
    /// <seealso cref="System.IO.StreamWriter"/>
    /// </remarks>
    /// <param name="employee">
    /// The employee to persist to a file</param>
    /// <date>January 1, 2000</date>
    public static void Store(Employee employee)
    {
        // ...
    }

    /** <summary>
     * Loads up an employee object.
     * </summary>
     * <remarks>
     * This method uses <seealso cref="System.IO.FileStream"/>
     * in addition to
     * <seealso cref="System.IO.StreamReader"/>
     * </remarks>
     * <param name="firstName">
     * The first name of the employee</param>
     * <param name="lastName">
     * The last name of the employee</param>
     * <returns>
     * The employee object corresponding to the names
     * </returns>
     * <date>January 1, 2000</date> **/
    public static Employee Load(string firstName, string lastName)
    {
        // ...
    }
}

class Program
{
    // ...
}
```

Listing 10.12 uses both XML-delimited comments that span multiple lines and single-line XML comments in which each line requires a separate three-forward-slash delimiter (///).

Given that XML comments are designed to document the API, they are intended for use only in association with C# declarations, such as the class or method shown in Listing 10.12. Any attempt to place an XML comment inline with the code, unassociated with a declaration, will result in a warning by the compiler. The compiler makes the association simply because the XML comment appears immediately before the declaration.

Although C# allows any XML tag to appear in comments, the C# standard explicitly defines a set of tags to be used. `<seealso cref="System.IO.StreamWriter"/>` is an example of using the `seealso` tag. This tag creates a link between the text and the `System.IO.StreamWriter` class.

Generating an XML Documentation File

The compiler checks that the XML comments are well formed and issues a warning if they are not. To generate the XML file, add a `DocumentationFile` element to the `ProjectProperties` element:

```
<DocumentationFile>$(OutputPath)\$(TargetFramework)\$(AssemblyName).x
</DocumentationFile>
```

This element causes an XML file to be generated during the build into the output directory using the `<assemblyname>.xml` as the filename. Using the `CommentSamples` class listed earlier and the compiler options listed here, the resultant `CommentSamples.XML` file appears as shown in Listing 10.13.

Listing 10.13: `Comments.xml`

```
<?xml version="1.0"?>
<doc>
    <assembly>
        <name>DataStorage</name>
    </assembly>
    <members>
        <member name="T:DataStorage">
            <summary>
                DataStorage is used to persist and retrieve
```

```
            employee data from the files.
        </summary>
    </member>
    <member name="M:DataStorage.Store(Employee)">
        <summary>
            Save an employee object to a file
            named with the Employee name.
        </summary>
        <remarks>
            This method uses
            <seealso cref="T:System.IO.FileStream"/>
            in addition to
            <seealso cref="T:System.IO.StreamWriter"/>
        </remarks>
        <param name="employee">
            The employee to persist to a file
        </param>
        <date>January 1, 2000</date>
    </member>
    <member name="M:DataStorage.Load(
             System.String,System.String)">
        <summary>
            Loads up an employee object
        </summary>
        <remarks>
            This method uses
            <seealso cref="T:System.IO.FileStream"/>
            in addition to
            <seealso cref="T:System.IO.StreamReader"/>
        </remarks>
        <param name="firstName">
            The first name of the employee
        </param>
        <param name="lastName">
            The last name of the employee
        </param>
        <returns>
            The employee object corresponding to the names
        </returns>
        <date>January 1, 2000</date>*
    </member>
  </members>
</doc>
```

The resultant file includes only the amount of metadata that is necessary to associate an element back to its corresponding C# declaration. This is important because, in general, it is necessary to use the XML output in combination with the generated assembly to produce any meaningful documentation. Fortunately, tools such as the free GhostDoc[6] and the open source project NDoc[7] can generate documentation.

Guidelines

DO provide XML comments on public APIs when they provide more context than the API signature alone. This includes member descriptions, parameter descriptions, and examples of calling the API.

Garbage Collection and Weak References

Garbage collection is obviously a core function of the runtime. Its purpose is to restore memory consumed by objects that are no longer referenced. The emphasis in this statement is on memory and references: The garbage collector is responsible only for restoring memory; it does not handle other resources such as database connections, handles (files, windows, etc.), network ports, and hardware devices such as serial ports. Also, the garbage collector determines what to clean up, based on whether any references remain. Implicitly, this means that the garbage collector works with reference objects and restores memory on the heap only. Additionally, it means that maintaining a reference to an object will delay the garbage collector from reusing the memory consumed by the object.

---

6. See https://submain.com/ to learn more about GhostDoc.
7. See https://ndoc.sourceforge.net/ to learn more about NDoc.

ADVANCED TOPIC

Garbage Collection in .NET

Many details about the garbage collector pertain to the specific CLI framework and therefore could vary. This section discusses the Microsoft .NET framework implementations because they are the most prevalent.

In .NET, the garbage collector uses a mark-and-compact algorithm. At the beginning of an iteration, it identifies all **root references** to objects. Root references are any references from static variables, CPU registers, and local variables or parameter instances (and f-reachable objects, as described later in this section). Given this list, the garbage collector is able to walk through the tree identified by each root reference and determine recursively all the objects to which the root references point. In this manner, the garbage collector creates a graph of all reachable objects.

Instead of enumerating all the inaccessible objects, the garbage collector performs garbage collection by compacting all reachable objects next to one another, thereby overwriting any memory consumed by objects that are inaccessible (and thus qualify as garbage).

Locating and moving all reachable objects requires that the system maintain a consistent state while the garbage collector runs. To achieve this, all managed threads within the process are halted during garbage collection. Obviously, this behavior can result in brief pauses in an application, which are generally insignificant unless a particularly large garbage collection cycle is necessary or done quite often. To reduce the likelihood of a garbage collection cycle occurring at an inopportune time, the `System.GC` object includes a `Collect()` method, which can be called immediately before the critical performing code. This method does not prevent the garbage collector from running, but it does reduce the probability that it will run, assuming no intense memory utilization occurs during the critical performance code.

One perhaps surprising aspect of .NET garbage collection behavior is that not all garbage is necessarily cleaned up during an iteration. Studies of object lifetimes reveal that recently created objects are more likely to need garbage collection than long-standing objects. Capitalizing on this behavior, the .NET garbage collector is generational, attempting to clean up short-lived objects more frequently than objects that have already survived a previous garbage collection iteration. Specifically, objects are organized into three generations. Each time an object survives a garbage collection cycle, it is moved to the next generation, until it ends up in generation 2 (counting starts from zero). The garbage collector, then, runs more frequently for objects in generation 0 than it does for objects in generation 2.

Over time, in spite of the trepidation that .NET stirred during its early beta releases when compared with unmanaged code, .NET's garbage collection has proved extremely efficient. More important, the gains realized in development productivity have far outweighed the costs in development for the few cases where managed code is dropped to optimize particular algorithms.

All references discussed so far are **strong references** because they maintain an object's accessibility and prevent the garbage collector from cleaning up the memory consumed by the object. The framework also supports the concept of **weak references**. Weak references do not prevent garbage collection on an object, but they do maintain a reference so that if the garbage collector does not clean up the object, it can be reused.

Weak references are designed for reference objects that are expensive to create, yet too expensive to keep around. Consider, for example, a large list of objects loaded from a database and displayed to the user. The loading of this list is potentially expensive, and once the user closes the list, it should be available for garbage collection. However, if the user requests the list multiple times, a second expensive load call will always be required. With weak references, it becomes possible to use code to check whether the list has been cleaned up, and if not, to re-reference the same list. In this way, weak references serve as a memory cache for objects. Objects within the cache are retrieved quickly, but if the garbage collector has recovered the memory of these objects, they will need to be re-created.

Once a reference object (or collection of objects) is recognized as worthy of potential weak reference consideration, it needs to be assigned to `System.WeakReference` (see Listing 10.14).

LISTING 10.14: Using a Weak Reference

```
public static class ByteArrayDataSource
{
    static private byte[] LoadData()
```

```
    {
        // Imagine a much lager number
        byte[] data = new byte[1000];
        // Load data
        // ...
        return data;
    }

    static private WeakReference<byte[]>? Data { get; set; }

    static public byte[] GetData()
    {
        byte[]? target;
        if (Data is null)
        {
            target = LoadData();
            Data = new WeakReference<byte[]>(target);
            return target;
        }
        else if (Data.TryGetTarget(out target))
        {
            return target;
        }
        else
        {
            // Reload the data and assign it (creating a strong
            // reference) before setting WeakReference's Target
            // and returning it.
            target = LoadData();
            Data.SetTarget(target);
            return target;
        }
    }
}

// ...
```

Admittedly, this code uses generics, which aren't discussed in this book until Chapter 12. However, you can safely ignore the `<byte[]>` text both when declaring the `Data` property and when assigning it. While there is a nongeneric version of `WeakReference`, there is little reason to consider it.[8]

8. Unless programming with .NET Framework 4.5 or earlier.

The bulk of the logic appears in the GetData() method. The purpose of this method is to always return an instance of the data—whether from the cache or by reloading it. GetData() begins by checking whether the Data property is null. If it is, the data is loaded and assigned to a local variable called target. This creates a reference to the data so that the garbage collector will not clear it. Next, we instantiate a WeakReference and pass a reference to the loaded data so that the WeakReference object has a handle to the data (its target); then, if requested, such an instance can be returned. Do not pass an instance that does not have a local reference to WeakReference, because it might get cleaned up before you have a chance to return it (i.e., do not call new WeakReference<byte[]>(LoadData())).

If the Data property already has an instance of WeakReference, then the code calls TryGetTarget() and, if there is an instance, assigns target, thus creating a reference so that the garbage collector will no longer clean up the data.

Lastly, if WeakReference's TryGetTarget() method returns false, we load the data, assign the reference with a call to SetTarget(), and return the newly instantiated object.

Resource Cleanup

Garbage collection is a key responsibility of the runtime. Nevertheless, it is important to recognize that the garbage collection process centers on the code's memory utilization. It is not about the cleaning up of file handles, database connection strings, ports, or other limited resources.

Finalizers

Finalizers allow developers to write code that will clean up a class's resources. Unlike constructors that are called explicitly using the new operator, finalizers cannot be called explicitly from within the code. There is no new equivalent such as a delete operator. Rather, the garbage collector is responsible for calling a finalizer on an object instance. Therefore, developers cannot determine at compile time exactly when the finalizer will execute. All they know is that the finalizer will run sometime between when an object was last used and generally when the application shuts down normally. The deliberate injection of incertitude with the word "Generally" highlights the fact that finalizers might not execute. This possibility is obvious when you consider that a process might terminate abnormally. For instance, events such as the computer being turned off or a forced termination of the process, such as when debugging the process, will prevent the finalizer from running. However, with .NET Core, even under normal circumstances, finalizers may not get processed before the application shuts down. As we shall see in the next section, it thus may be necessary to take additional action to register finalization activities with other mechanisms.

NOTE

You cannot determine at compile time exactly when the finalizer will execute.

The finalizer declaration is identical to the destructor syntax of C#'s predecessor —that is, C++. As shown in Listing 10.15, the finalizer declaration is prefixed with a tilde before the name of the class.

Listing 10.15: Defining a Finalizer

```
using System.IO;

public class TemporaryFileStream
{
    public TemporaryFileStream(string fileName)
    {
        File = new FileInfo(fileName);
        // For a preferable solution use FileOptions.DeleteOnClose.
        Stream = new FileStream(
            File.FullName, FileMode.OpenOrCreate,
            FileAccess.ReadWrite);
    }

    public TemporaryFileStream()
        : this(Path.GetTempFileName())
    { }

    // Finalizer
    ~TemporaryFileStream()
```

```
    {
        try
        {
            Close();
        }
        catch (Exception )
        {
            // Write event to logs or UI
            // ...
        }
    }

    public FileStream? Stream { get; private set; }
    public FileInfo? File { get; private set; }

    public void Close()
    {
        Stream?.Dispose();
        try
        {
            File?.Delete();
        }
        catch(IOException exception)
        {
            Console.WriteLine(exception);
        }
        Stream = null;
        File = null;
    }
}
```

Finalizers do not allow any parameters to be passed, so they cannot be overloaded. Furthermore, finalizers cannot be called explicitly—that is, only the garbage collector can invoke a finalizer. Access modifiers on finalizers are therefore meaningless, and as such, they are not supported. Finalizers in base classes will be invoked automatically as part of an object finalization call.

> **NOTE**
>
> Finalizers cannot be called explicitly; only the garbage collector can invoke a finalizer.

Because the garbage collector handles all memory management, finalizers are not responsible for de-allocating memory. Rather, they are responsible for freeing up resources such as database connections and file handles—resources that require an explicit activity that the garbage collector doesn't know about.

In the finalizer shown in Listing 10.15, we start by disposing of the `FileStream`. This step is optional because the `FileStream` has its own finalizer that provides the same functionality as `Dispose()`. The purpose of invoking `Dispose()` now is to ensure that it is cleaned up when `TemporaryFileStream` is finalized, since the latter is responsible for instantiating the former. Without the explicit invocation of `Stream?.Dispose()`, the garbage collector will clean it up independently from the `TemporaryFileStream` once the `TemporaryFileStream` object is garbage collected and releases its reference on the `FileStream` object. That said, if we didn't need a finalizer for resource cleanup anyway, it would not make sense to define a finalizer just for invoking `FileStream.Dispose()`. In fact, limiting the need for a finalizer to only objects that need resource cleanup that the runtime isn't already aware of (resources that don't have finalizers) is an important guideline that significantly reduces the number of scenarios where it is necessary to implement a finalizer.

In Listing 10.15, the purpose of the finalizer is to delete the file[9]—an unmanaged resource in this case. Hence we have the call to `File?.Delete()`. Now, when the finalizers are executed, the file will get cleaned up.

Finalizers execute on an unspecified thread, making their execution even less deterministic. This indeterminate nature makes an unhandled exception within a finalizer (outside of the debugger) likely to crash the application—and the source of this problem is difficult to diagnose because the circumstances that led to the exception are not clear. From the user's perspective, the unhandled exception will be thrown relatively randomly and with little regard for any action the user was performing. For this reason, you should take care to avoid exceptions within finalizers. Instead, you should use defensive programming techniques such as checking for `null` (refer to the use of the null-conditional operator in Listing 10.15).

9. Listing 10.20 is somewhat a contrived example because there is a `FileOptions.DeleteOnClose` option when instantiating the `FileStream`, which triggers the file's deletion when the `FileStream` closes.

In fact, it is advisable to catch all exceptions in the finalizer and report them via an alternative means (such as logging or via the user interface) rather than keeping them as unhandled exceptions. This guideline leads to the try/catch block surrounding the `Delete()` invocation.

Another potential option to force finalizers to execute is to invoke `System.GC.WaitForPendingFinalizers()`. When this method is invoked, the current thread will be suspended until all finalizers for objects that are no longer referenced have executed.

Deterministic Finalization with the `using` Statement

The problem with finalizers on their own is that they don't support **deterministic finalization** (the ability to know when a finalizer will run). Rather, finalizers serve the important role of being a backup mechanism for cleaning up resources if a developer using a class neglects to call the requisite cleanup code explicitly.

For example, consider the `TemporaryFileStream`, which includes not only a finalizer but also a `Close()` method. This class uses a file resource that could potentially consume a significant amount of disk space. The developer using `TemporaryFileStream` can explicitly call `Close()` to restore the disk space.

Providing a method for deterministic finalization is important because it eliminates a dependency on the indeterminate timing behavior of the finalizer. Even if the developer fails to call `Close()` explicitly, the finalizer will take care of the call. In such a case, the finalizer will run later than if it was called explicitly.

Because of the importance of deterministic finalization, the base class library includes a specific interface for the pattern and C# integrates the pattern into the language. The `IDisposable` interface defines the details of the pattern with a single method called `Dispose()`, which developers call on a resource class to "dispose" of the consumed resources. Listing 10.16 demonstrates the `IDisposable` interface and some code for calling it.

Listing 10.16: Resource Cleanup with `IDisposable`

```
using System;
using System.IO;

public static class Program
```

```
{
    // ...
    public static void Search()
    {
        TemporaryFileStream fileStream =
            new();

        // Use temporary file stream
        // ...

        fileStream.Dispose();

        // ...
    }
}

class TemporaryFileStream : IDisposable
{
    public TemporaryFileStream(string fileName)
    {
        File = new FileInfo(fileName);
        Stream = new FileStream(
            File.FullName, FileMode.OpenOrCreate,
            FileAccess.ReadWrite);
    }

    public TemporaryFileStream()
        : this(Path.GetTempFileName()) { }

    ~TemporaryFileStream()
    {
        Dispose(false);
    }

    public FileStream? Stream { get; private set; }
    public FileInfo? File { get; private set; }

    #region IDisposable Members
    public void Dispose()
    {
        Dispose(true);

        //unregister from the finalization queue.
        System.GC.SuppressFinalize(this);
    }
    #endregion
    public void Dispose(bool disposing)
```

```
    {
        // Do not dispose of an owned managed object (one with a
        // finalizer) if called by member finalize,
        // as the owned managed objects finalize method
        // will be (or has been) called by finalization queue
        // processing already
        if (disposing)
        {
            Stream?.Dispose();
        }
        try
        {
            File?.Delete();
        }
        catch (IOException exception)
        {
            Console.WriteLine(exception);
        }
        Stream = null;
        File = null;
    }
}
```

Begin 8.0

From `Program.Search()`, there is an explicit call to `Dispose()` after using the `TemporaryFileStream`. `Dispose()` is the method responsible for cleaning up the resources (in this case, a file) that are not related to memory and therefore are subject to cleanup implicitly by the garbage collector. Nevertheless, the execution here contains a hole that would prevent execution of `Dispose()`—namely, the chance that an exception will occur between the time when `TemporaryFileStream` is instantiated and the time when `Dispose()` is called. If this happens, `Dispose()` will not be invoked and the resource cleanup will have to rely on the finalizer. To avoid this problem, callers need to implement a try/finally block. Instead of requiring programmers to code such a block explicitly, C# provides a `using` statement expressly for the purpose (see Listing 10.17).

Listing 10.17: Invoking the `using` Statement

```
public static class Program
{
    public static void Search()
    {
        // C# 8.0
```

```
        using TemporaryFileStream fileStream1 = new();

        // Prior to C# 8.0
        using (TemporaryFileStream fileStream2 =
            new(),
            fileStream3 = new())
        {
            // Use temporary file stream;
        }
    }
}
```

In the first highlighted code snippet, the resultant CIL code is identical to the code that would be created if the programmer specified an explicit try/finally block, where `fileStream.Dispose()` is called in the finally block. The `using` statement, however, provides a syntax shortcut for the try/finally block.

Within this `using` statement, you can instantiate more than one variable by separating each variable from the others with a comma. The key considerations are that all variables must be of the same type, the type must implement `IDisposable`, and initialization occurs at the time of declaration. To enforce the use of the same type, the data type is specified only once rather than before each variable declaration.

C# 8.0 introduces a potential simplification with regard to resource cleanup. As shown in the second highlighted snippet of Listing 10.17, you can prefix the declaration of a disposable resource (one that implements `IDisposable`) with the `using` keyword. As is the case with the `using` statement, this will generate the try/finally behavior, with the finally block placed just before the variable goes out of scope (in this case, before the closing curly brace of the `Search()` method). One additional constraint on the `using` declaration is that the variable is read-only, so it can't be assigned a different value.

End 8.0

Garbage Collection, Finalization, and `IDisposable`

There are several additional noteworthy items to point out in Listing 10.16. First, the `IDisposable.Dispose()` method contains an important call to `System.GC.SuppressFinalize()`. Its purpose is to remove the `TemporaryFileStream` class instance from the **finalization (f-reachable) queue.** This is possible because all cleanup was done in the `Dispose()` method rather than waiting for the finalizer to execute.

Without the call to `SuppressFinalize()`, the instance of the object will be included in the f-reachable queue—a list of all the objects that are mostly ready for garbage collection, except they also have finalization implementations. The runtime cannot garbage-collect objects with finalizers until after their finalization methods have been called. However, garbage collection itself does not call the finalization method. Rather, references to finalization objects are added to the f-reachable queue and are processed by an additional thread at a time deemed appropriate based on the execution context. In an ironic twist, this approach delays garbage collection for the managed resources—when it is most likely that these very resources should be cleaned up earlier. The reason for the delay is that the f-reachable queue is a list of "references"; as such, the objects are not considered garbage until after their finalization methods are called and the object references are removed from the f-reachable queue.

NOTE

Objects with finalizers that are not explicitly disposed will end up with an extended object lifetime. Even after all explicit references have gone out of scope, the f-reachable queue will have references, keeping the object alive until the f-reachable queue processing is complete.

For this reason, `Dispose()` invokes `System.GC.SuppressFinalize`. Invoking this method informs the runtime that it should not add this object to the finalization queue, but instead should allow the garbage collector to de-allocate the object when it no longer has any references (including any f-reachable references).

Second, `Dispose()` calls `Dispose(bool disposing)` with an argument of `true`. The result is that the `Dispose()` method on `Stream` is invoked (cleaning up its resources and suppressing its finalization). Next, the temporary file itself is deleted immediately upon calling `Dispose()`. This important call eliminates the need to wait for the finalization queue to be processed before cleaning up potentially expensive resources.

Third, rather than calling `Close()`, the finalizer now calls `Dispose(bool disposing)` with an argument of `false`. The result is that `Stream` is not closed (disposed) even though the file is deleted. The condition around closing `Stream` ensures that if `Dispose(bool disposing)` is called from the finalizer, the `Stream` instance itself will also be queued up for finalization processing (or possibly it would have already run depending on the order). Therefore, when executing the finalizer, objects owned by the managed resource should not be cleaned up, as this action will be the responsibility of the finalization queue.

Fourth, you should use caution when creating both a `Close()` type and a `Dispose()` method. It is not clear by looking at only the API that `Close()` calls `Dispose()`, so developers will be left wondering whether they need to explicitly call `Close()` and `Dispose()`.

Fifth, to increase the probability that the functionality defined in the finalizer will execute before a process shuts down even in .NET Core, you should register the code with the `AppDomain.CurrentDomain.ProcessExit` event handler. Any finalization code registered with this event handler will be invoked, barring an abnormal process termination (discussed in the next section).

Guidelines

DO implement the dispose pattern on objects with resources that are scarce or expensive.

DO implement `IDisposable` to support possible deterministic finalization on classes with finalizers.

DO implement finalizer methods only on objects with resources that don't have finalizers but still require cleanup.

DO refactor a finalization method to call the same code as `IDisposable`, perhaps simply by calling the `Dispose()` method.

DO NOT throw exceptions from finalizer methods.

CONSIDER registering the finalization code with the `AppDomain.ProcessExit` to increase the probability that resource cleanup will execute before the process exits.

DO unregister any `AppDomain.ProcessExit` events during dispose.

DO call `System.GC.SuppressFinalize()` from `Dispose()` to avoid repeating resource cleanup and delaying garbage collection on an object.

DO ensure that `Dispose()` is idempotent (it should be possible to call `Dispose()` multiple times).

DO keep `Dispose()` simple, focusing on the resource cleanup required by finalization.

AVOID calling `Dispose()` on owned objects that have a finalizer. Instead, rely on the finalization queue to clean up the instance.

AVOID referencing other objects that are not being finalized during finalization.

DO invoke a base class's `Dispose()` method when overriding `Dispose()`.

CONSIDER ensuring that an object becomes unusable after `Dispose()` is called. After an object has been disposed, methods other than `Dispose()` (which could potentially be called multiple times) should throw an `ObjectDisposedException`.

DO implement `IDisposable` on types that own disposable fields (or properties) and dispose of those instances.

DO invoke a base class's `Dispose()` method from the `Dispose(bool disposing)` method if one exists.

Language Contrast: C++—Deterministic Destruction

Although finalizers are similar to destructors in C++, the fact that their execution cannot be determined at compile time makes them distinctly different. The garbage collector calls C# finalizers sometime after they were last used but before the program shuts down; C++ destructors are automatically called when the object (not a pointer) goes out of scope.

Although running the garbage collector can be a relatively expensive process, the fact that garbage collection is intelligent enough to delay running until process utilization is somewhat reduced offers an advantage over deterministic destructors, which will run at compile-time–defined locations, even when a processor is in high demand.

ADVANCED TOPIC

Forcing Resource Cleanup before Process Exit

Starting with .NET Core, the finalizers may not execute when a process is shutting down. To increase the likelihood of execution, the finalization activities should be registered to execute when the process[10] shuts down. For this reason, notice the statement involving `ProcessExit` in the `SampleUnmanagedResource` constructor in Listing 10.18, with Output 10.3 showing the result when no arguments are passed to the program. (The code involves LINQ, event registration, and special attributes,[11] which aren't covered until Chapters 12, 14, and 18, respectively.)

LISTING 10.18: Registering with Process Exit

```
using System.IO;
using System.Linq;
using System.Runtime.CompilerServices;
using static ConsoleLogger;

public static class Program
{
    public static void Main(string[] args)
    {
        WriteLine("Starting...");
        DoStuff();
        if (args.Any(arg => arg.ToLower() == "-gc"))
        {
            GC.Collect();
            GC.WaitForPendingFinalizers();
        }
        WriteLine("Exiting...");
    }

    public static void DoStuff()
    {
        // ...

        WriteLine("Starting...");
```

10. Technically the app domain, at least for .NET Framework projects.
11. See the accompanying source code.

```
        SampleUnmanagedResource? sampleUnmanagedResource = null;

        try
        {
            sampleUnmanagedResource =
                new SampleUnmanagedResource();
            // Use unmanaged Resource
            // ...
        }
        finally
        {
            if (Environment.GetCommandLineArgs().Any(
            arg => arg.ToLower() == "-dispose"))
            {
                sampleUnmanagedResource?.Dispose();
            }
        }

        WriteLine("Exiting...");

        // ...
    }
}

class SampleUnmanagedResource : IDisposable
{
    public SampleUnmanagedResource(string fileName)
    {
        WriteLine("Starting...",
            $"{nameof(SampleUnmanagedResource)}.ctor");

        WriteLine("Creating managed stuff...",
            $"{nameof(SampleUnmanagedResource)}.ctor");
        WriteLine("Creating unmanaged stuff...",
            $"{nameof(SampleUnmanagedResource)}.ctor");

        WeakReference<IDisposable> weakReferenceToSelf =
             new(this);
        ProcessExitHandler = (_, __) =>
        {
            WriteLine("Starting...", "ProcessExitHandler");
            if (weakReferenceToSelf.TryGetTarget(
                out IDisposable? self))
            {
                self.Dispose();
            }
            WriteLine("Exiting...", "ProcessExitHandler");
```

```
    };
    AppDomain.CurrentDomain.ProcessExit
        += ProcessExitHandler;
    WriteLine("Exiting...",
        $"{nameof(SampleUnmanagedResource)}.ctor");
}

// Stores the process exit delegate so that we can remove it
// if Dispose() or Finalize() is called already.
private EventHandler ProcessExitHandler { get; }

public SampleUnmanagedResource()
    : this(Path.GetTempFileName()) { }

~SampleUnmanagedResource()
{
    WriteLine("Starting...");
    Dispose(false);
    WriteLine("Exiting...");
}

public void Dispose()
{
    Dispose(true);
    // ...
}

public void Dispose(bool disposing)
{
    WriteLine("Starting...");

    // Do not dispose of an owned managed object (one with a
    // finalizer) if called by member finalize,
    // as the owned managed objects finalize method
    // will be (or has been) called by finalization queue
    // processing already
    if (disposing)
    {
        WriteLine("Disposing managed stuff...");
    }

    AppDomain.CurrentDomain.ProcessExit -=
        ProcessExitHandler;

    WriteLine("Disposing unmanaged stuff...");

    WriteLine("Exiting...");
```

```
    }
}
```

OUTPUT 10.3

```
Main: Starting...
DoStuff: Starting...
SampleUnmanagedResource.ctor: Starting...
SampleUnmanagedResource.ctor: Creating managed stuff...
SampleUnmanagedResource.ctor: Creating unmanaged stuff...
SampleUnmanagedResource.ctor: Exiting...
DoStuff: Exiting...
Main: Exiting...
ProcessExitHandler: Starting...
Dispose: Starting...
Dispose: Disposing managed stuff...
Dispose: Disposing unmanaged stuff...
Dispose: Exiting...
ProcessExitHandler: Exiting...
```

Ignoring the `WriteLine()` statements throughout, the code begins with an invocation of `DoStuff()`, which instantiates the `SampleUnmanagedResource`.

When instantiating `SampleUnmanagedResource`, we simulate the instantiation of both managed and unmanaged resources using simple `WriteLine()` invocations. Next, we declare a delegate—called a handler—that will execute when the process exits. The handler leverages a `WeakReference` to the `SampleUnmanagedResource` instance and invokes `Dispose()` on the instance if there is still an instance to invoke. The `WeakReference` is necessary to ensure that `ProcessExit` doesn't maintain a reference to the instance, thereby preventing the garbage collector from cleaning up the unmanaged resource after it goes out of scope and finalization has run. The handler is registered with `AppDomain.CurrentDomain.ProcessExit` and saved into the `ProcessExitHandler` property. The latter step is necessary so that we can remove the handler from the `AppDomain.CurrentDomain.ProcessExit` event when `Dispose()` executes, rather than have `Dispose()` execute repeatedly and unnecessarily.

Back in the `DoStuff()` method, we check whether the command-line argument `-Dispose` is specified as an argument when starting the program. If it is, then `Dispose()` would be invoked and neither the finalizer nor the `ProcessExit` handler will get invoked. Upon the exit from `DoStuff()`, the instance of

`SampleUnmanagedResource` no longer has a root reference. However, when the garbage collector runs, it sees the finalizer and adds the resource to the finalization queue.

When the process begins to shut down, and assuming neither `Dispose()` nor the finalizer has executed on the `SampleUnmanagedResource` instance as yet, the `AppDomain.CurrentDomain.ProcessExit` event fires and invokes the handler, which in turn invokes `Dispose()`. The key difference in the `Dispose()` method from Listing 10.16 is that we unregister from `AppDomain.CurrentDomain.ProcessExit` so that `Dispose()` doesn't get invoked again during the process exit if it was invoked earlier.

Note that while you can invoke `GC.Collect()` followed by `GC.WaitForPendingFinalizers()` to force all finalizers for objects without root references to run, and you could theoretically even do this right before the process exits, doing so is fallible. The first caveat is that library projects can't invoke these methods immediately before the process exits because there is no instance of `Main()`. The second caveat is that even simple things like static references will be root references, so that static object instances will not be cleaned up. For this reason, using the `ProcessExit` handler is the preferred approach.

ADVANCED TOPIC

Exception Propagating from Constructors

Even when an exception propagates out of a constructor, the object is still instantiated, although no new instance is returned by the new operator. If the type defines a finalizer, the method will run when the object becomes eligible for garbage collection (providing additional motivation to ensure the finalize method can run on partially constructed objects). Also note that if a constructor prematurely shares its `this` reference, it will still be accessible even if the constructor throws an exception. Do not allow this scenario to occur.

ADVANCED TOPIC

Resurrecting Objects

By the time an object's finalization method is called, all references to the object have disappeared and the only step before garbage collection is running the finalization code. Even so, it is possible to add a reference inadvertently for a finalization object back into the root reference's graph. In such a case, the re-referenced object will no longer be inaccessible; in turn, it will not be ready for garbage collection. However, if the finalization method for the object has already run, it will not run again unless it is explicitly marked for finalization (using the `GC.ReRegisterFinalize()` method).

Obviously, resurrecting objects in this manner is peculiar behavior, and you should generally avoid it. Finalization code should be simple and should focus on cleaning up only the resources that it references.

Lazy Initialization

In the preceding section, we discussed how to deterministically dispose of an object with a `using` statement and how the finalization queue will dispose of resources in the event that no deterministic approach is used.

A related pattern is called **lazy initialization** or **lazy loading**. Using lazy initialization, you can create (or obtain) objects when you need them rather than beforehand—the latter can be an especially problematic situation when those objects are never used. Consider the `FileStream` property of Listing 10.19.

Listing 10.19: Lazy Loading a Property

```
class DataCache
{
    // ...

    public TemporaryFileStream FileStream =>
        InternalFileStream ??=
            new TemporaryFileStream();

    private TemporaryFileStream? InternalFileStream
        { get; set; } = null;
```

```
    // ...
}
```

In the `FileStream` expression bodied property, we check whether `InternalFileStream` is `null` before returning its value directly. If `InternalFileStream` is `null`, we first instantiate the `TemporaryFileStream` object and assign it to `InternalFileStream` before returning the new instance. Thus, the `TemporaryFileStream` required in the `FileStream` property is created only when the getter on the property is called. If the getter is never invoked, the `TemporaryFileStream` object would not be instantiated and we would save whatever execution time such an instantiation would cost. Obviously, if the instantiation is negligible or inevitable (and postponing the inevitable is less desirable), simply assigning it during declaration or in the constructor makes sense.

ADVANCED TOPIC

Lazy Loading with Generics and Lambda Expressions

Listing 10.20 demonstrates how to use `System.Lazy<T>` to assist with lazy initialization.[12]

Listing 10.20: Lazy Loading a Property with `System.Lazy<T>`

```
class DataCache
{
    // ...

    public TemporaryFileStream FileStream =>
        InternalFileStream.Value;
    private Lazy<TemporaryFileStream> InternalFileStream { get; }
        = new Lazy<TemporaryFileStream>(
            () => new TemporaryFileStream() );
```

12. Class added to the CLR starting with C# 4.0 and Microsoft .NET Framework 4.0.

```
    // ...
}
```

The System.Lazy<T> class takes a type parameter (T) that identifies which type the Value property on System.Lazy<T> will return. Instead of assigning a fully constructed TemporaryFileStream to the _FileStream field, an instance of Lazy<TemporaryFileStream> is assigned (a lightweight call), delaying the instantiation of the TemporaryFileStream itself until the Value property (and therefore the FileStream property) is accessed.

If you use delegates in addition to type parameters (generics), you can even provide a function for how to initialize an object when the Value property is accessed. Listing 10.20 demonstrates passing the delegate—a lambda expression in this case—into the constructor for System.Lazy<T>.

Note that the lambda expression itself, () => new TemporaryFileStream(FileStreamName), does not execute until Value is called. Rather, the lambda expression provides a means of passing the instructions for what will happen; it does not actually execute those instructions until explicitly requested to do so.

One obvious question is when you should use the System.Lazy<T> rather than the approach outlined in Listing 10.19. The difference is negligible: In fact, Listing 10.19 may actually be simpler. That is, it is simpler until multiple threads are involved, such that a race condition might occur regarding the instantiation. In Listing 10.19, more than one check for null might potentially occur before instantiation, resulting in multiple instances being created. In contrast, System.Lazy<T> provides a thread-safe mechanism ensuring that one and only one object will be created.

Summary

This chapter provided a whirlwind tour of many topics related to building solid class libraries. All the topics pertain to internal development as well, but they are much more critical to building robust classes. Ultimately, the focus here was on forming more robust and programmable APIs. In the category of robustness, we can include namespaces and garbage collection. Both of these topics fit in the programmability category as well, along with overriding `object`'s virtual members, operator overloading, and XML comments for documentation.

Exception handling heavily depends on inheritance, by defining an exception hierarchy and enforcing custom exceptions to fit within this hierarchy. Furthermore, the C# compiler uses inheritance to verify catch block order. In Chapter 11, you will see why inheritance is such a core part of exception handling.

11 ■

Exception Handling

Chapter 5 discussed using the try/catch/finally blocks for standard exception handling. In that chapter, the catch block always caught exceptions of type `System.Exception`. This chapter defines some additional details of exception handling—specifically, details surrounding additional exception types, defining custom exceptions, and multiple catch blocks for handling each type. This chapter also details exceptions because of their reliance on inheritance.

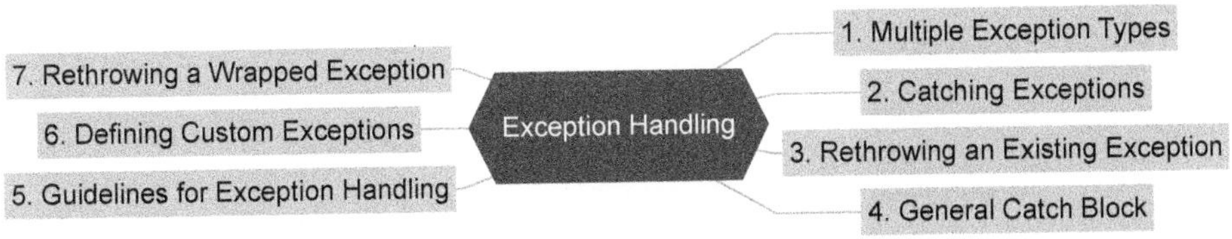

Multiple Exception Types

Listing 11.1 throws a `System.ArgumentException`, not the `System.Exception` type demonstrated in Chapter 5. C# allows code to throw any type that derives (perhaps indirectly) from `System.Exception`. To throw an exception, you simply prefix the exception instance with the keyword `throw`. The type of exception used is obviously the type that best describes the circumstances surrounding the error that caused the exception. For example, consider the `TextNumberParser.Parse()` method in Listing 11.1.

Listing 11.1: Throwing an Exception

```
public sealed class TextNumberParser
{
    public static int Parse(string textDigit)
    {
        string[] digitTexts =
            { "zero", "one", "two", "three", "four",
              "five", "six", "seven", "eight", "nine" };

        int result = Array.IndexOf(
            digitTexts,
            // Leveraging C# 2.0's null-coalescing operator
            (textDigit ??
              // Leveraging C# 7.0's throw expression
              throw new ArgumentNullException(nameof(textDigit))
            ).ToLower());

        if (result < 0)
        {
            // Leveraging C# 6.0's nameof operator
            throw new ArgumentException(
                "The argument did not represent a digit",
↪nameof(textDigit));
        }
        return result;
    }
}
```

In the call to `Array.IndexOf()`, we leverage a `throw` expression[1] when the `textDigit` argument is `null`.

Instead of throwing `System.Exception`, it is more appropriate to throw `ArgumentException` because the type itself indicates what went wrong and includes special parameters for identifying which parameter was at fault.

Two similar exceptions are `ArgumentNullException` and `NullReferenceException`. `ArgumentNullException` should be thrown for the inappropriate passing of `null` arguments. This is a special case of an invalid

1. Starting with C# 7.0.

argument exception that would more generally (when it isn't `null`) be thrown as an `ArgumentException` or an `ArgumentOutOfRangeException`.

`NullReferenceException` is generally an exception that the underlying runtime will throw only with an attempt to dereference a `null` value—that is, an attempt to call a member on an object whose value is `null`. Instead of triggering a `NullReferenceException` to be thrown, programmers should check parameters for `null` before accessing them and then throw an `ArgumentNullException`, which can provide more contextual information, such as the parameter name. If there is an innocuous way to proceed even if an argument is `null`, be sure to use the null-conditional operator[2] when dereferencing to avoid the runtime throwing a `NullReferenceException`.

One important characteristic of the argument exception types (including `ArgumentException`, `ArgumentNullException`, and `ArgumentOutOfRangeException`) is that each has a constructor parameter that allows identification of the argument name as a string.[3] The general guideline is to always use the `nameof` operator for the parameter name of an argument type exception. Chapter 18 provides a full explanation for the `nameof` operator. Until then, it is sufficient to understand that `nameof` simply returns the name of the argument identified.

Several other exceptions are intended only for the runtime and derive (sometimes indirectly) from `System.SystemException`. They include `System.StackOverflowException`, `System.OutOfMemoryException`, `System.Runtime.InteropServices.COMException`, `System.ExecutionEngineException`, and `System.Runtime.InteropServices.SEHException`. Do not throw exceptions of these types. Similarly, you should avoid throwing a `System.Exception` or `System.ApplicationException`, as these exceptions are so general that they provide little indication of the cause of or resolution to the problem. Instead, throw the most derived exception that fits the scenario. Obviously, developers should avoid creating APIs that could potentially result in a system failure. However, if the executing code reaches a certain state such

---

2. Starting in C# 6.0.
3. Prior to C# 6.0, this meant hard-coding a magic string to identify the parameter name.

that continuing to execute is unsafe or unrecoverable, it should call `System.Environment.FailFast()`. This will immediately terminate the process after potentially writing a message to standard error and, on Microsoft Windows, the Windows Application event log.

Guidelines

DO throw an `ArgumentException` or one of its subtypes if bad arguments are passed to a member. Prefer the most derived exception type (e.g., `ArgumentNullException`), if applicable.

DO NOT throw a `System.SystemException` or an exception type that derives from it.

DO NOT throw a `System.Exception`, `System.NullReferenceException`, or `System.ApplicationException`.

CONSIDER terminating the process by calling `System.Environment.FailFast()` if the program encounters a scenario where it is unsafe to continue execution.

DO use `nameof` for the `paramName` argument passed into argument exception types that take such a parameter. Examples of such exceptions include `ArgumentException`, `ArgumentOutOfRangeException`, and `ArgumentNullException`.

Catching Exceptions

Throwing a particular exception type enables the catcher to use the exception's type itself to identify the problem. It is not necessary, in other words, to catch the exception and use a `switch` statement on the exception message to determine which action to take in light of the exception. Instead, C# allows for multiple catch blocks, each targeting a specific exception type, as Listing 11.2 shows.

Listing 11.2: Catching Different Exception Types

```
using System;

public sealed class Program
{
```

```
    public static void Main(string[] args)
    {
        try
        {
            // ...
            throw new InvalidOperationException(
                "Arbitrary exception");
            // ...
        }
        catch(Win32Exception exception)
            when(exception.NativeErrorCode  == 42)
        {
            // Handle Win32Exception where
            // ErrorCode is 42
        }
        catch(ArgumentException exception)
        {
            // Handle ArgumentException
        }
        catch(InvalidOperationException exception)
        {
            bool exceptionHandled = false;
            // Handle InvalidOperationException
            // ...
            if(!exceptionHandled)
            {
                throw;
            }
        }
        catch(Exception exception)
        {
            // Handle Exception
        }
        finally
        {
            // Handle any cleanup code here as it runs
            // regardless of whether there is an exception
        }
    }
}
```

Listing 11.2 includes five catch blocks, each handling a different type of exception. When an exception occurs, the execution jumps to the catch block with the exception type that most closely matches the exception. The closeness of a match is determined by the inheritance chain. For example, even though the exception thrown is of type `System.Exception`, this "is a" relationship occurs through inheritance because `System.InvalidOperationException` ultimately derives from `System.Exception`. Since the exception type `InvalidOperationException` most closely matches the exception thrown, the `catch(InvalidOperationException...)` block catches the exception and not the `catch(Exception...)` block.

An additional conditional expression is available for catch blocks. Instead of limiting whether a catch block matches based only on an exception type match, there is also a conditional clause. This `when` clause allows you to supply a Boolean expression; the catch block handles the exception only if the condition is true. In Listing 11.2, this is an equality comparison operator. For more complex logic, you could make a method call to check for a condition.

Of course, you could also simply place the conditional check as an `if` block within the catch body. However, doing so causes the catch block to become the handler for the exception before the condition is checked. It is difficult to write code that allows a different catch block to handle the exception in the scenario where the condition is not met. However, with the **exception condition**,[4] it is now possible to examine the program state (including the exception) without having to catch and rethrow the exception.

Use conditional clauses with caution: If the conditional expression itself throws an exception, then that new exception will be ignored and the condition will be treated as false. For this reason, you should avoid throwing exceptions for the exception conditional expression.

Catch blocks must appear in order, from most specific to most general, to avoid a compile-time error. For example, moving the `catch(Exception...)` block before any of the other exceptions will result in a compile error, since all prior exceptions derive from `System.Exception` at some point in their inheritance chain.

As shown with the catch `(SystemException){ }`) block, a named parameter for the catch block is not required. In fact, a final catch without even the type parameter is allowable, as you will see in the next section.

---

4. Starting with C# 6.0.

Rethrowing an Existing Exception

In the `InvalidOperationException` catch block, a `throw` statement appears without any identification of the exception to `throw` (`throw` is on its own), even though an exception instance (`exception`) appears in the catch block scope that could be rethrown. Throwing a specific exception would update all the stack information to match the new throw location. As a result, all the stack information indicating the call site where the exception originally occurred would be lost, making it significantly more difficult to diagnose the problem. For this reason, C# supports a `throw` statement or expression without the explicit exception reference as long as it occurs within a catch block.[5] This way, code can examine the exception to determine if it is possible to fully handle it and, if not, rethrow the exception (even though not specified explicitly) as though it was never caught and without replacing any stack information.

ADVANCED/BEGINNER TOPIC

Throwing Existing Exceptions without Replacing Stack Information

There is a mechanism that enables the throwing of a previously thrown exception without losing the stack trace information in the original exception.[6] This allows you to rethrow exceptions, for example, even from outside a catch block and, therefore, without using `throw;`. Although it is fairly rare to need to do this, occasionally exceptions are wrapped or saved until the program execution moves outside the catch block. For example, multithreaded code might wrap an exception with an `AggregateException`. The `System.Runtime.ExceptionServices.ExceptionDispatchInfo` class is specifically designed to handle this scenario through the use of its static `Capture()` and instance `Throw()` methods. Listing 11.3 demonstrates rethrowing the exception without resetting the stack trace information or using an empty `throw` statement.

5. C# 7.0 or later.
6. Starting in C# 5.0.

LISTING 11.3: Using `ExceptionDispatchInfo` to Rethrow an Exception

```
using System;
using System.Runtime.ExceptionServices;
using System.Threading.Tasks;
using System.Net;
using System.Linq;
using System.IO;
// ...
        Task task = WriteWebRequestSizeAsync(url);
        try
        {
            while (!task.Wait(100))
            {
                Console.Write(".");
            }
        }
        catch (AggregateException exception)
        {
            exception = exception.Flatten();
            ExceptionDispatchInfo.Capture(
                exception.InnerException??exception).Throw();
        }
```

With the `ExceptionDispatchInfo.Throw()` method, the compiler doesn't treat the code as a return statement in the same way that it might a normal `throw` statement. For example, if the method signature returned a value but no value was returned from the code path with `ExceptionDispatchInfo.Throw()`, the compiler would issue an error indicating no value was returned. On occasion, therefore, developers may be forced to follow `ExceptionDispatchInfo.Throw()` with a return statement even though such a statement would never execute at runtime—the exception would be thrown instead.

Language Contrast: Java—Exception Specifiers

C# has no equivalent to Java's exception specifiers. With exception specifiers, the Java compiler is able to verify that all possible exceptions thrown within a function (or a function's call hierarchy) are either caught or declared as possibly rethrown. The C# team considered this option and concluded that the maintenance burden that it imposed was not worth the perceived benefit. Therefore, it is not necessary to maintain a list of all possible exceptions throughout a particular call stack, but neither is it feasible to easily determine the possible exceptions. (As it turns out, this wasn't possible for Java, either. Calling virtual methods or using late binding, such as reflection, made it impossible to fully resolve at compile time which exceptions a method could possibly throw.)

General Catch Block

C# requires that any object that code throws must derive from `System.Exception`. However, this requirement is not universal to all languages. C++, for example, allows any object type to be thrown, including managed exceptions that don't derive from `System.Exception`. All exceptions, whether derived from `System.Exception` or not, will propagate into C# assemblies as derived from `System.Exception`.[7] The result is that `System.Exception` catch blocks will catch all exceptions not caught by earlier blocks.

C# also supports a **general catch block** (`catch{ }`) that behaves identically to the `catch(System.Exception exception)` block, except that there is no type or variable name. Also, the general catch block must appear last within the list of catch blocks. Since the general catch block is identical to the `catch(System.Exception exception)` block and the general catch block must appear last, the compiler issues a warning if both exist within the same try/catch statement because the general catch block will never be invoked.

---

7. Starting with C# 2.0.

ADVANCED TOPIC

General Catch Block Internals

The Common Intermediate Language (CIL) code corresponding to a general catch block is, in fact, a `catch(object)` block. Thus, regardless of the type thrown, the general catch block will catch it. Interestingly, it is not possible to explicitly declare a `catch(object)` exception block within C# code. Therefore, there is no means of catching a non–`System.Exception`-derived exception and having an exception instance to scrutinize.

In fact, unmanaged exceptions from languages such as C++ generally result in `System.Runtime.InteropServices.SEHException`-type exceptions, which derive from the `System.Exception` type. Therefore, not only can the unmanaged type exceptions be caught using a general catch block, but the non–`System.Exception`-managed types that are thrown can be caught as well—for instance, types such as `string`.

Guidelines for Exception Handling

Exception handling provides much-needed structure to the error-handling mechanisms that preceded it. However, it can still lead to some unwieldy results if used haphazardly. The following guidelines offer some best practices for exception handling.

- *Catch only the exceptions that you can handle.*

  It is generally possible to handle some types of exceptions but not others. For example, opening a file for exclusive read-write access may throw a `System.IO.IOException` because the file is already in use. In catching this type of exception, the code can report to the user that the file is in use and allow the user the option of canceling the operation or retrying it. Only exceptions for which there is a known action should be caught. Other exception types should be left for callers higher in the call stack.

- *Don't hide (bury) exceptions you don't fully handle.*

New programmers are often tempted to catch all exceptions and then continue executing instead of reporting an unhandled exception to the user. However, this practice may result in a critical system problem going undetected. Unless code takes explicit action to handle an exception or explicitly determines certain exceptions to be innocuous, catch blocks should rethrow exceptions instead of catching them and hiding them from the caller. In most cases, `catch(System.Exception)` and general catch blocks should occur higher in the call stack unless the block ends by rethrowing the exception.

- *Use* `System.Exception` *and general catch blocks rarely.*

  Almost all exceptions derive from `System.Exception`. However, the best way to handle some `System.Exceptions` is to allow them to go unhandled or to gracefully shut down the application sooner rather than later. These exceptions include cases such as `System.OutOfMemoryException` and `System.StackOverflowException`. Fortunately, such exceptions default to a nonrecoverable state, such that catching them without rethrowing them would cause the CLR to rethrow them anyway.[8] These exceptions are runtime exceptions that the developer cannot write code to recover from. Therefore, the best course of action is to shut down the application—something the runtime forces.

- *Avoid exception reporting or logging lower in the call stack.*

  Often, programmers are tempted to log exceptions or report exceptions to the user at the soonest possible location in the call stack. However, these locations are seldom able to handle the exception fully; instead, they resort to rethrowing the exception. Such catch blocks should not log the exception or report it to a user while in the bowels of the call stack. If the exception is logged and rethrown, the callers higher in the call stack may do the same, resulting in duplicate log entries of the exception. Worse, displaying the exception to the user may not be appropriate for the type of application. (Using `System.Console.WriteLine()` in a Windows application will never be seen by the user, for example, and displaying a dialog in an unattended command-line process may go unnoticed and freeze the application.) Logging- and exception-related user interfaces should be reserved for use higher up in the call stack.

8. Starting with Common Language Runtime (CLR) 4. Prior to CLR 4, code should catch such exceptions only to run cleanup or emergency code (such as saving any volatile data) before shutting down the application or rethrowing the exception with `throw;`.

- *Use* throw; *rather than* throw <exception object> *inside a catch block.*

  It is possible to rethrow an exception inside a catch block. For example, the implementation of catch(ArgumentNullException exception) could include a call to throw exception. However, rethrowing the exception like this will reset the stack trace to the location of the rethrown call instead of reusing the original throw point location. Therefore, unless you are rethrowing with a different exception type or intentionally hiding the original call stack, use throw; to allow the same exception to propagate up the call stack.

- *Favor exception conditions to avoid rethrowing an exception inside a catch block.*

  On occasions when you find yourself catching an exception that you can't actually handle appropriately and therefore need to rethrow, favor using an exception condition to avoid catching the exception in the first place.

- *Avoid throwing exceptions from exception filters.*

  When providing an exception filter, avoid code that throws an exception. Throwing an exception from an exception filter will result in a false condition, and the exception occurrence will be ignored. For this reason, you should consider placing complicated conditional checks into a separate method that is wrapped in a try/catch block that handles the exception explicitly.

- *Avoid exception conditionals that might change over time.*

  If an exception filter evaluates conditions such as exception messages that could potentially change with localization or changed message, the expected exception condition will not get caught, unexpectedly changing the business logic. For this reason, you should ensure exception conditions are valid over time.

- *Use caution when rethrowing different exceptions.*

  From inside a catch block, rethrowing a different exception will not only reset the call stack but also hide the original exception. To preserve the original exception, set the new exception's InnerException property, generally assignable via the constructor. Rethrowing a different exception should be reserved for the following situations:

1. *Changing the exception type clarifies the problem.*

   For example, in a call to `Logon(User user)`, rethrowing a different exception type is perhaps more appropriate than propagating `System.IO.IOException` when the file with the user list is inaccessible.

2. *Private data is part of the original exception.*

   In the preceding scenario, if the file path is included in the original `System.IO.IOException`, thereby exposing private security information about the system, the exception should be wrapped. This assumes, of course, that `InnerException` is not set with the original exception. (Funnily enough, a very early version of CLR version 1 [pre-alpha, even] had an exception that said something like "Security exception: You do not have permission to determine the path of `c:\temp\foo.txt`".)

3. *The exception type is too specific for the caller to handle appropriately.*

   For example, instead of throwing an exception specific to a particular database system, use a more generic exception so that database-specific code higher in the call stack can be avoided.

Guidelines

AVOID exception reporting or logging lower in the call stack.

DO NOT over-catch. Exceptions should be allowed to propagate up the call stack unless it is clearly understood how to programmatically address those errors lower in the stack.

CONSIDER catching a specific exception when you understand why it was thrown in a given context and can respond to the failure programmatically.

AVOID catching `System.Exception` or `System.SystemException` except in top-level exception handlers that perform final cleanup operations before rethrowing the exception.

DO use `throw;` rather than `throw <exception object>` inside a catch block.

DO use exception filters to avoid rethrowing an exception from within a catch block.

DO use caution when rethrowing different exceptions.

AVOID throwing exceptions from exception filters.

AVOID exception filters with logic that might implicitly change over time.

Defining Custom Exceptions

Once throwing an exception becomes the best course of action, it is preferable to use framework exceptions because they are well established and understood. Instead of throwing a custom invalid argument exception, for example, it is preferable to use the `System.ArgumentException` type. However, if the developers using a particular API will take special action—the exception-handling logic will vary to handle a custom exception type, for instance—it is appropriate to define a custom exception. For example, if a mapping API receives an address for which the ZIP code is invalid, instead of throwing `System.ArgumentException`, it may be better to throw a custom `InvalidAddressException`. The key is whether the caller is likely to write a specific `InvalidAddressException` catch block with special handling rather than just a generic `System.ArgumentException` catch block.

Defining a custom exception simply involves deriving from `System.Exception` or some other exception type. Listing 11.4 provides an example.

LISTING 11.4: Creating a Custom Exception

```
class DatabaseException : Exception
{
    public DatabaseException(
        string? message,
        System.Data.SqlClient.SQLException? exception)
        : base(message, innerException: exception)
    {
        // ...
    }

    public DatabaseException(
        string? message,
```

```
        System.Data.OracleClient.OracleException? exception)
        : base(message, innerException: exception)
    {
        // ...
    }

    public DatabaseException()
    {
        // ...
    }

    public DatabaseException(string? message)
        : base(message)
    {
        // ...
    }

    public DatabaseException(
        string? message, Exception? exception)
        : base(message, innerException: exception)
    {
        // ...
    }
    // ...
}
```

This custom exception might be created to wrap proprietary database exceptions. Since Oracle and SQL Server (for example) throw different exceptions for similar errors, an application could define a custom exception that standardizes the database-specific exceptions into a common exception wrapper that the application can handle in a standard manner. That way, whether the application was using an Oracle or a SQL Server back-end database, the same catch block could be used to handle the error higher up the stack.

The only requirement for a custom exception is that it derives from `System.Exception` or one of its descendants. Other good practices for custom exceptions are as follows:

- All exceptions should use the "Exception" suffix. This way, their purpose is easily established from their name.
- Generally, all exceptions should include constructors that take no parameters, a string parameter, and a parameter set consisting of a string and an inner

exception. Furthermore, since exceptions are usually constructed within the same statement in which they are thrown, any additional exception data should be allowed as part of the constructor. (The obvious exception to creating all these constructors is if certain data is required and a constructor would circumvent the requirements.)

- The inheritance chain should be kept relatively shallow (with fewer than approximately five levels).

The inner exception serves an important purpose when rethrowing an exception that is different from the one that was caught. For example, if a `System.Data.SqlClient.SqlException` is thrown by a database call but is caught within the data access layer and will be rethrown as a `DatabaseException`, the `DatabaseException` constructor that takes the `SqlException` (or inner exception) will save the original `SqlException` in the `InnerException` property. That way, if they require additional details about the original exception, developers can retrieve the exception from the `InnerException` property (e.g., `exception.InnerException`).

Guidelines

AVOID deep exception hierarchies.

DO NOT create a new exception type if the exception would not be handled differently than an existing CLR exception. Throw the existing framework exception instead.

DO create a new exception type to communicate a unique program error that cannot be communicated using an existing CLR exception and that can be programmatically handled in a different way than any other existing CLR exception type.

DO provide a parameterless constructor on all custom exception types. Also provide constructors that take a message and an inner exception.

DO name exception classes with the "Exception" suffix.

DO make exceptions runtime-serializable.

CONSIDER providing exception properties for programmatic access to extra information relevant to the exception.

ADVANCED TOPIC

Serializable Exceptions

Serializable objects are objects that the runtime can persist into a stream—a file stream, for example—and that can then be reinstantiated out of the stream. In the case of exceptions, this behavior may be necessary for certain distributed communication technologies. To support serialization, exception declarations should either include the `System.SerializableAttribute` attribute or implement `ISerializable`. Furthermore, they must include a constructor that takes `System.Runtime.Serialization.SerializationInfo` and `System.Runtime.Serialization.StreamingContext`. Listing 11.5 shows an example of using `System.SerializableAttribute`.

Listing 11.5: Defining a Serializable Exception

```
// Supporting serialization via an attribute
[Serializable]
class DatabaseException : Exception
{
    // ...

    // Used for deserialization of exceptions
    public DatabaseException(
        SerializationInfo serializationInfo,
        StreamingContext context)
        : base(serializationInfo, context)
    {
        //...
    }
}
```

The preceding `DatabaseException` example demonstrates both the attribute and the constructor requirement for making an exception serializable.

For .NET Core, `System.SerializableAttribute` was not available until .NET Standard 2.0. If you are writing code that will compile across multiple frameworks including a .NET Standard version prior to 2.0, consider defining your own `System.SerializableAttribute` as a **polyfill**. A polyfill is code that fills a hole in a particular version of technology, thereby adding the functionality or at least providing a shim for what is missing.

Rethrowing a Wrapped Exception

On occasion, an exception thrown at a lower level in the stack will no longer make sense when caught at a higher level. For example, consider a `System.IO.IOException` that occurs because a system is out of disk space on the server. A client catching such an exception would not necessarily be able to understand the context of why there was even I/O activity. Similarly, consider a geographic coordinate request API that throws a `System.UnauthorizedAccessException` (an exception totally unrelated to the API called). In this second example, the caller has no context for understanding what the API call has to do with security. From the perspective of the code that invokes the API, these exceptions cause more confusion than they help diagnose. Instead of exposing such exceptions to the client, it might make sense to first catch the exception and then throw a different exception, such as `InvalidOperationException` (or even perhaps a custom exception), as a means of communicating that the system is in an invalid state. In such scenarios, be sure to set the `InnerException` property of the wrapping exception (generally via a constructor call such as `new InvalidOperationException(string, Exception)`) so that there is additional context that can be used for diagnostic purposes by someone closer to the framework that was invoked.

An important detail to remember when considering whether to wrap and rethrow an exception is the fact that the original stack trace—which provides the context of where the exception was thrown—will be replaced with the new stack trace of where the wrapping exception is thrown (assuming `ExceptionDispatchInfo` is not used). Fortunately, when the original exception is embedded into the wrapping exception, the original stack trace is still available.

Ultimately, the intended recipient of the exception is the programmer writing code that calls your API—possibly incorrectly. Therefore, you should provide as much information as possible to them to indicate both what the programmer did wrong and—perhaps more important—how to fix it. The exception type is a critical piece of the communication mechanism, so you must choose it wisely.

Guidelines

CONSIDER wrapping specific exceptions thrown from the lower layer in a more appropriate exception if the lower-layer exception does not make sense in the context of the higher-layer operation.

DO specify the inner exception when wrapping exceptions.

DO target developers as the audience for exceptions, identifying both the problem and the mechanism to resolve it, where possible.

BEGINNER TOPIC

Checked and Unchecked Conversions

As we first discussed in a Chapter 2 Advanced Topic, C# provides special keywords for marking a code block with instructions to the runtime for what should happen if the target data type is too small to contain the assigned data. By default, if the target data type cannot contain the assigned data, the data will be truncated during assignment. For an example, see Listing 11.6 with Output 11.1.

LISTING 11.6: Overflowing an Integer Value

```
using System;
public class Program
{
    public static void Main()
    {
        // int.MaxValue equals 2147483647
        int n = int.MaxValue;
        n = n + 1;
        Console.WriteLine(n);
    }
}
```

OUTPUT 11.1

```
-2147483648
```

The code in Listing 11.6 writes the value `-2147483648` to the console. However, placing the code within a checked block or using the `checked` option when running the compiler will cause the runtime to throw an exception of type `System.OverflowException`. The syntax for a checked block uses the `checked` keyword, as shown in Listing 11.7 with Output 11.2. If the calculation involves only constants, the calculation will be checked by default.

LISTING 11.7: A Checked Block Example

```
using System;
public class Program
{
    public static void Main()
    {
        checked
        {
            // int.MaxValue equals 2147483647
            int n = int.MaxValue;
            n = n + 1;
            Console.WriteLine(n);
        }
    }
}
```

OUTPUT 11.2

```
Unhandled Exception: OverflowException: Arithmetic operation
resulted in an overflow. at Program.Main() in ...Program.cs:line 12
```

As shown in Output 11.2, an exception is thrown if, within the checked block, an overflow assignment occurs at runtime.[9] Note that the location information in Output 11.2 (`Program.cs:line X`) appears only in debug compilations—that is, compilations using the `/Debug` option of the compiler.

9. In addition to Output 11.2, if the .NET Framework debugger is installed, a dialog may appear that prompts the user to send an error message to Microsoft, check for a solution, or debug the application.

To change an entire project to be unchecked or checked, set the `CheckForOverflowUnderflow` property to `false` or `true`, respectively.

```
<PropertyGroup>
<CheckForOverflowUnderflow>true</CheckForOverflowUnderflow>
</PropertyGroup>
```

C# also supports an unchecked block that truncates the data instead of throwing an exception for assignments within the block (see Listing 11.8 with Output 11.3).

Listing 11.8: An Unchecked Block Example

```
using System;
public class Program
{
    public static void Main()
    {
        unchecked
        {
            // int.MaxValue equals 2147483647
            int n = int.MaxValue;
            n = n + 1;
            Console.WriteLine(n);
        }
    }
}
```

Output 11.3

```
-2147483648
```

Even if the checked option is on during compilation, the `unchecked` keyword in the code in Listing 11.8 will prevent the runtime from throwing an exception during execution.

Equivalent `checked` and `unchecked` expressions are available for cases where statements are not allowed. For example, a field initializer may consist of an expression rather than a statement:

```
int number = unchecked(int.MaxValue + 1);
```

Summary

Throwing an exception produces a significant performance hit. A single exception causes lots of runtime stack information to be loaded and processed—data that would not otherwise be loaded—and it takes a considerable amount of time to handle. As pointed out in Chapter 5, you should use exceptions only to handle exceptional circumstances; APIs should provide mechanisms to check whether an exception will be thrown instead of forcing a particular API to be called to determine whether an exception will be thrown.

The next chapter introduces generics.[10] In fact, it essentially deprecates any use of the `System.Collections` namespace, which was formerly used in nearly every project.

---

10. A feature starting in C# 2.0.

12

Generics

As your projects become more sophisticated, you will need a better way to reuse and customize existing software. To facilitate code reuse, especially the reuse of algorithms, C# includes a feature called **generics**.

Generics are lexically like generic types in Java and templates in C++. In all three languages, these features enable the implementation of algorithms and patterns once, rather than requiring separate implementations for each type that the algorithm or pattern operates on. However, C# generics are very different from both Java generics and C++ templates in the details of their implementation and impact on the type system of their respective languages. Just as methods are powerful because they can take arguments, so types and methods that take type arguments have significantly more functionality.

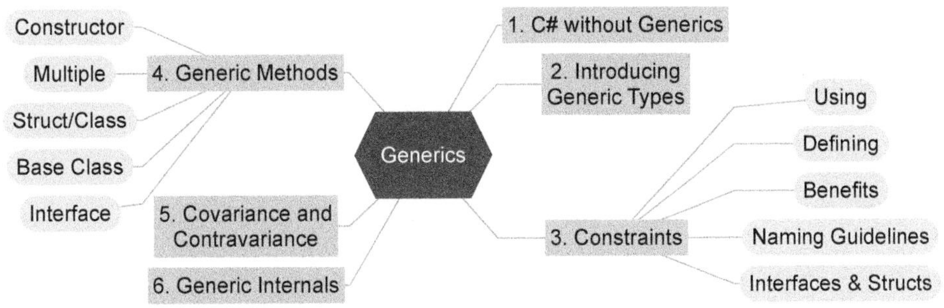

Generics were added to the runtime and C# in version 2.0.

C# without Generics

We begin the discussion of generics by examining a class that does not use generics. This class, `System.Collections.Stack`, represents a collection of objects such that the last item to be added to the collection is the first item retrieved from the collection (last in, first out [LIFO]). `Push()` and `Pop()`, the two main methods of the `Stack` class, add items to the stack and remove them from the stack, respectively. The declarations for the methods on the `Stack` class appear in Listing 12.1.

Listing 12.1: The `System.Collections.Stack` Method Signatures

```
public class Stack
{
    public virtual object Pop()
    {
        // ...
    }

    public virtual void Push(object obj)
    {
        // ...
    }
    // ...
}
```

Programs frequently use stack type collections to facilitate multiple undo operations. For example, Listing 12.2, with results shown in Output 12.1, uses the `System.Collections.Stack` class for undo operations within a program that simulates an Etch A Sketch toy.

Listing 12.2: Supporting Undo in a Program Similar to an Etch A Sketch Toy

```
using System.Collections.Generic;

public class Program
{
    // ...

    public static void Sketch()
    {
        Stack<Cell> path = new();
```

```
    Cell currentPosition;
    ConsoleKeyInfo key;
    // ...

    do
    {
        // Etch in the direction indicated by the
        // arrow keys that the user enters
        key = Move();

        switch(key.Key)
        {
            case ConsoleKey.Z:
                // Undo the previous Move
                if(path.Count >= 1)
                {
                    currentPosition = (Cell)path.Pop();
                    Console.SetCursorPosition(
                        currentPosition.X, currentPosition.Y);
                    // ...
                    Undo();
                }
                break;
            case ConsoleKey.DownArrow:
                // ...
            case ConsoleKey.UpArrow:
                // ...
            case ConsoleKey.LeftArrow:
                // ...
            case ConsoleKey.RightArrow:
                // SaveState()
                if(Console.CursorLeft < Console.WindowWidth - 2)
                {
                    currentPosition = new Cell(
                        Console.CursorLeft + 1, Console.CursorTop);
                }
                path.Push(currentPosition);
                // ...
                break;

            default:
                Console.Beep();
                break;
        }
    }
    while(key.Key != ConsoleKey.X);  // Use X to quit.
}
```

```
    // ...
}

public struct Cell
{
    public int X { get; }
    public int Y { get; }

    public Cell(int x, int y)
    {
        X = x;
        Y = y;
    }
}
```

Output 12.1

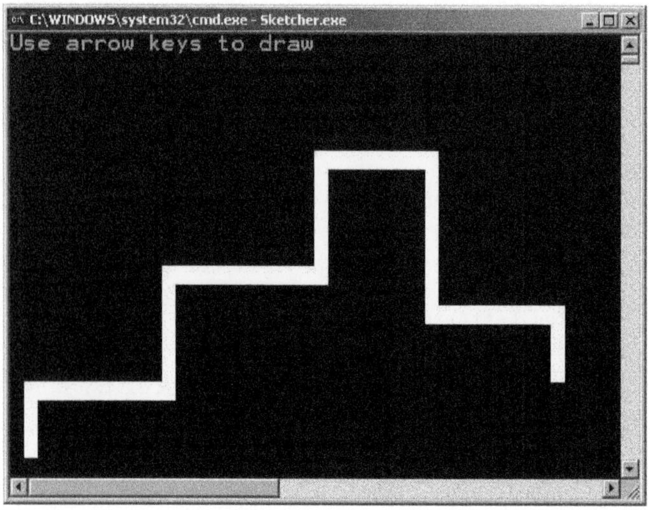

Using the variable `path`, which is declared as a `System.Collections.Stack`, you save the previous move by passing a custom type, `Cell`, into the `Stack.Push()` method using `path.Push(currentPosition)`. If the user enters a *Z* (or presses Ctrl+Z), you undo the previous move by retrieving it from the stack using a `Pop()` method, setting the cursor position to be the previous position, and calling `Undo()`.

Although this code is functional, the `System.Collections.Stack` class has a fundamental shortcoming. As shown in Listing 12.1, the `Stack` class collects values of type `object`. Because every object in the Common Language Runtime

(CLR) derives from `object`, `Stack` provides no validation that the elements you place into it are homogenous or are of the intended type. For example, instead of passing `currentPosition`, you can pass a string in which `X` and `Y` are concatenated with a decimal point between them. However, the compiler must allow the inconsistent data types because the stack class is written to take any object, regardless of its more specific type.

Furthermore, when retrieving the data from the stack using the `Pop()` method, you must cast the return value to a `Cell`. But if the type of the value returned from the `Pop()` method is not `Cell`, an exception is thrown. By deferring type checking until runtime by using a cast, you make the program more brittle. The fundamental problem with creating classes that can work with multiple data types without generics is that they must work with a common base class (or interface), usually `object`.

Using value types, such as a struct or an integer, with classes that use `object` exacerbates the problem. If you pass a value type to the `Stack.Push()` method, for example, the runtime automatically boxes it. Similarly, when you retrieve a value type, you need to explicitly unbox the data and cast the `object` reference you obtain from the `Pop()` method into a value type. Casting a reference type to a base class or interface has a negligible performance impact, but the box operation for a value type introduces more overhead, because it must allocate memory, copy the value, and then later garbage-collect that memory.

C# is a language that encourages *type safety*: The language is designed so that many type errors, such as assigning an integer to a variable of type `string`, can be caught at compile time. The fundamental problem is that the `Stack` class is not as type-safe as one expects a C# program to be. To change the `Stack` class to enforce type safety by restricting the contents of the stack to be a particular data type (without using generic types), you must create a specialized `stack` class, as in Listing 12.3.

Listing 12.3: Defining a Specialized Stack Class

```
public class CellStack
{
    public virtual Cell Pop() { return new Cell(); } // would return
                                                      // that last cell
↪added and remove it from the list
```

```
    public virtual void Push(Cell cell) { }
    // ...
}
```

Because CellStack can store only objects of type Cell, this solution requires a custom implementation of the stack methods, which is less than ideal. Implementing a type-safe stack of integers would require yet another custom implementation; each implementation would look remarkably like every other one. There would be lots of duplicated, redundant code.

BEGINNER TOPIC

Another Example: Nullable Value Types

Chapter 3 introduced the capability of declaring variables that could contain null by using the nullable modifier, ?, when declaring a value type variable. C# began supporting this functionality only in version 2.0, because the right implementation required generics. Prior to the introduction of generics, programmers faced essentially two options.

The first option was to declare a nullable data type for each value type that needs to handle null values, as shown in Listing 12.4.

Listing 12.4: Declaring Versions of Various Value Types That Store null

```
struct NullableInt
{
    /// <summary>
    /// Provides the value when HasValue returns true
    /// </summary>
    public int Value { get; private set; }

    /// <summary>
    /// Indicates whether there is a value or whether
    /// the value is "null"
    /// </summary>
    public bool HasValue { get; private set; }

    // ...
}

struct NullableGuid
```

```
{
    /// <summary>
    /// Provides the value when HasValue returns true
    /// </summary>
    public Guid Value { get; private set; }

    /// <summary>
    /// Indicates whether there is a value or whether
    /// the value is "null"
    /// </summary>
    public bool HasValue { get; private set; }

    // ...
}

// ...
```

Listing 12.4 shows possible implementations of `NullableInt` and `NullableGuid`. If a program required additional nullable value types, you would have to create yet another struct with the properties modified to use the desired value type. Any improvement of the implementation (e.g., adding a user-defined implicit conversion from the underlying type to the nullable type) would require modifying all the nullable type declarations.

An alternative strategy for implementing a nullable type without generics is to declare a single type with a `Value` property of type `object`, as shown in Listing 12.5.

Listing 12.5: Declaring a Nullable Type That Contains a `Value` Property of Type `object`

```
struct Nullable
{
    /// <summary>
    /// Provides the value when HasValue returns true.
    /// </summary>
    public object Value { get; private set; }

    /// <summary>
    /// Indicates whether there is a value or whether
    /// the value is "null"
    /// </summary>
    public bool HasValue { get; private set; }
```

```
    // ...
}
```

Although this option requires only one implementation of a nullable type, the runtime always boxes value types when setting the `Value` property. Furthermore, retrieving the underlying value from the `Value` property requires a cast operation, which might potentially be invalid at runtime.

Neither option is particularly attractive. To eliminate this problem, generics[1] were added to C#. (And, in fact, nullable types are implemented as the generic type `Nullable<T>`.)

Introducing Generic Types

Generics provide a facility for creating data structures that can be specialized to handle specific types. Programmers define these **parameterized types** so that each variable of a particular generic type has the same internal algorithm, but the types of data and method signatures can vary on the basis of the type arguments provided for the type parameters.

To minimize the learning curve for developers, the C# designers chose syntax that superficially resembles C++ templates. In C#, the syntax for generic classes and structures uses angle brackets to both declare the generic type parameters in the type declaration and specify the generic type arguments when the type is used.

Using a Generic Class

Listing 12.6 shows how you can specify the actual type argument used by the generic class. You instruct the `path` variable to be the "Stack of Cell" type by specifying `Cell` within angle bracket notation in both the object creation expression and the declaration statement. In other words, when declaring a variable (`path` in this case) using a generic data type, C# requires the developer to identify the actual type arguments used by the generic type. Listing 12.6 with Output 12.2 illustrates this process with the new generic `Stack` class.

1. Introduced in C# 2.0.

Listing 12.6: Implementing Undo with a Generic `Stack` Class

```
using System;
using System.Collections.Generic;

public class Program
{
    // ...

    public static void Sketch()
    {
        Stack<Cell> path = new();
        Cell currentPosition;
        ConsoleKeyInfo key;
        // ...

        do
        {
            // Etch in the direction indicated by the
            // arrow keys that the user enters
            key = Move();

            switch(key.Key)
            {
                case ConsoleKey.Z:
                    // Undo the previous Move
                    if(path.Count >= 1)
                    {
                        // No cast required
                        currentPosition = path.Pop();
                        Console.SetCursorPosition(
                            currentPosition.X, currentPosition.Y);
                        FillCell(currentPosition, ConsoleColor.Black);
                        Undo();
                    }
                    break;
                case ConsoleKey.DownArrow:
                    // ...
                case ConsoleKey.UpArrow:
                    // ...
                case ConsoleKey.LeftArrow:
                    // ...
                case ConsoleKey.RightArrow:
                    // SaveState()
                    if(Console.CursorLeft < Console.WindowWidth - 2)
                    {
                        currentPosition = new Cell(
```

```
                              Console.CursorLeft + 1, Console.CursorTop);
                      }
                      // Only type Cell allowed in call to Push()
                      path.Push(currentPosition);
                      FillCell(currentPosition);
                      break;

                  default:
                      Console.Beep();
                      break;
              }

          }
          while(key.Key != ConsoleKey.X);  // Use X to quit
      }
      // ...
}
```

Output 12.2

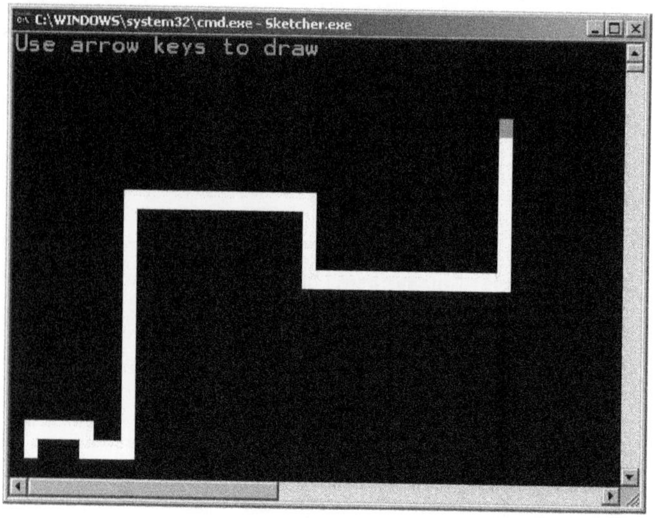

In the `path` declaration shown in Listing 12.6, you declare a variable and initialize it with a new instance of the `System.Collections.Generic.Stack<Cell>` class. You specify in angle brackets that the data type of the stack's elements is `Cell`. As a result, every object added to and retrieved from `path` is of type `Cell`. In turn, you no longer need to cast the return of `path.Pop()` or ensure that only `Cell` type objects are added to `path` in the `Push()` method.

Defining a Simple Generic Class

Generics allow you to author algorithms and patterns and to reuse the code for different data types. Listing 12.7 creates a generic `Stack<T>` class similar to the `System.Collections.Generic.Stack<T>` class used in the code in Listing 12.6. You specify a **type parameter** (in this case, `T`) within angle brackets after the class name. The generic `Stack<T>` can then be supplied with a single type argument that is substituted everywhere `T` appears in the class. Thus, the stack can store items of any stated type, without duplicating code or converting the item to type `object`. The type parameter `T` is a placeholder that must be supplied with a type argument. In Listing 12.7, you can see that the type parameter will be used for the `InternalItems` array, the type for the parameter to the `Push()` method, and the return type for the `Pop()` method.

Listing 12.7: Declaring a Generic Class, `Stack<T>`

```
public class Stack<T>
{
    public Stack(int maxSize)
    {
        InternalItems = new T[maxSize];
    }

    private T[] InternalItems { get; }

    public void Push(T data)
    {
        //...
    }

    public T Pop()
    {
        // ...
    }
}
```

Benefits of Generics

There are several advantages of using a generic class rather than a nongeneric version (such as the `System.Collections.Generic.Stack<T>` class used earlier instead of the original `System.Collections.Stack` type):

1. Generics facilitate increased type safety, preventing data types other than those explicitly intended by the members within the parameterized class. In Listing 12.7, the parameterized stack class restricts you to the `Cell` data type when using `Stack<Cell>`. For example, the statement `path.Push("garbage")` produces a compile-time error indicating that there is no overloaded method for `System.Collections.Generic.Stack<T>.Push(T)` that can work with the string, because it cannot be converted to a `Cell`.

2. Compile-time type checking reduces the likelihood of `InvalidCastException` type errors at runtime.

3. Using value types with generic class members no longer causes a boxing conversion to `object`. For example, `path.Pop()` and `path.Push()` do not require an item to be boxed when added or unboxed when removed.

4. Generics in C# reduce code bloat. Generic types retain the benefits of specific class versions, without the overhead. For example, it is no longer necessary to define a class such as `CellStack`.

5. Performance improves because casting from an object is no longer required, thereby eliminating a type check operation. Also, performance improves because boxing is no longer necessary for value types.

6. Generics reduce memory consumption by avoiding boxing and thus consuming less memory on the heap.

7. Code becomes more readable because of fewer casting checks and because of the need for fewer type-specific implementations.

8. Editors that assist coding via some type of IntelliSense work directly with return parameters from generic classes. There is no need to cast the return data for IntelliSense to work.

At their core, generics offer the ability to code pattern implementations and then reuse those implementations wherever the patterns appear. Patterns describe problems that occur repeatedly within code, and templates provide a single implementation for these repeating patterns.

Type Parameter Naming Guidelines

Just as when naming a method's formal parameter, so you should be as descriptive as possible when naming a type parameter. Furthermore, to distinguish the parameter as being a type parameter, its name should include a *T* prefix. For example, in defining a class such as `EntityCollection<TEntity>`, you would use the type parameter name `TEntity`.

The only time you would not use a descriptive type parameter name is when such a description would not add any value. For example, using *T* in the `Stack<T>` class is appropriate, since the indication that *T* is a type parameter is sufficiently descriptive; the stack works for any type.

In the next section, you will learn about constraints. It is a good practice to use constraint-descriptive type names. For example, if a type parameter must implement `IComponent`, consider using a type name of `TComponent`.

Guidelines

DO choose meaningful names for type parameters and prefix the name with *T*.

CONSIDER indicating a constraint in the name of a type parameter.

Generic Interfaces and Structs

C# supports the use of generics throughout the language, including interfaces and structs. The syntax is identical to that used by classes. To declare an interface with a type parameter, place the type parameter in angle brackets immediately after the interface name, as shown in the example of `IPair<T>` in Listing 12.8.

Listing 12.8: Declaring a Generic Interface

```
interface IPair<T>
{
    T First { get; set; }
    T Second { get; set; }
}
```

This interface represents pairs of like objects, such as the coordinates of a point, a person's genetic parents, or nodes of a binary tree. The type contained in the pair is the same for both items.

To implement the interface, you use the same syntax as you would for a nongeneric class. Note that it is legal—indeed, common—for the type argument for one generic type to be a type parameter of another generic type, as shown in Listing 12.9. The type argument of the interface is the type parameter declared by the class. In addition, this example uses a struct rather than a class, demonstrating that C# supports custom generic value types.

Listing 12.9: Implementing a Generic Interface

```
public struct Pair<T> : IPair<T>
{
    public T First { get; set; }
    public T Second { get; set; }
}
```

Support for generic interfaces is especially important for collection classes, where generics are most prevalent. Before generics were available in C#, developers relied on a series of interfaces within the `System.Collections` namespace. Like their implementing classes, these interfaces worked only with type `object`, and as a result, the interface forced all access to and from these collection classes to require a cast. By using type-safe generic interfaces, you can avoid cast operations.

ADVANCED TOPIC

Implementing the Same Interface Multiple Times on a Single Class

Two different constructions of the same generic interface are considered different types. Consequently, "the same" generic interface can be implemented multiple times by a class or struct. Consider the example in Listing 12.10.

Listing 12.10: Duplicating an Interface Implementation on a Single Class

```
public interface IContainer<T>
{
    ICollection<T> Items { get; set; }
}

public class Person : IContainer<Address>,
    IContainer<Phone>, IContainer<Email>
{
    ICollection<Address> IContainer<Address>.Items
    {
        get
        {
            // ...
        }
        set
        {
            //...
        }
    }
    ICollection<Phone> IContainer<Phone>.Items
    {
        get
        {
            // ...
        }
        set
        {
            //...
        }
    }
    ICollection<Email> IContainer<Email>.Items
    {
        get
        {
            // ...
```

```
        }
        set
        {
            //...
        }
    }
}
```

In this example, the `Items` property appears multiple times using an explicit interface implementation with a varying type parameter. Without generics, this would not be possible; instead, the compiler would allow only one explicit `IContainer.Items` property.

However, this technique of implementing multiple versions of the same interface is considered by many developers to be a "bad code smell" because it is potentially confusing (particularly if the interface permits covariant or contravariant conversions). Moreover, the `Person` class here seems potentially badly designed; one does not normally think of a person as being "a thing that can provide a set of email addresses." When you feel tempted to make a class implement three versions of the same interface, consider whether it might be better to make it instead implement three properties—for example, `EmailAddresses`, `PhoneNumbers`, and `MailingAddresses`—each of which returns the appropriate construction of the generic interface.

Guidelines

AVOID implementing multiple constructions of the same generic interface in one type.

Defining a Constructor and a Finalizer

Perhaps surprisingly, the constructors (and finalizer) of a generic class or struct do not require type parameters; in other words, they do not require `Pair<T>(){...}`. In the pair example in Listing 12.11, the constructor is declared using `public Pair(T first, T second)`.

Listing 12.11: Declaring a Generic Type's Constructor

```
public struct Pair<T> : IPair<T>
{
    public Pair(T first, T second)
    {
        First = first;
        Second = second;
    }

    public T First { get; set; }
    public T Second { get; set; }
}
```

Specifying a Default Value with the `default` operator

Listing 12.11 included a constructor that takes the initial values for both `first` and `second` and assigns them to `First` and `Second`. Since `Pair<T>` is a struct, any constructor you provide must initialize all fields and automatically implemented properties. This presents a problem, however.

Consider a constructor for `Pair<T>` that initializes only half of the pair at instantiation time. Defining such a constructor, as shown in Listing 12.12, causes a compile-time error because the field `Second` is still uninitialized at the end of the constructor. Providing initialization for `Second` presents a problem because you don't know the data type of `T`. If it is a nullable type, `null` would work, but this approach would not work if `T` were a non-nullable type.

Listing 12.12: Not Initializing All Fields, Causing a Compile-Time Error

```
public struct Pair<T> : IPair<T>
{
    // ERROR:  Field 'Pair<T>.Second' must be fully assigned
    //         before control leaves the constructor
    // public Pair(T first)
    // {
    //     First = first;
    // }

    // ...
}
```

To deal with this scenario, C# provides the `default` operator. The default value of `int`, for example,[2] could be specified with `default`. In the case of `T`, which `Second` requires, you can use `default`, as shown in Listing 12.13.

Listing 12.13: Initializing a Field with the `default` Operator

```
public struct Pair<T> : IPair<T>
{
    public Pair(T first)
    {
        First = first;
        // ...
        Second = default;
        // ...
    }
    // ...
}
```

The `default` operator can provide the default value for any type, including type parameters.

It's possible to use `default` without specifying a parameter if it is possible to infer the data type.[3] For example, with variable initialization or assignment, you can use `Pair<T> pair = default` in place of `Pair<T> pair = default(Pair<T>)`. Furthermore, if a method returns an `int`, it is possible to simply use `return default` and have the compiler infer a `default(int)` from the return of the method. Other scenarios where such inference is possible are default parameter (optional) values and method call arguments.

Begin 8.0

Note that all nullable types have `null` as their default value, as do nullable generic types such as `default(T?)`. Furthermore, the default value for all reference types is `null`. As a result, if nullable reference types are enabled with C# 8.0, assigning `default` to a non-nullable reference type will result in a warning. Prior to C# 8.0 (and obviously after it), you should avoid assigning `default` or `null` to reference types unless `null` is expected to be a valid value.[4] Where possible, favor leaving the variable uninitialized until a valid value is available for

2. Assuming C# 7.1.
3. Introduced in C# 7.1.
4. Assigning `default` to a reference type in C# 7.0 or earlier produces a warning.

assignment. In cases like Listing 12.13, where an appropriate value for `Second` is unknown in the constructor, `Second` will inevitably be `null` for a reference type or a nullable value type; thus, a warning appears when assigning `default` (which is potentially `null`) to a property of generic type `T`. To appropriately handle the warning, you will need to declare the `Second` property to be of type `T?` and identify whether `T` is a reference type or a value type with a class/struct constraint as described in the "`struct`/`class` Constraints" section. (In fact, this leads to the more general guideline not to assign default on a generic type unless the type assigned is constrained to a class or a struct.)

End 8.0

Multiple Type Parameters

Generic types may declare any number of type parameters. The initial `Pair<T>` example contained only one type parameter. To enable support for storing a dichotomous pair of objects, such as a name/value pair, you could create a new version of the type that declares two type parameters, as shown in Listing 12.14.

Listing 12.14: Declaring a Generic with Multiple Type Parameters

```
interface IPair<TFirst, TSecond>
{
    TFirst First { get; set; }
    TSecond Second { get; set; }
}

public struct Pair<TFirst, TSecond> : IPair<TFirst, TSecond>
{
    public Pair(TFirst first, TSecond second)
    {
        First = first;
        Second = second;
    }

    public TFirst First { get; set; }
    public TSecond Second { get; set; }
}
```

When you use the Pair<TFirst, TSecond> class, you supply multiple type parameters within the angle brackets of the declaration and instantiation statements; you then supply matching types to the parameters of the methods when you call them. Listing 12.15 illustrates this approach.

Listing 12.15: Using a Type with Multiple Type Parameters

```
Pair<int, string> historicalEvent =
    new(1914,
        "Shackleton leaves for South Pole on ship Endurance");

Console.WriteLine("{0}: {1}",
    historicalEvent.First, historicalEvent.Second);
```

The number of type parameters—that is, the **arity**—uniquely distinguishes the class from others of the same name. Because of this arity variation, it is possible to define both Pair<T> and Pair<TFirst, TSecond> within the same namespace. Furthermore, because of their close semantic relationship, generics that differ only by arity should be placed into the same C# file.

Guidelines

DO place multiple generic semantically equivalent classes into a single file if they differ only by the number of generic parameters.

BEGINNER TOPIC

Tuples: An Abundance of Arity

Internally, the underlying type that implements the tuple syntax is, in fact, a generic—specifically a System.ValueTuple. As with Pair<...>, it is possible to reuse the same name because of the variation in arity (each class has a different number of type parameters), as shown in Listing 12.16.

Listing 12.16: Using Arity to Overload a Type Definition

```
public class Tuple
{
    // ...
}
public class Tuple<T1> // : IStructuralEquatable,
                       // IStructuralComparable, IComparable
{
    // ...
}
public class Tuple<T1, T2> // : IStructuralEquatable,
                           // IStructuralComparable, IComparable
{
    // ...
}
public class Tuple<T1, T2, T3> // : IStructuralEquatable,
                               // IStructuralComparable, IComparable
{
    // ...
}
public class Tuple<T1, T2, T3, T4> // : IStructuralEquatable,
                                   // IStructuralComparable, IComparable
{
    // ...
}
public class Tuple<T1, T2, T3, T4, T5> // : IStructuralEquatable,
                                       // IStructuralComparable,
                                       // IComparable
{
    // ...
}
public class Tuple<T1, T2, T3, T4, T5, T6>
    // : IStructuralEquatable, IStructuralComparable, IComparable
{
    // ...
}
public class Tuple<T1, T2, T3, T4, T5, T6, T7>
    // : IStructuralEquatable, IStructuralComparable, IComparable
{
    // ...
}
public class Tuple<T1, T2, T3, T4, T5, T6, T7, TRest>
    // : IStructuralEquatable, IStructuralComparable, IComparable
{
```

```
    // ...
}
```

The `ValueTuple<...>` set of classes was designed for the same purpose as the `Pair<T>` and `Pair<TFirst, TSecond>` classes, except that together they can handle eight type arguments. In fact, using the last `ValueTuple` shown in Listing 12.16, `TRest` can be used to store another `ValueTuple`, making the number of elements of the tuple practically unlimited.

Another interesting member of the tuple family of classes is the nongeneric `ValueTuple` class. This class has eight static factory methods for instantiating the various generic tuple types. Although each generic type could be instantiated directly using its constructor, the `ValueTuple` type's factory methods allow for inference of the type arguments via the `Create()` method. Listing 12.17 demonstrates using the `Create()` method in combination with type inference.[5]

Listing 12.17: Comparing `System.ValueTuple` Instantiation Approaches

```
#if !PRECSHARP7
(string, Contact) keyValuePair;
keyValuePair =
    ("555-55-5555", new Contact("Inigo Montoya"));
#else // Use System.ValueTupe<string,Contact> prior to C# 7.0
ValueTuple<string, Contact> keyValuePair;
keyValuePair =
    ValueTuple.Create(
        "555-55-5555", new Contact("Inigo Montoya"));
keyValuePair =
    new ValueTuple<string, Contact>(
        "555-55-5555", new Contact("Inigo Montoya"));
#endif // !PRECSHARP7
```

Obviously, when the `ValueTuple` gets large, the number of type parameters to specify could be cumbersome without the `Create()` factory methods.[6]

5. Simpler for C# 6.0.
6. Similar tuple class added in C# 4.0: `System.Tuple`.

As you might have deduced from the fact that the framework libraries declare eight different generic `System.ValueTuple` types,[7] there is no support in the CLR type system for *variadic* generic types. Methods can take an arbitrary number of arguments by using *parameter arrays*, but there is no corresponding technique for generic types; every generic type must be of a specific arity. (See "Beginner Topic: Tuples: An Abundance of Arity" for an example where you might imagine such a feature.)

Nested Generic Types

Type parameters on a containing generic type will "cascade" down to any nested types automatically. If the containing type declares a type parameter `T`, for example, all nested types will also be generic, and type parameter `T` will be available on the nested type as well. If the nested type includes its own type parameter named `T`, this will hide the type parameter within the containing type, and any reference to `T` in the nested type will refer to the nested `T` type parameter. Fortunately, reuse of the same type parameter name within the nested type will cause a compiler warning to prevent accidental overlap (see Listing 12.18).

Listing 12.18: Nested Generic Types

```
public class Container<T, U>
{
    // Nested classes inherit type parameter
    // Reusing a type parameter name will cause
    // a warning
    public class Nested<U>
    {
        static void Method(T param0, U param1)
        {
        }
    }
}
```

7. Created due to C# 7.0's abundant tuple syntax.

The containing type's type parameters are accessible in the nested type in the same way that members of the containing type are also accessible from the nested type. The rule is simply that a type parameter is available anywhere within the body of the type that declares it.

> **Guidelines**
>
> **AVOID** shadowing a type parameter of an outer type with an identically named type parameter of a nested type.

Constraints

Generics support the ability to define constraints on type parameters. These constraints ensure that the types provided as type arguments conform to various rules. Take, for example, the BinaryTree<T> class shown in Listing 12.19.

Listing 12.19: Declaring a BinaryTree<T> Class with No Constraints

```
public class BinaryTree<T>
{
    public BinaryTree(T item)
    {
        Item = item;
    }

    public T Item { get; set; }
    public Pair<BinaryTree<T>> SubItems { get; set; }
}
```

(An interesting side note is that BinaryTree<T> uses Pair<T> internally, which is possible because Pair<T> is simply another type.)

Suppose you want the tree to sort the values within the Pair<T> value as it is assigned to the SubItems property. To achieve the sorting, the SubItems set accessor uses the CompareTo() method of the supplied key, as shown in Listing 12.20.

At compile time, the type parameter T is an unconstrained generic. When the code is written as shown in Listing 12.20, the compiler assumes that the only members available on T are those inherited from the base type `object`, since every

Listing 12.20: Needing the Type Parameter to Support an Interface

```
public class BinaryTree<T>
{
    public BinaryTree(T item)
    {
        Item = item;
    }

    public T Item { get; set; }
    public Pair<BinaryTree<T>> SubItems
    {
        get { return _SubItems; }
        set
        {
            IComparable<T> first;
            // ERROR: Cannot implicitly convert type...
            //first = value.First;  // Explicit cast required

            //if(first.CompareTo(value.Second) < 0)
            //{
            //    // first is less than second
            //    //...
            //}
            //else
            //{
            //    // first and second are the same or
            //    // second is less than first
            //    //...
            //}
            _SubItems = value;
        }
    }
    private Pair<BinaryTree<T>> _SubItems;
}
```

type has `object` as a base class. Only methods such as `ToString()`, therefore, are available to call on an instance of the type parameter T. As a result, the compiler displays a compilation error because the `CompareTo()` method is not defined on type `object`.

You can cast the T parameter to the `IComparable<T>` interface to access the `CompareTo()` method, as shown in Listing 12.21.

Listing 12.21: Needing the Type Parameter to Support an Interface or Exception Thrown

```
public class BinaryTree<T>
{
    public BinaryTree(T item)
    {
        Item = item;
    }

    public T Item { get; set; }
    public Pair<BinaryTree<T>?>? SubItems
    {
        get { return _SubItems; }
        set
        {
            switch (value)
            {
                // Null handling removed for elucidation

                // Using C# 8.0 Pattern Matching. Switch to
                // checking for null prior to C# 8.0
                // ...
                case
                {
                        First: {Item: IComparable<T> first },
                        Second: {Item: T second } }:
                    if (first.CompareTo(second) < 0)
                    {
                        // first is less than second
                    }
                    else
                    {
                        // second is less than or equal to first
                    }
                    break;
                default:
                    throw new InvalidCastException(
                        @$"Unable to sort the items as {
                            typeof(T) } does not support IComparable<T>.
↪");
            };
            _SubItems = value;
        }
    }
private Pair<BinaryTree<T>?>? _SubItems;
}
```

Unfortunately, if you now declare a `BinaryTree<SomeType>` class variable but the type argument (`SomeType`) does not implement the `IComparable<SomeType>` interface, there is no way to sort the items; in turn, we throw an `InvalidCastException`, indicating the type doesn't support the requisite interface. This eliminates a key reason for having generics in the first place: to improve type safety.

To avoid this exception and instead generate a compile-time error if the type argument does not implement the interface, C# allows you to supply an optional list of **constraints** for each type parameter declared in the generic type. A constraint declares the characteristics that the generic type requires of the type argument supplied for each type parameter. You declare a constraint using the `where` keyword, followed by a parameter–requirements pair, where the parameter must be one of those declared in the generic type. The requirements describe one of three things: the class or interfaces to which the type argument must be convertible, the presence of a default constructor, or a reference/value type restriction.

Interface Constraints

To ensure that a binary tree has its nodes correctly ordered, you can use the `CompareTo()` method in the `BinaryTree` class. To do this most effectively, you should impose a constraint on the `T` type parameter. That is, you need the `T` type parameter to implement the `IComparable<T>` interface. The syntax for declaring this constraint appears in Listing 12.22.

Listing 12.22: Declaring an Interface Constraint

```
public class BinaryTree<T>
    where T : System.IComparable<T>
{
    public BinaryTree(T item)
    {
        Item = item;
    }

    public T Item { get; set; }
    public Pair<BinaryTree<T>?> SubItems
    {
        get { return _SubItems; }
        set
```

```
        {
            switch (value)
            {
                // Null handling removed for elucidation

                // Using C# 8.0 Pattern Matching. Switch to
                // checking for null prior to C# 8.0
                // ...
                case
                {
                    First: { Item: T first },
                    Second: { Item: T second }
                }:
                    if (first.CompareTo(second) < 0)
                    {
                        // first is less than second
                    }
                    else
                    {
                        // second is less than or equal to first
                    }
                    break;
                default:
                    throw new InvalidCastException(
                        @$"Unable to sort the items as {
                            typeof(T) } does not support IComparable<T>.
↪");
            };
            _SubItems = value;
        }
    }
    private Pair<BinaryTree<T>?> _SubItems;
}
```

While the code change in this example is minor, it moves the error identification to the compiler rather than at runtime, and this is an important difference. When given the interface constraint addition in Listing 12.22, the compiler ensures that each time you use the `BinaryTree<T>` class, you specify a type parameter that implements the corresponding construction of the `IComparable<T>` interface. Furthermore, you no longer need to explicitly cast the variable to an `IComparable<T>` interface before calling the `CompareTo()` method. Casting is not even required to access members that use explicit interface implementation, which in other contexts would hide the member without a cast. When calling a method on a value typed as a generic type parameter, the compiler checks whether the method matches any method on any of the interfaces declared as constraints.

If you tried to create a `BinaryTree<T>` variable using `System.Text.StringBuilder` as the type parameter, you would receive a compiler error because `StringBuilder` does not implement `IComparable<StringBuilder>`. The error is similar to the one shown in Output 12.3.

Output 12.3

```
error CS0311: The type 'System.Text.StringBuilder' cannot be used as
type
parameter 'T' in the generic type or method 'BinaryTree<T>'. There is no
implicit reference conversion from 'System.Text.StringBuilder' to
'System.IComparable<System.Text.StringBuilder>'.
```

To specify an interface for the constraint, you declare an **interface type constraint**. This constraint even circumvents the need to cast to call an explicit interface member implementation.

Type Parameter Constraints

Sometimes you might want to constrain a type argument to be convertible to a particular type. You do this using a **type parameter constraint**, as shown in Listing 12.23.

Listing 12.23: Declaring a Class Type Constraint

```
public class EntityDictionary<TKey, TValue>
    : System.Collections.Generic.Dictionary<TKey, TValue>
    where TKey : notnull
    where TValue : EntityBase
{
    // ...
}
```

In Listing 12.23, `EntityDictionary<TKey, TValue>` requires that all type arguments provided for the type parameter `TValue` be implicitly convertible to the `EntityBase` class. By requiring the conversion, it becomes possible to use the members of `EntityBase` on values of type `TValue` within the generic implementation, because the constraint will ensure that all type arguments can be implicitly converted to the `EntityBase` class.

The syntax for the class type constraint is the same as that for the interface type constraint, except that class type constraints must appear before any interface type constraints (just as the base class must appear before implemented interfaces in a class declaration). However, unlike interface constraints, multiple base class constraints are not allowed, since it is not possible to derive from multiple unrelated classes. Similarly, base class constraints cannot specify sealed classes or non-class types. For example, C# does not allow a type parameter to be constrained to `string` or `System.Nullable<T>` because there would then be only one possible type argument for that type parameter—that's hardly "generic." If the type parameter is constrained to a single type, there is no need for the type parameter in the first place; just use that type directly.

Certain "special" types are not legal as class type constraints. See "Advanced Topic: Constraint Limitations," later in this chapter, for details.

You can use `System.Enum` as a constraint, thereby ensuring a type parameter is an enum.[8] However, you cannot specify type `System.Array` as a constraint. The latter restriction has minimal impact, however, as other collection types and interfaces are preferable anyway; see Chapter 15.

ADVANCED TOPIC

Delegate Constraints

Using `System.Delegate` and `System.MulticastDelegate` allows for combining (using the static `Combine()` method) and separating (using the static `Remove()` method) delegates in a type-safe manner.[9] There isn't a strongly typed way for a generic type to invoke a delegate, but the `DynamicInvoke()` method can accomplish this. Internally, it uses reflection. Even though the generic type can't invoke the delegate directly (without going through `DynamicInvoke()`), it is possible via a direct reference to `T` at compile time. For example, you could invoke a

8. Starting with C# 7.3.
9. Support added in C# 7.3.

`Combine()` method and cast to the expected type, as shown with the pattern matching in Listing 12.24.

Listing 12.24: Declaring a Generic with a `MulticastDelegate` Constraint

```
static public object? InvokeAll<TDelegate>(
    object?[]? args, params TDelegate[] delegates)
    // Constraint of type Action/Func not allowed
    where TDelegate : System.MulticastDelegate
{
  switch (Delegate.Combine(delegates))
  {
      case Action action:
          action();
          return null;
      case TDelegate result:
          return result.DynamicInvoke(args);
      default:
          return null;
  };
}
```

In this example, we attempt to cast to `Action` before invoking the result. If that effort is not successful, we cast to `TDelegate` and invoke the result using `DynamicInvoke()`.

Note that outside the generic we would know the type of `T`, so we could invoke it directly after calling `Combine()`:

```
Action? result =
(Action?)Delegate.Combine(actions);
result?.Invoke();
```

Note the comment in Listing 12.24. While `System.Delegate` and `System.MulticastDelegate` are supported, you cannot specify a specific delegate type such as `Action`, `Func<T>`, or one of the related types.

unmanaged Constraint

The unmanaged constraint[10] limits the type parameter to be of type sbyte, byte, short, ushort, int, uint, long, ulong, char, float, double, decimal, bool, an enum, a pointer, or any struct where all fields are unmanaged. This allows you to do things like use the sizeof (or stackalloc, as discussed in Chapter 22) operator on an unmanaged constrained type parameter.

Begin 8.0

Prior to C# 8.0, the unmanaged constraint restricted type parameters to **constructed struct types**—that is, value types that were not generic. However, C# 8.0 removed this constraint. You can now declare a variable of type Thing<Thing<int>> even if Thing<T> had an unmanaged constraint for T.

notnull Constraint

In Listing 12.23, there is a second constraint: the non-null constraint using the contextual keyword notnull. This constraint triggers a warning if a nullable type is specified for the type parameter decorated with notnull. In this case, for example, declaring EntityDictionary<string?, EntityBase> will lead to the following warning: Nullability of type argument 'string?' doesn't match 'notnull' constraint.

The notnull keyword cannot be combined with the struct or class constraints, which are not nullable by default (as we describe next).

struct/class Constraints

Another valuable generic constraint is the ability to restrict type arguments to be any non-nullable value type or any reference type. Rather than specifying a class from which T must derive, you simply use the keyword struct or class, as shown in Listing 12.25.

Listing 12.25: Specifying the Type Parameter as a Value Type

```
public struct Nullable<T> :
    IFormattable, IComparable,
    IComparable<Nullable<T>>, INullable
    where T : struct
```

10. Introduced in C# 7.3.

```
{
    // ...
    public static implicit operator Nullable<T>(T value) => new(value);
    public static explicit operator T(Nullable<T> value) => value!.Value;
    // ...
}
```

Note that the `class` constraint restricts the type parameter to reference types including interface, delegate, or array types (and not, as the keyword might seem to imply, only class types).

In C# 8.0, a `class` constraint defaults to not nullable (assuming, of course, that nullable reference types are enabled). Specifying a nullable reference type parameter will trigger a warning by the compiler. You can change the generic type to allow nullable reference types by including the nullable modifier on the `class` constraint. Consider the `WeakReference<T>` class introduced in Chapter 10. Since only reference types are garbage collected, this type includes the `class` constraint as follows:

```
public sealed partial class WeakReference<T> : ISerializable
where T : class?
{ ... }
```

This restricts the type parameter, `T`, to be a reference type—which may be nullable.

In contrast to the `class` constraint, the `struct` constraint does not allow the nullable modifier. Instead, you can specify nullability when using the parameter. In Listing 12.25, for example, the implicit and explicit conversion operators, for example, use `T` and `T?` to identify whether a non-nullable or nullable version of `T` is allowed. As such, the type parameter is constrained when it is used in member declarations, rather than with a type constraint.

Because a class type constraint requires a reference type, using a `struct` constraint with a class type constraint would be contradictory. Therefore, you cannot combine `struct` and `class` constraints.

The `struct` constraint has one special characteristic: Nullable value types do not satisfy the constraint. Why? Nullable value types are implemented as the generic type `Nullable<T>`, which itself applies the `struct` constraint to T. If nullable value types satisfied that constraint, it would be possible to define the nonsense type

End 8.0

Nullable<Nullable<int>>. A doubly nullable integer is confusing to the point of being meaningless. (As expected, the shorthand syntax int?? is also disallowed.)

Multiple Constraints

For any given type parameter, you may specify any number of interface type constraints, but no more than one class type constraint (just as a class may implement any number of interfaces but inherit from only one other class). Each new constraint is declared in a comma-delimited list following the generic type parameter and a colon. If there is more than one type parameter, each must be preceded by the where keyword. In Listing 12.26, the generic EntityDictionary class declares two type parameters: TKey and TValue. The TKey type parameter has two interface type constraints, and the TValue type parameter has one class type constraint.

Listing 12.26: Specifying Multiple Constraints

```
public class EntityDictionary<TKey, TValue>
    : Dictionary<TKey, TValue>
    where TKey : IComparable<TKey>, IFormattable
    where TValue : EntityBase
{
    // ...
}
```

In this case, there are multiple constraints on TKey itself and an additional constraint on TValue. When specifying multiple constraints on one type parameter, an AND relationship is assumed. If a type C is supplied as the type argument for TKey, C must implement IComparable<C> and IFormattable, for example.

Notice there is no comma between each where clause.

Constructor Constraints

In some cases, it is desirable to create an instance of the type argument's type inside the generic class. In Listing 12.27, for example, the MakeValue() method for the EntityDictionary<TKey, TValue> class must create an instance of the type argument corresponding to type parameter TValue.

Because not all objects are guaranteed to have public default constructors, the compiler does not allow you to call the default constructor on an unconstrained type parameter. To override this compiler restriction, you can add the text `new()` after all

Listing 12.27: Requiring a Default Constructor Constraint

```
public class EntityBase<TKey>
    where TKey: notnull
{
    public EntityBase(TKey key)
    {
        Key = key;
    }

    public TKey Key { get; set; }
}

public class EntityDictionary<TKey, TValue> :
    Dictionary<TKey, TValue>
    where TKey : IComparable<TKey>, IFormattable
    where TValue : EntityBase<TKey>, new()
{
    public TValue MakeValue(TKey key)
    {
        TValue newEntity = new()
        {
            Key = key
        };
        Add(newEntity.Key, newEntity);
        return newEntity;
    }

    // ...
}
```

other constraints are specified. This text, called a **constructor constraint**, requires the type argument corresponding to the constrained type parameter to have a public or internal default constructor. Only the default constructor constraint is available. You cannot specify a constraint that ensures that the type argument supplied provides a constructor that takes formal parameters.

Listing 12.27 includes a constructor constraint that forces the type argument supplied for `TValue` to provide a public parameterless constructor. There is no constraint to force the type argument to provide a constructor that takes other formal parameters. For example, you might want to constrain `TValue` so that the type argument provided for it must provide a constructor that takes the type argument provided for TKey, but this is not possible. Listing 12.28 demonstrates the invalid code.

Listing 12.28: Constructor Constraints Can Be Specified Only for Default Constructors

```
public TValue New(TKey key)
{
    // Error: 'TValue': Cannot provide arguments
    // when creating an instance of a variable type
    TValue newEntity = null;
    // newEntity = new TValue(key);
    Add(newEntity.Key, newEntity);
    return newEntity;
}
```

One way to circumvent this restriction is to supply a factory interface that includes a method for instantiating the type. The factory implementing the interface takes responsibility for instantiating the entity rather than the EntityDictionary itself (see Listing 12.29).

Listing 12.29: Using a Factory Interface in Place of a Constructor Constraint

```
public class EntityBase<TKey>
{
    public EntityBase(TKey key)
    {
        Key = key;
    }
    public TKey Key { get; set; }
}

public class EntityDictionary<TKey, TValue, TFactory> :
  Dictionary<TKey, TValue>
    where TKey : IComparable<TKey>, IFormattable
    where TValue : EntityBase<TKey>
    where TFactory : IEntityFactory<TKey, TValue>, new()
{
    // ...

    public TValue New(TKey key)
    {
        TFactory factory = new();
        TValue newEntity = factory.CreateNew(key);
```

```
        Add(newEntity.Key, newEntity);
        return newEntity;
    }
    //...
}

public interface IEntityFactory<TKey, TValue>
{
    TValue CreateNew(TKey key);
}
```

A declaration such as this allows you to pass the new `key` to a `TValue` factory method that takes parameters, rather than forcing you to rely on the default constructor. It no longer uses the constructor constraint on `TValue` because `TFactory` is responsible for instantiating value. (One modification to the code in Listing 12.29 would be to cache a reference to the factory method—possibly leveraging `Lazy<T>` if multithreaded support was needed. This would enable you to reuse the factory method instead of reinstantiating it every time.)

A declaration for a variable of type `EntityDictionary<TKey, TValue, TFactory>` would result in an entity declaration similar to the `Order` entity in Listing 12.30.

Listing 12.30: Declaring an Entity to Be Used in `EntityDictionary<...>`

```
public class Order : EntityBase<Guid>
{
    public Order(Guid key) :
        base(key)
    {
        // ...
    }
}

public class OrderFactory : IEntityFactory<Guid, Order>
{
    public Order CreateNew(Guid key)
    {
        return new Order(key);
    }
}
```

Constraint Inheritance

Neither generic type parameters nor their constraints are inherited by a derived class, because generic type parameters are not members. (Remember, class inheritance is the property that the derived class has all the members of the base class.) It is a common practice to make new generic types that inherit from other generic types. In such a case, because the type parameters of the derived generic type become the type arguments of the generic base class, the type parameters must have constraints equal to (or stronger than) those on the base class. Confused? Consider Listing 12.31.

Listing 12.31: Inherited Constraints Specified Explicitly

```
public class EntityBase<T> where T : IComparable<T>
{
    // ...
}

// ERROR:
// The type 'U' must be convertible to 'System.IComparable<U>'
// to use it as parameter 'T' in the generic type or
// method
// class Entity<U> : EntityBase<U>
// {
//     ...
// }
```

In Listing 12.31, `EntityBase<T>` requires that the type argument `U` supplied for `T` by the base class specifier `EntityBase<U>` implement `IComparable<U>`. Therefore, the `Entity<U>` class needs to require the same constraint on `U`. Failure to do so will result in a compile-time error. This pattern increases a programmer's awareness of the base class's type constraint in the derived class, avoiding the confusion that might otherwise occur if the programmer uses the derived class and discovers the constraint but does not understand where it comes from.

We have not covered generic methods yet; we'll get to them later in this chapter. For now, simply recognize that methods may also be generic and may also place constraints on the type arguments supplied for their type parameters. How, then, are constraints handled when a virtual generic method is inherited and overridden? In contrast to the situation with type parameters declared on a generic class, constraints on overriding virtual generic methods (or explicit interface) methods are inherited implicitly and may not be restated (see Listing 12.32).

Listing 12.32: Repeating Inherited Constraints on Virtual Members Is Prohibited

```
public class EntityBase
{
    public virtual void Method<T>(T t)
        where T : IComparable<T>
    {
        // ...
    }
}
public class Order : EntityBase
{
    public override void Method<T>(T t)
    //    Constraints may not be repeated on overriding
    //    members
    //    where T : IComparable<T>
    {
        // ...
    }
}
```

In the generic class inheritance case, the type parameter on the derived class can be further constrained by adding not only the constraints on the base class (required), but also other constraints. However, overriding virtual generic methods need to conform exactly to the constraints defined by the base class method. Additional constraints could break polymorphism, so they are not allowed, and the type parameter constraints on the overriding method are implied.

ADVANCED TOPIC

Constraint Limitations

Constraints are appropriately limited to avoid nonsensical code. For example, you cannot combine a class type constraint with a `struct` or `class` constraint, or `notnull` with either type of constraint. Also, you cannot specify constraints that restrict inheritance to special types such as `object`, arrays, or `System`

.ValueType.[11] You cannot have a constraint for a specific delegate type like Action, Func<T>, or related types.

In some cases, constraint limitations are perhaps more desirable, yet they are still not supported. Only having the ability to require a default constructor is perhaps one such limitation. The following subsections provide some additional examples of constraints that are not allowed.

Operator Constraints Are Not Allowed

All generics implicitly allow for == and != comparisons, along with implicit casts to object, because everything is an object. You cannot constrain a type parameter to a type that implements a particular method or operator (other than in the aforementioned cases), except via interface type constraints (for methods) or class type constraints (for methods and operators). Because of this, the generic Add() in Listing 12.33 does not work.

Listing 12.33: Constraint Expressions Cannot Require Operators

```
public abstract class MathEx<T>
{
    public static T Add(T first, T second)
    {
        // Error: Operator '+' cannot be applied to
        // operands of type 'T' and 'T'
        // return first + second;
    }
}
```

In this case, the method assumes that the + operator is available on all types that could be supplied as type arguments for T. But there is no constraint that prevents you from supplying a type argument that does not have an associated addition operator, so an error occurs. Unfortunately, there is no way to specify that an addition operator is required within a constraint, aside from using a class type constraint where the class type implements an addition operator.

More generally, there is no way to constrain a type to have a static method.

---

11. System.Enum (enum), System.Delegate, and System.MulticastDelegate are supported starting in C# 7.3.

OR Criteria Are Not Supported

If you supply multiple interfaces or class constraints for a type parameter, the compiler always assumes an AND relationship between constraints. For example, `where T : IComparable<T>, IFormattable` requires that both `IComparable<T>` and `IFormattable` are supported. There is no way to specify an OR relationship between constraints. Hence, code equivalent to Listing 12.34 is not supported.

Listing 12.34: Combining Constraints Using an OR Relationship Is Not Allowed

```
public class BinaryTree<T>
    // Error: OR is not supported
    // where T: System.IComparable<T> || System.IFormattable
{
    // ...
}
```

Supporting this functionality would prevent the compiler from resolving which method to call at compile time.

Generic Methods

Earlier, you saw that it is a relatively simple matter to add a method to a type when the type is generic; such a method can use the generic type parameters declared by the type. You did this, for example, in the generic class examples we have seen so far.

Generic methods use generic type parameters, much as generic types do. They can be declared in generic or nongeneric types. If declared in a generic type, their type parameters are distinct from those of their containing generic type. To declare a generic method, you specify the generic type parameters the same way you do for generic types: Add the type parameter declaration syntax immediately following the method name, as shown in the `MathEx.Max<T>` and `MathEx.Min<T>` examples in Listing 12.35.

In this example, the method is static, although this is not required.

Listing 12.35: Defining Generic Methods

```
public static class MathEx
{
    public static T Max<T>(T first, params T[] values)
        where T : IComparable<T>
    {
        T maximum = first;
        foreach(T item in values)
        {
            if(item.CompareTo(maximum) > 0)
            {
                maximum = item;
            }
        }
        return maximum;
    }

    public static T Min<T>(T first, params T[] values)
        where T : IComparable<T>
    {
        T minimum = first;

        foreach(T item in values)
        {
            if(item.CompareTo(minimum) < 0)
            {
                minimum = item;
            }
        }
        return minimum;
    }
}
```

Generic methods, like generic types, can include more than one type parameter. The arity (the number of type parameters) is an additional distinguishing characteristic of a method signature. That is, it is legal to have two methods with identical names and formal parameter types, as long as they differ in method type parameter arity.

Generic Method Type Inference

Just as type arguments are provided after the type name when using a generic type, so the method type arguments are provided after the method type name. The code used to call the `Min<T>` and `Max<T>` methods looks like that shown in Listing 12.36 with Output 12.4.

Listing 12.36: Specifying the Type Parameter Explicitly

```
Console.WriteLine(
    MathEx.Max<int>(7, 490));
Console.WriteLine(
    MathEx.Min<string>("R.O.U.S.", "Fireswamp"));
```

OUTPUT 12.4

```
490
Fireswamp
```

Not surprisingly, the type arguments, `int` and `string`, correspond to the actual types used in the generic method calls. However, specifying the type arguments is redundant because the compiler can infer the type parameters from the formal parameters passed to the method. Clearly, the caller of `Max` in Listing 12.36 intends the type argument to be `int` because both of the method arguments are of type `int`. To avoid redundancy, you can exclude the type parameters from the call in all cases when the compiler is able to logically infer which type arguments you must have intended. An example of this practice, which is known as **method type inference**, appears in Listing 12.37 with Output 12.5.

Listing 12.37: Inferring the Type Argument from the Arguments

```
Console.WriteLine(
    MathEx.Max(7, 490)); // No type arguments!
Console.WriteLine(
    MathEx.Min("R.O.U.S'", "Fireswamp"));
```

OUTPUT 12.5

```
490
Fireswamp
```

For method type inference to succeed, the types of the arguments must be "matched" with the formal parameters of the generic method in such a way that the desired type arguments can be inferred. An interesting question to consider is what happens when contradictory inferences are made. For example, when you call the `Max<T>` method using `MathEx.Max(7.0, 490)`, the compiler could deduce from the first argument that the type argument should be `double`, and it could deduce from the second argument that the type argument is `int`—a contradiction. A more sophisticated analysis would notice that the contradiction can be resolved because every `int` can be converted to a `double`, so `double` is the best choice for the type argument.[12]

In cases where method type inference is still not sophisticated enough to deduce the type arguments, you can resolve the error either by inserting casts on the arguments that clarify to the compiler the argument types that should be used in the inferences or by giving up on type inferencing and including the type arguments explicitly.

Notice that the method type inference algorithm, when making its inferences, considers only the arguments, the arguments' types, and the formal parameter types of the generic method. Other factors that could, in practice, be used in the analysis—such as the return type of the generic method, the type of the variable to which the method's returned value is being assigned, or the constraints on the method's generic type parameters—are not considered at all by this algorithm.

Specifying Constraints

Type parameters of generic methods may be constrained in the same way that type parameters of generic types are constrained. For example, you can restrict a method's type parameter to implement an interface or to be convertible to a class type. The constraints are specified between the parameter list and the method body, as shown in Listing 12.38.

---

12. This discrepancy produced an error in C# 2.0. C# 3.0 and C# 4.0 introduced improvements to the method type inferencing algorithm.

Listing 12.38: Specifying Constraints on Generic Methods

```
public class ConsoleTreeControl
{
    // Generic method Show<T>
    public static void Show<T>(BinaryTree<T> tree, int indent)
        where T : IComparable<T>
    {
        Console.WriteLine("\n{0}{1}",
            "+ --".PadLeft(5 * indent, ' '),
            tree.Item.ToString());
        if(tree.SubItems.First != null)
            Show(tree.SubItems.First, indent + 1);
        if(tree.SubItems.Second != null)
            Show(tree.SubItems.Second, indent + 1);
    }
}
```

Here, the `Show<T>` implementation itself does not directly use any member of the `IComparable<T>` interface, so you might wonder why the constraint is required. Recall, however, that the `BinaryTree<T>` class did require this constraint (see Listing 12.39).

Listing 12.39: `BinaryTree<T>` **Requiring** `IComparable<T>` **Type Parameters**

```
public class BinaryTree<T>
    where T : System.IComparable<T>
{
    //...
}
```

Because the `BinaryTree<T>` class requires this constraint on its `T`, and because `Show<T>` uses its `T` as a type argument corresponding to a constrained type parameter, `Show<T>` needs to ensure that the constraint on the class's type parameter is met on its method type argument.

ADVANCED TOPIC

Casting inside a Generic Method

Sometimes you should be wary of using generics—for instance, when using them specifically to bury a cast operation. Consider the following method, which converts a stream into an object of a given type:

```
public static T Deserialize<T>(
Stream stream, IFormatter formatter)
{
return (T)formatter.Deserialize(stream);
}
```

The `formatter` is responsible for removing data from the stream and converting it to an object. The `Deserialize()` call on the formatter returns data of type `object`. A call to use the generic version of `Deserialize()` looks something like this:

```
string greeting =
Deserialization.Deserialize<string>(stream, formatter);
```

The problem with this code is that to the caller of the method, `Deserialize<T>()` appears to be type-safe. However, a cast operation is still performed on behalf of the caller, as in the case of the nongeneric equivalent:

```
string greeting =
(string)Deserialization.Deserialize(stream, formatter);
```

The cast could fail at runtime; the method might not be as type-safe as it appears. The `Deserialize<T>` method is generic solely so that it can hide the existence of the cast from the caller, which seems dangerously deceptive. It might be better for the method to be nongeneric and return `object`, making the caller aware that it is not type-safe. Developers should use care when casting in generic methods if there are no constraints to verify cast validity.

Guidelines

AVOID misleading the caller with generic methods that are not as type-safe as they appear.

Covariance and Contravariance

A question often asked by new users of generic types is why an expression of type `List<string>` may not be assigned to a variable of type `List<object>`: If a `string` may be converted to type `object`, surely a list of strings is similarly compatible with a list of objects. In reality, this is not, generally speaking, either type-safe or legal. If you declare two variables with different type parameters using the same generic class, the variables are not type-compatible, even if they are assigning from a more specific type to a more generic type—in other words, they are not **covariant**.

Covariant is a technical term from category theory, but its underlying idea is straightforward: Suppose two types `X` and `Y` have a special relationship—namely, that every value of the type `X` may be converted to the type `Y`. If the types `I<X>` and `I<Y>` always also have that same special relationship, we say, "`I<T>` is covariant in `T`." When dealing with simple generic types with only one type parameter, the type parameter can be understood such that we simply say, "`I<T>` is covariant." The conversion from `I<X>` to `I<Y>` is called a **covariant conversion**.

For example, two instances of a generic class, `Pair<Contact>` and `Pair<PdaItem>`, are not type-compatible even when the type arguments are themselves compatible. In other words, the compiler prevents the conversion (implicit or explicit) of `Pair<Contact>` to `Pair<PdaItem>`, even though `Contact` derives from `PdaItem`. Similarly, converting `Pair<Contact>` to the interface type `IPair<PdaItem>` will fail. See Listing 12.40 for an example.

Listing 12.40: Conversion between Generics with Different Type Parameters

```
// ...
// Error: Cannot convert type ...
Pair<PdaItem> pair = (Pair<PdaItem>)new Pair<Contact>();
IPair<PdaItem> duple = (IPair<PdaItem>)new Pair<Contact>();
```

But why is this not legal? Why are `List<T>` and `Pair<T>` not covariant? Listing 12.41 shows what would happen if the C# language allowed unrestricted generic covariance.

Listing 12.41: Preventing Covariance Maintains Homogeneity

```
// ...
Contact contact1 = new("Princess Buttercup");
Contact contact2 = new("Inigo Montoya");
Pair<Contact> contacts = new(contact1, contact2);

// This gives an error: Cannot convert type ...
// But suppose it did not
IPair<PdaItem> pdaPair = (IPair<PdaItem>) contacts;
// This is perfectly legal, but not type-safe
pdaPair.First = new Address("123 Sesame Street");
```

An `IPair<PdaItem>` can contain an address, but the object is really a `Pair<Contact>` that can contain only contacts, not addresses. Type safety is completely violated if unrestricted generic covariance is allowed.

Now it should also be clear why a list of strings may not be used as a list of objects. You cannot insert an integer into a list of strings, but you can insert an integer into a list of objects; thus it must be illegal to cast a list of strings to a list of objects—an error the compiler can enforce.

Enabling Covariance with the `out` Type Parameter Modifier

You might have noticed that both problems described earlier as consequences of unrestricted covariance arise because the generic pair and the generic list allow their contents to be written. Suppose we eliminated this possibility by creating a read-only `IReadOnlyPair<T>` interface that exposes `T` only as coming "out" of the interface (i.e., used as the return type of a method or read-only property) and never going "into" it (i.e., used as a formal parameter or writeable property type). If we restricted ourselves to an "out-only" interface with respect to `T`, the covariance problem just described would not occur (see Listing 12.42).[13]

Listing 12.42: Possible Covariance

```
interface IReadOnlyPair<T>
{
    T First { get; }
    T Second { get; }
```

13. This capability was introduced in C# 4.0.

```
}

interface IPair<T>
{
    T First { get; set; }
    T Second { get; set; }
}

public struct Pair<T> : IPair<T>, IReadOnlyPair<T>
{
    // ...
}

public class Program
{
    static void Main()
    {
        // Only possible with out type parameter
        //Pair<Contact> contacts =
        //    new Pair<Contact>(
        //        new Contact("Princess Buttercup"),
        //        new Contact("Inigo Montoya"));
        //IReadOnlyPair<PdaItem> pair = contacts;
        //PdaItem pdaItem1 = pair.First;
        //PdaItem pdaItem2 = pair.Second;
    }
}
```

When we restrict the generic type declaration to expose data only as it comes out of the interface, there is no reason for the compiler to prevent covariance. All operations on an `IReadOnlyPair<PdaItem>` instance would convert `Contacts` (from the original `Pair<Contact>` object) up to the base class `PdaItem`—a perfectly valid conversion. There is no way to "write" an address into the object that is really a pair of contacts, because the interface does not expose any writeable properties.

The code in Listing 12.42 still does not compile.[14] To indicate that a generic interface is intended to be covariant in one of its type parameters, you can declare the type parameter with the `out` type parameter modifier. Listing 12.43 shows how to modify the interface declaration to indicate that it should be allowed to be covariant.

14. Support for safe covariance was added to C# 4.0.

Listing 12.43: Covariance Using the `out` Type Parameter Modifier

```
interface IReadOnlyPair<out T>
{
    T First { get; }
    T Second { get; }
}
```

Modifying the type parameter on the `IReadOnlyPair<out T>` interface with `out` will cause the compiler to verify that `T` is, indeed, used only for "outputs"—method return types and read-only property return types—and never for formal parameters or property setters. From then on, the compiler will allow any covariant conversions involving the interface to succeed. When this modification is made to the code in Listing 12.42, it will compile and execute successfully.

Several important restrictions are placed on covariant conversions:

- Only generic interfaces and generic delegates (described in Chapter 13) may be covariant. Generic classes and structs are never covariant.
- The varying type arguments of both the source and target generic types must be reference types, not value types. That is, an `IReadOnlyPair<string>` may be converted covariantly to `IReadOnlyPair<object>` because both `string` and `IReadOnlyPair<object>` are reference types. An `IReadOnlyPair<int>` may not be converted to `IReadOnlyPair<object>` because `int` is not a reference type.
- The interface or delegate must be declared as supporting covariance, and the compiler must be able to verify that the annotated type parameters are, in fact, used in only "output" positions.

Enabling Contravariance with the `in` Type Parameter Modifier

Covariance that "goes backward" is called **contravariance**. Again, suppose two types `X` and `Y` are related such that every value of the type `X` may be converted to the type `Y`. If the types `I<X>` and `I<Y>` always have that same special relationship "backward"—that is, every value of the type `I<Y>` can be converted to the type `I<X>`—we say that "`I<T>` is contravariant in `T`."

Most people find that contravariance is much harder to comprehend than covariance is. The canonical example of contravariance is a comparer. Suppose you have a derived type, `Apple`, and a base type, `Fruit`. Clearly, they have the special relationship: Every value of type `Apple` may be converted to `Fruit`.

Now suppose you have an interface `ICompareThings<T>` that has a method `bool FirstIsBetter(T t1, T t2)` that takes two `T`s and returns a `bool` saying whether the first one is better than the second one.

What happens when we provide type arguments? An `ICompareThings<Apple>` has a method that takes two `Apples` and compares them. An `ICompareThings<Fruit>` has a method that takes two `Fruits` and compares them. But since every `Apple` is a `Fruit`, clearly a value of type `ICompareThings<Fruit>` can be safely used anywhere that an `ICompareThings<Apple>` is needed. The direction of the convertibility has been reversed—hence the term *contravariance*.

Perhaps unsurprisingly, the opposite restrictions to those placed on a covariant interface are necessary to ensure safe contravariance. An interface that is contravariant in one of its type parameters must use that type parameter only in input positions such as formal parameters (or in the types of write-only properties, which are extremely rare). You can mark an interface as being contravariant by declaring the type parameter with the `in` modifier,[15] as shown in Listing 12.44.

Listing 12.44: Contravariance Using the `in` Type Parameter Modifier

```
class Fruit { }
class Apple : Fruit { }
class Orange : Fruit { }

interface ICompareThings<in T>
{
    bool FirstIsBetter(T t1, T t2);
}

public class Program
{

    private class FruitComparer : ICompareThings<Fruit>
```

15. Introduced in C# 4.0.

```
        {
            // ...
        }
        static void Main()
        {
            ICompareThings<Fruit> fc = new FruitComparer();

            Apple apple1 = new();
            Apple apple2 = new();
            Orange orange = new();

            // A fruit comparer can compare apples and oranges:
            bool b1 = fc.FirstIsBetter(apple1, orange);
            // or apples and apples:
            bool b2 = fc.FirstIsBetter(apple1, apple2);
            // This is legal because the interface is
            // contravariant.
            ICompareThings<Apple> ac = fc;
            // This is really a fruit comparer, so it can
            // still compare two apples
            bool b3 = ac.FirstIsBetter(apple1, apple2);
        }
}
```

Like covariance support, contravariance uses a type parameter modifier: `in`, which appears in the interface's type parameter declaration. This instructs the compiler to check that `T` never appears on a property getter or as the return type of a method, thereby enabling contravariant conversions for this interface.

Contravariant conversions have all the analogous restrictions as described earlier for covariant conversions: They are valid only for generic interface and delegate types, the varying type arguments must be reference types, and the compiler must be able to verify that the interface is safe for the contravariant conversions.

An interface can be covariant in one type parameter and contravariant in another, although this case seldom arises in practice except with delegates. The `Func<A1, A2, ..., R>` family of delegates, for example, are covariant in the return type, `R`, and contravariant in all the argument types.

Lastly, note that the compiler will check the validity of the covariance and contravariance type parameter modifiers throughout the source. Consider the `IPairInitializer<in T>` interface in Listing 12.45.

Listing 12.45: Compiler Validation of Variance

```
// ERROR:  Invalid variance: the type parameter 'T' is not
//         invariantly valid
interface IPairInitializer<in T>
{
    void Initialize(IPair<T> pair);
}
// Suppose the code above were legal, and see what goes
//  wrong:
public class FruitPairInitializer : IPairInitializer<Fruit>
{
    // Let's initialize  our pair of fruits  with an
    // apple and an orange:
    public void Initialize(IPair<Fruit> pair)
    {
        pair.First = new Orange();
        pair.Second = new Apple();
    }
}

// ... later ...
// ...
        var f = new FruitPairInitializer();
        // This would be legal if contravariance were legal:
        IPairInitializer<Apple> a = f;
        // And now we write an orange into a pair of apples:
        a.Initialize(new Pair<Apple>());
        // ...
```

A casual observer might be tempted to think that since `IPair<T>` is used only as an input formal parameter, the contravariant `in` modifier on `IPairInitializer` is valid. However, the `IPair<T>` interface cannot safely vary, so it cannot be constructed with a type argument that can vary. As you can see, this would not be type-safe and, in turn, the compiler disallows the `IPairInitializer<T>` interface from being declared as contravariant in the first place.

Support for Unsafe Covariance in Arrays

So far, we have described covariance and contravariance as being properties of generic types. Of all the nongeneric types, arrays are most like generics; that is, just as we think of a generic "list of T" or a generic "pair of T," so we can think of an "array of T" as demonstrating the same sort of pattern. Since arrays clearly support both reading and writing, given what you know about covariance and contravariance, you probably would suppose that arrays may be neither safely contravariant nor covariant. That is, you might imagine that an array can be safely covariant only if it is never written to and safely contravariant only if it is never read from—though neither seems like a realistic restriction.

Unfortunately, C# does support array covariance, even though doing so is not type-safe. For example, Fruit[] fruits = new Apple[10]; is perfectly legal in C#. If you then include the expression fruits[0] = new Orange();, the runtime will issue a type-safety violation in the form of an exception. It is deeply disturbing that it is not always legal to assign an Orange into an array of Fruit because it might really be an array of Apples, but that is the situation not just in C# but in all CLR languages that use the runtime's implementation of arrays.

You should try to avoid using unsafe array covariance. Every array is convertible to the read-only (and therefore safely covariant) interface IEnumerable<T>; that is, IEnumerable<Fruit> fruits = new Apple[10] is both safe and legal because there is no way to insert an Orange into the array if all you have is the read-only interface.

Guidelines

AVOID unsafe array covariance. Instead, **CONSIDER** converting the array to the read-only interface IEnumerable<T>, which can be safely converted via covariant conversions.

Generic Internals

Given the discussions in earlier chapters about the prevalence of objects within the CLI type system, it should come as no surprise to learn that generics are also objects. In fact, the type parameter on a generic class becomes metadata that the runtime uses to build appropriate classes when needed. Generics, therefore, support inheritance, polymorphism, and encapsulation. With generics, you can define methods, properties, fields, classes, interfaces, and delegates.

To achieve this, generics require support from the underlying runtime. In turn, the addition of generics to the C# language is a feature of both the compiler and the framework. To avoid boxing, for example, the implementation of generics is different for value-based type parameters than for generics with reference type parameters.

ADVANCED TOPIC

CIL Representation of Generics

When a generic class is compiled, it is not significantly different from a nongeneric class. The result of the compilation consists of just metadata and CIL. The CIL is parameterized to accept a user-supplied type somewhere in code. As an example, suppose you had a simple `Stack` class declared as shown in Listing 12.46.

Listing 12.46: `Stack<T>` **Declaration**

```
public class Stack<T> where T : IComparable
{
    private T[] _Items;
    // rest of the class here
    // ...
}
```

When you compile the class, the generated CIL is parameterized and looks something like Listing 12.47.

Listing 12.47: CIL Code for `Stack<T>`

```
.class private auto ansi beforefieldinit
Stack'1<([mscorlib]System.IComparable)T>
extends [mscorlib]System.Object
{
    ...
}
```

The first notable item is the `'1` that appears following `Stack` on the second line. That number is the arity of the generic types: It declares the number of type parameters for which the generic class will require type arguments. A declaration such as `EntityDictionary<TKey, TValue>` would have an arity of 2.

The second line of the generated CIL shows the constraints imposed upon the class. The `T` type parameter is decorated with an interface declaration for the `IComparable` constraint.

If you continue looking through the CIL, you will find that the item's array declaration of type `T` is altered to contain a type parameter using *exclamation point notation*, which is featured in the generics-capable version of the CIL. The exclamation point denotes the presence of the first type parameter specified for the class, as shown in Listing 12.48.

Listing 12.48: CIL with Exclamation Point Notation to Support Generics

```
.class public auto ansi beforefieldinit
 'Stack'1'<([mscorlib]System.IComparable) T>
 extends [mscorlib]System.Object
{
    .field private !0[ ] _Items
    ...
}
```

Beyond the inclusion of the arity and type parameter in the class header and the type parameter denoted with exclamation points in code, there is little difference between the CIL generated for a generic class and the CIL generated for a nongeneric class.

ADVANCED TOPIC

Instantiating Generics Based on Value Types

When a generic type is first constructed with a value type as a type parameter, the runtime creates a specialized generic type with the supplied type parameter(s) placed appropriately in the CIL. Therefore, the runtime creates new specialized generic types for each new parameter value type.

For example, suppose some code declared a `Stack` constructed of integers, as shown in Listing 12.49.

Listing 12.49: `Stack<int>` **Definition**

```
Stack<int> stack;
```

When using this type, `Stack<int>`, for the first time, the runtime generates a specialized version of the `Stack` class with the type argument `int` substituted for its type parameter. From then on, whenever the code uses a `Stack<int>`, the runtime reuses the generated specialized `Stack<int>` class. In Listing 12.50, you declare two instances of a `Stack<int>`, both using the code already generated by the runtime for a `Stack<int>`.

Listing 12.50: Declaring Variables of Type `Stack<T>`

```
Stack<int> stackOne = new();
Stack<int> stackTwo = new();
```

If, later in the code, you create another `Stack` with a different value type substituted for the type parameter (such as a `long` or a user-defined `struct`), the runtime will generate another version of the generic type. The benefit of specialized value type classes is better performance. Furthermore, the code can avoid conversions and boxing because each specialized generic class natively contains the value type.

ADVANCED TOPIC

Instantiating Generics Based on Reference Types

Generics work slightly differently for reference types. The first time a generic type is constructed with a reference type, the runtime creates a specialized generic type with `object` references substituted for type parameters in the CIL, rather than a specialized generic type based on the type argument. Each subsequent time a constructed type is instantiated with a reference type parameter, the runtime reuses the previously generated version of the generic type, even if the reference type is different from the first reference type.

For example, suppose you have two reference types: a Customer class and an Order class. Next, you create an EntityDictionary of Customer types:

```
EntityDictionary<Guid, Customer> customers;
```

Prior to accessing this class, the runtime generates a specialized version of the EntityDictionary class that, instead of storing Customer as the specified data type, stores object references. Suppose the next line of code creates an EntityDictionary of another reference type, called Order:

```
EntityDictionary<Guid, Order> orders =
new EntityDictionary<Guid, Order>();
```

Unlike with value types, no new specialized version of the EntityDictionary class is created for the EntityDictionary that uses the Order type. Instead, an instance of the version of EntityDictionary that uses object references is instantiated, and the orders variable is set to reference it.

To still gain the advantage of type safety, for each object reference substituted in place of the type parameter, an area of memory for an Order type is specifically allocated and the pointer is set to that memory reference. Suppose you then encountered a line of code to instantiate an EntityDictionary of a Customer type as follows:

```
customers = new EntityDictionary<Guid, Customer>();
```

As with the previous use of the EntityDictionary class created with the Order type, another instance of the specialized EntityDictionary class (the one based on object references) is instantiated, and the pointers contained therein are set to reference a Customer type specifically. This implementation of generics greatly reduces code bloat by ensuring that the compiler creates only one specialized class for generic classes of reference types.

Even though the runtime uses the same internal generic type definition when the type parameter on a generic reference type varies, this behavior is superseded if the type parameter is a value type. Dictionary<int, Customer>, Dictionary<Guid, Order>, and Dictionary<long, Order> will require new internal type definitions, for example.

Language Contrast: Java—Generics

The implementation of generics in Java occurs entirely within the compiler, not within the Java Virtual Machine. Sun Microsystems, which originally developed Java (long before Oracle took it over), adopted this approach to ensure that no updated Java Virtual Machine would need to be distributed because generics were used.

The Java implementation uses syntax like the templates in C++ and the generics in C#, including type parameters and constraints. Because it does not treat value types differently from reference types, however, the unmodified Java Virtual Machine cannot support generics for value types. As such, generics in Java do not offer the same gains in execution efficiency as they do in C#. Indeed, whenever the Java compiler needs to return data, it injects automatic downcasts from the specified constraint, if one is declared, or the base `Object` type, if a constraint is not declared. Further, the Java compiler generates a single specialized type at compile time, which it then uses to instantiate any constructed type. Finally, because the Java Virtual Machine does not support generics natively, there is no way to ascertain the type parameter for an instance of a generic type at execution time, and other uses of reflection are severely limited.

Summary

In modern C# programs, using `object` (particularly in the context of any collection type) should make you consider whether the problem would be better solved with generics. The increased type safety enabled by the elimination of casts, the elimination of the boxing performance penalty, and the reduction of repeated code are all significant improvements.

Chapter 15 looks more at the most pervasive generic namespaces, `System.Collections.Generic`. As its name implies, this namespace is composed almost exclusively of generic types. It provides clear examples of how some types that originally used objects were then converted to use generics. However, before we tackle these topics, we will investigate expressions, which provide a significant improvement[16] for working with collections.

---

16. Starting in C# 3.0.

13

Delegates and Lambda Expressions

Previous chapters discussed extensively how to create classes to encapsulate data and operations on data. As you create more and more classes, you will see common patterns in the relationships among them. One common pattern is to pass an object to a method solely so that the method can, in turn, call a method on the object. For example, if you pass an `IComparer<int>` reference to a method, odds are good that the called method will itself call the `Compare()` method on the object you provided. In this case, the interface is nothing more than a way to pass a reference to a single method that can be invoked. Consider a second example in which you invoke a new process. Rather than blocking or repeatedly checking (polling) when the process has completed, ideally you would like to have the method run asynchronously and then invoke a **callback** function, which the called method will invoke to notify the caller when the asynchronous invocation completes.

It seems unnecessary to have to define a new interface every time you want to pass a method around. In this chapter, we describe how to create and use a special kind of class called a *delegate* that enables you to treat references to methods as you would any other data. We then show how to create custom delegate instances quickly and easily with *lambda expressions*.

This chapter includes Advanced Topic blocks that describe how to use anonymous methods should you need to work with legacy C# 2.0 code[1]; you can largely ignore these sections if you are working only with newer code.

We conclude the chapter with a discussion of *expression trees*, which enable you to use the compiler's analysis of a lambda expression at execution time.

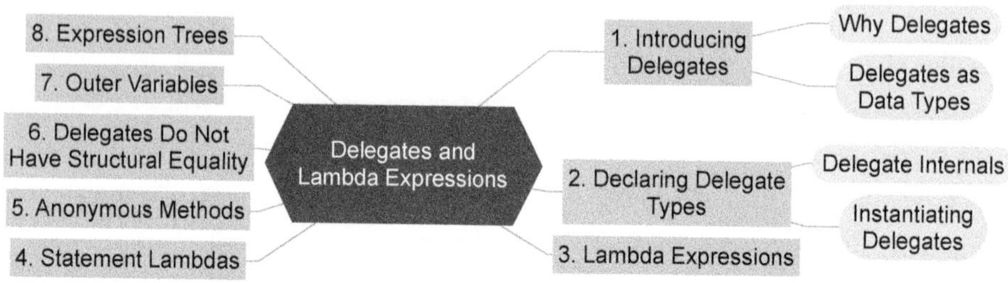

Introducing Delegates

Veteran C and C++ programmers have long used function pointers as a mechanism for passing a reference to one method as an argument to another method. C# achieves similar functionality by using **delegates**. Delegates allow you to capture a reference to a method and pass it around like any other object, and to call the captured method like any other method. Let's consider an example illustrating how this technique might be useful.

Defining the Scenario

Although it is not very efficient, one of the simplest sort routines is the bubble sort. Listing 13.1 shows the `BubbleSort()` method.

LISTING 13.1: `BubbleSort()` **Method**

```
public static class SimpleSort1
{
```

1. Lambda expressions added in C# 3.0. Anonymous methods used in C# 2.0 and prior for custom delegate creation.

```
    public static void BubbleSort(int[] items)
    {
        int i;
        int j;
        int temp;

        if(items == null)
        {
            return;
        }

        for(i = items.Length - 1; i >= 0; i--)
        {
            for(j = 1; j <= i; j++)
            {
                if(items[j - 1] > items[j])
                {
                    temp = items[j - 1];
                    items[j - 1] = items[j];
                    items[j] = temp;
                }
            }
        }
    }
    // ...
}
```

This method will sort an array of integers in ascending order.

Suppose you need to sort the integers in Listing 13.1 in either ascending or descending order. You could duplicate the code and replace the greater-than operator with a less-than operator, but it seems like a bad idea to replicate several dozen lines of code merely to change a single operator. As a less verbose alternative, you could pass in an additional parameter indicating how to perform the sort, as shown in Listing 13.2.

Listing 13.2: `BubbleSort()` **Method, Ascending or Descending**

```
public class SimpleSort2
{
    public enum SortType
    {
        Ascending,
        Descending
    }
```

```
    public static void BubbleSort(int[] items, SortType sortOrder)
    {
        int i;
        int j;
        int temp;

        if(items == null)
        {
            return;
        }

        for(i = items.Length - 1; i >= 0; i--)
        {
            for(j = 1; j <= i; j++)
            {

                bool swap = false;
                switch(sortOrder)
                {
                    case SortType.Ascending:
                        swap = items[j - 1] > items[j];
                        break;

                    case SortType.Descending:
                        swap = items[j - 1] < items[j];
                        break;
                }

                if(swap)
                {
                    temp = items[j - 1];
                    items[j - 1] = items[j];
                    items[j] = temp;
                }
            }
        }
    }
    // ...
}
```

However, this code handles only two of the possible sort orders. If you want to sort them lexicographically (that is, 1, 10, 11, 12, 2, 20, ...), or order them via some other criterion, it would not take long before the number of `SortType` values and the corresponding switch cases would become cumbersome.

Delegate Data Types

To increase flexibility and reduce code duplication in the previous code listings, you can make the comparison method a parameter to the `BubbleSort()` method. To pass a method as an argument, a data type is required to represent that method; this data type is generally called a *delegate* because it "delegates" the call to another method. You can use the name of a method as a delegate instance. You can also use a lambda expression as a delegate, to express a short piece of code "in place" rather than creating a method for it.[2] Listing 13.3 includes a modification to the `BubbleSort()` method that takes a lambda expression parameter.[3] Here, the delegate data type is `Func<int, int, bool>`.

LISTING 13.3: `BubbleSort()` **with Delegate Parameter**

```
public class DelegateSample
{
    // ...

    public static void BubbleSort(
        int[] items, Func<int, int, bool> compare)
    {
        int i;
        int j;
        int temp;

        if(compare == null)
        {
            throw new ArgumentNullException(nameof(compare));
        }

        if(items == null)
        {
            return;
        }

        for(i = items.Length - 1; i >= 0; i--)
        {
            for(j = 1; j <= i; j++)
            {
                if (compare(items[j - 1], items[j]))
```

2. Starting in C# 3.0.
3. In C# 7.0, you can create a local function and then use the function name for the delegate as well.

```
                    {
                        temp = items[j - 1];
                        items[j - 1] = items[j];
                        items[j] = temp;
                    }
                }
            }
        }
        // ...
    }
```

The delegate of type Func<int, int, bool> represents a method that compares two integers. Within the BubbleSort() method, you then use the instance of the Func<int, int, bool>, referred to by the compare parameter, to determine which integer is greater. Since compare represents a method, the syntax to invoke the method is identical to calling any other method. In this case, the Func<int, int, bool> delegate takes two integer parameters and returns a Boolean value that indicates whether the first integer is greater than the second one:

```
if (compare(items[j - 1], items[j])) { ... }
```

Note that the Func<int, int, bool> delegate is strongly typed to represent a method that accepts exactly two integer parameters and returns a bool. Just as with any other method call, the call to a delegate is strongly typed, and if the data types for the arguments are not compatible with the parameters, the C# compiler reports an error.

Declaring Delegate Types

You just saw how to define a method that uses a delegate, and you learned how to invoke a call to the delegate simply by treating the delegate variable as a method. However, you have yet to learn how to declare a delegate type. To declare a delegate type, you use the delegate keyword and follow it with what looks like a method declaration. The signature of that method is the signature of the method that the delegate can refer to, and the name of the delegate type appears where the name of the method would appear in a method declaration. The Func<...> delegate in Listing 13.3, for example, is declared as[4]

```
public delegate TResult Func<in T1, in T2, out TResult>(
in T1 arg1, in T2 arg2)
```

General-Purpose Delegate Types: System.Func and System.Action

Fortunately,[5] it turns out you rarely, if ever, need to declare your own delegates. The need to define your own custom delegate types was effectively eliminated with the .NET 3.5 runtime library[6] because it included a set of general-purpose delegates, most of them generic. The System.Func family of delegates is for referring to methods that return a value; the System.Action family of delegates is for referring to void-returning methods. The signatures for these delegates are shown in Listing 13.4.

LISTING 13.4: Func **and** Action **Delegate Declarations**

```
public delegate void Action();
public delegate void Action<in T>(T arg);
public delegate void Action<in T1, in T2>(
    T1 arg1, T2 arg2);
public delegate void Action<in T1, in T2, in T3>(
    T1 arg1, T2 arg2, T3 arg3);
public delegate void Action<in T1, in T2, in T3, in T4>(
    T1 arg1, T2 arg2, T3 arg3, T4 arg4);

 ...

public delegate void Action<
    in T1, in T2, in T3, in T4, in T5, in T6, in T7, in T8,
    in T9, in T10, in T11, in T12, in T13, in T14, in T15, in T16>(
        T1 arg1, T2 arg2, T3 arg3, T4 arg4,
        T5 arg5, T6 arg6, T7 arg7, T8 arg8,
        T9 arg9, T10 arg10, T11 arg11, T12 arg12,
        T13 arg13, T14 arg14, T15 arg15, T16 arg16);
```

4. in/out type modifiers were not added until C# 4.0.
5. Starting with C# 3.0.
6. Corresponds to C# 3.0.

```
public delegate TResult Func<out TResult>();
public delegate TResult Func<in T, out TResult>(T arg);
public delegate TResult Func<in T1, in T2, out TResult>(
    T1 arg1, T2 arg2);
public delegate TResult Func<in T1, in T2, in T3, out TResult>(
    T1 arg1, T2 arg2, T3 arg3);
public delegate TResult Func<in T1, in T2, in T3, in T4,
    out TResult>(T1 arg1, T2 arg2, T3 arg3, T4 arg4);

...

public delegate TResult Func<
    in T1, in T2, in T3, in T4, in T5, in T6, in T7, in T8,
    in T9, in T10, in T11, in T12, in T13, in T14, in T15, in T16,
    out TResult>(
        T1 arg1, T2 arg2, T3 arg3, T4 arg4,
        T5 arg5, T6 arg6, T7 arg7, T8 arg8,
        T9 arg9, T10 arg10, T11 arg11, T12 arg12,
        T13 arg13, T14 arg14, T15 arg15, T16 arg16);

public delegate bool Predicate<in T>( T obj)
```

Since the delegate definitions described in Listing 13.4 are generic, you can use them instead of defining your own custom delegate.

The first delegate type in Listing 13.4 is `Action<...>`. It is used to represent a method for which there is no return and supports methods with up to 16 parameters. For delegates that need to return a result, there is the `Func<...>` delegate. The last type parameter of `Func<...>` is `TResult`—the type of the return. The other type parameters on `Func<...>` correspond in sequence to the types of the delegate parameters. The `BubbleSort` method in Listing 13.3, for example, requires a delegate that returns `bool` and takes two `int` parameters.

The last delegate in Listing 13.4 is `Predicate<in T>`. When a lambda is used to return a `bool`, the lambda is called a **predicate**. However, this predicate is generally used to filter or identify items from a collection—you pass it an item and it returns true or false to indicate whether or not to filter the item. In contrast, our `BubbleSort()` example accepted two parameters for the purpose of comparing them, so `Func<int, int, bool>` was used instead of a predicate type.

Guidelines

CONSIDER whether the readability benefit of defining your own delegate type outweighs the convenience of using a predefined generic delegate type.

ADVANCED TOPIC

Declaring a Delegate Type

In many cases, the inclusion of `Func` and `Action` delegates in Microsoft .NET Framework 3.5, and later in the .NET Standard, virtually eliminates the need to define your own delegate types. However, you should consider declaring your own delegate types when doing so significantly increases the readability of the code. A delegate named `Comparer`, for example, provides an explicit indication of what the delegate is used for, whereas using `Func<int, int, bool>` only identifies a delegate's parameters and return type. Listing 13.5 shows how to declare the `Comparer` delegate type to require two integers and return a Boolean value.

Listing 13.5: Declaring a Delegate Type

```
public delegate bool Comparer(
    int first, int second);
```

Given the new delegate data type, you can update Listing 13.3 with a signature that replaces `Func<int, int, bool>` with `Comparer`:

```
public static void BubbleSort(int[] items, Comparer compare)
```

Just as classes can be nested in other classes, so delegates can also be nested in classes. If the delegate declaration appeared within another class, the delegate type would be a nested type, as shown in Listing 13.6.

Listing 13.6: Declaring a Nested Delegate Type

```
public class DelegateSample
{
    public delegate bool ComparisonHandler(
```

```
        int first, int second);
}
```

In this case, the data type would be `DelegateSample.ComparisonHandler` because it is defined as a nested type within `DelegateSample`. Nesting should be considered when utilization is expected to be needed only from within the containing class.

Instantiating a Delegate

In the final step of implementing the `BubbleSort()` method with a delegate, you will call the method and pass a delegate instance—specifically, an instance of type `Func<int, int, bool>`. To instantiate a delegate, you need a method with parameters and a return type that matches the signature of the delegate type itself. The name of the method need not match the name of the delegate, but the rest of the method signature must be compatible with the delegate signature. Listing 13.7 shows the code for a greater-than method compatible with the delegate type.

LISTING 13.7: Declaring a `Func<int, int, bool>`-Compatible Method

```
public class DelegateSample
{
    public static void BubbleSort(
        int[] items, Func<int, int, bool> compare)
    // ...
    public static bool GreaterThan(int first, int second)
    {
        return first > second;
    }

    // ...
}
```

With this method defined, you can call `BubbleSort()` and supply as the argument the name of the method that is to be captured by the delegate, as shown in Listing 13.8.

LISTING 13.8: Using a Method Name as an Argument

```
public class DelegateSample
{
    public static void BubbleSort(
        int[] items, Func<int, int, bool> compare)
    // ...
    public static bool GreaterThan(int first, int second)
    {
        return first > second;
    }

    public static void Main()
    {
        int[] items = new int[5];

        for(int i = 0; i < items.Length; i++)
        {
            Console.Write("Enter an integer: ");
            string? text = Console.ReadLine();
            if (!int.TryParse(text, out items[i]))
            {
                Console.WriteLine($"'{text}' is not a valid integer.");
                return;
            }
        }

        BubbleSort(items, GreaterThan);

        for (int i = 0; i < items.Length; i++)
        {
            Console.WriteLine(items[i]);
        }
    }
}
```

Note that delegates are reference types, but you do not necessarily use `new` to instantiate them. The conversion from the **method group**—the expression that names the method—to the delegate type automatically creates a new delegate object.[7]

7. Starting in C# 2.0.

ADVANCED TOPIC

Delegate Instantiation in C# 1.0

In Listing 13.8, the delegate was instantiated by simply passing the name of the desired method, GreaterThan, as an argument to the call to the BubbleSort() method. The first version of C# required instantiation of the delegate, using the more verbose syntax shown in Listing 13.9.

LISTING 13.9: Passing a Delegate as a Parameter in C# 1.0

```
BubbleSort(items,
    new Comparer(GreaterThan));
```

In this case, we use Comparer rather than Func<int, int, bool> because the latter wasn't available in C# 1.0.

Later versions support both syntaxes; throughout the remainder of the book, we will show only the modern, concise syntax.

ADVANCED TOPIC

Delegate Internals

A delegate is actually a special kind of class. Although the C# standard does not specify exactly what the class hierarchy is, a delegate must always derive directly or indirectly from System.Delegate. In fact, in .NET, delegate types always derive from System.MulticastDelegate, which in turn derives from System.Delegate, as shown in Figure 13.1.

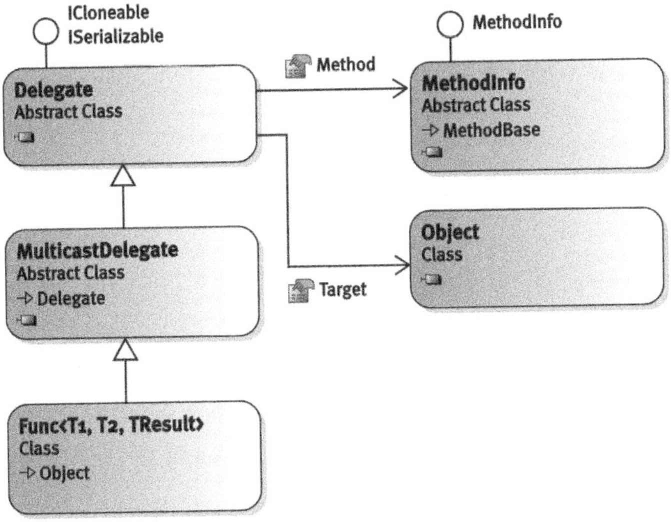

FIGURE 13.1: Delegate types object model

The first property is of type `System.Reflection.MethodInfo`. `MethodInfo` describes the signature of a method, including its name, parameters, and return type. In addition to `MethodInfo`, a delegate needs the instance of the object containing the method to invoke. This is the purpose of the second property, `Target`. In the case of a static method, `Target` is `null`. The purpose of the `MulticastDelegate` class is discussed in Chapter 14.

Note that all delegates are immutable; that is, you cannot change a delegate once you have created it. If you have a variable that contains a reference to a delegate and you want it to refer to a different method, you must create a new delegate and assign it to the variable.

Although all delegate data types derive indirectly from `System.Delegate`, the C# compiler does not allow you to declare a class that derives directly or indirectly from `System.Delegate` or `System.MulticastDelegate`. As a consequence, the code shown in Listing 13.10 is not valid.

LISTING 13.10: `System.Delegate` **Cannot Explicitly Be a Base Class**

```
// ERROR: Func<T1, T2, TResult> cannot
// inherit from special class 'System.Delegate'
public class Func<T1, T2, TResult>: System.Delegate
{
//    ...
}
```

Passing the delegate to specify the sort order is a significantly more flexible strategy than using the approach described at the beginning of this chapter. By passing a delegate, you can change the sort order to be alphabetical simply by adding an alternative delegate to convert integers to strings as part of the comparison. Listing 13.11 shows a full listing that demonstrates alphabetical sorting, and Output 13.1 shows the results.

LISTING 13.11: Using a Different `Func<int, int, bool>` **Compatible Method**

```
using System;

public class DelegateSample
{
    public static void BubbleSort(
        int[] items, Func<int, int, bool> compare)
    {
        int i;
        int j;
        int temp;

        for(i = items.Length - 1; i >= 0; i--)
        {
            for(j = 1; j <= i; j++)
            {
                if(compare(items[j - 1], items[j]))
                {
                    temp = items[j - 1];
                    items[j - 1] = items[j];
                    items[j] = temp;
                }
            }
        }
    }
```

```
    public static bool GreaterThan(int first, int second)
    {
        return first > second;
    }

    public static bool AlphabeticalGreaterThan(
        int first, int second)
    {
        int comparison;
        comparison = (first.ToString().CompareTo(
            second.ToString()));

        return comparison > 0;
    }

    public static void Main()
    {
        int[] items = new int[5];

        for(int i = 0; i < items.Length; i++)
        {
            Console.Write("Enter an integer: ");
            string? text = Console.ReadLine();
            if (!int.TryParse(text, out items[i]))
            {
                Console.WriteLine($"'{text}' is not a valid integer.");
                return;
            }
        }

        BubbleSort(items, AlphabeticalGreaterThan);

        for (int i = 0; i < items.Length; i++)
        {
            Console.WriteLine(items[i]);
        }
    }
}
```

Output 13.1

```
Enter an integer: 1
Enter an integer: 12
Enter an integer: 13
Enter an integer: 5
Enter an integer: 4
```

```
1
12
13
4
5
```

The alphabetical order is different from the numeric order. Even so, notice how simple it was to add this additional sort mechanism compared to the process used at the beginning of the chapter. The only changes to create the alphabetical sort order were the addition of the `AlphabeticalGreaterThan` method and then passing that method into the call to `BubbleSort()`.

Lambda Expressions

In Listing 13.7 and Listing 13.11, we saw that you can convert the expressions `GreaterThan` and `AlphabeticalGreaterThan` to a delegate type that is compatible with the parameter types and the return type of the named method. You might have noticed that the declaration of the `GreaterThan` method—the code that says it is a public, static, `bool`-returning method with two parameters of type `int` named `first` and `second`—was considerably larger than the body of the method, which simply compared its two parameters and returned the result. It is unfortunate that so much ceremony must surround such a simple method merely so that it can be converted to a delegate type.

To address this concern, compact syntax exists for creating a delegate. When referring generally to **anonymous methods** or **lambda expressions**, we'll refer to them as **anonymous functions**. Both syntaxes are still legal, but for new code, the lambda expression syntax is preferred over the anonymous method syntax.[8]

Lambda expressions are themselves divided into two types: **statement lambdas** and **expression lambdas**. Figure 13.2 shows the hierarchical relationship between these terms.

---

8. Throughout this book, we generally use the lambda expression syntax except when specifically describing C# 2.0 anonymous methods.

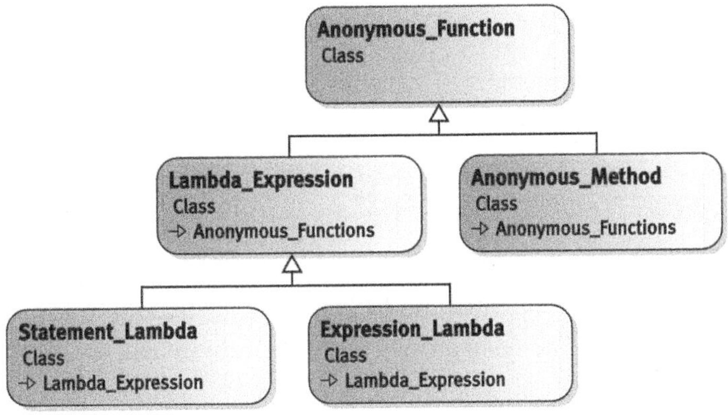

FIGURE 13.2: Anonymous function terminology

Statement Lambdas

The purpose of a lambda expression is to eliminate the hassle of declaring an entirely new member when you need to make a delegate from a very simple method. Several different forms of lambda expressions exist. A statement lambda, for example, consists of a formal parameter list, followed by the lambda operator `=>`, followed by a code block.

Listing 13.12 shows equivalent functionality to the call to `BubbleSort` from Listing 13.8, except that Listing 13.12 uses a statement lambda to represent the comparison method rather than creating a `GreaterThan` method. As you can see, much of the information that appeared in the `GreaterThan` method declaration is now included in the statement lambda; the formal parameter declarations and the block are the same, but the method name and its modifiers are missing.

LISTING 13.12: Creating a Delegate with a Statement Lambda

```
//...

BubbleSort(items,
    (int first, int second) =>
    {
        return first < second;
    }
);
```

```
//...
```

When reading code that includes a lambda operator, you would replace the lambda operator with the words *go/goes to*. For example, in Listing 13.12, you would read the second `BubbleSort()` parameter as "integers `first` and `second` go to returning the result of `first` less than `second`."

Notice that the syntax in Listing 13.12 is almost identical to that in Listing 13.8, apart from the fact that the comparison method is now found lexically where it is converted to the delegate type rather than being found elsewhere and looked up by name. The name of the method is missing, which explains why such methods are called *anonymous functions*. The return type is missing, but the compiler can infer that the lambda expression is being converted to a delegate whose signature requires the return type `bool`. The compiler verifies that the expressions of every `return` statement in the statement lambda's block would be legal in a `bool`-returning method. The `public` modifier is missing; given that the method is no longer an accessible member of the containing class, there is no need to describe its accessibility. Similarly, the `static` modifier is no longer necessary. The amount of ceremony around the method is already greatly reduced.

The syntax is still needlessly verbose, however. We have deduced from the delegate type that the lambda expression must be `bool`-returning; we can similarly deduce that both parameters must be of type `int`, as shown in Listing 13.13.

Listing 13.13: Omitting Parameter Types from Statement Lambdas

```
//...
DelegateSample.BubbleSort(items,
    (first, second) =>
    {
        return first < second;
    }
);
//...
```

In general, explicitly declared parameter types are optional in all lambda expressions if the compiler can infer the types from the delegate that the lambda expression is being converted to. For situations when specifying the type makes code more readable, however, C# enables you to do so. In cases where inference is not possible, the C# language requires that the lambda parameter types be stated explicitly. If one lambda parameter type is specified explicitly, then all of them must be specified explicitly, and they must all match the delegate parameter types exactly.

Guidelines

CONSIDER omitting the types from lambda formal parameter lists when the types are obvious to the reader or when they are an insignificant detail.

One other means of reducing the syntax is possible, as shown in Listing 13.14: A lambda expression that has exactly one parameter whose type is inferred may omit the parentheses around the parameter list. If there are zero parameters or more than one parameter, or if the single parameter is explicitly typed, the lambda must have parentheses around the parameter list.

LISTING 13.14: Statement Lambdas with a Single Input Parameter

```
using System.Collections.Generic;
using System.Diagnostics;
using System.Linq;

// ...
    IEnumerable<Process> processes = Process.GetProcesses().Where(
        process => { return process.WorkingSet64 > 1000000000; });
    // ...
```

In Listing 13.14, the `Where()` method returns a query for processes that have a physical memory utilization greater than 1 billion bytes.

Starting in C# 9.0, you can use discards (_) for one or more parameters for all anonymous functions assuming they are not needed for implementation.[9] Begin 9.0 End 9.0

Contrast this with Listing 13.15, which has a parameterless statement lambda. The empty parameter list requires parentheses. Also note that in Listing 13.15, the body of the statement lambda includes multiple statements inside the statement block

9. If there is only one parameter, then the underscore will result in a variable declaration for backwards compatibility.

(via curly braces). Although a statement lambda can contain any number of statements, typically a statement lambda uses only two or three statements in its statement block.

LISTING 13.15: Parameterless Statement Lambdas

```
//...
Func<string> getUserInput =
    () =>
    {
        string? input;
        do
        {
            input = Console.ReadLine();
        }
        while(!string.IsNullOrWhiteSpace(input));
        return input!;
    };
//...
```

Expression Lambdas

The statement lambda syntax is already much less verbose than the corresponding method declaration; as we've seen, it need not declare the method's name, accessibility, return type, or parameter types. Nevertheless, we can get even less verbose by using an expression lambda. In Listing 13.12, Listing 13.13, and Listing 13.14, we saw statement lambdas whose blocks consisted of a single return statement. What if we eliminated the ceremony around that? The only relevant information in such a lambda block is the expression that is returned. An expression lambda contains only that returned expression, with no statement block at all. Listing 13.16 is the same as Listing 13.12, except that it uses an expression lambda rather than a statement lambda.

LISTING 13.16: Passing a Delegate with an Expression Lambda

```
//...
DelegateSample.BubbleSort
```

```
    (items, (first, second) => first < second);
//...
```

Generally, you would read the lambda operator `=>` in an expression lambda the same way as you would a statement lambda: as *goes to* or *becomes*, although, in those cases where the delegate is a predicate, it is common to read the lambda operator as *such that* or *where*. Thus, you might read the lambda in Listing 13.16 as "`first` and `second` such that `first` is less than `second`."

Like the `null` literal, an anonymous function does not have any type associated with it; rather, its type is determined by the type it is being converted to. In other words, the lambda expressions we've seen so far are not intrinsically of the `Func<int, int, bool>` (or `Comparer`) type, but they are compatible with that type and may be converted to it. As a result, you cannot use the `typeof()` operator on an anonymous method, and calling `GetType()` is possible only after you convert the anonymous method to a particular type.

Table 13.1 provides additional lambda expression characteristics.

Begin 9.0

Begin 10.0

TABLE 13.1: Lambda Expression Notes, Errors, and Examples

Statement	Example
Starting with C# 9.0, lambda expressions supported discard parameters. (For backwards compatibility, a single discard results in a variable declaration named _.)	`Action<int, int> x = (_,_)=>` `Console.WriteLine("This is a test.");`

Starting with C# 10.0, a lambda expression has a definite type, so they can be used with an anonymous type declaration.	`// You can assign lambda`
	`// expression to an implicitly`
	`// typed local variable starting C# 10.`
	`var v = (int x) => x;`

Starting with C# 10.0, lambda expressions may have a return type, even a return type of `void`. This is especially helpful when the delegate type cannot be inferred—such as when returning `null`.	`Action action = void () => { };`
	`var func`
	`= short? (long number) =>`
	`number<=short.MaxValue?`
	`(short)number:null;`

TABLE 13.1: Lambda Expression Notes, Errors, and Examples (continued)

Statement	Example

There are no members that can be accessed directly from a lambda expression—not even the methods of `object`.	`// ERROR: Operator "." cannot be applied to`
	`// operand of type "lambda expression"`
	`string s = ((int x) => x).ToString();`

Lambda expressions do not have a type and so cannot appear to the left of an `is` operator.	`// ERROR: The first operand of an "is" or "as"`
	`// operator may not be a lambda expression or`
	`// anonymous method`
	`bool b = ((int x) => x) is Func<int, int>;`

A lambda expression can be converted only to a compatible delegate type; here an `int`-returning lambda may not be converted to a delegate type that represents a `bool`-returning method.	`// ERROR: Lambda expression is not compatible`
	`// with Func<int, bool> type`
	`Func<int, bool> f = (int x) => x;`

Jump statements (`break`, `goto`, `continue`) inside lambda expressions cannot be used to jump to locations outside the lambda expression, and vice versa. Here the `break` statement inside the lambda would jump to the end of the `switch` statement outside the lambda.	`// ERROR: Control cannot leave the body of an`
	`// anonymous method or lambda expression`
	`string[] args;`
	`Func<string> f;`
	`switch(args[0])`
	`{`
	`case "/File":`
	`f = () =>`
	`{`
	`if (!File.Exists(args[1]))`
	`break;`
	`return args[1];`
	`};`
	`// ...`
	`}`

Parameters and locals introduced by a lambda expression are in scope only within the lambda body.	`// ERROR: The name "first" does not`
	`// exist in the current context`
	`Func<int, int, bool> expression =`
	`(first, second) => first > second;`
	`first++;`

The compiler's definite assignment analysis is unable to detect initialization of "outer" local variables in lambda expressions.	`int number;`
	`Func<string, bool> f =`
	`text => int.TryParse(text, out number);`
	`if (f("1"))`
	`{`
	`   // ERROR: Use of unassigned local variable`
	`System.Console.Write(number);`
	`}`

TABLE 13.1: Lambda Expression Notes, Errors, and Examples (continued)

Statement	Example

	`int number;`
	`Func<int, bool> isFortyTwo =`
	`x => 42 == (number = x);`
	`if (isFortyTwo(42))`
	`{`
	`    // ERROR: Use of unassigned local variable`
	`Console.Write(number);`
	`}`

End 10.0

End 9.0

Anonymous Methods

An anonymous method is like a statement lambda,[10] but without many of the features that make lambdas so compact. An anonymous method must explicitly type every parameter, and it must have a statement block. Rather than using the lambda operator `=>` between the parameter list and the code block, an anonymous method puts the keyword `delegate` before the parameter list, emphasizing that the anonymous method must be converted to a delegate type. Listing 13.17 shows the code from Listing 13.7, Listing 13.12, and Listing 13.15 rewritten to use an anonymous method.

LISTING 13.17: Passing an Anonymous Method in C# 2.0

```
//...
DelegateSample.BubbleSort(items,
    delegate(int first, int second)
    {
        return first < second;
    }
);
//...
```

Anonymous methods support one small feature that is not supported in lambda expressions: Anonymous methods may omit their parameter list entirely in some circumstances.

10. Lambda expressions were not yet available in C# 2.0.

Guidelines

AVOID the anonymous method syntax in new code; prefer the more compact lambda expression syntax.

ADVANCED TOPIC

Parameterless Anonymous Methods

Unlike lambda expressions, anonymous methods may omit the parameter list entirely provided that the anonymous method body does not use any parameter and the delegate type requires only "value" parameters (i.e., it does not require the parameters to be marked as `out` or `ref`). For example, the anonymous method expression `delegate { return Console.ReadLine() != ""; }` is convertible to any delegate type that requires a return type of `bool` regardless of the number of parameters the delegate requires. This feature is not used frequently, but you might encounter it when reading legacy code.

ADVANCED/BEGINNER TOPIC

Why "Lambda" Expressions?

It is fairly obvious why anonymous methods are so named: They look very similar to method declarations but do not have a declared name associated with them. But where did the *lambda* in "lambda expressions" come from?

The idea of lambda expressions comes from the work of the logician Alonzo Church, who in the 1930s invented a technique called the *lambda calculus* for studying functions. In Church's notation, a function that takes a parameter *x* and results in an expression *y* is notated by prefixing the entire expression with a small Greek letter lambda and separating the parameter from the value with a dot. The C# lambda expression `x=>y` would be notated `λx.y` in Church's notation. Because it is inconvenient to use Greek letters in C# programs and because the dot already has many meanings in C#, the designers of C# chose to use the "fat arrow" notation rather than the original notation. The name lambda expression indicates that the theoretical underpinnings of the idea of anonymous functions are based on the lambda calculus, even though no letter lambda actually appears in the text.

Delegates Do Not Have Structural Equality

Delegate types in .NET do not exhibit **structural equality**. That is, you cannot convert a reference to an object of one delegate type to an unrelated delegate type, even if the formal parameters and return types of both delegates are identical. For example, you cannot assign a reference to a `Comparer` to a variable of type `Func<int, int, bool>`, even though both delegate types represent methods that take two `int` parameters and return a `bool`. Unfortunately, the only way to use a delegate of a given type when a delegate of a structurally identical but unrelated delegate type is needed is to create a new delegate that refers to the `Invoke` method of the old delegate. For example, if you have a variable `c` of type `Comparer`, and you need to assign its value to a variable `f` of type `Func<int, int, bool>`, you can say `f = c.Invoke;`.

However, thanks to variance support,[11] it is possible to make reference conversions between some delegate types. Consider the following contravariant example: Because `void Action<in T>(T arg)` has the `in` type parameter modifier, it is possible to assign a reference to a delegate of type `Action<object>` to a variable of type `Action<string>`.

Many people find delegate contravariance confusing. It may help to remember that an action that can act on every object can be used as an action that acts on any string. But the opposite is not true: An action that can act only on strings cannot act on every object. Similarly, every type in the `Func` family of delegates is covariant in its return type, as indicated by the `out` type parameter modifier on `TResult`. Therefore, it is possible to assign a reference to a delegate of type `Func<string>` to a variable of type `Func<object>`.

Listing 13.18 shows examples of delegate covariance and contravariance.

11. Added in C# 4.0.

Listing 13.18: Using Variance for Delegates

```
// Contravariance
Action<object> broadAction =
    (object data) =>
    {
        Console.WriteLine(data);
    };

Action<string> narrowAction = broadAction;

// Covariance
Func<string?> narrowFunction =
    () => Console.ReadLine();
Func<object?> broadFunction = narrowFunction;

// Contravariance and covariance combined
Func<object, string?> func1 =
    (object data) => data.ToString();

Func<string, object?> func2 = func1;
```

The last part of the listing combines both variance concepts into a single example, demonstrating how they can occur simultaneously if both `in` and `out` type parameters are involved.

Allowing reference conversions on generic delegate types was a key motivating scenario for adding covariant and contravariant conversions.[12] (The other was support for covariance to `IEnumerable<out T>`.)

ADVANCED TOPIC

Lambda Expression and Anonymous Method Internals

Lambda expressions (and anonymous methods) are not intrinsically built into the CLR. Rather, when the compiler encounters an anonymous function, it translates it into special hidden classes, fields, and methods that implement the desired semantics. The C# compiler generates the implementation code for this pattern so that developers do not have to code it themselves. When given the code in Listing 13.12,

12. Added to C# 4.0.

Listing 13.13, Listing 13.16, or Listing 13.17, the C# compiler generates CIL code that is similar to the C# code shown in Listing 13.19.

Listing 13.19: C# Equivalent of CIL Generated by the Compiler for Lambda Expressions

```
public class DelegateSample
{
    // ...

    public static void Main()
    {
        int[] items = new int[5];

        for(int i = 0; i < items.Length; i++)
        {
            Console.Write("Enter an integer: ");
            string? text = Console.ReadLine();
            if (!int.TryParse(text, out items[i]))
            {
                Console.WriteLine($"'{text}' is not a valid integer.");
                return;
            }
        }

        BubbleSort(items,
            __AnonymousMethod_00000000);


        for (int i = 0; i < items.Length; i++)
        {
            Console.WriteLine(items[i]);
        }

    }
    private static bool __AnonymousMethod_00000000(
        int first, int second)
    {
        return first < second;
    }
}
```

In this example, the compiler transforms an anonymous function into a separately declared static method, which is then instantiated as a delegate and passed as a parameter. Unsurprisingly, the compiler generates code that looks remarkably like the original code in Listing 13.8, which the anonymous function syntax was intended to streamline. However, the code transformation performed by the compiler can be considerably more complex than merely rewriting the anonymous function as a static method if outer variables are involved.

Outer Variables

Local variables declared outside a lambda expression (including parameters of the containing method) are called the **outer variables** of that lambda. (The `this` reference, though technically not a variable, is also considered to be an outer variable.) When a lambda body uses an outer variable, the variable is said to be **captured** (or, equivalently, **closed over**) by the lambda. In Listing 13.20, we use an outer variable to count how many times `BubbleSort()` performs a comparison. Output 13.2 shows the results of this listing.

LISTING 13.20: Using an Outer Variable in a Lambda Expression

```
public class Program
{
    public static void Main()
    {
        int[] items = new int[5];
        int comparisonCount = 0;

        for (int i = 0; i < items.Length; i++)
        {
            Console.Write("Enter an integer:");
            string? text = Console.ReadLine();
            if (!int.TryParse(text, out items[i]))
            {
                Console.WriteLine($"'{text}' is not a valid integer.");
                return;
            }
        }

        DelegateSample.BubbleSort(items,
            (int first, int second) =>
            {
                comparisonCount++;
                return first < second;
```

```
            }
        );

        for (int i = 0; i < items.Length; i++)
        {
            Console.WriteLine(items[i]);
        }

        Console.WriteLine("Items were compared {0} times.",
            comparisonCount);
    }
}
```

Output 13.2

```
Enter an integer:5
Enter an integer:1
Enter an integer:4
Enter an integer:2
Enter an integer:3
5
4
3
2
1
Items were compared 10 times.
```

Note that `comparisonCount` appears outside the lambda expression and is incremented inside it. After calling the `BubbleSort()` method, `comparisonCount` is printed out to the console.

Normally, the lifetime of a local variable is tied to its scope; when control leaves the scope, the storage location associated with the variable is no longer valid. But a delegate created from a lambda that captures an outer variable might have a longer (or shorter) lifetime than the local variable normally would, and the delegate must be able to safely access the outer variable every time the delegate is invoked. Therefore, the lifetime of a captured variable is extended: It is guaranteed to live at least as long as the longest-lived delegate object capturing it. (And it may live even longer than that—precisely how the compiler generates the code that ensures outer variable lifetimes are extended is an implementation detail and subject to change.)

The C# compiler takes care of generating CIL code that shares `comparisonCount` between the anonymous method and the method that declares it.

Begin 9.0

Static Anonymous Functions

To avoid any unintended consequences with captured data from outside the anonymous function, C# 9.0 enables a static modifier on the declaration. This causes the compiler to verify there is no closure over data captured from outside the anonymous function declaration. (It has nothing to do with whether the function is instance or static.) To observe the behavior, see Listing 13.21.

LISTING 13.21: Declaring a Static Anonymous Function

```
int comparisonCount = 0;

DelegateSample.BubbleSort(items,
    static (int first, int second) =>
    {
        // Error CS8820: A static anonymous function
        // cannot contain a reference to comparisonCount.
        comparisonCount++;
        return first < second;
    }
);

for (int i = 0; i < items.Length; i++)
{
    Console.WriteLine(items[i]);
}

Console.WriteLine("Items were compared {0} times.",
    comparisonCount);
    }
}
```

In general, consider using static local function declarations by default, and only switching to the less restrictive version when needed, thereby increasing the intentionality of the closure.

End 9.0

ADVANCED TOPIC

Outer Variable CIL Implementation

The CIL code generated by the C# compiler for anonymous functions that capture outer variables is more complex than the code for a simple anonymous function that captures nothing. Listing 13.22 shows the C# equivalent of the CIL code used to implement outer variables for the code in Listing 13.20.

LISTING 13.22: C# Equivalent of CIL Code Generated by Compiler for Outer Variables

```
public class Program
{
    // ...
    private sealed class __LocalsDisplayClass_00000001
    {
        public int comparisonCount;
        public bool __AnonymousMethod_00000000(
            int first, int second)
        {
            comparisonCount++;
            return first < second;
        }
    }

    public static void Main()
    {
        __LocalsDisplayClass_00000001 locals = new();
        locals.comparisonCount = 0;
        int[] items = new int[5];

        for (int i = 0; i < items.Length; i++)
        {
            Console.Write("Enter an integer: ");
            string? text = Console.ReadLine();
            if (!int.TryParse(text, out items[i]))
            {
                Console.WriteLine($"'{text}' is not a valid integer.");
                return;
            }
        }

        DelegateSample.BubbleSort
            (items, locals.__AnonymousMethod_00000000);
        for (int i = 0; i < items.Length; i++)
        {
```

```
                Console.WriteLine(items[i]);
            }

        Console.WriteLine("Items were compared {0} times.",
            locals.comparisonCount);
    }
}
```

Notice that the captured local variable is never "passed" or "copied" anywhere. Rather, the captured local variable (`comparisonCount`) is a single variable whose lifetime the compiler has extended by implementing it as an instance field rather than as a local variable. All usages of the local variable are rewritten to be usages of the field.

The generated class, `__LocalsDisplayClass`, is a data structure (a class in C#) that contains an expression and the variables (public fields in C#) necessary to evaluate the expression.

ADVANCED TOPIC

Accidentally Capturing Loop Variables

What do you think the output of Listing 13.23 should be?

LISTING 13.23: Capturing Loop Variables in C# 5.0

```
public class CaptureLoop
{
    public static void Main()
    {
        var items = new string[] { "Moe", "Larry", "Curly" };
        var actions = new List<Action>();
        foreach(string item in items)
        {
            actions.Add(() => { Console.WriteLine(item); });
        }
        foreach(Action action in actions)
        {
            action();
        }
```

```
    }
}
```

Most people expect that the output will be that shown in Output 13.3, and in C# 5.0 it is. In previous versions of C#, however, the output is that shown in Output 13.4.

Output 13.3: C# 5.0 Output

```
Moe
Larry
Curly
```

Output 13.4: C# 4.0 Output

```
Curly
Curly
Curly
```

A lambda expression captures a variable and always uses the latest value of the variable; it does not capture and preserve the value that the variable had when the delegate was created. This is normally what you want—after all, the whole point of capturing `comparisonCount` in Listing 13.20 was to ensure that its latest value would be used when it was incremented. Loop variables are no different; when you capture a loop variable, every delegate captures the same loop variable. When the loop variable changes, every delegate that captured this loop variable sees the change. The C# 4.0 behavior is therefore justified—but is almost never what the author of the code wants.

In C# 5.0, the C# language was changed so that the loop variable of a `foreach` loop is now considered to be a fresh variable every time the loop iterates; therefore, each delegate creation captures a different variable, rather than all iterations sharing the same variable. This change was not applied to the `for` loop, however: If you write similar code using a `for` loop, any loop variable declared in the header of the `for` statement will be considered a single outer variable when captured. If you need to write code that works the same in both C# 5.0 and previous C# versions, use the pattern shown in Listing 13.24.

Listing 13.24: Loop Variable Capture Workaround before C# 5.0

```
public class DoNotCaptureLoop
{
    public static void Main()
    {
        var items = new string[] { "Moe", "Larry", "Curly" };
        var actions = new List<Action>();
        foreach(string item in items)
        {
            string _item = item;
            actions.Add(
                () => { Console.WriteLine(_item); });
        }
        foreach(Action action in actions)
        {
            action();
        }
    }
}
```

Now there is clearly one fresh variable per loop iteration; each delegate is, in turn, closed over a different variable.

Guidelines

AVOID capturing loop variables in anonymous functions.

Expression Trees

Thus far we've seen that lambda expressions are a succinct syntax for declaring an "inline" method that can be converted to a delegate type. Expression lambdas (but not statement lambdas or anonymous methods) can also be converted to **expression trees**. A delegate is an object that enables you to pass around a method like any other object and invoke it at any time. An expression tree is an object that enables you to pass around the compiler's analysis of the lambda expression. But why would you ever need that capability? Obviously, the compiler's analysis is useful to the compiler when generating the CIL, but why is it useful to the developer to have an object representing that analysis at execution time? Let's take a look at an example.

Using Lambda Expressions as Data

Consider the lambda expression in the following code:

```
persons.Where(
person => person.Name.ToUpper() == "INIGO MONTOYA");
```

Suppose that `persons` is an array of `Persons`, and the formal parameter of the `Where` method that corresponds to the lambda expression argument is of the delegate type `Func<Person, bool>`. The compiler emits a method that contains the code in the body of the lambda. It generates code that creates a delegate to the emitted method and passes the delegate to the `Where` method. The `Where` method returns a query object that, when executed, applies the delegate to each member of the array to determine the query results.

Now suppose that `persons` is not an array of `Persons`, but rather an object that represents a remote database table containing data on millions of people. Information about each row in the table can be streamed from the server to the client, and the client can then create a `Person` object corresponding to that row. The call to `Where` returns an object that represents the query. When the results of that query are requested on the client, how are the results determined?

One technique would be to transmit several million rows of data from the server to the client. You could create a `Person` object from each row, create a delegate from the lambda, and execute the delegate on every `Person`. This is conceptually no different from the array scenario, but it is far, far more expensive.

A second, much better technique is to somehow send the meaning of the lambda ("filter out every row that names a person other than Inigo Montoya") to the server. Database servers are optimized to rapidly perform this sort of filtering. The server can then choose to stream only the tiny number of matching rows to the client. Thus, instead of creating millions of `Person` objects and rejecting almost all of them, the client creates only those objects that already match the query, as determined by the server. But how does the meaning of the lambda get sent to the server?

This scenario is the motivation for adding expression trees to the language. Lambda expressions converted to expression trees become objects that represent data describing the lambda expression rather than compiled code implementing an anonymous function. Since the expression tree represents data rather than compiled code, it is possible to analyze the lambda at execution time and use that information to construct a query that executes on a database, for example. The expression tree received by `Where()` might be converted into a SQL query that is passed to a database, as shown in Listing 13.25.

LISTING 13.25: Converting an Expression Tree to a SQL `where` Clause

```
EXPRESSION TREE:
    persons.Where(person => person.Name.ToUpper() == "INIGO MONTOYA");

SQL WHERE CLAUSE:
    select * from Person where upper(Name) = 'INIGO MONTOYA';
```

The expression tree passed to the `Where()` call says that the lambda argument consists of the following elements:

- A read of the `Name` property of a `Person` object
- A call to a `string` method called `ToUpper()`
- A constant value, `"INIGO MONTOYA"`
- An equality operator, `==`

The `Where()` method takes this data and converts it to the SQL `where` clause by examining the data and building a SQL query string. However, SQL is just one possibility; you can build an expression tree evaluator that converts expressions to any query language.

Expression Trees Are Object Graphs

At execution time, a lambda converted to an expression tree becomes an object graph containing objects from the `System.Linq.Expressions` namespace. The root object in the graph represents the lambda itself. This object refers to objects representing the parameters, a return type, and body expression, as shown in Figure 13.3. The object graph contains all the information that the compiler deduced about the lambda. That information can then be used at execution time to create a query. Alternatively, the root lambda expression has a method, `Compile`, that generates CIL on the fly and creates a delegate that implements the described lambda.

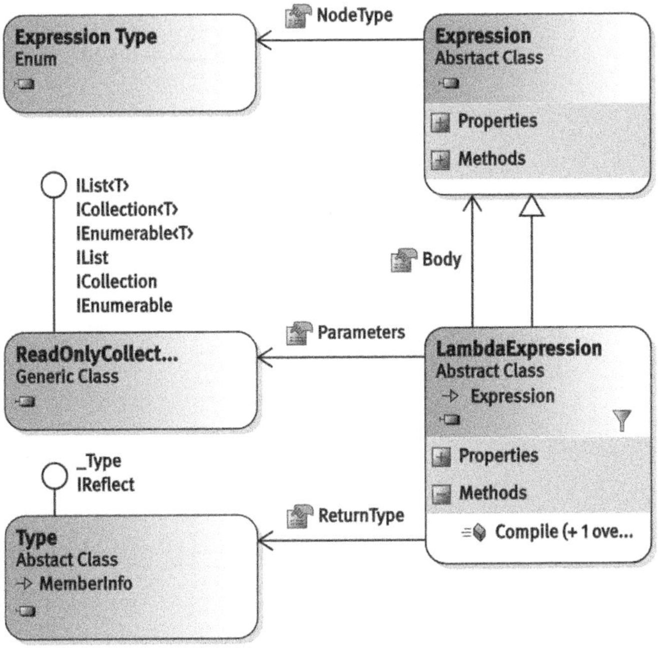

FIGURE 13.3: The lambda expression tree type

Figure 13.4 shows the types found in object graphs for unary and binary expressions in the body of a lambda.

A `UnaryExpression` represents an expression such as `-count`. It has a single child, `Operand`, of type `Expression`. A `BinaryExpression` has two child expressions, `Left` and `Right`. Both types have a `NodeType` property that identifies the specific operator, and both inherit from the base class `Expression`. Another 30 or so expression types, such as `NewExpression`, `ParameterExpression`, `MethodCallExpression`, and `LoopExpression`, are available that represent (almost) every possible expression in C# and Visual Basic.

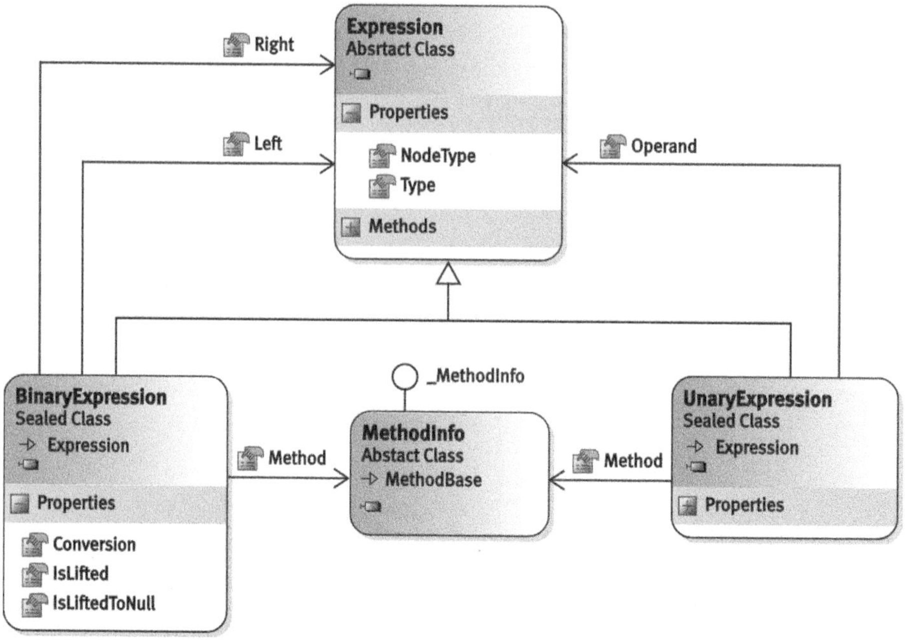

FIGURE 13.4: Unary and binary expression tree types

Delegates versus Expression Trees

The validity of a lambda expression is verified at compile time with a full semantic analysis, whether it is converted to a delegate or an expression tree. A lambda that is converted to a delegate causes the compiler to emit the lambda as a method and generates code that creates a delegate to that method at execution time. A lambda that is converted to an expression tree causes the compiler to generate code that creates an instance of `LambdaExpression` at execution time. But when using the Language Integrated Query (LINQ) API, how does the compiler know whether to generate a delegate, to execute a query locally, or to generate an expression tree so that information about the query can be sent to the remote database server?

The methods used to build LINQ queries, such as `Where()`, are extension methods. The versions of those methods that extend the `IEnumerable<T>` interface take delegate parameters; the methods that extend the `IQueryable<T>` interface take expression tree parameters. The compiler, therefore, can use the type of the collection that is being queried to determine whether to create delegates or expression trees from lambdas supplied as arguments.

Consider, for example, the `Where()` method in the following code:

```
persons.Where( person => person.Name.ToUpper() ==
"INIGO MONTOYA");
```

The extension method signature declared in the `System.Linq.Enumerable` class is

```
public IEnumerable<TSource> Where<TSource>(
this IEnumerable<TSource> collection,
Func<TSource, bool> predicate);
```

The extension method signature declared in the `System.Linq.Queryable` class is

```
public IQueryable<TSource> Where<TSource>(
this IQueryable<TSource> collection,
Expression<Func<TSource, bool>> predicate);
```

The compiler decides which extension method to use on the basis of the compile-time type of `persons`; if it is a type convertible to `IQueryable<Person>`, the method from `System.Linq.Queryable` is chosen. It converts the lambda to an expression tree. At execution time, the object referred to by `persons` receives the expression tree data and might use that data to build a SQL query, which is then passed to the database when the results of the query are requested. The result of the call to `Where` is an object that, when asked for query results, sends the query to the database and produces the results.

If `persons` cannot be converted implicitly to `IQueryable<Person>` but can be converted implicitly to `IEnumerable<Person>`, the method from `System.Linq.Enumerable` is chosen, and the lambda is converted to a delegate. The result of the call to `Where` is an object that, when asked for query results, applies the generated delegate as a predicate to every member of the collection and produces the results that match the predicate.

Examining an Expression Tree

Converting a lambda expression to an `Expression<TDelegate>` creates an expression tree rather than a delegate, as noted previously. Earlier in this chapter, we also explored how to convert a lambda such as `(x,y)=>x>y` to a delegate type such as `Func<int, int, bool>`. To turn this same lambda into an expression tree, we simply convert it to `Expression<Func<int, int, bool>>`, as shown in Listing 13.26. We can then examine the generated object and display information about its structure, as well as that of a more complex expression tree.

LISTING 13.26: Examining an Expression Tree

```
using System;
using System.Linq.Expressions;
using static System.Linq.Expressions.ExpressionType;

public class Program
{
    public static void Main()
    {
        Expression<Func<int, int, bool>> expression;
        expression = (x, y) => x > y;
        Console.WriteLine("------------- {0} -------------",
            expression);
        PrintNode(expression.Body, 0);
        Console.WriteLine();
        Console.WriteLine();
        expression = (x, y) => x * y > x + y;
        Console.WriteLine("------------- {0} -------------",
            expression);
        PrintNode(expression.Body, 0);
    }

    public static void PrintNode(Expression expression,
        int indent)
    {
        if (expression is BinaryExpression binaryExpression)
            PrintNode(binaryExpression, indent);
        else
            PrintSingle(expression, indent);
    }

    private static void PrintNode(BinaryExpression expression,
      int indent)
    {
```

```
        PrintNode(expression.Left, indent + 1);
        PrintSingle(expression, indent);
        PrintNode(expression.Right, indent + 1);
    }

    private static void PrintSingle(
            Expression expression, int indent) =>
        Console.WriteLine("{0," + indent * 5 + "}{1}",
          "", NodeToString(expression));

    private static string NodeToString(Expression expression) =>
        expression.NodeType switch
        {
            // using static ExpressionType
            Multiply => "*",
            Add => "+",
            Divide => "/",
            Subtract => "-",
            GreaterThan => ">",
            LessThan => "<",
            _ => expression.ToString() +
                " (" + expression.NodeType.ToString() + ")",
        };
```

Note that passing an instance of the expression tree to `Console.WriteLine()` automatically converts the expression tree to a descriptive string form; the objects generated for expression trees all override `ToString()` so that you can see the contents of an expression tree at a glance when debugging.

In Output 13.5, we see that the `Console.WriteLine()` statements within `Main()` print out the body of the expression trees as text.

Output 13.5

```
------------- (x, y) => (x > y) -------------
     x (Parameter)
>
     y (Parameter)


------------- (x, y) => ((x * y) > (x + y)) -------------
          x (Parameter)
     *
          y (Parameter)
>
          x (Parameter)
```

```
    +
        y (Parameter)
```

The important point to note is that an expression tree is a collection of data, and by iterating over the data, it is possible to convert the data to another format. In this case, we convert the expression tree to descriptive strings, but it could also be converted to expressions in another query language.

Using recursion, the `PrintNode()` function demonstrates that nodes in an expression tree are themselves trees containing zero or more child expression trees. The root tree that represents the lambda refers to the expression that is the body of the lambda with its `Body` property. Every expression tree node includes a `NodeType` property of enumerated type `ExpressionType` that describes what kind of expression it is. Numerous types of expressions exist: `BinaryExpression`, `ConditionalExpression`, `LambdaExpression`, `MethodCallExpression`, `ParameterExpression`, and `ConstantExpression` are examples. Each type derives from `Expression`.

Although the expression tree library now contains objects to represent most of the statements of C# and Visual Basic, neither of these languages actually supports the conversion of statement lambdas to expression trees. Only expression lambdas can be converted to expression trees.

Summary

This chapter began with a discussion of delegates and their use as references to methods or callbacks. This powerful concept enables you to pass a set of instructions to call in a different location, rather than immediately, when coding the instructions.

The concept of lambda expressions is a syntax that supersedes (but does not eliminate) the anonymous method syntax.[13] These constructs allow programmers to assign a set of instructions to a variable directly, without defining an explicit method that contains the instructions. This construct provides significant flexibility for

13. As used in C# 2.0.

programming instructions dynamically within the method—a powerful concept that greatly simplifies the programming of collections through the LINQ API.

The chapter ended with a discussion of the concept of expression trees and a consideration of how they compile into objects that represent the semantic analysis of a lambda expression rather than the delegate implementation itself. This important feature supports such libraries as the Entity Framework and LINQ to XML—that is, libraries that interpret the expression tree and use it within contexts other than anonymous functions.

Lambda expressions encompass both *statement lambdas* and *expression lambdas.* In other words, both statement lambdas and expression lambdas are types of lambda expressions.

One thing that the chapter mentioned but did not elaborate on was multicast delegates. The next chapter investigates multicast delegates in detail and explains how they enable the publish–subscribe pattern with events.

14

Events

In Chapter 13, you saw how to reference a method with an instance of a delegate type and invoke that method via the delegate. Delegates are the building blocks of a larger pattern called *publish–subscribe* or *observer*. The use of delegates for the publish–subscribe pattern is the focus of this chapter. Almost everything described in this chapter can be done using delegates alone. However, the event constructs that this chapter highlights provide additional encapsulation, making the publish–subscribe pattern easier to implement and less error-prone.

In Chapter 13, all delegates referenced a single method. More broadly, a single delegate value can reference a whole collection of methods to be called in sequence; such a delegate is called a **multicast delegate**. Its application enables scenarios where notifications of single events, such as a change in object state, are published to multiple subscribers.

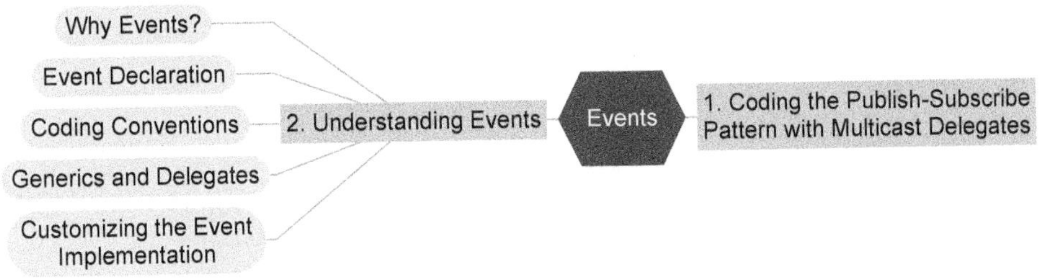

Generics significantly changed coding conventions because using a generic delegate data type meant that it was no longer necessary to declare a delegate for every possible event signature.[1]

Coding the Publish–Subscribe Pattern with Multicast Delegates

Consider a temperature control, where a heater and a cooler are hooked up to the same thermostat. For each unit to turn on and off appropriately, you must notify the units of changes in temperature. One thermostat publishes temperature changes to multiple subscribers—the heating and cooling units. The next section investigates the code.[2]

Defining Subscriber Methods

Begin by defining the `Heater` and `Cooler` objects (see Listing 14.1).

LISTING 14.1: `Heater` **and** `Cooler` **Event Subscriber Implementations**

```
public class Cooler
{
    public Cooler(float temperature)
    {
        Temperature = temperature;
    }

    // Cooler is activated when ambient temperature
    // is higher than this
    public float Temperature { get; set; }

    // Notifies that the temperature changed on this instance
    public void OnTemperatureChanged(float newTemperature)
    {
        if(newTemperature > Temperature)
        {
            System.Console.WriteLine("Cooler: On");
        }
```

1. The current chapter assumes a minimum of C# 2.0 throughout.
2. In this example, we use the term thermostat because people more commonly think of it in the context of heating and cooling systems. Technically, *thermometer* would be more appropriate.

```
        else
        {
            System.Console.WriteLine("Cooler: Off");
        }
    }
}

public class Heater
{
    public Heater(float temperature)
    {
        Temperature = temperature;
    }

    // Heater is activated when ambient temperature
    // is lower than this
    public float Temperature { get; set; }

    // Notifies that the temperature changed on this instance
    public void OnTemperatureChanged(float newTemperature)
    {
        if(newTemperature < Temperature)
        {
            System.Console.WriteLine("Heater: On");
        }
        else
        {
            System.Console.WriteLine("Heater: Off");
        }
    }
}
```

The two classes are essentially identical except for the temperature comparison. (In fact, you could eliminate one of the classes if you used a delegate to a comparison method within the `OnTemperatureChanged` method.) Each class stores the temperature at which the unit should be turned on. In addition, both classes provide an `OnTemperatureChanged()` method. Calling the `OnTemperatureChanged()` method is the means to indicate to the `Heater` and `Cooler` classes that the temperature has changed. The method implementation uses `newTemperature` to compare against the stored trigger temperature to determine whether to turn on the device.

The `OnTemperatureChanged()` methods are the subscriber (also called *listener*) methods. They must have the parameters and a return type that matches the delegate from the `Thermostat` class, which we discuss next.

Defining the Publisher

The `Thermostat` class is responsible for reporting temperature changes to the `heater` and `cooler` object instances. The `Thermostat` class code appears in Listing 14.2.

LISTING 14.2: Defining the Event Publisher, `Thermostat`

```
public class Thermostat
{
    // Define the event publisher (initially without the sender)
    public Action<float>? OnTemperatureChange { get; set; }

    public float CurrentTemperature { get; set; }
```

The `Thermostat` includes a property called `OnTemperatureChange` that is of the `Action<float>` delegate type. `OnTemperatureChange` stores a list of subscribers. Notice that only one delegate property is required to store all the subscribers. In other words, both the `Cooler` and the `Heater` instances receive notifications of a change in the temperature from this single publisher.

The last member of `Thermostat` is the `CurrentTemperature` property. This property sets and retrieves the value of the current temperature reported by the `Thermostat` class.

Hooking Up the Publisher and Subscribers

Finally, we put all these pieces together in a `Main()` method. Listing 14.3 shows a sample of what `Main()` could look like.

LISTING 14.3: Connecting the Publisher and Subscribers

```
public class Program
{
    public static void Main()
    {
        Thermostat thermostat = new();
```

```
        Heater heater = new(60);
        Cooler cooler = new(80);

        thermostat.OnTemperatureChange +=
            heater.OnTemperatureChanged;
        thermostat.OnTemperatureChange +=
            cooler.OnTemperatureChanged;

        Console.Write("Enter temperature: ");
        string? temperature = Console.ReadLine();
        if (!int.TryParse(temperature, out int currentTemperature))
        {
            Console.WriteLine($"'{temperature}' is not a valid integer.
↪");
            return;
        }
        thermostat.CurrentTemperature = currentTemperature;
    }
}
```

The code in this listing has registered two subscribers (`heater.OnTemperatureChanged` and `cooler.OnTemperatureChanged`) to the `OnTemperatureChange` delegate by directly assigning them using the `+=` operator.

By taking the temperature value the user has entered as input, you can set the `CurrentTemperature` of `thermostat`. However, you have not yet written any code to publish the change temperature event to subscribers.

Invoking a Delegate

Every time the `CurrentTemperature` property on the `Thermostat` class changes, you want to **invoke the delegate** to notify the subscribers (`heater` and `cooler`) of the change in temperature. To achieve this goal, you must modify the `CurrentTemperature` property to save the new value and publish a notification to each subscriber. The code modification appears in Listing 14.4.

LISTING 14.4: Invoking a Delegate without Checking for `null`

```
public class Thermostat
{
    // ...
    public float CurrentTemperature
```

```
    {
        get { return _CurrentTemperature; }
        set
        {
            if (value != CurrentTemperature)
            {
                _CurrentTemperature = value;

                // Call subscribers
                // Incomplete, check for null needed
                // ...
                OnTemperatureChange(value);
                // ...
            }
        }
    }
    private float _CurrentTemperature;
}
```

Now the assignment of `CurrentTemperature` includes some special logic to notify subscribers of changes in `CurrentTemperature`. The call to notify all subscribers is simply the single C# statement, `OnTemperatureChange(value)`. This single statement publishes the temperature change to both the `cooler` and `heater` objects. Here, you see in practice that the ability to notify multiple subscribers using a single call is why delegates are more specifically known as multicast delegates, as discussed later in the chapter.

Begin 8.0

In C# 8.0, however, invoking the `CurrentTemperature` delegate directly triggers a nullable dereference warning, indicating that a null check is required.

End 8.0

Check for `null`

One important part of event publishing code is missing from Listing 14.4. If no subscriber has registered to receive the notification, `OnTemperatureChange` would be `null`, and executing the `OnTemperatureChange(value)` statement would throw a `NullReferenceException`. To avoid this scenario, it is necessary to check for `null` before firing the event. Listing 14.5 demonstrates how to do this using the null-conditional operator before calling `Invoke()`.[3]

3. Used in C# 6.0.

LISTING 14.5: Invoking a Delegate

```
public class Thermostat
{
    // Define the event publisher
    public Action<float>? OnTemperatureChange { get; set; }

    public float CurrentTemperature
    {
        get { return _CurrentTemperature; }
        set
        {
            if(value != CurrentTemperature)
            {
                _CurrentTemperature = value;
                // If there are any subscribers,
                // notify them of changes in
                // temperature by invoking said subscribers
                OnTemperatureChange?.Invoke(value);       // C# 6.0
            }
        }
    }

    private float _CurrentTemperature;
}
```

Notice the call to the `Invoke()` method that follows the null-conditional operator. Although this method may be called using only a dot operator, there is little point, since that is the equivalent of calling the delegate directly (see `OnTemperatureChange(value)` in Listing 14.4). An important advantage underlying the use of the null-conditional operator is special logic to ensure that after checking for `null`, there is no possibility that a subscriber might invoke a stale handler (one that has changed after checking for `null`), leaving the delegate `null` again.

Guidelines

DO check that the value of a delegate is not `null` before invoking it.

DO use the null-conditional operator prior to calling `Invoke()` starting in C# 6.0.

ADVANCED TOPIC

The -= Operator for a Delegate Returns a New Instance

Given that a delegate is a reference type, it is perhaps somewhat surprising that assigning a local variable and then using that local variable is sufficient for making the `null` check thread-safe. Since `localOnChange` refers to the same location as `OnTemperatureChange` does, you might imagine that any changes in `OnTemperatureChange` would be reflected in `localOnChange` as well.

This is not the case because, effectively, any calls made to `OnTemperatureChange -= <subscriber>` will not simply remove a delegate from `OnTemperatureChange` so that it contains one less delegate than before. Rather, such a call will assign an entirely new multicast delegate without having any effect on the original multicast delegate to which `localOnChange` also refers.

ADVANCED TOPIC

Thread-Safe Delegate Invocation

If subscribers can be added and removed from the delegate on different threads, it is wise (as noted earlier) to conditionally invoke the delegate or copy the delegate reference into a local variable before checking it for `null`. Although this approach prevents the invocation of a `null` delegate, it does not avoid all possible race conditions. For example, one thread could make the copy, and then another thread could reset the delegate to `null`, and then the original thread could invoke the previous value of the delegate, thereby notifying a subscriber that is no longer on the list of subscribers. Subscribers in multithreaded programs should ensure that their code remains robust in this scenario; it is always possible that a "stale" subscriber will be invoked.

Delegate Operators

To combine the two subscribers in the `Thermostat` example, you used the `+=` operator. This operator takes the first delegate and adds the second delegate to the chain. Now, after the first delegate's method returns, the second delegate is called. To remove delegates from a delegate chain, use the -= operator, as shown in Listing 14.6 with Output 14.1.

Listing 14.6: Using the += and -= Delegate Operators

```
//...
Thermostat thermostat = new();
Heater heater = new(60);
Cooler cooler = new(80);

Action<float> delegate1;
Action<float> delegate2;
Action<float>? delegate3;

delegate1 = heater.OnTemperatureChanged;
delegate2 = cooler.OnTemperatureChanged;

Console.WriteLine("Invoke both delegates:");
delegate3 = delegate1;
delegate3 += delegate2;
delegate3(90);

Console.WriteLine("Invoke only delegate2");
delegate3 -= delegate1;
delegate3!(30);
//...
```

Output 14.1

```
Invoke both delegates:
Heater: Off
Cooler: On
Invoke only delegate2
Cooler: Off
```

You can also use the + and – operators to combine delegates, as shown in Listing 14.7.

Begin 8.0

Listing 14.7: Using the + and - Delegate Operators

```
//...
Thermostat thermostat = new();
Heater heater = new(60);
Cooler cooler = new(80);
```

```
Action<float> delegate1;
Action<float> delegate2;
Action<float> delegate3;

delegate1 = heater.OnTemperatureChanged;
delegate2 = cooler.OnTemperatureChanged;

Console.WriteLine("Combine delegates using + operator:");
delegate3 = delegate1 + delegate2;
delegate3(60);

Console.WriteLine("Uncombine delegates using - operator:");
delegate3 = (delegate3 - delegate2)!;
delegate3(60);
//...
```

Using the assignment operator clears out all previous subscribers and allows you to replace them with new subscribers. This is an unfortunate characteristic of a delegate. It is simply too easy to mistakenly code an assignment when, in fact, the `+=` operator is intended. The solution, called events, is described in the "Understanding Events" section later in this chapter.

Both the `+` and `-` operators and their assignment equivalents, `+=` and `-=`, are implemented internally using the static methods `System.Delegate.Combine()` and `System.Delegate.Remove()`, respectively. These methods take two parameters of type `delegate`. The first method, `Combine()`, joins the two parameters so that the first parameter refers to the second within the list of delegates. The second, `Remove()`, searches through the chain of delegates specified in the first parameter and then removes the delegate specified by the second parameter. And, since the `Remove()` method could potentially return `null`, we use the C# 8.0 null-forgiveness operator to tell the compiler to assume a valid delegate instance remains.

End 8.0

One interesting thing to note about the `Combine()` method is that either or both of its parameters can be `null`. If one of them is `null`, `Combine()` returns the non-`null` parameter. If both are `null`, `Combine()` returns `null`. This explains why you can call `thermostat.OnTemperatureChange += heater.OnTemperatureChanged;` and not throw an exception, even if the value of `thermostat.OnTemperatureChange` is still `null`.

Sequential Invocation

Figure 14.1 highlights the sequential notification of both `heater` and `cooler`.

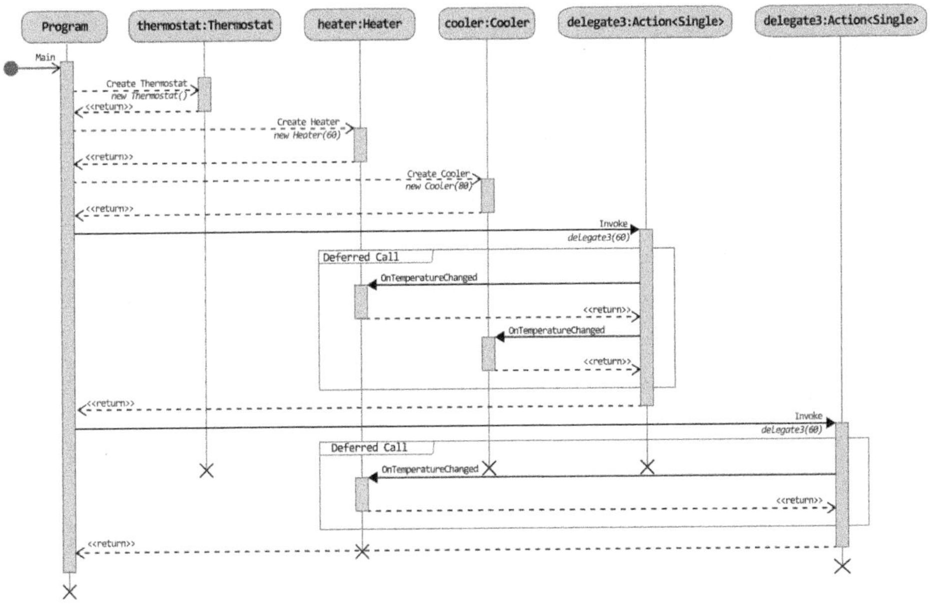

FIGURE 14.1: Delegate invocation sequence diagram

Although you coded only a single call to `OnTemperatureChange()`, the call is broadcast to both subscribers. Thus, with just one call, both `cooler` and `heater` are notified of the change in temperature. If you added more subscribers, they, too, would be notified by `OnTemperatureChange()`.

Although a single call, `OnTemperatureChange()`, caused the notification of each subscriber, the subscribers are still called sequentially, not simultaneously, because they are all called on the same thread of execution.

ADVANCED TOPIC

Multicast Delegate Internals

To understand how events work, you need to revisit the first examination of the `System.Delegate` type internals. Recall that the `delegate` keyword is an alias for a type derived from System.MulticastDelegate. In turn, System.MulticastDelegate is derived from System.Delegate, which, for its part, is composed of an object reference (needed for nonstatic methods) and a method reference. When you create a delegate, the compiler automatically employs the System.MulticastDelegate type rather than the System.Delegate type. The MulticastDelegate class includes an object reference and a method reference, just like its Delegate base class, but it also contains a reference to another System.MulticastDelegate object.

When you add a method to a multicast delegate, the MulticastDelegate class creates a new instance of the delegate type, stores the object reference and the method reference for the added method into the new instance, and adds the new delegate instance as the next item in a list of delegate instances. In effect, the MulticastDelegate class maintains a list of Delegate objects. Conceptually, you can represent the thermostat example as shown in Figure 14.2.

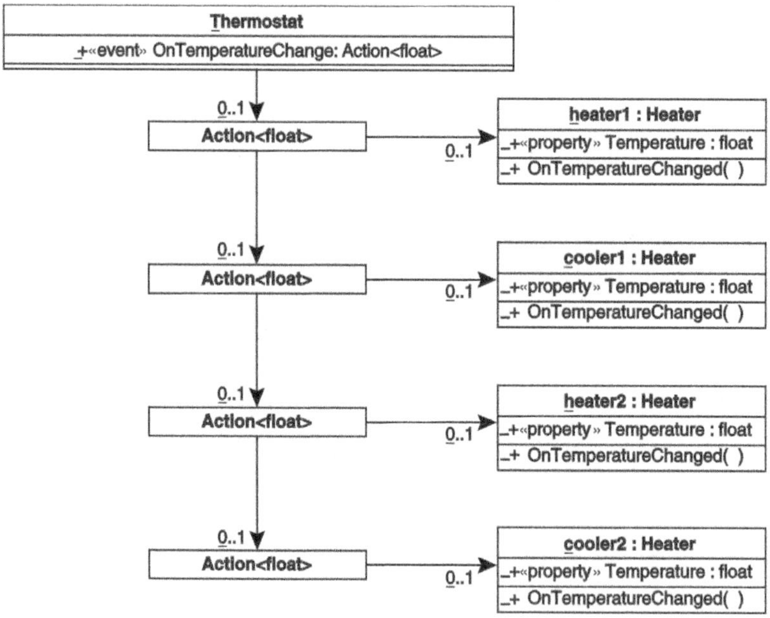

FIGURE 14.2: Multicast delegates chained together

When invoking a multicast delegate, each delegate instance in the list is called sequentially. Generally, delegates are called in the order they were added, but this behavior is not specified within the Common Language Infrastructure (CLI) specification. Furthermore, it can be overridden. Therefore, programmers should not depend on the invocation order.

Error Handling

Error handling makes awareness of the sequential notification critical. If one subscriber throws an exception, later subscribers will not receive the notification. Consider, for example, what would happen if you changed `Heater`'s `OnTemperatureChanged()` method so that it threw an exception, as shown in Listing 14.8.

LISTING 14.8: `OnTemperatureChanged()` **Throwing an Exception**

```
public class Program
{
    public static void Main()
    {
        Thermostat thermostat = new();
        Heater heater = new(60);
        Cooler cooler = new(80);

        thermostat.OnTemperatureChange +=
            heater.OnTemperatureChanged;
        thermostat.OnTemperatureChange +=
            (newTemperature) =>
                {
                    throw new InvalidOperationException();
                };
        thermostat.OnTemperatureChange +=
            cooler.OnTemperatureChanged;

        Console.Write("Enter temperature: ");
        string? temperature = Console.ReadLine();
        if (!int.TryParse(temperature, out int currentTemperature))
        {
            Console.WriteLine($"'{temperature}' is not a valid integer.
↪");
            return;
        }
```

```
            thermostat.CurrentTemperature = currentTemperature;
        }
    }
```

Figure 14.3 shows an updated sequence diagram. Even though `cooler` and `heater` subscribed to receive messages, the lambda expression exception terminates the chain and prevents the `cooler` object from receiving notification.

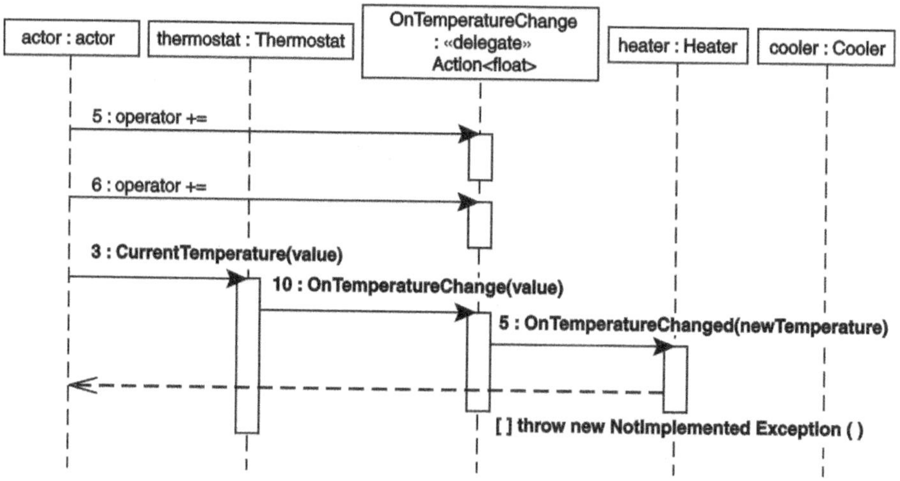

FIGURE 14.3: Delegate invocation with exception sequence diagram

To avoid this problem so that all subscribers receive notification, regardless of the behavior of earlier subscribers, you must manually enumerate through the list of subscribers and call them individually. Listing 14.9 shows the updates required in the `CurrentTemperature` property. The results appear in Output 14.2.

LISTING 14.9: Handling Exceptions from Subscribers

```
public class Thermostat
{
    // Define the event publisher
    public Action<float>? OnTemperatureChange;

    public float CurrentTemperature
    {
        get { return _CurrentTemperature; }
```

```
        set
        {
            if(value != CurrentTemperature)
            {
                _CurrentTemperature = value;
                Action<float>? onTemperatureChange
                    = OnTemperatureChange;
                if (onTemperatureChange != null)
                {
                    List<Exception> exceptionCollection =
                        new();
                    foreach(
                        Delegate handler in
                        onTemperatureChange.GetInvocationList())
                    {
                        try
                        {
                            ((Action<float>)handler)(value);
                        }
                        catch(Exception exception)
                        {
                            exceptionCollection.Add(exception);
                        }
                    }
                    if(exceptionCollection.Count > 0)
                    {
                        throw new AggregateException(
                            "There were exceptions thrown by " +
                            "OnTemperatureChange Event subscribers.",
                            exceptionCollection);
                    }
                }
            }
        }
    }
    private float _CurrentTemperature;
}
```

OUTPUT 14.2

```
Enter temperature: 45
Heater: On
Cooler: Off
There were exceptions thrown by OnTemperatureChange Event subscribers.
(Operation is not valid due to the current state of the object.)
```

Listing 14.9 demonstrates that you can retrieve a list of subscribers from a delegate's `GetInvocationList()` method. Enumerating over each item in this list returns the individual subscribers. If you then place each invocation of a subscriber within a try/catch block, you can handle any error conditions before continuing with the enumeration loop. In this example, even though the delegate subscriber throws an exception, `cooler` still receives notification of the temperature change. After all notifications have been sent, Listing 14.9 reports any exceptions by throwing an `AggregateException`, which wraps a collection of exceptions that are accessible by the `InnerExceptions` property. In this way, all exceptions are still reported and, at the same time, all subscribers are notified.

Method Returns and Pass-by-Reference

There is another scenario in which it is useful to iterate over the delegate invocation list instead of simply invoking a delegate directly. This scenario relates to delegates that either do not return `void` or have `ref` or `out` parameters. In the thermostat example, the `OnTemperatureChange` delegate is of type `Action<float>`, which returns `void` and has no `out` or `ref` parameters. As a result, no data is returned to the publisher. This consideration is important, because an invocation of a delegate potentially triggers notification to multiple subscribers. If each of the subscribers returns a value, it is ambiguous as to which subscriber's return value would be used.

If you changed `OnTemperatureChange` to return an enumeration value indicating whether the device was on because of the temperature change, the new delegate would be of type `Func<float, Status>`, where `Status` was an enum with elements `On` and `Off`. All subscriber methods would have to use the same method signature as the delegate, and thus each would be required to return a status value. Also, since `OnTemperatureChange` might potentially correspond to a chain of delegates, it is necessary to follow the same pattern that you used for error handling. In other words, you must iterate through each delegate invocation list, using the `GetInvocationList()` method, to retrieve each individual return value. Similarly, delegate types that use `ref` and `out` parameters need special consideration. However, although it is possible to use this approach in exceptional circumstances, the best advice is to avoid this scenario entirely by only returning `void`.

Understanding Events

There are two key problems with the delegates as you have used them so far in this chapter. To overcome these issues, C# uses the keyword `event`. In this section, you will see why you would use events and how they work.

Why Events?

This chapter and the preceding one covered all you need to know about how delegates work. Unfortunately, weaknesses in the delegate structure may inadvertently allow the programmer to introduce a bug. These issues relate to encapsulation that neither the subscription nor the publication of events can sufficiently control. Specifically, using events restricts external classes from doing anything other than adding subscribing methods to the publisher via the `+=` operator and then unsubscribing using the `-=` operator. In addition, they restrict classes, other than the containing class, from invoking the event.

Encapsulating the Subscription

As demonstrated earlier, it is possible to assign one delegate to another using the assignment operator. Unfortunately, this capability introduces a common source of bugs. Consider Listing 14.10.

Listing 14.10: Using the Assignment Operator `=` Rather Than `+=`

```
public class Program
{
    public static void Main()
    {
        Thermostat thermostat = new();
        Heater heater = new(60);
        Cooler cooler = new(80);

        thermostat.OnTemperatureChange =
            heater.OnTemperatureChanged;
```

```
        // Bug: Assignment operator overrides
        // previous assignment
        thermostat.OnTemperatureChange =
            cooler.OnTemperatureChanged;

        Console.Write("Enter temperature: ");
        string? temperature = Console.ReadLine();
        if (!int.TryParse(temperature, out int currentTemperature))
        {
            Console.WriteLine($"'{temperature}' is not a valid integer.
↪");
            return;
        }
        thermostat.CurrentTemperature = currentTemperature;
    }
}
```

Listing 14.10 is almost identical to Listing 14.6, except that instead of using the `+=` operator, you use a simple assignment operator. As a result, when the code assigns `cooler.OnTemperatureChanged` to `OnTemperatureChange`, `heater.OnTemperatureChanged` is cleared out because an entirely new chain is assigned to replace the previous one. The potential for mistakenly using an assignment operator, when the `+=` assignment was intended, is so high that it would be preferable if the assignment operator were not even supported for objects except within the containing class. The `event` keyword provides this additional encapsulation so that you cannot inadvertently cancel other subscribers.

Encapsulating the Publication

The second important difference between delegates and events is that events ensure that only the containing class can trigger an event notification. Consider Listing 14.11.

Listing 14.11: Firing the Event from Outside the Events Container

```
public class Program
{
    public static void Main()
    {
        Thermostat thermostat = new();
        Heater heater = new(60);
        Cooler cooler = new(80);
```

```
        thermostat.OnTemperatureChange +=
            heater.OnTemperatureChanged;

        thermostat.OnTemperatureChange +=
            cooler.OnTemperatureChanged;

        // Bug: Should not be allowed
        thermostat.OnTemperatureChange(42);
    }
}
```

In Listing 14.11, `Program` can invoke the `OnTemperatureChange` delegate even though the `CurrentTemperature` on `thermostat` did not change. `Program`, therefore, triggers a notification to all `thermostat` subscribers that the temperature changed, even though the `thermostat` temperature did not change. As before, the problem with the delegate is insufficient encapsulation. `Thermostat` should prevent any other class from being able to invoke the `OnTemperatureChange` delegate.

Declaring an Event

C# provides the `event` keyword to deal with both problems. Although seemingly like a field modifier, `event` defines a new type of member (see Listing 14.12).

Listing 14.12: Using the `event` Keyword with the Event-Coding Pattern

```
public class Thermostat
{
    public class TemperatureArgs : System.EventArgs
    {
        public TemperatureArgs(float newTemperature)
        {
            NewTemperature = newTemperature;
        }

        public float NewTemperature { get; set; }
    }

    // Define the event publisher
    public event EventHandler<TemperatureArgs> OnTemperatureChange =
        delegate { };
```

```
    public float CurrentTemperature
    // ...
    private float _CurrentTemperature;
}
```

The new Thermostat class has four changes relative to the original class. First, the OnTemperatureChange property has been removed, and OnTemperatureChange has instead been declared as a public field. This seems contrary to solving the earlier encapsulation problem. It would make more sense to increase the encapsulation, not decrease it by making a field public. However, the second change was to add the event keyword immediately before the field declaration. This simple change provides all the encapsulation needed. By adding the event keyword, you prevent the use of the assignment operator on a public delegate field (e.g., thermostat.OnTemperatureChange = cooler .OnTemperatureChanged). In addition, only the containing class is able to invoke the delegate that triggers the publication to all subscribers (e.g., disallowing thermostat.OnTemperatureChange(42) from outside the class). In other words, the event keyword provides the needed encapsulation that prevents any external class from publishing an event or unsubscribing previous subscribers it did not add. This resolves the two previously mentioned issues with plain delegates and is one of the key reasons for the inclusion of the event keyword in C#.

Another potential pitfall with plain delegates is that it is all too easy to forget to check for null[4] before invoking the delegate. This omission may result in an unexpected NullReferenceException. Fortunately, the encapsulation that the event keyword provides an alternative possibility during declaration (or within the constructor), as shown in Listing 14.12. Notice that when declaring the event, we assign delegate { }—a non-null delegate, which does nothing. By assigning the empty delegate, we can raise the event without checking whether there are any subscribers. (This behavior is similar to assigning an array of zero items to a variable. Doing so allows the invocation of an array member without first checking whether the variable is null.) Of course, if there is any chance that the delegate could be reassigned to have a null value, a check is still required. However, because the

4. Using the null conditional operator in C# 6.0.

event keyword restricts assignment to occur only within the class, any reassignment of the delegate could occur only from within the class. Assuming null is never assigned, there will be no need to check for null whenever the code invokes the delegate.[5]

Coding Conventions

All you need to do to gain the desired functionality is to change the original delegate variable declaration to a field and add the event keyword. With these two changes, you provide the necessary encapsulation; all other functionality remains the same. However, an additional change occurs in the delegate declaration in the code in Listing 14.12. To follow standard C# coding conventions, you should replace Action<float> with a new delegate type: EventHandler<TemperatureArgs>, a Common Language Runtime (CLR) type whose declaration is shown in Listing 14.13.

Listing 14.13: The Generic Event Handler Type

```
public delegate void EventHandler<TEventArgs>(
    object sender, TEventArgs e)
    where TEventArgs : EventArgs;
```

The result is that the single temperature parameter in the Action<TEventArgs> delegate type is replaced with two new parameters—one for the publisher or "sender" and a second for the event data. This change is not something that the C# compiler will enforce, but passing two parameters of these types is the norm for a delegate intended for an event.

The first parameter, sender, contains an instance of the class that invoked the delegate. This is especially helpful if the same subscriber method registers with multiple events—for example, if the heater.OnTemperatureChanged event subscribes to two different Thermostat instances. In such a scenario, either Thermostat instance can trigger a call to heater.OnTemperatureChanged. To determine which instance of Thermostat triggered the event, you use the sender parameter from inside Heater.OnTemperatureChanged(). If the

5. While rare, note that this pattern doesn't work when the event is contained within a struct.

event is static, this option will not be available, so you would pass `null` for the `sender` argument value.

The second parameter, `TEventArgs e`, is specified as type `Thermostat.TemperatureArgs`. The important thing about `TemperatureArgs`, at least as far as the coding convention goes, is that it derives from `System.EventArgs`. (In fact, derivation from `System.EventArgs` is something that the framework forced with a generic constraint until Microsoft .NET Framework 4.5.) The only significant property on `System.EventArgs` is `Empty`, which is used to indicate that there is no event data. When you derive `TemperatureArgs` from `System.EventArgs`, however, you add an additional property, `NewTemperature`, to pass the temperature from the thermostat to the subscribers.

Let's summarize the coding convention for events: The first argument, `sender`, is of type `object` and contains a reference to the object that invoked the delegate or `null` if the event is static. The second argument is of type `System.EventArgs` or something that derives from `System.EventArgs` but contains additional data about the event. You invoke the delegate exactly as before, except for the additional parameters. Listing 14.14 shows an example.

Listing 14.14: Firing the Event Notification

```
public class Thermostat
// ...

    public float CurrentTemperature
    {
        get { return _CurrentTemperature; }
        set
        {
            if(value != CurrentTemperature)
            {
                _CurrentTemperature = value;
                // If there are any subscribers,
                // notify them of changes in
                // temperature by invoking said subscribers
                OnTemperatureChange?.Invoke(
                    this, new TemperatureArgs(value));
            }
        }
    }
```

```
    private float _CurrentTemperature;
}
```

You usually specify the sender using the container class (`this`) because it is the only class that can invoke the delegate for events.

In this example, the subscriber could cast the sender parameter to `Thermostat` and access the current temperature that way, as well as via the `TemperatureArgs` instance. However, the current temperature on the `Thermostat` instance may change via a different thread. When events may occur due to state changes, passing the previous value along with the new value is a pattern frequently used to control which state transitions are allowable.

Guidelines

DO check that the value of a delegate is not `null` before invoking it (possibly by using the null-conditional operator in C# 6.0).

DO pass the instance of the class as the value of the sender for nonstatic events.

DO pass `null` as the sender for static events.

DO NOT pass `null` as the value of the `eventArgs` argument.

DO use `System.EventArgs` or a type that derives from `System.EventArgs` for a `TEventArgs` type.

CONSIDER using a subclass of `System.EventArgs` as the event argument type (`TEventArgs`) unless you are sure the event will never need to carry any data.

ADVANCED TOPIC

Event Internals

As mentioned earlier, events provide encapsulation that restricts external classes to only subscribing and unsubscribing methods to the publisher via the `+=` and `-=` operators respectively. In addition, they restrict classes, other than the containing class, from invoking the event. To do so, the C# compiler takes the public delegate variable with its `event` keyword modifier and declares the delegate as private. In addition, it adds a couple of methods and two special event blocks. Essentially, the `event` keyword is a C# shortcut for generating the appropriate encapsulation logic. Consider the example in the event declaration shown in Listing 14.15.

Listing 14.15: Declaring the `OnTemperatureChange` Event

```
public class Thermostat
// ...
    public event EventHandler<TemperatureArgs>? OnTemperatureChange;
}
```

When the C# compiler encounters the `event` keyword, it generates CIL code equivalent to the C# code shown in Listing 14.16.

Listing 14.16: C# Conceptual Equivalent of the Event CIL Code Generated by the Compiler

```
public class Thermostat
// ...
    // Declaring the delegate field to save the
    // list of subscribers
    private EventHandler<TemperatureArgs>? _OnTemperatureChange;

    public void add_OnTemperatureChange(
        EventHandler<TemperatureArgs> handler)
    {
        System.Delegate.Combine(_OnTemperatureChange, handler);
    }

    public void remove_OnTemperatureChange(
        EventHandler<TemperatureArgs> handler)
    {
        System.Delegate.Remove(_OnTemperatureChange, handler);
    }

    #if ConceptualEquivalentCode
    public event EventHandler<TemperatureArgs> OnTemperatureChange
    {
        //Would cause a compiler error
        add
        {
            add_OnTemperatureChange(value);
        }
        //Would cause a compiler error
```

```
        remove
        {
            remove_OnTemperatureChange(value);
        }
    }
    #endif // ConceptualEquivalentCode
```

In other words, the code shown in Listing 14.15 is (conceptually) the C# shorthand that the compiler uses to trigger the code expansion shown in Listing 14.16. (The "conceptually" qualifier is needed because some details regarding thread synchronization have been eliminated for elucidation.)

The C# compiler first takes the original event definition and defines a private delegate variable in its place. As a result, the delegate becomes unavailable to any external class—even to classes derived from it.

Next, the C# compiler defines two methods, `add_OnTemperatureChange()` and `remove_OnTemperatureChange()`, in which the `OnTemperatureChange` suffix is taken from the original name of the event. These methods are responsible for implementing the `+=` and `-=` assignment operators, respectively. As Listing 14.16 shows, these methods are implemented using the static `System.Delegate.Combine()` and `System.Delegate.Remove()` methods, discussed earlier in the chapter. The first parameter passed to each of these methods is the private `EventHandler<TemperatureArgs>` delegate instance, `OnTemperatureChange`.

Perhaps the most curious part of the code generated from the `event` keyword is the last segment. The syntax is very similar to that of a property's getter and setter methods, except that the methods are called `add` and `remove`, respectively. The `add` block takes care of handling the `+=` operator on the event by passing the call to `add_OnTemperatureChange()`. In a similar manner, the `remove` block operator handles the `-=` operator by passing the call on to `remove_OnTemperatureChange`.

Take careful note of the similarities between this code and the code generated for a property. Recall that the C# implementation of a property is to create `get_<propertyname>` and `set_<propertyname>` and then to pass calls to the `get` and `set` blocks on to these methods. Clearly, the event syntax in such cases is very similar.

Another important characteristic to note about the generated CIL code is that the CIL equivalent of the `event` keyword remains in the CIL. In other words, an event is something that the CIL code recognizes explicitly; it is not just a C# construct. By keeping an equivalent `event` keyword in the CIL code, all languages and editors can provide special functionality because they can recognize the event as a special class member.

Customizing the Event Implementation

You can customize the code that the compiler generates for `+=` and `-=`. Consider, for example, changing the scope of the `OnTemperatureChange` delegate so that it is protected rather than private. This, of course, would allow classes derived from `Thermostat` to access the delegate directly instead of being limited to the same restrictions as external classes. To enable this behavior, C# allows the same property as the syntax shown in Listing 14.17. In other words, C# allows you to define custom `add` and `remove` blocks to provide a unique implementation for each aspect of the event encapsulation.

LISTING 14.17: Custom `add` and `remove` Handlers

```
public class Thermostat
{
    public class TemperatureArgs : System.EventArgs
    // ...
    // Define the event publisher
    public event EventHandler<TemperatureArgs> OnTemperatureChange
    {
        add
        {
            _OnTemperatureChange =
                (EventHandler<TemperatureArgs>)
                    System.Delegate.Combine(value, _OnTemperatureChange);
        }
        remove
        {
            _OnTemperatureChange =
                (EventHandler<TemperatureArgs>?)
                    System.Delegate.Remove(_OnTemperatureChange, value);
        }
    }
```

```
    protected EventHandler<TemperatureArgs>? _OnTemperatureChange;

    public float CurrentTemperature
    // ...
    private float _CurrentTemperature;
}
```

Here, the delegate that stores each subscriber, `_OnTemperatureChange`, was changed to `protected`. In addition, implementation of the `add` block switches around the delegate storage so that the last delegate added to the chain is the first delegate to receive a notification. However, code should not rely on this implementation.

Summary

Now that we have described events, we note that, in general, method references are the only cases where it is advisable to work with a delegate variable outside the context of an event. In other words, given the additional encapsulation features of an event and the ability to customize the implementation when necessary, the best practice is always to use events for the publish–subscribe pattern.

It may take a little practice before you can code events from scratch without referring to sample code. However, events are a critical foundation for the asynchronous, multithreaded coding described in later chapters of this book.

15

Collection Interfaces with Standard Query Operators

Through a set of extension methods and lambda expressions, the programming API called **Language Integrated Query (LINQ)** provides a far superior API for working with collections.[1] In fact, in earlier editions of this book, the chapter on collections came immediately after the chapter on generics and just before the one on delegates. However, lambda expressions were so fundamental to LINQ that it is no longer possible to cover collections without first covering delegates (the basis of lambda expressions). Now that you have a solid foundation in lambda expressions from the preceding two chapters, we can delve into the details of collections—a topic that spans three chapters. In this chapter, the focus begins with **standard query operators**—a means of leveraging LINQ via direct invocation of extension methods.

After introducing collection initializers, this chapter covers the various collection interfaces and explores how they relate to one another. This is the basis for understanding collections, so you should cover the material with diligence. The section on collection interfaces includes coverage of the `IEnumerable<T>` extension methods[2] that implement the standard query operators.

There are two categories of collection-related classes and interfaces: those that support generics and those that don't. This chapter primarily discusses the generic

1. Significant features added in C# 3.0 in collections attributable to LINQ.
2. Added in C# 3.0.

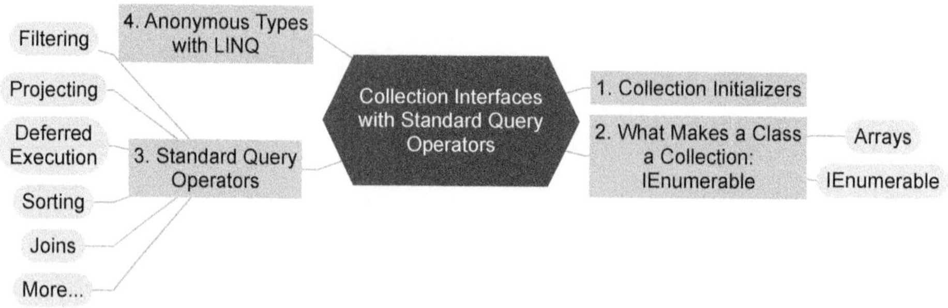

collection interfaces. You should use collection classes that don't support generics only when you are writing components that need to interoperate with earlier versions of the runtime. This is because everything that was available in the nongeneric form has a generic replacement that is strongly typed. Although the concepts still apply to both forms, we do not explicitly discuss the nongeneric versions.[3]

The chapter concludes with an in-depth discussion of anonymous types—topics that we covered only briefly in a few Advanced Topic sections in Chapter 3. The interesting thing about anonymous types is that they have been eclipsed by tuples[4] —a topic we discuss further at the end of the chapter.

Collection Initializers

A **collection initializer** allows programmers to construct a collection with an initial set of members at instantiation time in a manner similar to array declaration. Before collection initialization was available, elements had to be explicitly added to a collection after the collection was instantiated—using something like `System.Collections.Generic.ICollection<T>`'s `Add()` method. With collection initialization, the `Add()` calls are generated by the C# compiler rather than explicitly coded by the developer. Listing 15.1 shows how to initialize the collection using a collection initializer.

3. In fact, .NET Standards and .NET Core don't even include the nongeneric collections.
4. Starting in C# 7.0.

LISTING 15.1: Collection Initialization

```
using System;
using System.Collections.Generic;

public class Program
{
    public static void Main()
    {
        List<string> sevenWorldBlunders;
        sevenWorldBlunders = new List<string>()
        {
            // Quotes from Gandhi
            "Wealth without work",
            "Pleasure without conscience",
            "Knowledge without character",
            "Commerce without morality",
            "Science without humanity",
            "Worship without sacrifice",
            "Politics without principle"
        };

        Print(sevenWorldBlunders);
    }

    private static void Print<T>(IEnumerable<T> items)
    {
        foreach(T item in items)
        {
            Console.WriteLine(item);
        }
    }
}
```

The syntax is similar not only to the array initialization but also to an object initializer with the curly braces following the constructor. If no parameters are passed in the constructor, the parentheses following the data type are optional (as they are with object initializers).

A few basic requirements are needed for a collection initializer to compile successfully. Ideally, the collection type to which a collection initializer is applied would be of a type that implements `System.Collections.Generic.ICollection<T>`. This ensures that the collection includes an `Add()` method that the compiler-generated code can invoke. However, a relaxed version of the requirement also exists that simply demands one or more `Add()` methods exist either as an extension method[5] or as an instance method on a type that implements `IEnumerable`—even if the collection doesn't implement `ICollection<T>`. The `Add()` methods need to take parameters that are compatible with the values specified in the collection initializer.

For dictionaries, the collection initializer syntax is slightly more complex, because each element in the dictionary requires both the key and the value. This syntax is shown in Listing 15.2.

Listing 15.2: Initializing a `Dictionary<>` with a Collection Initializer

```
using System;
using System.Collections.Generic;
// ...
#if !PRECSHARP6
        Dictionary<string, ConsoleColor> colorMap = new()
            {
                ["Error"] = ConsoleColor.Red,
                ["Warning"] = ConsoleColor.Yellow,
                ["Information"] = ConsoleColor.Green,
                ["Verbose"] = ConsoleColor.White
            };
#else
        Dictionary<string, ConsoleColor> colorMap =
            new Dictionary<string, ConsoleColor>
            {
                {"Error", ConsoleColor.Red },
                {"Warning", ConsoleColor.Yellow },
                {"Information", ConsoleColor.Green },
                {"Verbose", ConsoleColor.White}
            };
#endif
```

Listing 15.2 includes two different versions of the initialization. The first demonstrates a new syntax,[6] which expresses the intent of a name/value pair by allowing the assignment operator to express which value is associated with which key. The second syntax[7] pairs the name and the value together using curly brackets.

5. Starting in C# 6.0.
6. Introduced in C# 6.0.
7. Works in C# 6.0 and later.

Allowing initializers on collections that don't support `ICollection<T>` was important for two reasons. First, most collections (types that implement `IEnumerable<T>`) do not also implement `ICollection<T>`, which significantly reduces the usefulness of collection initializers. Second, matching on the method name and signature compatibility with the collection initializer items enables greater diversity in the items initialized into the collection. For example, the initializer now can support `new DataStore(){ a, {b, c}}` as long as there is one `Add()` method whose signature is compatible with `a` and a second `Add()` method whose signature is compatible with `b, c`.

What Makes a Class a Collection: `IEnumerable`

By definition, a collection within .NET is a class that, at a minimum, implements `IEnumerable`. This interface is critical because implementing the methods of `IEnumerable` is the minimum needed to support iterating over the collection.

Chapter 4 showed how to use a `foreach` statement to iterate over an array of elements. This syntax is simple and avoids the complication of having to know how many elements there are. The runtime does not directly support the `foreach` statement, however. Instead, the C# compiler transforms the code as described in this section.

`foreach` with Arrays

Listing 15.3 demonstrates a simple `foreach` loop iterating over an array of integers and then printing out each integer to the console.

LISTING 15.3: `foreach` **with Arrays**

```
int[] array = new int[] { 1, 2, 3, 4, 5, 6 };

foreach(int item in array)
{
    Console.WriteLine(item);
}
```

From this code, the C# compiler creates a CIL equivalent of the `for` loop, as shown in Listing 15.4.

LISTING 15.4: Compiled Implementation of `foreach` with Arrays

```
int[] tempArray;
int[] array = new int[] { 1, 2, 3, 4, 5, 6 };

tempArray = array;
for(int counter = 0; (counter < tempArray.Length); counter++)
{
    int item = tempArray[counter];

    Console.WriteLine(item);
}
```

In this example, note that `foreach` relies on support for the `Length` property and the index operator (`[]`). With the `Length` property, the C# compiler can use the `for` statement to iterate through each element in the array.

`foreach` with `IEnumerable<T>`

Although the code shown in Listing 15.4 works well on arrays where the length is fixed and the index operator is always supported, not all types of collections have a known number of elements. Furthermore, many of the collection classes, including the `Stack<T>`, `Queue<T>`, and `Dictionary<TKey, TValue>` classes, do not support retrieving elements by index. Therefore, a more general approach of iterating over collections of elements is needed. The iterator pattern provides this capability. Assuming you can determine the first and next elements, knowing the count and supporting retrieval of elements by index are unnecessary.

The `System.Collections.Generic.IEnumerator<T>` and nongeneric `System.Collections.IEnumerator` interfaces are designed to enable the iterator pattern for iterating over collections of elements, rather than the length–index pattern shown in Listing 15.4. A class diagram of their relationships appears in Figure 15.1.

`IEnumerator`, which `IEnumerator<T>` derives from, includes three members. The first is `bool MoveNext()`. Using this method, you can move from one element within the collection to the next, while at the same time detecting when you have enumerated through every item. The second member, a read-only property called `Current`, returns the element currently in process. `Current` is overloaded in `IEnumerator<T>`, providing a type-specific implementation of it. With these

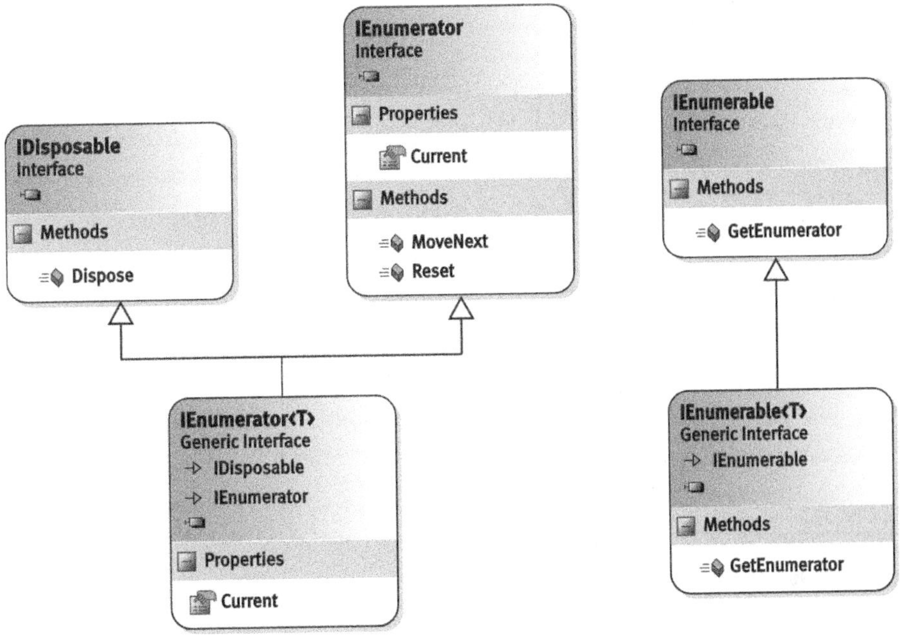

FIGURE 15.1: A class diagram of the `IEnumerator<T>` and `IEnumerator` interfaces

two members of the collection class, it is possible to iterate over the collection by simply using a `while` loop, as demonstrated in Listing 15.5. (The `Reset()` method usually throws a `NotImplementedException`, so it should never be called. If you need to restart an enumeration, just create a fresh enumerator.)

LISTING 15.5: Iterating over a Collection Using `while`

```
System.Collections.Generic.Stack<int> stack = new();
int number;
// ...

// This code is conceptual, not the actual code
#if ConceptualCode
while(stack.MoveNext())
{
    number = stack.Current();
    Console.WriteLine(number);
}
```

```
#endif // ConceptualCode
```

In Listing 15.5, the `MoveNext()` method returns `false` when it moves past the end of the collection. This replaces the need to count elements while looping.

Listing 15.5 uses a `System.Collections.Generic.Stack<T>` as the collection type. Numerous other collection types exist; this is just one example. The key trait of `Stack<T>` is its design as a last in, first out (LIFO) collection. Notice that the type parameter `T` identifies the type of all items within the collection. Collecting one type of object within a collection is a key characteristic of a generic collection. The programmer must know the data type within the collection when adding, removing, or accessing items within the collection.

The preceding example shows the gist of the C# compiler output, but it doesn't actually compile that way because it omits two important details concerning the implementation: interleaving and error handling.

State Is Shared

The problem with an implementation such as Listing 15.5 is that if two such loops interleaved each other—one `foreach` inside another, both using the same collection—the collection must maintain a state indicator of the current element so that when `MoveNext()` is called, the next element can be determined. In such a case, one interleaving loop can affect the other. (The same is true of loops executed by multiple threads.)

To overcome this problem, the collection classes do not support `IEnumerator<T>` and `IEnumerator` interfaces directly. Instead, as shown in Figure 15.1, there is a second interface, called `IEnumerable<T>`, whose only method is `GetEnumerator()`. The purpose of this method is to return an object that supports `IEnumerator<T>`. Instead of the collection class maintaining the state, a different class—usually a nested class, so that it has access to the internals of the collection—will support the `IEnumerator<T>` interface and will keep the state of the iteration loop. The enumerator is like a "cursor" or a "bookmark" in the sequence. You can have multiple bookmarks, and moving each of them enumerates over the collection independently of the others. Using this pattern, the C# equivalent of a `foreach` loop will look like the code shown in Listing 15.6.

Listing 15.6: A Separate Enumerator Maintaining State during an Iteration

```
System.Collections.Generic.Stack<int> stack =
    new();
int number;
System.Collections.Generic.Stack<int>.Enumerator
  enumerator;

// ...

// If IEnumerable<T> is implemented explicitly,
// then a cast is required
// ((IEnumerable<int>)stack).GetEnumerator();
enumerator = stack.GetEnumerator();
while(enumerator.MoveNext())
{
    number = enumerator.Current;
    Console.WriteLine(number);
}
```

ADVANCED/BEGINNER TOPIC

Cleaning Up Following Iteration

Given that the classes that implement the `IEnumerator<T>` interface maintain the state, sometimes you need to clean up the state after it exits the loop (because either all iterations have completed or an exception is thrown). To achieve this, the `IEnumerator<T>` interface derives from `IDisposable`. Enumerators that implement `IEnumerator` do not necessarily implement `IDisposable`, but if they do, `Dispose()` will be called as well. This means that `Dispose()` can be called after the `foreach` loop exits. The C# equivalent of the final Common Intermediate Language (CIL) code, therefore, looks like Listing 15.7.

Listing 15.7: Compiled Result of `foreach` on Collections

```
System.Collections.Generic.Stack<int> stack = new();
System.Collections.Generic.Stack<int>.Enumerator enumerator;
IDisposable disposable;

enumerator = stack.GetEnumerator();
try
{
```

```
        int number;
        while(enumerator.MoveNext())
        {
            number = enumerator.Current;
            Console.WriteLine(number);
        }
    }
    finally
    {
        // Explicit cast used for IEnumerator<T>
        disposable = (IDisposable)enumerator;
        disposable.Dispose();

        // IEnumerator will use the as operator unless IDisposable
        // support is known at compile time
        // disposable = (enumerator as IDisposable);
        // if (disposable != null)
        // {
        //     disposable.Dispose();
        // }
    }
```

Notice that because the `IDisposable` interface is supported by `IEnumerator<T>`, the `using` statement can simplify the code in Listing 15.7 to that shown in Listing 15.8.

Listing 15.8: Error Handling and Resource Cleanup with `using`

```
System.Collections.Generic.Stack<int> stack = new();
int number;

using (
    System.Collections.Generic.Stack<int>.Enumerator
        enumerator = stack.GetEnumerator())
{
    while (enumerator.MoveNext())
    {
        number = enumerator.Current;
        Console.WriteLine(number);
    }
}
```

However, recall that the CIL does not directly support the `using` keyword. For this reason, the code in Listing 15.7 is actually a more accurate C# representation of the `foreach` CIL code.

Begin 9.0

ADVANCED TOPIC

`foreach` without `IEnumerable`

C# doesn't require that `IEnumerable/IEnumerable<T>` be implemented to iterate over a data type using `foreach`. Rather, the compiler uses a concept known as **duck typing**: It looks for a `GetEnumerator()` method that returns a type with a `Current` property and a `MoveNext()` method. Duck typing involves searching by name rather than relying on an interface or explicit method call to the method. (The name "duck typing" comes from the whimsical idea that to be treated as a duck, the object must merely implement a `Quack()` method; it need not implement an `IDuck` interface.) If duck typing fails to find a suitable implementation of the enumerable pattern, the compiler checks whether the collection implements the interfaces. Furthermore, even if neither the method nor the interface exist, starting in C# 9.0, the compiler will look for an extension method that implements the `GetEnumerator()` signature, and will use that if it is available.

End 9.0

Do Not Modify Collections during `foreach` Iteration

Chapter 4 showed that the compiler prevents assignment of the `foreach` variable (`number`). As is demonstrated in Listing 15.7, an assignment to `number` would not change the collection element itself, so the C# compiler prevents such an assignment altogether.

In addition, neither the element count within a collection nor the items themselves can generally be modified during the execution of a `foreach` loop. If, for example, you called `stack.Push(42)` inside the `foreach` loop, it would be ambiguous whether the `iterator` should ignore or incorporate the change to `stack`—in other words, whether `iterator` should iterate over the newly added item or ignore it and assume the same state as when it was instantiated.

Because of this ambiguity, an exception of type System.InvalidOperationException is generally thrown upon accessing the enumerator if the collection is modified within a foreach loop. This exception reports that the collection was modified after the enumerator was instantiated.

Standard Query Operators

Besides the methods on System.Object, any type that implements IEnumerable<T> is required to implement only one other method, GetEnumerator(). Yet, doing so makes more than 50 methods available to all types implementing IEnumerable<T>, not including any overloading—and this happens without needing to explicitly implement any method except the GetEnumerator() method. The additional functionality is provided through extension methods[8] and resides in the class System.Linq.Enumerable. Therefore, including the using declarative for System.Linq is all it takes to make these methods available.

Each method on IEnumerable<T> is a **standard query operator**; it provides querying capability over the collection on which it operates. In the following sections, we examine some of the most prominent of these standard query operators. Many of these examples depend on an Inventor and/or Patent class, both of which are defined in Listing 15.9 with Output 15.1.

Listing 15.9: Sample Classes for Use with Standard Query Operators

```
using System;
using System.Collections.Generic;

public class Program
{
    public static void Main()
    {
        IEnumerable<Patent> patents = PatentData.Patents;
        Print(patents);

        Console.WriteLine();
```

8. Starting in C# 3.0.

```
        IEnumerable<Inventor> inventors = PatentData.Inventors;
        Print(inventors);
    }

    private static void Print<T>(IEnumerable<T> items)
    {
        foreach(T item in items)
        {
            Console.WriteLine(item);
        }
    }
}
```

Output 15.1

```
Bifocals (1784)
Phonograph (1877)
Kinetoscope (1888)
Electrical Telegraph (1837)
Flying Machine (1903)
Steam Locomotive (1815)
Droplet Deposition Apparatus (1989)
Backless Brassiere (1914)

Benjamin Franklin (Philadelphia, PA)
Orville Wright (Kitty Hawk, NC)
Wilbur Wright (Kitty Hawk, NC)
Samuel Morse (New York, NY)
George Stephenson (Wylam, Northumberland)
John Michaelis (Chicago, IL)
Mary Phelps Jacob (New York, NY)
```

Filtering with `Where()`

To filter out data from a collection, we need to provide a filter method that returns `true` or `false`, indicating whether or not a particular element should be included. A delegate expression that takes an argument and returns a Boolean value is called a **predicate**, and a collection's `Where()` method depends on predicates for identifying filter criteria, as shown in Listing 15.10. (Technically, the result of the `Where()` method is an **object** that encapsulates the operation of filtering a given sequence with a given predicate.) The results appear in Output 15.2.

LISTING 15.10: Filtering with `System.Linq.Enumerable.Where()`

```
using System;
using System.Collections.Generic;
using System.Linq;

public class Program
{
    public static void Main()
    {
        IEnumerable<Patent> patents = PatentData.Patents;
        patents = patents.Where(
            patent => patent.YearOfPublication.StartsWith("18"));
        Print(patents);
    }
    // ...
}
```

OUTPUT 15.2

```
Phonograph (1877)
Kinetoscope (1888)
Electrical Telegraph (1837)
Steam Locomotive (1815)
```

Notice that the code assigns the output of the `Where()` call back to `IEnumerable<T>`. In other words, the output of `IEnumerable<T>.Where()` is a new `IEnumerable<T>` collection. In Listing 15.10, it is `IEnumerable<Patent>`.

Less obvious is that the `Where()` expression argument has not necessarily been executed at assignment time. This is true for many of the standard query operators. In the case of `Where()`, for example, the expression is passed into the collection and "saved" but not executed. Instead, execution of the expression occurs only when it is necessary to begin iterating over the items within the collection. For example, a `foreach` loop, such as the one in `Print()` (in Listing 15.9), can trigger the expression to be evaluated for each item within the collection. At least conceptually, the `Where()` method should be understood as a means of specifying the query regarding what appears in the collection, not the actual work involved with iterating over the items to produce a new collection with potentially fewer items.

Projecting with Select()

Since the output from the IEnumerable<T>.Where() method is a new IEnumerable<T> collection, it is possible to again call a standard query operator on the same collection. For example, rather than just filtering the data from the original collection, we could transform the data (see Listing 15.11).

Listing 15.11: Projection with System.Linq.Enumerable.Select()

```
using System;
using System.Collections.Generic;
using System.Linq;

public class Program
{
    public static void Main()
    {
        IEnumerable<Patent> patents = PatentData.Patents;
        IEnumerable<Patent> patentsOf1800 = patents.Where(
            patent => patent.YearOfPublication.StartsWith("18"));
        IEnumerable<string> items = patentsOf1800.Select(
            patent => patent.ToString());

        Print(items);
    }
    // ...
}
```

In Listing 15.11, we create a new IEnumerable<string> collection. In this case, it just so happens that adding the Select() call doesn't change the output—but only because Print()'s Console.WriteLine() call used ToString() anyway. Obviously, a transform still occurred on each item from the Patent type of the original collection to the string type of the items collection.

Consider the example using System.IO.FileInfo in Listing 15.12.

Listing 15.12: Projection with System.Linq.Enumerable.Select() and new

```
//...
IEnumerable<string> fileList = Directory.EnumerateFiles(
    rootDirectory, searchPattern);
IEnumerable<FileInfo> files = fileList.Select(
```

```
    file => new FileInfo(file));
//...
```

Here `fileList` is of type `IEnumerable<string>`. However, using the projection offered by `Select`, we can transform each item in the collection to a `System.IO.FileInfo` object.

Lastly, capitalizing on tuples, we can create an `IEnumerable<T>` collection where T is a tuple (see Listing 15.13 and Output 15.3).

Listing 15.13: Projection to Tuple

```
//...
IEnumerable<string> fileList = Directory.EnumerateFiles(
rootDirectory, searchPattern);
IEnumerable<(string FileName, long Size)> items = fileList.Select(
    file =>
    {
        FileInfo fileInfo = new(file);
        return (
            FileName: fileInfo.Name,
            Size: fileInfo.Length
        );
    });
//...
```

Output 15.3

```
FileName = AssemblyInfo.cs, Size = 1704
FileName = CodeAnalysisRules.xml, Size = 735
FileName = CustomDictionary.xml, Size = 199
FileName = EssentialCSharp.sln, Size = 40415
FileName = EssentialCSharp.suo, Size = 454656
FileName = EssentialCSharp.vsmdi, Size = 499
FileName = EssentialCSharp.vssscc, Size = 256
FileName = intelliTechture.ConsoleTester.dll, Size = 24576
FileName = intelliTechture.ConsoleTester.pdb, Size = 30208
```

The output of an anonymous type automatically shows the property names and their values as part of the generated `ToString()` method associated with the anonymous type.

Projection using the `Select()` method is very powerful. We already saw how to filter a collection vertically (reducing the number of items in the collection) using the

Where() standard query operator. Now, via the Select() standard query operator, we can also reduce the collection horizontally (making fewer columns) or transform the data entirely. In combination, Where() and Select() provide a means for extracting only those pieces of the original collection that are desirable for the current algorithm. These two methods alone provide a powerful collection manipulation API that would otherwise result in significantly more—and less readable—code.

ADVANCED TOPIC

Running LINQ Queries in Parallel

With the widespread availability of computers having multiple processors and multiple cores within those processors, the ability to easily take advantage of the additional processing power becomes far more important. To do so, programs need to support multiple threads so that work can happen simultaneously on different CPUs within the computer. Listing 15.14 demonstrates one way to do this using Parallel LINQ (PLINQ).

LISTING 15.14: Executing LINQ Queries in Parallel

```
//...
IEnumerable<string> fileList = Directory.EnumerateFiles(
    rootDirectory, searchPattern);
var items = fileList.AsParallel().Select(
    file =>
    {
        FileInfo fileInfo = new(file);
        return new
        {
            FileName = fileInfo.Name,
            Size = fileInfo.Length
        };
    });
//...
```

As Listing 15.14 shows, only a minimal change in code is needed to enable parallel support. All that this example uses is a Microsoft .NET Framework 4–introduced standard query operator, AsParallel(), on the static class System

.Linq.ParallelEnumerable. Using this simple extension method, the runtime begins executing over the items within the fileList collection and returning the resultant objects in parallel. Each parallel operation in this case isn't particularly expensive (although it is relative to the other execution taking place), but consider the burden imposed by CPU-intensive operations such as encryption or compression. Running the query in parallel across multiple CPUs can decrease execution time by a factor corresponding to the number of CPU cores.

An important caveat to be aware of (and the reason why AsParallel() appears as an Advanced Topic rather than in the standard text) is that parallel execution can introduce race conditions, such that an operation on one thread can be intermingled with an operation on a different thread, causing data corruption. To avoid this problem, synchronization mechanisms are required on data with shared access from multiple threads to force the operations to be atomic where necessary. Synchronization itself, however, can introduce deadlocks that freeze the execution, further complicating the effective parallel programming.

More details on this and additional multithreading topics are provided in Chapters 19 through 22.

Counting Elements with Count()

Another query frequently performed on a collection of items is to retrieve the count. To support this type of query, LINQ includes the Count() extension method.

Listing 15.15 demonstrates that Count() is overloaded to simply count all elements (no parameters) or to take a predicate that counts only items identified by the predicate expression.

LISTING 15.15: Counting Items with Count()

```
using System;
using System.Collections.Generic;
using System.Linq;

public class Program
{
    public static void Main()
    {
        IEnumerable<Patent> patents = PatentData.Patents;
```

```
    Console.WriteLine($"Patent Count: { patents.Count() }");
    Console.WriteLine($@"Patent Count in 1800s: {
        patents.Count(patent =>
            patent.YearOfPublication.StartsWith("18"))}");
```

In spite of the apparent simplicity of the `Count()` statement, `IEnumerable<T>` has not changed, so the executed code still iterates over all the items in the collection. Whenever a `Count` property is directly available on the collection, it is preferable to use that rather than LINQ's `Count()` method (a subtle difference). Fortunately, `ICollection<T>` includes the `Count` property, so code that calls the `Count()` method on a collection that supports `ICollection<T>` casts the collection and call `Count` directly. However, if `ICollection<T>` is not supported, `Enumerable.Count()` proceeds to enumerate all the items in the collection rather than call the built-in `Count` mechanism. If the purpose of checking the count is just to see whether it is greater than zero (`if(patents.Count() > 0){...}`), the preferred approach would be to use the `Any()` operator (`if(patents.Any()){...}`). `Any()` attempts to iterate over only one of the items in the collection to return a true result, rather than iterating over the entire sequence.

Guidelines

DO use `System.Linq.Enumerable.Any()` rather than calling `patents.Count()` when checking whether there are more than zero items.

DO use a collection's `Count` property (if available) instead of calling the `System.Linq.Enumerable.Count()` method.

Deferred Execution

One of the most important concepts to remember when using LINQ is deferred execution. Consider the code in Listing 15.16 and the corresponding output in Output 15.4.

Listing 15.16: Filtering with `System.Linq.Enumerable.Where()`

```
using System;
using System.Collections.Generic;
```

```
using System.Linq;
// ...
        IEnumerable<Patent> patents = PatentData.Patents;
        bool result;
        patents = patents.Where(
            patent =>
            {
                if(result =
                    patent.YearOfPublication.StartsWith("18"))
                {
                    // Side effects like this in a predicate
                    // are used here to demonstrate a
                    // principle and should generally be
                    // avoided
                    Console.WriteLine("\t" + patent);
                }
                return result;
            });

        Console.WriteLine("1. Patents prior to the 1900s are:");
        foreach(Patent patent in patents)
        {
        }

        Console.WriteLine();
        Console.WriteLine(
            "2. A second listing of patents prior to the 1900s:");
        Console.WriteLine(
            $@"   There are { patents.Count()
                } patents prior to 1900.");


        Console.WriteLine();
        Console.WriteLine(
            "3. A third listing of patents prior to the 1900s:");
        patents = patents.ToArray();
        Console.Write("   There are ");
        Console.WriteLine(
            $"{ patents.Count() } patents prior to 1900.");

        //...
```

Output 15.4

```
1. Patents prior to the 1900s are:
        Phonograph (1877)
        Kinetoscope (1888)
```

```
        Electrical Telegraph (1837)
        Steam Locomotive (1815)

2. A second listing of patents prior to the 1900s:
        Phonograph (1877)
        Kinetoscope (1888)
        Electrical Telegraph (1837)
        Steam Locomotive (1815)
   There are 4 patents prior to 1900.

3. A third listing of patents prior to the 1900s:
        Phonograph (1877)
        Kinetoscope (1888)
        Electrical Telegraph (1837)
        Steam Locomotive (1815)
   There are 4 patents prior to 1900.
```

Notice that `Console.WriteLine("1. Patents prior...)` executes before the lambda expression. This characteristic is very important to recognize because it is not obvious to those who are unaware of its importance. In general, predicates should do exactly one thing—evaluate a condition—and should not have any side effects (even printing to the console, as in this example).

To understand what is happening, recall that lambda expressions are delegates—references to methods—that can be passed around. In the context of LINQ and standard query operators, each lambda expression forms part of the overall query to be executed.

At the time of declaration, lambda expressions are not executed. In fact, it isn't until the lambda expressions are invoked that the code within them begins to execute. Figure 15.2 shows the sequence of operations.

As Figure 15.2 shows, three calls in Listing 15.14 trigger the lambda expression, and each time it is fairly implicit. If the lambda expression were expensive (such as a call to a database), it would therefore be important to minimize the lambda expression's execution.

First, the execution is triggered within the `foreach` loop. As described earlier in the chapter, the `foreach` loop breaks down into a `MoveNext()` call, and each call results in the lambda expression's execution for each item in the original collection. While iterating, the runtime invokes the lambda expression for each item to determine whether the item satisfies the predicate.

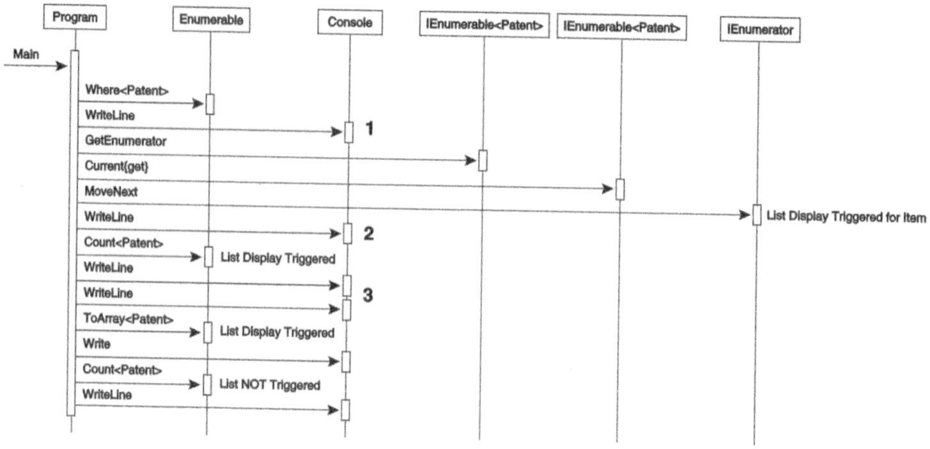

FIGURE 15.2: Sequence of operations invoking lambda expressions

Second, a call to `Enumerable`'s `Count()` (the function) triggers the lambda expression for each item once more. Again, this is subtle behavior because `Count` (the property) is very common on collections that have not been queried with a standard query operator.

Third, the call to `ToArray()` (or `ToList()`, `ToDictionary()`, or `ToLookup()`) evaluates the lambda expression for each item. However, converting the collection with one of these "To" methods is extremely helpful. Doing so returns a collection on which the standard query operator has already executed. In Listing 15.14, the conversion to an array means that when `Length` is called in the final `Console.WriteLine()`, the underlying object pointed to by `patents` is, in fact, an array (which obviously implements `IEnumerable<T>`); in turn, `System.Array`'s implementation of `Length` is called rather than `System.Linq.Enumerable`'s implementation. Consequently, following a conversion to one of the collection types returned by a "To" method, it is generally safe to work with the collection (until another standard query operator is called). However, be aware that this will bring the entire result set into memory (it may have been backed by a database or file prior to this step). Furthermore, the "To" method will take a snapshot of the underlying data, so that no fresh results will be returned upon requerying the "To" method result.

We strongly encourage you to review the sequence diagram in Figure 15.2 along with the corresponding code and recognize that the deferred execution of standard query operators can result in extremely subtle triggering of the standard query operators; therefore, developers should use caution and seek to avoid unexpected calls. The query object represents the query, not the results. When you ask the query for the results, the whole query executes (perhaps even again) because the query object doesn't know that the results will be the same as they were during a previous execution (if one existed).

NOTE

To avoid such repeated execution, you must cache the data retrieved by the executed query. To do so, assign the data to a local collection using one of the "To" collection methods. During the assignment call of a "To" method, the query obviously executes. However, iterating over the assigned collection after that point will not involve the query expression any further. In general, if you want the behavior of an in-memory collection snapshot, it is a best practice to assign a query expression to a cached collection to avoid unnecessary iterations.

Sorting with `OrderBy()` and `ThenBy()`

Another common operation on a collection is to sort it. Sorting involves a call to `System.Linq.Enumerable`'s `OrderBy()`, as shown in Listing 15.17 and Output 15.5.

LISTING 15.17: Ordering with `System.Linq.Enumerable.OrderBy()`/`ThenBy()`

```
using System;
using System.Collections.Generic;
using System.Linq;
// ...
        IEnumerable<Patent> items;
        Patent[] patents = PatentData.Patents;
        items = patents.OrderBy(
                patent => patent.YearOfPublication)
            .ThenBy(
```

```
            patent => patent.Title);
    Print(items);
    Console.WriteLine();

    items = patents.OrderByDescending(
            patent => patent.YearOfPublication)
        .ThenByDescending(
            patent => patent.Title);
    Print(items);

    //...
```

OUTPUT 15.5

```
Bifocals (1784)
Steam Locomotive (1815)
Electrical Telegraph (1837)
Phonograph (1877)
Kinetoscope (1888)
Flying Machine (1903)
Backless Brassiere (1914)
Droplet Deposition Apparatus (1989)

Droplet Deposition Apparatus (1989)
Backless Brassiere (1914)
Flying Machine (1903)
Kinetoscope (1888)
Phonograph (1877)
Electrical Telegraph (1837)
Steam Locomotive (1815)
Bifocals (1784)
```

The `OrderBy()` call takes a lambda expression that identifies the key on which to sort. In Listing 15.17, the initial sort uses the year in which the patent was published.

Notice that the `OrderBy()` call takes only a single parameter, `keySelector`, to sort on. To sort on a second column, it is necessary to use a different method: `ThenBy()`. Similarly, code would use `ThenBy()` for any additional sorting.

`OrderBy()` returns an `IOrderedEnumerable<T>` interface, not an `IEnumerable<T>`. Furthermore, `IOrderedEnumerable<T>` derives from `IEnumerable<T>`, so all the standard query operators (including `OrderBy()`) are available on the `OrderBy()` return. However, repeated calls to `OrderBy()` would undo the work of the previous call such that the end result would sort by only the keySelector in the final OrderBy() call. For this reason, you should be careful not to call OrderBy() on a previous OrderBy() call.

Instead, you should specify additional sorting criteria using ThenBy(). Although ThenBy() is an extension method, it is not an extension of IEnumerable<T> but rather of IOrderedEnumerable<T>. The method, also defined on System.Linq.Extensions.Enumerable, is declared as follows:

```
public static IOrderedEnumerable<TSource>
ThenBy<TSource, TKey>(
this IOrderedEnumerable<TSource> source,
Func<TSource, TKey> keySelector)
```

In summary, use OrderBy() first, followed by zero or more calls to ThenBy() to provide additional sorting "columns." The methods OrderByDescending() and ThenByDescending() provide the same functionality except that they sort items in descending order. Mixing and matching ascending and descending methods is not a problem, but if sorting items further, you would use a ThenBy() call (either ascending or descending).

Two more important notes about sorting are warranted. First, the actual sort doesn't occur until you begin to access the members in the collection, at which point the entire query is processed. You can't sort unless you have all the items to sort, because you can't determine whether you have the first item. The fact that sorting is delayed until you begin to access the members is due to deferred execution, as described earlier in this chapter. Second, each subsequent call to sort the data (e.g., Orderby() followed by ThenBy() followed by ThenByDescending()) does involve additional calls to the keySelector lambda expression of the earlier sorting calls. In other words, a call to OrderBy() calls its corresponding keySelector lambda expression once you iterate over the collection. Furthermore, a subsequent call to ThenBy() again makes calls to OrderBy()'s keySelector.

Guidelines

DO NOT call an OrderBy() following a prior OrderBy() method call. Use ThenBy() to sequence items by more than one value.

BEGINNER TOPIC

Join Operations

Consider two collections of objects as shown in the Venn diagram in Figure 15.3. The left circle in the diagram includes all inventors, and the right circle contains all patents. The intersection includes both inventors and patents, and a line is formed for each case where there is a match of inventors to patents. As the diagram shows, each inventor may have multiple patents and each patent can have one or more inventors. Each patent has an inventor, but in some cases, inventors do not yet have patents.

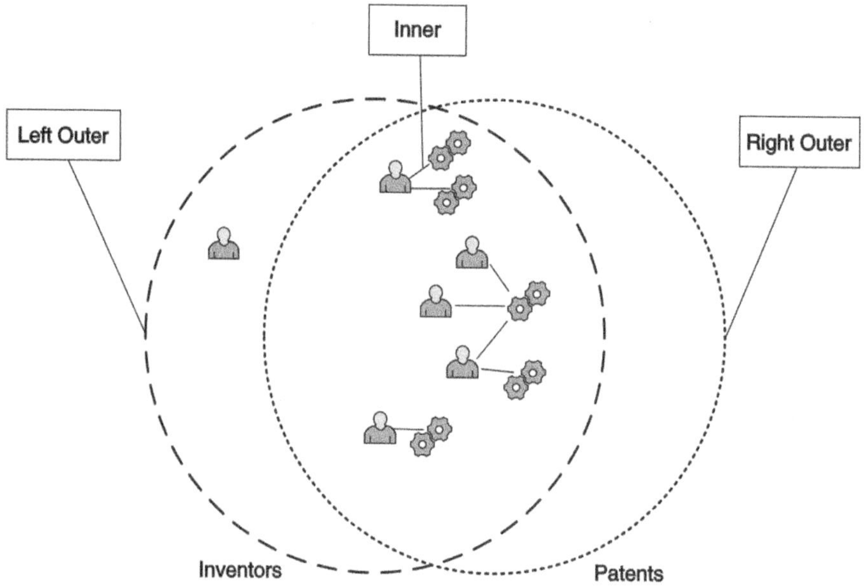

FIGURE 15.3: Venn diagram of inventor and patent collections

Matching up inventors within the intersection to patents is an **inner join**. The result is a collection of inventor/patent pairs in which both patents and inventions exist for a pair. A **left outer join** includes all the items within the left circle regardless of whether they have a corresponding patent. In this particular example, a **right outer join** would be the same as an inner join because there are no patents without inventors. Furthermore, the designation of left versus right is arbitrary, so there is really no distinction between left and outer joins. A **full outer join**, however, would include records from both outer sides; it is relatively rare to perform a full outer join.

Another important characteristic in the relationship between inventors and patents is that it is a **many-to-many** relationship. Each individual patent can have one or more inventors (e.g., the flying machine's invention by both Orville and Wilbur Wright). Furthermore, each inventor can have one or more patents (e.g., Benjamin Franklin's invention of both bifocals and the phonograph).

Another common relationship is a **one-to-many** relationship. For example, a company department may have many employees. However, each employee can belong to only one department at a time. (However, as is common with one-to-many relationships, adding the factor of time can transform them into many-to-many relationships. A particular employee may move from one department to another so that, over time, they could potentially be associated with multiple departments, making another many-to-many relationship.)

Listing 15.18 provides a sample listing of employee and department data, and Output 15.6 shows the results.

LISTING 15.18: Sample Employee and Department Data

```
public class Program
{
    public static void Main()
    {
        IEnumerable<Department> departments =
            CorporateData.Departments;
        Print(departments);

        Console.WriteLine();

        IEnumerable<Employee> employees =
            CorporateData.Employees;
        Print(employees);
    }

    private static void Print<T>(IEnumerable<T> items)
    {
        foreach(T item in items)
        {
            Console.WriteLine(item);
        }
```

```
    }
}
```

Output 15.6

```
Corporate
Human Resources
Engineering
Information Technology
Philanthropy
Marketing

Mark Michaelis (Chief Computer Nerd)
Michael Stokesbary (Senior Computer Wizard)
Brian Jones (Enterprise Integration Guru)
Anne Beard (HR Director)
Pat Dever (Enterprise Architect)
Kevin Bost (Programmer Extraordinaire)
Thomas Heavey (Software Architect)
Eric Edmonds (Philanthropy Coordinator)
```

We use this data in the example in the following section on joining data.

Performing an Inner Join with `Join()`

In the world of objects on the client side, relationships between objects are generally already set up. For example, the relationship between files and the directories in which they reside are preestablished with the `DirectoryInfo.GetFiles()` method and the `FileInfo.Directory` method, respectively. Frequently, however, this is not the case with data being loaded from nonobject stores. Instead, the data needs to be joined together so that you can navigate from one type of object to the next in a way that makes sense for the data.

Consider the example of employees and company departments. In Listing 15.19, we join each employee to their department and then list each employee with their corresponding department. Since each employee belongs to only one (and exactly one) department, the total number of items in the list is equal to the total number of employees—each employee appears only once (each employee is said to be **normalized**). Output 15.7 shows the results.

Listing 15.19: An Inner Join Using `System.Linq.Enumerable.Join()`

```
using System;
using System.Collections.Generic;
using System.Linq;
// ...
        Department[] departments = CorporateData.Departments;
        Employee[] employees = CorporateData.Employees;

        IEnumerable<(int Id, string Name, string Title,
            Department Department)> items =
            employees.Join(
                departments,
                employee => employee.DepartmentId,
                department => department.Id,
                (employee, department) => (
                    employee.Id,
                    employee.Name,
                    employee.Title,
                    department
                ));


        foreach ((int Id, string Name, string Title, Department
↪Department) item in items)
        {
            Console.WriteLine(
                $"{item.Name} ({item.Title})");
            Console.WriteLine("\t" + item.Department);
        }
    }
    //...
```

Output 15.7

```
Mark Michaelis (Chief Computer Nerd)
        Corporate
Michael Stokesbary (Senior Computer Wizard)
        Engineering
Brian Jones (Enterprise Integration Guru)
        Engineering
Anne Beard (HR Director)
        Human Resources
Pat Dever (Enterprise Architect)
        Information Technology
Kevin Bost (Programmer Extraordinaire)
        Engineering
Thomas Heavey (Software Architect)
```

```
        Engineering
Eric Edmonds (Philanthropy Coordinator)
        Philanthropy
```

The first parameter for `Join()` has the name `inner`. It specifies the collection, `departments`, that `employees` joins to. The next two parameters are lambda expressions that specify how the two collections will connect. `employee => employee.DepartmentId` (with a parameter name of `outerKeySelector`) identifies that on each `employee`, the key will be `DepartmentId`. The next lambda expression (`department => department.Id`) specifies the `Department`'s `Id` property as the key—in other words, for each employee, join a department where `employee.DepartmentId` equals `department.Id`. The last parameter is the resultant item that is selected. In this case, it is a tuple with `Employee`'s `Id`, `Name`, and `Title`, as well as a `Department` property with the joined `department` object.

Notice in the output that *Engineering* appears multiple times—once for each employee in `CorporateData`. In this case, the `Join()` call produces a **Cartesian product** between all the departments and all the employees, such that a new record is created for every case where a record exists in both collections and the specified department IDs are the same. This type of join is an inner join.

The data could also be joined in reverse, such that `department` joins to each `employee` to list each department-to-employee match. Notice that the output includes more records than there are departments: There are multiple employees for each department, and the output is a record for each match. As we saw before, the Engineering department appears multiple times, once for each employee.

The code in Listing 15.20 (which produces Output 15.8) is similar to that in Listing 15.19, except that the objects, `Departments` and `Employees`, are reversed. The first parameter to `Join()` is `employees`, indicating what `departments` joins to. The next two parameters are lambda expressions that specify how the two collections will connect: `department => department.Id` for `departments` and `employee => employee.DepartmentId` for `employees`. As before, a join occurs whenever `department.Id` equals `employee.EmployeeId`. The final tuple parameter specifies a class with `int`

`Id`, `string Name`, and `Employee Employee items`. (Specifying the names in the expression is optional but used here for clarity.)

Listing 15.20: Another Inner Join with `System.Linq.Enumerable.Join()`

```
using System;
using System.Collections.Generic;
using System.Linq;
// ...
        Department[] departments = CorporateData.Departments;
        Employee[] employees = CorporateData.Employees;

        IEnumerable<(long Id, string Name, Employee Employee)> items =
            departments.Join(
                employees,
                department => department.Id,
                employee => employee.DepartmentId,
                (department, employee) => (
                    department.Id,
                    department.Name,
                    Employee: employee)
                );


        foreach ((long Id, string Name, Employee Employee) item in items)
        {
            Console.WriteLine(item.Name);
            Console.WriteLine("\t" + item.Employee);
        }
        //...
```

Output 15.8

```
Corporate
        Mark Michaelis (Chief Computer Nerd)
Human Resources
        Anne Beard (HR Director)
Engineering
        Michael Stokesbary (Senior Computer Wizard)
Engineering
        Brian Jones (Enterprise Integration Guru)
Engineering
        Kevin Bost (Programmer Extraordinaire)
Engineering
        Thomas Heavey (Software Architect)
Information Technology
        Pat Dever (Enterprise Architect)
```

```
Philanthropy
        Eric Edmonds (Philanthropy Coordinator)
```

In addition to ordering and joining a collection of objects, you might want to group objects with like characteristics. For the employee data, you might want to group employees by department, region, job title, and so forth. Listing 15.21 shows an example of how to do this with the `GroupBy()` standard query operator (see Output 15.9 to view the results).

Listing 15.21: Grouping Items Using `System.Linq.Enumerable.GroupBy()`

```
using System;
using System.Collections.Generic;
using System.Linq;
// ...
        IEnumerable<Employee> employees = CorporateData.Employees;

        IEnumerable<IGrouping<int, Employee>> groupedEmployees =
            employees.GroupBy((employee) => employee.DepartmentId);

        foreach(IGrouping<int, Employee> employeeGroup in
            groupedEmployees)
        {
            Console.WriteLine();
            foreach(Employee employee in employeeGroup)
            {
                Console.WriteLine(employee);
            }
            Console.WriteLine(
              "\tCount: " + employeeGroup.Count());
        }
        //...
```

Output 15.9

```
Mark Michaelis (Chief Computer Nerd)
    Count: 1

Michael Stokesbary (Senior Computer Wizard)
Brian Jones (Enterprise Integration Guru)
Kevin Bost (Programmer Extraordinaire)
Thomas Heavey (Software Architect)
    Count: 4

Anne Beard (HR Director)
```

```
    Count: 1

Pat Dever (Enterprise Architect)
    Count: 1

Eric Edmonds (Philanthropy Coordinator)
    Count: 1
```

Note that the items output from a `GroupBy()` call are of type `IGrouping<TKey, TElement>`, which has a property for the key that the query is grouping on (`employee.DepartmentId`). However, it does not have a property for the items within the group. Rather, `IGrouping<TKey, TElement>` derives from `IEnumerable<T>`, allowing for enumeration of the items within the group using a `foreach` statement or for aggregating the data into something such as a count of items (`employeeGroup.Count()`).

Implementing a One-to-Many Relationship with `GroupJoin()`

Listing 15.19 and Listing 15.20 are virtually identical. Either `Join()` call could have produced the same output just by changing the tuple definition. When trying to create a list of employees, Listing 15.19 provides the correct result. `Department` ends up as an item of both tuples representing the joined employee. However, Listing 15.20 is not ideal. Given support for collections, a more preferable representation of a department would have a collection of employees rather than a single tuple for each department–employee relationship. Listing 15.22 demonstrates the creation of such a child collection; Output 15.10 shows the preferred output.

Listing 15.22: Creating a Child Collection with `System.Linq.Enumerable.GroupJoin()`

```
using System;
using System.Collections.Generic;
using System.Linq;
// ...
        Department[] departments = CorporateData.Departments;
        Employee[] employees = CorporateData.Employees;

        IEnumerable<(long Id, string Name, IEnumerable<Employee>
↪Employees)> items =
            departments.GroupJoin(
                employees,
```

```
                department => department.Id,
                employee => employee.DepartmentId,
                (department, departmentEmployees) => (
                    department.Id,
                    department.Name,
                    departmentEmployees
                ));

        foreach (
            (_, string name, IEnumerable<Employee> employeeCollection)
↪in items)
        {
            Console.WriteLine(name);
            foreach (Employee employee in employeeCollection)
            {
                Console.WriteLine("\t" + employee);
            }
        }
        //...
```

Output 15.10

```
Corporate
        Mark Michaelis (Chief Computer Nerd)
Human Resources
        Anne Beard (HR Director)
Engineering
        Michael Stokesbary (Senior Computer Wizard)
        Brian Jones (Enterprise Integration Guru)
        Kevin Bost (Programmer Extraordinaire)
        Thomas Heavey (Software Architect)
Information Technology
        Pat Dever (Enterprise Architect)
Philanthropy
        Eric Edmonds (Philanthropy Coordinator)
```

To achieve the preferred result, we use `System.Linq.Enumerable`'s `GroupJoin()` method. The parameters are the same as those in Listing 15.19, except for the final tuple selected. In Listing 15.19, the lambda expression is of type `Func<Department, IEnumerable<Employee>, (long Id, string Name, IEnumerable<Employee> Employees)>`. Notice that we use the second type argument (`IEnumerable<Employee>`) to project the collection of employees for each department onto the resultant department tuple; thus each department in the resulting collection includes a list of the employees.

(Readers familiar with SQL will notice that, unlike `Join()`, `GroupJoin()` doesn't have a SQL equivalent because the data returned by SQL is record based, not hierarchical.)

ADVANCED TOPIC

Implementing an Outer Join with `GroupJoin()`

The earlier inner joins are *equi-joins* because they are based on an equivalent evaluation of the keys. Records appear in the resultant collection only if there are objects in both collections. On occasion, however, you might want to create a record even if the corresponding object doesn't exist. For example, rather than leaving the Marketing department out from the final department list simply because it doesn't have any employees, it would be preferable if we included it with an empty employee list. To accomplish this, we perform a left outer join using a combination of both `GroupJoin()` and `SelectMany()`, along with `DefaultIfEmpty()`. This is demonstrated in Listing 15.23 and Output 15.11.

LISTING 15.23: Implementing an Outer Join Using `GroupJoin()` with `SelectMany()`

```
using System;
using System.Linq;
// ...
        Department[] departments = CorporateData.Departments;
        Employee[] employees = CorporateData.Employees;

        var items = departments.GroupJoin(
            employees,
            department => department.Id,
            employee => employee.DepartmentId,
            (department, departmentEmployees) => new
            {
                department.Id,
                department.Name,
                Employees = departmentEmployees
            }).SelectMany(
                departmentRecord =>
                    departmentRecord.Employees.DefaultIfEmpty(),
                (departmentRecord, employee) => new
                {
                    departmentRecord.Id,
```

```
                    departmentRecord.Name,
                    departmentRecord.Employees
                }).Distinct();

        foreach (var item in items)
        {
            Console.WriteLine(item.Name);
            foreach (Employee employee in item.Employees)
            {
                Console.WriteLine("\t" + employee);
            }
        }
        //...
```

OUTPUT 15.11

```
Corporate
        Mark Michaelis (Chief Computer Nerd)
Human Resources
        Anne Beard (HR Director)
Engineering
        Michael Stokesbary (Senior Computer Wizard)
        Brian Jones (Enterprise Integration Guru)
        Kevin Bost (Programmer Extraordinaire)
        Thomas Heavey (Software Architect)
Information Technology
        Pat Dever (Enterprise Architect)
Philanthropy
        Eric Edmonds (Philanthropy Coordinator)
Marketing
```

Calling `SelectMany()`

On occasion, you may have collections of collections. Listing 15.24 provides an example of such a scenario. The `teams` array contains two teams, each with a string array of players.

LISTING 15.24: Calling `SelectMany()`

```
using System;
using System.Collections.Generic;
using System.Linq;
// ...
        (string Team, string[] Players)
```

```
    [] worldCup2006Finalists = new[]
{
    (
        TeamName: "France",
        Players: new string[]
        {
            "Fabien Barthez", "Gregory Coupet",
            "Mickael Landreau", "Eric Abidal",
            "Jean-Alain Boumsong", "Pascal Chimbonda",
            "William Gallas", "Gael Givet",
            "Willy Sagnol", "Mikael Silvestre",
            "Lilian Thuram", "Vikash Dhorasoo",
            "Alou Diarra", "Claude Makelele",
            "Florent Malouda", "Patrick Vieira",
            "Zinedine Zidane", "Djibril Cisse",
            "Thierry Henry", "Franck Ribery",
            "Louis Saha", "David Trezeguet",
            "Sylvain Wiltord",
        }
    ),
    (
        TeamName: "Italy",
        Players: new string[]
        {
            "Gianluigi Buffon", "Angelo Peruzzi",
            "Marco Amelia", "Cristian Zaccardo",
            "Alessandro Nesta", "Gianluca Zambrotta",
            "Fabio Cannavaro", "Marco Materazzi",
            "Fabio Grosso", "Massimo Oddo",
            "Andrea Barzagli", "Andrea Pirlo",
            "Gennaro Gattuso", "Daniele De Rossi",
            "Mauro Camoranesi", "Simone Perrotta",
            "Simone Barone", "Luca Toni",
            "Alessandro Del Piero", "Francesco Totti",
            "Alberto Gilardino", "Filippo Inzaghi",
            "Vincenzo Iaquinta",
        }
    )
};

IEnumerable<string> players =
    worldCup2006Finalists.SelectMany(
        team => team.Players);

Print(players);
//...
```

The output from this listing has each player's name displayed on its own line in the order in which it appears in the code. The difference between `Select()` and `SelectMany()` is that `Select()` would return two items, one corresponding to each item in the original collection. `Select()` may project out a transform from the original type, but the number of items would not change. For example, `teams.Select(team => team.Players)` will return an `IEnumerable<string[]>`.

In contrast, `SelectMany()` iterates across each item identified by the lambda expression (the array selected by `Select()` earlier) and hoists out each item into a new collection that includes a union of all items within the child collection. Instead of two arrays of players, `SelectMany()` combines each array selected and produces a single collection of all items.

More Standard Query Operators

Listing 15.25 shows code that uses some of the simpler APIs enabled by `Enumerable`; Output 15.12 shows the results.

Listing 15.25: More `System.Linq.Enumerable` Method Calls

```
using System;
using System.Collections.Generic;
using System.Linq;

public class Program
{
    public static void Main()
    {
        IEnumerable<object> stuff =
            new object[] { new object(), 1, 3, 5, 7, 9,
                "\"thing\"", Guid.NewGuid() };
        Print("Stuff: {0}", stuff);

        IEnumerable<int> even = new int[] { 0, 2, 4, 6, 8 };
        Print("Even integers: {0}", even);

        IEnumerable<int> odd = stuff.OfType<int>();
        Print("Odd integers: {0}", odd);

        IEnumerable<int> numbers = even.Union(odd);
        Print("Union of odd and even: {0}", numbers);
```

```
        Print("Union with even: {0}", numbers.Union(even));
        Print("Concat with odd: {0}", numbers.Concat(odd));
        Print("Intersection with even: {0}",
            numbers.Intersect(even));
        Print("Distinct: {0}", numbers.Concat(odd).Distinct());

        if (!numbers.SequenceEqual(
            numbers.Concat(odd).Distinct()))
        {
            throw new Exception("Unexpectedly unequal");
        }
        else
        {
            Console.WriteLine(
                @"Collection ""SequenceEquals""" +
                $" {nameof(numbers)}.Concat(odd).Distinct())");
        }
        Print("Reverse: {0}", numbers.Reverse());
        Print("Average: {0}", numbers.Average());
        Print("Sum: {0}", numbers.Sum());
        Print("Max: {0}", numbers.Max());
        Print("Min: {0}", numbers.Min());
    }

    private static void Print<T>(
            string format, IEnumerable<T> items)
            where T : notnull =>
        Console.WriteLine(format, string.Join(
            ", ", items));
    // ...
}
```

Output 15.12

```
Stuff: System.Object, 1, 3, 5, 7, 9, "thing"
24c24a41-ee05-41b9-958e-50dd12e3981e
Even integers: 0, 2, 4, 6, 8
Odd integers: 1, 3, 5, 7, 9
Union of odd and even: 0, 2, 4, 6, 8, 1, 3, 5, 7, 9
Union with even: 0, 2, 4, 6, 8, 1, 3, 5, 7, 9
Concat with odd: 0, 2, 4, 6, 8, 1, 3, 5, 7, 9, 1, 3, 5, 7, 9
Intersection with even: 0, 2, 4, 6, 8
Distinct: 0, 2, 4, 6, 8, 1, 3, 5, 7, 9
Collection "SequenceEquals" numbers.Concat(odd).Distinct())
Reverse: 9, 7, 5, 3, 1, 8, 6, 4, 2, 0
Average: 4.5
Sum: 45
```

```
Max: 9
Min: 0
```

None of the API calls in Listing 15.25 requires a lambda expression. Table 15.1 and Table 15.2 describe each method and provide an example. Included in `System.Linq.Enumerable` is a collection of aggregate functions that enumerate the collection and calculate a result (shown in Table 15.2). `Count` is one example of an aggregate function already shown in the chapter.

TABLE 15.1: Simpler Standard Query Operators

Comment Type	Description
`OfType<T>()`	Forms a query over a collection that returns only the items of a particular type, where the type is identified in the type parameter of the `OfType<T>()` method call.
`Union()`	Combines two collections to form a superset of all the items in both collections. The final collection does not include duplicate items even if the same item existed in both collections.
`Concat()`	Combines two collections to form a superset of both collections. Duplicate items are not removed from the resultant collection. `Concat()` will preserve the ordering. That is, concatenating `{A, B}` with `{C, D}` will produce `{A, B, C, D}`.
`Intersect()`	Extracts the collection of items that exist in both original collections.
`Distinct()`	Filters out duplicate items from a collection so that each item within the resultant collection is unique.
`SequenceEquals()`	Compares two collections and returns a Boolean indicating whether the collections are identical, including the order of items within the collection. (This is a very helpful message when testing expected results.)
`Reverse()`	Reverses the items within a collection so that they occur in reverse order when iterating over the collection.

TABLE 15.2: Aggregate Functions on `System.Linq.Enumerable`

Comment Type	Description
`Count()`	Provides a total count of the number of items within the collection
`Average()`	Calculates the average value for a numeric collection
`Sum()`	Computes the sum values within a numeric collection
`Max()`	Determines the maximum value among a collection of numeric values
`Min()`	Determines the minimum value among a collection of numeric values

Note that each method listed in Table 15.1 and Table 15.2 will trigger deferred execution.

ADVANCED TOPIC

`Queryable` Extensions for `IQueryable<T>`

One virtually identical interface to `IEnumerable<T>` is `IQueryable<T>`. Because `IQueryable<T>` derives from `IEnumerable<T>`, it has all the members of `IEnumerable<T>` that are declared directly (e.g., `GetEnumerator()`). Extension methods are not inherited, however, so `IQueryable<T>` doesn't have any of the `Enumerable` extension methods. Nevertheless, it does have a similar extending class called `System.Linq.Queryable` that adds to `IQueryable<T>` almost all of the same methods that `Enumerable` added to `IEnumerable<T>`. Therefore, it provides a very similar programming interface.

What makes `IQueryable<T>` unique is that it enables custom LINQ providers. A LINQ provider subdivides expressions into their constituent parts. Once divided, the expression can be translated into another language, serialized for remote execution, injected with an asynchronous execution pattern, and much more. Essentially, LINQ providers allow for an interception mechanism into a standard collection API; behavior relating to the queries and collection can be injected via this seemingly limitless functionality.

For example, LINQ providers allow for the translation of a query expression from C# into SQL that is then executed on a remote database. In so doing, the C# programmer can remain in their primary object-oriented language and leave the translation to SQL to the underlying LINQ provider. Through this type of expression, programming languages can span the impedance mismatch between the object-oriented world and the relational database.

In the case of `IQueryable<T>`, vigilance regarding deferred execution is even more critical. Imagine, for example, a LINQ provider that returns data from a database. Rather than retrieving the data from a database regardless of the selection criteria, the lambda expression would provide an implementation of `IQueryable<T>` that possibly includes context information such as the connection string, but not the data itself. The data retrieval wouldn't occur until the call to `GetEnumerator()` or even `MoveNext()`. However, the `GetEnumerator()` call is generally implicit, such as when iterating over the collection with `foreach` or calling an `Enumerable` method such as `Count<T>()` or `Cast<T>()`. Obviously, cases such as this require developers to be wary of the subtle and repeated calls to any expensive operation that deferred execution might involve. For example, if calling `GetEnumerator()` involves a distributed call over the network to a database, it would be wise to avoid unintentional duplicate calls to iterations with `Count()` or `foreach`.

Anonymous Types with LINQ

To support LINQ, an advanced API, only eight new language enhancements were made.[9] Two of these enhancements were anonymous types and implicit local variables. Even so, anonymous types have essentially been eclipsed by the introduction of C# tuple syntax.[10] In fact, with the sixth edition of this book, all the LINQ examples that previously leveraged anonymous types were updated to use tuples instead.

9. Starting in C# 3.0.
10. Starting in C# 7.0.

The remainder of the chapter covers the topic of anonymous types so that you can still make sense of the anonymous type language feature if you are working with code written prior to C# 7.0.

Anonymous Types

Anonymous types are data types that are declared by the compiler rather than through the explicit class definitions introduced in Chapter 6. As with anonymous functions, when the compiler sees an anonymous type, it does the work to make that class for you and then lets you use it as though you had declared it explicitly. Listing 15.26 shows such a declaration. The corresponding output is shown in Output 15.13.

Listing 15.26: Implicit Local Variables with Anonymous Types

```
using System;

public class Program
{
    public static void Main()
    {
        var patent1 =
            new
            {
                Title = "Bifocals",
                YearOfPublication = "1784"
            };
        var patent2 =
            new
            {
                Title = "Phonograph",
                YearOfPublication = "1877"
            };
        var patent3 =
            new
            {
                patent1.Title,
                // Renamed to show property naming
                Year = patent1.YearOfPublication
            };

        Console.WriteLine(
            $"{ patent1.Title } ({ patent1.YearOfPublication })");
        Console.WriteLine(
            $"{ patent2.Title } ({ patent2.YearOfPublication })");
```

```
            Console.WriteLine();
            Console.WriteLine(patent1);
            Console.WriteLine(patent2);

            Console.WriteLine();
            Console.WriteLine(patent3);
        }
    }
```

Output 15.13

```
Bifocals (1784)
Phonograph (1784)

{ Title = Bifocals, YearOfPublication = 1784 }
{ Title = Phonograph, YearOfPublication = 1877 }

{ Title = Bifocals, Year = 1784 }
```

Anonymous types are purely a C# feature, not a new kind of type in the runtime. When the compiler encounters the anonymous type syntax, it generates a CIL class with properties corresponding to the named values and data types in the anonymous type declaration.

BEGINNER TOPIC

Implicitly Typed Local Variables Reviewed (`var`)

Because an anonymous type has no name, it is not possible to declare a local variable as explicitly being of an anonymous type. Rather, the local variable's type is replaced with `var`. However, by no means does this indicate that implicitly typed variables are untyped. On the contrary, they are fully typed to the data type of the value they are assigned. If an implicitly typed variable is assigned an anonymous type, the underlying CIL code for the local variable declaration is of the type generated by the compiler. Similarly, if the implicitly typed variable is assigned a `string`, its data type in the underlying CIL is a `string`. In fact, there is no difference in the resultant CIL code for implicitly typed variables whose assignment is not an anonymous type (such as `string`) and those that are declared with an explicit type. If the declaration statement is string text = "This is a test of the...", the resultant CIL code is identical to an implicitly typed declaration, var text = "This is a test of the...".

The compiler determines the data type of the implicitly typed variable from the expression assigned. In an explicitly typed local variable with an initializer (string s = "hello";), the compiler first determines the type of s from the declared type on the left-hand side, then analyzes the right-hand side and verifies that the expression on the right-hand side is assignable to that type. In an implicitly typed local variable, the process is in some sense reversed. First, the right-hand side is analyzed to determine its type, and then the var is logically replaced with that type.

Although C# does not include a name for the anonymous type, it is strongly typed as well. For example, the properties of the type are fully accessible. In Listing 15.26, patent1.Title and patent2.YearOfPublication are called within the Console.WriteLine statement. Any attempts to call nonexistent members will result in compile-time errors. Even IntelliSense in IDEs such as Visual Studio works with the anonymous type.

You should use implicitly typed variable declarations sparingly. Obviously, for anonymous types, it is not possible to specify the data type, and the use of var is required. However, if the data type is not an anonymous type, it is frequently preferable to use the explicit data type.

As is the case generally, you should focus on making the semantics of the code more readable while also using the compiler to verify that the resultant variable is of the type you expect. To accomplish this with implicitly typed local variables, use them only when the type assigned to the implicitly typed variable is entirely obvious. For example, in var items = new Dictionary<string, List<Account>>();, the resultant code is more succinct and readable. In contrast, when the type is not obvious, such as when a method return is assigned, developers should favor an explicit variable type declaration such as the following:

```
Dictionary<string, List<Account>> dictionary = GetAccounts();
```

Selecting into Anonymous Types with LINQ

Lastly, capitalizing on anonymous types, we could create an `IEnumerable<T>` collection where T is an anonymous type (see Listing 15.27 and Output 15.14).

LISTING 15.27: Projection to an Anonymous Type

```
//...
IEnumerable<string> fileList = Directory.EnumerateFiles(
    rootDirectory, searchPattern);
var items = fileList.Select(
    file =>
    {
        FileInfo fileInfo = new(file);
        return new
        {
            FileName = fileInfo.Name,
            Size = fileInfo.Length
        };
    });
//...
```

OUTPUT 15.14

```
{ FileName = AssemblyInfo.cs, Size = 1704 }
{ FileName = CodeAnalysisRules.xml, Size = 735 }
{ FileName = CustomDictionary.xml, Size = 199 }
{ FileName = EssentialCSharp.sln, Size = 40415 }
{ FileName = EssentialCSharp.suo, Size = 454656 }
{ FileName = EssentialCSharp.vsmdi, Size = 499 }
{ FileName = EssentialCSharp.vssscc, Size = 256 }
{ FileName = intelliTechture.ConsoleTester.dll, Size = 24576 }
{ FileName = intelliTechture.ConsoleTester.pdb, Size = 30208 }
```

The output of an anonymous type automatically shows the property names and their values as part of the generated `ToString()` method associated with the anonymous type.

Projection using the `Select()` method is very powerful. We already saw how to filter a collection vertically (reducing the number of items in the collection) using the `Where()` standard query operator. Now, by using the `Select()` standard query operator, we can also reduce the collection horizontally (making fewer columns) or transform the data entirely. By adding support of anonymous types, we can `Select()` an arbitrary "object" by extracting only those pieces of the original collection that are desirable for the current algorithm but without having to declare a class to contain them.

More about Anonymous Types and Implicit Local Variables

In Listing 15.26, member names for the anonymous types are explicitly identified using the assignment of the value to the name for `patent1` and `patent2` (e.g., `Title = "Phonograph"`). However, if the value assigned is a property or field call, the name may default to the name of the field or property rather than explicitly specifying the value. For example, `patent3` is defined using a property named `Title` rather than an assignment to an explicit name. As Output 15.13 shows, the resultant property name is determined, by the compiler, to match the property from where the value was retrieved.

Both `patent1` and `patent2` have the same property names with the same data types. Therefore, the C# compiler generates only one data type for these two anonymous declarations. In contrast, `patent3` forces the compiler to create a second anonymous type because the property name for the patent year is different from that in `patent1` and `patent2`. Furthermore, if the order of the properties were switched between `patent1` and `patent2`, these two anonymous types would not be type-compatible. In other words, the requirements for two anonymous types to be type-compatible within the same assembly are a match in property names, data types, and order of properties. If these criteria are met, the types are compatible, even if they appear in different methods or classes. Listing 15.28 demonstrates the type incompatibilities.

LISTING 15.28: Type Safety and Immutability of Anonymous Types

```
public class Program
{
    public static void Main()
    {
        var patent1 =
            new
            {
                Title = "Bifocals",
                YearOfPublication = "1784"
            };

        var patent2 =
```

```
            new
            {
                YearOfPublication = "1877",
                Title = "Phonograph"
            };

        var patent3 =
            new
            {
                patent1.Title,
                Year = patent1.YearOfPublication
            };

        // ERROR: Cannot implicitly convert type
        //        'AnonymousType#1' to 'AnonymousType#2'
        //patent1 = patent2; //won't compile if uncommented
        // ERROR: Cannot implicitly convert type
        //        'AnonymousType#1' to 'AnonymousType#3'
        //patent1 = patent3; //won't compile if uncommented

        // ERROR: Property or indexer 'AnonymousType#1.Title'
        //        cannot be assigned to -- it is read-only'
        //patent1.Title = "Swiss Cheese";
            //won't compile if uncommented
    }
}
```

The first two compile-time errors assert that the types are not compatible, so they will not successfully convert from one to the other. The third compile-time error is caused by the reassignment of the `Title` property. Anonymous types are immutable, so it is a compile-time error to change a property on an anonymous type once it has been instantiated.

Although not shown in Listing 15.28, it is not possible to declare a method with an implicit data type parameter (`var`). Therefore, instances of anonymous types can be passed outside the method in which they are created in only two ways. First, if the method parameter is of type `object`, the anonymous type instance may be passed outside the method because the anonymous type will convert implicitly. A second way is to use method type inference, whereby the anonymous type instance is passed as a method type parameter that the compiler can successfully infer. Thus, calling `void Method<T>(T parameter)` using `Function(patent1)` would succeed, although the available operations on `parameter` within `Function()` are limited to those supported by `object`.

Although C# allows anonymous types such as the ones shown in Listing 15.26, it is generally not recommended that you define them in this way. Anonymous types provide critical functionality with support for projections,[11] such as joining/associating collections, as we discuss later in the chapter. Nevertheless, you should generally reserve anonymous type definitions for circumstances where they are required, such as aggregation of data from multiple types.

At the time that anonymous types were introduced, they were a breakthrough that solved an important problem: declaring a temporary type on the fly without the ceremony of having to declare a full type. Even so, they have several drawbacks, as detailed earlier. Fortunately, tuples[12] avoid these drawbacks and, in fact, essentially obviate the need for using anonymous types altogether. Specifically, tuples have the following advantages over anonymous types:

- Provide a named type that can be used anywhere a type can be used, including declarations and type parameters
- Available outside the method in which they are instantiated
- Avoid type "pollution" with types that are generated but rarely used

One way in which tuples differ from anonymous types is that anonymous types are reference types and tuples are value types. Whether this difference is advantageous to one approach or the other depends on the performance characteristics needed. If the tuple type is frequently copied and its memory footprint is more than 128 bits, a reference type is likely preferable. Otherwise, using a tuple will most likely be more performant—and a better choice to default to.

---

11. Starting in C# 3.0.
12. Starting in C# 7.0.

ADVANCED TOPIC

Anonymous Type Generation

Even though `Console.WriteLine()`'s implementation is to call `ToString()`, notice in Listing 15.26 that the output from `Console.WriteLine()` is not the default `ToString()`, which writes out the fully qualified data type name. Rather, the output is a list of `PropertyName = value` pairs, one for each property on the anonymous type. This occurs because the compiler overrides `ToString()` in the anonymous type code generation, so as to format the `ToString()` output as shown. Similarly, the generated type includes overriding implementations for `Equals()` and `GetHashCode()`.

The implementation of `ToString()` on its own is an important reason that variation in the order of properties causes a new data type to be generated. If two separate anonymous types, possibly in entirely separate types and even in separate namespaces, were unified and then the order of properties changed, changes in the order of properties on one implementation would have noticeable and possibly unacceptable effects on the other's `ToString()` results. Furthermore, at execution time, it is possible to reflect back on a type and examine the members of a type—even to call one of these members dynamically (determining at runtime which member to call). A variation in the order of members of two seemingly identical types could then trigger unexpected results. To avoid this problem, the C# designers decided to generate two different types.

ADVANCED TOPIC

Collection Initializers with Anonymous Types

You cannot have a collection initializer for an anonymous type, since the collection initializer requires a constructor call, and it is impossible to name the constructor. The workaround is to define a method such as `static List<T> CreateList<T>(T t) { return new List<T>(); }`. Method type inference allows the type parameter to be implied rather than specified explicitly, so this workaround successfully allows for the creation of a collection of anonymous types.

Another approach to initializing a collection of anonymous types is to use an array initializer. As it is not possible to specify the data type in the constructor, array initialization syntax allows for anonymous array initializers using `new[]` (see Listing 15.29).

Listing 15.29: Initializing Anonymous Type Arrays

```
using System;
using System.Collections.Generic;

public class Program
{
    public static void Main()
    {
        var worldCup2006Finalists = new[]
        {
            new
            {
                TeamName = "France",
                Players = new string[]
                {
                    "Fabien Barthez", "Gregory Coupet",
                    "Mickael Landreau", "Eric Abidal",
                    // ...
                }
            },
            new
            {
                TeamName = "Italy",
                Players = new string[]
                {
                    "Gianluigi Buffon", "Angelo Peruzzi",
                    "Marco Amelia", "Cristian Zaccardo",
                    // ...
                }
            }
        };

        Print(worldCup2006Finalists);
    }

    private static void Print<T>(IEnumerable<T> items)
    {
```

```
            foreach(T item in items)
            {
                Console.WriteLine(item);
            }
        }
    }
```

The resultant variable is an array of the anonymous type items, which must be homogeneous because it is an array.

Summary

This chapter described the internals of how the `foreach` loop works and explained which interfaces are required for its execution. In addition, developers frequently filter a collection so that there are fewer items and project the collection so that the items take a different form. Toward that end, this chapter discussed the details of how to use the standard query operators—LINQ introduced collection extension methods on the `System.Linq.Enumerable` class—to perform collection manipulation.

In the introduction to standard query operators, we detailed the process of deferred execution and emphasized how developers should take care to avoid unintentionally re-executing an expression via a subtle call that enumerates over the collection contents. The deferred execution and resultant implicit execution of standard query operators is a significant factor in code efficiency, especially when the query execution is expensive. Programmers should treat the query object as the query object, not the results, and should expect the query to execute fully even if it executed already. The query object doesn't know that the results will be the same as they were during a previous execution.

Listing 15.23 appeared in an Advanced Topic section because of the complexity of calling multiple standard query operators one after the other. Although requirements for similar execution may be commonplace, it is not necessary to rely on standard query operators directly. Query expressions,[13] a SQL-like syntax for

13. Starting in C# 3.0.

manipulating collections in a way that is frequently easier to code and read, are shown in the next chapter.

The chapter ended with a detailed look at anonymous types and explained why tuples are, in fact, a preferable approach if you have C# 7.0 or later.

16

LINQ with Query Expressions

The end of Chapter 15 showed a query using standard query operators for `GroupJoin()`, `SelectMany()`, and `Distinct()`. The result was a statement that spanned multiple lines and was rather more complex and difficult to comprehend than statements typically written using only features of earlier versions of C#. Modern programs, which manipulate rich data sets, often require such complex queries; it would therefore be advantageous if the language made them easier to read. Domain-specific query languages such as SQL make it much easier to read and understand a query but lack the full power of the C# language. That is why the C# language designers added **query expressions** syntax.[1] With query expressions, many standard query operator expressions are transformed into more readable code, much like SQL.

In this chapter, we introduce query expressions and use them to express many of the queries from Chapter 15.

1. Starting in C# 3.0.

Introducing Query Expressions

Two of the operations that developers most frequently perform are **filtering** the collection to eliminate unwanted items and **projecting** the collection so that the items take a different form. For example, given a collection of files, we could filter it to create a new collection of only the files with a `.cs` extension or only the files larger than 1 million bytes. We could also project the file collection to create a new collection that would contain both the path to the directory and the corresponding directory size. Query expressions provide straightforward syntaxes for both of these common operations. Listing 16.1 shows a query expression that filters a collection of strings; Output 16.1 shows the results.

LISTING 16.1: Simple Query Expression

```
public static class CSharp
{
    public static readonly ReadOnlyCollection<string> Keywords =
        new(
            new string[]
            {
                "abstract","add*","alias*","as","ascending*",
                "async*","await*","base","bool","break",
                "by*","byte","case","catch","char","checked",
                "class","const","continue","decimal","default",
                "delegate","descending*","do","double","dynamic*",
                "else","enum","equals*","event","explicit",
                "extern","false","finally","fixed","float","for",
                "foreach","from*","get*","global*","goto","group*",
                "if","implicit","in","int","interface","internal",
                "into*","is","join*","let*","lock","long",
                "nameof*", "namespace","new","nonnull*","null",
                "object","on*","operator","orderby*","out",
                "override","params","partial*","private",
                "protected","public","readonly","ref","remove*",
                "return","sbyte","sealed","select*","set*","short",
                "sizeof","stackalloc","static","string","struct",
                "switch","this","throw","true","try","typeof",
                "uint","ulong","unchecked","unsafe","ushort",
                "using","value*","var*","virtual","void","volatile",
                "when*","where*","while","yield*"
            }
        );
}
```

```
// ...
using System;
using System.Collections.Generic;
using System.Linq;
// ...
    private static void ShowContextualKeywords()
    {
        IEnumerable<string> selection =
            from word in CSharp.Keywords
            where !word.Contains('*')
            select word;

        foreach (string keyword in selection)
        {
            Console.Write(keyword + " ");
        }
    }
    //...
```

Output 16.1

```
abstract as base bool break byte case catch char checked class const
continue decimal default delegate do double else enum event explicit
extern false finally fixed float for foreach goto if implicit in int
interface internal is lock long namespace new null object operator out
override params private protected public readonly ref return sbyte
sealed short sizeof stackalloc static string struct switch this throw
true try typeof uint ulong unchecked unsafe ushort using virtual void
volatile while
```

In this query expression, `selection` is assigned the collection of C# reserved keywords. The query expression in this example includes a `where` clause that filters out the noncontextual keywords.

Query expressions always begin with a `from` clause and end with a `select` clause or a `group` clause, identified by the `from`, `select`, or `group` contextual keyword, respectively. The identifier `word` in the `from` clause is called a **range variable**; it represents each item in the collection, much as the loop variable in a `foreach` loop represents each item in a collection.

Developers familiar with SQL will notice that query expressions have a syntax that is similar to that of SQL. This design was deliberate—it was intended that programmers who already know SQL should find it easy to learn LINQ. However, there are some obvious differences. The first difference that most SQL-experienced developers will notice is that the C# query expression shown here has the clauses in the following order: `from`, then `where`, then `select`. The equivalent SQL query puts the `SELECT` clause first, followed by the `FROM` clause, and finally the `WHERE` clause.

One reason for this change in sequence is to enable use of IntelliSense, the feature of the IDE whereby the editor produces helpful user interface elements such as drop-down lists that describe the members of a given object. Because `from` appears first and identifies the string array `Keywords` as the data source, the code editor can deduce that the range variable `word` is of type `string`. When you are entering the code into the editor and reach the dot following `word`, the editor displays only the members of `string`.

If the `from` clause appeared after the `select`, like it does in SQL, as you were typing in the query the editor would not know what the data type of `word` was, so it would not be able to display a list of `word`'s members. In Listing 16.1, for example, it wouldn't be possible to predict that `Contains()` is a possible member of `word`.

The C# query expression order also more closely matches the order in which operations are logically performed. When evaluating the query, you begin by identifying the collection (described by the `from` clause), then filter out the unwanted items (with the `where` clause), and finally describe the desired result (with the `select` clause).

Finally, the C# query expression order ensures that the rules for "where" (range) variables are in scope are mostly consistent with the scoping rules for local variables. For example, a (range) variable must be declared by a clause (typically a `from` clause) before the variable can be used, much as a local variable must always be declared before it can be used.

Projection

The result of a query expression is a collection of type `IEnumerable<T>` or `IQueryable<T>`.[2] The actual type `T` is inferred from the `select` or `group by`

2. The result of a query expression is, as a practical matter, almost always `IEnumerable<T>` or a type derived from it. It is legal, though somewhat perverse, to create an implementation of the query methods that return other types; there is no requirement in the language that the result of a query expression be convertible to `IEnumerable<T>`.

clause. In Listing 16.1, for example, the compiler knows that `Keywords` is of type `string[]`, which is convertible to `IEnumerable<string>`, and it deduces that `word` is therefore of type `string`. The query ends with `select word`, which means the result of the query expression must be a collection of strings, so the type of the query expression is `IEnumerable<string>`.

In this case, the "input" and the "output" of the query are both a collection of strings. However, the output type can be quite different from the input type if the expression in the `select` clause is of an entirely different type. Consider the query expression in Listing 16.2 and its corresponding output in Output 16.2.

Listing 16.2: Projection Using Query Expressions

```
using System;
using System.Collections.Generic;
using System.IO;
using System.Linq;
// ...
    public static void List1
        (string rootDirectory, string searchPattern)
    {
        IEnumerable<string> fileNames = Directory.GetFiles(
            rootDirectory, searchPattern);

        IEnumerable<FileInfo> fileInfos =
            from fileName in fileNames
            select new FileInfo(fileName);

        foreach (FileInfo fileInfo in fileInfos)
        {
            Console.WriteLine(
                $@".{ fileInfo.Name } ({
                    fileInfo.LastWriteTime })");
        }
    }
    //...
```

Output 16.2

```
Account.cs (11/22/2011 11:56:11 AM)
Bill.cs (8/10/2011 9:33:55 PM)
Contact.cs (8/19/2011 11:40:30 PM)
Customer.cs (11/17/2011 2:02:52 AM)
```

```
Employee.cs (8/17/2011 1:33:22 AM)
Person.cs (10/22/2011 10:00:03 PM)
```

This query expression results in an `IEnumerable<FileInfo>` rather than the `IEnumerable<string>` data type returned by `Directory.GetFiles()`. The `select` clause of the query expression can potentially project out a data type that differs from that collected by the `from` clause expression.

In this example, the type `FileInfo` was chosen because it has the two relevant fields needed for the desired output: the filename and the last write time. There might not be such a convenient type if you needed other information not captured in the `FileInfo` object. Tuples[3] provide a convenient and concise way to project the exact data you need without having to find or create an explicit type. Listing 16.3 provides output similar to that in Listing 16.2, but uses tuple syntax rather than `FileInfo`.

Listing 16.3: Tuples within Query Expressions

```
using System;
using System.IO;
using System.Linq;
// ...
    public static void List2
        (string rootDirectory, string searchPattern)
    {
        var fileNames = Directory.EnumerateFiles(
            rootDirectory, searchPattern);
        var fileResults =
            from fileName in fileNames
            select
            (
                Name: fileName,
                LastWriteTime: File.GetLastWriteTime(fileName)
            );

        foreach (var fileResult in fileResults)
        {
            Console.WriteLine(
                $@"{ fileResult.Name } ({
                    fileResult.LastWriteTime })");
```

3. Anonymous types used prior to C# 7.0.

```
        }
    }
    //...
```

In this example, the query projects out only the filename and its last file write time. A projection such as the one in Listing 16.3 makes little difference when working with something small, such as `FileInfo`. However, "horizontal" projection that filters down the amount of data associated with each item in the collection is extremely powerful when the amount of data is significant and retrieving it (perhaps from a different computer over the Internet) is expensive. Rather than retrieving all the data when a query executes, the use of a tuple enables the capability of storing and retrieving only the required data into the collection.

Imagine, for example, a large database that has tables with 30 or more columns. If there were no tuples, developers would be required either to use objects containing unnecessary information or to define small, specialized classes useful only for storing the specific data required. Instead, tuples enable support for types to be defined by the compiler—types that contain only the data needed for their immediate scenario. Other scenarios can have a different projection of only the properties needed for that scenario.

BEGINNER TOPIC

Deferred Execution with Query Expressions

Queries written using query expression notation exhibit deferred execution, just as the queries written in Chapter 15 did. Consider again the assignment of a query object to variable `selection` in Listing 16.1. The creation of the query and the assignment to the variable do not execute the query; rather, they simply build an object that represents the query. The method `word.Contains("*")` is not called when the query object is created. Instead, the query expression saves the selection criteria to be used when iterating over the collection identified by the `selection` variable.

To demonstrate this point, consider Listing 16.4 and the corresponding output (Output 16.3).

LISTING 16.4: Deferred Execution and Query Expressions (Example 1)

```
using System;
using System.Collections.Generic;
using System.Linq;
// ...
    private static void ShowContextualKeywords2()
    {
        IEnumerable<string> selection = from word in CSharp.Keywords
                                        where IsKeyword(word)
                                        select word;
        Console.WriteLine("Query created.");
        foreach(string keyword in selection)
        {
            // No space output here
            Console.Write(keyword);
        }
    }

    // The side effect of console output is included
    // in the predicate to demonstrate deferred execution;
    // predicates with side effects are a poor practice in
    // production code
    private static bool IsKeyword(string word)
    {
        if(word.Contains('*'))
        {
            Console.Write(" ");
            return true;
        }
        else
        {
            return false;
        }
    }
    //...
```

OUTPUT 16.3

```
Query created.
 add* alias* ascending* async* await* by* descending* dynamic*
equals* from* get* global* group* into* join* let* nameof* nonnull*
on* orderby* partial* remove* select* set* value* var* where* when*
yield*
```

In Listing 16.4, no space is output within the `foreach` loop. The side effect of printing a space when the predicate `IsKeyword()` is executed happens when the query is iterated over—not when the query is created. Thus, although `selection` is a collection (it is of type `IEnumerable<T>`, after all), at the time of assignment everything following the `from` clause serves as the selection criteria. Not until we begin to iterate over `selection` are the criteria applied.

Now consider a second example (see Listing 16.5 and Output 16.4).

Listing 16.5: Deferred Execution and Query Expressions (Example 2)

```
using System;
using System.Collections.Generic;
using System.Linq;
// ...
    private static void CountContextualKeywords()
    {
        int delegateInvocations = 0;
        string func(string text)
        {
            delegateInvocations++;
            return text;
        }

        IEnumerable<string> selection =
            from keyword in CSharp.Keywords
            where keyword.Contains('*')
            select func(keyword);


        Console.WriteLine(
            $"1. delegateInvocations={ delegateInvocations }");

        // Executing count should invoke func once for
        // each item selected
        Console.WriteLine(
            $"2. Contextual keyword count={ selection.Count() }");

        Console.WriteLine(
            $"3. delegateInvocations={ delegateInvocations }");

        // Executing count should invoke func once for
        // each item selected
        Console.WriteLine(
            $"4. Contextual keyword count={ selection.Count() }");
```

```
        Console.WriteLine(
            $"5. delegateInvocations={ delegateInvocations }");

        // Cache the value so future counts will not trigger
        // another invocation of the query
        List<string> selectionCache = selection.ToList();

        Console.WriteLine(
            $"6. delegateInvocations={ delegateInvocations }");

        // Retrieve the count from the cached collection
        Console.WriteLine(
            $"7. selectionCache count={ selectionCache.Count }");

        Console.WriteLine(
            $"8. delegateInvocations={ delegateInvocations }");
    }
    //...
```

OUTPUT 16.4

```
1. delegateInvocations=0
2. Contextual keyword count=28
3. delegateInvocations=28
4. Contextual keyword count=28
5. delegateInvocations=56
6. delegateInvocations=84
7. selectionCache count=28
8. delegateInvocations=84
```

Rather than defining a separate method, Listing 16.5 uses a statement lambda that counts the number of times the method is called.

Two things in the output are remarkable. First, after `selection` is assigned, `DelegateInvocations` remains at zero. At the time of assignment to `selection`, no iteration over `Keywords` is performed. If `Keywords` were a property, the property call would run—in other words, the `from` clause executes at the time of assignment. However, neither the projection, nor the filtering, nor anything after the `from` clause will execute until the code iterates over the values within `selection`. It is as though at the time of assignment, `selection` would more appropriately be called "query."

Once we call `ToList()`, however, a term such as `selection` or `Items` or something that indicates a container or collection is appropriate because we begin to count the items within the collection. In other words, the variable `selection` serves the dual purpose of saving the query information and acting like a container from which the data is retrieved.

A second important characteristic of Output 16.4 is that calling `Count()` a second time causes `func` to again be invoked once on each item selected. Given that `selection` behaves both as a query and as a collection, requesting the count requires that the query be executed again by iterating over the `IEnumerable<string>` collection that `selection` refers to and counting the items. The C# compiler does not know whether anyone has modified the strings in the array such that the count would now be different, so the counting has to happen anew every time to ensure that the answer is correct and up-to-date. Similarly, a `foreach` loop over `selection` would trigger `func` to be called again for each item. The same is true of all the other extension methods provided via `System.Linq.Enumerable`.

ADVANCED TOPIC

Implementing Deferred Execution

Deferred execution is implemented by using delegates and expression trees. A delegate provides the ability to create and manipulate a reference to a method that contains an expression that can be invoked later. An expression tree similarly provides the ability to create and manipulate information about an expression that can be examined and manipulated later.

In Listing 16.5, the predicate expressions of the `where` clauses and the projection expressions of the `select` clauses are transformed by the compiler into expression lambdas, and then the lambdas are transformed into delegate creations. The result of the query expression is an object that holds references to these delegates. Only when the query results are iterated over does the query object actually execute the delegates.

Filtering

In Listing 16.1, a `where` clause filters out reserved keywords but not contextual keywords. This clause filters the collection "vertically": If you think of the collection as a vertical list of items, the `where` clause makes that vertical list shorter so that the collection holds fewer items. The filter criteria are expressed with a **predicate**—a lambda expression that returns a `bool` such as `word.Contains()` (as in Listing 16.1) or `File.GetLastWriteTime(fileName) < DateTime.Now.AddMonths(-1)`. The latter is shown in Listing 16.6, whose output appears in Output 16.5.

LISTING 16.6: Query Expression Filtering Using `where`

```
using System;
using System.Collections.Generic;
using System.IO;
using System.Linq;
// ...
    public static void FindMonthOldFiles(
        string rootDirectory, string searchPattern)
    {
        IEnumerable<FileInfo> files =
            from fileName in Directory.EnumerateFiles(
                rootDirectory, searchPattern)
            where File.GetLastWriteTime(fileName) <
                DateTime.Now.AddMonths(-1)
            select new FileInfo(fileName);

        foreach(FileInfo file in files)
        {
            // As a simplification, the current directory is
            // assumed to be a subdirectory of
            // rootDirectory
            string relativePath = file.FullName.Substring(
                Directory.GetCurrentDirectory().Length);
            Console.WriteLine(
                $".{ relativePath } ({ file.LastWriteTime })");
        }
    }
    //...
```

Output 16.5

```
.\TestData\Bill.cs (8/10/2011 9:33:55 PM)
.\TestData\Contact.cs (8/19/2011 11:40:30 PM)
.\TestData\Employee.cs (8/17/2011 1:33:22 AM)
.\TestData\Person.cs (10/22/2011 10:00:03 PM)
```

Sorting

To order the items using a query expression, you can use the `orderby` clause, as shown in Listing 16.7.

Listing 16.7: Sorting Using a Query Expression with an `orderby` Clause

```
using System;
using System.Collections.Generic;
using System.Linq;
using System.IO;
// ...
    public static void ListByFileSize1(
        string rootDirectory, string searchPattern)
    {
        IEnumerable<string> fileNames =
            from fileName in Directory.EnumerateFiles(
                rootDirectory, searchPattern)
            orderby (new FileInfo(fileName)).Length descending,
                fileName
            select fileName;

        foreach(string fileName in fileNames)
        {
            Console.WriteLine(fileName);
        }
    }
    //...
```

Listing 16.7 uses the `orderby` clause to sort the files returned by `Directory.GetFiles()` first by file size in descending order, and then by filename in ascending order. Multiple sort criteria are separated by commas, such that first the items are ordered by size, and then, if the size is the same, they are ordered by filename. `ascending` and `descending` are contextual keywords indicating the sort order direction. Specifying the order as ascending or descending is optional; if the direction is omitted (as it is here on `filename`), the default is `ascending`.

The `let` Clause

Listing 16.8 includes a query that is very similar to the query in Listing 16.7, except that the type argument of `IEnumerable<T>` is `FileInfo`. This query has a problem, however: We have to redundantly create a `FileInfo` twice, in both the `orderby` clause and the `select` clause.

Listing 16.8: Projecting a `FileInfo` Collection and Sorting by File Size

```
using System;
using System.Collections.Generic;
using System.Linq;
using System.IO;
// ...
    public static void ListByFileSize2(
        string rootDirectory, string searchPattern)
    {
        IEnumerable<FileInfo> files =
            from fileName in Directory.EnumerateFiles(
                rootDirectory, searchPattern)
            orderby new FileInfo(fileName).Length, fileName
            select new FileInfo(fileName);

        foreach (FileInfo file in files)
        {
            //  As a simplification, the current directory
            //  is assumed to be a subdirectory of
            //  rootDirectory
            string relativePath = file.FullName.Substring(
                Directory.GetCurrentDirectory().Length);
            Console.WriteLine(
                $".{ relativePath }({ file.Length })");
        }
    }
    //...
```

Unfortunately, although the end result is correct, Listing 16.8 ends up instantiating a `FileInfo` object twice for each item in the source collection, which is wasteful and unnecessary. To avoid this kind of unnecessary and potentially expensive overhead, you can use a `let` clause, as demonstrated in Listing 16.9.

The `let` clause introduces a new range variable that can hold the value of an expression that is used throughout the remainder of the query expression. You can add as many `let` clauses as you like; simply insert each as an additional clause to

LISTING 16.9: Ordering the Results in a Query Expression

```
//...
IEnumerable<FileInfo> files =
    from fileName in Directory.EnumerateFiles(
        rootDirectory, searchPattern)
    let file = new FileInfo(fileName)
    orderby file.Length, fileName
    select file;
//...
```

the query after the first `from` clause but before the final `select`/`group by` clause.

Grouping

A common data manipulation scenario is the grouping of related items. In SQL, this generally involves aggregating the items to produce a summary or total or some other aggregate value. LINQ, however, is notably more expressive. LINQ expressions allow for individual items to be grouped into a series of subcollections, and those groups can then be associated with items in the collection being queried. For example, Listing 16.10 and Output 16.6 demonstrate how to group together the contextual keywords and the regular keywords.

LISTING 16.10: Grouping Together Query Results

```
using System;
using System.Collections.Generic;
using System.Linq;
// ...
    private static void GroupKeywords1()
    {
        IEnumerable<IGrouping<bool, string>> selection =
            from word in CSharp.Keywords
            group word by word.Contains('*');

        foreach(IGrouping<bool, string> wordGroup
            in selection)
        {
            Console.WriteLine(Environment.NewLine + "{0}:",
                wordGroup.Key ?
                    "Contextual Keywords" : "Keywords");
            foreach(string keyword in wordGroup)
```

```
            {
                Console.Write(" " +
                    (wordGroup.Key ?
                        keyword.Replace("*", null) : keyword));
            }
        }
    }
    //...
```

Output 16.6

```
Keywords:
abstract as base bool break byte case catch char checked class
const continue decimal default delegate do double else enum event
explicit extern false finally fixed float for foreach goto if
implicit in int interface internal is lock long namespace new null
operator out override object params private protected public
readonly ref return sbyte sealed short sizeof stackalloc static
string struct switch this throw true try typeof uint ulong unsafe
ushort using virtual unchecked void volatile while
Contextual Keywords:
 add alias ascending async await by descending dynamic equals from
get global group into join let nameof nonnull on orderby partial remove
select set value var where yield
```

There are several things to note in Listing 16.10. First, the query result is a sequence of elements of type `IGrouping<bool, string>`. The first type argument indicates that the "group key" expression following `by` was of type `bool`, and the second type argument indicates that the "group element" expression following `group` was of type `string`. That is, the query produces a sequence of groups where the Boolean key is the same for each `string` in the group.

Because a query with a `group by` clause produces a sequence of collections, the common pattern for iterating over the results is to create nested `foreach` loops. In Listing 16.10, the outer loop iterates over the groupings and prints out the type of keyword as a header. The nested `foreach` loop prints each keyword in the group as an item below the header.

The result of this query expression is itself a sequence, which you can then query like any other sequence. Listing 16.11 and Output 16.7 show how to create an additional query that adds a projection onto a query that produces a sequence of groups. (The next section, on query continuations, shows a more pleasant syntax for adding more query clauses to a complete query.)

Listing 16.11: Selecting a Tuple Following the `group` Clause

```
using System;
using System.Collections.Generic;
using System.Linq;
// ...
    private static void GroupKeywords1()
    {
        IEnumerable<IGrouping<bool, string>> keywordGroups =
            from word in CSharp.Keywords
            group word by word.Contains('*');

        IEnumerable<(bool IsContextualKeyword,
            IGrouping<bool, string> Items)> selection =
            from groups in keywordGroups
            select
            (
                IsContextualKeyword: groups.Key,
                Items: groups
            );

        foreach (
            (bool isContextualKeyword, IGrouping<bool, string> items)
                in selection)
        {

            Console.WriteLine(Environment.NewLine + "{0}:",
                isContextualKeyword ?
                    "Contextual Keywords" : "Keywords");
            foreach (string keyword in items)
            {
                Console.Write(" " + keyword.Replace("*", null));
            }
        }
    }
    //...
```

Output 16.7

```
Keywords:
 abstract as base bool break byte case catch char checked class
const continue decimal default delegate do double else enum
event explicit extern false finally fixed float for foreach goto if
implicit in int interface internal is lock long namespace new null
operator out override object params private protected public
readonly ref return sbyte sealed short sizeof stackalloc static
string struct switch this throw true try typeof uint ulong unsafe
```

```
ushort using virtual unchecked void volatile while
Contextual Keywords:
 add alias ascending async await by descending dynamic equals from
get global group into join let nameof nonnull on orderby partial remove
select set value var where yield
```

The `group` clause results in a query that produces a collection of `IGrouping<TKey, TElement>` objects—just as the `GroupBy()` standard query operator did (see Chapter 15). The `select` clause in the subsequent query uses a tuple to effectively rename `IGrouping<TKey, TElement>.Key` to `IsContextualKeyword` and to name the subcollection property `Items`. With this change, the nested `foreach` loop uses `wordGroup.Items` rather than `wordGroup` directly, as shown in Listing 16.10. Another potential item to add to the tuple would be a count of the items within the subcollection. This functionality is already available through LINQ's `wordGroup.Items.Count()` method, however, so the benefit of adding it to the anonymous type directly is questionable.

Query Continuation with `into`

As you saw in Listing 16.11, you can use an existing query as the input to a second query. However, it is not necessary to write an entirely new query expression when you want to use the results of one query as the input to another. You can extend any query with a **query continuation clause** using the contextual keyword `into`. A query continuation is nothing more than syntactic sugar for creating two queries and using the first as the input to the second. The range variable introduced by the `into` clause (`groups` in Listing 16.11) becomes the range variable for the remainder of the query; any previous range variables are logically a part of the earlier query and cannot be used in the query continuation. Listing 16.12 rewrites the code of Listing 16.11 to use a query continuation instead of two queries.

Listing 16.12: Selecting without the Query Continuation

```
using System;
using System.Collections.Generic;
using System.Linq;
// ...
    private static void GroupKeywords1()
    {
        IEnumerable<(bool IsContextualKeyword,
```

```
            IGrouping<bool, string> Items)> selection =
            from word in CSharp.Keywords
            group word by word.Contains('*')
                into groups
                select
                (
                    IsContextualKeyword: groups.Key,
                    Items: groups
                );
        // ...
    }
    //...
```

The ability to run additional queries on the results of an existing query using `into` is not specific to queries ending with `group` clauses, but rather can be applied to all query expressions. Query continuation is simply a shorthand for writing query expressions that consume the results of other query expressions. You can think of `into` as a "pipeline operator," because it "pipes" the results of the first query into the second query. You can arbitrarily chain together many queries in this way.

Flattening Sequences of Sequences with Multiple `from` Clauses

It is often desirable to "flatten" a sequence of sequences into a single sequence. For example, each member of a sequence of customers might have an associated sequence of orders, or each member of a sequence of directories might have an associated sequence of files. The `SelectMany` sequence operator (discussed in Chapter 15) concatenates together all the subsequences; to do the same thing with query expression syntax, you can use multiple `from` clauses, as shown in Listing 16.13.

Listing 16.13: Multiple Selection

```
var selection =
    from word in CSharp.Keywords
    from character in word
    select character;
```

The preceding query will produce the sequence of characters `a`, `b`, `s`, `t`, `r`, `a`, `c`, `t`, `a`, `d`, `d`, `*`, `a`, `l`, `i`, `a`, ...

Multiple `from` clauses can also be used to produce a **Cartesian product**—the set of all possible combinations of several sequences—as shown in Listing 16.14.

LISTING 16.14: Cartesian Product

```
var numbers = new[] { 1, 2, 3 };
IEnumerable<(string Word, int Number)> product =
    from word in CSharp.Keywords
    from number in numbers
    select (word, number);
```

This query would produce a sequence of pairs (`abstract`, `1`), (`abstract`, `2`), (`abstract`, `3`), (`as`, `1`), (`as`, `2`), ...

BEGINNER TOPIC

Distinct Members

Often, it is desirable to return only distinct (i.e., unique) items from within a collection, discarding any duplicates. Query expressions do not have an explicit syntax for distinct members, but such functionality is available via the query operator `Distinct()`, which was introduced in Chapter 15. To apply a query operator to a query expression, the expression must be enclosed in parentheses so that the compiler does not think that the call to `Distinct()` is a part of the `select` clause. Listing 16.15 gives an example; Output 16.8 shows the results.

LISTING 16.15: Obtaining Distinct Members from a Query Expression

```
using System;
using System.Linq;
using System.Collections.Generic;
// ...
    public static void ListMemberNames()
    {
        IEnumerable<string> enumerableMethodNames = (
            from method in typeof(Enumerable).GetMembers(
                System.Reflection.BindingFlags.Static |
                System.Reflection.BindingFlags.Public)
                orderby method.Name
                select method.Name).Distinct();
        foreach(string method in enumerableMethodNames)
```

```
        {
            Console.Write($"{ method }, ");
        }
    }
    //...
```

Output 16.8

```
Aggregate, All, Any, Append, AsEnumerable, Average, Cast, Chunk,
Concat, Contains, Count, DefaultIfEmpty, Distinct, DistinctBy,
ElementAt, ElementAtOrDefault, Empty, Except, ExceptBy, First,
FirstOrDefault, GroupBy, GroupJoin, Intersect, IntersectBy, Join,
Last, LastOrDefault, LongCount, Max, MaxBy, Min, MinBy, OfType,
Order, OrderBy, OrderByDescending, OrderDescending, Prepend,
Range, Repeat, Reverse, Select, SelectMany, SequenceEqual, Single,
SingleOrDefault, Skip, SkipLast, SkipWhile, Sum, Take, TakeLast,
TakeWhile, ThenBy, ThenByDescending, ToArray, ToDictionary,
ToHashSet, ToList, ToLookup, TryGetNonEnumeratedCount, Union,
UnionBy, Where, Zip,
```

In this example, `typeof(Enumerable).GetMembers()` returns a list of all the members (methods, properties, and so on) for `System.Linq.Enumerable`. However, many of these members are overloaded, sometimes more than once. Rather than displaying the same member multiple times, `Distinct()` is called from the query expression. This eliminates the duplicate names from the list. (We cover the details of `typeof()` and reflection [where methods like `GetMembers()` are available] in Chapter 18.)

Query Expressions Are Just Method Invocations

Somewhat surprisingly, adding query expressions[4] required no changes to the Common Language Runtime (CLR) or to the Common Intermediate Language (CIL). Rather, the C# compiler simply translates query expressions into a series of method calls. Consider, for example, the query expression from Listing 16.1, a portion of which appears in Listing 16.16.

4. Starting in C# 3.0.

LISTING 16.16: Simple Query Expression

```
private static void ShowContextualKeywords1()
{
    IEnumerable<string> selection =
        from word in CSharp.Keywords
        where !word.Contains('*')
        select word;
    // ...
}
```

After compilation, the expression from Listing 16.16 is converted to an `IEnumerable<T>` extension method call from `System.Linq.Enumerable`, as shown in Listing 16.17.

LISTING 16.17: Query Expression Translated to Standard Query Operator Syntax

```
private static void ShowContextualKeywords2()
{
    IEnumerable<string> selection =
        CSharp.Keywords.Where(word => !word.Contains('*'));
    // ...
}
```

As discussed in Chapter 15, the lambda expression is then itself translated by the compiler to emit a method with the body of the lambda, and its usage entails allocation of a delegate to that method.

Every query expression can (and must) be translated into method calls, but not every sequence of method calls has a corresponding query expression. For example, there is no query expression equivalent for the extension method `TakeWhile<T>(Func<T, bool> predicate)`, which repeatedly returns items from the collection as long as the predicate returns `true`.

For those queries that do have both a method call form and a query expression form, which is better? This is a judgment call. Some queries are better suited for query expressions, whereas others are more readable as method invocations.

Guidelines

DO use query expression syntax to make queries easier to read, particularly if they involve complex `from`, `let`, `join`, or `group` clauses.

CONSIDER using the standard query operators (method call form) if the query involves operations that do not have a query expression syntax, such as `Count()`, `TakeWhile()`, or `Distinct()`.

Summary

This chapter introduced a new syntax—namely, query expressions. Readers familiar with SQL will immediately see the similarities between query expressions and SQL. However, query expressions also introduce additional functionality, such as grouping into a hierarchical set of new objects, which is unavailable with SQL. All of the functionality of query expressions was already available via standard query operators, but query expressions frequently provide a simpler syntax for expressing such a query. Whether standard query operators or query expression syntax is used, however, the end result is a significant improvement in the way developers can code against collection APIs—an improvement that ultimately provides a paradigm shift in the way object-oriented languages are able to interface with relational databases.

In the next chapter, we continue our discussion of collections by investigating some of the .NET framework collection types and exploring how to define custom collections.

17

Building Custom Collections

Chapter 15 covered the standard query operators—that is, the extension methods on `IEnumerable<T>` that provide methods common to all collections. However, these operators do not make all collections equally suited for all tasks; there is still a need for different collection types. Some collections are better suited to searching by key, whereas others are better suited to accessing items by position. Some collections act like queues: The first element in is the first out. Others are more like stacks: The first element in is the last out. Others are not ordered at all.

The .NET frameworks provide a plethora of collection types suited to many of the scenarios in which collections are needed. This chapter introduces some of these collection types and the interfaces they implement. It also describes how to create custom-built collections that support standard functionality, such as indexing. In addition, it explores the use of the `yield return` statement to create classes and methods that implement `IEnumerable<T>`. This feature[1] greatly simplifies implementation of collections that can be enumerated with the `foreach` statement.

Many nongeneric collection classes and interfaces are available in the Microsoft .NET Framework, but in general, these exist today only for backward compatibility with code written before generics came into use. The generic collection types are both faster, because they avoid boxing costs, and more type-safe than the nongeneric collections. Thus, new code should almost always use the generic collection types

1. Starting in C# 2.0.

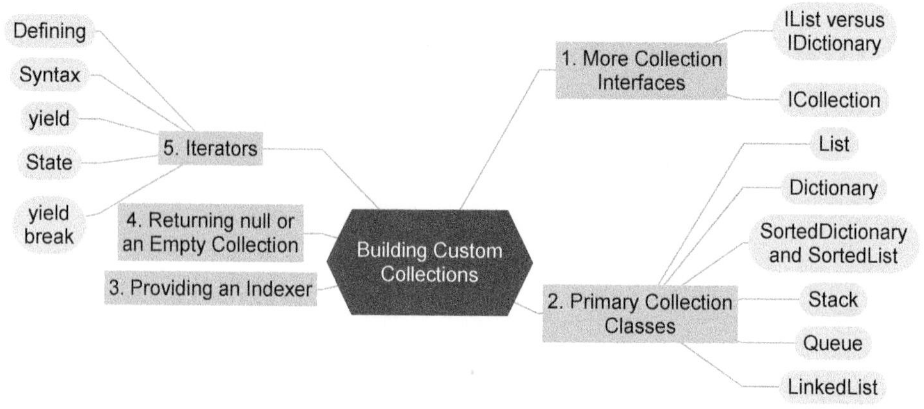

exclusively. Throughout this book, we assume that you are primarily using generic collection types.

More Collection Interfaces

We've already seen how collections implement `IEnumerable<T>`, the primary interface that enables iteration over the elements of a collection. Many additional interfaces exist that are implemented by more complex collections. Figure 17.1 shows the hierarchy of interfaces implemented by collection classes.

These interfaces provide a standard way to perform common tasks such as iterating, indexing, and counting elements in a collection. This section examines these interfaces (at least all of the generic ones), starting at the bottom of Figure 17.1 and moving upward.

`IList<T>` versus `IDictionary<TKey, TValue>`

An English-language dictionary can be thought of as a collection of definitions. A specific definition can be rapidly accessed by looking up its associated "key"—that is, the word being defined. A dictionary collection class is similarly a collection of values, in which each value can be rapidly accessed by using its associated unique key. Note, however, that a language dictionary typically stores the definitions sorted alphabetically by key; a dictionary class might choose to do so but typically does not. Dictionary collections are best thought of as an unordered list of keys and associated

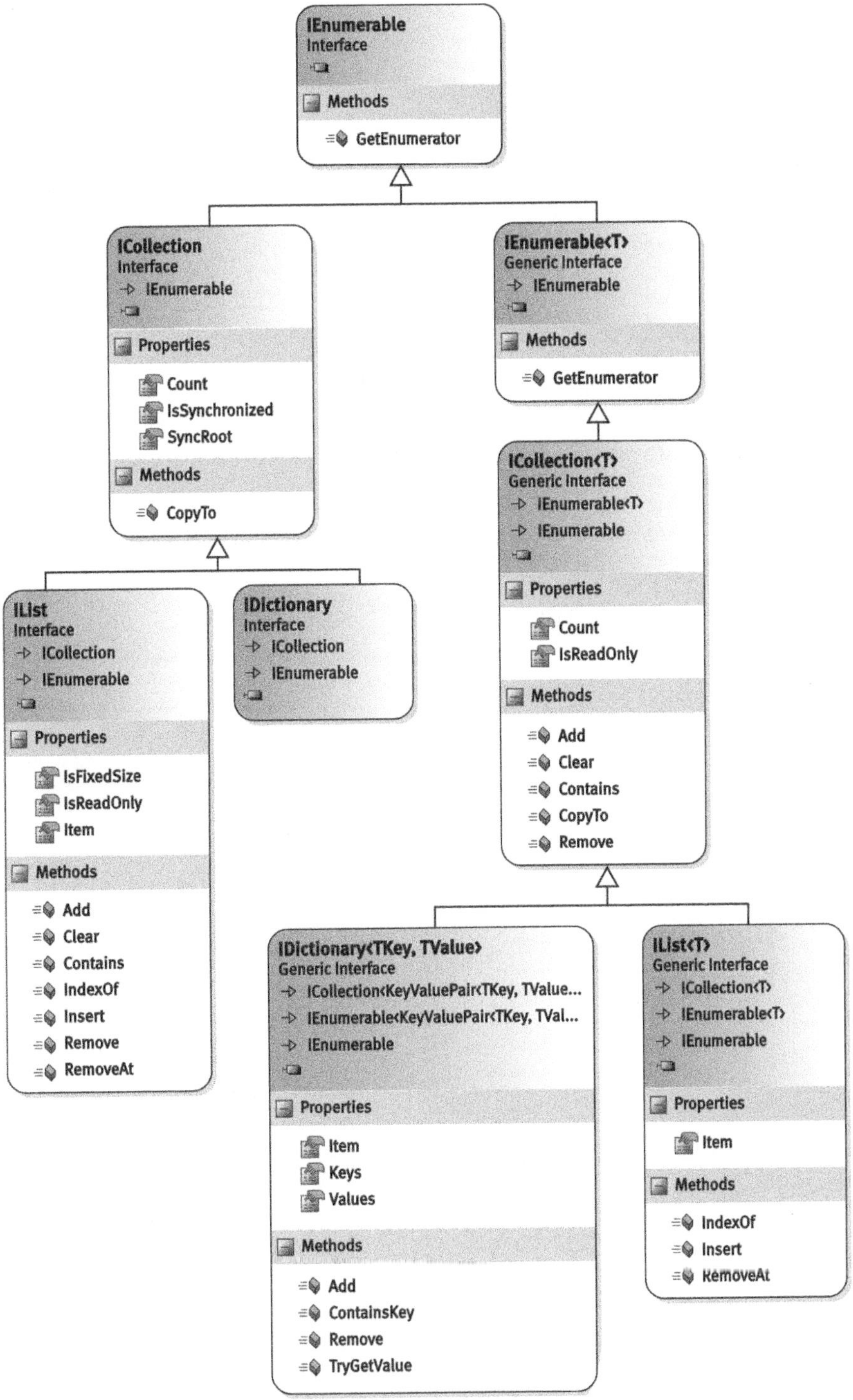

FIGURE 17.1: Collection class hierarchy

values unless specifically documented as being ordered. Similarly, one does not normally think of looking up "the sixth definition in the dictionary"; dictionary classes usually provide indexing only by key, not by position.

A list, by contrast, stores values in a specific order and accesses them by their position. In a sense, lists are just the special case of dictionaries where the "key" is always an integer and the "key set" is always a contiguous set of non-negative integers starting with zero. Nevertheless, that is a strong enough difference that it is worth having an entirely different type to represent it.

Thus, when selecting a collection class to solve some data storage or retrieval problem, the first two interfaces to look for are `IList<T>` and `IDictionary<TKey, TValue>`. These interfaces indicate whether the collection type is focused on retrieval of a value when given its positional index or retrieval of a value when given its associated key.

Both of these interfaces require that a class that implements them provide an indexer. In the case of `IList<T>`, the operand of the indexer corresponds to the position of the element being retrieved: The indexer takes an integer and gives you access to the *n*th element in the list. In the case of the `IDictionary<TKey, TValue>` interface, the operand of the indexer corresponds to the key associated with a value and gives you access to that value.

`ICollection<T>`

Both `IList<T>` and `IDictionary<TKey, TValue>` implement `ICollection<T>`. A collection that does not implement either `IList<T>` or `IDictionary<TKey, TValue>` will more than likely implement `ICollection<T>` (although not necessarily, because collections could implement the lesser requirement of `IEnumerable` or `IEnumerable<T>`). `ICollection<T>` is derived from `IEnumerable<T>` and includes two members: `Count` and `CopyTo()`.

- The `Count` property returns the total number of elements in the collection. Initially, it might appear that this would be sufficient to iterate through each element in the collection using a `for` loop, but, in fact, the collection would also need to support retrieval by index, which the `ICollection<T>` interface does not include (although `IList<T>` does include it).

- The CopyTo() method provides the ability to convert the collection into an array. This method includes an index paramcter so that you can specify where to insert elements in the target array. To use the method, you must initialize the array target with sufficient capacity, starting at the index, to contain all the elements in ICollection<T>.

Primary Collection Classes

Five key categories of collection classes exist, and they differ from one another in terms of how data is inserted, stored, and retrieved. Each generic class is located in the System.Collections.Generic namespace, and their nongeneric equivalents are found in the System.Collections namespace.

List Collections: List<T>

The List<T> class has properties similar to an array. The key difference is that these classes automatically expand as the number of elements increases. (In contrast, an array size is constant.) Furthermore, lists can shrink via explicit calls to TrimToSize() or Capacity (see Figure 17.2).

These classes are categorized as **list collections** whose distinguishing functionality is that each element can be individually accessed by index, just like an array. Therefore, you can set and access elements in the list collection classes using the index operator, where the index parameter value corresponds to the position of an element in the collection. Listing 17.1 shows an example, and Output 17.1 shows the results.

LISTING 17.1: Using List<T>

```
using System;
using System.Collections.Generic;

public class Program
{
    public static void Main()
    {
        List<string> list = new() { "Sneezy", "Happy", "Dopey",  "Doc",
                                    "Sleepy", "Bashful",  "Grumpy"};
```

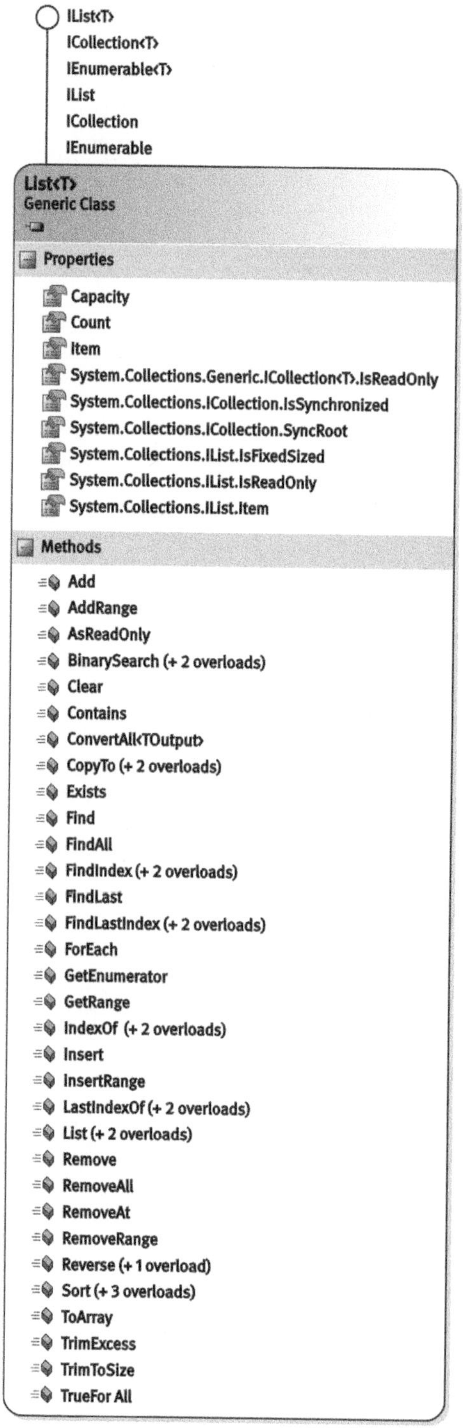

FIGURE 17.2: `List<>` class diagrams

```
            list.Sort();

            Console.WriteLine(
                $"In alphabetical order { list[0] } is the "
                + $"first dwarf while { list[^1] } is the last.");

            list.Remove("Grumpy");
        }
    }
```

OUTPUT 17.1

```
In alphabetical order Bashful is the first dwarf while Sneezy is the
last.
```

C# is zero-index based; therefore, index 0 in Listing 17.1 corresponds to the first element and index 6 indicates the seventh element. Retrieving elements by index does not involve a search. Rather, it entails a quick and simple "jump" operation to a location in memory.

A `List<T>` is an ordered collection; the `Add()` method appends the given item to the end of the list. Before the call to `Sort()` in Listing 17.1, `"Sneezy"` is first and `"Grumpy"` is last; after the call, the list is sorted into alphabetical order rather than the order in which items were added. Some collections automatically sort elements as they are added, but `List<T>` is not one of them; an explicit call to `Sort()` is required for the elements to be sorted.

To remove an element, you use the `Remove()` or `RemoveAt()` method to either remove a given element or remove whatever element is at a particular index, respectively.

ADVANCED TOPIC

Customizing Collection Sorting

You might have wondered how the `List<T>.Sort()` method in Listing 17.1 knew how to sort the elements of the list into alphabetical order. The `string` type implements the `IComparable<string>` interface, which has one method, `CompareTo()`. It returns an integer indicating whether the element passed is greater than, less than, or equal to the current element. If the element type implements the generic `IComparable<T>` interface (or the nongeneric `IComparable` interface), the sorting algorithm will, by default, use it to determine the sorted order.

But what if either the element type does not implement `IComparable<T>` or the default logic for comparing two things does not meet your needs? To specify a nondefault sort order, you can call the overload of `List<T>.Sort()`, which takes `IComparer<T>` as an argument.

The difference between `IComparable<T>` and `IComparer<T>` is subtle but important. The first interface means, "I know how to compare *myself* to another instance of my type." The latter means, "I know how to compare *two things* of a given type."

The `IComparer<T>` interface is typically used when there are many different possible ways of sorting a data type and none is obviously the best. For example, you might have a collection of `Contact` objects that you sometimes want to sort by name, by location, by birthday, by geographic region, or by any number of other possibilities. Rather than choosing a sorting strategy and making the `Contact` class implement `IComparable<Contact>`, it might be wiser to create several different classes that implement `IComparer<Contact>`. Listing 17.2 shows a sample implementation of a `LastName, FirstName` comparison.

LISTING 17.2: Implementing `IComparer<T>`

```
using System;
using System.Collections.Generic;
// ...
public class Contact
{
    public string FirstName { get; private set; }
    public string LastName { get; private set; }

    public Contact(string firstName, string lastName)
    {
        this.FirstName = firstName;
        this.LastName = lastName;
    }
}
public class NameComparison : IComparer<Contact>
{
```

```
    public int Compare(Contact? x, Contact? y)
    {
        if(Object.ReferenceEquals(x, y))
            return 0;
        if(x == null)
            return 1;
        if(y == null)
            return -1;
        int result = StringCompare(x.LastName, y.LastName);
        if(result == 0)
            result = StringCompare(x.FirstName, y.FirstName);
        return result;
    }

    private static int StringCompare(string? x, string? y)
    {
        if(Object.ReferenceEquals(x, y))
            return 0;
        if(x == null)
            return 1;
        if(y == null)
            return -1;
        return x.CompareTo(y);
    }
}
```

To sort a `List<Contact>` by last name and then first name, you can call `contactList.Sort(new NameComparer())`.

Total Ordering

You are required to produce a **total order** when implementing `IComparable<T>` or `IComparer<T>`. Your implementation of `CompareTo` must provide a fully consistent ordering for any possible pair of items. This ordering is required to have a number of basic characteristics. For example, every element is required to be considered equal to itself. If an element X is considered to be equal to element Y, and element Y is considered to be equal to element Z, then all three elements X, Y, and Z must be considered equal to one another. If an element X is considered to be greater than Y, Y must be considered to be less than X. And there must be no "transitivity paradoxes"—that is, you cannot have X greater than Y, Y greater than Z, and Z greater than X. If you fail to provide a total ordering, the action of the sort algorithm is undefined; it may produce a crazy ordering, it may crash, it may go into an infinite loop, and so on.

Notice, for example, how the comparer in Listing 17.2 ensures a total order, even if the arguments are `null` references. It would not be legal to say, "If either element is `null`, then return zero," for example, because then two non-`null` things could be equal to `null` but not equal to each other.

Guidelines

DO ensure that custom comparison logic produces a consistent "total order."

Searching a `List<T>`

To search `List<T>` for a particular element, you use the `Contains()`, `IndexOf()`, `LastIndexOf()`, and `BinarySearch()` methods. The first three methods search through the array, starting at the first element (or the last element for `LastIndexOf()`), and examine each element until the desired one is found. The execution time for these algorithms is proportional to the number of elements searched before a hit occurs. (Be aware that the collection classes do not require that all the elements within the collection are unique. If two or more elements in the collection are the same, `IndexOf()` returns the first index and `LastIndexOf()` returns the last index.)

`BinarySearch()` uses a much faster binary search algorithm but requires that the elements be sorted. A useful feature of the `BinarySearch()` method is that if the element is not found, a negative integer is returned. The bitwise complement (~) of this value is the index of the next element larger than the element being sought, or the total element count if there is no greater value. This provides a convenient means to insert new values into the list at the specific location so as to maintain sorting. Listing 17.3 provides an example.

Beware that if the list is not first sorted, this code will not necessarily find an element, even if it is in the list. The results of Listing 17.3 appear in Output 17.2.

Listing 17.3: Using the Bitwise Complement of the `BinarySearch()` Result

```
using System;
using System.Collections.Generic;

public class Program
{
    public static void Main()
    {
        List<string> list = new();
        int search;

        list.Add("public");
        list.Add("protected");
        list.Add("private");

        list.Sort();

        search = list.BinarySearch("protected internal");
        if(search < 0)
        {
            list.Insert(~search, "protected internal");
        }

        foreach(string accessModifier in list)
        {
            Console.WriteLine(accessModifier);
        }
    }
}
```

Output 17.2

```
private
protected
protected internal
public
```

ADVANCED TOPIC

Finding Multiple Items with `FindAll()`

Sometimes you must find multiple items within a list, and your search criteria are more complex than merely looking for specific values. To support this scenario,

System.Collections.Generic.List<T> includes a FindAll() method. FindAll() takes a parameter of type Predicate<T>, which is a delegate (a reference to a method). Listing 17.4 demonstrates how to use the FindAll() method.

Listing 17.4: Demonstrating FindAll() and Its Predicate Parameter

```
using System;
using System.Collections.Generic;

public class Program
{
    public static void Main()
    {
        List<int> list = new();
        list.Add(1);
        list.Add(2);
        list.Add(3);
        list.Add(2);

        List<int> results = list.FindAll(Even);

        foreach (int number in results)
        {
            Console.WriteLine(number);
        }
    }
    public static bool Even(int value) =>
        (value % 2) == 0;
}
```

In Listing 17.4's call to FindAll(), you pass a delegate instance, Even(). This method returns true when the integer argument value is even. FindAll() takes the delegate instance and calls into Even() for each item within the list.[2] Each time the return value is true, it adds it to a new List<T> instance and then returns this instance once it has checked each item within list. A complete discussion of delegates occurs in Chapter 13.

2. This listing uses C# 2.0's delegate type inferencing.

Dictionary Collections: Dictionary<TKey, TValue>

Another category of collection classes is the dictionary classes—specifically, Dictionary<TKey, TValue> (see Figure 17.3). Unlike the list collections, dictionary classes store name/value pairs. The name functions as a unique key that can be used to look up the corresponding element in a manner similar to that of using a primary key to access a record in a database. This adds some complexity to the access of dictionary elements, but because lookups by key are efficient operations, this is a useful collection. Note that the key may be any data type, not just a string or a numeric value.

One option for inserting elements into a dictionary is to use the Add() method, passing both the key and the value as arguments, as shown in Listing 17.5.

LISTING 17.5: Adding Items to a Dictionary<TKey, TValue>

```
using System;
using System.Collections.Generic;

public class Program
{
    public static void Main()
    {
        var colorMap = new Dictionary<string, ConsoleColor>
        {
            ["Error"] = ConsoleColor.Red,
            ["Warning"] = ConsoleColor.Yellow,
            ["Information"] = ConsoleColor.Green
        };
        colorMap.Add("Verbose", ConsoleColor.White);
        // ...
    }
}
```

After initializing the dictionary with a dictionary initializer[3] (see the section "Collection Initializers" in Chapter 15), Listing 17.5 inserts the string a ConsoleColor of White for the key of "Verbose". If an element with the same key has already been added, an exception is thrown.

An alternative for adding elements is to use the indexer, as shown in Listing 17.6.

3. Starting with C# 6.0.

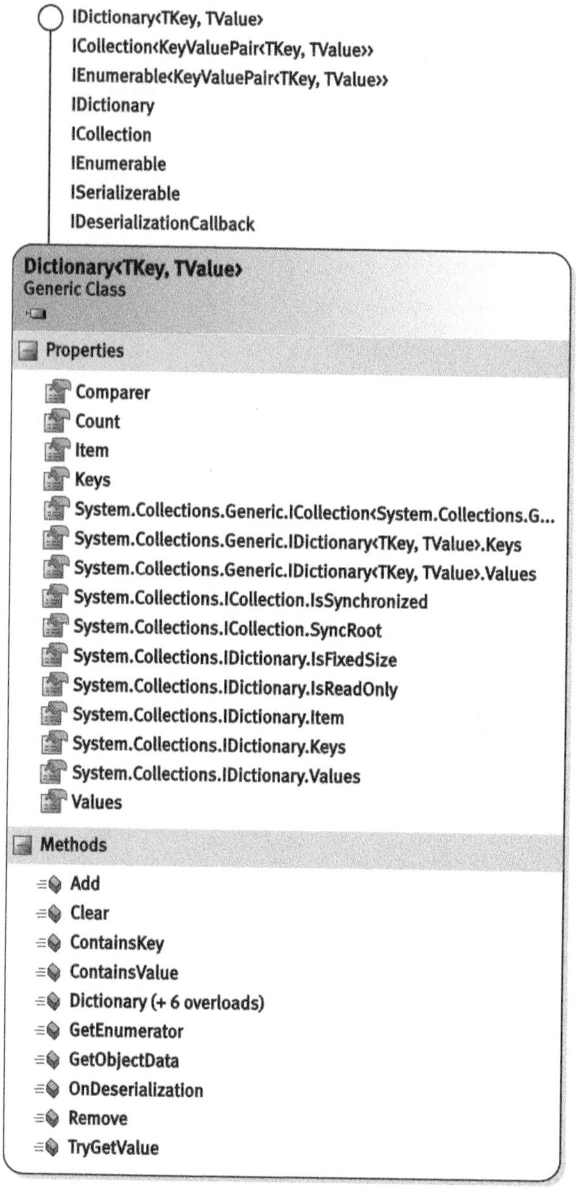

FIGURE 17.3: `Dictionary` class diagrams

Listing 17.6: Inserting Items in a `Dictionary<TKey, TValue>` Using the Index Operator

```
using System;
using System.Collections.Generic;

public class Program
{
    public static void Main()
    {
        var colorMap = new Dictionary<string, ConsoleColor>
            {
                ["Error"] = ConsoleColor.Red,
                ["Warning"] = ConsoleColor.Yellow,
                ["Information"] = ConsoleColor.Green
            };

        colorMap["Verbose"] = ConsoleColor.White;
        colorMap["Error"] = ConsoleColor.Cyan;

        // ...
    }
}
```

The first thing to observe in Listing 17.6 is that the index operator does not require an integer. Instead, the index operand type is specified by the first type argument (`string`), and the type of the value that is set or retrieved by the indexer is specified by the second type argument (`ConsoleColor`).

The second thing to notice in Listing 17.6 is that the same key (`"Error"`) is used twice. In the first assignment, no dictionary value corresponds to the given key. When this happens, the dictionary collection classes insert a new value with the supplied key. In the second assignment, an element with the specified key already exists. Instead of inserting an additional element, the prior `ConsoleColor` value for the `"Error"` key is replaced with `ConsoleColor.Cyan`.

Attempting to read a value from a dictionary with a nonexistent key throws a `KeyNotFoundException`. The `ContainsKey()` method allows you to check whether a particular key is used before accessing its value, thereby avoiding the exception.

The `Dictionary<TKey, TValue>` is implemented as a *hash table*; this data structure provides extremely fast access when searching by key, regardless of the number of values stored in the dictionary. By contrast, checking whether there is a particular value in the dictionary collections is a time-consuming operation with linear performance characteristics, much like searching an unsorted list. To do this, you use the `ContainsValue()` method, which searches sequentially through each element in the collection.

You remove a dictionary element using the `Remove()` method, passing the key, not the element value, as the argument.

Because both the key and the value are required to add a value to the dictionary, the loop variable of a `foreach` loop that enumerates elements of a dictionary must be `KeyValuePair<TKey, TValue>`. Listing 17.7 shows a snippet of code demonstrating the use of a `foreach` loop to enumerate the keys and values in a dictionary. The output appears in Output 17.3.

LISTING 17.7: Iterating over `Dictionary<TKey, TValue>` with `foreach`

```
using System;
using System.Collections.Generic;

public class Program
{
    public static void Main()
    {
        var colorMap = new Dictionary<string, ConsoleColor>
            {
                ["Error"] = ConsoleColor.Red,
                ["Warning"] = ConsoleColor.Yellow,
                ["Information"] = ConsoleColor.Green,
                ["Verbose"] = ConsoleColor.White
            };

        Print(colorMap);
  }

    private static void Print(
      IEnumerable<KeyValuePair<string, ConsoleColor>> items)
    {
        foreach (KeyValuePair<string, ConsoleColor> item in items)
        {
            Console.ForegroundColor = item.Value;
          Console.WriteLine(item.Key);
      }
```

```
    }
}
```

OUTPUT 17.3

```
Error
Warning
Information
Verbose
```

Note that the order of the items shown here is the order in which the items were added to the dictionary, just as if they had been added to a list. Implementations of dictionaries will often enumerate the keys and values in the order in which they were added to the dictionary, but this feature is neither required nor documented, so you should not rely on it.

Guidelines

DO NOT make any unwarranted assumptions about the order in which elements of a collection will be enumerated. If the collection is not documented as enumerating its elements in a particular order, it is not guaranteed to produce elements in any particular order.

If you want to deal only with keys or only with elements within a dictionary class, they are available via the `Keys` and `Values` properties, respectively. The data type returned from these properties is of type `ICollection<T>`. The data returned by these properties is a reference to the data within the original dictionary collection rather than a copy; changes within the dictionary are automatically reflected in the collection returned by the `Keys` and `Values` properties.

ADVANCED TOPIC

Customizing Dictionary Equality

To determine whether a given key matches any existing key in the dictionary, the dictionary must be able to compare two keys for equality. This is analogous to the way that lists must be able to compare two items to determine their order. (For an example, see "Advanced Topic: Customizing Collection Sorting" earlier in this chapter.) By default, two instances of a value type are compared by checking whether they contain exactly the same data, and two instances of a reference type are compared to see whether both reference the same object. However, it is occasionally necessary to be able to compare two instances as equal even if they are not exactly the same value or exactly the same reference.

For example, suppose you wish to create a `Dictionary<Contact, string>` using the `Contact` type from Listing 17.2. However, you want any two `Contact` objects to compare as equal if they have the same first and last names, regardless of whether the two objects are reference equal. Much as you can provide an implementation of `IComparer<T>` to sort a list, so you can provide an implementation of `IEqualityComparer<T>` to determine if two keys are to be considered equal. This interface requires two methods: one that returns whether two items are equal and one that returns a "hash code" that the dictionary can use to facilitate fast indexing. Listing 17.8 shows an example.

LISTING 17.8: Implementing `IEqualityComparer<T>`

```
using System.Collections.Generic;

public class ContactEquality : IEqualityComparer<Contact>
{
    public bool Equals(Contact? x, Contact? y)
    {
        if(object.ReferenceEquals(x, y))
            return true;
        if(x == null || y == null)
            return false;
        return x.LastName == y.LastName &&
            x.FirstName == y.FirstName;
    }

    public int GetHashCode(Contact x)
    {
        if(x is null)
            return 0;

        int h1 = x.FirstName == null ? 0 : x.FirstName.GetHashCode();
        int h2 = x.LastName == null ? 0 : x.LastName.GetHashCode();
        return h1 * 23 + h2;
```

```
    }
}
```

To create a dictionary that uses this equality comparer, you can use the constructor `new Dictionary<Contact, string>(new ContactEquality)`.

BEGINNER TOPIC

Requirements of Equality Comparisons

As discussed in Chapter 10, several important rules apply to the equality and hash code algorithms. Conformance to these rules is critical in the context of collections. Just as correctly sorting a list requires a custom ordering comparison to provide a total order, so, too, does a hash table require certain guarantees to be met by a custom equality comparison. The most important requirement is that if `Equals()` returns `true` for two objects, `GetHashCode()` must return the same value for those two objects. Note that the converse is not true: Two unequal items may have the same hash code. (Indeed, there *must* be two unequal items that have the same hash code because there are only 2^{32} possible hash codes but many more than that number of unequal objects!)

The second-most important requirement is that two calls to `GetHashCode()` on the same item must produce the same result for at least as long as the item is in the hash table. Note, however, that two objects that "look equal" are not required to give the same hash code in two separate runs of a program. For example, it is perfectly legal for a given contact to be assigned one hash code today and, two weeks later when you run the program a second time, for "the same" contact to be given a different hash code. Do not persist hash codes into a database and expect them to remain stable across different runs of a program.

Ideally, the result of `GetHashCode()` should appear to be random. That is, small changes to the input should cause large changes to the output, and the result should be distributed roughly evenly across all possible integer values. It is difficult, however, to devise a hash algorithm that is extremely fast and produces extremely well-distributed output; try to find a good middle ground.

Finally, `GetHashCode()` and `Equals()` must not throw exceptions. Notice how the code in Listing 17.8 is careful to never dereference a `null` reference, for example.

To summarize, here are the key principles:

- Equal objects must have equal hash codes.
- The hash code of an object should not change for the life of the instance (at least while it is in the hash table).
- The hashing algorithm should quickly produce a well-distributed hash.

The hashing algorithm should avoid throwing exceptions in all possible object states.

Sorted Collections: `SortedDictionary<TKey, TValue>` and `SortedList<T>`

The sorted collection classes (see Figure 17.4) store their elements sorted by key for `SortedDictionary<TKey, TValue>` and by value for `SortedList<T>`. If we change the code in Listing 17.7 to use a `SortedDictionary<string, string>` instead of a `Dictionary<string, string>`, the output of the program is as appears in Output 17.4.

OUTPUT 17.4

```
Error
Information
Verbose
Warning
```

Note that the elements are sorted into order by key, not by value.

Because sorted collections must do extra work to maintain the sorted order of their elements, insertion and removal are typically slightly slower than insertion and removal of values in an unordered dictionary.

Because sorted collections must store their items in a particular order, it is possible to access values both by key and by index. To access a key or value by its index in the sorted list, use the `Keys` and `Values` properties. They return

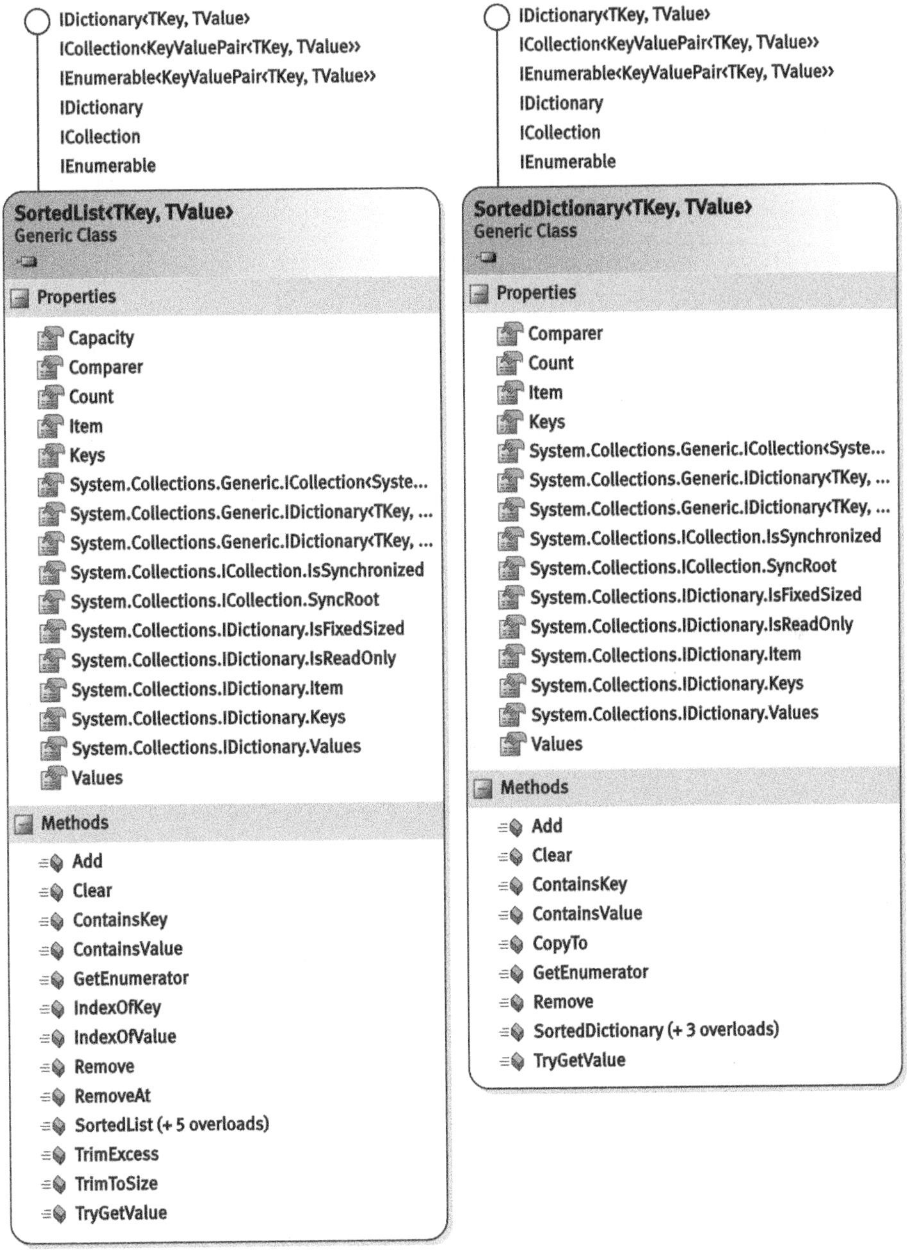

FIGURE 17.4: Sorted Collections

IList<TKey> and IList<TValue> instances, respectively; the resultant collection can be indexed like any other list.

Stack Collections: Stack<T>

Chapter 12 discussed the stack collection classes (see Figure 17.5). The stack collection classes are designed as last in, first out (LIFO) collections. The two key methods are Push() and Pop():

- Push() inserts elements into the collection. The elements do not have to be unique.
- Pop() removes elements in the reverse order in which they were added.

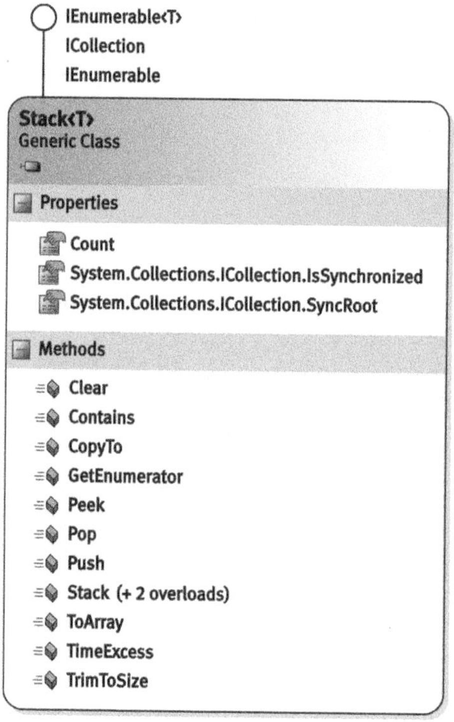

FIGURE 17.5: Stack<T> class diagram

To access the elements on the stack without modifying the stack, you use the `Peek()` and `Contains()` methods. The `Peek()` method returns the next element that `Pop()` will retrieve.

As with most collection classes, you use the `Contains()` method to determine whether an element exists anywhere in the stack. As with all collections, it is also possible to use a `foreach` loop to iterate over the elements in a stack. This allows you to access values from anywhere in the stack. Note, however, that accessing a value via the `foreach` loop does not remove it from the stack—only `Pop()` provides this functionality.

Queue Collections: `Queue<T>`

Queue collection classes, shown in Figure 17.6, are identical to stack collection classes, except that they follow the ordering pattern of first in, first out (FIFO). Instead of the `Pop()` and `Push()` methods, they use the `Enqueue()` and `Dequeue()` methods, respectively. The queue collection behaves like a pipe: You place objects into the queue at one end using the `Enqueue()` method and remove them from the other end using the `Dequeue()` method. As with stack collection classes, the objects do not have to be unique, and queue collection classes automatically increase in size as required. As a queue shrinks, it does not necessarily reclaim the storage space previously used, because that would make inserting a new element potentially more expensive. If you happen to know that a queue will remain the same size for a long time, however, you can hint to it that you would like to reclaim storage space by using the `TrimToSize()` method.

Linked Lists: `LinkedList<T>`

`System.Collections.Generic` also supports a linked list collection that enables both forward and reverse traversal. Figure 17.7 shows the class diagram. (There is no corresponding nongeneric type.)

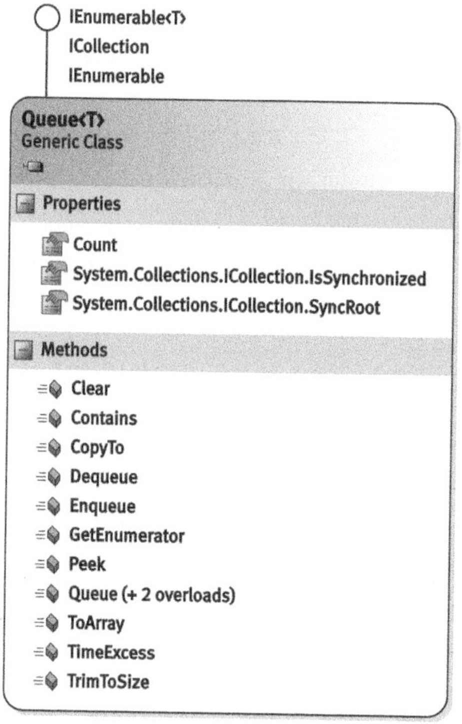

FIGURE 17.6: Queue<T> class diagram

Span<T> and ReadOnlySpan<T>

Another collection type worth reviewing is `Span<T>`. It's a special collection type that is used for accessing a sequence of elements from an existing array without reallocating all the memory required for each element in the array. For example, given an `int[]` instance, you can create a `Span<int>` instance referring to a slice of the original array without copying each of the elements into the `Span<int>` collection. This makes `Span<int>` an efficient way of working with slices of existing collections. The memory consumed by the slice essentially overlaps much of the memory of the original array—the `Span<T>` refers to the elements in the original collection without copying them to a new collection. Listing 17.9 provides an example and demonstrates how `Span<T>` references the same data pointed to by the original array.

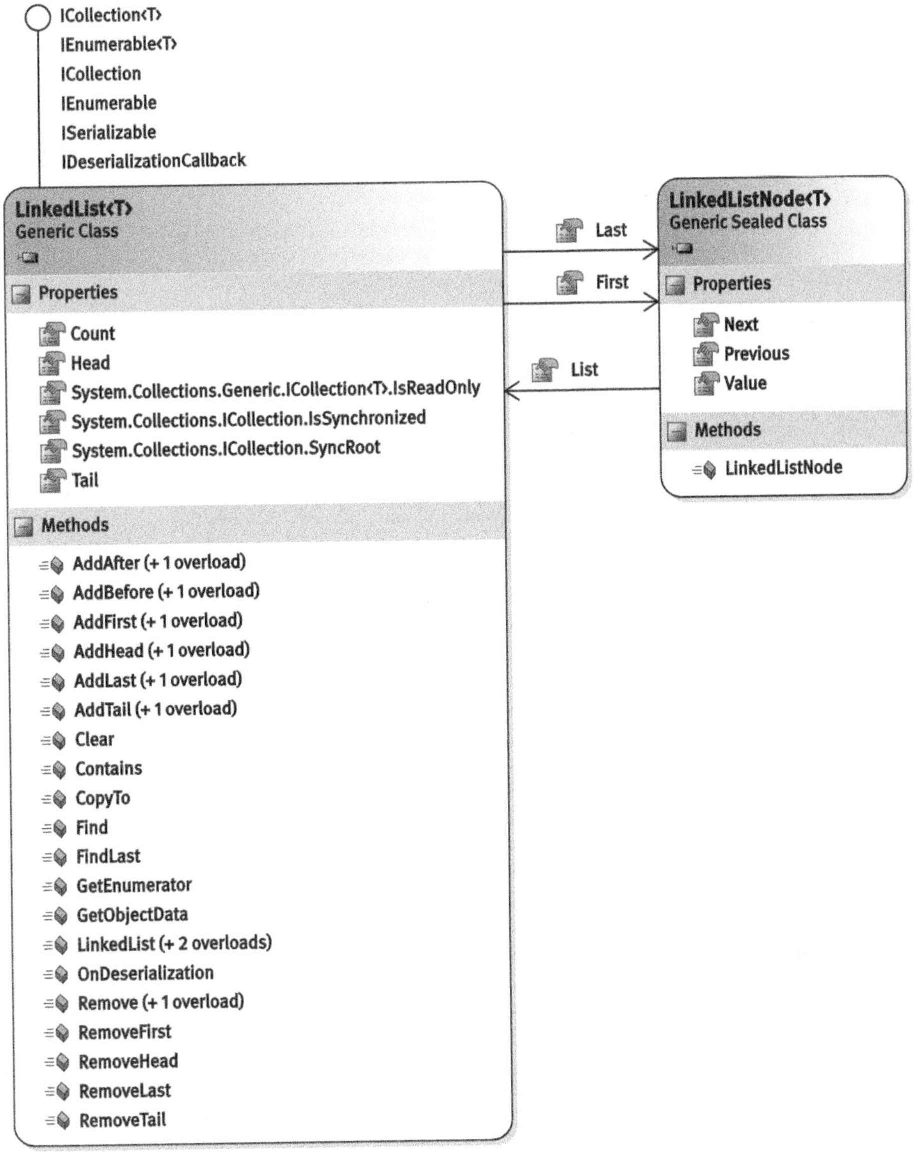

FIGURE 17.7: `LinkedList<T>` and `LinkedListNode<T>` class diagrams

LISTING 17.9: `Span<T>` **Examples**

```
string[] languages = new [] {
    "C#", "COBOL", "Java",
    "C++", "TypeScript", "Python",};

// Create a Span<string> from the arrays first 3 elements.
Span<string> languageSpan = languages.AsSpan(0, 2);
languages[0] = "R";
Assert(languages[0] == languageSpan[0]);
Assert("R" == languageSpan[0]);
languageSpan[0] = "Lisp";
Assert(languages[0] == languageSpan[0]);
Assert("Lisp" == languages[0]);

int[] numbers = languages.Select(item => item.Length).ToArray();
// Create a Span<string> from the arrays first 3 elements.
Span<int> numbersSpan = numbers.AsSpan(0, 2);
Assert(numbers[1] == numbersSpan[1]);
numbersSpan[1] = 42;
Assert(numbers[1] == numbersSpan[1]);
Assert(42 == numbers[1]);

const string bigWord = "supercalifragilisticexpialidocious";
// Create a Span<char> from a suffix portion of the word.
#if NET8_0_OR_GREATER
ReadOnlySpan<char> expialidocious = bigWord.AsSpan(20..);
#else // NET8_0_OR_GREATER
ReadOnlySpan<char> expialidocious = bigWord.AsSpan(20, 14);
#endif // NET8_0_OR_GREATER
Assert(expialidocious.ToString() == "expialidocious");
```

To demonstrate the behavior of shared memory, review how we can assign a new value to `languages[0]` and the corresponding element in `languagesSpan` will also update, and vice versa. Furthermore, this behavior applies whether using a collection of reference types or value types.

There is also a `ReadOnlySpan<T>`, which allows using the same construct on an immutable array such as a `string`, rather than allocating an entirely new string. With `ReadOnlySpan<T>` we can have a new string that points to a slice of the old string, a significantly more performance-based approach when a slice of the original array is all that is needed.

Internally, Span<T> uses a ref struct (added in C# 7.2). That means it can only live on the stack but never on the heap. As a result, it can be used as a local variable but not as a static or instance member on a class or normal struct. For similar functionality but without the same restriction, use a Memory<T> type.

Providing an Indexer

Arrays, dictionaries, and lists all provide an **indexer** as a convenient way to get or set a member of a collection based on a key or index. As we've seen, to use the indexer, you simply put the index (or indices) in square brackets after the collection name. It is possible to define your own indexer; Listing 17.10 shows an example using Pair<T>.

Listing 17.10: Defining an Indexer

```
interface IPair<T>
{
    T First { get; }
    T Second { get; }
    T this[PairItem index] { get; }
}

public enum PairItem
{
    First,
    Second
}

public struct Pair<T> : IPair<T>
{
    public Pair(T first, T second)
    {
        First = first;
        Second = second;
    }

    public T First { get; }
    public T Second { get; }

    public T this[PairItem index]
    {
        get
```

```
        {
            switch (index)
            {
                case PairItem.First:
                    return First;
                case PairItem.Second:
                    return Second;
                default:
                    throw new NotImplementedException(
                        $"The enum { index.ToString() } has not been
↪implemented");

            }
        }
        // ...
    }
}
```

An indexer is declared much as a property is declared, except that instead of the name of the property, you use the keyword `this` followed by a parameter list in square brackets. The body is also like a property, with `get` and `set` blocks. As Listing 17.10 shows, the parameter does not have to be an `int`. In fact, the index can take multiple parameters and can even be overloaded. This example uses an `enum` to reduce the likelihood that callers will supply an index for a nonexistent item.

The Common Intermediate Language (CIL) code that the C# compiler creates from an index operator is a special property called `Item` that takes an argument. Properties that accept arguments cannot be created explicitly in C#, so the `Item` property is unique in this aspect. Any additional member with the identifier `Item`, even if it has an entirely different signature, will conflict with the compiler-created member, so it will not be allowed.

ADVANCED TOPIC

Assigning the Indexer Property Name Using `IndexerName`

As indicated earlier, the CIL property name for an indexer defaults to `Item`. Using the `IndexerNameAttribute`, you can specify a different name, however. Listing 17.11, for example, changes the name to `"Entry"`.

Listing 17.11: Changing the Indexer's Default Name

```
[System.Runtime.CompilerServices.IndexerName("Entry")]
public T this[PairItem index]
{
    // ...
}
```

This makes no difference to C# callers of the index, but it specifies the name for languages that do not support indexers directly.

The `IndexerNameAttribute` is merely an instruction to the compiler to use a different name for the indexer; the attribute is not actually emitted into metadata by the compiler, so it is not available via reflection.

ADVANCED TOPIC

Defining an Index Operator with Variable Parameters

An index operator can also take a variable parameter list. For example, Listing 17.12 defines an index operator for `BinaryTree<T>`, discussed in Chapter 12 (and again in the next section).

Listing 17.12: Defining an Index Operator with Variable Parameters

```
using System;

public class BinaryTree<T>
{
    // ...
    public BinaryTree<T> this[params PairItem[]? branches]
    {
        get
        {
            BinaryTree<T> currentNode = this;

            // Allow either an empty array or null
            // to refer to the root node
            int totalLevels = branches?.Length ?? 0;
            int currentLevel = 0;
```

```
            while (currentLevel < totalLevels)
            {
                System.Diagnostics.Debug.Assert(branches != null,
                    $"{ nameof(branches) } != null");

                currentNode = currentNode.SubItems[
                    branches[currentLevel]];
                if (currentNode == null)
                {
                    // The binary tree at this location is null
                    throw new IndexOutOfRangeException();
                }
                currentLevel++;
            }
            return currentNode;
        }
    }
    // ...
}
```

Each item within `branches` is a `PairItem` and indicates which branch to navigate down in the binary tree. For example,

```
tree[PairItem.Second, PairItem.First].Value
```

will retrieve the value located at the second item in the first branch, followed by the first branch within that branch.

Returning `null` or an Empty Collection

When returning an array or collection, you must indicate that there are zero items by returning either `null` or a collection instance with no items. The better choice, in general, is to return a collection instance with no items. In so doing, you avoid forcing the caller to check for `null` before iterating over the items in the collection. For example, given a zero-size `IEnumerable<T>` collection, the caller can immediately and safely use a `foreach` loop over the collection without concern that the generated call to `GetEnumerator()` will throw a `NullReferenceException`. Consider using the `Enumerable.Empty<T>()` method to easily generate an empty collection of a given type.

One of the few times to deviate from this guideline is when `null` is intentionally indicating something different from zero items. For example, a collection of user names for a website might be `null` to indicate that an up-to-date collection could not be obtained for some reason; that is semantically different from an empty collection.

> **Guidelines**
>
> **DO NOT** represent an empty collection with a `null` reference.
>
> **CONSIDER** using the `Enumerable.Empty<T>()` method instead.

Iterators

Chapter 15 went into detail on the internals of the `foreach` loop. This section discusses how to use **iterators** to create your own implementation of the `IEnumerator<T>`, `IEnumerable<T>`, and corresponding nongeneric interfaces for custom collections. Iterators provide clean syntax for specifying how to iterate over data in collection classes, especially using the `foreach` loop. The iterator allows end users of a collection to navigate its internal structure without knowledge of that structure.

ADVANCED TOPIC

Origin of Iterators

In 1972, Barbara Liskov and a team of scientists at MIT began researching programming methodologies, focusing on user-defined data abstractions. To prove much of their work, they created a language called CLU that had a concept called "clusters" (*CLU* being the first three letters of this term). Clusters were predecessors to the primary data abstraction that programmers use today: objects.

During their research, the team realized that although they were able to use the CLU language to abstract some data representation away from end users of their types, they consistently found themselves having to reveal the inner structure of their data to allow others to intelligently consume it. The result of their consternation was the creation of a language construct called an *iterator*. (The CLU language offered many insights into what would eventually be popularized as object-oriented programming.)

If classes want to support iteration using the `foreach` loop construct, they must implement the enumerator pattern. As Chapter 15 describes, in C# the `foreach` loop construct is expanded by the compiler into the `while` loop construct based on the `IEnumerator<T>` interface that is retrieved from the `IEnumerable<T>` interface.

The problem with the enumeration pattern is that it can be cumbersome to implement manually, because it must maintain all the state necessary to describe the current position in the collection. This internal state may be simple for a list collection type class; the index of the current position usually suffices. In contrast, for data structures that require recursive traversal, such as binary trees, the state can be quite complicated.[4]

Defining an Iterator

Iterators are a means to implement methods of a class, and they are syntactic shortcuts for the more complex enumerator pattern. When the C# compiler encounters an iterator, it expands its contents into CIL code that implements the enumerator pattern. As such, there are no runtime dependencies for implementing iterators. Because the C# compiler handles implementation through CIL code generation, there is no real runtime performance benefit from using iterators. However, a substantial programmer productivity gain may be realized by choosing iterators over the manual implementation of the enumerator pattern. To understand how this improvement arises, we must first consider how an iterator is defined in code.

4. C# 2.0 included a construct that makes it easier for a class to dictate how the `foreach` loop iterates over its contents.

Iterator Syntax

An iterator provides a shorthand implementation of iterator interfaces, the combination of the `IEnumerable<T>` and `IEnumerator<T>` interfaces. Listing 17.13 declares an iterator for the generic `BinaryTree<T>` type by creating a `GetEnumerator()` method. Next, you add support for the iterator interfaces.

Listing 17.13: Iterator Interfaces Pattern

```
using System.Collections;
using System.Collections.Generic;

public class BinaryTree<T> :
IEnumerable<T>
{
    public BinaryTree(T value)
    {
        Value = value;
    }

    #region IEnumerable<T>
    public IEnumerator<T> GetEnumerator()
    {
        // ...
    }
    #endregion IEnumerable<T>

    public T Value { get; }
    public Pair<BinaryTree<T>> SubItems { get; set; }
}

public struct Pair<T>
{
    public Pair(T first, T second) : this()
    {
        First = first;
        Second = second;
    }
    public T First { get; }
    public T Second { get; }
}
```

As Listing 17.13 shows, we need to provide an implementation for the `GetEnumerator()` method.

Yielding Values from an Iterator

Iterators are like functions, but instead of returning a single value, they *yield* a sequence of values, one at a time. In the case of `BinaryTree<T>`, the iterator yields a sequence of values of the type argument provided for `T`. If the nongeneric version of `IEnumerator` is used, the yielded values are instead of type `object`.

To correctly implement the iterator pattern, you need to maintain some internal state to keep track of where you are while enumerating the collection. In the `BinaryTree<T>` case, you track which elements within the tree have already been enumerated and which are still to come. Iterators are transformed by the compiler into a "state machine" that keeps track of the current position and knows how to "move itself" to the next position.

The `yield return` statement yields a value each time an iterator encounters it; control immediately returns to the caller that requested the item. (An interesting point here is that control really does *immediately* return, unlike, ironically, the `return` statement. A `return` statement runs `finally` blocks along the way; `yield return` does not.) When the caller requests the next item, the code begins to execute immediately following the previously executed `yield return` statement. In Listing 17.14, you return the C# built-in data type keywords sequentially. Results are shown in Output 17.5.

Listing 17.14: Yielding Some C# Keywords Sequentially

```
using System;
using System.Collections.Generic;

public class CSharpBuiltInTypes : IEnumerable<string>
{
    public IEnumerator<string> GetEnumerator()
    {
        yield return "object";
        yield return "byte";
        yield return "uint";
        yield return "ulong";
        yield return "float";
        yield return "char";
        yield return "bool";
        yield return "ushort";
        yield return "decimal";
        yield return "int";
```

```
            yield return "sbyte";
            yield return "short";
            yield return "long";
            yield return "void";
            yield return "double";
            yield return "string";
        }

        // The IEnumerable.GetEnumerator method is also required
        // because IEnumerable<T> derives from IEnumerable
        System.Collections.IEnumerator
            System.Collections.IEnumerable.GetEnumerator()
        {
            // Invoke IEnumerator<string> GetEnumerator() above
            return GetEnumerator();
        }
    }
    public class Program
    {
        public static void Main()
        {
            var keywords = new CSharpBuiltInTypes();
            foreach (string keyword in keywords)
            {
                Console.WriteLine(keyword);
            }
        }
    }
```

Output 17.5

```
object
byte
uint
ulong
float
char
bool
ushort
decimal
int
sbyte
short
long
void
double
string
```

The output from this listing is a listing of the C# built-in types.

Iterators and State

When `GetEnumerator()` is first called in a `foreach` statement, such as `foreach (string keyword in keywords)` in Listing 17.14, an iterator object is created and its state is initialized to a special "start" state that represents the fact that no code has executed in the iterator and, therefore, no values have been yielded yet. The iterator maintains its state as long as the `foreach` statement at the call site continues to execute. Every time the loop requests the next value, control enters the iterator and continues where it left off the previous time around the loop; the state information stored in the iterator object is used to determine where control must resume. When the `foreach` statement at the call site terminates, the iterator's state is no longer saved.

It is always safe to call `GetEnumerator()` again; "fresh" enumerator objects will be created when necessary.

Figure 17.8 shows a high-level sequence diagram of what takes place. Remember that the `MoveNext()` method appears on the `IEnumerator<T>` interface.

In Listing 17.13, the `foreach` statement at the call site initiates a call to `GetEnumerator()` on the `CSharpBuiltInTypes` instance called `keywords`. Given the iterator instance (referenced by `iterator`), `foreach` begins each iteration with a call to `MoveNext()`. Within the iterator, you yield a value back to the `foreach` statement at the call site. After the `yield return` statement, the `GetEnumerator()` method seemingly pauses until the next `MoveNext()` request. Back at the loop body, the `foreach` statement displays the yielded value on the screen. It then loops back around and calls `MoveNext()` on the iterator again. Notice that the second time, control picks up at the second `yield return` statement. Once again, the `foreach` displays on the screen what `CSharpBuiltInTypes` yielded and starts the loop again. This process continues until there are no more `yield return` statements within the iterator. At that point, the `foreach` loop at the call site terminates because `MoveNext()` returns `false`.

More Iterator Examples

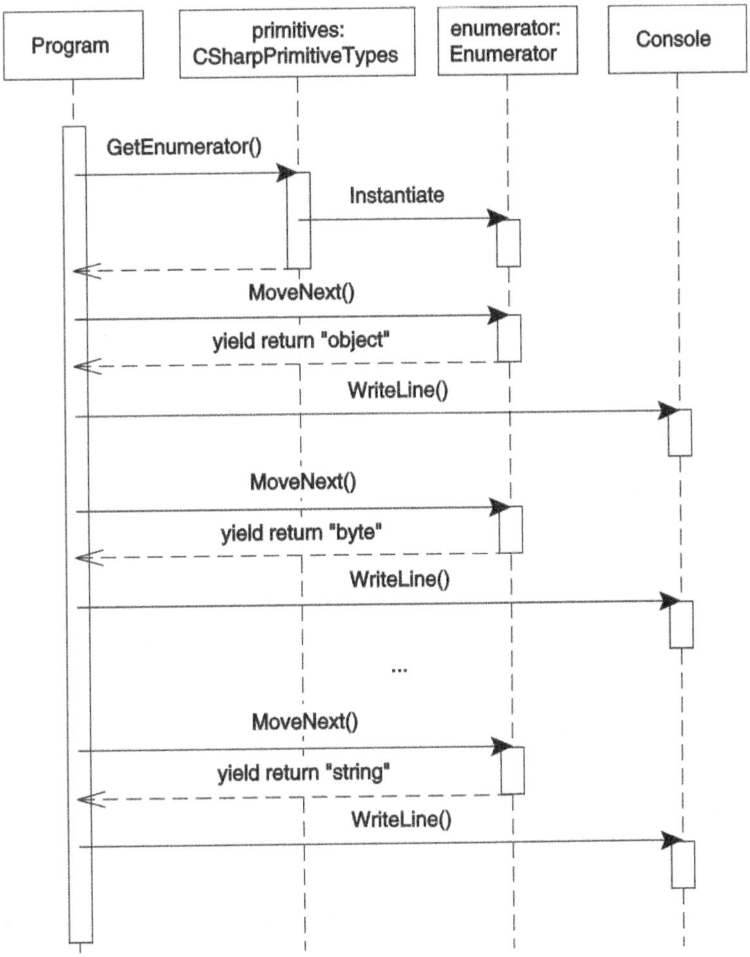

FIGURE 17.8: Sequence diagram with `yield return` application

Before you modify `BinaryTree<T>`, you must modify `Pair<T>` to support the `IEnumerable<T>` interface using an iterator. Listing 17.15 is an example that yields each element in `Pair<T>`.

In Listing 17.15, the iteration over the `Pair<T>` data type loops twice: first through `yield return First` and then through `yield return Second`. Each time the `yield return` statement within `GetEnumerator()` is encountered, the state is saved and execution appears to "jump" out of the `GetEnumerator()`

LISTING 17.15: Using `yield` to Implement `BinaryTree<T>`

```
public struct Pair<T> : IPair<T>,
IEnumerable<T>
{
    public Pair(T first, T second) : this()
    {
        First = first;
        Second = second;
    }
    public T First { get; }
    public T Second { get; }
    // ...
    #region IEnumerable<T>
    public IEnumerator<T> GetEnumerator()
    {
        yield return First;
        yield return Second;
    }
    #endregion IEnumerable<T>

    #region IEnumerable Members
    System.Collections.IEnumerator
        System.Collections.IEnumerable.GetEnumerator()
    {
        return GetEnumerator();
    }
    #endregion IEnumerable Members
}
```

method context and into the loop body. When the second iteration starts, `GetEnumerator()` begins to execute again with the `yield return Second` statement.

`System.Collections.Generic.IEnumerable<T>` inherits from `System.Collections.IEnumerable`. Therefore, when implementing `IEnumerable<T>`, it is also necessary to implement `IEnumerable`. In Listing 17.15, you do so explicitly, and the implementation simply involves a call to `IEnumerable<T>`'s `GetEnumerator()` implementation. This call from `IEnumerable.GetEnumerator()` to `IEnumerable<T>.GetEnumerator()`

will always work because of the type compatibility (via inheritance) between `IEnumerable<T>` and `IEnumerable`. Since the signatures for both versions of `GetEnumerator()` are identical (the return type does not distinguish a signature), one or both implementations must be explicit. Given the additional type safety offered by `IEnumerable<T>`'s version, you implement `IEnumerable`'s implementation explicitly.

Listing 17.16 uses the `Pair<T>.GetEnumerator()` method and displays `"Inigo"` and `"Montoya"` on two consecutive lines.

LISTING 17.16: Using `Pair<T>.GetEnumerator()` via `foreach`

```
var fullName = new Pair<string>("Inigo", "Montoya");
foreach(string name in fullName)
{
    Console.WriteLine(name);
}
```

Notice that the call to `GetEnumerator()` is implicit within the `foreach` loop.

Placing a `yield return` within a Loop

It is not necessary to hardcode each `yield return` statement, as you did in both `CSharpBuiltInTypes` and `Pair<T>`. Using the `yield return` statement, you can return values from inside a loop construct. Listing 17.17 uses a `foreach` loop. Each time the `foreach` within `GetEnumerator()` executes, it returns the next value.

LISTING 17.17: Placing `yield return` Statements within a Loop

```
public class BinaryTree<T> :
  IEnumerable<T>
{
    // ...
    #region IEnumerable<T>
    public IEnumerator<T> GetEnumerator()
    {
        // Return the item at this node
        yield return Value;

        // Iterate through each of the elements in the pair
        foreach (BinaryTree<T>? tree in SubItems)
```

```
            {
                if(tree != null)
                {
                    // Since each element in the pair is a tree,
                    // traverse the tree and yield each
                    // element
                    foreach(T item in tree)
                    {
                        yield return item;
                    }
                }
            }
        }
        #endregion IEnumerable<T>

        #region IEnumerable Members
        System.Collections.IEnumerator
            System.Collections.IEnumerable.GetEnumerator()
        {
            return GetEnumerator();
        }
        #endregion
        // ...
}
```

In Listing 17.17, the first iteration returns the root element within the binary tree. During the second iteration, you traverse the pair of subelements. If the subelement pair contains a non-`null` value, you traverse into that child node and yield its elements. Note that `foreach (T item in tree)` is a recursive call to a child node.

As observed with `CSharpBuiltInTypes` and `Pair<T>`, you can now iterate over `BinaryTree<T>` using a `foreach` loop. Listing 17.18 demonstrates this process, and Output 17.6 shows the results.

LISTING 17.18: Using `foreach` with `BinaryTree<string>`

```
// JFK
var jfkFamilyTree = new BinaryTree<string>(
    "John Fitzgerald Kennedy")
{
    SubItems = new Pair<BinaryTree<string>>(
        new BinaryTree<string>("Joseph Patrick Kennedy")
        {
```

```
            // Grandparents (Father's side)
            SubItems = new Pair<BinaryTree<string>>(
                new BinaryTree<string>("Patrick Joseph Kennedy"),
                new BinaryTree<string>("Mary Augusta Hickey"))
        },
        new BinaryTree<string>("Rose Elizabeth Fitzgerald")
        {
            // Grandparents (Mother's side)
            SubItems = new Pair<BinaryTree<string>>(
                new BinaryTree<string>("John Francis Fitzgerald"),
                new BinaryTree<string>("Mary Josephine Hannon"))
        })
};

foreach (string name in jfkFamilyTree)
{
    Console.WriteLine(name);
}
```

OUTPUT 17.6

```
John Fitzgerald Kennedy
Joseph Patrick Kennedy
Patrick Joseph Kennedy
Mary Augusta Hickey
Rose Elizabeth Fitzgerald
John Francis Fitzgerald
Mary Josephine Hannon
```

ADVANCED TOPIC

The Dangers of Recursive Iterators

The code in Listing 17.17 creates new "nested" iterators as it traverses the binary tree. As a consequence, when the value is yielded by a node, the value is yielded by the node's iterator, and then yielded by its parent's iterator, and then yielded by its parent's iterator, and so on, until it is finally yielded to the original loop by the root's iterator. A value that is *n* levels deep must actually pass its value up a chain of *n* iterators. If the binary tree is relatively shallow, this is not typically a problem; however, an imbalanced binary tree can be extremely deep and therefore expensive to iterate recursively.

Guidelines

CONSIDER using nonrecursive algorithms when iterating over potentially deep data structures.

ADVANCED/BEGINNER TOPIC

`struct` versus `class`

An interesting side effect of defining `Pair<T>` as a `struct` rather than as a `class` is that `SubItems.First` and `SubItems.Second` cannot be assigned directly, even if the setter were public. If you modify the setter to be public, the following code produces a compile error indicating that `SubItems` cannot be modified "because it is not a variable":

```
jfkFamilyTree.SubItems.First =
new BinaryTree<string>(
"Joseph Patrick Kennedy");
```

The issue is that `SubItems` is a property of type `Pair<T>`, a `struct`. Therefore, when the property returns the value, a copy of `SubItems` is made, and assigning `First` on a copy that is promptly lost at the end of the statement would be misleading. Fortunately, the C# compiler prevents this error.

To overcome the issue, don't assign `First` (see the approach in Listing 17.18), use `class` rather than `struct` for `Pair<T>`, don't create a `SubItems` property and instead use a field, or provide properties in `BinaryTree<T>` that give direct access to `SubItems` members.

Canceling Further Iteration: `yield break`

Sometimes you might want to cancel further iteration. You can do so by including an `if` statement so that no further statements within the code are executed. However, you can also use `yield break` to cause `MoveNext()` to return `false` and control to return immediately to the caller and end the loop. Listing 17.19 shows an example of such a method.

Listing 17.19: Escaping Iteration via `yield break`

```
public System.Collections.Generic.IEnumerable<T> GetNotNullEnumerator()
{
    if ((First == null) || (Second == null))
    {
        yield break;
    }
    yield return Second;
    yield return First;
}
```

This method cancels the iteration if either of the elements in the `Pair<T>` class is `null`.

A `yield break` statement is similar to placing a `return` statement at the top of a function when it is determined that there is no work to do. It is a way to exit from further iterations without surrounding all remaining code with an `if` block. As such, it allows multiple exits. Use it with caution, because a casual reading of the code may overlook the early exit.

ADVANCED TOPIC

How Iterators Work

When the C# compiler encounters an iterator, it expands the code into the appropriate CIL for the corresponding enumerator design pattern. In the generated code, the C# compiler first creates a nested private class to implement the `IEnumerator<T>` interface, along with its `Current` property and a `MoveNext()` method. The `Current` property returns a type corresponding to the return type of the iterator. In Listing 17.15 of `Pair<T>`, an iterator returns a `T` type. The C# compiler examines the code contained within the iterator and creates the necessary code within the `MoveNext` method and the `Current` property to mimic its behavior. For the `Pair<T>` iterator, the C# compiler generates roughly equivalent code (see Listing 17.20).

Listing 17.20: C# Equivalent of Compiler-Generated C# Code for Iterators

```
using System;
using System.Collections;
using System.Collections.Generic;
// ...
    [NullableContext(1)]
    [Nullable(0)]
    public struct Pair<[Nullable(2)] T> : IPair<T>, IEnumerable<T>,
↪IEnumerable
    {
        public Pair(T first, T second)
        {
            First = first;
            Second = second;
        }

        public T First { get; }

        public T Second { get; }

        public T this[PairItem index]
        {
            get
            {
                PairItem pairItem = index;
                PairItem pairItem2 = pairItem;
                T result;
                if (pairItem2 != PairItem.First)
                {
                    if (pairItem2 != PairItem.Second)
                    {
                        throw new NotImplementedException(
                            string.Format(
                                "The enum {0} has not been implemented",
                                index.ToString()));
                    }
                    result = Second;
                }
                else
                {
                    result = First;
                }
                return result;
            }
        }
```

```
        public IEnumerator<T> GetEnumerator()
        {
            yield return First;
            yield return Second;
            yield break;
        }

        IEnumerator IEnumerable.GetEnumerator()
        {
            return GetEnumerator();
        }
    }
}
```

Because the compiler takes the `yield return` statement and generates classes that correspond to what you probably would have written manually, iterators in C# exhibit the same performance characteristics as classes that implement the enumerator design pattern manually. Although there is no performance improvement, the gains in programmer productivity are significant.

ADVANCED TOPIC

Contextual Keywords

Many C# keywords are "reserved" and cannot be used as identifiers unless preceded with an `@` sign. The `yield` keyword is a contextual keyword, not a reserved keyword; thus, it is legal (though confusing) to declare a local variable called `yield`. In fact, all the keywords added to C# after version 1.0 have been contextual keywords; this helps prevent accidental breakages when upgrading existing programs to use new versions of the language.

Had the C# designers chosen to use `yield value;` instead of `yield return value;` as the syntax for an iterator to yield, a possible ambiguity would have been introduced: `yield(1+2);` now might be yielding a value, or it might be passing the value as an argument to a method called `yield`.

Since it was previously never legal to have the identifier `yield` appear immediately before `return` or `break`, the C# compiler knows that such a usage of `yield` must be as a keyword, not an identifier.

Creating Multiple Iterators in a Single Class

Previous iterator examples implemented `IEnumerable<T>.GetEnumerator()`, the method that `foreach` seeks implicitly. Sometimes you might want different iteration sequences, such as iterating in reverse, filtering the results, or iterating over an object projection other than the default. You can declare additional iterators in the class by encapsulating them within properties or methods that return `IEnumerable<T>` or `IEnumerable`. If you want to iterate over the elements of `Pair<T>` in reverse, for example, you could provide a `GetReverseEnumerator()` method, as shown in Listing 17.21.

Listing 17.21: Using `yield return` in a Method That Returns `IEnumerable<T>`

```
public struct Pair<T> : IPair<T>, IEnumerable<T>
{
    // ...
    public IEnumerable<T> GetReverseEnumerator()
    {
        yield return Second;
        yield return First;
    }
    // ...
    public static void Main()
    {
        var game = new Pair<string>("Redskins", "Eagles");
        foreach (string name in game.GetReverseEnumerator())
        {
            Console.WriteLine(name);
        }
    }
```

Note that you return `IEnumerable<T>`, not `IEnumerator<T>`. This is different from `IEnumerable<T>.GetEnumerator()`, which returns `IEnumerator<T>`. The code in `Main()` demonstrates how to call `GetReverseEnumerator()` using a `foreach` loop.

`yield` Statement Requirements

You can use the `yield return` statement only in members that return an `IEnumerator<T>` or `IEnumerable<T>` type, or their nongeneric equivalents. Members whose bodies include a `yield return` statement may not have a simple `return`. If the member uses the `yield return` statement, the C# compiler generates the necessary code to maintain the state of the iterator. In contrast, if the member uses the `return` statement instead of `yield return`, the programmer is responsible for maintaining his own state machine and returning an instance of one of the iterator interfaces. Further, just as all code paths in a method with a return type must contain a `return` statement accompanied by a value (assuming they don't throw an exception), so all code paths in an iterator must contain a `yield return` statement if they are to return any data.

The following additional restrictions on the `yield` statement result in compiler errors if they are violated:

- The `yield` statement may appear only inside a method, a user-defined operator, or the `get` accessor of an indexer or property. The member must not take any `ref` or `out` parameter.
- The `yield` statement may not appear anywhere inside an anonymous method or lambda expression (see Chapter 13).
- The `yield` statement may not appear inside the `catch` and `finally` clauses of the `try` statement. Furthermore, a `yield` statement may appear in a try block only if there is no catch block.

Summary

In this chapter, we reviewed the key collection classes and considered how they fit into categories according to the interfaces that they support. Each class focuses on inserting items into and retrieving items from the collection, using mechanisms such as by key, by index, or by FIFO or LIFO, to name a few examples. We also explored how to iterate over the collection. In addition, the chapter explained how to define custom collections with custom iterators for enumerating through items within the collection. (Iterators involve a contextual keyword, `yield`, that C# uses to generate the underlying CIL code that implements the iterator pattern used by the `foreach` loop.)

In Chapter 18, we explore reflection, a topic briefly touched on earlier, albeit with little to no explanation. Reflection allows us to examine the structure of a type within CIL code at runtime.

18

Reflection, Attributes, and Dynamic Programming

Attributes are a means of inserting additional metadata into an assembly and associating the metadata with a programming construct such as a class, method, or property. This chapter investigates the details surrounding attributes that are built into the framework and describes how to define custom attributes. To take advantage of custom attributes, it is necessary to identify them. This is handled through reflection.

This chapter begins with a look at reflection, including how you can use it to dynamically bind at execution time based on member invocation by name (or metadata) at compile time. Reflection is frequently leveraged within tools such as a code generator. In addition, reflection is used at execution time when the call target is unknown.

The chapter ends with a discussion of dynamic programming,[1] a feature that greatly simplifies working with data that is dynamic and requires execution-time rather than compile-time binding.

Reflection

Using reflection, it is possible to do the following:

1. Added in C# 4.0.

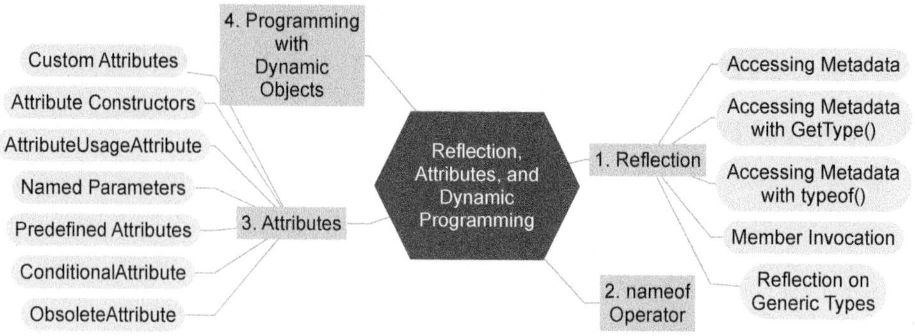

- Access the metadata for types within an assembly. This includes constructs such as the full type name, member names, and any attributes decorating the construct.
- Dynamically invoke a type's members at runtime using the metadata, rather than a compile-time–defined binding.

Reflection is the process of examining the metadata within an assembly. Traditionally, when code compiles down to a machine language, all the metadata (such as type and method names) about the code is discarded. In contrast, when C# compiles into the Common Intermediate Language (CIL), it maintains most of the metadata about the code. Furthermore, using reflection, it is possible to enumerate through all the types within an assembly and search for those that match certain criteria. You access a type's metadata through instances of `System.Type`, and this object includes methods for enumerating the type instance's members. Additionally, it is possible to invoke those members on objects that are of the examined type.

The facility for reflection enables a host of new paradigms that otherwise are unavailable. For example, reflection enables you to enumerate over all the types within an assembly, along with their members, and in the process create stubs for documentation of the assembly API. To create the API documentation, you can then combine the metadata retrieved from reflection with the XML document created from XML comments (using the `/doc` switch). Similarly, programmers can use reflection metadata to generate code for persisting (serializing) business objects into a database. It can also be used in a list control that displays a collection of objects. Given the collection, a list control could use reflection to iterate over all the properties of an object in the collection, defining a column within the list for each property. Furthermore, by invoking each property on each object, the list control could populate each row and column with the data contained in the object, even though the data type of the object is unknown at compile time.

`XmlSerializer`, `ValueType`, and the Microsoft .NET Framework's `DataBinder` are a few of the classes in the framework that use reflection for portions of their implementation as well.

Accessing Metadata Using `System.Type`

The key to reading a type's metadata is to obtain an instance of `System.Type` that represents the target type instance. `System.Type` provides all the methods for retrieving the information about a type. You can use it to answer questions such as the following:

- What is the type's name (`Type.Name`)?
- Is the type public (`Type.IsPublic`)?
- What is the type's base type (`Type.BaseType`)?
- Does the type support any interfaces (`Type.GetInterfaces()`)?
- Which assembly is the type defined in (`Type.Assembly`)?
- What are a type's properties, methods, fields, and so on (`Type.GetProperties()`, `Type.GetMethods()`, `Type.GetFields()`, and so on)?
- Which attributes decorate a type (`Type.GetCustomAttributes()`)?

There are more such members, but all of them provide information about a particular type. The key is to obtain a reference to a type's `Type` object, and the two primary ways to do so are through `object.GetType()` and `typeof()`.

Note that the `GetMethods()` call does not return extension methods. These methods are available only as static members on the implementing type.

GetType()

`object` includes a `GetType()` member, so all types necessarily include this function. You call `GetType()` to retrieve an instance of `System.Type` corresponding to the original object. Listing 18.1 demonstrates this process, using a `Type` instance from `DateTime`. Output 18.1 shows the results.

LISTING 18.1: Using `Type.GetProperties()` to Obtain an Object's Public Properties

```
DateTime dateTime = new();

Type type = dateTime.GetType();
foreach(
    System.Reflection.PropertyInfo property in
        type.GetProperties())
{
    Console.WriteLine(property.Name);
}
```

OUTPUT 18.1

```
Date
Day
DayOfWeek
DayOfYear
Hour
Kind
Millisecond
Minute
Month
Now
UtcNow
Second
Ticks
TimeOfDay
Today
Year
```

After calling `GetType()`, you iterate over each `System.Reflection.PropertyInfo` instance returned from `Type.GetProperties()` and display the property names. The key to calling `GetType()` is that you must have an object instance. However, sometimes no such instance is available. Static classes, for example, cannot be instantiated, so there is no way to call `GetType()` with them.

typeof()

Another way to retrieve a `Type` object is with the `typeof` expression. `typeof` binds at compile time to a particular `Type` instance, and it takes a type directly as a parameter. The exception is for the type parameter on a generic type, as it isn't determined until runtime. Listing 18.2 demonstrates the use of `typeof` with `Enum.Parse()`.

Listing 18.2: Using `typeof()` to create a `System.Type` instance

```
using System.Diagnostics;
// ...
        ThreadPriorityLevel priority;
        priority = (ThreadPriorityLevel)Enum.Parse(
                typeof(ThreadPriorityLevel), "Idle");
        //...
```

In this listing, `Enum.Parse()` takes a `Type` object identifying an enum and then converts a string to the specific enum value. In this case, it converts `"Idle"` to `System.Diagnostics.ThreadPriorityLevel.Idle`.

Similarly, Listing 18.3 in the next section uses the `typeof` expression inside the `CompareTo(object obj)` method to verify that the type of the `obj` parameter was indeed what was expected:

```
if(obj.GetType() != typeof(Contact)) { ... }
```

The `typeof` expression is resolved at compile time such that a type comparison—perhaps comparing the type returned from a call to `GetType()`—can determine if an object is of a specific type.

Member Invocation

The possibilities with reflection don't stop with retrieving the metadata. You can also take the metadata and dynamically invoke the members it identifies. Consider the possibility of defining a class to represent an application's command line.[2] The difficulty with a `CommandLineInfo` class such as this relates to populating the class with the actual command-line data that started the application. However, using reflection, you can map the command-line options to property names and then dynamically set the properties at runtime. Listing 18.3 demonstrates this process.

LISTING 18.3: Dynamically Invoking a Member

```
using System.Diagnostics;
using System.IO;
using System.Reflection;

public partial class Program
{
    public static void Main(string[] args)
    {
        CommandLineInfo commandLine = new();
        if(!CommandLineHandler.TryParse(
            args, commandLine, out string? errorMessage))
        {
            Console.WriteLine(errorMessage);
            DisplayHelp();
        }
        else if (commandLine.Help || string.
↪IsNullOrWhiteSpace(commandLine.Out))
        {
            DisplayHelp();
        }
        else
        {
            if(commandLine.Priority !=
                ProcessPriorityClass.Normal)
            {
                // Change thread priority
            }
            // ...
        }
    }

    private static void DisplayHelp()
```

2. The .NET Standard 1.6 added the `CommandLineUtils NuGet` package, which also provides a command-line parsing mechanism. For more information, see my MSDN article on the topic at http://itl.tc/sept2016.

```
    {
        // Display the command-line help.
        Console.WriteLine(
            "Compress.exe /Out:< file name > /Help "
            + "/Priority:RealTime | High | "
            + "AboveNormal | Normal | BelowNormal | Idle");

    }
}

public partial class Program
{
    private class CommandLineInfo
    {
        public bool Help { get; set; }

        public string? Out { get; set; }

        public ProcessPriorityClass Priority { get; set; }
            = ProcessPriorityClass.Normal;
    }

}

public class CommandLineHandler
{
    public static void Parse(string[] args, object commandLine)
    {
        if (!TryParse(args, commandLine, out string? errorMessage))
        {
            throw new InvalidOperationException(errorMessage);
        }
    }

    public static bool TryParse(string[] args, object commandLine,
        out string? errorMessage)
    {
        bool success = false;
        errorMessage = null;
        foreach(string arg in args)
        {
            string option;
            if(arg[0] == '/' || arg[0] == '-')
            {
                string[] optionParts = arg.Split(
                    new char[] { ':' }, 2);
```

```
        // Remove the slash|dash
        option = optionParts[0].Remove(0, 1);
        PropertyInfo? property =
            commandLine.GetType().GetProperty(option,
                BindingFlags.IgnoreCase |
                BindingFlags.Instance |
                BindingFlags.Public);
        if(property != null)
        {
            if(property.PropertyType == typeof(bool))
            {
                // Last parameters for handling indexers
                property.SetValue(
                    commandLine, true, null);
                success = true;
            }
            else if(
                property.PropertyType == typeof(string))
            {
                property.SetValue(
                    commandLine, optionParts[1], null);
                success = true;
            }
            else if (
                // property.PropertyType.IsEnum also available
                property.PropertyType ==
                    typeof(ProcessPriorityClass))
            {
                try
                {
                    property.SetValue(commandLine,
                        Enum.Parse(
                            typeof(ProcessPriorityClass),
                            optionParts[1], true),
                        null);
                    success = true;
                }
                catch (ArgumentException)
                {
                    success = false;
                    errorMessage =
                        $@"The option '{
                            optionParts[1]
                            }' is invalid for '{
                            option }'";
                }
            }
```

```
                    else
                    {
                        success = false;
                        errorMessage =
                            $@"Data type '{
                                property.PropertyType }' on {
                                commandLine.GetType() } is not
↪supported.";
                    }
                }
                else
                {
                    success = false;
                    errorMessage =
                      $"Option '{ option }' is not supported.";
                }
            }
        }
        return success;
    }
}
```

Although Listing 18.3 is long, the code is relatively simple. `Main()` begins by instantiating a `CommandLineInfo` class. This type is defined specifically to contain the command-line data for this program. Each property corresponds to a command-line option for the program, where the command line is as shown in Output 18.2.

Output 18.2

```
Compress.exe /Out:<file name> /Help
/Priority:RealTime|High|AboveNormal|Normal|BelowNormal|Idle
```

The `CommandLineInfo` object is passed to the `CommandLineHandler`'s `TryParse()` method. This method begins by enumerating through each option and separating out the option name (e.g., `Help` or `Out`). Once the name is determined, the code reflects on the `CommandLineInfo` object, looking for an instance property with the same name. If it finds such a property, it assigns the property using a call to `SetValue()` and specifies the data corresponding to the property type. (For arguments, this call accepts the object on which to set the value, the new value, and an additional `index` parameter that is `null` unless the property is an indexer.) This listing handles three property types: Boolean, string, and enum. In the case of enums, you parse the option value and assign the text's enum equivalent to the property. Assuming the `TryParse()` call was successful, the method exits and the `CommandLineInfo` object is initialized with the data from the command line.

Interestingly, although `CommandLineInfo` is a private class nested within `Program`, `CommandLineHandler` has no trouble reflecting over it and even invoking its members. In other words, reflection can circumvent accessibility rules as long as appropriate permissions are established. For example, if `Out` was private, the `TryParse()` method could still assign it a value. Because of this, it would be possible to move `CommandLineHandler` into a separate assembly and share it across multiple programs, each with its own `CommandLineInfo` class.

In this example, you invoke a member on `CommandLineInfo` using `PropertyInfo.SetValue()`. Not surprisingly, `PropertyInfo` also includes a `GetValue()` method for retrieving data from the property. For a method, however, there is a `MethodInfo` class with an `Invoke()` member. Both `MethodInfo` and `PropertyInfo` derive from `MemberInfo` (albeit indirectly), as shown in Figure 18.1.

Reflection on Generic Types

The introduction of generic types in version 2.0 of the Common Language Runtime (CLR) necessitated additional reflection features. Runtime reflection on generics determines whether a class or method contains a generic type and any type parameters or arguments it may include.

Determining the Type of Type Parameters

In the same way that you can use a `typeof` operator with nongeneric types to retrieve an instance of `System.Type`, so you can use the `typeof` operator on type parameters in a generic type or generic method. Listing 18.4 applies the `typeof` operator to the type parameter in the `Add` method of a `Stack` class.

LISTING 18.4: Declaring the `Stack<T>` Class

```
public class Stack<T>
{
    //...
```

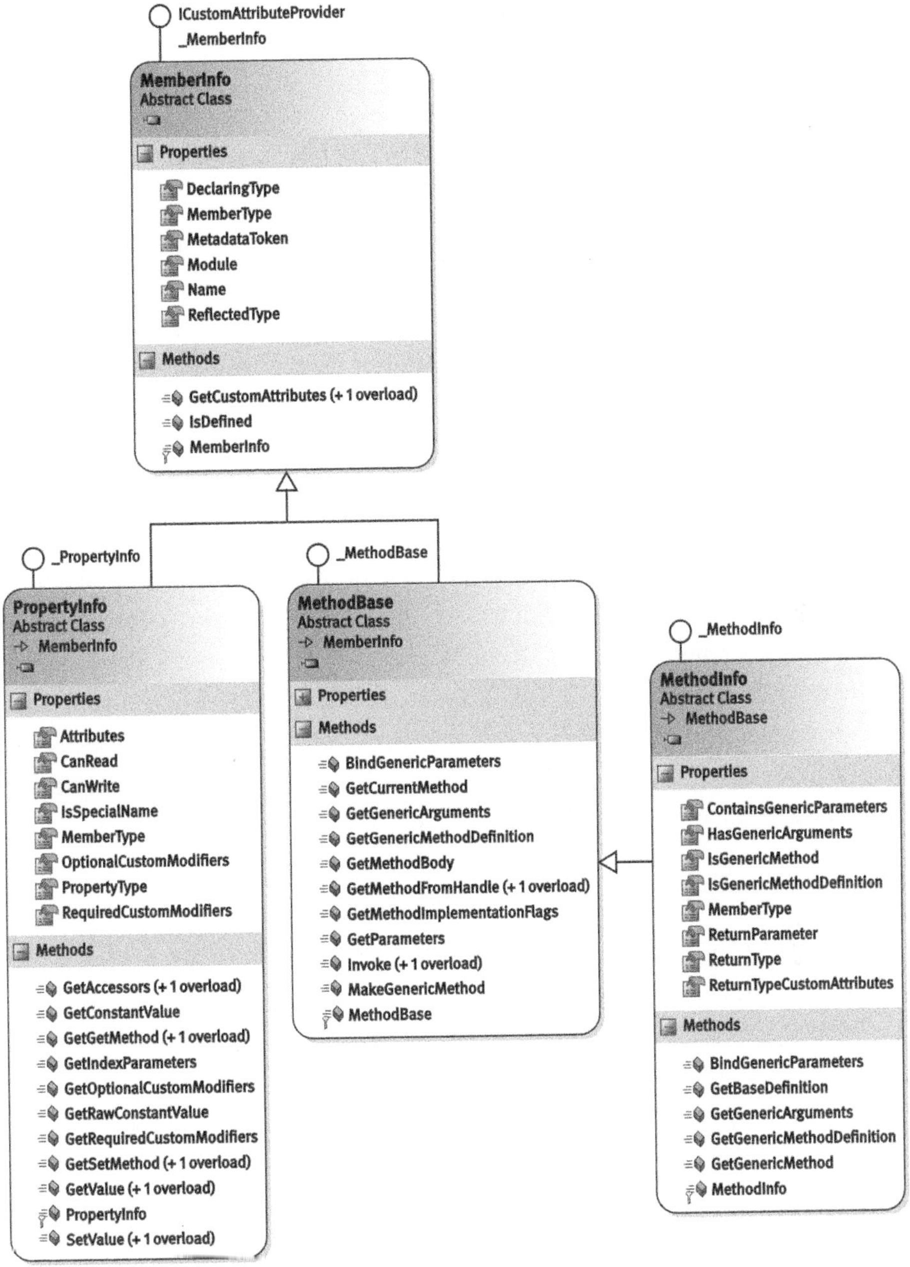

FIGURE 18.1: `MemberInfo` derived classes

```
    public void Add(T i)
    {
        //...
        Type t = typeof(T);
        //...
    }
    //...
}
```

Once you have an instance of the Type object for the type parameter, you may then use reflection on the type parameter itself to determine its behavior and tailor the Add method to the specific type more effectively.

Determining Whether a Class or Method Supports Generics

In the System.Type class for the version 2.0 release of the CLR, a handful of methods were added that determine whether a given type supports generic parameters and arguments. A generic argument is a type parameter supplied when a generic class is instantiated. You can determine whether a class or method contains generic parameters that have not yet been set by querying the Type .ContainsGenericParameters property, as demonstrated in Listing 18.5 with Output 18.3.

LISTING 18.5: Reflection with Generics

```
public class Program
{
    public static void Main()
    {
        Type type;
        type = typeof(System.Nullable<>);
        Console.WriteLine(type.ContainsGenericParameters);
        Console.WriteLine(type.IsGenericType);

        type = typeof(System.Nullable<DateTime>);
        Console.WriteLine(type.ContainsGenericParameters);
        Console.WriteLine(type.IsGenericType);
    }
}
```

OUTPUT 18.3

```
True
True
False
True
```

`Type.IsGenericType` is a Boolean property that evaluates whether a type is generic.

Obtaining Type Parameters for a Generic Class or Method

You can obtain a list of generic arguments, or type parameters, from a generic class by calling the `GetGenericArguments()` method. The result is an array of `System.Type` instances that corresponds to the order in which they were declared as type parameters of the generic class. Listing 18.6 reflects into a generic type and obtains each type parameter; Output 18.4 shows the results.

LISTING 18.6: Using Reflection with Generic Types

```
public class Program
{
    public static void Main()
    {
        Stack<int> s = new();

        Type t = s.GetType();

        foreach(Type type in t.GetGenericArguments())
        {
            System.Console.WriteLine(
                "Type parameter: " + type.FullName);
        }
        //...
    }
}
```

OUTPUT 18.4

```
Type parameter: System.Int32
```

nameof Operator

We briefly touched on the `nameof` operator in Chapter 11, where it was used to provide the name of a parameter in an argument exception:

```
throw new ArgumentException(
"The argument did not represent a digit", nameof(textDigit));
```

This contextual keyword[3] produces a constant string containing the unqualified name of whatever program element is specified as an argument. In this case, `textDigit` is a parameter to the method, so `nameof(textDigit)` returns "`textDigit`." (Given that this activity happens at compile time, `nameof` is not technically reflection. We include it here because ultimately it receives data about the assembly and its structure.)

You might ask what advantage is gained by using `nameof(textDigit)` over simply `"textDigit"` (especially given that the latter might even seem easier to use to some programmers). The advantages are twofold:

- The C# compiler ensures that the argument to the `nameof` operator is, in fact, a valid program element. This helps prevent errors when a program element name is changed, helps prevent misspellings, and so on.
- IDE tools work better with the `nameof` operator than with literal strings. For example, the "find all references" tool will find program elements mentioned in a `nameof` expression but not in a literal string. The automatic refactoring also works better, and so on.

Begin 11.0

In the snippet given earlier, `nameof(textDigit)` produces the name of a parameter. In reality, the `nameof` operator works with any program element that is in scope. In fact, starting in C# 11, you can even use `nameof` with parameter names of the method an attribute is decorating. For example, Listing 18.7 uses `nameof` to pass the property name to `INotifyPropertyChanged.PropertyChanged`.

End 11.0

3. Introduced in C# 6.0.

Listing 18.7: Dynamically Invoking a Member

```
using System.ComponentModel;

public class Person : INotifyPropertyChanged
{
    public event PropertyChangedEventHandler? PropertyChanged;
    public Person(string name)
    {
        Name = name;
    }
    private string _Name = string.Empty;
    public string Name
    {
        get { return _Name; }
        set
        {
            if (_Name != value)
            {
                _Name = value;
                PropertyChanged?.Invoke(
                    this,
                    new PropertyChangedEventArgs(
                        nameof(Name)));
            }
        }
    }
    // ...
}
```

No matter whether only the unqualified "Name" is provided (because it's in scope) or the fully (or partially) qualified name such as `Person.Name` is used, the result is only the final identifier (the last element in a dotted name).

You can still use the `CallerMemberName` parameter attribute[4] to obtain a property's name; see http://itl.tc/CallerMemberName for an example.

Attributes

Before delving into the details of how to program attributes, we should consider a use case that demonstrates their utility. In the `CommandLineHandler` example in

4. Starting in C# 5.0.

Listing 18.3, you dynamically set a class's properties based on the command-line option matching the property name. This approach is insufficient, however, when the command-line option is an invalid property name. The command-line option /?, for example, cannot be supported. Furthermore, this mechanism doesn't provide any way of identifying which options are required versus which are truly optional.

Instead of relying on an exact match between the option name and the property name, you can use attributes to identify additional metadata about the decorated construct—in this case, the option that the attribute decorates. With attributes, you can decorate a property as `Required` and provide a `/?` option alias. In other words, attributes are a means of associating additional data with a property (and other constructs).

Attributes appear within square brackets preceding the construct they decorate. For example, you can modify the `CommandLineInfo` class to include attributes, as shown in Listing 18.8.

LISTING 18.8: Decorating a Property with an Attribute

```
public class CommandLineInfo
{
    [CommandLineSwitchAlias("?")]
    public bool Help { get; set; }

    [CommandLineSwitchRequired]
    public string? Out { get; set; }

    public System.Diagnostics.ProcessPriorityClass Priority
    { get; set; } =
        System.Diagnostics.ProcessPriorityClass.Normal;
}
```

In Listing 18.8, the `Help` and `Out` properties are decorated with attributes. These attributes have two purposes: They allow an alias of `/?` for `/Help`, and they indicate that `/Out` is a required parameter. The idea is that from within the `CommandLineHandler.TryParse()` method, you enable support for option aliases and, assuming the parsing was successful, you check that all required switches were specified.

Attributes may be associated with the same construct in two ways. First, you can separate the attributes with commas within the same square brackets. Alternatively, you can place each attribute within its own square brackets. Listing 18.9 provides examples.

Listing 18.9: Decorating a Property with Multiple Attributes

```
[CommandLineSwitchRequired,
CommandLineSwitchAlias("FileName")]
public string? Out { get; set; }

public System.Diagnostics.ProcessPriorityClass Priority
    { get; set; } =
        System.Diagnostics.ProcessPriorityClass.Normal;
}
```

In addition to decorating properties, developers can use attributes to decorate assemblies, classes, constructors, delegates, enums, events, fields, generic parameters, interfaces, methods, modules, parameters, properties, return values, and structs. For the majority of these cases, applying an attribute involves the same square brackets syntax shown in Listing 18.9. However, this syntax doesn't work for return values, assemblies, and modules.

Assembly attributes are used to add metadata about the assembly. Visual Studio's Project Wizard for .NET Framework projects, for example, generates an `AssemblyInfo.cs` file that includes numerous attributes about the assembly. Listing 18.10 is an example of such a file.

Listing 18.10: Assembly Attributes within `AssemblyInfo.cs`

```
using System.Reflection;
using System.Runtime.CompilerServices;
using System.Runtime.InteropServices;

// General information about an assembly is controlled
// through the following set of attributes. Change these
// attribute values to modify the information
// associated with an assembly.
[assembly: AssemblyTitle("CompressionLibrary")]
[assembly: AssemblyDescription("")]
[assembly: AssemblyConfiguration("")]
[assembly: AssemblyCompany("IntelliTect")]
```

```
[assembly: AssemblyProduct("Compression Library")]
[assembly: AssemblyCopyright("Copyright© IntelliTect 2006-2018")]
[assembly: AssemblyTrademark("")]
[assembly: AssemblyCulture("")]

// Setting ComVisible to false makes the types in this
// assembly not visible to COM components. If you need to
// access a type in this assembly from COM, set the ComVisible
// attribute to true on that type.
[assembly: ComVisible(false)]

// The following GUID is for the ID of the typelib
// if this project is exposed to COM
[assembly: Guid("417a9609-24ae-4323-b1d6-cef0f87a42c3")]

// Version information for an assembly consists
// of the following four values:
//
//      Major Version
//      Minor Version
//      Build Number
//      Revision
//
// You can specify all the values or you can
// default the Revision and Build Numbers
// by using the '*' as shown below:
// [assembly: AssemblyVersion("1.0.*")]
[assembly: AssemblyVersion("1.0.0.0")]
[assembly: AssemblyFileVersion("1.0.0.0")]
```

The `assembly` attributes define things such as the company, product, and assembly version number. Similar to using `assembly`, identifying an attribute usage as `module` requires prefixing it with `module:`. The restriction on `assembly` and `module` attributes is that they must appear after the `using` directive but before any namespace or class declarations. The attributes in Listing 18.10 are generated by the Visual Studio Project Wizard and should be included in all projects to mark the resultant binaries with information about the contents of the executable or dynamic link library (DLL).

Return attributes, such as the one shown in Listing 18.11, appear before a method declaration but use the same type of syntax structure.

Listing 18.11: Specifying a Return Attribute

```
[return: Description(
   "Returns true if the object is in a valid state.")]
public bool IsValid()
{
    // ...
    return true;
}
```

In addition to `assembly:` and `return:`, C# allows for explicit target identifications of `module:`, `class:`, and `method:`, corresponding to attributes that decorate the module, class, and method, respectively. `class:` and `method:`, however, are optional, as demonstrated earlier.

One of the conveniences of using attributes is that the language takes into consideration the attribute naming convention, which calls for `Attribute` to appear at the end of the name. However, in all the attribute *uses* in the preceding listings, no such suffix appears, even though each attribute used follows the naming convention. This is because although the full name (`DescriptionAttribute`, `AssemblyVersionAttribute`, and so on) is allowed when applying an attribute, C# makes the suffix optional. Generally, no such suffix appears when *applying* an attribute; rather, it appears only when defining one or using the attribute inline (such as `typeof(DescriptionAttribute)`).

Note that instead of generating an `AssemblyInfo.cs` file, .NET Core–based projects allow specification of the assembly information within the `*.CSPROJ` file. Listing 18.12, for example, injects corresponding assembly attributes into the assembly at compile time. The results are shown in Output 18.5.

Listing 18.12: Defining a Custom Attribute

```
<Project>
  <PropertyGroup>
    <Company>Addison Wesley</Company>
    <Copyright>Copyright © Addison Wesley 2020</Copyright>
    <Product>Essential C# 8.0</Product>
    <Version>8.0</Version>
  </PropertyGroup>
</Project>
```

Output 18.5

```
[assembly: AssemblyCompany("Addison Wesley")]
[assembly: AssemblyCopyright("Copyright © Addison Wesley 2020")]
[assembly: AssemblyFileVersion("8.0.0.0")]
[assembly: AssemblyInformationalVersion("8.0")]
[assembly: AssemblyProduct("Essential C# 8.0")]
[assembly: AssemblyVersion("8.0.0.0")]
```

Guidelines

DO apply `AssemblyVersionAttribute` to assemblies with public types.

CONSIDER applying `AssemblyFileVersionAttribute` and `AssemblyCopyrightAttribute` to provide additional information about the assembly.

DO apply the following information assembly attributes: `System.Reflection.AssemblyCompanyAttribute`, `System.Reflection.AssemblyCopyrightAttribute`, `System.Reflection.AssemblyDescriptionAttribute`, and `System.Reflection.AssemblyProductAttribute`.

Custom Attributes

Defining a custom attribute is relatively trivial. Attributes are objects; therefore, to define an attribute, you need to define a class. The characteristic that turns a general class into an attribute is that it derives from `System.Attribute`. Consequently, you can create a `CommandLineSwitchRequiredAttribute` class, as shown in Listing 18.13.

Listing 18.13: Defining a Custom Attribute

```
public class CommandLineSwitchRequiredAttribute : Attribute
{
}
```

With that simple definition, you now can use the attribute as demonstrated in Listing 18.8. So far, no code responds to the attribute; therefore, the `Out` property that includes the attribute will have no effect on command-line parsing.

Guidelines

DO name custom attribute classes with the suffix `Attribute`.

Looking for Attributes

In addition to providing properties for reflecting on a type's members, `Type` includes methods to retrieve the `Attributes` decorating that type. Similarly, all the reflection types (e.g., `PropertyInfo` and `MethodInfo`) include members for retrieving a list of attributes that decorate a type. Listing 18.14 defines a method to return a list of required switches that are missing from the command line.

Listing 18.14: Retrieving a Custom Attribute

```
using System.Reflection;
using System.Collections.Generic;

public class CommandLineSwitchRequiredAttribute : Attribute
{
    public static string[] GetMissingRequiredOptions(
        object commandLine)
    {
        List<string> missingOptions = new();
        PropertyInfo[] properties =
            commandLine.GetType().GetProperties();

        foreach(PropertyInfo property in properties)
        {
            Attribute[] attributes =
                 (Attribute[])property.GetCustomAttributes(
                    typeof(CommandLineSwitchRequiredAttribute),
                    false);
            if (attributes.Length > 0 &&
                property.GetValue(commandLine, null) == null)
            {
                missingOptions.Add(property.Name);
            }
        }
        return missingOptions.ToArray();
    }
}
```

The code that checks for an attribute is relatively simple. Given a `PropertyInfo` object (obtained via reflection), you call `GetCustomAttributes()` and specify the attribute sought, then indicate whether to check any overloaded methods. (Alternatively, you can call the `GetCustomAttributes()` method without the attribute type to return all of the attributes.)

Although it is possible to place code for finding the `CommandLineSwitchRequiredAttribute` attribute within the `CommandLineHandler`'s code directly, it makes for better object encapsulation to place the code within the `CommandLineSwitchRequiredAttribute` class itself. This is frequently the pattern for custom attributes. What better location to place code for finding an attribute than in a static method on the attribute class?

Initializing an Attribute through a Constructor

The call to `GetCustomAttributes()` returns an array of objects that can be cast to an `Attribute` array. Because the attribute in our example didn't have any instance members, the only metadata information that it provided in the returned attribute was whether it appeared. Attributes can also encapsulate data, however. Listing 18.15 defines a `CommandLineAliasAttribute` attribute—a custom attribute that provides alias command-line options. For example, you can provide command-line support for `/Help` or `/?` as an abbreviation. Similarly, `/S` could provide an alias to `/Subfolders` that indicates the command should traverse all the subdirectories.

LISTING 18.15: Providing an Attribute Constructor

```
public class CommandLineSwitchAliasAttribute : Attribute
{
    public CommandLineSwitchAliasAttribute(string alias)
    {
        Alias = alias;
    }
    public string Alias { get; }
}
public class CommandLineInfo
{
    [CommandLineSwitchAlias("?")]
    public bool Help { get; set; }
```

```
    // ...
}
```

To support this functionality, you need to provide a constructor for the attribute. Specifically, for the alias, you need a constructor that takes a string argument. (Similarly, if you want to allow multiple aliases, you need to define an attribute that has a `params string` array for a parameter.)

When applying an attribute to a construct, only constant values and `typeof()` expressions are allowed as arguments. This constraint is required to enable their serialization into the resultant CIL. It implies that an attribute constructor should require parameters of the appropriate types; creating a constructor that takes arguments of type `System.DateTime` would be of little value, as there are no `System.DateTime` constants in C#.

The objects returned from `PropertyInfo.GetCustomAttributes()` will be initialized with the specified constructor arguments, as demonstrated in Listing 18.16.

LISTING 18.16: Retrieving a Specific Attribute and Checking Its Initialization

```
PropertyInfo property =
    typeof(CommandLineInfo).GetProperty("Help")!;
CommandLineSwitchAliasAttribute? attribute =
    (CommandLineSwitchAliasAttribute?)
        property.GetCustomAttribute(
        typeof(CommandLineSwitchAliasAttribute), false);
if(attribute?.Alias == "?")
{
    Console.WriteLine("Help(?)");
};
```

Furthermore, as Listing 18.17 and Listing 18.18 demonstrate, you can use similar code in a `GetSwitches()` method on `CommandLineAliasAttribute` that returns a dictionary collection of all the switches, including those from the property names, and associate each name with the corresponding attribute on the command-line object.

Listing 18.17: Retrieving Custom Attribute Instances

```
using System.Reflection;
using System.Collections.Generic;

public class CommandLineSwitchAliasAttribute : Attribute
{
    public CommandLineSwitchAliasAttribute(string alias)
    {
        Alias = alias;
    }

    public string Alias { get; set; }

    public static Dictionary<string, PropertyInfo> GetSwitches(
        object commandLine)
    {
        PropertyInfo[] properties;
        Dictionary<string, PropertyInfo> options = new();

        properties = commandLine.GetType().GetProperties(
            BindingFlags.Public | BindingFlags.Instance);
        foreach(PropertyInfo property in properties)
        {
            options.Add(property.Name, property);
            foreach (CommandLineSwitchAliasAttribute attribute in
                property.GetCustomAttributes(
                typeof(CommandLineSwitchAliasAttribute), false))
            {
                options.Add(attribute.Alias.ToLower(), property);
            }
        }
        return options;
    }
}
```

Listing 18.18: Updating `CommandLineHandler.TryParse()` to Handle Aliases

```
using System.Reflection;
using System.Collections.Generic;
using System.Diagnostics;

public class CommandLineHandler
{
    // ...
    public static bool TryParse(
```

```
        string[] args, object commandLine,
        out string? errorMessage)
    {
        bool success = false;
        errorMessage = null;

        Dictionary<string, PropertyInfo> options =
            CommandLineSwitchAliasAttribute.GetSwitches(
                commandLine);

        foreach (string arg in args)
        {
            string option;
            if(arg[0] == '/' || arg[0] == '-')
            {
                string[] optionParts = arg.Split(
                    new char[] { ':' }, 2);
                option = optionParts[0].Remove(0, 1).ToLower();

                if (options.TryGetValue(option, out PropertyInfo?
↪property))
                {
                    success = SetOption(
                        commandLine, property,
                        optionParts, ref errorMessage);
                }
                else
                {
                    success = false;
                    errorMessage =
                        $"Option '{option}' is not supported.";
                }
            }
        }
        return success;
    }

    private static bool SetOption(
        object commandLine, PropertyInfo property,
        string[] optionParts, ref string? errorMessage)
    {
        bool success;

        if(property.PropertyType == typeof(bool))
        {
            // Last parameters for handling indexers
            property.SetValue(
```

```
                    commandLine, true, null);
                success = true;
            }
            else
            {

                if (optionParts.Length < 2
                    || optionParts[1] == "")
                {
                    // No setting was provided for the switch.
                    success = false;
                    errorMessage =
                        $"You must specify the value for the { property.
↪Name } option.";
                }
                else if(
                    property.PropertyType == typeof(string))
                {
                    property.SetValue(
                        commandLine, optionParts[1], null);
                    success = true;
                }
                else if(
                    // property.PropertyType.IsEnum also available
                    property.PropertyType ==
                        typeof(ProcessPriorityClass))
                {
                    success = TryParseEnumSwitch(
                        commandLine, optionParts,
                        property, ref errorMessage);
                }
                else
                {
                    success = false;
                    errorMessage =
                        $@"Data type '{ property.PropertyType.ToString() }'
↪on {
                        commandLine.GetType().ToString() } is not supported.
↪";
                }
            }
            return success;
        }
```

Guidelines

DO provide get-only properties (without public setters) on attributes with required property values.

DO provide constructor parameters to initialize properties on attributes with required properties. Each parameter should have the same name (albeit with different casing) as the corresponding property.

AVOID providing constructor parameters to initialize attribute properties corresponding to the optional arguments (and, therefore, avoid overloading custom attribute constructors).

`System.AttributeUsageAttribute`

Most attributes are intended to decorate only particular constructs. For example, it makes no sense to allow `CommandLineOptionAttribute` to decorate a class or an assembly, as the attribute would be meaningless in those contexts. To avoid inappropriate use of an attribute, custom attributes can be decorated with `System.AttributeUsageAttribute` (yes, an attribute is decorating a custom attribute declaration). Listing 18.19 (for `CommandLineOptionAttribute`) demonstrates how to do this.

Listing 18.19: Restricting the Constructs an Attribute Can Decorate

```
[AttributeUsage(AttributeTargets.Property)]
public class CommandLineSwitchAliasAttribute : Attribute
{
    // ...
}
```

If the attribute is used inappropriately, as it is in Listing 18.20, it will cause a compile-time error, as Output 18.6 demonstrates.

Listing 18.20: `AttributeUsageAttribute` Restricting Where to Apply an Attribute

```
// ERROR: The attribute usage is restricted to properties
[CommandLineSwitchAlias("?")]
class CommandLineInfo
```

```
{
}
```

OUTPUT 18.6

```
...Program+CommandLineInfo.cs(24,17): error CS0592: Attribute
'CommandLineSwitchAlias' is not valid on this declaration type. It is
valid on 'property, indexer' declarations only.
```

`AttributeUsageAttribute`'s constructor takes an `AttributeTargets` flag. This enum provides a list of all possible targets that the runtime allows an attribute to decorate. For example, if you also allowed `CommandLineSwitchAliasAttribute` on a field, you would update the `AttributeUsageAttribute` class, as shown in Listing 18.21.

LISTING 18.21: Limiting an Attribute's Usage with `AttributeUsageAttribute`

```
// Restrict the attribute to properties and methods
[AttributeUsage(
  AttributeTargets.Field | AttributeTargets.Property)]
public class CommandLineSwitchAliasAttribute : Attribute
{
    // ...
}
```

> **Guidelines**
>
> **DO** apply the `AttributeUsageAttribute` class to custom attributes.

Named Parameters

In addition to restricting what an attribute can decorate, `AttributeUsageAttribute` provides a mechanism for allowing duplicates of the same attribute on a single construct. The syntax appears in Listing 18.22.

This syntax is different from the constructor initialization syntax discussed earlier. The `AllowMultiple` parameter is a **named parameter**, similar to the named parameter syntax used for optional method parameters.[5] Named parameters provide a mechanism for setting specific public properties and fields within the

LISTING 18.22: Using a Named Parameter

```
[AttributeUsage(AttributeTargets.Property, AllowMultiple = true)]
public class CommandLineSwitchAliasAttribute : Attribute
{
    // ...
}
```

attribute constructor call, even though the constructor includes no corresponding parameters. The named attributes are optional designations, but they provide a means of setting additional instance data on the attribute without providing a constructor parameter for the purpose. In this case, `AttributeUsageAttribute` includes a public member called `AllowMultiple`; you can set this member using a named parameter assignment when you use the attribute. Assigning named parameters must occur as the last portion of a constructor, following any explicitly declared constructor parameters.

Named parameters allow for assigning attribute data without providing constructors for every conceivable combination of which attribute properties are specified and which are not. Given that many of an attribute's properties may be optional, this is a useful construct in many cases.

BEGINNER TOPIC

`FlagsAttribute`

Chapter 9 introduced enums and included an Advanced Topic covering `FlagsAttribute`. This framework-defined attribute targets enums that represent flag type values. The Beginner Topic here also addresses `FlagsAttribute`, starting with the sample code shown in Listing 18.23 with Output 18.7.

5. Starting in C# 4.0.

Listing 18.23: Using `FlagsAttribute`

```
/*
[Flags]
public enum FileAttributes
{
    ReadOnly = 0x0001,
    Hidden   = 0x0002,
    // ...
}
*/

public class Program
{
    public static void Main()
    {
        // ...
        string fileName = @"enumtest.txt";
        FileInfo file = new(fileName);

        file.Attributes = FileAttributes.Hidden |
            FileAttributes.ReadOnly;

        Console.WriteLine("\"{0}\" outputs as \"{1}\"",
            file.Attributes.ToString().Replace(",", " |"),
            file.Attributes);

        FileAttributes attributes =
            (FileAttributes)Enum.Parse(typeof(FileAttributes),
            file.Attributes.ToString());

        Console.WriteLine(attributes);

        // ...
    }
}
```

Output 18.7

```
"ReadOnly | Hidden" outputs as "ReadOnly, Hidden"
```

The flag documents that the enumeration values can be combined. Furthermore, it changes the behavior of the `ToString()` and `Parse()` methods. For example, calling `ToString()` on an enumeration that is decorated with `FlagsAttribute` writes out the strings for each enumeration flag that is set. In Listing 18.23, `file.Attributes.ToString()` returns `"ReadOnly, Hidden"` rather than the `3` it would have returned without the `FlagsAttribute` flag. If two enumeration values are the same, the `ToString()` call would return the first one. As mentioned earlier, however, you should use caution when relying on this outcome because it is not localizable.

Parsing a value from a string to the enumeration also works, provided that each enumeration value identifier is separated by a comma.

Note that `FlagsAttribute` does not automatically assign the unique flag values or check that flags have unique values. The values of each enumeration item still must be assigned explicitly.

Predefined Attributes

The `AttributeUsageAttribute` attribute has a special characteristic that you haven't seen yet in the custom attributes you have created in this book. This attribute affects the behavior of the compiler, causing it to sometimes report an error. Unlike the reflection code that you wrote earlier for retrieving `CommandLineRequiredAttribute` and `CommandLineSwitchAliasAttribute`, `AttributeUsageAttribute` has no runtime code; instead, it has built-in compiler support.

`AttributeUsageAttribute` is a predefined attribute. Not only do such attributes provide additional metadata about the constructs they decorate, but the runtime and compiler also behave differently to facilitate these attributes' functionality. Attributes such as `AttributeUsageAttribute`, `FlagsAttribute`, `ObsoleteAttribute`, and `ConditionalAttribute` are examples of predefined attributes. They implement special behavior that only the CLI provider or compiler can offer because there are no extension points for additional noncustom attributes. In contrast, custom attributes are entirely passive. Listing 18.23 includes a couple of predefined attributes; Chapter 19 includes a few more.

System.ConditionalAttribute

Within a single assembly, the `System.Diagnostics.ConditionalAttribute` attribute behaves a little like the `#if/#endif` preprocessor identifier. However, instead of eliminating the CIL code from the assembly, `System.Diagnostics.ConditionalAttribute` will optionally cause the call to behave like a **no-op**, an instruction that does nothing. Listing 18.24 demonstrates the concept, and Output 18.8 shows the results.

Listing 18.24: Using `ConditionalAttribute` to Eliminate a Call

```
#define CONDITION_A
// ...
using System.Diagnostics;

public class Program
{
    public static void Main()
    {
        Console.WriteLine("Begin...");
        MethodA();
        MethodB();
        Console.WriteLine("End...");
    }

    [Conditional("CONDITION_A")]
    public static void MethodA()
    {
        Console.WriteLine("MethodA() executing...");
    }

    [Conditional("CONDITION_B")]
    public static void MethodB()
    {
        Console.WriteLine("MethodB() executing...");
    }
}
```

Output 18.8

```
Begin...
MethodA() executing...
End...
```

This example defined CONDITION_A, so MethodA() executed normally. CONDITION_B, however, was not defined either through #define or by using the csc.exe /Define option. As a result, all calls to Program.MethodB() from within this assembly will do nothing.

Functionally, ConditionalAttribute is similar to placing an #if/#endif around the method invocation. The syntax is cleaner, however, because developers create the effect by adding the ConditionalAttribute attribute to the target method without making any changes to the caller itself.

The C# compiler notices the attribute on a called method during compilation; assuming the preprocessor identifier exists, it then eliminates any calls to the method. ConditionalAttribute, however, does not affect the compiled CIL code on the target method itself (besides the addition of the attribute metadata). Instead, it affects the call site during compilation by removing the calls. This further distinguishes ConditionalAttribute from #if/#endif when calling across assemblies. Because the decorated method is still compiled and included in the target assembly, the determination of whether to call a method is based not on the preprocessor identifier in the *callee's* assembly, but rather on the *caller's* assembly. In other words, if you create a second assembly that defines CONDITION_B, any calls to Program.MethodB() from the second assembly will execute. This is a useful characteristic in many tracing and testing scenarios. In fact, calls to System.Diagnostics.Trace and System.Diagnostics.Debug use this trait with ConditionalAttributes on TRACE and DEBUG preprocessor identifiers.

Because methods don't execute whenever the preprocessor identifier is not defined, ConditionalAttribute may not be used on methods that include an out parameter or specify a return other than void. Doing so causes a compile-time error. This makes sense because potentially none of the code within the decorated method will execute, so it is unknown what to return to the caller. Similarly, properties cannot be decorated with ConditionalAttribute. The AttributeUsage (see the section titled "System.AttributeUsageAttribute" earlier in this chapter) for ConditionalAttribute[6] is decorated with the AttributeTargets.Class

6. A feature introduced in Microsoft .NET Framework 2.0.

and `AttributeTargets.Method`, which allow the attribute to be used on either a method or a class, respectively. However, the class usage is special because `ConditionalAttribute` is allowed only on `System.Attribute`-derived classes.

When `ConditionalAttribute` decorates a custom attribute, the latter can be retrieved via reflection only if the conditional string is defined in the calling assembly. Without such a conditional string, reflection that looks for the custom attribute will fail to find it.

System.ObsoleteAttribute

As mentioned earlier, predefined attributes affect the compiler's and/or the runtime's behavior. `ObsoleteAttribute` provides another example of attributes affecting the compiler's behavior. Its purpose is to help with versioning of code by providing a means of indicating to callers that a member or type is no longer current. Listing 18.25 provides an example of `ObsoleteAttribute`'s use. As Output 18.9 shows, any callers that compile code that invokes a member marked with `ObsoleteAttribute` will cause a compile-time warning and, optionally, an error.

LISTING 18.25: Using `ObsoleteAttribute`

```
public class Program
{
    public static void Main()
    {
        ObsoleteMethod();
    }

    [Obsolete]
    public static void ObsoleteMethod()
    {
    }
}
```

OUTPUT 18.9

```
c:\SampleCode\ObsoleteAttributeTest.cs(24,17): warning CS0612:
Program.ObsoleteMethod()' is obsolete
```

In this case, `ObsoleteAttribute` simply displays a warning. However, the attribute has two additional constructors. The first constructor, `ObsoleteAttribute(string message)`, appends the additional message argument to the compiler's obsolete message. The best practice for this message is to provide direction on what replaces the obsolete code. The second constructor is a `bool error` parameter that forces the warning to be recorded as an error instead.

`ObsoleteAttribute` allows third parties to notify developers of deprecated APIs. The warning (not an error) allows the original API to continue to work until the developer is able to update the calling code.

Begin 11.0

Generic Attributes

Starting with C# 11.0, C# supports generic attributes. For example, consider the custom attribute `ExpectedException<TException>` shown in Listing 18.26.

Listing 18.26: Generic Attributes

```
public class SampleTests
{
    [ExpectedException<DivideByZeroException>]
    public static void ThrowDivideByZeroExceptionTest()
    {
        var result = 1/"".Length;
    }
}

[AttributeUsage(AttributeTargets.Method)]
public class ExpectedException<TException> :
    Attribute where TException : Exception
{
    public static TException AssertExceptionThrown(Action testMethod)
    {
        try
        {
            testMethod();
            throw new InvalidOperationException(
                $"The expected exception, {
                    typeof(TException).FullName }, was not thrown.");
        }
        catch (TException exception)
        {
            return exception;
        }
```

```
    }

    // Attribute detection
    // ...
}
```

Here we have a generic attribute that is used to decorate a test method. For this test method to pass, it must throw an exception of type `TException`. In Listing 18.26, `ThrowsDivideByZeroExceptionTest()` is expected to throw a `DivideByZeroException` and is identified by the `ExpectedException<DivideByZeroException>` that decorates it.

Begin 10.0

`Caller*` Attributes

In C# 10.0, `Caller*` Attributes (frequently referred to as CallerArgumentExpression attributes) were added. With these attributes, the compiler injects argument values of the caller for the invoked method. Consider, for example, the invocation of the `AssertExceptionThrown()` method:

```
ExpectedException<DivideByZeroException>.AssertExceptionThrown(
() => throw new Exception(),
"() => throw new Exception()",
nameof(Method),
"./FileName.cs");
```

Notice that in addition to the type argument for the expected exception type, there is also an expression and a repeat of the expression as a string, along with the method name and file name of the caller. Without any additional language support, all these arguments are required if the `AssertExceptionThrown()` method is to include complete diagnostics when the expected exception it not thrown. Even though all the values other than the initial expression are obviously trivial to determine automatically. (In this case, the duplication of the expression as a string is especially annoying.) Nonetheless, they all still need to be specified for the called method to have all the necessary information to provide a detailed error message (see Listing 18.27).

Notice that all the parameters, other than `testAction`, have 1) an attribute and 2) a default value. The attributes provide metadata to the compiler that the parameter values, which should not be specified by the caller, should be provided by the

Listing 18.27: `CallerArgumentExpression` **Attributes Example**

```
public class SampleTests
{
    [ExpectedException<DivideByZeroException>]
    public static void ThrowArgumentNullExceptionTest()
    {
        var result = 1/"".Length;
    }
}

[AttributeUsage(AttributeTargets.Method)]
public class ExpectedException<TException> :
    Attribute where TException : Exception
{
    public static TException AssertExceptionThrown(
        Action testAction,
        [CallerArgumentExpression(nameof(testAction))]
            string testExpression = null!,
        [CallerMemberName]string testActionMemberName = null!,
        [CallerFilePath]string testActionFileName = null!
        )
    {
        try
        {
            testAction();
            throw new InvalidOperationException(
                $"The expected exception, {
                    typeof(TException).FullName }, was not thrown" +
                    $" by the expression '{
                        testExpression }' in the method '{
                        testActionMemberName }' and file '{
                        testActionFileName }'.");
        }
        catch (TException exception)
        {
            return exception;
        }
    }

    // Attribute detection
    // ...
}
```

compiler. As a result, the invocation for the method is simplified significantly as shown in Listing 18.28.

LISTING 18.28: INVOKING A `Caller*` ATTRIBUTES METHOD

```
ExpectedException<DivideByZeroException>.AssertExceptionThrown(
    () => throw new DivideByZeroException());
```

Now, even though no argument is specified in the source code for the `testActionMemberName` parameter (for example), the string value "Method" still is injected and available in the `AssertExceptionThrown()` method. Obviously, there is a limited set of such `Caller*` attributes as shown in Table 18.1.

TABLE 18.1: Caller* Attributes[7]

Attribute	Description	Type
`CallerFilePathAttribute`	Full path of the source file that contains the caller. The full path is the path at compile time.	`string`
`CallerLineNumberAttribute`	Line number in the source file from which the method is called.	`System.Int32`
`CallerMemberNameAttribute`	Method name or property name of the caller.	`string`
`CallerArgumentExpressionAttribute`	String representation of the argument expression.	`string`

All the `Caller*` attributes are limited to use on parameter constructs and mostly self-explanatory from Listing 18.27. The one exception is the `CallerArgumentExpressionAttrribute` since it requires its own parameter. The `CallerArgumentExpressionAttrribute` identifies (as text) the expression used for another parameter within the method. For example, in Listing 18.27 the expression `() => throw new Exception()` is for the value of `testAction`. And, since the `CallerArgumentExpressionAttrribute` decorating the `testExpression` parameter has `nameof(testAction)` as a parameter for the

7. https://learn.microsoft.com /dotnet/csharp/language-reference/attributes/caller-information

attribute (thus identifying the `testAction` parameter), the compiler injects the string "() => throw new Exception()" as the value for the `testExpression` parameter. (Allowing `nameof` as an attribute parameter to refer to a parameter in the same method signature was added in C# 11.) In summary, the `CallerArgumentExpressionAttrribute` decorates parameter `testExpression` and takes a parameter of its own—a string that identifies `testAction` as the parameter for which it should extract the expression and provide it as text for the `testExpression` argument. (If the parameter that `CallerArgumentExpressionAttrribute` is pointing to is an extension method, `this` is an allowable value.)

Note that for the compiler to allow `Caller*` attribute decorated parameters to not require arguments, it is necessary to provide a default value. Even though the data types on the parameters should be non-nullable – deterring a caller from explicitly providing a null value and usurping the compiler injecting a value – the only reasonable value to specify for the default is null. In a somewhat contradiction, therefore, the string parameters decorated by the `Caller*` attributes are non-nullable but assigned null values with a null forgiveness operator. This is done because the compiler is expected to appropriately provide values for all of these arguments.

Guidelines

DO NOT **explicitly pass arguments for `Caller*` attribute decorated parameters.**

DO **use non-nullable string for the data type of `Caller*` attribute decorated string parameters.**

DO **assign `null!` for the default value of `Caller*` attribute decorated string parameters.**

End 10.0

End 11.0

Programming with Dynamic Objects

The introduction of dynamic objects[8] simplified a host of programming scenarios and enabled several new ones previously not available. At its core, programming with dynamic objects enables developers to code operations using a dynamic dispatch mechanism that the runtime will resolve at execution time, rather than having the compiler verify and bind to it at compile time.

Why? Many times, objects are inherently not statically typed. Examples include loading data from an XML/CSV file, a database table, the Internet Explorer DOM, or COM's `IDispatch` interface, or calling code in a dynamic language such as an IronPython object. `Dynamic` object support provides a common solution for talking to runtime environments that don't necessarily have a compile-time–defined structure. In the initial implementation of dynamic objects, four binding methods are available:

1. Using reflection against an underlying CLR type
2. Invoking a custom `IDynamicMetaObjectProvider` that makes available a `DynamicMetaObject`
3. Calling through the `IUnknown` and `IDispatch` interfaces of COM
4. Calling a type defined by dynamic languages such as IronPython

Of these four approaches, we will delve into the first two. The principles underlying them translate seamlessly to the remaining cases—COM interoperability and dynamic language interoperability.

Invoking Reflection Using `dynamic`

One of the key features of reflection is the ability to dynamically find and invoke a member on a type based on an execution-time identification of the member name or some other quality, such as an attribute (see Listing 18.3). However, dynamic objects

8. Introduced in C# 4.0.

provide a simpler way of invoking a member by reflection, assuming compile-time knowledge of the member signature. To reiterate, this restriction states that at compile time we need to know the member name along with the signature (the number of parameters and whether the specified parameters will be type-compatible with the signature). Listing 18.29 (with Output 18.10) provides an example.

LISTING 18.29: Dynamic Programming Using Reflection

```
// ...
dynamic data =
  "Hello!  My name is Inigo Montoya";
Console.WriteLine(data);
data = (double)data.Length;
data = data * 3.5 + 28.6;
if(data == 2.4 + 112 + 26.2)
    // The distance (in miles) for the swim, bike, and
    // run portions of an Ironman triathlon, respectively
{
    Console.WriteLine(
        $"{data} makes for a long triathlon.");
}
else
{
    data.NonExistentMethodCallStillCompiles();
}
// ...
```

OUTPUT 18.10

```
Hello!  My name is Inigo Montoya
140.6 makes for a long triathlon.
```

In this example, there is no explicit code for determining the object type, finding a particular `MemberInfo` instance, and then invoking it. Instead, `data` is declared as type `dynamic` and methods are called against it directly. At compile time, there is no check of whether the members specified are available or even which type underlies the `dynamic` object. Hence, it is possible at compile time to make any call, so long as the syntax is valid. At compile time, it is irrelevant whether there is really a corresponding member.

However, type safety is not abandoned altogether. For standard CLR types (such as those used in Listing 18.29), the same type checker normally used at compile time for non-`dynamic` types is instead invoked at execution time for the `dynamic` type. Therefore, at execution time, if no such member is available, the call will result in a `Microsoft.CSharp.RuntimeBinder.RuntimeBinderException`.

Note that this capability is not nearly as flexible as the reflection described earlier in the chapter, although the API is undoubtedly simpler. The key difference when using a dynamic object is that it is necessary to identify the signature at compile time rather than determine things such as the member name at runtime (as we did when parsing the command-line arguments).

`dynamic` Principles and Behaviors

Listing 18.29 and the accompanying text reveal several characteristics of the `dynamic` data type:

- `dynamic` *is a directive to the compiler to generate code.*

  `dynamic` involves an interception mechanism so that when a dynamic call is encountered by the runtime, it can compile the request to CIL and then invoke the newly compiled call. (See "Advanced Topic: `dynamic` Uncovered" later in this chapter for more details.)

  The principle at work when a type is assigned to `dynamic` is to conceptually "wrap" the original type so that no compile-time validation occurs. Additionally, when a member is invoked at runtime, the wrapper intercepts the call and dispatches it appropriately (or rejects it). Calling `GetType()` on the `dynamic` object reveals the type underlying the dynamic instance—it does not return `dynamic` as a type.

- *Any type*[9] *will convert to* `dynamic`.

  In Listing 18.29, we successfully cast both a value type (`double`) and a reference type (`string`) to `dynamic`. In fact, all types can successfully be converted into a `dynamic` object. There is an implicit conversion from any reference type to `dynamic`, an implicit conversion (a boxing conversion) from a value type to `dynamic`, and an implicit conversion from `dynamic` to

9. Technically, it is restricted to any type that converts to an object—which excludes unsafe pointers, lambdas, and method groups.

`dynamic`. This is perhaps obvious, but with `dynamic`, this process is more complicated than simply copying the "pointer" (address) from one location to the next.

- *Successful conversion from* `dynamic` *to an alternative type depends on support in the underlying type.*

  Conversion from a `dynamic` object to a standard CLR type is an explicit cast (e.g., `(double)data.Length`). Not surprisingly, if the target type is a value type, an unboxing conversion is required. If the underlying type supports the conversion to the target type, the conversion from `dynamic` will also succeed.

- *The type underlying the* `dynamic` *type can change from one assignment to the next.*

  Unlike an implicitly typed variable (`var`), which cannot be reassigned to a different type, `dynamic` involves an interception mechanism for compilation before the underlying type's code is executed. Therefore, it is possible to successfully swap out the underlying type instance to an entirely different type. This will result in another interception call site that will need to be compiled before invocation.

- *Verification that the specified signature exists on the underlying type doesn't occur until runtime—but it does occur.*

  The compiler makes almost no verification of operations on a `dynamic` type, as the method call to `data.NonExistentMethodCallStillCompiles()` demonstrates. This step is left entirely to the work of the runtime when the code executes. Moreover, if the code never executes, even though surrounding code does (as with `data.NonExistentMethodCallStillCompiles()`), no verification and binding to the member will ever occur.

- *The result of any* `dynamic` *member invocation is of compile-time type* `dynamic`.

  A call to any member on a `dynamic` object will return a `dynamic` object. Therefore, calls such as `data.ToString()` will return a `dynamic` object rather than the underlying `string` type. However, at execution time, when `GetType()` is called on the `dynamic` object, an object representing the runtime type is returned.

- *If the member specified does not exist at runtime, the runtime will throw a* `Microsoft.CSharp.RuntimeBinder.RuntimeBinderException` *exception.*

If an attempt to invoke a member at execution time does occur, the runtime will verify that the member call is truly valid (e.g., that the signatures are type-compatible in the case of reflection). If the method signatures are not compatible, the runtime will throw a `Microsoft.CSharp.RuntimeBinder.RuntimeBinderException`.

- `dynamic` *with reflection does not support extension methods.*

  As is the case for reflection using `System.Type`, reflection using `dynamic` does not support extension methods. Invocation of extension methods is still available on the implementing type (e.g., `System.Linq.Enumerable`), just not on the `dynamic` type directly.

- *At its core,* `dynamic` *is a* `System.Object`.

  Given that any object can be successfully converted to `dynamic`, and that `dynamic` may be explicitly converted to a different object type, `dynamic` behaves like `System.Object`. Like `System.Object`, it even returns `null` for its default value (`default(dynamic)`), indicating it is a reference type. The special dynamic behavior of `dynamic` that distinguishes it from a `System.Object` appears only at compile time.

ADVANCED TOPIC

`dynamic` Uncovered

The CIL disassembler reveals that within the CIL, the `dynamic` type is actually a `System.Object`. In fact, without any invocations, declaration of the `dynamic` type is indistinguishable from `System.Object`. However, the difference becomes apparent when invoking a member.

To invoke the member, the compiler declares a variable of type `System.Runtime.CompilerServices.CallSite<T>`. `T` varies on the basis of the member signature, but something simple, such as the invocation of `ToString()`, would require instantiation of the type `CallSite<Func<CallSite, object, string>>`, along with a method call with parameters of `CallSite site`, `object dynamicTarget`, and `string result`. `site` is the call site itself, `dynamicTarget` is the `object` on which the method call is invoked, and `result` is the underlying return value from the `ToString()` method call. Rather than instantiate `CallSite<Func<CallSite _site, object dynamicTarget,`

string result>> directly, a Create() factory method is available for instantiating it; this method takes a parameter of type Microsoft.CSharp.RuntimeBinder.CSharpConvertBinder. Given an instance of CallSite<T>, the final step involves a call to CallSite<T>.Target() to invoke the actual member.

Under the covers at execution time, the framework uses reflection to look up members and to verify that the signatures match. Next, the runtime builds an expression tree that represents the dynamic expression as defined by the call site. Once the expression tree is compiled, we have a CIL method body that is similar to what the compiler would have generated had the call not been dynamic. This CIL code is then cached in the call site, and the invocation occurs via a delegate. As the CIL is now cached at the call site, the next invocation doesn't require all the reflection and compilation overhead again.

Why Dynamic Binding?

In addition to reflection, we can define custom types that we invoke dynamically. We might consider using dynamic invocation to retrieve the values of an XML element, for example. Rather than using the strongly typed syntax of Listing 18.30, using dynamic invocation we could call person.FirstName and person.LastName.

LISTING 18.30: Runtime Binding to XML Elements without dynamic

```
using System.Xml.Linq;

// ...
        XElement person = XElement.Parse(
            @"<Person>
                    <FirstName>Inigo</FirstName>
                    <LastName>Montoya</LastName>
                  </Person>");

        Console.WriteLine($"{ person.Descendants("FirstName").First().
↪Value }" +
        $"{ person.Descendants("LastName").First().Value }");
        //...
```

Although the code in Listing 18.30 is not overly complex, compare it to Listing 18.31—an alternative approach that uses a dynamically typed object.

LISTING 18.31: Runtime Binding to XML Elements with `dynamic`

```
dynamic person = DynamicXml.Parse(
 @"<Person>
        <FirstName>Inigo</FirstName>
        <LastName>Montoya</LastName>
       </Person>");

Console.WriteLine(
    $"{ person.FirstName } { person.LastName }");
//...
```

The advantages are clear, but does that mean dynamic programming is preferable to static compilation?

Static Compilation versus Dynamic Programming

In Listing 18.31, we have the same functionality as in Listing 18.30, albeit with one very important difference: Listing 18.30 is entirely statically typed. Thus, at compile time, all types and their member signatures are verified with this approach. Method names are required to match, and all parameters are checked for type compatibility. This is a key feature of C#—and something we have highlighted throughout the book.

In contrast, Listing 18.31 has virtually no statically typed code; the variable `person` is instead `dynamic`. As a result, there is no compile-time verification that `person` has a `FirstName` or `LastName` property—or any other members, for that matter. Furthermore, when coding within an IDE, no IntelliSense is available to identify the members on `person`.

The loss of typing would seem to result in a significant decrease in functionality. Why, then, is such a possibility even available in C#?[10]

To understand this apparent paradox, let's reexamine Listing 18.31. Notice the call to retrieve the `"FirstName"` element:

10. Functionality added in C# 4.0.

```
Element.Descendants("LastName").FirstOrDefault().Value
```

The listing uses a `string` (`"LastName"`) to identify the element name, but no compile-time verification occurs to ensure that the string is correct. If the casing was inconsistent with the element name or if there was a space, the compile would still succeed, even though a `NullReferenceException` would occur with the call to the `Value` property. Furthermore, the compiler does not attempt to verify that the `"FirstName"` element even exists; if it doesn't, we would also get the `NullReferenceException` message. In other words, in spite of all the type-safety advantages, type safety doesn't offer many benefits when you're accessing the dynamic data stored within the XML element.

Listing 18.31 is no better than Listing 18.30 when it comes to compile-time verification of the element retrieval. If a case mismatch occurs or if the `FirstName` element doesn't exist, an exception would still be thrown.[11] However, compare the call to access the first name in Listing 18.31 (`person.FirstName`) with the corresponding call in Listing 18.30. The call in the latter listing is undoubtedly significantly simpler.

In summary, in some situations type safety doesn't—and likely can't—make certain checks. In those cases, code that makes a dynamic call that is verified only at runtime, rather than also being verified at compile time, is significantly more readable and succinct. Obviously, if compile-time verification is possible, statically typed programming is preferred because readable and succinct APIs can accompany it. However, in the cases where it isn't effective, dynamic capabilities[12] enable programmers to write simpler code rather than emphasizing the purity of type safety.

Implementing a Custom Dynamic Object

Listing 18.31 included a method call to `DynamicXml.Parse(...)` that was essentially a factory method call for `DynamicXml`—a custom type rather than one built into the CLR framework. However, `DynamicXml` doesn't implement a

---

11. You cannot use a space in the `FirstName` property call—but XML doesn't support spaces in element names, so let's just ignore this fact.
12. Starting in C# 4.0.

FirstName or LastName property. To do so would break the dynamic support for retrieving data from the XML file at execution time rather than fostering compile-time–based implementation of the XML elements. In other words, DynamicXml does not use reflection for accessing its members but rather dynamically binds to the values based on the XML content.

The key to defining a custom dynamic type is implementation of the System.Dynamic.IDynamicMetaObjectProvider interface. Rather than implementing the interface from scratch, however, the preferred approach is to derive the custom dynamic type from System.Dynamic.DynamicObject. This provides default implementations for a host of members and allows you to override the ones that don't fit. Listing 18.32 shows the full implementation.

Listing 18.32: Implementing a Custom Dynamic Object

```
using System.Dynamic;
using System.Linq;
using System.Xml.Linq;

public class DynamicXml : DynamicObject
{
    private XElement Element { get; set; }

    public DynamicXml(System.Xml.Linq.XElement element)
    {
        Element = element;
    }

    public static DynamicXml Parse(string text)
    {
        return new DynamicXml(XElement.Parse(text));
    }

    public override bool TryGetMember(
        GetMemberBinder binder, out object? result)
    {
        bool success = false;
        result = null;
        XElement? firstDescendant =
            Element.Descendants(binder.Name).FirstOrDefault();
        if(firstDescendant != null)
        {
            if(firstDescendant.Descendants().Any())
            {
```

```
                result = new DynamicXml(firstDescendant);
            }
            else
            {
                result = firstDescendant.Value;
            }
            success = true;
        }
        return success;
    }

    public override bool TrySetMember(
        SetMemberBinder binder, object? value)
    {
        bool success = false;
        XElement? firstDescendant =
            Element.Descendants(binder.Name).FirstOrDefault();
        if(firstDescendant != null)
        {
            if(value?.GetType() == typeof(XElement))
            {
                firstDescendant.ReplaceWith(value);
            }
            else
            {
                firstDescendant.Value = value?.ToString() ?? string.
↪Empty;
            }
            success = true;
        }
        return success;
    }
}
```

The key dynamic implementation methods for this use case are `TryGetMember()` and `TrySetMember()` (assuming you want to assign the elements as well). Only these two method implementations are necessary to support the invocation of the dynamic getter and setter properties. Furthermore, the implementations are straightforward. First, they examine the contained `XElement`, looking for an element with the same name as the `binder.Name`—the name of the member invoked. If a corresponding XML element exists, the value is retrieved (or set). The return value is set to `true` if the element exists and `false` if it doesn't. A return value of `false` will immediately cause the runtime to throw a

`Microsoft.CSharp.RuntimeBinder.RuntimeBinderException` at the call site of the dynamic member invocation.

`System.Dynamic.DynamicObject` supports additional virtual methods if more dynamic invocations are required. Listing 18.33 produces a list of all overridable members.

LISTING 18.33: Overridable Members on `System.Dynamic.DynamicObject`

```
using System.Collections.Generic;
using System.Dynamic;

public class DynamicObject : IDynamicMetaObjectProvider
{
    protected DynamicObject();

    public virtual IEnumerable<string> GetDynamicMemberNames();
    public virtual DynamicMetaObject GetMetaObject(
        Expression parameter);
    public virtual bool TryBinaryOperation(
        BinaryOperationBinder binder, object arg,
            out object result);
    public virtual bool TryConvert(
        ConvertBinder binder, out object result);
    public virtual bool TryCreateInstance(
        CreateInstanceBinder binder, object[] args,
            out object result);
    public virtual bool TryDeleteIndex(
        DeleteIndexBinder binder, object[] indexes);
    public virtual bool TryDeleteMember(
        DeleteMemberBinder binder);
    public virtual bool TryGetIndex(
        GetIndexBinder binder, object[] indexes,
            out object result);
    public virtual bool TryGetMember(
        GetMemberBinder binder, out object result);
    public virtual bool TryInvoke(
        InvokeBinder binder, object[] args, out object result);
    public virtual bool TryInvokeMember(
        InvokeMemberBinder binder, object[] args,
            out object result);
    public virtual bool TrySetIndex(
        SetIndexBinder binder, object[] indexes, object value);
    public virtual bool TrySetMember(
        SetMemberBinder binder, object value);
    public virtual bool TryUnaryOperation(
```

```
        UnaryOperationBinder binder, out object result);
}
```

As Listing 18.33 shows, there are member implementations for everything—from casts and various operations, to index invocations. In addition, there is a method for retrieving all the possible member names: `GetDynamicMemberNames()`.

Summary

This chapter discussed the use of reflection to read the metadata that is compiled into the CIL. Using reflection, it is possible to provide a late binding in which the code to call is defined at execution time rather than at compile time. Although reflection is entirely feasible for deploying a dynamic system, it executes considerably more slowly than statically linked (compile-time), defined code. This tends to make it more prevalent and useful in development tools when performance is potentially not as critical.

Reflection also enables the retrieval of additional metadata decorating various constructs in the form of attributes. Typically, custom attributes are sought using reflection. You can define your own custom attributes that insert additional metadata of your own choosing into the CIL. At runtime, you can then retrieve this metadata and use it within the programming logic.

Many programmers view attributes as a precursor to a concept known as aspect-oriented programming, in which you add functionality through constructs such as attributes instead of manually implementing the functionality wherever it is needed. It will take some time before you see true aspects within C# (if ever); however, attributes provide a clear steppingstone in that direction, without creating a significant risk to the stability of the language.

Finally, this chapter explored dynamic programming using the new type `dynamic`.[13] This coverage included a discussion of why static binding, although preferred when the API is strongly typed, has limitations when you are working with dynamic data.

13. Introduced in C# 4.0.

The next chapter looks at multithreading, where attributes are used for synchronization.

19

Introducing Multithreading

Two significant trends of the past decade have had an enormous effect on the field of software development. First, the continued decrease in the cost of performing computations is no longer driven by increases in clock speed and transistor density, as illustrated by Figure 19.1. Rather, the cost of computation is now falling because it has become economical to make hardware containing multiple CPUs.

Second, computations now routinely involve enormous **latency**. Latency is, simply put, the amount of time required to obtain a desired result. There are two principal causes of latency. **Processor-bound latency** occurs when the computational task is complex; if a computation requires performing 12 billion arithmetic operations and the total processing power available is only 6 billion operations per second, at least 2 seconds of processor-bound latency will be incurred between asking for the result and obtaining it. **I/O-bound latency**, by contrast, is latency incurred by the need to obtain data from an external source such as a disk drive, web server, and so on. Any computation that requires fetching data from a web server physically located far from the client machine will incur latency equivalent to millions of processor cycles.

These two trends together create an enormous challenge for modern software developers. Given that machines have more computing power than ever, how are we to make effective use of that power to deliver results to the user quickly and without compromising on the user experience? How do we avoid creating frustrating user interfaces that freeze up when a high-latency operation is triggered? Moreover, how

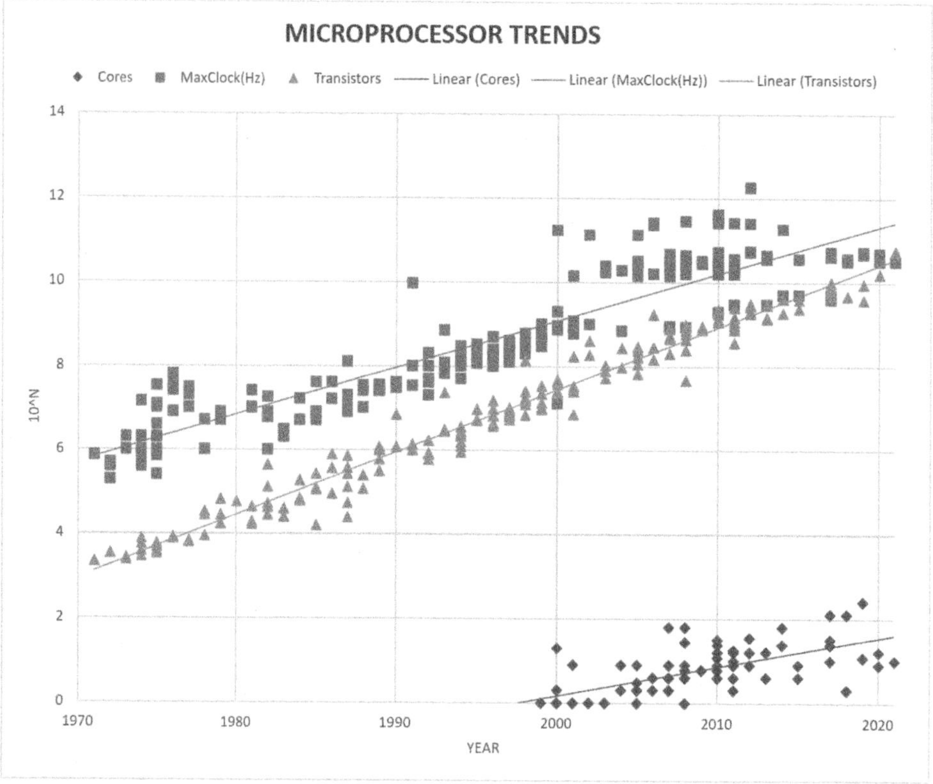

FIGURE 19.1: Clock speeds over time

do we go about splitting CPU-bound work among multiple processors to decrease the time required for the computation?

The standard technique for engineering software that keeps the user interface responsive and CPU utilization high is to write **multithreaded** programs that perform multiple computations in parallel. Unfortunately, multithreading logic is notoriously difficult to get right; we spend the next four chapters exploring what makes multithreading difficult and learning how to use higher-level abstractions and new language features to ease that burden.

The first higher-level abstraction was the Parallel Extensions library, which was released with .NET 4.0. It includes the **Task Parallel Library (TPL)**, which is discussed in this chapter, and the **Parallel LINQ (PLINQ)**, which is discussed in

Chapter 21. The second higher-level abstraction is the **Task-based Asynchronous Pattern (TAP)** and its accompanying language support.[1]

Although we strongly encourage you to use these higher-level abstractions, we also cover some of the lower-level threading APIs from previous versions of the .NET runtime at the end of this chapter.[2] Thus, if you want to fully understand the resources from multithreaded programming without the later features, you still have access to that material.

We begin this chapter with a few beginner topics in case you are new to multithreading.

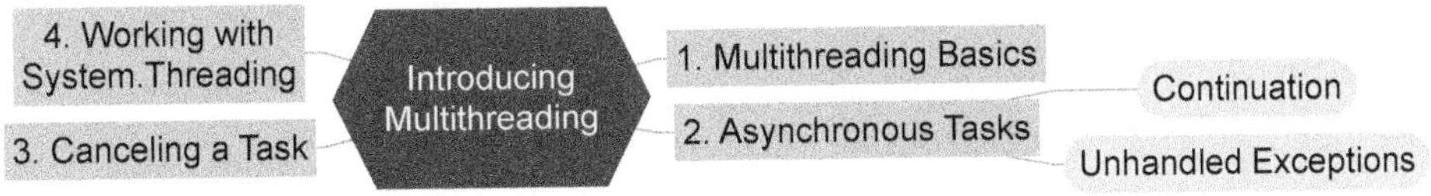

Multithreading Basics

BEGINNER TOPIC

Multithreading Jargon

There is a lot of confusing jargon associated with multithreading, so let's define a few terms.

A **CPU** (central processing unit) or **core**[3] is the unit of hardware that actually executes a given program. Every machine has at least one CPU, though today multiple CPU machines are common. Many modern CPUs support **simultaneous**

1. Starting in C# 5.0.
2. Additional multithreading patterns prior to C# 5.0 are available for download at https://intellitect.com/EssentialCSharp, along with the chapters from *Essential C# 3.0*.
3. Technically, we ought to say that CPU always refers to the physical chip, and core may refer to a physical or virtual CPU. This distinction is unimportant for the purposes of this book, so we use these terms interchangeably.

multithreading (which Intel trademarks as **Hyper-Threading**), a mode whereby a single CPU can appear as multiple "virtual" CPUs.

A **process** is a currently executing instance of a given program; the fundamental purpose of the operating system is to manage processes. Each process contains one or more threads. A process may be accessed programmatically by an instance of the `Process` class in the `System.Diagnostics` namespace.

C# programming at the level of statements and expressions is fundamentally about describing **flow of control**. Thus far in this book, we've made the implicit assumption that a given program has only a single point of control. You can imagine the point of control as being a cursor that enters the text of your program at the `Main` method when you start it up, and then moves around the program as the various conditions, loops, method calls, and so on, are executed. A **thread** is this point of control. The `System.Threading` namespace contains the API for manipulating a thread—specifically, the `System.Threading.Thread` class.

A **single-threaded** program is one in which there is only one thread in the process. A **multithreaded** program has two or more threads in the process.

A piece of code is said to be **thread safe** if it behaves correctly when used in a multithreaded program. The **threading model** of a piece of code is the set of requirements that the code places upon its caller in exchange for guaranteeing thread safety. For example, the threading model of many classes is "static methods may be called from any thread, but instance methods may be called only from the thread that allocated the instance."

A **task** is a unit of potentially high-latency work that produces a resultant value or desired side effect. The distinction between tasks and threads is as follows: A task represents a job that needs to be performed, whereas a thread represents the worker that does the job. A task is useful only for its side effects and is represented by an instance of the `Task` class. A task used to produce a value of a given type is represented by the `Task<T>` class, which derives from the nongeneric `Task` type. These can be found in the `System.Threading.Tasks` namespace.

A **thread pool** is a collection of threads, along with logic for determining how to assign work to those threads. When your program has a task to perform, it can delegate a worker thread from the pool, assign the thread to perform the task, and then de-allocate it when the work completes, thereby making it available the next time additional work is requested.

BEGINNER TOPIC

The Why and How of Multithreading

There are two principal scenarios for multithreading: enabling multitasking and dealing with latency.

Users think nothing of running dozens of processes at the same time. They might have presentations and spreadsheets open for editing while at the same time they are browsing documents on the Internet, listening to music, receiving instant messages and email arrival notifications, and watching the little clock in the corner. Each of these processes must continue to do its job even though it is not the only task the machine has to attend to. This kind of multitasking is usually implemented at the process level, but in some situations, you want to do this sort of multitasking within a single process.

For the purposes of this book, we will mostly consider multithreading as a technique for dealing with latency. For example, to import a large file while simultaneously allowing a user to click Cancel, a developer creates an additional thread to perform the import. By performing the import on a different thread, the user can request cancellation instead of freezing the user interface until the import completes.

If enough cores are available so that each thread can be assigned a core, each thread essentially gets its own little machine. However, often there are more threads than cores. Even the relatively common multicore machines of today still have only a handful of cores, while each process could quite possibly run dozens of threads.

To overcome the discrepancy between the numerous threads and the handful of cores, an operating system simulates multiple threads running concurrently by **time slicing**. The operating system switches execution from one thread to the next so quickly that it appears the threads are executing simultaneously. The time that the processor executes a thread before switching to another is the **time slice** or

quantum. The act of changing which thread is executing on a core is called a **context switch**.

The effect is like that of a fiber-optic telephone line in which the fiber-optic line represents the processor and each conversation represents a thread. A (single-mode) fiber-optic telephone line can send only one signal at a time, but many people can hold simultaneous conversations over the line. The fiber-optic channel is fast enough to switch between conversations so quickly that each conversation appears uninterrupted. Similarly, each thread of a multithreaded process appears to run continuously with other threads.

If two operations are running in parallel, via either true multicore parallelism or simulated parallelism using time slicing, they are said to be **concurrent**. To implement such concurrency, you invoke it **asynchronously**, such that both the execution and the completion of the invoked operation are separate from the control flow that invoked it. Concurrency, therefore, occurs when work dispatched asynchronously executes in parallel with the current control flow. **Parallel programming** is the act of taking a single problem and splitting it into pieces, whereby you **asynchronously** initiate the process of each piece such that the pieces can all be processed concurrently.

BEGINNER TOPIC

Performance Considerations

A thread that is servicing an I/O-bound operation can essentially be ignored by the operating system until the result is available from the I/O subsystem; switching away from an I/O-bound thread to a processor-bound thread results in more efficient processor utilization because the CPU is not idle while waiting for the I/O operation to complete.

However, context switching is not free; the current internal state of the CPU must be saved to memory, and the state associated with the new thread must be loaded. Similarly, if thread A is doing lots of work with one piece of memory, and thread B is doing lots of work with another piece of memory, context switching between them will likely mean that all of the data that was loaded into the cache from thread A will get replaced with the data from thread B (or vice versa). If there are too many threads, the switching overhead can begin to noticeably affect performance. Adding more threads will likely decrease performance further, to the point where the processor spends more time switching from one thread to another than it does accomplishing the work of each thread.

Even if we ignore the cost of context switching, time slicing itself can have a huge impact on performance. Suppose, for example, that you have two processor-bound high-latency tasks, each working out the average of two lists of 1 billion numbers each. Suppose the processor can perform 1 billion operations per second. If the two tasks are each associated with a thread, and the two threads each have their own core, obviously we can get both results in 1 second.

If, however, the two threads share a single processor, time slicing performs a few hundred thousand operations on one thread, then switches to the other thread, then switches back, and so on. Each task consumes a total of 1 second of processor time, and the results of both are available after 2 seconds, leading to an average completion time of 2 seconds. (Again, we are ignoring the cost of context switching.)

If we assigned those two tasks to a single thread that performed the first task and did not even start the second until after the first was completed, the result of the first task would be obtained in 1 second and the result of the subsequent task would be obtained 1 second after that, leading to an average time of 1.5 seconds (a task completes in either 1 or 2 seconds and therefore, on average, completes in 1.5 seconds).

Guidelines

DO NOT fall into the common error of believing that more threads always make code faster.

DO carefully measure performance when attempting to speed up processor-bound problems through multithreading.

BEGINNER TOPIC

Threading Problems

We've said several times that writing multithreaded programs is complex and difficult, but we have not said why. In a nutshell, the problem is that many of our reasonable assumptions that are true for single-threaded programs are violated in multithreaded programs. The issues include a lack of atomicity, race conditions, complex memory models, and deadlocks.

Most Operations Are Not Atomic

An atomic operation is one that always is observed to be either not started or already completed. Its state is never externally visible as "in progress." Consider, for example, this code fragment:

```
if (bankAccounts.Checking.Balance >= 1000.00m)
{
bankAccounts.Checking.Balance -= 1000.00m;
bankAccounts.Savings.Balance += 1000.00m;
}
```

This operation—checking for available funds and then conditionally debiting one account and crediting another—needs to be atomic. In other words, for it to execute correctly, we must ensure that there is never a moment when the operation can be observed to be partially completed. Imagine, for example, that two threads are running in this code concurrently. It is possible that both threads verify that there are sufficient funds in the account, and then both threads do a transfer of funds, even if there are only sufficient funds in the account to do the transfer once. And, in fact, the situation is considerably worse: There are *no* operations in this code fragment that are atomic! Even operations like compound addition/subtraction or reading and writing a property of decimal type are non-atomic operations in C#. As such, they can all be observed to be "partially complete" in multithreaded scenarios—only partially incremented or decremented. The observation of inconsistent state due to partially completed non-atomic operations is a special case of a more general problem, called a **race condition**.

Uncertainty Caused by Race Conditions

As we discussed earlier, concurrency is often simulated by time slicing. In the absence of special thread synchronization (which we discuss in detail in Chapter 22), the operating system can switch contexts between any two threads at any time of its choosing. As a consequence, when two threads are accessing the same object, which thread wins the race and gets to run first is unpredictable. If there are two threads running in the code fragment given previously, for example, it is possible that one thread might win the race and get all the way to the end before the second thread gets a chance to run. It is also possible that the context switch might happen after the first thread does the balance check, and the second thread might then win the race to get all the way to the end first.

The behavior of code that contains race conditions depends on the timing of context switches. This dependency introduces uncertainty concerning program execution. The order in which one instruction will execute relative to an instruction in a different thread is unknown. The worst of it is that code containing race conditions often behaves correctly 99.9 percent of the time, and then one time in a thousand a different thread wins the race due to an accident of timing. This unpredictability is what makes multithreaded programming so difficult.

Because such race conditions are difficult to replicate in the laboratory, much of the quality assurance of multithreaded code depends on long-running stress tests, specially designed code analysis tools, and a significant investment in code analysis and code review by experts. Perhaps more important than any of these is the discipline of keeping things as simple as possible. Often, in the name of hypothetical performance, a developer will try to avoid the simple approach of using a lock and go for lower-level primitives such as interlocked operations and volatiles, which makes it much more likely that their code is wrong. "Keep it simple" is possibly one of the most important guidelines of good multithreaded programming.

Chapter 22 is about techniques for dealing with race conditions.

Memory Models Are Complex

The existence of race conditions, where two points of control can "race" through a piece of code at unpredictable and inconsistent speeds, is bad enough, but it gets worse. Consider two threads that are running on two different processors but are accessing the same fields of some object. Modern processors do not actually access main memory every time you use a variable. Rather, they make a local copy in special cache memory on the processor; these caches are then periodically synchronized with main memory. This means that two threads that read from and write to the same location on two different processors can, in fact, be failing to observe each other's updates to that memory or observing inconsistent results. Essentially what we have here is a race condition that depends on when processors choose to synchronize their caches.

Locking Leads to Deadlocks

Clearly there must exist mechanisms to make non-atomic operations into atomic operations, to instruct the operating system to schedule threads so as to avoid races, and to ensure that processor caches are synchronized when necessary. The primary mechanism used to solve all these problems in C# programs is the `lock` statement. This statement allows the developer to identify a section of code as "critical" code that only one thread may be in at one time; if multiple threads try to enter the critical section, the operating system will suspend[4] all but one. The operating system also ensures that processor caches are synchronized properly upon encountering a lock.

However, locks introduce problems of their own (along with performance overhead). Most notably, if the order of lock acquisition between threads varies, a **deadlock** could occur such that threads freeze, each waiting for the other to release its lock.

For example, consider Figure 19.2.

---

4. Either by putting the thread to sleep, spinning the thread, or spinning the thread before putting it back into sleep mode and repeating.

Time ↓

Thread A	Thread B
Acquires a lock on A	Acquires a lock on B
Requests a lock on B	Requests a lock on A
Deadlocks, waiting for B	Deadlocks, waiting for A

FIGURE 19.2: Deadlock timeline

At this point, each thread is waiting on the other thread before proceeding, so each thread is blocked, leading to an overall deadlock in the execution of that code.

We discuss various locking techniques in detail in Chapter 22.

Guidelines

DO NOT make an unwarranted assumption that any operation that is seemingly atomic in single-threaded code will be atomic in multithreaded code.

DO NOT assume that all threads will observe all side effects of operations on shared memory in a consistent order.

DO ensure that code that concurrently acquires multiple locks always acquires them in the same order.

AVOID all race conditions—that is, conditions where program behavior depends on how the operating system chooses to schedule threads.

Asynchronous Tasks

Multithreaded programming includes the following complexities:

1. *Monitoring an asynchronous operation state for completion:* This includes determining when an asynchronous operation has completed, preferably not by polling the thread's state or by blocking and waiting.

2. *Thread pooling:* This avoids the significant cost of starting and tearing down threads. In addition, thread pooling avoids the creation of too many threads, such that the system spends more time switching threads than running them.

3. *Avoiding deadlocks:* This involves preventing the occurrence of deadlocks while attempting to protect the data from simultaneous access by two different threads.

4. *Providing atomicity across operations and synchronizing data access:* Adding synchronization around groups of operations ensures that operations execute as a single unit and that they are appropriately interrupted by another thread. Locking is provided so that two different threads do not access the data simultaneously.

Furthermore, anytime a method is long running, multithreaded programming will probably be required—that is, invoking the long-running method asynchronously.[5]

However, as developers wrote more multithreaded code, a common set of scenarios and programming patterns for handling those scenarios emerged. And, to simplify the programming model, a new threading type `System.Threading.Tasks.Task` was introduced,[6] which greatly enhanced the programmability of one such pattern—TAP[7]—by leveraging the TPL[8] from .NET 4.0 and enhancing the C# language with new constructs to support it. This and the following section delve into the details of the TPL on its own and then the TPL with the `async/await` contextual keywords that simplify TAP programming.

Why the TPL?

Creating a thread is a relatively expensive operation, and each thread consumes a large amount (1 megabyte, by default, on Windows, for example) of virtual memory. It is likely more efficient to use a thread pool to allocate threads when needed, assign asynchronous work to the thread, run the work to completion, and then reuse the

5. Multithreaded programming prior to C# 5.0 required using with a relatively low-level `System.Threading.Thread` class.
6. Starting in C# 5.0.
7. As a reminder, TAP = Task-based Asynchronous Pattern.
8. As a reminder, TPL = Task Parallel Library.

thread for subsequent asynchronous work rather than destroying the thread when the work is complete and creating a new one later.

In .NET Framework 4 and later, instead of creating an operating system thread each time asynchronous work is started, the TPL creates a `Task` and tells the **task scheduler** that there is asynchronous work to perform. A task scheduler might use many different strategies to fulfill this purpose, but by default it requests a worker thread from the thread pool. The thread pool might decide that it is more efficient to run the task later, after some currently executing tasks have completed, or it might decide to schedule the task's worker thread on a particular processor. The thread pool determines whether it is more efficient to create an entirely new thread or to reuse an existing thread that previously finished executing.

By abstracting the concept of asynchronous work into the `Task` object, the TPL provides an object that represents asynchronous work and provides an object-oriented API for interacting with that work. Moreover, by providing an object that represents the unit of work, the TPL enables programmatically building up workflows by composing small tasks into larger ones, as we'll see.

A task is an object that encapsulates work that executes asynchronously. This should sound familiar: A *delegate* is also an object that represents code. The difference between a task and a delegate is that delegates are **synchronous** and tasks are **asynchronous**. Executing a delegate—say, an `Action`—immediately transfers the point of control of the current thread to the delegate's code; control does not return to the caller until the delegate is finished. By contrast, starting a task almost immediately returns control to the caller, no matter how much work the task must perform. The task executes asynchronously, typically on another thread (though, as we will discuss in Chapter 20, it is possible and even beneficial to execute tasks asynchronously with only one thread). A task essentially transforms a delegate from a synchronous to an asynchronous execution pattern.

Introducing Asynchronous Tasks

You know when a delegate is done executing on the current thread because the caller cannot do anything until the delegate is done. But how do you know when a task is done, and how do you get the result, if there is one? Consider the example of turning a synchronous delegate into an asynchronous task. The worker thread writes plus signs to the console, while the main thread writes hyphens.

Starting the task obtains a thread from the thread pool, creating a second point of control, and executes the delegate on that thread. As shown in Listing 19.1, the point of control on the main thread continues normally after the call to start the task (`Task.Run()`).

Listing 19.1: Invoking an Asynchronous Task

```
using System;
using System.Threading.Tasks;

public class Program
{
    public static void Main()
    {
        const int repetitions = 10000;
        // Use Task.Factory.StartNew<string>() for
        // TPL prior to .NET 4.5
        Task task = Task.Run(() =>
            {
                for(int count = 0; count < repetitions; count++)
                {
                    Console.Write('-');
                }
            });
        for(int count = 0; count < repetitions; count++)
        {
            Console.Write('+');
        }

        // Wait until the Task completes
        task.Wait();
    }
}
```

The code that is to run in a new thread is defined in the delegate (of type `Action` in this case) passed to the `Task.Run()` method. This delegate (in the form of a lambda expression) prints out hyphens to the console repeatedly. The loop that follows the starting of the task is almost identical, except that it displays plus signs.

Notice that following the call to `Task.Run()`, the `Action` passed as the argument immediately starts executing. The `Task` is said to be "hot," meaning that it has already been triggered to start executing—as opposed to a "cold" task, which needs to be explicitly started before the asynchronous work begins.

Although a `Task` can also be instantiated in a cold state via the `Task` constructor, doing so is generally appropriate only as an implementation detail internal to an API that returns an already running (hot) `Task`, one triggered by a call to `Task.Start()`.

Notice that the exact state of a hot task is indeterminate immediately following the call to `Run()`. The behavior is determined by a combination of the operating system, its load, and the accompanying task library. The combination determines whether `Run()` chooses to execute the task's worker thread immediately or delay it until additional resources are available. In fact, it is possible that the hot task may have already finished by the time the code on the calling thread gets its turn to execute again. The call to `Wait()` forces the main thread to wait until all the work assigned to the task has completed executing.

In this scenario, we have a single task, but it is also possible for many tasks to be running asynchronously. It is common to have a set of tasks where you want to wait for all of them to complete, or for any one of them to complete, before continuing execution of the current thread. The `Task.WaitAll()` and `Task.WaitAny()` methods, respectively, do just that.

So far, we've seen how a task can take an `Action` and run it asynchronously. But what if the work executed in the task returns a result? We can use the `Task<T>` type to run a `Func<T>` asynchronously. When executing a delegate synchronously, we know that control will not return until the result is available. When executing a `Task<T>` asynchronously, we can poll it from one thread to see if it is done, and fetch the result when it is.[9] Listing 19.2 demonstrates how to do so in a console

9. Exercise caution when using this polling technique. When creating a task from a delegate, as we have here, the task will be scheduled to run on a worker thread from the thread pool. As a consequence, the current thread will loop until the work is complete on the worker thread. This technique works, but it might consume CPU resources unnecessarily. Such a polling technique is dangerously broken if, instead of scheduling the task to run on a worker thread, you schedule the task to execute in the future on the current thread. Since the current thread is in a loop polling the task, it will loop forever because the task will not complete until the current thread exits the loop.

application. Note that this sample uses a `PiCalculator.Calculate()` method that we will delve into further in the section "Executing Loop Iterations in Parallel" in Chapter 21.

LISTING 19.2: Polling a `Task<T>`

```
using System;
using System.Threading.Tasks;
using AddisonWesley.Michaelis.EssentialCSharp.Shared;

public class Program
{
    public static void Main()
    {
        // Use Task.Factory.StartNew<string>() for
        // TPL prior to .NET 4.5
        Task<string> task =
            Task.Run<string>(
                () => PiCalculator.Calculate(100));

        foreach(
            char busySymbol in Utility.BusySymbols())
        {
            if(task.IsCompleted)
            {
                Console.Write('\b');
                break;
            }
            Console.Write(busySymbol);
        }

        Console.WriteLine();

        Console.WriteLine(task.Result);
        if (!task.IsCompleted)
        {
            throw new Exception("Task Should Be Completed");
        }
    }
}
// ...
public class PiCalculator
{
    public static string Calculate(int digits = 100)
    {
        //...
```

```
    }
}
public class Utility
{
    public static IEnumerable<char> BusySymbols()
    {
        string busySymbols = @"-\|/-\|/";
        int next = 0;
        while(true)
        {
            yield return busySymbols[next];
            next = next + 1) % busySymbols.Length;
            yield return '\b';
        }
    }
}
 // ...
```

This listing shows that the data type of the task is `Task<string>`. The generic type includes a `Result` property from which to retrieve the value returned by the `Func<string>` that the `Task<string>` executes.

Note that Listing 19.2 does not make a call to `Wait()`. Instead, reading from the `Result` property automatically causes the current thread to block until the result is available, if it isn't already; in this case, we know that it will already be complete when the result is fetched.

In addition to the `IsCompleted` and `Result` properties on `Task<T>`, several others are worth noting:

- The `IsCompleted` property is set to `true` when a task completes, whether it completed normally or faulted (i.e., ended because it threw an exception). More detailed information on the status of a task can be obtained by reading the `Status` property, which returns a value of type `TaskStatus`. Possible values are `Created`, `WaitingForActivation`, `WaitingToRun`, `Running`, `WaitingForChildrenToComplete`, `RanToCompletion`, `Canceled`, and `Faulted`. `IsCompleted` is `true` whenever the `Status` is `RanToCompletion`, `Canceled`, or `Faulted`. Of course, if the task is running on another thread and you read the status as running, the status could change to completed at any time, including immediately after you read the value of the property. The same is true of many other states—even `Created` could potentially change if a different thread starts it. Only

RanToCompletion, Canceled, and Faulted can be considered final states that no longer can be transitioned.

- A task can be uniquely identified by the value of the Id property. The static Task.CurrentId property provides the identifier for the currently executing Task (i.e., the task that is executing the Task.CurrentId call). These properties are especially useful when debugging.
- You can use the AsyncState to associate additional data with a task. For example, imagine a List<T> whose values will be computed by various tasks. Each task could contain the index of the value in the AsyncState property. This way, when the task completes, the code can index into the list using the AsyncState (first casting it to an int).[10]

We discuss other useful properties later in this chapter under "Canceling a Task."

Task Continuation

We've talked several times about the control flow of a program without ever saying what the most fundamental nature of control flow is: *Control flow determines what happens next.* When you have a simple control flow like Console.WriteLine(x .ToString());, the control flow tells you that when ToString completes normally, the next thing that will happen is a call to WriteLine with the value returned as the argument. The concept of "what happens next" is called **continuation**; each point in a control flow has a continuation. In our example, the continuation of ToString is WriteLine (and the continuation of WriteLine is whatever code runs in the next statement). The idea of continuation is so elementary to C# programming that most programmers don't even think about it; it's part of the invisible air that they breathe. The act of C# programming is the act of constructing continuation upon continuation until the control flow of the entire program is complete.

Notice that the continuation of a given piece of code in a normal C# program will be executed *immediately* upon the completion of that code. When ToString() returns, the point of control on the current thread immediately does a synchronous

10. Be careful when using tasks to asynchronously mutate collections. The tasks might be running on worker threads, and the collection might not be thread safe. It is safer to fill in the collection from the main thread after the tasks are completed.

call to `WriteLine`. Notice also that there are actually two possible continuations of a given piece of code: the *normal* continuation and the *exceptional* continuation that will be executed if the current piece of code throws an exception.

Asynchronous method calls, such as starting a `Task`, add an additional dimension to the control flow. With an asynchronous `Task` invocation, the control flow goes immediately to the statement after the `Task.Start()`, while at the same time, it begins executing within the body of the `Task` delegate. In other words, what happens next when asynchrony is involved is multidimensional. Unlike with exceptions, where the continuation is just a different path, continuation is an additional, parallel path with asynchrony.

Asynchronous tasks also allow composition of larger tasks out of smaller tasks by describing asynchronous continuations. Just as with regular control flow, a task can have different continuations to handle error situations, and tasks can be melded together by manipulating their continuations. There are several techniques for doing so, the most explicit of which is the `ContinueWith()` method (see Listing 19.3 and its corresponding output, Output 19.1).

Listing 19.3: Calling `Task.ContinueWith()`

```
using System;
using System.Threading.Tasks;

public class Program
{
    public static void Main()
    {
        Console.WriteLine("Before");
        // Use Task.Factory.StartNew<string>() for
        // TPL prior to .NET 4.5
        Task taskA =
            Task.Run(() =>
                 Console.WriteLine("Starting..."))
            .ContinueWith(antecedent =>
                 Console.WriteLine("Continuing A..."));
        Task taskB = taskA.ContinueWith(antecedent =>
            Console.WriteLine("Continuing B..."));
        Task taskC = taskA.ContinueWith(antecedent =>
            Console.WriteLine("Continuing C..."));
        Task.WaitAll(taskB, taskC);
        Console.WriteLine("Finished!");
```

```
    }
}
```

OUTPUT 19.1

```
Before
Starting...
Continuing A...
Continuing C...
Continuing B...
Finished!
```

The `ContinueWith()` method enables "chaining" two tasks together, such that when the predecessor task—the **antecedent task**—completes, the second task—the **continuation task**—is automatically started asynchronously. In Listing 19.3, for example, `Console.WriteLine("Starting...")` is the antecedent task body and `Console.WriteLine("Continuing A...")` is its continuation task body. The continuation task takes a `Task` as its argument (`antecedent`), thereby allowing the continuation task's code to access the antecedent task's completion state. When the antecedent task is completed, the continuation task starts automatically, asynchronously executing the second delegate and passing the just-completed antecedent task as an argument to that delegate. Furthermore, since the `ContinueWith()` method returns a `Task` as well, that `Task` can be used as the antecedent of yet another `Task`, and so on, forming a continuation chain of `Task`s that can be arbitrarily long.

If you call `ContinueWith()` twice on the same antecedent task (as Listing 19.3 shows with `taskB` and `taskC` representing continuation tasks for `taskA`), the antecedent task (`taskA`) has two continuation tasks, and when the antecedent task completes, both continuation tasks will be executed asynchronously. Notice that the order of execution of the continuation tasks from a single antecedent is indeterminate at compile time. Output 19.1 happens to show `taskC` executing before `taskB`, but in a second execution of the program, the order might be reversed. However, `taskA` will always execute before `taskB` and `taskC` because the latter are continuation tasks of `taskA` and therefore can't start before `taskA` completes. Similarly, the `Console.WriteLine("Starting...")` delegate will always execute to completion before `taskA` (`Console.WriteLine("Continuing A...")`)

because the latter is a continuation task of the former. Furthermore, `Finished!` will always appear last because of the call to `Task.WaitAll(taskB, taskC)` that blocks the control flow from continuing until both `taskB` and `taskC` complete.

Many different overloads of `ContinueWith()` are possible, and some of them take a `TaskContinuationOptions` value to tweak the behavior of the continuation chain. These values are flags, so they can be combined using the logical OR operator (`|`). A brief description of some of the possible flag values appears in Table 19.1; see the online documentation[11] for more details.

TABLE 19.1: List of Available `TaskContinuationOptions` Enums

Enum	Description
`None`	This is the default behavior. The continuation task will be executed when the antecedent task completes, regardless of its task status.
`PreferFairness`	If two tasks were both asynchronously started, one before the other, there is no guarantee that the one that was started first actually gets to run first. This flag asks the task scheduler to try to increase the likelihood that the first task started is the first task to execute—something that is particularly relevant when the two tasks you describe are created from different thread pool threads.
`LongRunning`	This tells the task scheduler that the task is likely to be an I/O-bound high-latency task. The scheduler can then allow other queued work to be processed rather than starved because of the long-running task. This option should be used sparingly.
`AttachedToParent`	This specifies that a task should attempt to attach to a parent task within the task hierarchy.
`DenyChildAttach` (.NET 4.5)	This throws an exception if creation of a child task is attempted. If code within the continuation tries to use `AttachedToParent`, it will behave as if there was no parent.
`NotOnRanToCompletion*`	This specifies that the continuation task should not be scheduled if its antecedent ran to completion. This option is not valid for multitask continuations.

11. Microsoft .NET Docs, https://docs.microsoft.com/dotnet/api/system.threading.tasks.taskcontinuationoptions.

Table 19.1: List of Available `TaskContinuationOptions` Enums (continued)

Enum	Description
`NotOnFaulted*`	This specifies that the continuation task should not be scheduled if its antecedent threw an unhandled exception. This option is not valid for multitask continuations.
`OnlyOnCanceled*`	This specifies that the continuation task should be scheduled only if its antecedent was canceled. This option is not valid for multitask continuations.
`NotOnCanceled*`	This specifies that the continuation task should not be scheduled if its antecedent was canceled. This option is not valid for multitask continuations.
`OnlyOnFaulted*`	This specifies that the continuation task should be scheduled only if its antecedent threw an unhandled exception. This option is not valid for multitask continuations.
`OnlyOnRanToCompletion*`	This specifies that the continuation task should be scheduled only if its antecedent ran to completion. This option is not valid for multitask continuations.
`ExecuteSynchronously`	This specifies that the continuation task should be executed synchronously. With this option specified, the continuation that the schedule will attempt to execute the work on is the same thread that causes the antecedent task to transition into its final state. If the antecedent is already complete when the continuation is created, the continuation will run on the thread creating the continuation.
`HideScheduler` (.NET 4.5)	This prevents the ambient scheduler from being seen as the current scheduler in the created task. This means that operations like `Run`/`StartNew` and `ContinueWith` that are performed in the created task will see `TaskScheduler.Default` (`null`) as the current scheduler. This is useful when continuation should run on a particular scheduler, but the continuation is calling out to additional code that should not schedule work on the same scheduler.
`LazyCancellation` (.NET 4.5)	This causes the continuation to delay monitoring the supplied cancellation token for a cancellation request until the antecedent has completed. Consider tasks t1, t2, and t3, where the latter is a continuation of the former. If t2 is canceled before t1 completes, it is possible that t3 could start before t1 completes. Setting `LazyCancellation` avoids this.

TABLE 19.1: List of Available `TaskContinuationOptions` Enums (continued)

Enum	Description
`RunContinuationsAsynchronously` (.NET 4.6)	When a task is created with the `RunContinuationsAsynchronously` option, that tells the task that it should force its continuations to run asynchronously. Even if the task is itself a continuation, this option does not affect how that task is run—only how continuations from it are run. A continuation task can be created with both `TaskContinuationOptions.ExecuteSynchronously` and `TaskContinuationOptions.RunContinuationsAsynchronously`. The former causes the continuation to execute synchronously when its antecedent completes and causes the continuation's continuations to run asynchronously when the continuation completes.

In Table 19.1, the items denoted with a star (*) indicate under which conditions the continuation task will be executed; thus they are particularly useful for creating continuations that act like event handlers for the antecedent task's behavior. Listing 19.4 demonstrates how an antecedent task can be given multiple continuations that execute conditionally, depending on how the antecedent task completed.

LISTING 19.4: Registering for Notifications of Task Behavior with `ContinueWith()`

```
using System;
using System.Threading.Tasks;
using AddisonWesley.Michaelis.EssentialCSharp.Shared;

public class Program
{
    public static void Main()
    {
        // Use Task.Factory.StartNew<string>() for
        // TPL prior to .NET 4.5
        Task<string> task =
            Task.Run<string>(
                () => PiCalculator.Calculate(10));
        Task faultedTask = task.ContinueWith(
            (antecedentTask) =>
            {
                if(!antecedentTask.IsFaulted)
                {
                    throw new Exception("Antecedent Task Should Be
```

```
↪Faulted");
                }
                Console.WriteLine(
                    "Task State: Faulted");
            },
            TaskContinuationOptions.OnlyOnFaulted);

        Task canceledTask = task.ContinueWith(
            (antecedentTask) =>
            {
                if (!antecedentTask.IsCanceled)
                {
                    throw new Exception("Antecedent Task Should Be
↪Canceled");
                }
                Console.WriteLine(
                    "Task State: Canceled");
            },
            TaskContinuationOptions.OnlyOnCanceled);

        Task completedTask = task.ContinueWith(
            (antecedentTask) =>
            {
                if (!antecedentTask.IsCompleted)
                {
                    throw new Exception("Antecedent Task Should Be
↪Completed");
                }
                Console.WriteLine(
                    "Task State: Completed");
            }, TaskContinuationOptions.
                    OnlyOnRanToCompletion);

        completedTask.Wait();
    }
}
```

In this listing, we effectively register *listeners* for *events* on the antecedent's task so that when the task completes normally or abnormally, the particular "listening" task will begin executing. This is a powerful capability, particularly if the original task is a fire-and-forget task—that is, a task that we start, hook up to continuation tasks, and then never refer to again.

In Listing 19.4, notice that the final `Wait()` call is on `completedTask`, not on `task`—the original antecedent task created with `Task.Run()`. Although each delegate's `antecedentTask` is a reference to the antecedent task (`task`), from outside the delegate listeners we can effectively discard the reference to the original `task`. We can then rely solely on the continuation tasks that begin executing asynchronously without any need for follow-up code that checks the status of the original `task`.

In this case, we call `completedTask.Wait()` so that the main thread does not exit the program before the completed output appears (see Output 19.2).

Output 19.2

```
Task State: Completed
```

In this case, invoking `completedTask.Wait()` is somewhat contrived because we know that the original task will complete successfully. However, invoking `Wait()` on `canceledTask` or `faultedTask` will result in an exception. Those continuation tasks run only if the antecedent task is canceled or throws an exception; given that will not happen in this program, those tasks will never be scheduled to run, and waiting for them to complete would throw an exception. The continuation options in Listing 19.1 happen to be mutually exclusive, so when the antecedent task runs to completion and the task associated with `completedTask` executes, the task scheduler automatically cancels the tasks associated with `canceledTask` and `faultedTask`. The canceled tasks end with their state set to `Canceled`. Therefore, calling `Wait()` (or any other invocation that would cause the current thread to wait for a task completion) on either of these tasks will throw an exception indicating that they are canceled. A less contrived approach might be to call `Task.WaitAny(completedTask, canceledTask, faultedTask)`, which will throw an `AggregateException` that then needs to be handled.

Unhandled Exception Handling on Task with `AggregateException`

When calling a method synchronously, we can wrap it in a try block with a catch clause to identify to the compiler which code we want to execute when an exception occurs. This does not work with an asynchronous call, however. We cannot simply wrap a try block around a call to `Start()` to catch an exception, because control immediately returns from the call, and control will then leave the try block, possibly long before the exception occurs on the worker thread. One solution is to wrap the body of the task delegate with a try/catch block. Exceptions thrown on and subsequently caught by the worker thread will consequently not present problems, as a try block will work normally on the worker thread. This is not the case, however, for unhandled exceptions—those that the worker thread does not catch.

Generally (starting with version 2.0[12] of the CLR), unhandled exceptions on any thread are treated as fatal, trigger the operating system error reporting dialog, and cause the application to terminate abnormally. All exceptions on all threads must be caught; if they are not, the application is not allowed to continue to run. (For some advanced techniques for dealing with unhandled exceptions, see the upcoming "Advanced Topic: Dealing with Unhandled Exceptions on a Thread.") Fortunately, this is not the case for unhandled exceptions in an asynchronously running task. In such a case, the task scheduler inserts a catchall exception handler around the delegate so that if the task throws an otherwise unhandled exception, the catchall handler will catch it and record the details of the exception in the task, avoiding any trigger of the CLR automatically terminating the process.

As we saw in Listing 19.4, one technique for dealing with a faulted task is to explicitly create a continuation task that is the fault handler for that task; the task scheduler will automatically schedule the continuation when it detects that the antecedent task threw an unhandled exception. If no such handler is present, however, and `Wait()` (or an attempt to get the `Result`) executes on a faulted task, an `AggregateException` will be thrown (see Listing 19.5 and Output 19.3).

LISTING 19.5: Handling a Task's Unhandled Exception

```
using System;
using System.Threading.Tasks;

public static class Program
{
    public static void Main()
    {
```

12. In version 1.0 of the CLR, an unhandled exception on a worker thread terminated the thread but not the application. As a result, it was possible for a buggy program to have all its worker threads die, but the main thread would continue to run, even though the program was no longer doing any work. This is a confusing situation for users to be in; it is better to signal to the user that the application is in a bad state and terminate it before it can do any more harm.

```
            // Use Task.Factory.StartNew<string>() for
            // TPL prior to .NET 4.5
            Task task = Task.Run(() =>
            {
                throw new InvalidOperationException();
            });

            try
            {
                task.Wait();
            }
            catch(AggregateException exception)
            {
                exception.Handle(eachException =>
                {
                    Console.WriteLine(
                        $"ERROR: { eachException.Message }");
                    return true;
                });
            }
        }
    }
```

OUTPUT 19.3

```
ERROR: Operation is not valid due to the current state of the object.
```

The aggregate exception is so called because it may contain many exceptions collected from one or more faulted tasks. Imagine, for example, asynchronously executing ten tasks in parallel and five of them throwing exceptions. To report all five exceptions and have them handled in a single catch block, the framework uses the `AggregateException` as a means of collecting the exceptions and reporting them as a single exception. Furthermore, since it is unknown at compile time whether a worker task will throw one or more exceptions, an unhandled faulted task will always throw an `AggregateException`. Listing 19.5 and Output 19.3 demonstrate this behavior. Even though the unhandled exception thrown on the worker thread was of type `InvalidOperationException`, the type of the exception caught on the main thread is still an `AggregateException`. Also, as expected, to catch the exception requires an `AggregateException` catch block.

A list of the exceptions contained within an AggregateException is available from the InnerExceptions property. As a result, you can iterate over this property to examine each exception and determine the appropriate course of action. Alternatively, and as shown in Listing 19.5, you can use the AggregateException.Handle() method, specifying an expression to execute against each individual exception contained within the AggregateException. One important characteristic of the Handle() method to consider, however, is that it is a predicate. As such, the predicate should return true for any exceptions that the Handle() delegate successfully addresses. If any exception handling invocation returns false for an exception, the Handle() method will throw a new AggregateException that contains the composite list of such corresponding exceptions.

You can also observe the state of a faulted task without causing the exception to be rethrown on the current thread by simply looking at the Exception property of the task. Listing 19.6 demonstrates this approach by waiting for the completion of a fault continuation of a task[13] that we know will throw an exception.

LISTING 19.6: Observing Unhandled Exceptions on a Task Using ContinueWith()

```
using System;
using System.Threading.Tasks;

public class Program
{
    public static void Main()
    {
        bool parentTaskFaulted = false;
        Task task = new(() =>
            {
                throw new InvalidOperationException();
            });
        Task continuationTask = task.ContinueWith(
            (antecedentTask) =>
            {
                parentTaskFaulted =
                    antecedentTask.IsFaulted;
            }, TaskContinuationOptions.OnlyOnFaulted);
```

13. As we discussed earlier, waiting for a fault continuation to complete is a strange thing to do because most of the time it will never be scheduled to run in the first place. This code is provided for illustrative purposes only.

```
        task.Start();
        continuationTask.Wait();
        if (!parentTaskFaulted)
        {
            throw new Exception("Parent task should be faulted");
        }
        if (!task.IsFaulted)
        {
            throw new Exception("Task should be faulted");
        }

        task.Exception!.Handle(eachException =>
        {
            Console.WriteLine(
                $"ERROR: { eachException.Message }");
            return true;
        });
    }
}
```

Notice that to retrieve the unhandled exception on the original task, we use the `Exception` property (as well as dereferencing with the null-forgiveness operator, because we know the value will not be `null`). The result is output identical to Output 19.3.

If an exception that occurs within a task goes entirely unobserved—that is, (1) it isn't caught from within the task; (2) the completion of the task is never observed, via `Wait()`, `Result`, or accessing the `Exception` property, for example; and (3) the faulted `ContinueWith()` is never observed—then the exception is likely to go unhandled entirely, resulting in a process-wide unhandled exception. In .NET 4.0, such a faulted task would get rethrown by the finalizer thread and likely crash the process. In contrast, in .NET 4.5, the crashing has been suppressed (although the CLR can be configured for the crashing behavior if preferred).

In either case, you can register for an unhandled task exception via the `TaskScheduler.UnobservedTaskException` event.

ADVANCED TOPIC

Dealing with Unhandled Exceptions on a Thread

As we discussed earlier, an unhandled exception on any thread by default causes the application to shut down. An unhandled exception is a fatal, unexpected bug, and the exception may have occurred because a crucial data structure is corrupt. Since you have no idea what the program could possibly be doing, the safest thing to do is to shut down the whole thing immediately.

Ideally, no programs would ever throw unhandled exceptions on any thread; programs that do so have bugs, and the best course of action is to find and fix the bug before the software is shipped to customers. However, rather than shutting down an application as soon as possible when an unhandled exception occurs, it is often desirable to save any working data and/or log the exception for error reporting and future debugging. This requires a mechanism to register notifications of unhandled exceptions.

With both the Microsoft .NET Framework and .NET Core 2.0 (or later), every AppDomain provides such a mechanism, and to observe the unhandled exceptions that occur in an AppDomain, you must add a handler to the `UnhandledException` event. The `UnhandledException` event will fire for all unhandled exceptions on threads within the application domain, whether it is the main thread or a worker thread. Note that the purpose of this mechanism is notification; it does not permit the application to recover from the unhandled exception and continue executing. After the event handlers run, the application will display the operating system's error reporting dialog, and then the application will exit. (For console applications, the exception details will also appear on the console.)

In Listing 19.7, we show how to create a second thread that throws an exception, which is then handled by the application domain's unhandled exception event handler. For demonstration purposes, to ensure that thread timing issues do not come into play, we insert some artificial delays using `Thread.Sleep`. Output 19.4 shows the results.

Listing 19.7: Registering for Unhandled Exceptions

```
using System;
using System.Diagnostics;
using System.Threading;
```

```
public class Program
{
    private static Stopwatch Clock { get; } = new Stopwatch();

    public static void Main()
    {
        try
        {
            Clock.Start();
            // Register a callback to receive notifications
            // of any unhandled exception

            AppDomain.CurrentDomain.UnhandledException +=
              (s, e) =>
              {
                  Message("Event handler starting");
                  Delay(4000);
              };
            Thread thread = new(() =>
            {
                Message("Throwing exception.");
                throw new Exception();
            });
            thread.Start();

            Delay(2000);
        }
        finally
        {
            Message("Finally block running.");
        }
    }

    static void Delay(int i)
    {
        Message($"Sleeping for {i} ms");
        Thread.Sleep(i);
        Message("Awake");
    }

    static void Message(string text)
    {
        Console.WriteLine("{0}:{1:0000}:{2}",
            Thread.CurrentThread.ManagedThreadId,
            Clock.ElapsedMilliseconds, text);
```

```
    }
}
```

OUTPUT 19.4

```
3:0047:Throwing exception.
3:0052:Unhandled exception handler starting.
3:0055:Sleeping for 4000 ms
1:0058:Sleeping for 2000 ms
1:2059:Awake
1:2060:Finally block running.
3:4059:Awake
Unhandled Exception: System.Exception: Exception of type 'System.
Exception' was thrown.
```

As you can see in Output 19.4, the new thread is assigned thread ID 3 and the main thread is assigned thread ID 1. The operating system schedules thread 3 to run for a while; it throws an unhandled exception, the event handler is invoked, and it goes to sleep. Soon thereafter, the operating system realizes that thread 1 can be scheduled, but its code immediately puts it to sleep. Thread 1 wakes up first and runs the finally block, and then 2 seconds later thread 3 wakes up, and the unhandled exception finally crashes the process.

This sequence of events—the event handler executing, and the process crashing after it is finished—is typical but not guaranteed. The moment there is an unhandled exception in your program, all bets are off; the program is now in an unknown and potentially very unstable state, so its behavior can be unpredictable. In this case, as you can see, the CLR allows the main thread to continue running and executing its finally block, even though it knows that by the time control gets to the finally block, another thread is in the AppDomain's unhandled exception event handler.

To emphasize this fact, try changing the delays so that the main thread sleeps longer than the event handler. In that scenario, the finally block will never execute! The process will be destroyed by the unhandled exception before thread 1 wakes up. You can also get different results depending on whether the exception-throwing thread is or is not created by the thread pool. The best practice, therefore, is to avoid all possible unhandled exceptions, whether they occur in worker threads or in the main thread.

How does this pertain to tasks? What if there are unfinished tasks hanging around the system when you want to shut it down? We look at task cancellation in the next section.

Guidelines

AVOID writing programs that produce unhandled exceptions on any thread.

CONSIDER registering an unhandled exception event handler for debugging, logging, and emergency shutdown purposes.

DO cancel unfinished tasks rather than allowing them to run during application shutdown.

Canceling a Task

Earlier in this chapter, we described why it's a bad idea to rudely abort a thread so as to cancel a task being performed by that thread. The TPL uses **cooperative cancellation**, a far more polite, robust, and reliable technique for safely canceling a task that is no longer needed. A task that supports cancellation monitors a `CancellationToken` object (found in the `System.Threading` namespace) by periodically polling it to see if a cancellation request has been issued. Listing 19.8 demonstrates both the cancellation request and the response to the request. Output 19.5 shows the results.

Listing 19.8: Canceling a Task Using `CancellationToken`

```
using System;
using System.Threading;
using System.Threading.Tasks;
using AddisonWesley.Michaelis.EssentialCSharp.Shared;

public class Program
{
    public static void Main()
    {
        string stars =
```

```
            "*".PadRight(Console.WindowWidth - 1, '*');
        Console.WriteLine("Push ENTER to exit.");

        CancellationTokenSource cancellationTokenSource = new();
        // Use Task.Factory.StartNew<string>() for
        // TPL prior to .NET 4.5
        Task task = Task.Run(
            () =>
                WritePi(cancellationTokenSource.Token),
                    cancellationTokenSource.Token);

        // Wait for the user's input
        Console.ReadLine();

        cancellationTokenSource.Cancel();
        Console.WriteLine(stars);
        task.Wait();
        Console.WriteLine();
    }

    private static void WritePi(
        CancellationToken cancellationToken)
    {
        const int batchSize = 1;
        string piSection = string.Empty;
        int i = 0;

        while (!cancellationToken.IsCancellationRequested
            || i == int.MaxValue)
        {
            piSection = PiCalculator.Calculate(
                batchSize, (i++) * batchSize);
            Console.Write(piSection);
        }
    }
}
```

Output 19.5

```
Push ENTER to exit.
3.141592653589793238462643383279502884197169399375105820974944592307816
406286208998628034825342117067982148086513282306647093844609550582231725
359408128481117450
*******************************************************************
2
```

After starting the task, a `Console.Read()` blocks the main thread. At the same time, the task continues to execute, calculating the next digit of pi and printing it out. Once the user presses Enter, the execution encounters a call to `CancellationTokenSource.Cancel()`. In Listing 19.8, we split the call to `task.Cancel()` from the call to `task.Wait()` and print out a line of asterisks in between. The purpose of this step is to show that quite possibly an additional iteration will occur before the cancellation token is observed—hence the additional 2 in Output 19.5 following the stars. The 2 appears because the `CancellationTokenSource.Cancel()` doesn't rudely stop the task from executing. The task keeps on running until it checks the token, and politely shuts down when it sees that the owner of the token is requesting cancellation of the task.

The `Cancel()` call effectively sets the `IsCancellationRequested` property on all cancellation tokens copied from `CancellationTokenSource.Token`. There are a few things to note, however:

- A `CancellationToken`, not a `CancellationTokenSource`, is given to the asynchronous task. A `CancellationToken` enables polling for a cancellation request; the `CancellationTokenSource` provides the token and signals it when it is canceled (see Figure 19.3). By passing the `CancellationToken` rather than the `CancellationTokenSource`, we don't have to worry about thread synchronization issues on the `CancellationTokenSource` because the latter remains accessible to only the original thread.
- A `CancellationToken` is a struct, so it is copied by value. The value returned by `CancellationTokenSource.Token` produces a copy of the token. The fact that `CancellationToken` is a value type and a copy is created results in thread-safe access to `CancellationTokenSource.Token`—it is available only from within the `WritePi()` method.

To monitor the `IsCancellationRequested` property, a copy of the `CancellationToken` (retrieved from `CancellationTokenSource.Token`) is passed to the task. In Listing 19.7, we then occasionally check the `IsCancellationRequested` property on the `CancellationToken` parameter; in this case, we check after each digit calculation. If `IsCancellationRequested` returns `true`, the `while` loop exits. Unlike a thread abort, which would throw an exception at essentially a random point, we exit the loop using normal control flow.

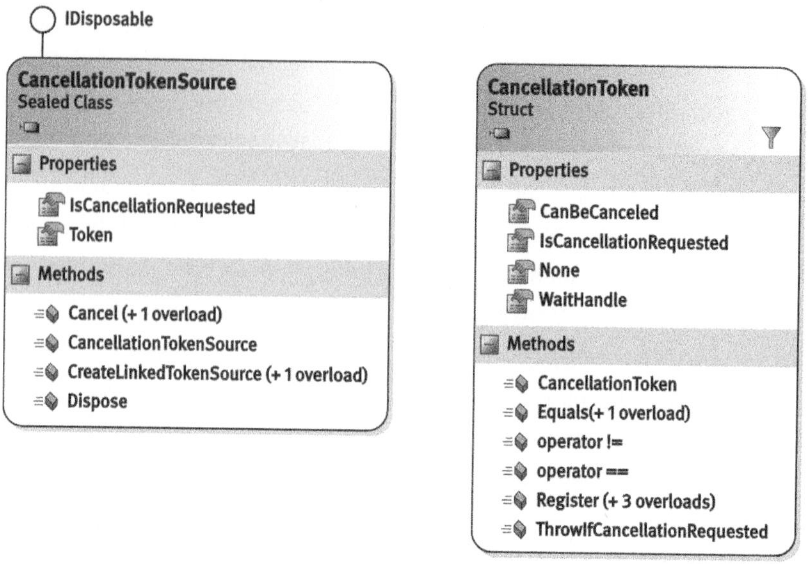

FIGURE 19.3: `CancellationTokenSource` **and** `CancellationToken` **class diagrams**

We guarantee that the code is responsive to cancellation requests by polling frequently.

One other point to note about the `CancellationToken` is the overloaded `Register()` method. Via this method, you can register an action that will be invoked whenever the token is canceled. In other words, calling the `Register()` method subscribes to a listener delegate on the corresponding `CancellationTokenSource`'s `Cancel()`.

Given that canceling before completing is the expected behavior in this program, the code in Listing 19.7 does not throw a `System.Threading.Tasks.TaskCanceledException`. As a consequence, `task.Status` will return `TaskStatus.RanToCompletion`—providing no indication that the work of the task was, in fact, canceled. In this example, there is no need for such an indication; however, the TPL does include the capability to do this. If the cancel call were disruptive in some way—preventing a valid result from returning, for example—throwing a `TaskCanceledException` (which derives from `System.OperationCanceledException`) would be the TPL pattern for reporting it. Instead of throwing the exception explicitly, `CancellationToken` includes a

ThrowIfCancellationRequested() method to report the exception more easily, assuming an instance of CancellationToken is available.

If you attempt to call Wait() (or obtain the Result) on a task that threw TaskCanceledException, the behavior is the same as if any other exception had been thrown in the task: The call will throw an AggregateException. The exception is a means of communicating that the state of execution following the task is potentially incomplete. Unlike a successfully completed task in which all expected work executed successfully, a canceled task potentially has partially completed work —the state of the work is untrusted.

This example demonstrates how a long-running processor-bound operation (calculating pi almost indefinitely) can monitor for a cancellation request and respond if one occurs. There are some cases, however, when cancellation can occur without explicitly coding for it within the target task. For example, the Parallel class, discussed in Chapter 21, offers such a behavior by default.

Guidelines

DO cancel unfinished tasks rather than allowing them to run during application shutdown.

Task.Run(): A Shortcut and Simplification to Task.Factory.StartNew()

In .NET 4.0, the general practice for obtaining a task was to call Task.Factory.StartNew(). In .NET 4.5, a simpler calling structure was provided in Task.Run(). Like Task.Run(), Task.Factory.StartNew() could be used[14] to invoke CPU-intensive methods that require an additional thread to be created.

Given .NET 4.5, Task.Run() should be used by default unless it proves insufficient. For example, if you need to control the task with TaskCreationOptions, if you need to specify an alternative scheduler, or if, for performance reasons, you want to pass in object state, you should consider using Task.Factory.StartNew(). Only in rare cases, where you need to separate

14. Starting in C# 4.0.

creation from scheduling, should constructor instantiation followed by a call to `Start()` be considered.

Listing 19.9 provides an example of using `Task.Factory.StartNew()`.

Listing 19.9: Using `Task.Factory.StartNew()`

```
public static Task<string> CalculatePiAsync(int digits)
{
    return Task.Factory.StartNew<string>(
        () => Program.CalculatePi(digits));
}

private static string CalculatePi(int digits)
{
    // ...
}
```

Long-Running Tasks

The thread pool assumes that work items will be processor bound and relatively short-lived; it makes these assumptions to effectively throttle the number of threads created. This prevents both overallocation of expensive thread resources and oversubscription of processors that would lead to excessive context switching and time slicing.

But what if the developer knows that a task will be long-running and, therefore, will hold on to an underlying thread resource for a long time? In this case, the developer can notify the scheduler that the task is unlikely to complete its work anytime soon. This has two effects. First, it hints to the scheduler that perhaps a dedicated thread ought to be created specifically for this task rather than attempting to use a thread from the thread pool. Second, it hints to the scheduler that perhaps this would be a good time to allow more tasks to be scheduled than there are processors to handle them. This will cause more time slicing to happen, which is a good thing. We do not want one long-running task to hog an entire processor and prevent shorter-running tasks from using it. The short-running tasks will be able to use their time slices to finish a large percentage of their work, and the long-running task is unlikely to notice the relatively slight delays caused by sharing a processor with other tasks. To accomplish this, use the `TaskCreationOptions`

`.LongRunning` option when calling `StartNew()`, as shown in Listing 19.10. (`Task.Run()` does not support a `TaskCreationOptions` parameter.)

Listing 19.10: Cooperatively Executing Long-Running Tasks

```
using System.Threading.Tasks;
// ...
        Task task = Task.Factory.StartNew(
            () => WritePi(cancellationTokenSource.Token),
                TaskCreationOptions.LongRunning);

        //...
```

> **Guidelines**
>
> **DO** inform the task factory that a newly created task is likely to be long-running so that it can manage it appropriately.
>
> **DO** use `TaskCreationOptions.LongRunning` sparingly.

Tasks Are Disposable

Note that `Task` also supports `IDisposable`. This is necessary because `Task` may allocate a `WaitHandle` when waiting for it to complete; since `WaitHandle` supports `IDisposable`, `Task` also supports `IDisposable` in accordance with best practices. However, note that the preceding code samples do not include a `Dispose()` call, nor do they rely on such a call implicitly via the `using` statement. Instead, the listings rely on an automatic `WaitHandle` finalizer invocation when the program exits.

This approach leads to two notable results. First, the handles live longer and hence consume more resources than they ought to. Second, the garbage collector is slightly less efficient because finalized objects survive into the next generation. However, both of these concerns are inconsequential in the `Task` case unless an extraordinarily large number of tasks are being finalized. Therefore, even though technically speaking all code should be disposing of tasks, you needn't bother to do so unless performance metrics require it and it's easy—that is, if you're certain that `Tasks` have completed and no other code is using them.

Working with System.Threading

The Parallel Extensions library is extraordinarily useful because it allows you to manipulate a higher-level abstraction—the task—rather than working directly with threads. Sometimes, however, you might need to work with code written before the TPL and PLINQ were available (prior to .NET 4.0), or you might have a programming problem not directly addressed by them. To do this, you can leverage the `Thread` class and related API in `System.Threading`. `System.Threading.Thread` represents a point of control in the program, wrapping operating system threads while the namespace provides additional managed APIs to manage those threads.

One common method in `Thread` is `Sleep()`; however, in spite of its convenience, it should be avoided. `Thread.Sleep()` puts the current thread to sleep, essentially telling the operating system not to schedule any time slices to this thread until (at least) the given amount of time has passed. This might sound like a sensible thing to do, but it is a "bad code smell" that indicates the design of the program could probably be better. Putting a thread to sleep is a bad programming practice because the whole point of allocating an expensive resource like a thread is to get work out of that resource. (You wouldn't pay an employee to sleep; likewise, you shouldn't pay the price of allocating an expensive thread only to put it to sleep for millions or billions of processor cycles.) That said, there are a couple of valid use cases.

The first use case is to put a thread to sleep with a time delay of zero to indicate to the operating system that "the current thread is politely giving up the rest of its quantum to another thread if there is one that can use it." The polite thread will then be scheduled normally, without any further delay. The second use case is in test code to simulate a thread that is working on some high-latency operation, but without actually having to burn a processor doing some pointless arithmetic. Other uses in production code should be reviewed carefully to ensure that a better way to obtain the desired effect is not available.

Another type in `System.Threading` is the `ThreadPool`, which is designed to limit an excess number of threads that might negatively impact performance.

Threads are expensive resources, thread context switching is not free, and running two jobs in simulated parallelism via time slicing can be significantly slower than running them one after the other. And while the thread pool does its job well, it does not provide services to deal with long-running jobs or jobs that need to be synchronized with the main thread or with one another. What we really need to do is build a higher-level abstraction that can use threads and thread pools as an implementation detail. Since TPL provides precisely that abstraction, `ThreadPool` can essentially be deprecated entirely in favor of the TPL-based APIs.

For more details on other techniques for managing worker threads that were commonly used prior to .NET 4, see the *Essential C# 3.0* multithreading chapters at https://intellitect.com/EssentialCSharp.

Guidelines

AVOID calling `Thread.Sleep()` in production code.

DO use tasks and related APIs in favor of `System.Theading` classes such as `Thread` and `ThreadPool`.

For more information on `System.Threading.ThreadPool`'s and `System.Threading.Thread`'s `Sleep()` methods, see https://intellitect.com/legacy-system-threading.

Summary

At the beginning of this chapter, we glossed over some of the difficult problems that developers often face when writing multithreaded programs: atomicity problems, deadlocks, and other race conditions that introduce uncertainty and bad behavior into multithreaded programs. We then delved into the Task Parallel Library (TPL) and its Task-based Asynchronous Pattern (TAP), a new API for creating and scheduling units of work represented by `Task` objects, and we saw how they simplify multithreaded programming by enabling you to automatically rewrite your programs to manage the continuation "wiring" that composes larger tasks out of smaller tasks. In Chapters 20 and 21, we introduce additional high-level abstractions that cover additional scenarios and simplify TAP even further.

In Chapter 22, we switch over to cover how to avoid atomicity problems with synchronized access to shared resources without introducing deadlocks.

20

Programming the Task-Based Asynchronous Pattern

As we saw in Chapter 19, tasks provide an abstraction for the manipulation of asynchronous work. Tasks are automatically scheduled to the right number of threads, and large tasks can be composed by chaining together small tasks, just as large programs can be composed from multiple small methods.

However, there are some drawbacks to tasks. The principal difficulty with tasks is that they turn your program logic "inside out." To illustrate this, we begin the chapter with a synchronous method that is blocked on an I/O-bound, high-latency operation—a web request. We then revise this method by leveraging the `async`/`await` contextual keywords,[1] demonstrating a significant simplification in authoring and readability of asynchronous code.

We finish the chapter with a look at asynchronous streams—a C# 8.0–introduced feature for defining and leveraging asynchronous iterators.

Synchronously Invoking a High-Latency Operation

In Listing 20.1, the code uses a `HttpClient` to download a web page and search for the number of times some text appears. Output 20.1 shows the results.

---

1. Introduced in C# 5.0.

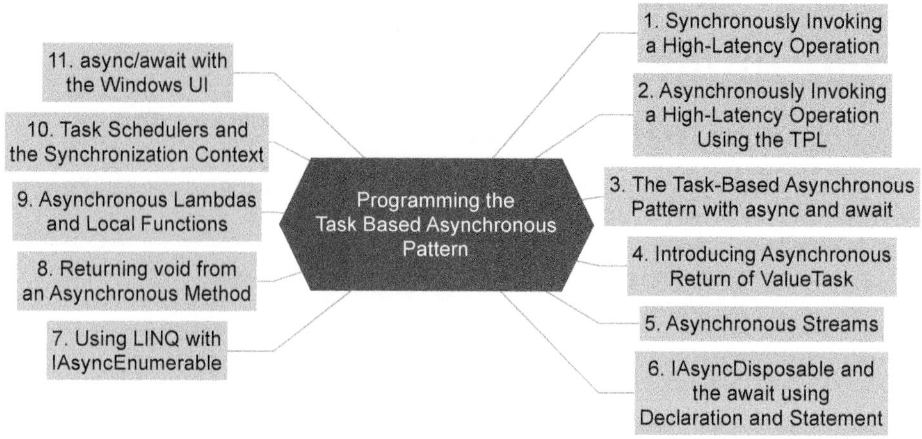

Listing 20.1: A Synchronous Web Request

```
using System;
using System.IO;
using System.Net;

public static class Program
{
    public static HttpClient HttpClient { get; set; } = new();
    public const string DefaultUrl = "https://IntelliTect.com";

    public static void Main(string[] args)
    {
        if (args.Length == 0)
        {
            Console.WriteLine("ERROR: No findText argument specified.");
            return;
        }
        string findText = args[0];

        string url = DefaultUrl;
        if (args.Length > 1)
        {
            url = args[1];
            // Ignore additional parameters
        }
        Console.WriteLine(
            $"Searching for '{findText}' at URL '{url}'.");
```

```
        Console.WriteLine("Downloading...");
        byte[] downloadData =
            HttpClient.GetByteArrayAsync(url).Result;

        Console.WriteLine("Searching...");
        int textOccurrenceCount = CountOccurrences(
            downloadData, findText);

        Console.WriteLine(
            @$"'{findText}' appears {
                textOccurrenceCount} times at URL '{url}'.");
    }

    private static int CountOccurrences(byte[] downloadData, string
↪findText)
    {
        int textOccurrenceCount = 0;

        using MemoryStream stream = new(downloadData);
        using StreamReader reader = new(stream);

        int findIndex = 0;
        int length = 0;
        do
        {
            char[] data = new char[reader.BaseStream.Length];
            length = reader.Read(data);
            for (int i = 0; i < length; i++)
            {
                if (findText[findIndex] == data[i])
                {
                    findIndex++;
                    if (findIndex == findText.Length)
                    {
                        // Text was found
                        textOccurrenceCount++;
                        findIndex = 0;
                    }
                }
                else
                {
                    findIndex = 0;
                }
            }
        }
        while (length != 0);
```

```
            return textOccurrenceCount;
        }
    }
```

Output 20.1

```
Searching for 'IntelliTect'...
http://www.IntelliTect.com
Downloading...
Searching...
'IntelliTect' appears 35 times at URL 'http://www.IntelliTect.com'.
```

The logic in Listing 20.1 is relatively straightforward—using common C# idioms. After determining the `url` and `findText` values, `Main()`, using an existing `HttpClient` instance, it invokes the asynchronous method `GetByteArrayAsync()` to download the content. It calls .Result to force the asynchronous method to execute synchronously and return the result. This approach to making asynchronous methods run synchronously is not recommend as it can cause deadlocks. Given the downloaded data, it passes this data to `CountOccurrences()`, which loads it into a `MemoryStream` and leverages a `StreamReader`'s `Read()` method to retrieve a block of data and search it for the `findText` value. (We use the `GetByteArrayAsync()` method rather than the simpler `GetStringAsync()` method so that we can demonstrate an additional asynchronous invocation when reading from a stream in Listing 20.2 and Listing 20.3.)

The problem with this approach is, of course, that the calling thread is blocked until the I/O operation completes; this is wasting a thread that could be doing useful work while the operation executes. For this reason, we cannot, for example, execute any other code, such as code that asynchronously indicates progress. In other words, "Download..." and "Searching..." are invoked *before* their corresponding operations, not *during* the operation. While doing so would be irrelevant here, imagine that we wanted to concurrently execute additional work or, at a minimum, provide an animated busy indicator.

Asynchronously Invoking a High-Latency Operation Using the TPL

To address this problem of executing other work in parallel, Listing 20.2 takes a similar approach but instead uses task-based asynchrony with the TPL.

Listing 20.2: An Asynchronous Web Request

```
using System;
using System.IO;
using System.Net;
using System.Runtime.ExceptionServices;
using System.Threading.Tasks;

public static class Program
{
    public static HttpClient HttpClient { get; set; } = new();
    public const string DefaultUrl = "https://IntelliTect.com";

    public static void Main(string[] args)
    {
        if (args.Length == 0)
        {
            Console.WriteLine("ERROR: No findText argument specified.");
            return;
        }
        string findText = args[0];

        string url = DefaultUrl;
        if (args.Length > 1)
        {
            url = args[1];
            // Ignore additional parameters
        }
        Console.WriteLine(
            $"Searching for '{findText}' at URL '{url}'.");

        Console.Write("Downloading...");
        Task task = HttpClient.GetByteArrayAsync(url)
            .ContinueWith(antecedent =>
            {
                byte[] downloadData = antecedent.Result;
                Console.Write($"{Environment.NewLine}Searching...");
                return CountOccurrencesAsync(
                    downloadData, findText);
            })
```

```
            .Unwrap()
            .ContinueWith(antecedent =>
            {
                int textOccurrenceCount = antecedent.Result;
                Console.WriteLine(
                     @$"{Environment.NewLine}'{findText}' appears {
                        textOccurrenceCount} times at URL '{url}'.");

            });

        try
        {
            while (!task.Wait(100))
            {
                Console.Write(".");
            }
        }
        catch (AggregateException exception)
        {
            exception = exception.Flatten();
            try
            {
                exception.Handle(innerException =>
                {
                    // Rethrowing rather than using
                    // if condition on the type
                    ExceptionDispatchInfo.Capture(
                        innerException)
                        .Throw();
                    return true;
                });
            }
            catch (HttpRequestException)
            {
                // ...
            }
            catch (IOException)
            {
                // ...
            }
        }
    }


    private static async Task<int> CountOccurrencesAsync(
        byte[] downloadData, string findText)
    {
```

```
        // ...
    }
}
```

The associated output is essentially the same as Output 20.1, except that additional periods are expected following "Downloading…" and "Searching…", depending on how long those operations take to execute.

When Listing 20.2 executes, it prints "Downloading…" with additional periods to the console while the page is downloading; much the same occurs with "Searching…". The result is that instead of simply printing four periods (`....`) to the console, Listing 20.2 is able to continuously print periods for as long as it takes to download the file and search its text.

Unfortunately, this asynchrony comes at the cost of complexity. Interspersed throughout the code is TPL-related code that interrupts the flow. Rather than simply following the `HttpClient.GetByteArrayAsync(url)` call with statements that count the occurrences (invocation of an asynchronous version of `CountOccurrences()`), the asynchronous version of the code requires `ContinueWith()` statements, `Unwrap()` invocations for simplicity, and a complicated try/catch handling system. The details are outlined in "Advanced Topic: The Complexity of Asynchronous Requests with TPL." Suffice it to say, you will be grateful for the task-based asynchronous pattern with `async`/`await`.[2]

ADVANCED TOPIC

The Complexity of Asynchronous Requests with TPL

The first `ContinueWith()` statement identifies what to execute after the `HttpClient.GetByteArrayAsync(url)`. Notice that the `return` statement in the first `ContinueWith()` statement returns `CountOccurrencesAsync(downloadData, findText)`, which returns another task, specifically `Task<int>`. The return type of the first `ContinueWith()` statement, therefore, is a `Task<Task<byte[]>`.

2. Introduced in C# 5.0.

Hence we have the Unwrap() invocation: Without it, the antecedent in the second ContinueWith() statement is also Task<Task<byte[]>>, which by itself indicates the complexity. As a result, it would be necessary to call Result twice—once on the antecedent directly, and a second time on the Task<byte[]>.Result property that antecedent.Result returned. The latter invocation blocks subsequent execution until the GetByteArrayAsync() operation completes. To avoid the Task<Task<TResult>> structure, we preface the second invocation of ContinueWith() with a call to Unwrap(), thereby shedding the outer Task and appropriately handling any errors or cancellation requests.

The complexity doesn't stop with Tasks and ContinueWith(), however: The exception handling adds an entirely new dimension to the complexity. As mentioned earlier, the TPL generally throws an AggregateException exception because of the possibility that an asynchronous operation could encounter multiple exceptions. However, because we are calling the Result property from within ContinueWith() blocks, potentially we might also throw an AggregateException inside the worker thread.

As you learned in earlier chapters, there are multiple ways to handle these exceptions:

1. We can add continuation tasks to all *Async methods that return a task along with each ContinueWith() method call. However, doing so would prevent us from using the fluid API in which the ContinueWith() statements are chained together one after the other. Furthermore, this would force us to deeply embed error-handling logic into the control flow rather than simply relying on exception handling.

2. We can surround each delegate body with a try/catch block so that no exceptions go unhandled from the task. Unfortunately, this approach is also less than ideal. First, some exceptions (like those triggered when calling `antecedent.Result`) will throw an `AggregateException`, from which we will need to unwrap the `InnerException`(s) to handle them individually. Upon unwrapping them, we either rethrow them to catch a specific type or conditionally check for the type of the exception separately from any other catch blocks (even catch blocks for the same type). Second, each delegate body requires its own separate try/catch handler, even if some of the exception types between blocks are the same. Third, `Main`'s call to `task.Wait()` could still throw an exception because `HttpClient.GetByteArrayAsync()` or `CountOccurrencesAsync()` could potentially throw an exception, and there is no way to surround the latter with a try/catch block. Therefore, there is no way to eliminate the try/catch block in `Main` that surrounds `task.Wait()`.

3. In Listing 20.2, we don't catch any exceptions thrown from `GetByteArrayAsync()` but instead rely solely on the try/catch block that surrounds `Main`'s `task.Wait()`. Given that we know the exception will be an `AggregateException`, there is a catch for only that exception. Within the catch block, we handle the exception by calling `AggregateException.Handle()` and throwing each exception using the `ExceptionDispatchInfo` object so as not to lose the original stack trace. These exceptions are then caught by the expected exception handlers and addressed accordingly. Notice, however, that before handling the `AggregateException`'s `InnerExceptions`, we first call `AggregateException.Flatten()`. This step addresses the issue of an `AggregateException` wrapping inner exceptions that are also of type `Aggregate Exception` (and so on). By calling `Flatten()`, we ensure that all exceptions are moved to the first level and all contained `AggregateExceptions` are removed.

As shown in Listing 20.2, option 3 is probably the preferred approach because it keeps the exception handling outside the control flow for the most part. This doesn't eliminate the error-handling complexity entirely; rather, it simply minimizes the occasions on which it is interspersed within the regular control flow.

In conclusion, although the asynchronous version in Listing 20.2 has almost the same logical control flow as the synchronous version in Listing 20.1, both versions attempt to download a resource from a server. If the download succeeds, the result is returned. If the download fails, the exception's type is interrogated to determine the right course of action. Clearly, the asynchronous version of Listing 20.2 is significantly more difficult to read, understand, and change than the corresponding synchronous version in Listing 20.1. Unlike the synchronous version, which uses standard control flow statements, the asynchronous version is forced to create multiple lambda expressions to express the continuation logic in the form of delegates.

And this is a relatively simple example, especially since we don't list the implementation of `CountOccurrencesAsync()`! Imagine what the asynchronous code would look like if, for example, the synchronous code contained a loop that retried the operation three times if it failed, if it tried to contact multiple different servers, if it took a collection of resources rather than a single one, or if all of these possible features occurred together. Adding those features to the synchronous version would be straightforward, but it is not at all clear how to do so in the asynchronous version. Rewriting synchronous methods into asynchronous methods by explicitly specifying the continuation of each task gets very complicated very quickly even if the synchronous continuations are what appear to be very simple control flows.

The Task-Based Asynchronous Pattern with `async` and `await`

To address the complexity problem, Listing 20.3 also provides asynchronous execution but instead uses task-based asynchrony, which leverages an `async/await` feature.[3] With `async/await`, the compiler takes care of the complexity, allowing the developer to focus on the business logic. Rather than worrying about chaining `ContinueWith()` statements, retrieving `antecedents.Results`, `Unwrap()` invocations, complex error handling, and the like, `async/await` allows you to just decorate the code with simple syntax that informs the compiler that it should handle the complexity. In addition, when a task completes and additional

3. Introduced in C# 5.0.

code needs to execute, the compiler automatically takes care of invoking the remaining code on the appropriate thread. You cannot have two different threads interacting with a single threaded UI platform, for example, and `async/await` addresses this issue. (See the section on the use of the `async/await` feature with the Windows UI later in the chapter.)

In other words, the `async/await` syntax tells the compiler to reorganize the code at compile time, even though it is written relatively simply, and to address the myriad of complexities that developers would otherwise have to consider explicitly —see Listing 20.3.

Listing 20.3: Asynchronous High-Latency Invocation with the Task-Based Asynchronous Pattern

```
using System;
using System.IO;
using System.Threading.Tasks;

public static class Program
{
    public static HttpClient HttpClient { get; set; } = new();
    public const string DefaultUrl = "https://IntelliTect.com";

    public static async Task Main(string[] args)
    {
        if (args.Length == 0)
        {
            Console.WriteLine("ERROR: No findText argument specified.");
            return;
        }
        string findText = args[0];

        string url = DefaultUrl;
        if (args.Length > 1)
        {
            url = args[1];
            // Ignore additional parameters
        }
        Console.WriteLine(
            $"Searching for '{findText}' at URL '{url}'.");

        Task<byte[]> taskDownload =
            HttpClient.GetByteArrayAsync(url);
```

```
        Console.Write("Downloading...");
        while (!taskDownload.Wait(100))
        {
            Console.Write(".");
        }

        byte[] downloadData = await taskDownload;

        Task<int> taskSearch = CountOccurrencesAsync(
         downloadData, findText);

        Console.Write($"{Environment.NewLine}Searching...");

        while (!taskSearch.Wait(100))
        {
            Console.Write(".");
        }

        int textOccurrenceCount = await taskSearch;

        Console.WriteLine(
            @$"{Environment.NewLine}'{findText}' appears {
                textOccurrenceCount} times at URL '{url}'.");
    }


    private static async Task<int> CountOccurrencesAsync(
        byte[] downloadData, string findText)
    {
        int textOccurrenceCount = 0;
        using MemoryStream stream = new(downloadData);
        using StreamReader reader = new(stream);

        int findIndex = 0;
        int length = 0;
        do
        {
            char[] data = new char[reader.BaseStream.Length];
            length = await reader.ReadAsync(data);
            for (int i = 0; i < length; i++)
            {
                if (findText[findIndex] == data[i])
                {
                    findIndex++;
                    if (findIndex == findText.Length)
                    {
                        // Text was found
```

```
                        textOccurrenceCount++;
                        findIndex = 0;
                    }
                }
                else
                {
                    findIndex = 0;
                }
            }
        }
        while (length != 0);

        return textOccurrenceCount;
    }
}
```

Notice there are relatively small differences between Listing 20.1 and Listing 20.3. Furthermore, while the number of periods will vary between executions, the output should match that from Listing 20.2. This is one of the key points about the `async/await` pattern: It lets you write code with only minor modifications from the way you would write it synchronously.

Begin 8.0

To understand the pattern, focus first on the `CountOccurrencesAsync()` method and the differences from Listing 20.1. First, we change the signature of the `CountOccurrences()` method declaration by adding the new contextual `async` keyword as a modifier on the signature. Next, we return a `Task<int>` rather than just `int`. Any method decorated with the `async` keyword must return a **valid async return type**. This can be a `void`, `Task`, `Task<T>`, `ValueTask<T>`,[4] or `IAsyncEnumerable<T>/IasyncEnumerator<T>` (as of C# 8.0).[5] In this case, since the body of the method does not return any data but we still want the ability to return information about the asynchronous activity to the caller, `CountOccurrencesAsync()` returns `Task`. By returning a task, the caller has access to the state of the asynchronous invocation and the result (the `int`) when it completes. Next, the method name is suffixed with "Async" by convention, to indicate that it can be invoked with an `await` method. Finally, everywhere that we

4. Starting in C# 7.0.
5. Technically, you can also return any type that implements a `GetAwaiter()` method. See "Advanced Topic: Valid Async Return Types Expanded" later in the chapter.

need to asynchronously wait for a task of an asynchronous method within `CountOccurrencesAsync()`, we include the `await` operator. In this case, this occurs only for the invocation of `reader.ReadAsync()`. Like `CountOccurrencesAsync()`, `StreamReader.ReadAsync()` is an `async` method with the same characteristics.

End 8.0

Back in `Main()`, the same sorts of differences occur. When we invoke the new `CountOccurencesAsync()` method, we do so with the `await` contextual keyword. In so doing, we can write code that is neutered of the explicit task complexities. When we add the `await` method, we can assign the result to an `int` (rather than a `Task<int>`) or assume there is no return if the invoked method returns a `Task`.

For emphasis, remember that the signature for `CountOccurrencesAsync()` is as follows:

```
private static async Task<int> CountOccurrencesAsync(
byte[] downloadData, string findText)
```

Even though it returns a `Task<int>`, the `await` invocation of `CountOccurrencesAsync()` would return an `int`:

```
int textOccurrenceCount = await CountOccurrencesAsync(
downloadData, findText);
```

This example shows some of the magic of the `await` feature: It unwraps the result from task and returns it directly.

If you wish to execute code while the asynchronous operation is executing, you can postpone the `await` invocation until the parallel work (writing to the console) has completed. The code prior to invoking `CountOccurrencesAsync()` invokes `HttpClient.GetByteArrayAsync(url)` similarly. Rather than assigning a `byte[]` and leveraging the `await` operator, the `await` invocation is also postponed while periods are written to the console in parallel.

```
Task<byte[]> taskDownload =
HttpClient.GetByteArrayAsync(url);
while (!taskSearch.Wait(100)){Console.Write(".");}
byte[] downloadData = await taskDownload;
```

In addition to unwrapping the Task, the await operator will tell the C# compiler to generate code for ensuring the code following the await invocation will execute on the appropriate thread. This is a critical benefit that avoids what can be challenging defects to find.

To better explain the control flow, Figure 20.1 shows each task in a separate column along with the execution that occurs on each task.

There are a couple of important misconceptions that Figure 20.1 helps to dismiss:

- **Misconception #1: A method decorated with the async keyword is automatically executed on a worker thread when called.** This is absolutely not true; the method is executed normally, on the calling thread, and if the implementation doesn't await any incomplete awaitable tasks, it will complete synchronously on the same thread. The method's implementation is responsible for starting any asynchronous work. Just using the async keyword does not change on which thread the method's code executes. Also, there is nothing unusual about a call to an async method from the caller's perspective; it is a method typed as returning one of the valid async return types and it is called normally. In Main(), for example, the return from CountOccurrencesAsync() is assigned a Task<int>, just like it would for a non-async method. We then await the task.
- **Misconception #2: The await keyword causes the current thread to block until the awaited task is completed.** That is also absolutely not true. If you have no other choice except for the current thread to block until the task completes, call the Wait() method (while being careful to avoid a deadlock), as we have described in Chapter 19. The await keyword evaluates the expression that follows it, a valid async return type such as Task, Task<T>, or ValueTask<T>; adds a continuation to the resultant task; and then *immediately* returns control to the caller. The creation of the task has started asynchronous work; the await keyword means that the developer wants the caller of this method to continue executing its work on this thread while the asynchronous work is processed. At some point after that asynchronous work is complete, execution will resume at the point of control following the await expression.

In fact, the principal reasons why the async keyword exists in the first place are twofold. First, it makes it crystal clear to the reader of the code that the compiler will automatically rewrite the method that follows. Second, it informs the compiler that

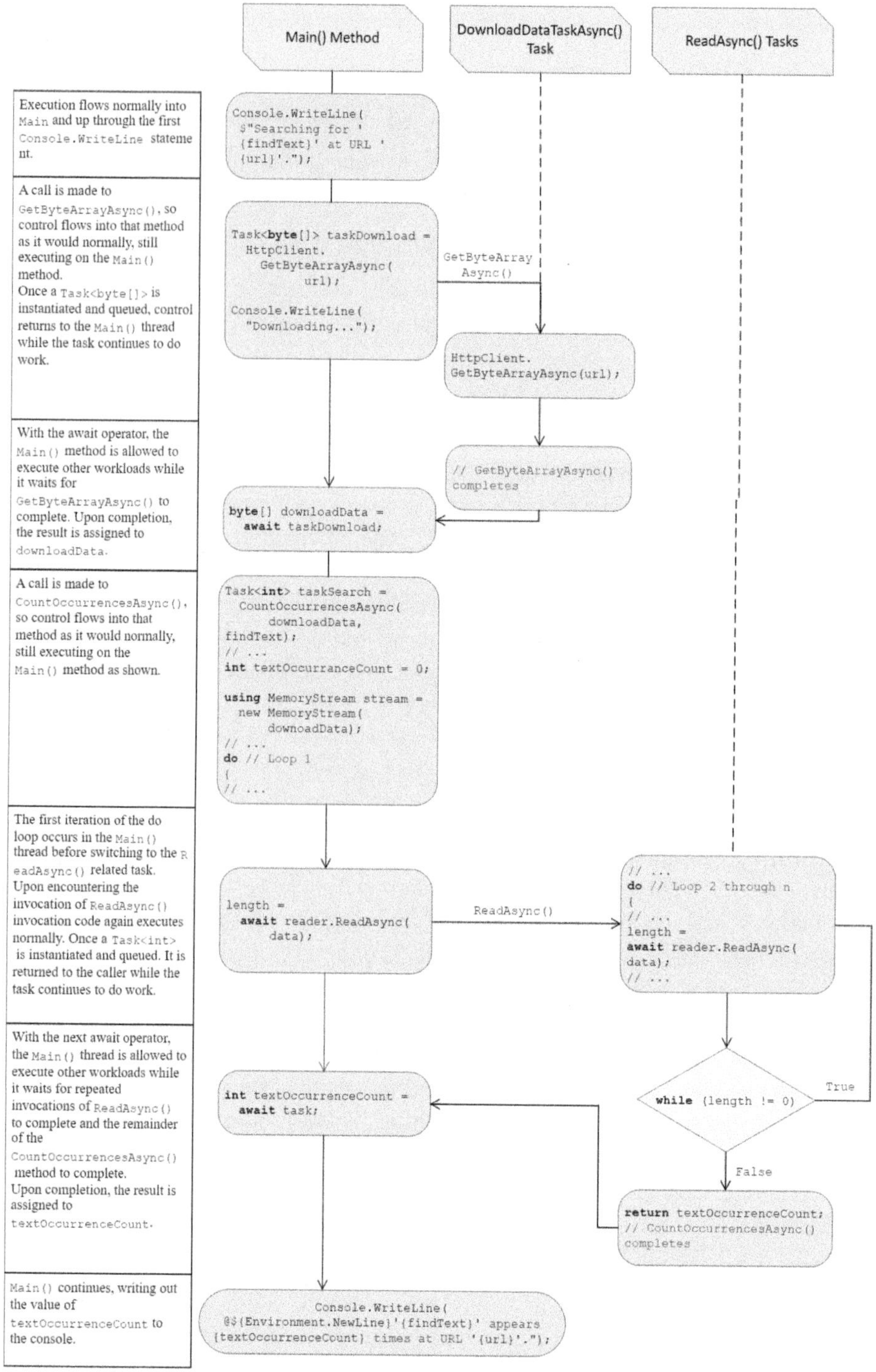

FIGURE 20.1: Control flow within each task

usages of the await contextual keyword in the method are to be treated as asynchronous control flow and not as an ordinary identifier.

It is possible to have an async Main method.[6] As a result, Listing 20.3's Main signature is public static async Task Main(string[] args). This allows the user of the await operator to invoke the asynchronous methods. Without an async Main() method, we would have to rely on working with valid async return types explicitly, along with explicitly waiting for the task completion before exiting the program, to avoid unexpected behavior.[7]

Introducing Asynchronous Return of ValueTask<T>

We use asynchronous methods for long-running, high-latency operations. And (obviously), since Task/Task<T> is the return, we always need to obtain an instance of one of these objects to return. The alternative, to return null, would force callers to always check for null before accessing the Task—an unreasonable and frustrating API from a usability perspective. Generally, the cost to create a Task/Task<T> is insignificant in comparison to the long-running, high-latency operation.

What happens, though, if the operation can be short-circuited and a result returned immediately? Consider, for example, compressing a buffer. If the amount of data is significant, performing the operation asynchronously makes sense. If, however, data is zero-length, then the operation can return immediately, and obtaining a (cached or new instance of) Task/Task<T> is pointless because there is no need for a task when the operation completes immediately. What is needed is a task-like object that can manage the asynchrony but not require the expense of a full Task/Task<T> when it isn't needed. Support for additional valid async return

---

6. Starting with C# 7.1.
7. C# 5.0 and 6.0 included a restriction that await operators couldn't appear within exception handling catch or finally statements. However, this restriction was removed starting with C# 7.0.

types was added[8]—that is, types that support a `GetAwaiter()` method, as detailed in "Advanced Topic: Valid Async Return Types Expanded."[9]

Listing 20.4 provides an example of file compression but escaping via `ValueTask<T>` if the compression can be short-circuited.

Listing 20.4: Returning `ValueTask<T>` from an `async` Method

```
using System.IO;
using System.Text;
using System.Threading.Tasks;

public static class Program
{
    public static async ValueTask<byte[]> CompressAsync(byte[] buffer)
    {
        if (buffer.Length == 0)
        {
            return buffer;
        }
        using MemoryStream memoryStream = new();
        using System.IO.Compression.GZipStream gZipStream =
            new(
                memoryStream,
                    System.IO.Compression.CompressionMode.Compress);
        await gZipStream.WriteAsync(buffer.AsMemory(0, buffer.Length));

        return memoryStream.ToArray();
    }
    // ...
}
```

Notice that even though an asynchronous method, such as `GZipStream.WriteAsync()`, might return `Task<T>`, the `await` implementation still works within a `ValueTask<T>` returning method. In Listing 20.4, for example, changing the return from `ValueTask<T>` to `Task<T>` involves no other code changes.

The availability of `ValueTask<T>` raises the question of when to use it versus `Task/Task<T>`. If your operation doesn't return a value, just use `Task` (there is

8. Starting in C# 7.0.

9. C# 7.0–related .NET frameworks include `ValueTask<T>`, a value type that scales down to support lightweight instantiation when a long-running operation can be short-circuited or that can be converted to a full `Task` otherwise.

no nongeneric `ValueTask<T>` because it has no benefit). Likewise, if your operation is likely to complete asynchronously, or if it's not possible to cache tasks for common result values, `Task<T>` is preferred. For example, there's generally no benefit to returning `ValueTask<bool>` instead of `Task<bool>`, because you can easily cache a `Task<bool>` for both `true` and `false` values—and in fact, the `async` infrastructure does this automatically. In other words, when returning an asynchronous `Task<bool>` method that completes synchronously, a cached result `Task<bool>` will return regardless. If, however, the operation is likely to complete synchronously and you can't reasonably cache all common return values, `ValueTask<T>` might be appropriate.

BEGINNER TOPIC

Common Async Return Types Explained

The expression that follows the `await` keyword is most frequently of type `Task`, `Task<T>`, or `ValueTask<T>`. From a syntax perspective, an `await` operating on type `Task` is essentially the equivalent of an expression that returns `void`. In fact, because the compiler does not even know whether the task has a result, much less which type it is, such an expression is classified in the same way as a call to a `void`-returning method; that is, you can use it only in a statement context. Listing 20.5 shows some `await` expressions used as statement expressions.

Listing 20.5: An `await` Expression May Be a Statement Expression

```
public async Task<int> DoStuffAsync()
{
    await DoSomethingAsync();
    await DoSomethingElseAsync();
    return await GetAnIntegerAsync() + 1;
}
```

Here we presume that the first methods return a `Task` rather than a `Task<T>` or `ValueTask<T>`. Since there is no result value associated with the first two tasks, awaiting them produces no value; thus the expression must appear as a statement.

The third task is presumably of type `Task<int>`, and its value can be used in the computation of the value of the task returned by `DoStuffAsync()`.

Begin 8.0

Asynchronous Streams

C# 8.0 introduced the ability to program **async streams**, essentially the ability to leverage the async pattern with iterators. As discussed in Chapter 15, collections in C# are all built on the `IEnumerable<T>` and `IEnumerator<T>`, the former with a single `GetEnumerator<T>()` function that returns an `IEnumerator<T>` over which you can iterate. And, when building an iterator with `yield return`, the method needs to return `IEnumerable<T>` or `IEnumerator<T>`. In contrast, valid async return types must support a `GetAwaiter()` method,[10] just as `Task`, `Task<T>`, and `ValueTask<T>` do. The conflict, therefore, is that you can't have both an `async` method and an iterator. When invoking an `async` method while iterating over a collection, for example, you can't yield the results to a calling function prior to the completion of all expected iterations.

To address these problems, the C# team added asynchronous streams (async streams) support in C# 8.0. This feature is specifically designed to enable asynchronous iteration and the building of asynchronous collections and enumerable type methods using `yield return`.

For example, imagine encrypting content with an `async` method, `EncryptFilesAsync()`, given a directory (defaulting to the current directory). Listing 20.6 provides the code.

Listing 20.6: Async Streams

```
using System.IO;
using System.Linq;
using System.Threading.Tasks;
using System.Collections.Generic;
using System.Threading;
using System.Runtime.CompilerServices;
using AddisonWesley.Michaelis.EssentialCSharp.Shared;
```

10. Or `void`.

```
public static class Program
{
    public static async void Main(params string[] args)
    {
        string directoryPath = Directory.GetCurrentDirectory();
        string searchPattern = "*";
        // ...
        using Cryptographer cryptographer = new();

        IEnumerable<string> files = Directory.EnumerateFiles(
            directoryPath, searchPattern);

        // Create a cancellation token source to cancel
        // if the operation takes more than a minute.
        using CancellationTokenSource cancellationTokenSource =
            new(1000*60);

        await foreach ((string fileName, string encryptedFileName)
            in EncryptFilesAsync(files, cryptographer)
            .Zip(files.ToAsyncEnumerable())
            .WithCancellation(cancellationTokenSource.Token)
            )
        {
            Console.WriteLine($"{fileName}=>{encryptedFileName}");
        }
    }

    public static async IAsyncEnumerable<string> EncryptFilesAsync(
        IEnumerable<string> files, Cryptographer cryptographer,
        [EnumeratorCancellation] CancellationToken cancellationToken =
↪default)
    {
        foreach (string fileName in files)
        {
            yield return await EncryptFileAsync(fileName, cryptographer);
            cancellationToken.ThrowIfCancellationRequested();
        }
    }

    private static async ValueTask<string> EncryptFileAsync(
        string fileName, Cryptographer cryptographer)
    {
        string encryptedFileName = $"{fileName}.encrypt";
        await using FileStream outputFileStream =
            new(encryptedFileName, FileMode.Create);
```

```
        string data = await File.ReadAllTextAsync(fileName);

        await cryptographer.EncryptAsync(data, outputFileStream);

        return encryptedFileName;
    }
    // ...
}
```

Listing 20.6 begins with a `Main()` method, inside of which there is a C# 8.0–introduced `async foreach` statement iterating over an asynchronous method, `EncryptFilesAsync()`. (We will address the `WithCancellation()` invocation shortly.) The `EncryptFilesAsync()` method iterates over each of the specified files with a `foreach` loop. Inside the `foreach` loop are two `async` method invocations. The first is a call to `File.ReadAllTextAsync()`, which reads in all the content of the file. Once the content is available in memory, the code invokes the `EncryptAsync()` method to encrypt it before returning the encrypted filename via a `yield return` statement. Thus, the method provides an example of the need to provide an asynchronous iterator to the caller. The key to making this possible is the `EncryptFilesAsync()`'s decoration with `async` and its return of `IAsyncEnumerable<T>` (where T is a string in this case).

Given a method returning `IAsyncEnumerable<T>`, you can consume it using an `await foreach` statement as demonstrated in the `Main` method of Listing 20.6. Thus, this listing is both producing and consuming an async stream.

The signature for `GetAsyncEnumerator()` includes a `CancellationToken` parameter. Because the `await foreach` loop generates the code that calls `GetAsyncEnumerator()`, the way to inject a cancellation token and provide cancellation is via the `WithCancellation()` extension method. As Figure 20.2 shows, there's no `WithCancellation()` method on `IAsyncEnumerable<T>` directly. To support cancellation in an async stream method, add an optional `CancellationToken` with an `EnumeratorCancellationAttribute` as demonstrated by the `EncryptFilesAsunc` method declaration:

```
static public async IAsyncEnumerable<string>
EncryptFilesAsync(
string directoryPath = null,
string searchPattern = "*",
[EnumeratorCancellation] CancellationToken
```

```
    cancellationToken = default)
    { ... }
```

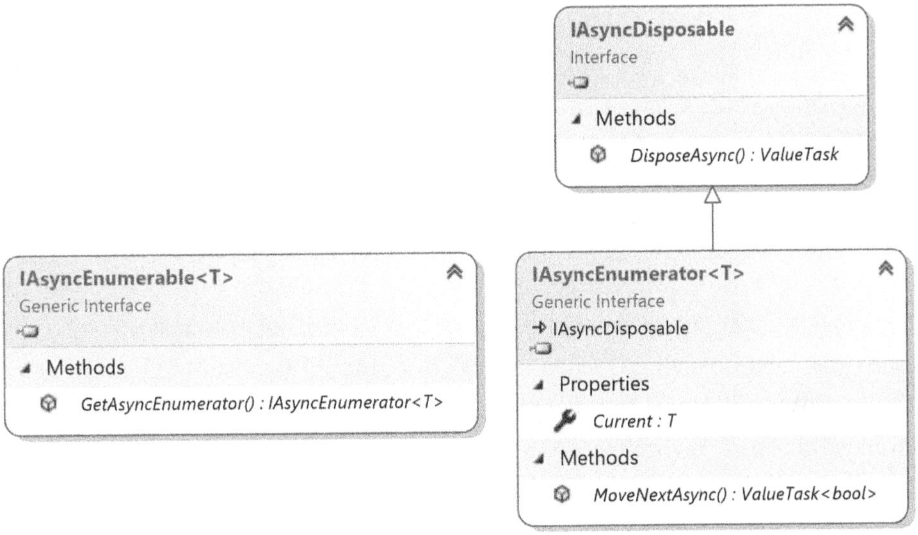

FIGURE 20.2: IAsycnEnumerable<T> and related interfaces

In Listing 20.6, you provide an async stream method that returns the `IAsyncEnumerable<T>` interface. As with the non-`async` iterators, however, you can also implement the `IAsyncEnumerable<T>` interface with its `GetAsyncEnumerator()` method. Of course, any class implementing the interface can then be iterated over with an `await foreach` statement, as shown in Listing 20.7.

LISTING 20.7: Async Streams Invocation with `await foreach`

```
public class AsyncEncryptionCollection : IAsyncEnumerable<string>
{
    public async IAsyncEnumerator<string> GetAsyncEnumerator(
        CancellationToken cancellationToken = default)
    {
        // ...
    }

    public static async Task Main()
```

```
    {
        AsyncEncryptionCollection collection =
            new();
        // ...

        await foreach (string fileName in collection)
        {
            Console.WriteLine(fileName);
        }
    }
}
```

One point of caution: Remember that declaring an `async` method doesn't automatically cause the execution to run in parallel. Just because the `EncryptFilesAsync()` method is asynchronous, that doesn't mean iterating over each file and invoking `File.ReadAllTextAsync()` and `Cryptographer.EncryptAsync()` will happen in parallel. To guarantee that behavior, you need to leverage a `Task` invocation or something like a `System.Threading.Tasks.Parallel.ForEach()` (Chapter 21).

The `IAsyncEnumerable<T>` interface, along with its partner `IAsyncEnumerator<T>`, are C# 8.0 additions shown in Figure 20.2 that match their synchronous equivalents. Note that both the `IAsyncDisposable.DisposeAsync()` and `IAsyncEnumerator<T>.MoveNextAsync()` methods are asynchronous versions of `IEnumerators<T>` equivalent methods. The `Current` property isn't asynchronous. (Also, there's no `Reset()` method in the asynchronous implementations.)

`IAsyncDisposable` and the `await using` Declaration and Statement

`IAsyncDisposable` is the asynchronous equivalent of `IDisposable`, so it can be invoked using C# 8.0's new `await using` **statement** or `await using` **declaration**. In Listing 20.6, we use the latter when declaring `outputFileStream` because, like `IAsyncEnumerable<T>`, `FileStream` also implements `IAsyncDisposable`. As with the `using` declarative, you can't reassign a variable declared with `async using`.

Not surprisingly, the `await using` statement follows the same syntax as the common `using` statement:

```
await using FileStream outputFileStream =
new FileStream(encryptedFileName, FileMode.Create);
{ ... }
```

Both can be used anytime the type implements `IAsyncDisposable` or simply has a `DisposeAsync()` method. The result is that the C# compiler injects a try/finally block around the declaration and before the variable goes out of scope, and then it invokes `await DisposeAsync()` within the finally block.[11] This approach ensures that all resources are cleaned up.

Note that `IAsyncDisposable` and `IDisposable` are not related to each other via inheritance. In consequence, their implementations are not dependent, either: One can be implemented without the other.

Using LINQ with IAsyncEnumerable

In the `await foreach` statement of Listing 20.6, we invoke the LINQ `AsyncEnumberable.Zip()` method to pair the original filename with the encrypted filename.

```
await foreach (
(string fileName, string encryptedFileName) in
EncryptFilesAsync(files)
.Zip(files.ToAsyncEnumerable()))
{
Console.WriteLine($"{fileName}=>{encryptedFileName}");
}
```

`AsyncEnumerable` provides the LINQ functionality for `IAsyncEnumerable<T>`, as you might expect. However, the library is not available in the BCL.[12] Instead, to access the asynchronous LINQ capabilities, you need to add a reference to the `System.Linq.Async` NuGet package.

---

11. Using `await` inside a finally block was added in C# 6.0.
12. At least at the time of this writing—per .NET Core 3.0 and 3.1.

`AsyncEnumerable` is defined in `System.Linq` (not a different unique namespace with `async` functionality). Not surprisingly, it includes asynchronous versions of the standard LINQ operators such as `Where()`, `Select()`, and the `Zip()` method used in the aforementioned listing. They are considered "asynchronous versions" because they are extension methods on `IAsyncEnumerable` rather than `IEnumerable<T>`. In addition, `AsyncEnumerable` includes a series of `*Async()`, `*AwaitAsync()`, and `*AwaitWithCancellationAsync()` methods. The `Select*()` versions of each of these methods are shown in Listing 20.8.

LISTING 20.8: Signatures of `AsyncEnumerable Select*()`[13] Methods

```
namespace System.Linq
// ...
public static class AsyncEnumerable
{
    // ...
    public static IAsyncEnumerable<TResult> Select<TSource?, TResult?>(
    this IAsyncEnumerable<TSource> source,
    Func<TSource, TResult> selector);
    public static IAsyncEnumerable<TResult> SelectAwait<TSource?,
↪TResult?>(
            this IAsyncEnumerable<TSource> source,
            Func<TSource, ValueTask<TResult>>? selector);
    public static
        IAsyncEnumerable<TResult> SelectAwaitWithCancellation<
        TSource?, TResult?>(
            this IAsyncEnumerable<TSource> source,
            Func<TSource, CancellationToken,
                ValueTask<TResult>> selector);
    // ...
}
```

The method name that matches the `Enumerable` equivalent—`Select()` in this case—has a similar "instance" signature, but the `TResult` and `TSource` are different. Both signatures with "Await" in the name take asynchronous signatures that include a selector that returns a `ValueTask<T>`. For example, you could

13. Excluding the `SelectMany()` category of methods.

invoke Listing 20.6's EncryptFileAsync() method from SelectAwait() as follows:

```
IAsyncEnumerable<string> items = files.ToAsyncEnumerable();
items = items.SelectAwait(
(text, id) => EncryptFileAsync(text));
```

The important thing to note is that EncyryptFileAsync() method returns a ValueTask<T>, which is what both *Await() and *AwaitWithCancellationAsync() require. The latter, of course, also allows for specification of a cancellation token.

Another asynchronous LINQ method worthy of mention is the ToAsyncEnumerable() method used in Listing 20.6. Since asynchronous LINQ methods work with IAsyncEnumerable<T> interfaces, ToAsyncEnumerable() takes care of converting IEnumerable<T> to IAsyncEnumerable<T>. Similarly, a ToEnumerable() method makes the opposite conversion. (Admittedly, using files.ToAsyncEnumerable() in the snippet is a contrived example for retrieving an IAsyncEnumerable<string>.)

The scalar versions of the asynchronous LINQ methods similarly match the IEnumerable<T>—with a *Await(), *AwaitAsync(), and *AwaitWithCancellation() set of members. The key difference is that they all return a ValueTask<T>. The following snippet provides an example of using the AverageAsync() method:

```
double average = await AsyncEnumerable.Range(
0, 999).AverageAsync();
```

As such, we can use await to treat the return as a double rather than a ValueTask<double>.

End 8.0

Returning void from an Asynchronous Method

We've already looked at several valid async return types, including Task, Task<T>, ValueTask<T>, and now IAsyncEnumerable<T>, all of which support a GetAwaiter() method. There is one allowable return type (or non-type) that does not support the GetAwaiter(). This return option, which is available for an async method, is void—a method henceforth referred to as an async void **method**. In most cases, async void methods should be avoided and might more accurately be considered a non-option. Unlike when returning a GetAwaiter() supporting type, when there is a void return it is indeterminate when a method completes executing. If an exception occurs, returning void means there is no such container to report an exception. In such a case, any exception thrown on an async void method is likely to end up on the UI SynchronizationContext—effectively becoming an unhandled exception (see "Advanced Topic: Dealing with Unhandled Exceptions on a Thread" in Chapter 19).

If async void methods should be generally avoided, why are they allowed in the first place? It's because async void methods can be used to enable async event handlers. As discussed in Chapter 14, an event should be declared as an EventHandler<T>, where EventHandler<T> has a signature of the following form:

```
void EventHandler<TEventArgs>(object sender, TEventArgs e)
```

Thus, to fit the convention of an event matching the EventHandler<T> signature, an async event needs to return void. One might suggest changing the convention, but (as discussed in Chapter 14) there could be multiple subscribers, and retrieving the return from multiple subscribers is nonintuitive and cumbersome. For this reason, the guideline is to avoid async void methods unless they are subscribers to an event handler—in which case they should not throw exceptions. Alternatively, you should provide a synchronization context to receive notifications of synchronization events such as the scheduling of work (e.g., Task.Run()) and, perhaps more important, unhandled exceptions. Listing 20.9 and the accompanying Output 20.2 provide an example of how to do this.

Listing 20.9: Catching an Exception from an async void Method

```
using System;
using System.Threading;
using System.Threading.Tasks;

public class AsyncSynchronizationContext : SynchronizationContext
{
    public Exception? Exception { get; set; }
```

```
    public ManualResetEventSlim ResetEvent { get; } = new();

    public override void Send(SendOrPostCallback callback, object? state)
    {
        try
        {
            Console.WriteLine($@"Send notification invoked...(Thread ID:
↪ {
                Thread.CurrentThread.ManagedThreadId})");
            callback(state);
        }
        catch (Exception exception)
        {
            Exception = exception;
        }
        finally
        {
            ResetEvent.Set();
        }
    }

    public override void Post(SendOrPostCallback callback, object? state)
    {
        try
        {
            Console.WriteLine($@"Post notification invoked...(Thread ID:
↪ {
                Thread.CurrentThread.ManagedThreadId})");
            callback(state);
        }
        catch (Exception exception)
        {
            Exception = exception;
        }
        finally
        {
            ResetEvent.Set();
        }
    }
}

public static class Program
{
    public static bool EventTriggered { get; set; }

    public const string ExpectedExceptionMessage = "Expected Exception";
```

```
    public static void Main()
    {
        SynchronizationContext? originalSynchronizationContext =
            SynchronizationContext.Current;
        try
        {
            AsyncSynchronizationContext synchronizationContext = new();
            SynchronizationContext.SetSynchronizationContext(
                synchronizationContext);

            OnEvent(typeof(Program), EventArgs.Empty);

            synchronizationContext.ResetEvent.Wait();

            if (synchronizationContext.Exception != null)
            {
                Console.WriteLine($@"Throwing expected exception...
↪.(Thread ID: {
                Thread.CurrentThread.ManagedThreadId})");
                System.Runtime.ExceptionServices.ExceptionDispatchInfo.
↪Capture(
                    synchronizationContext.Exception).Throw();
            }
        }
        catch (Exception exception)
        {
            Console.WriteLine($@"{exception} thrown as expected.(Thread
↪ID: {
                Thread.CurrentThread.ManagedThreadId})");
        }
        finally
        {
            SynchronizationContext.SetSynchronizationContext(
                originalSynchronizationContext);
        }
    }

    private static async void OnEvent(object sender, EventArgs eventArgs)
    {
        Console.WriteLine($@"Invoking Task.Run...(Thread ID: {
                Thread.CurrentThread.ManagedThreadId})");
        await Task.Run(() =>
        {
            EventTriggered = true;
            Console.WriteLine($@"Running task... (Thread ID: {
                Thread.CurrentThread.ManagedThreadId})");
            throw new Exception(ExpectedExceptionMessage);
```

```
        });
    }
}
```

OUTPUT 20.2

```
Invoking Task.Run...(Thread ID: 8)
Running task... (Thread ID: 9)
Post notification invoked...(Thread ID: 8)
Post notification invoked...(Thread ID: 8)
Throwing expected exception....(Thread ID: 8)
System.Exception: Expected Exception
   at
AddisonWesley.Michaelis.EssentialCSharp.Chapter20.Listing20_09.Program.M
ain()
...Listing20.09.AsyncVoidReturn.cs:line 80 thrown as expected.(Thread
ID: 8)
```

The code in Listing 20.9 executes procedurally up until the `await Task.Run()` invocation within `OnEvent()` starts. Following its completion, control is passed to the `Post()` method within `AsyncSynchronizationContext`. After the execution and completion of the `Post()` invocation, the `Console.WriteLine("throw Exception...")` method executes, and then an exception is thrown. This exception is captured by the `AsyncSynchronizationContext.Post()` method and passed back into `Main()`.

In this example, we use a `Task.Delay()` call to ensure the program doesn't end before the `Task.Run()` invocation. In the real world, as shown in Chapter 22, a `ManualResetEventSlim` would be the preferred approach.

Begin 8.0

ADVANCED TOPIC

Valid Async Return Types Expanded

Generally, the expression that follows the `await` keyword is of type `Task`, `Task<T>`, `ValueTask<T>`, occasionally `void`, or in C# 8.0, `IAsyncEnumerable<T>/IAsyncEnumerator<string>`. The word *Generally*, however, is a deliberate injection of incertitude. In fact, the exact rule regarding the return type that `await` requires is more generic than just these types. Additionally, it allows the type to be an awaitable type—supporting a `GetAwaiter()` method.

This method produces an object that has certain properties and methods needed by the compiler's rewriting logic—specifically, an object that supports the `INotifyCompletion` interface with the addition of a `GetResult()` method. By allowing an awaitable type, the system is extensible by third parties. In other words, if you want to design your own non-`Task`-based asynchrony system that uses some other type to represent asynchronous work, you can do so and still use the `await` syntax.

Prior to C# 8.0, it was not possible to make `async` methods return something other than `void`, `Task`, or `Task<T>` or `ValueTask<T>`, no matter which type is awaited inside the method. However, leveraging the more general `GetAwaiter()` approach, C# 8.0 introduced the `IAsyncEnumerable<T>`/`IAsyncEnumerator<string>` async return described earlier in the chapter.

End 8.0

Asynchronous Lambdas and Local Functions

Just as a lambda expression converted to a delegate can be used as a concise syntax for declaring a normal method, lambdas containing `await` expressions can be converted to delegates.[14] To do so, just precede the lambda expression with the `async` keyword. In Listing 20.10, we first assign an `async` lambda to a `Func<string, Task> writeWebRequestSizeAsync` variable. We then use the `await` operator to invoke it.

LISTING 20.10: An Asynchronous Client-Server Interaction as a Lambda Expression

```
using System;
using System.IO;
using System.Net;
using System.Linq;
using System.Threading.Tasks;

public class Program
{

    public static void Main(string[] args)
```

14. Starting in C# 5.0.

```
    {
        string url = "http://www.IntelliTect.com";
        if(args.Length > 0)
        {
            url = args[0];
        }

        Console.Write(url);

        Func<string, Task> writeWebRequestSizeAsync =
            async (string webRequestUrl) =>
            {
                // Error handling omitted for
                // elucidation
                WebRequest webRequest =
                   WebRequest.Create(url);

                WebResponse response =
                    await webRequest.GetResponseAsync();

                // Explicitly counting rather than invoking
                // webRequest.ContentLength to demonstrate
                //  multiple await operators
                using (StreamReader reader =
                    new(response.GetResponseStream()))
                {
                    string text =
                        (await reader.ReadToEndAsync());
                    Console.WriteLine(
                        FormatBytes(text.Length));
                }
            };

        Task task = writeWebRequestSizeAsync(url);

        while (!task.Wait(100))
        {
            Console.Write(".");
        }
    }
    // ...
}
```

Similarly, the same effect can be achieved with a local function.[15] For example, in Listing 20.10, you could change the lambda expression header (everything up to and including the => operator) to

```
async Task WriteWebRequestSizeAsync(string webRequestUrl)
```

leaving everything in the body, including the curly braces, unchanged.

Note that an `async` lambda expression has the same restrictions as the named `async` method:

- An `async` lambda expression must be converted to a delegate whose return type is a valid async return type.
- The lambda is rewritten so that `return` statements become signals that the task returned by the lambda has completed with the given result.
- Execution within the lambda expression occurs synchronously until the first `await` on an incomplete awaitable is executed.
- All instructions following the `await` will execute as continuations on the return from the invoked asynchronous method (or, if the awaitable is already complete, simply will be executed synchronously rather than as continuations).
- An `async` lambda expression can be invoked with an `await` operator (not shown in Listing 20.10).

ADVANCED/BEGINNER TOPIC

Implementing a Custom Asynchronous Method

Implementing an asynchronous method by relying on other asynchronous methods (which, in turn, rely on more asynchronous methods) is relatively easy with the `await` keyword. However, at some point in the call hierarchy, it becomes necessary to write a "leaf" asynchronous `Task`-returning method. Consider, for example, an asynchronous method for running a command-line program with the eventual goal that the output could be accessed. Such a method would be declared as follows:

15. Starting in C# 7.0.

```
public static Task<Process> RunProcessAsync(string filename)
```

The simplest implementation would, of course, be to rely on `Task.Run()` again and call both the `System.Diagnostics.Process`'s `Start()` and `WaitForExit()` methods. However, creating an additional thread in the current process is unnecessary when the invoked process itself will have its own collection of one or more threads. To implement the `RunProcessAsync()` method and return to the caller's synchronization context when the invoked process completes, we can rely on a `TaskCompletionSource<T>` object, as shown in Listing 20.11.

Listing 20.11: Implementing a Custom Asynchronous Method

```
using System.Diagnostics;
using System.Threading;
using System.Threading.Tasks;

public class Program
{
    public static Task<Process> RunProcessAsync(
        string fileName,
        string arguments = "",
        CancellationToken cancellationToken = default)
    {
        TaskCompletionSource<Process> taskCS =
                      new();

        Process process = new()
        {
            StartInfo = new ProcessStartInfo(fileName)
            {
                UseShellExecute = false,
                Arguments = arguments
            },
            EnableRaisingEvents = true
        };

        process.Exited += (sender, localEventArgs) =>
        {
            taskCS.SetResult(process);
        };

        cancellationToken
            .ThrowIfCancellationRequested();
```

```
        process.Start();

        cancellationToken.Register(() =>
        {
            Process.GetProcessById(process.Id).Kill();
        });

        return taskCS.Task;
    }
    // ...
}
```

Ignore the highlighting for the moment and instead focus on the pattern of using an event for notification when the process completes. Since `System.Diagnostics.Process` includes a notification upon exit, we register for this notification and use it as a callback from which we can invoke `TaskCompletionSource.SetResult()`. The code in Listing 20.11 follows a fairly common pattern that you can use to create an asynchronous method without having to resort to `Task.Run()`.

Another important characteristic that an `async` method might require is cancellation. TAP relies on the same methods for cancellation as the TPL does—namely, a `System.Threading.CancellationToken`. Listing 20.11 highlights the code necessary to support cancellation. In this example, we allow for canceling before the process ever starts, as well as an attempt to close the application's main window (if there is one). A more aggressive approach would be to call `Process.Kill()`, but this method could potentially cause problems for the program that is executing.

Notice that we don't register for the cancellation event until after the process is started. This avoids any race conditions that might occur if cancellation is triggered before the process actually begins.

One last feature to consider supporting is a progress update. Listing 20.12 is the full version of `RunProcessAsync()` with just such an update.

Listing 20.12: Implementing a Custom Asynchronous Method with Progress Support

```
using System;
using System.Diagnostics;
using System.Threading;
using System.Threading.Tasks;
```

```
public class Program
{
    public static Task<Process> RunProcessAsync(
        string fileName,
        string arguments = "",
        IProgress<ProcessProgressEventArgs>? progress =
            null, object? objectState = null,
        CancellationToken cancellationToken =
            default(CancellationToken))
    {
        TaskCompletionSource<Process> taskCS = new();

        Process process = new()
        {
            StartInfo = new ProcessStartInfo(fileName)
            {
                UseShellExecute = false,
                Arguments = arguments,
                RedirectStandardOutput =
                   progress != null
            },
            EnableRaisingEvents = true
        };

        process.Exited += (sender, localEventArgs) =>
        {
            taskCS.SetResult(process);
        };

        if (progress != null)
        {
            process.OutputDataReceived +=
                (sender, localEventArgs) =>
            {
                progress.Report(
                    new ProcessProgressEventArgs(
                        localEventArgs.Data,
                        objectState));
            };
        }

        cancellationToken
            .ThrowIfCancellationRequested();

        process.Start();
```

```
        if (progress !=null)
        {
            process.BeginOutputReadLine();
        }

        cancellationToken.Register(() =>
        {
            Process.GetProcessById(process.Id).Kill();
        });

        return taskCS.Task;
    }

    // ...
}

public class ProcessProgressEventArgs
{
    // ...
}
```

Wrapping your head around precisely what is happening in an `async` method can be difficult, but it is far less difficult than trying to figure out what asynchronous code written with explicit continuations in lambdas is doing. The key points to remember are as follows:

- When control reaches an `await` keyword, the expression that follows it produces a task.[16] Control then returns to the caller so that it can continue to do work while the task completes asynchronously (assuming it hadn't already completed).
- Sometime after the task completes, control resumes at the point following the `await`. If the awaited task produces a result, that result is then obtained. If it faulted, the exception is thrown.
- A `return` statement in an `async` method causes the task associated with the method invocation to become completed; if the `return` statement has a value, the value returned becomes the result of the task.

16. Technically, it is an awaitable type, as described in the "Advanced Topic: Valid Async Return Types Expanded."

Task Schedulers and the Synchronization Context

On occasion, this chapter has mentioned the task scheduler and its role in determining how to assign work to threads efficiently. Programmatically, the task scheduler is an instance of the `System.Threading.Tasks.TaskScheduler`. This class, by default, uses the thread pool to schedule tasks appropriately, determining how to safely and efficiently execute them—when to reuse them, dispose them, or create additional ones.

It is possible to create your own task scheduler that makes different choices about how to schedule tasks by deriving a new type from the `TaskScheduler` class. You can obtain a `TaskScheduler` that will schedule a task to the current thread (or, more precisely, to the **synchronization context** associated with the current thread), rather than to a different worker thread, by using the static `FromCurrentSynchronizationContext()` method.

The synchronization context under which a task executes and, in turn, the continuation task(s) execute(s), is important because the awaiting task consults the synchronization context (assuming there is one) so that a task can execute efficiently and safely. Listing 20.13 (along with Output 20.3) is similar to Listing 19.3, except that it also prints out the thread ID when it displays the message.

Listing 20.13: Calling `Task.ContinueWith()`

```
using System;
using System.Threading;
using System.Threading.Tasks;

public class Program
{
    public static void Main()
    {
        DisplayStatus("Before");
        Task taskA =
            Task.Run(() =>
                 DisplayStatus("Starting..."))
            .ContinueWith(antecedent =>
                 DisplayStatus("Continuing A..."));
        Task taskB = taskA.ContinueWith(antecedent =>
      DisplayStatus("Continuing B..."));
        Task taskC = taskA.ContinueWith(antecedent =>
            DisplayStatus("Continuing C..."));
```

```
        Task.WaitAll(taskB, taskC);
        DisplayStatus("Finished!");
    }

    private static void DisplayStatus(string message)
    {
        string text =
                $@"{ Thread.CurrentThread.ManagedThreadId
                    }: { message }";


        Console.WriteLine(text);
    }
}
```

Output 20.3

```
1: Before
3: Starting...
4: Continuing A...
3: Continuing C...
4: Continuing B...
1: Finished!
```

What is noteworthy about this output is that the thread ID changes sometimes and gets repeated at other times. In this kind of plain console application, the synchronization context (accessible from `SynchronizationContext.Current`) is null—the default synchronization context causes the thread pool to handle thread allocation instead. This explains why the thread ID changes between tasks: Sometimes the thread pool determines that it is more efficient to use a new thread, and sometimes it decides that the best course of action is to reuse an existing thread.

Fortunately, the synchronization context gets set automatically for types of applications where that is critical. For example, if the code creating tasks is running in a thread created by ASP.NET, the thread will have a synchronization context of type `AspNetSynchronizationContext` associated with it. In contrast, if your code is running in a thread created in a Windows UI application—namely, Windows Presentation Foundation (WPF) or Windows Forms—the thread will have an instance of `DispatcherSynchronizationContext` or `WindowsFormsSynchronizationContext`, respectively. (For console applications and Windows Services, the thread will have an instance of the default

SynchronizationContext.) Since the TPL consults the synchronization context, and that synchronization context varies depending on the circumstances of the execution, the TPL is able to schedule continuations executing in contexts that are both efficient and safe.

To modify the code so that the synchronization context is leveraged instead, you must (1) set the synchronization context and (2) use async/await to ensure that the synchronization context is consulted.[17]

It is possible to define custom synchronization contexts and to work with existing synchronization contexts to improve their performance in some specific scenarios. However, describing how to do so is beyond the scope of this text.

async/await with the Windows UI

One place where synchronization is especially important is in the UI context. With the Windows UI, for example, a message pump processes messages such as mouse click and move events. Furthermore, the UI is single-threaded, so that interaction with any UI components (e.g., a text box) must always occur from the single UI thread. One of the key advantages of the async/await pattern is that it leverages the synchronization context to ensure that continuation work—work that appears after the await statement—will always execute on the same synchronization task that invoked the await statement. This approach is of significant value because it eliminates the need to explicitly switch back to the UI thread to update a control.

To better appreciate this benefit, consider the example of a UI event for a button click in WPF, as shown in Listing 20.14.

Listing 20.14: Synchronous High-Latency Invocation in WPF

```
private void PingButton_Click(
    object sender, RoutedEventArgs e)
{
    StatusLabel.Content = "Pinging...";
    UpdateLayout();
```

17. For a simple example of how to set the synchronization context of a thread and how to use a task scheduler to schedule a task to that thread, see Listing C.8 in "Multithreading Patterns Prior to C# 5.0," available at https://intellitect.com/EssentialCSharp.

```
        Ping ping = new Ping();
        PingReply pingReply =
            ping.Send("www.IntelliTect.com");
        StatusLabel.Text = pingReply.Status.ToString();
    }
```

Given that `StatusLabel` is a WPF `System.Windows.Controls.TextBlock` control and we have updated the `Content` property twice within the `PingButton_Click()` event subscriber, it would be a reasonable assumption that first “Pinging...” would be displayed until `Ping.Send()` returned, and then the label would be updated with the status of the `Send()` reply. As those experienced with Windows UI frameworks well know, this is not, in fact, what happens. Rather, a message is posted to the Windows message pump to update the content with “Pinging...,” but because the UI thread is busy executing the `PingButton_Click()` method, the Windows message pump is not processed. By the time the UI thread is freed and can look at the Windows message pump, a second `Text` property update request has been queued and the only message that the user is able to observe is the final status.

To fix this problem using TAP, we change the code highlighted in Listing 20.15.

Listing 20.15: Synchronous High-Latency Invocation in WPF Using `await`

```
private async void PingButton_Click(
    object sender, RoutedEventArgs e)
{
    StatusLabel.Content = "Pinging...";
    UpdateLayout();
    Ping ping = new Ping();
    PingReply pingReply =
        await ping.SendPingAsync("www.IntelliTect.com");
    StatusLabel.Text = pingReply.Status.ToString();
}
```

This change offers two advantages. First, the asynchronous nature of the ping call frees up the caller thread to return to the Windows message pump caller's synchronization context, and it processes the update to `StatusLabel.Content` so that “Pinging...” appears to the user. Second, when awaiting the completion of `ping.SendTaskAsync()`, it will always execute on the same synchronization context as the caller. Also, because the synchronization context is specifically appropriate for the Windows UI, it is single-threaded; thus, the return will always be to the same thread—the UI thread. In other words, rather than immediately executing the continuation task, the TPL consults the synchronization context, which instead posts a message regarding the continuation work to the message pump. Next, because the UI thread monitors the message pump, upon picking up the continuation work message, it invokes the code following the `await` call. (As a result, the invocation of the continuation code is on the same thread as the caller that processed the message pump.)

A key code readability feature is built into the TAP language pattern. Notice in Listing 20.15 that the call to return `pingReply.Status` appears to flow naturally after the `await` statement, providing a clear indication that it will execute immediately following the previous line. However, writing what really happens from scratch would be far less understandable for multiple reasons.

BEGINNER TOPIC

Reviewing `await` Operators

There is no limitation on the number of times that `await` can be placed into a single method. In fact, such statements are not limited to appearing one after another. Rather, `await` statements can be placed into loops and processed consecutively one after the other, thereby following a natural control flow that matches the way code appears. Consider the example in Listing 20.16.

LISTING 20.16: Iterating over an `await` Operation

```
private async void PingButton_Click(
object sender, RoutedEventArgs e)
{
    List<string> urls = new List<string>()
        {
            "www.habitat-spokane.org",
            "www.partnersintl.org",
            "www.iassist.org",
            "www.fh.org",
            "www.worldVision.org"
        };
    IPStatus status;
```

```
    Func<string, Task<IPStatus>> func =
        async (localUrl) =>
        {
            Ping ping = new Ping();
            PingReply pingReply =
                await ping.SendPingAsync(localUrl);
            return pingReply.Status;
        };

    StatusLabel.Content = "Pinging...";

    foreach (string url in urls)
    {
        status = await func(url);
        StatusLabel.Text =
            $@"{ url }: { status.ToString() } ({
                Thread.CurrentThread.ManagedThreadId })";
    }
}
```

Regardless of whether the `await` statements occur within an iteration or as separate entries, they will execute serially, one after the other and in the same order they were invoked from the calling thread. The underlying implementation is to string them together in the semantic equivalent of `Task.ContinueWith()` except that all of the code between the `await` operators will execute in the caller's synchronization context.

The need to support TAP from the UI is one of the key scenarios that led to TAP's creation. A second scenario takes place on the server, when a request comes in from a client to query an entire table's worth of data from the database. As querying the data could be time-consuming, a new thread should be created rather than consuming one from the limited number allocated to the thread pool. The problem with this approach is that the work to query from the database is executing entirely on another machine. There is no reason to block an entire thread, given that the thread is generally not active anyway.

To summarize, TAP was created to address these key problems:

- There is a need to allow long-running activities to occur without blocking the UI thread.

- Creating a new thread (or Task) for non–CPU-intensive work is relatively expensive when you consider that all the thread is doing is waiting for the activity to complete.
- When the activity completes (either by using a new thread or via a callback), it is frequently necessary to make a thread synchronization context switch back to the original caller that initiated the activity.

TAP provides a new pattern that works for both CPU-intensive and non–CPU-intensive asynchronous invocations—one that all .NET languages support explicitly.

Begin 8.0

Summary

The bulk of this chapter focused on task-based asynchronous pattern, which features the async/await syntax. It provided detailed examples demonstrating how much simpler it is to leverage TAP rather than to solely rely on TPL, especially when transforming code from a synchronous to an asynchronous implementation. In so doing, it detailed the requirements for the return type of an async method. In summary, the async/await feature makes programming complex workflows with Task objects much easier by automatically rewriting your programs to manage the continuation "wiring" that composes larger tasks out of smaller tasks.

Next, the chapter focused on async streams and the C# 8.0–introduced IAsyncEnumerable<T> data type. It considered how to leverage these capabilities to create asynchronous iterators and how to consume them with async foreach statements.

At this point, readers should have a firm foundation regarding how to write asynchronous code, except for parallel iterations (the topic of Chapter 21) and thread synchronization (which is covered in Chapter 22).

End 8.0

21

Iterating in Parallel

In Chapter 19, we mentioned how the cost of computation is falling, resulting in computers with faster CPUs, an increased number of CPUs, and an increased number of cores in each CPU. Collectively, these trends are making it increasingly more economical to boost the execution parallelization to take advantage of the increased computing power. In this chapter, we look at executing loops in parallel, which is one of the easiest ways to take advantage of the increased computing capability. Much of the chapter consists of Beginner and Advanced Topic blocks.

Executing Loop Iterations in Parallel

Consider the `for` loop statement and associated code shown in Listing 21.1 and the corresponding results in Output 21.1. The listing calls a method for calculating a section of the decimal expansion of pi, where the parameters are the number of digits and the digit to start with. The actual calculation is not germane to the discussion. What is interesting about this calculation is that it is *embarrassingly parallelizable*; that is, it is remarkably easy to split up a large task—say, computing 1 million decimal digits of pi—into any desired number of smaller tasks that can all be run in parallel. These types of computations are the easiest ones to speed up by adding parallelism.

Listing 21.1: A `for` Loop Synchronously Calculating Pi in Sections

```
using System;
using AddisonWesley.Michaelis.EssentialCSharp.Shared;

public class Program
{
    const int TotalDigits = 100;
    const int BatchSize = 10;

    public static void Main()
    {
        string pi = "";
        const int iterations = TotalDigits / BatchSize;
        for(int i = 0; i < iterations; i++)
        {
            pi += PiCalculator.Calculate(
                BatchSize, i * BatchSize);
        }

        Console.WriteLine(pi);
    }
}
// ...
using System;

public static class PiCalculator
{
    public static string Calculate(
        int digits, int startingAt)
    {
        //...
    }

    //...
}
// ...
```

The `for` loop executes each iteration synchronously and sequentially. However, because the pi calculation algorithm splits the pi calculation into independent pieces, it is not necessary to compute the pieces sequentially providing the results are

OUTPUT 21.1

```
>3.141592653589793238462643383279502884197169399375105820974944592307816
406286208998628034825342117067982148086513282306647093844609550582231725
359408128481117450284102701938521105559644622948954930381964428810975665
933446128475648233786783165271201909145648566923460348610454326648213393
607260249141273724587006606315588174881520920962829254091715364367892590
360011330530548820466521384146951941511609433057270365759591953092186117
38193261179310511854807446237996274956735188575272489122793818301194912
```

appended in the right order. Imagine what would happen if you could have all the iterations of this loop run concurrently: Each processor could take a single iteration and execute it in parallel with other processors executing other iterations. Given the simultaneous execution of iterations, we could decrease the execution time more and more based on the number of processors.

The Task Parallel Library (TPL) provides a convenient method, `Parallel.For()`, which does precisely that. Listing 21.2 shows how to modify the sequential, single-threaded program in Listing 21.1 to use the helper method.

LISTING 21.2: `For` Loop Calculating Pi in Sections in Parallel

```
using System;
using System.Threading.Tasks;
using AddisonWesley.Michaelis.EssentialCSharp.Shared;

//...

public class Program
{
    const int TotalDigits = 100;
    const int BatchSize = 10;

    public static void Main()
    {
        string pi = "";
        const int iterations = TotalDigits / BatchSize;
        string[] sections = new string[iterations];
        Parallel.For(0, iterations, i =>
        {
            sections[i] = PiCalculator.Calculate(
                BatchSize, i * BatchSize);
        });

        pi = string.Join("", sections);
        Console.WriteLine(pi);
```

```
    }
}
```

The output for Listing 21.2 is identical to Output 21.2; however, the execution time is significantly faster if you have multiple CPUs (and possibly slower if you do not). The `Parallel.For()` API is designed to look similar to a standard `for` loop. The first parameter is the `fromInclusive` value, the second is the `toExclusive` value, and the last is the `Action<int>` to perform as the loop body. When using an expression lambda for the action, the code looks similar to a `for` loop statement except that now each iteration may execute in parallel. As with the `for` loop, the call to `Parallel.For()` will not complete until all iterations are complete. In other words, by the time execution reaches the `string.Join()` statement, all sections of pi will have been calculated.

Note that the code for combining the various sections of pi no longer occurs inside the iteration (`action`) in Listing 21.2. As sections of the pi calculation will very likely not complete sequentially, appending a section whenever an iteration completes will likely append them out of order. Even if sequence was not a problem, there is still a potential race condition because the `+=` operator in Listing 21.1 is not atomic. To address both problems, each section of pi is stored into an array, and no two or more iterations will access a single element within the array simultaneously. Only once all sections of pi are calculated does `string.Join()` combine them. In other words, we postpone concatenating the sections until after the `Parallel.For()` loop has completed. This avoids any race condition caused by sections not yet calculated or sections concatenating out of order.

The TPL uses the same sorts of thread pooling techniques that it uses for task scheduling to ensure good performance of the parallel loop: It will try to ensure that CPUs are not overscheduled and so on.

Guidelines

DO use parallel loops when the computations performed can be easily split up into many mutually independent processor-bound computations that can be executed in any order on any thread.

The TPL also provides a similar parallel version of the `foreach` statement, as shown in Listing 21.3.

Listing 21.3: Parallel Execution of a `foreach` Loop

```
using System;
using System.Collections.Generic;
using System.IO;
using System.Threading.Tasks;

public class Program
{
    // ...
    public static void EncryptFiles(
        string directoryPath, string searchPattern)

    {
        IEnumerable<string> files = Directory.EnumerateFiles(
            directoryPath, searchPattern,
            SearchOption.AllDirectories);

        Parallel.ForEach(files, fileName =>
        {
            Encrypt(fileName);
        });
    }
    // ...
}
```

In this example, we call a method that encrypts each file within the `files` collection. It does so in parallel, executing as many threads as the TPL determines is efficient.

ADVANCED TOPIC

How the TPL Tunes Its Own Performance

The default scheduler within the TPL targets the thread pool, resulting in a variety of heuristics that try to ensure the right number of threads are executing at any one time. Two of the heuristics it uses are **hill climbing** and **work stealing**.

The hill-climbing algorithm involves creating threads to run tasks, and then monitoring the performance of those tasks to experimentally determine the point at which adding more threads begins making performance worse. Once that point is reached, the number of threads can then be decreased back to the number that produced the best performance.

The TPL does not associate top-level tasks that are waiting to be executed with any particular thread. If, however, a task running on a thread itself creates another task, the newly created task is associated with that thread automatically. When the new child task is eventually scheduled to run, it usually runs on the same thread as the task that created it. The work-stealing algorithm identifies threads that have an unusually large or unusually small amount of pending work; a thread that has too few tasks associated with it will sometimes "steal" not-yet-executed tasks from threads that have too many tasks waiting to run.

The key feature of these algorithms is that they enable the TPL to dynamically tune its own performance to mitigate processor overscheduling and underscheduling and to balance the work among the available processors.

The TPL generally does a good job of tuning its own performance, but you can help it do a better job by providing hints about the best course of action. Specifying the TPL `TaskCreationOptions.LongRunning` option described in the section "Long-Running Tasks" in Chapter 19 is an example of such a hint. You can also explicitly tell the task scheduler how many threads you think would be best to service a parallel loop; see "Advanced Topic: Parallel Loop Options" later in this chapter for more details.

BEGINNER TOPIC

Parallel Loop Exception Handling with `AggregateException`

The TPL catches and saves exceptions associated with tasks in an `AggregateException`, because a given task might have several exceptions obtained from its subtasks. This is also the case with parallel execution of loops: Each iteration could have produced an exception, so the exceptions need to be gathered up into one aggregating exception. Consider the example in Listing 21.4 and its results in Output 21.2.

Listing 21.4: Unhandled Exception Handling for Parallel Iterations

```
using System;
using System.Collections.Generic;
using System.IO;
using System.Threading.Tasks;

public static class Program
{
    // ...
    static void EncryptFiles(
        string directoryPath, string searchPattern)
    {
        IEnumerable<string> files = Directory.EnumerateFiles(
            directoryPath, searchPattern,
            SearchOption.AllDirectories);
        try
        {
            Parallel.ForEach(files, fileName =>
            {
                Encrypt(fileName);
            });
        }
        catch (AggregateException exception)
        {
            Console.WriteLine(
                "ERROR: {0}:",
                exception.GetType().Name);
            foreach(Exception item in
                exception.InnerExceptions)
            {
                Console.WriteLine("  {0} - {1}",
                    item.GetType().Name, item.Message);
            }
        }
    }
    // ...
}
```

Output 21.2

```
ERROR: AggregateException:
  UnauthorizedAccessException - Attempted to perform an unauthorized
operation.
  UnauthorizedAccessException - Attempted to perform an unauthorized
operation.
```

```
  UnauthorizedAccessException - Attempted to perform an unauthorized
operation.
```

Output 21.2 shows that three exceptions occurred while executing the `Parallel.ForEach<T>(...)` loop. However, the code shows only one catch, of type `System.AggregateException`. The `UnauthorizedAccessExceptions` were retrieved from the `InnerExceptions` property on the `AggregateException`. With a `Parallel.ForEach<T>()` loop, each iteration could potentially throw an exception, so the `System.AggregateException` thrown by the method call will contain each of those exceptions within its `InnerExceptions` property.

Canceling a Parallel Loop

Unlike a task, which requires an explicit call if it is to block until it completes, a parallel loop executes iterations in parallel but does not itself return until the entire parallel loop completes. Canceling a parallel loop, therefore, generally involves the invocation of the cancellation request from a thread other than the one executing the parallel loop. In Listing 21.5, we invoke `Parallel.ForEach<T>()` using `Task.Run()`. In this manner, not only does the query execute in parallel, but it also executes asynchronously, allowing the code to prompt the user to "Press any key to exit."

Listing 21.5: Canceling a Parallel Loop

```
using System;
using System.Collections.Generic;
using System.IO;
using System.Threading;
using System.Threading.Tasks;

public class Program
{
    // ...

    static void EncryptFiles(
        string directoryPath, string searchPattern)
    {
```

```
        string stars =
            "*".PadRight(Console.WindowWidth - 1, '*');

        IEnumerable<string> files = Directory.GetFiles(
           directoryPath, searchPattern,
           SearchOption.AllDirectories);

        CancellationTokenSource cts = new();
        ParallelOptions parallelOptions = new()
            { CancellationToken = cts.Token };
        cts.Token.Register(
            () => Console.WriteLine("Canceling..."));

        Console.WriteLine("Press ENTER to exit.");

        Task task = Task.Run(() =>
            {
                try
                {
                    Parallel.ForEach(
                        files, parallelOptions,
                        (fileName, loopState) =>
                        {
                            Encrypt(fileName);
                        });
                }
                catch(OperationCanceledException) { }
            });

        // Wait for the user's input
        Console.ReadLine();

        // Cancel the query
        cts.Cancel();
        Console.Write(stars);
        task.Wait();
    }
    // ...
}
```

The parallel loops use the same cancellation token pattern that tasks use. The token obtained from a `CancellationTokenSource` is associated with the parallel loop by calling an overload of the `ForEach()` method that has a parameter of type `ParallelOptions`. This object contains the cancellation token.

Note that if you cancel a parallel loop operation, any iterations that have not started yet are prevented from starting by checking the `IsCancellationRequested` property. Existing executing iterations run to their respective termination points. Furthermore, calling `Cancel()` even after all iterations have completed still causes the registered cancel event (via `cts.Token.Register()`) to execute.

The only means by which the `ForEach()` method is able to acknowledge that the loop has been canceled is via the `OperationCanceledException`. Given that cancellation in this example is expected, the exception is caught and ignored, allowing the application to display "Canceling...", followed by a line of stars before exiting.

ADVANCED TOPIC

Parallel Loop Options

Although not generally necessary, it is possible to control the maximum degree of parallelism (i.e., the number of threads that are scheduled to run at the same time) via the `ParallelOptions` parameter on overloads of both the `Parallel.For()` and `Parallel.ForEach<T>()` loops. In some specific cases, the developer may know more about the particular algorithm or circumstance such that changing the maximum degree of parallelism makes sense. These circumstances include the following:

- Scenarios where you want to disable parallelism to make debugging or analysis easier. Setting the maximum degree of parallelism to 1 ensures that the loop iterations do not run concurrently.
- Scenarios where you know ahead of time that the degree of parallelism will be gated on an external factor such as a hardware constraint. For example, if your parallel operation involves using multiple USB ports, there might be no point in creating more threads than there are available ports.
- Scenarios with really long-running loop iterations (e.g., minutes or hours). The thread pool can't distinguish long-running iterations from blocked operations, so it could end up introducing many new threads, all of which will be

consumed by the `for` loop. This can result in incremental thread growth over time, resulting in a huge number of threads in the process.

And so on. To control the maximum degree of parallelism, use the `MaxDegreeOfParallelism` property on the `ParallelOptions` object.

You can also use the `ParallelOptions` object's `TaskScheduler` property to specify a custom task scheduler to use when scheduling the tasks associated with each iteration. For example, you might have an asynchronous event handler that responds to the user's click of a Next button. If the user clicks the button several times, you might want to use a custom task scheduler that prioritizes the most recently created task rather than prioritizing the task that has waited the longest. The task scheduler provides a means of specifying how the tasks will execute in relation to one another.

The `ParallelOptions` object also has a `CancellationToken` property that provides a mechanism to communicate to the loop that no further iterations should start. Additionally, the body of an iteration can watch the cancellation token to determine if an early exit from the iteration is in order.

ADVANCED TOPIC

Breaking a Parallel Loop

Like a standard `for` loop, the `Parallel.For()` loop supports the concept of "breaking" to exit the loop and canceling any further iterations. In the context of parallel `for` execution, however, a break signifies that no *new* iterations following the breaking iteration should start. All currently executing iterations, however, will run to completion.

To break a parallel loop, you can provide a cancellation token and cancel it on another thread, as described in the preceding "Advanced Topic: Parallel Loop Options." You can also use an overload of the `Parallel.For()` method whose body delegate takes two parameters: the index and a `ParallelLoopState` object. An iteration that wishes to break the loop can call the `Break()` or `Stop()` method on the loop state object passed to the delegate. The `Break()` method indicates that no more iterations with index values higher than the current value need to execute; the `Stop()` method indicates that no more iterations need to run at all.

For example, suppose you have a `Parallel.For()` loop that is performing ten iterations in parallel. Some of those iterations might run faster than others, and the task scheduler does not guarantee that they will run in any particular order. Suppose the first iteration has completed; iterations 3, 5, 7, and 9 are "in flight," scheduled to four different threads; and iterations 5 and 7 both call `Break()`. In this scenario, iterations 6 and 8 never start, but iterations 2 and 4 are still scheduled to run. Iterations 3 and 9 run to completion because they had already started when the break happened.

The `Parallel.For()` and `Parallel.ForEach<T>()` methods return a reference to a `ParallelLoopResult` object that contains useful information about what happened during the loop. This result object has the following properties:

- `IsCompleted` returns a Boolean indicating whether all iterations started.
- `LowestBreakIteration` identifies the lowest iteration that executed a break. The value is of type `long?`, where a value of `null` indicates no break statement was encountered.

Returning to the ten-iteration example, the `IsCompleted` property returns `false` and the `LowestBreakIteration` returns a value of `5`.

Running LINQ Queries in Parallel

Just as it is possible to execute a loop in parallel using `Parallel.For()`, so it is also possible to execute LINQ queries in parallel using the Parallel LINQ API (PLINQ, for short). An example of a simple nonparallel LINQ expression is shown in Listing 21.6; in Listing 21.7, we modify it to run in parallel.

LISTING 21.6: LINQ `Select()`

```
using System.Collections.Generic;
using System.Linq;

public class Program
{
```

```
    // ...
    public static List<string>
      Encrypt(IEnumerable<string> data)
    {
        return data.Select(
            item => Encrypt(item)).ToList();
    }
    // ...
}
```

In Listing 21.6, a LINQ query uses the `Select()` standard query operator to encrypt each string within a sequence of strings and convert the resultant sequence to a list. This seems like an embarrassingly parallel operation; each encryption is likely to be a high-latency processor-bound operation that could be farmed out to a worker thread on another CPU.

Listing 21.7 shows how to modify Listing 21.6 so that the code that encrypts the strings is executed in parallel.

LISTING 21.7: Parallel LINQ `Select()`

```
using System.Linq;

public class Program
{
    // ...
    public static List<string>
      Encrypt(IEnumerable<string> data)
    {
        return data.AsParallel().Select(
            item => Encrypt(item)).ToList();
    }
    // ...
}
```

As Listing 21.7 shows, the change to enable parallel support is extremely small! All that it involves is a standard query operator, `AsParallel()`, which can be found on the static class `System.Linq.ParallelEnumerable`. This simple extension method tells the runtime that it can execute the query in parallel. The result is that on machines with multiple available CPUs, the total time taken to execute the query can be significantly shorter.

System.Linq.ParallelEnumerable, the engine that was introduced in Microsoft .NET Framework 4.0 to enable PLINQ, includes a superset of the query operators available on System.Linq.Enumerable. Thus, it provides the API that enables the possible performance improvements for all of the common query operators, including those used for sorting, filtering (Where()), projecting (Select()), joining, grouping, and aggregating. Listing 21.8 shows how to do a parallel sort.

LISTING 21.8: Parallel LINQ with Standard Query Operators

```
//...
OrderedParallelQuery<string> parallelGroups =
    data.AsParallel().OrderBy(item => item);

// Show the total count of items still
// matches the original count
if (data.Count() != parallelGroups.Sum(
        item => item.Length))
{
    throw new Exception("data.Count() != parallelGroups" +
        ".Sum(item => item.Count()");
}
// ...
```

As Listing 21.8 shows, invoking the parallel version simply involves a call to the AsParallel() extension method. Notice that the type of the result returned by the parallel standard query operators is either ParallelQuery<T> or OrderedParallelQuery<T>; both inform the compiler that it should continue to use the parallel versions of the standard query operations that are available.

Given that query expressions are simply a syntactic sugar for the method call form of the query used in Listing 21.5 and Listing 21.6, you can just as easily use AsParallel() with the expression form. Listing 21.9 shows an example of executing a grouping operation in parallel using query expression syntax.

LISTING 21.9: Parallel LINQ with Query Expressions

```
//...
ParallelQuery<IGrouping<char, string>> parallelGroups;
parallelGroups =
    from text in data.AsParallel()
```

```
    orderby text
    group text by text[0];

// Show the total count of items still
// matches the original count
if (data.Count() != parallelGroups.Sum(
        item => item.Count()))
{
    throw new Exception("data.Count() != parallelGroups" +
        ".Sum(item => item.Count()");
}
//...
```

As you saw in the previous examples, converting a query or iteration loop to execute in parallel is simple. There is one significant caveat, however: As we will discuss in depth in Chapter 22, you must take care not to allow multiple threads to inappropriately access and modify the same memory simultaneously. Doing so will cause a race condition.

As we saw earlier in this chapter, the `Parallel.For()` and `Parallel.ForEach<T>` methods gather up any exceptions thrown during the parallel iterations and then throw one aggregating exception containing all of the original exceptions. PLINQ operations are no different. That is, they also have the potential of returning multiple exceptions for exactly the same reason: When the query logic is run on each element in parallel, the code executing on each element can independently throw an exception. Unsurprisingly, PLINQ deals with this situation in exactly the same way as do parallel loops and the TPL: Exceptions thrown during parallel queries are accessible via the `InnerExceptions` property of the `AggregateException`. Therefore, wrapping a PLINQ query in a try/catch block with the exception type of `System.AggregateException` successfully handles any exceptions within each iteration that were unhandled.

Canceling a PLINQ Query

As expected, the cancellation request pattern is also available on PLINQ queries. Listing 21.10 (with Output 21.3) provides an example. Like the parallel loops, canceled PLINQ queries throw a `System.OperationCanceledException`. Also like the parallel loops, executing a PLINQ query is a synchronous operation on the invoking thread. Thus, a common technique is to wrap the parallel query in a task that runs on another thread so that the current thread can cancel it if necessary—the same solution used in Listing 21.5.

Listing 21.10: Canceling a PLINQ Query

```
using System;
using System.Collections.Generic;
using System.Linq;
using System.Threading;
using System.Threading.Tasks;

public static class Program
{
    public static List<string> ParallelEncrypt(
        List<string> data,
        CancellationToken cancellationToken)
    {
        int governor = 0;
        return data.AsParallel().WithCancellation(
            cancellationToken).Select(
                (item) =>
                {
                    if (Interlocked.CompareExchange(
                        ref governor, 0, 100) % 100 == 0)
                    {
                        Console.Write('.');
                    }
                    Interlocked.Increment(ref governor);
                    return Encrypt(item);
                }).ToList();
    }

    public static async Task Main()
    {
        ConsoleColor originalColor = Console.ForegroundColor;
        List<string> data = Utility.GetData(100000).ToList();

        using CancellationTokenSource cts = new();

        Task task = Task.Run(() =>
        {
            data = ParallelEncrypt(data, cts.Token);
        }, cts.Token);

        Console.WriteLine("Press any key to Exit.");
        Task<int> cancelTask = ConsoleReadAsync(cts.Token);
```

```
        try
        {
            Task.WaitAny(task, cancelTask);
            // Cancel whichever task has not finished.
            cts.Cancel();
            await task;

            Console.ForegroundColor = ConsoleColor.Green;
            Console.WriteLine("\nCompleted successfully");
        }
        catch (OperationCanceledException taskCanceledException)
        {
            Console.ForegroundColor = ConsoleColor.Red;
            Console.WriteLine(
                $"\nCancelled: { taskCanceledException.Message }");
        }
        finally
        {
            Console.ForegroundColor = originalColor;
        }
    }

    private static async Task<int> ConsoleReadAsync(
        CancellationToken cancellationToken = default)
    {
        return await Task.Run(async () =>
        {
            const int maxDelay = 1025;
            int delay = 0;
            while (!cancellationToken.IsCancellationRequested)
            {
                if (Console.KeyAvailable)
                {
                    return Console.Read();
                }
                else
                {
                    await Task.Delay(delay, cancellationToken);
                    if (delay < maxDelay) delay *= 2 + 1;
                }
            }
            cancellationToken.ThrowIfCancellationRequested();
            throw new InvalidOperationException(
                "Previous line should throw preventing this from ever
↪executing");
        }, cancellationToken);
```

```
    }

    private static string Encrypt(string item)
    {
        Cryptographer cryptographer = new();
        return System.Text.Encoding.UTF8.GetString(cryptographer.
↪Encrypt(item));
    }
}
```

Output 21.3

```
Press any key to Exit.
..........................................................................
..........................................................................
...............................................................
......................................
Cancelled: The query has been canceled via the token supplied to
WithCancellation.
```

As with a parallel loop or task, canceling a PLINQ query requires a `CancellationToken`, which is available from a `CancellationTokenSource`. However, rather than overloading every PLINQ query to support the cancellation token, the `ParallelQuery<T>` object returned by `IEnumerable`'s `AsParallel()` method includes a `WithCancellation()` extension method that simply takes a `CancellationToken`. As a result, calling `Cancel()` on the `CancellationTokenSource` object will request the parallel query to cancel—because it checks the `IsCancellationRequested` property on the `CancellationToken`.

As mentioned, canceling a PLINQ query throws an exception in place of returning the complete result. One common technique for dealing with a possibly canceled PLINQ query is to wrap the query in a try block and catch the `OperationCanceledException`. A second common technique, used in Listing 21.10, is to pass the `CancellationToken` both to `ParallelEncrypt()` and as a second parameter on `Run()`. This causes `task.Wait()` to throw an `AggregateException` whose `InnerException` property will be set to a `TaskCanceledException`. The aggregating exception can then be caught, just as you would catch any other exception from a parallel operation.

Summary

In this chapter, we discussed how to use the TPL `Parallel` class for both `for` and `foreach` type iterations. In addition, via the `AsParallel()` extension method included in `System.Linq`, we demonstrated how to execute LINQ queries in parallel. The ease with which this is accomplished should help you recognize that parallel iteration is one of the easiest ways to introduce parallel execution. Although it is still necessary to be aware of race conditions and deadlocks, these issues are far less likely to occur if you do not share data within the iterations of a parallel loop than if you work with tasks directly. All that remains is identifying the CPU-intensive code blocks that can benefit from parallel execution.

22

Thread Synchronization

In Chapter 21, we discussed the details of multithreaded programming using the Task Parallel Library (TPL) and Parallel LINQ (PLINQ). One topic we specifically avoided, however, was thread synchronization, which prevents race conditions while avoiding deadlocks. Thread synchronization is the topic of this chapter.

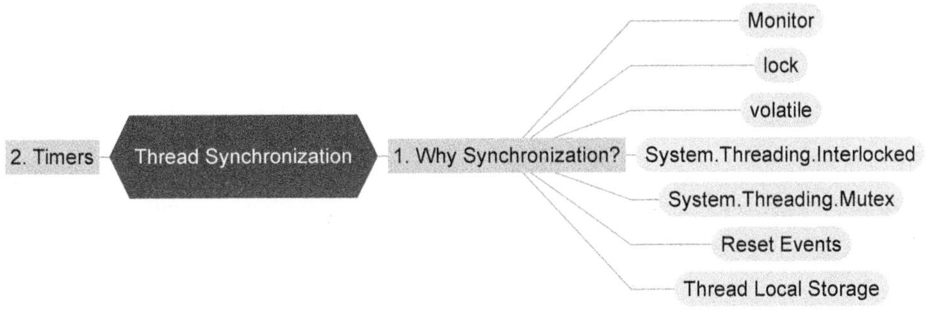

We begin with a multithreaded example with no thread synchronization around shared data—resulting in a race condition in which data integrity is lost. This discussion serves as the introduction for why we need thread synchronization. It is followed by coverage of myriad mechanisms and best practices for doing it.

Prior editions of this book included a significant section on additional multithreading patterns and another on various timer callback mechanisms. With the introduction of the `async/await` pattern, however, those approaches have essentially been replaced.[1]

This entire chapter uses the TPL, so the samples cannot be compiled on frameworks prior to Microsoft .NET Framework 4. However, unless specifically identified as a Microsoft .NET Framework 4 API, the only reason for the Microsoft .NET Framework 4 restriction is the use of the `System.Threading.Tasks.Task` class to execute the asynchronous operation. Modifying the code to instantiate a `System.Threading.Thread` and use a `Thread.Join()` to wait for the thread to execute will allow the vast majority of samples to compile on earlier frameworks.

That being said, the specific API for starting tasks throughout this chapter is the .NET 4.5 (or later) `System.Threading.Tasks.Task.Run()`. As we discussed in Chapter 19, this method is preferred over `System.Threading.Tasks.Task.Factory.StartNew()` because it is simpler and sufficient for the majority of scenarios. If you are limited to .NET 4, you can replace `Task.Run()` with `Task.Factory.StartNew()` without any additional modifications. (For this reason, the chapter does not explicitly highlight such code as .NET 4.5–specific code when only this method is used.)

Why Synchronization?

Running a new thread is a relatively simple programming task. What makes multithreaded programming difficult, however, is identifying which data multiple threads can safely access simultaneously. The program must synchronize such data to prevent simultaneous access, thereby creating the "safety." Consider Listing 22.1 with Output 22.1.

1. Pre–C# 5.0 material is still available from this book's website: https://intellitect.com/EssentialCSharp.

Listing 22.1: Unsynchronized State

```
using System;
using System.Threading.Tasks;

public class Program
{
    static int _Total = int.MaxValue;
    static int _Count = 0;

    public static int Main(string[] args)
    {
        if (args?.Length > 0) { _ = int.TryParse(args[0], out _Total); }

        Console.WriteLine("Increment and decrementing " +
            $"{_Total} times...");

        // Use Task.Factory.StartNew for .NET 4.0
        Task task = Task.Run(() => Decrement());

        // Increment
        for(int i = 0; i < _Total; i++)
        {
            _Count++;
        }

        task.Wait();
        Console.WriteLine($"Count = {_Count}");

        return _Count;
    }

    public static void Decrement()
    {
        // Decrement
        for(int i = 0; i < _Total; i++)
        {
            _Count--;
        }
    }
}
```

Output 22.1

```
Count = 113449949
```

The important thing to note about Listing 22.1 is that the output is not `0`. It would have been if `Decrement()` was called directly (sequentially). However, when calling `Decrement()` asynchronously, a race condition occurs because the individual steps within `_Count++` and `_Count--` statements intermingle. (As discussed in "Beginner Topic: Multithreading Jargon" in Chapter 19, a single statement in C# likely involves multiple steps.) Consider the sample execution in Table 22.1.

TABLE 22.1: Sample Pseudocode Execution

Main Thread	Decrement Thread	Count
...	...	...
Copy the value `0` out of `_Count`.		0
Increment the copied value (`0`), resulting in `1`.		0
Copy the resultant value (`1`) into `_Count`.		1
Copy the value `1` out of `_Count`.		1
	Copy the value `1` out of `_Count`.	1
Increment the copied value (`1`), resulting in `2`.		1
Copy the resultant value (`2`) into `_Count`.		2
	Decrement the copied value (`1`), resulting in `0`.	2
	Copy the resultant value (`0`) into `_Count`.	0
...	...	...

Table 22.1 shows a parallel execution (or a thread context switch) by the transition of instructions appearing from one column to the other. The value of `_Count` after a particular line has completed appears in the last column. In this example, `_Count++` executes twice and `_Count--` occurs once. However, the

resultant `_Count` value is `0`, not `1`. Copying a result back to `_Count` essentially wipes out any `_Count` value changes that have occurred since the read of `_Count` on the same thread.

The problem in Listing 22.1 is a race condition, where multiple threads have simultaneous access to the same data elements. As this example execution demonstrates, allowing multiple threads to access the same data elements is likely to undermine data integrity, even on a single-processor computer. To remedy this potential problem, the code needs synchronization around the data. Code or data synchronized for simultaneous access by multiple threads is **thread safe**.

There is one important point to note about atomicity of reading and writing to variables. The runtime guarantees that a type whose size is no bigger than a native (pointer-size) integer will not be read or written partially. With a 64-bit operating system, therefore, reads and writes to a `long` (64 bits) are atomic. However, reads and writes to a 128-bit variable such as `decimal` may not be atomic. Therefore, write operations to change a `decimal` variable may be interrupted after copying only 32 bits, resulting in the reading of an incorrect value, known as a **torn read**.

BEGINNER TOPIC

Multiple Threads and Local Variables

Note that it is not necessary to synchronize local variables. Local variables are loaded onto the stack, and each thread has its own logical stack. Therefore, each local variable has its own instance for each method call. By default, local variables are not shared across method calls; likewise, they are not shared among multiple threads.

However, this does not mean local variables are entirely without concurrency issues—after all, code could easily expose the local variable to multiple threads.[2] A parallel `for` loop that shares a local variable between iterations, for example, exposes the variable to concurrent access and a race condition (see Listing 22.2).

---

2. While at the C# level it's a local variable, at the Common Intermediate Language level it's a field —and fields can be accessed from multiple threads.

Listing 22.2: Unsynchronized Local Variables

```
using System;
using System.Threading.Tasks;

public class Program
{
    public static int Main(string[] args)
    {
        int total = int.MaxValue;
        if (args?.Length > 0) { _ = int.TryParse(args[0], out total); }
        Console.WriteLine("Increment and decrementing " +
            $"{total} times...");
        int x = 0;
        Parallel.For(0, total, i =>
        {
            x++;
            x--;
        });
        Console.WriteLine($"Count = {x}");
        return x;
    }
}
```

In this example, `x` (a local variable) is accessed within a parallel `for` loop, so multiple threads modify it simultaneously, creating a race condition very similar to that in Listing 22.1. The output is unlikely to yield the value `0`, even though `x` is incremented and decremented the same number of times.

Synchronization Using `Monitor`

To synchronize multiple threads so that they cannot execute particular sections of code simultaneously, you can use a **monitor** to block the second thread from entering a protected code section before the first thread has exited that section. The monitor functionality is part of a class called `System.Threading.Monitor`, and the beginning and end of protected code sections are marked with calls to the static methods `Monitor.Enter()` and `Monitor.Exit()`, respectively.

Listing 22.3 (results shown in Output 22.2) demonstrates synchronization using the `Monitor` class explicitly. As this listing shows, it is important that all code between calls to `Monitor.Enter()` and `Monitor.Exit()` are surrounded with a try/finally block. Without this block, an exception could occur within the protected section and `Monitor.Exit()` may never be called, thereby blocking other threads indefinitely.

Listing 22.3: Synchronizing with a Monitor Explicitly

```
using System;
using System.Threading;
using System.Threading.Tasks;

public class Program
{
    readonly static object _Sync = new();
    static int _Total = int.MaxValue;
    static int _Count = 0;

    public static int Main(string[] args)
    {
        if (args?.Length > 0) { _ = int.TryParse(args[0], out _Total); }
        Console.WriteLine("Increment and decrementing " +
            $"{_Total} times...");

        // Use Task.Factory.StartNew for .NET 4.0
        Task task = Task.Run(() => Decrement());

        // Increment
        for(int i = 0; i < _Total; i++)
        {
            bool lockTaken = false;
            try
            {
                Monitor.Enter(_Sync, ref lockTaken);
                _Count++;
            }
            finally
            {
                if(lockTaken)
                {
                    Monitor.Exit(_Sync);
                }
            }
        }

        task.Wait();
        Console.WriteLine($"Count = {_Count}");
```

```
            return _Count;
        }

        public static void Decrement()
        {
            for(int i = 0; i < _Total; i++)
            {
                bool lockTaken = false;
                try
                {
                    Monitor.Enter(_Sync, ref lockTaken);
                    _Count--;
                }
                finally
                {
                    if(lockTaken)
                    {
                        Monitor.Exit(_Sync);
                    }
                }
            }
        }
    }
```

OUTPUT 22.2

```
Count =
```

Note that calls to `Monitor.Enter()` and `Monitor.Exit()` are associated with each other by sharing the same object reference passed as the parameter (in this case, `_Sync`). The `Monitor.Enter()` overload method that takes the `lockTaken` parameter was added to the framework only in .NET 4.0. Before then, no such `lockTaken` parameter was available and there was no way to reliably catch an exception that occurred between the `Monitor.Enter()` and the try block. Placing the try block immediately following the `Monitor.Enter()` call was reliable in release code because the just-in-time compiler, or JIT, prevented any such asynchronous exception from sneaking in. However, anything other than a try block immediately following the `Monitor.Enter()`, including any instructions that the compiler might have injected within debug code, could prevent the JIT from reliably returning execution within the try block. Therefore, if an exception did occur, it would leak the lock (the lock remained acquired) rather than executing the finally block and releasing it—likely causing a deadlock when another thread tried to acquire the lock. In summary, in versions of the framework prior to .NET 4.0, you should always follow `Monitor.Enter()` with a try/finally `{Monitor.Exit(_Sync))}` block.

`Monitor` also supports a `Pulse()` method for allowing a thread to enter the *ready queue*, indicating it is up next for execution. This is a common means of synchronizing producer–consumer patterns so that no "consume" occurs until there has been a "produce." The producer thread that owns the monitor (by calling `Monitor.Enter()`) calls `Monitor.Pulse()` to signal the consumer thread (which may already have called `Monitor.Enter()`) that an item is available for consumption and that it should get ready. For a single `Pulse()` call, only one thread (the consumer thread, in this case) can enter the ready queue. When the producer thread calls `Monitor.Exit()`, the consumer thread takes the lock (`Monitor.Enter()` completes) and enters the critical section to begin consuming the item. Once the consumer processes the waiting item, it calls `Exit()`, thus allowing the producer (currently blocked with `Monitor.Enter()`) to produce again. In this example, only one thread can enter the ready queue at a time, ensuring that there is no consumption without production, and vice versa.

Using the `lock` Keyword

Because of the frequent need for synchronization using `Monitor` in multithreaded code, and because the try/finally block can easily be forgotten, C# provides a special keyword to handle this locking synchronization pattern. Listing 22.4 demonstrates the use of the `lock` keyword, and Output 22.3 shows the results.

LISTING 22.4: Synchronization Using the `lock` Keyword

```
using System;
using System.Threading.Tasks;

public class Program
{
    readonly static object _Sync = new();
    static int _Total = int.MaxValue;
    static int _Count = 0;

    public static int Main(string[] args)
```

```
    {
        if (args?.Length > 0) { _ = int.TryParse(args[0], out _Total); }
        Console.WriteLine("Increment and decrementing " +
            $"{_Total} times...");

        // Use Task.Factory.StartNew for .NET 4.0
        Task task = Task.Run(() => Decrement());

        // Increment
        for (int i = 0; i < _Total; i++)
        {
            lock (_Sync)
            {
                _Count++;
            }
        }

        task.Wait();
        Console.WriteLine($"Count = {_Count}");
        return _Count;
    }

    public static void Decrement()
    {
        for (int i = 0; i < _Total; i++)
        {
            lock (_Sync)
            {
                _Count--;
            }
        }
    }
}
```

Output 22.3

```
Count = 0
```

By locking the section of code accessing `_Count` (using either `lock` or `Monitor`), you make the `Main()` and `Decrement()` methods thread safe, meaning they can be safely called from multiple threads simultaneously.[3]

The price of synchronization is a reduction in performance. Listing 22.4, for example, takes an order of magnitude longer to execute than Listing 22.1 does, which demonstrates `lock`'s relatively slow execution compared to the execution of incrementing and decrementing the count.

Even when `lock` is insignificant in comparison with the work it synchronizes, programmers should avoid indiscriminate synchronization so as to avoid the possibility of deadlocks and unnecessary synchronization on multiprocessor computers that could instead be executing code in parallel. The general best practice for object design is to synchronize *mutable static* state, but not any instance data. (There is no need to synchronize something that never changes.) Programmers who allow multiple threads to access a particular object must provide synchronization for the object. Any class that explicitly deals with threads is likely to want to make instances thread safe to some extent.

BEGINNER TOPIC

`Task` Return with No `await`

In Listing 22.1, although `Task.Run(() => Decrement())` returns a `Task`, the `await` operator is not used. The reason for this is that prior to C# 7.1, `Main()` didn't support the use of `async`. Given C# 7.1, however, the code can be refactored to use the `async/await` pattern, as shown in Listing 22.5.

LISTING 22.5: `async Main()` **with C# 7.1**

```
using System;
using System.Threading.Tasks;

public class Program
{
```

3. Prior to C# 4.0, the concept was the same but the compiler-emitted code depended on the `lockTaken`-less `Monitor.Enter()` method, and the `Monitor.Enter()` called was emitted before the try block.

```
    readonly static object _Sync = new();
    static int _Total = int.MaxValue;
    static int _Count = 0;

    public static async Task<int> Main(string[] args)
    {
        if (args?.Length > 0) { _ = int.TryParse(args[0], out _Total); }
        Console.WriteLine("Increment and decrementing " +
            $"{_Total} times...");

        // Use Task.Factory.StartNew for .NET 4.0
        Task task = Task.Run(() => Decrement());

        // Increment
        for(int i = 0; i < _Total; i++)
        {
            lock(_Sync)
            {
                _Count++;
            }
        }

        await task;
        Console.WriteLine($"Count = {_Count}");
        return _Count;
    }

    static void Decrement()
    {
        for(int i = 0; i < _Total; i++)
        {
            lock(_Sync)
            {
                _Count--;
            }
        }
    }
}
```

Choosing a `lock` Object

Whether or not the `lock` keyword or the `Monitor` class is explicitly used, it is crucial that programmers carefully select the `lock` object.

In the previous examples, the synchronization variable, `_Sync`, is declared as both private and read-only. It is declared as read-only to ensure that the value is not changed between calls to `Monitor.Enter()` and `Monitor.Exit()`. This allows correlation between entering and exiting the synchronized block. Similarly, the code declares `_Sync` as private so that no synchronization block outside the class can synchronize the same object instance, causing the code to block.

If the data is public, the synchronization object may be public so that other classes can synchronize using the same object instance. However, this makes it harder to avoid deadlock. Fortunately, the need for this pattern is rare. For public data, it is instead preferable to leave synchronization entirely outside the class, allowing the calling code to take locks with its own synchronization object.

It's important that the synchronization object not be a value type. If the `lock` keyword is used on a value type, the compiler will report an error. (In the case of accessing the `System.Threading.Monitor` class explicitly [not via `lock`], no such error occurs at compile time. Instead, the code throws an exception with the call to `Monitor.Exit()`, indicating there was no corresponding `Monitor.Enter()` call.) The issue is that when using a value type, the runtime makes a copy of the value, places it in the heap (boxing occurs), and passes the boxed value to `Monitor.Enter()`. Similarly, `Monitor.Exit()` receives a boxed copy of the original variable. The result is that `Monitor.Enter()` and `Monitor.Exit()` receive different synchronization object instances so that no correlation between the two calls occurs.

Why to Avoid Locking on `this`, `typeof(type)`, and `string`

One seemingly reasonable pattern is to lock on the `this` keyword for instance data in a class and on the type instance obtained from `typeof(type)` (e.g., `typeof(MyType)`) for static data. Such a pattern provides a synchronization target for all states associated with a particular object instance when `this` is used and for all static data for a type when `typeof(type)` is used. The problem is that the synchronization target that `this` (or `typeof(type)`) points to could participate in the synchronization target for an entirely different synchronization block created in an unrelated block of code. In other words, although only the code within the instance itself can block using the `this` keyword, the caller that created the instance can pass that instance to a synchronization lock.

As a result, two different synchronization blocks that synchronize two entirely different sets of data could potentially block each other. Although perhaps unlikely, sharing the same synchronization target could have an unintended performance impact and, in extreme cases, could even cause a deadlock. Instead of locking on `this` or even `typeof(type)`, it is better to define a private, read-only field on which no one will block except for the class that has access to it.

Another lock type to avoid is `string` because of the risk associated with string interning. If the same `string` constant appears within multiple locations, it is likely that all locations refer to the same instance, making the scope of the lock much broader than expected.

In summary, you should use a per-synchronization context instance of type `object` for the lock target.

Guidelines

AVOID locking on `this`, `System.Type`, or a `string`.

DO declare a separate, read-only synchronization variable of type `object` for the synchronization target.

Avoid Synchronizing with `MethodImplAttribute`

One synchronization mechanism introduced in .NET 1.0 was the `MethodImplAttribute`. Used in conjunction with the `MethodImplOptions.Synchronized` method, this attribute marks a method as synchronized, so that only one thread can execute the method at a time. To achieve this, the JIT essentially treats the method as though it is surrounded by `lock(this)` or, in the case of a static method, locks on the type. Such an implementation means that, in fact, the method and all other methods on the same class, decorated with the same attribute and enum parameter, are synchronized—rather than each method being synchronized relative to itself. In other words, given two or more methods on the same class decorated with the attribute, only one of them will be able to execute at a time, and the method that is executing will block all calls by other threads to itself or to any other method in the class with the same decoration. Furthermore, since the synchronization is on `this` (or even worse, on the type), it suffers the same detriments as `lock(this)` (or worse, for the static case) discussed in the preceding section. As a result, it is a best practice to avoid `MethodImplAttribute` altogether.

Guidelines

AVOID using the `MethodImplAttribute` for synchronization.

Declaring Fields as `volatile`

On occasion, the compiler or CPU may optimize code in such a way that the instructions do not occur in the exact order they are coded or some instructions are optimized out. Such optimizations are innocuous when code executes on one thread. However, with multiple threads, such optimizations may have unintended consequences because the optimizations may change the order of execution of a field's read or write operations relative to an alternate thread's access to the same field.

One way to stabilize this behavior is to declare fields using the `volatile` keyword. This keyword forces all reads and writes to the volatile field to occur at the exact location identified by the code instead of at some other location produced by the optimization. The `volatile` modifier indicates that the field is susceptible to modification by the hardware, operating system, or another thread. As such, the data is "volatile," and the keyword instructs the compilers and runtime to handle it more exactly. (See https://docs.microsoft.com/dotnet/csharp/language-reference/keywords/volatile for further details.)

In general, the use of the `volatile` modifier is rare and fraught with complications that will likely lead to incorrect usage. Using `lock` is preferred to the `volatile` modifier unless you are absolutely certain about the `volatile` usage.

Using the System.Threading.Interlocked Class

The mutual exclusion pattern described so far provides the minimum set of tools for handling synchronization within a process (application domain). However, synchronization with System.Threading.Monitor is a relatively expensive operation, and an alternative solution that the processor supports directly targets specific synchronization patterns.

Listing 22.6 sets _Data to a new value as long as the preceding value was null. As indicated by the method name, this pattern is the compare/exchange pattern. Instead of manually placing a lock around behaviorally equivalent compare and exchange code, the Interlocked.CompareExchange() method provides a built-in method for a synchronous operation that does the same check for a value (null) and updates the first parameter if the value is equal to the second parameter. Table 22.2 shows other synchronization methods supported by Interlocked.

Listing 22.6: Synchronization Using System.Threading.Interlocked

```
public class SynchronizationUsingInterlocked
{
    private static object? _Data;

    // Initialize data if not yet assigned
    public static void Initialize(object newValue)
    {
        // If _Data is null then set it to newValue
        Interlocked.CompareExchange(
            ref _Data, newValue, null);
    }

    // ...
}
```

Table 22.2: Interlocked's Synchronization-Related Methods

Method Signature	Description

`public static T CompareExchange<T>(`
`T location,`
`T value,`
`T comparand`
`);`
	Checks location for the value in comparand. If the values are equal, it sets location to value and returns the original data stored in location.

TABLE 22.2: Interlocked's Synchronization-Related Methods (continued)

Method Signature	Description
`public static T Exchange<T>( T location, T value );`	Assigns `location` with `value` and returns the previous value.
`public static int Decrement( ref int location );`	Decrements `location` by 1. It is equivalent to the prefix `--` operator, except that `Decrement()` is thread safe.
`public static int Increment( ref int location );`	Increments `location` by 1. It is equivalent to the prefix `++` operator, except that `Increment()` is thread safe.
`public static int Add( ref int location, int value );`	Adds `value` to `location` and assigns `location` the result. It is equivalent to the `+=` operator.
`public static long Read( ref long location );`	Returns a 64-bit value in a single atomic operation.

Most of these methods are overloaded with additional data type signatures, such as support for `long`. Table 22.2 provides the general signatures and descriptions.

Note that you can use `Increment()` and `Decrement()` in place of the synchronized `++` and `--` operators from Listing 22.5, and doing so will yield better performance. Also note that if a different thread accessed `_Count` using a non-interlocked method, the two accesses would not be synchronized correctly.

Event Notification with Multiple Threads

One area where developers often overlook synchronization is when firing events. The unsafe thread code for publishing an event is similar to Listing 22.7.

LISTING 22.7: Firing an Event Notification

```
// Not thread safe
if (OnTemperatureChanged != null)
{
    // Call subscribers
    OnTemperatureChanged(
```

```
        this, new TemperatureEventArgs(value));
}
```

This code is valid as long as no race condition arises between this method and the event subscribers. However, the code is not atomic, so multiple threads could introduce a race condition. It is possible that between the time when `OnTemperatureChange` is checked for `null` and when the event is actually fired, `OnTemperatureChange` could be set to `null`, thereby throwing a `NullReferenceException`. In other words, if multiple threads could potentially access a delegate simultaneously, it is necessary to synchronize the assignment and firing of the delegate.

All that is necessary is to use the null-conditional operator:

```
OnTemperature?.Invoke(
this, new TemperatureEventArgs( value ) );
```

The null-conditional operator is specifically designed to be atomic, so this invocation of the delegate is, in fact, atomic. The key—obviously—is to remember to make use of the null-conditional operator.

Although it requires more code, thread-safe delegate invocation isn't especially difficult, either.[4] This approach works because the operators for adding and removing listeners are thread safe and static (operator overloading is done with static methods). To correct Listing 22.7 and make it thread safe, assign a copy, check the copy for `null`, and fire the copy (see Listing 22.8).

Listing 22.8: Thread-Safe Event Notification

```
//...
TemperatureChangedHandler localOnChange =
    OnTemperatureChanged;
if(localOnChange != null)
{
    // Call subscribers
    localOnChange(
      this, new TemperatureEventArgs(value));
```

4. Prior to C# 6.0.

```
}
//...
```

Given that a delegate is a reference type, it is perhaps surprising that assigning a local variable and then firing with the local variable is sufficient for making the `null` check thread safe. As `localOnChange` points to the same location that `OnTemperatureChange` points to, you might think that any changes in `OnTemperatureChange` would be reflected in `localOnChange` as well.

In fact, this is *not* the case: Any calls to `OnTemperatureChange += <listener>` will not add a new delegate to `OnTemperatureChange`, but rather will assign it an entirely new multicast delegate without having any effect on the original multicast delegate to which `localOnChange` also points. This makes the code thread safe because only one thread will access the `localOnChange` instance, and `OnTemperatureChange` will be an entirely new instance if listeners are added or removed.

Synchronization Design Best Practices

Along with the complexities of multithreaded programming come several best practices for handling those complexities.

Avoiding Deadlock

With the introduction of synchronization comes the potential for deadlock. Deadlock occurs when two or more threads wait for one another to release a synchronization lock. For example, suppose Thread 1 requests a lock on `_Sync1`, and then later requests a lock on `_Sync2` before releasing the lock on `_Sync1`. At the same time, Thread 2 requests a lock on `_Sync2`, followed by a lock on `_Sync1`, before releasing the lock on `_Sync2`. This sets the stage for the deadlock. The deadlock actually occurs if both Thread 1 and Thread 2 successfully acquire their initial locks (`_Sync1` and `_Sync2`, respectively) before obtaining their second locks.

For a deadlock to occur, four fundamental conditions must be met:

- *Mutual exclusion:* One thread (`Thread A`) exclusively owns a resource such that no other thread (`Thread B`) can acquire the same resource.

- *Hold and wait:* One thread (`Thread A`) with a mutual exclusion is waiting to acquire a resource held by another thread (`Thread B`).
- *No preemption:* The resource held by a thread (`Thread A`) cannot be forcibly removed (`Thread A` needs to release its own locked resource).
- *Circular wait condition:* Two or more threads form a circular chain such that they lock on the same two or more resources, and each waits on the resource held by the next thread in the chain.

Removing any one of these conditions prevents the deadlock.

One scenario likely to cause a deadlock is when two or more threads request exclusive ownership on the same two or more synchronization targets (resources) and the locks are requested in different orders. This situation can be avoided when developers are careful to ensure that multiple lock acquisitions always occur in the same order. Another potential cause of a deadlock is locks that are not **reentrant**. When a lock from one thread can block the same thread—that is, when it re-requests the same lock—the lock is not reentrant. For example, if `Thread A` acquires a lock and then re-requests the same lock but is blocked because the lock is already owned (by itself), the lock is not reentrant and the additional request will result in deadlock.

The code generated by the `lock` keyword (with the underlying `Monitor` class) is reentrant. However, as we shall see in the "More Synchronization Types" section, some lock types are not reentrant.

When to Provide Synchronization

As we discussed earlier, all static data should be thread safe. Therefore, synchronization needs to surround static data that is mutable. Generally, programmers should declare private static variables and then provide public methods for modifying the data. Such methods should internally handle the synchronization if multithreaded access is possible.

In contrast, instance state is not expected to include synchronization. Synchronization may significantly decrease performance and increase the chance of a lock contention or deadlock. With the exception of classes that are explicitly designed for multithreaded access, programmers sharing objects across multiple threads are expected to handle their own synchronization of the data being shared.

Avoiding Unnecessary Locking

Without compromising data integrity, programmers should avoid unnecessary synchronization where possible. For example, you should use immutable types between threads so that no synchronization is necessary (this approach has proved invaluable in functional programming languages such as F#). Similarly, you should avoid locking on thread-safe operations such as simple reads and writes of values smaller than a native (pointer-size) integer, as such operations are automatically atomic.

> **Guidelines**
>
> **DO NOT** request exclusive ownership of the same two or more synchronization targets in different orders.
>
> **DO** ensure that code that concurrently holds multiple locks always acquires them in the same order.
>
> **DO** encapsulate mutable static data in public APIs with synchronization logic.
>
> **AVOID** synchronization on simple reading or writing of values no bigger than a native (pointer-size) integer, as such operations are automatically atomic.

More Synchronization Types

In addition to `System.Threading.Monitor` and `System.Threading.Interlocked`, several more synchronization techniques are available.

Using `System.Threading.Mutex`

`System.Threading.Mutex` is similar in concept to the `System.Threading.Monitor` class (without the `Pulse()` method support), except that the `lock` keyword does not use it, and `Mutex`es can be named so that they support synchronization across multiple processes. Using the `Mutex` class, you can synchronize access to a file or some other cross-process resource. Since `Mutex` is a cross-process resource, .NET 2.0 added support to allow for setting the access control via a `System.Security.AccessControl.MutexSecurity` object. One use for the Mutex class is to limit an application so that it cannot run multiple times simultaneously, as Listing 22.9 demonstrates with Output 22.4.

Listing 22.9: Creating a Single Instance Application

```
using System;
using System.Reflection;
using System.Threading;

public class Program
{
    public static void Main()
    {
        // Obtain the mutex name from the full
        // assembly name.
        string mutexName =
            Assembly.GetEntryAssembly()!.FullName!;

        // firstApplicationInstance indicates
        // whether this is the first
        // application instance.
        using Mutex mutex = new(false, mutexName,
             out bool firstApplicationInstance);

        if (!firstApplicationInstance)
        {
            Console.WriteLine(
                "This application is already running.");
        }
        else
        {
            Console.WriteLine("ENTER to shut down");
            Console.ReadLine();
        }
    }
}
```

Output 22.4

```
ENTER to shut down
```

The results from running the second instance of the application while the first instance is still running appear in Output 22.5.

Output 22.5

```
This application is already running.
```

In this case, the application can run only once on the machine, even if it is launched by different users. To restrict the instances to once per user, add `System.Environment.UserName` (which requires the Microsoft .NET Framework or .NET Standard 2.0) as a suffix when assigning the `mutexName`.

`Mutex` derives from `System.Threading.WaitHandle`, so it includes the `WaitAll()`, `WaitAny()`, and `SignalAndWait()` methods. These methods allow it to acquire multiple locks automatically—something `Monitor` does not support.

WaitHandle

The base class for `Mutex` is `System.Threading.WaitHandle`. It is a fundamental synchronization class used by the `Mutex`, `EventWaitHandle`, and `Semaphore` synchronization classes. The key methods on a `WaitHandle` are the `WaitOne()` methods, which block execution until the `WaitHandle` instance is signaled or set. The `WaitOne()` methods include several overloads allowing for an indefinite wait: `void WaitOne()`, a millisecond-timed wait; `bool WaitOne(int milliseconds)`; and `bool WaitOne(TimeSpan timeout)`, a `TimeSpan` wait. The versions that return a Boolean will return a value of `true` whenever the `WaitHandle` is signaled before the timeout.

In addition to the `WaitHandle` instance methods, there are two key static members: `WaitAll()` and `WaitAny()`. Like their instance cousins, these static members support timeouts. In addition, they take a collection of `WaitHandles`, in the form of an array, so that they can respond to signals coming from within the collection.

Note that `WaitHandle` contains a handle (of type `SafeWaitHandle`) that implements `IDisposable`. As such, care is needed to ensure that `WaitHandles` are disposed when they are no longer needed.

Reset Events: ManualResetEvent and ManualResetEventSlim

One way to control uncertainty about when particular instructions in a thread will execute relative to instructions in another thread is by using reset events. In spite of the use of the term *events*, reset events have nothing to do with C# delegates and events. Instead, reset events are a way to force code to wait for the execution of another thread until the other thread signals. They are especially useful for testing multithreaded code because it is possible to wait for a particular state before verifying the results.

The reset event types are `System.Threading.ManualResetEvent` and the Microsoft .NET Framework 4–added lightweight version, `System.Threading.ManualResetEventSlim`. (As discussed in the upcoming "Advanced Topic: Favor `ManualResetEvent` and Semaphores over `AutoResetEvent`," there is a third type, `System.Threading.AutoResetEvent`, but programmers should avoid it in favor of one of the first two.) The key methods on the reset events are `Set()` and `Wait()` (called `WaitOne()` on `ManualResetEvent`). Calling the `Wait()` method causes a thread to block until a different thread calls `Set()` or until the wait period times out. Listing 22.10 demonstrates how this works, and Output 22.6 shows the results.

Listing 22.10: Waiting for `ManualResetEventSlim`

```
using System;
using System.Threading;
using System.Threading.Tasks;

public class Program
{
    // ...
    static ManualResetEventSlim _MainSignaledResetEvent;
    static ManualResetEventSlim _DoWorkSignaledResetEvent;
    // ...

    public static void DoWork()
    {
        Console.WriteLine("DoWork() started....");
        _DoWorkSignaledResetEvent.Set();
        _MainSignaledResetEvent.Wait();
        Console.WriteLine("DoWork() ending....");
```

```
    }

    public static void Main()
    {
        using(_MainSignaledResetEvent = new ())
        using(_DoWorkSignaledResetEvent = new ())
        {
            Console.WriteLine(
                "Application started....");
            Console.WriteLine("Starting task....");

            // Use Task.Factory.StartNew for .NET 4.0
            Task task = Task.Run(() => DoWork());

            // Block until DoWork() has started
            _DoWorkSignaledResetEvent.Wait();
            Console.WriteLine(
                " Waiting while thread executes...");
            _MainSignaledResetEvent.Set();
            task.Wait();
            Console.WriteLine("Thread completed");
            Console.WriteLine(
                "Application shutting down....");
        }
    }
}
```

Output 22.6

```
Application started....
Starting thread....
DoWork() started....
Waiting while thread executes...
DoWork() ending....
Thread completed
Application shutting down....
```

Listing 22.10 begins by instantiating and starting a new `Task`. Table 22.3 shows the execution path, where each column represents a thread. In cases where code appears on the same row, it is indeterminate which side executes first.

Table 22.3: Execution Path with `ManualResetEvent` Synchronization

`Main()`	`DoWork()`
`...`	
`Console.WriteLine( "Application started....");`	
`Task task = new Task(DoWork);`	
`Console.WriteLine( "Starting thread....");`	
`task.Start();`	
`_DoWorkSignaledResetEvent.Wait();`	`Console.WriteLine( "DoWork() started....");`
	`_DoWorkSignaledResetEvent.Set();`
`Console.WriteLine( "Thread executing...");`	`_MainSignaledResetEvent.Wait();`
`_MainSignaledResetEvent.Set();`	
`task.Wait();`	`Console.WriteLine( "DoWork() ending....");`
`Console.WriteLine( "Thread completed");`	
`Console.WriteLine( "Application exiting....");`	

Calling a reset event's `Wait()` method (for a `ManualResetEvent`, this method is called `WaitOne()`) blocks the calling thread until another thread signals and allows the blocked thread to continue. Instead of blocking indefinitely, `Wait()`/`WaitOne()` overrides include a parameter, either in milliseconds or as a `TimeSpan` object, for the maximum amount of time to block. When specifying a timeout period, the return from `WaitOne()` is `false` if the timeout occurs before the reset event is signaled. `ManualResetEvent.Wait()` also includes a version that takes a cancellation token, allowing for cancellation requests as discussed in Chapter 19.

The difference between `ManualResetEventSlim` and `ManualResetEvent` is that the latter uses kernel synchronization by default, whereas the former is optimized to avoid trips to the kernel except as a last resort. Thus, `ManualResetEventSlim` is more performant, even though it could possibly use more CPU cycles. For this reason, you should use `ManualResetEventSlim` in general, unless waiting on multiple events or across processes is required.

Notice that reset events implement `IDisposable`, so they should be disposed of when they are no longer needed. In Listing 22.10, we do this via a `using` statement. (`CancellationTokenSource` contains a `ManualResetEvent`, which is why it, too, implements `IDisposable`.)

Although not exactly the same, `System.Threading.Monitor`'s `Wait()` and `Pulse()` methods provide similar functionality to reset events in some circumstances.

ADVANCED TOPIC

Favor `ManualResetEvent` and Semaphores over `AutoResetEvent`

A third reset event, known as `System.Threading.AutoResetEvent`, like `ManualResetEvent`, allows one thread to signal (with a call to `Set()`) another thread that the first thread has reached a certain location in the code. The difference is that the `AutoResetEvent` unblocks only one thread's `Wait()` call: After the first thread passes through the auto-reset gate, it goes back to locked. With the auto-reset event, it is all too easy to mistakenly code the producer thread with more iterations than the consumer thread has. Therefore, the use of `Monitor`'s `Wait()`/`Pulse()` pattern or the use of a semaphore (if fewer than *n* threads can participate in a particular block) is generally preferred.

In contrast to an `AutoResetEvent`, the `ManualResetEvent` won't return to the unsignaled state until `Reset()` is called explicitly.

`Semaphore`/`SemaphoreSlim` and *`CountdownEvent`*

`Semaphore` and `SemaphoreSlim` have the same performance differences as `ManualResetEvent` and `ManualResetEventSlim`, respectively. Unlike `ManualResetEvent`/`ManualResetEventSlim`, which provide a lock (like a gate) that is either open or closed, semaphores restrict only *N* calls to pass within a critical section simultaneously. The semaphore essentially keeps a count of the pool of resources. When this count reaches zero, it blocks any further access to the pool until one of the resources is returned, making it available for the next blocked request that is queued.

CountdownEvent acts much like a semaphore, except that it achieves the opposite synchronization. That is, rather than preventing further access to a pool of resources that has been depleted, the CountdownEvent allows access only once the count reaches zero. Consider, for example, a parallel operation that downloads a multitude of stock quotes. Only when all of the quotes are downloaded can a particular search algorithm execute. The CountdownEvent may be used for synchronizing the search algorithm, decrementing the count as each stock is downloading, and then releasing the search to start once the count reaches zero.

Notice that SemaphoreSlim and CountdownEvent were introduced with Microsoft .NET Framework 4. In .NET 4.5, the former includes a SemaphoreSlim.WaitAsync() method so that the Task-based Asynchronous Pattern (TAP) can be used when waiting to enter the semaphore.

Concurrent Collection Classes

Another series of classes introduced with Microsoft .NET Framework 4 is the concurrent collection classes. These classes have been specially designed to include built-in synchronization code so that they can support simultaneous access by multiple threads without concern for race conditions. Table 22.4 describes the concurrent collection classes.

TABLE 22.4: Concurrent Collection Classes

Collection Class	Description
BlockingCollection<T>	Provides a blocking collection that enables producer/consumer scenarios in which producers write data into the collection while consumers read the data. This class provides a generic collection type that synchronizes add and remove operations without concern for the back-end storage (whether a queue, stack, list, or something else). BlockingCollection<T> provides blocking and bounding support for collections that implement the IProducerConsumerCollection<T> interface.
ConcurrentBag<T>*	A thread-safe unordered collection of T type objects.

TABLE 22.4: Concurrent Collection Classes (continued)

Collection Class	Description
`ConcurrentDictionary<TKey, TValue>`	A thread-safe dictionary; a collection of keys and values.
`ConcurrentQueue<T>*`	A thread-safe queue supporting first in, first out (FIFO) semantics on objects of type `T`.
`ConcurrentStack<T>*`	A thread-safe stack supporting first in, last out (FILO) semantics on objects of type `T`.

A common pattern enabled by concurrent collections is support for thread-safe access by producers and consumers. Classes that implement `IProducerConsumerCollection<T>` (identified by an asterisk in Table 22.4) are specifically designed to provide such support. This enables one or more classes to pump data into the collection while a different set of classes reads it out, removing the data. The order in which data is added and removed is determined by the individual collection classes that implement the `IProducerConsumerCollection<T>` interface.

Although it is not built into the out-of-the-box .NET/Dotnet Core Frameworks, an additional immutable collection library is available as a NuGet package reference, called `System.Collections.Immutable`. The advantage of the immutable collection is that it can be passed freely between threads without concern for either deadlocks or interim updates. As immutable collections cannot be modified, interim updates won't occur; thus such collections are automatically thread safe (so there is no need to lock access).

Thread Local Storage

In some cases, using synchronization locks can lead to unacceptable performance and scalability restrictions. In other instances, providing synchronization around a particular data element may be too complex, especially when it is added after the original coding.

One alternative solution to synchronization is isolation, and one method for implementing isolation is **thread local storage**. With thread local storage, each thread has its own dedicated instance of a variable. In this scenario, synchronization is not needed, as there is no point in synchronizing data that occurs within only a single thread's context. Two examples of thread local storage implementations are `ThreadLocal<T>` and `ThreadStaticAttribute`.

ThreadLocal<T>

Use of thread local storage with Microsoft .NET Framework 4 or later involves declaring a field (or variable, in the case of closure by the compiler) of type `ThreadLocal<T>`. The result is a different instance of the field for each thread, as demonstrated in Listing 22.11 and Output 22.7. Note that a different instance exists even if the field is static.

Listing 22.11: Using `ThreadLocal<T>` for Thread Local Storage

```
using System;
using System.Threading;

public class Program
{
    static ThreadLocal<double> _Count = new(() => 0.01134);
    public static double Count
    {
        get { return _Count.Value; }
        set { _Count.Value = value; }
    }

    public static void Main()
    {
        Thread thread = new(Decrement);
        thread.Start();

        // Increment
        for(double i = 0; i < short.MaxValue; i++)
        {
            Count++;
        }
        thread.Join();
        Console.WriteLine("Main Count = {0}", Count);
    }

    public static void Decrement()
    {
        Count = -Count;
        for(double i = 0; i < short.MaxValue; i++)
```

```
        {
            Count--;
        }
        Console.WriteLine(
            "Decrement Count = {0}", Count);
    }
}
```

Output 22.7

```
Decrement Count = -32767.01134
Main Count = 32767.01134
```

As Output 22.7 demonstrates, the value of `Count` for the thread executing `Main()` is never decremented by the thread executing `Decrement()`. For `Main()`'s thread, the initial value is `0.01134` and the final value is `32767.01134`. `Decrement()` has similar values, except that they are negative. As `Count` is based on the static field of type `ThreadLocal<T>`, the thread running `Main()` and the thread running `Decrement()` have independent values stored in `_Count.Value`.

Thread Local Storage with `ThreadStaticAttribute`

Decorating a static field with a `ThreadStaticAttribute`, as in Listing 22.12 (results shown in Output 22.8), is a second way to designate a static variable as an instance per thread. This technique has a few caveats relative to `ThreadLocal<T>`, but also has the advantage of being available prior to Microsoft .NET Framework 4. (Also, since `ThreadLocal<T>` is based on the `ThreadStaticAttribute`, it would consume less memory and give a slight performance advantage given frequently enough repeated small iterations.)

Listing 22.12: Using `ThreadStaticAttribute` for Thread Local Storage

```
using System;
using System.Threading;

public class Program
{
    [ThreadStatic]
    static double _Count = 0.01134;
    public static double Count
```

```
        {
            get { return Program._Count; }
            set { Program._Count = value; }
        }

        public static void Main()
        {
            Thread thread = new(Decrement);
            thread.Start();

            // Increment
            for(int i = 0; i < short.MaxValue; i++)
            {
                Count++;
            }

            thread.Join();
            Console.WriteLine("Main Count = {0}", Count);
        }

        public static void Decrement()
        {
            for(int i = 0; i < short.MaxValue; i++)
            {
                Count--;
            }
            Console.WriteLine("Decrement Count = {0}", Count);
        }
    }
```

OUTPUT 22.8

```
Decrement Count = -32767
Main Count = 32767.01134
```

As in Listing 22.11, the value of `Count` for the thread executing `Main()` is never decremented by the thread executing `Decrement()`. For `Main()`'s thread, the initial value is a negative `_Total` and the final value is `0`. In other words, with `ThreadStaticAttribute` the value of `Count` for each thread is specific to the thread and not accessible across threads.

Notice that unlike in Listing 22.11, the value displayed for the decrement count does not have any decimal digits, indicating it was never initialized to `0.01134`. Although the value of `_Count` is assigned during declaration—`private double`

`_Count = 0.01134` in this example—only the thread static instance associated with the thread running the static constructor will be initialized. In Listing 22.12, only the thread executing `Main()` will have a thread local storage variable initialized to `0.01134`. The value of `_Count` that `Decrement()` decrements will always be initialized to `0` (`default(double)` since `_Count` is a `double`). Similarly, if a constructor initializes a thread local storage field, only the constructor calling that thread will initialize the thread local storage instance. For this reason, it is a good practice to initialize a thread local storage field within the method that each thread initially calls. However, this is not always reasonable, especially in connection with `async`: Different pieces of computation might run on different threads, resulting in unexpectedly differing thread local storage values on each piece.

The decision to use thread local storage requires some degree of cost–benefit analysis. For example, consider using thread local storage for a database connection. Depending on the database management system, database connections are relatively expensive, so creating a connection for every thread could be costly. Similarly, locking a connection so that all database calls are synchronized places a significantly lower ceiling on scalability. Each pattern has its costs and benefits, and the best choice depends largely on the individual implementation.

Another reason to use thread local storage is to make commonly needed context information available to other methods without explicitly passing the data via parameters. For example, if multiple methods in the call stack require user security information, you can pass the data using thread local storage fields instead of as parameters. This technique keeps APIs cleaner while still making the information available to methods in a thread-safe manner. Such an approach requires that you ensure the thread local data is always set—a step that is especially important on `Tasks` or other thread pool threads because the underlying threads are reused.

Timers

On occasion, it is necessary to delay code execution for a specific period of time or to register for a notification after a specific period of time. Examples include refreshing the screen at specific time intervals, rather than immediately, when frequent data changes occur. One approach to implementing timers is to leverage the async/await pattern[5] and the Task.Delay() method added in .NET 4.5. As we pointed out in Chapter 19, one key feature of TAP is that the code executing after an async call will continue in a supported thread context, thereby avoiding any UI cross-threading issues. Listing 22.13 provides an example of how to use the Task.Delay() method.

Listing 22.13: Using Task.Delay() as a Timer

```
using System;
using System.Threading.Tasks;

public class Pomodoro
{
    // ...

    private static async Task TickAsync(
        System.Threading.CancellationToken token)
    {
        for(int minute = 0; minute < 25; minute++)
        {
            DisplayMinuteTicker(minute);
            for(int second = 0; second < 60; second++)
            {
                await Task.Delay(1000, token);
                if(token.IsCancellationRequested)
                    break;
                DisplaySecondTicker();
            }
            if(token.IsCancellationRequested)
                break;
        }
    }
    // ...
}
```

The call to Task.Delay(1000) will set a countdown timer that triggers after 1 second and executes the continuation code that appears after it.

Fortunately, TAP's use of the synchronization context[6] specifically addressed executing UI-related code exclusively on the UI thread. Prior to that, it was necessary

5. Starting in C# 5.0.
6. In C# 5.0.

to use specific timer classes that were UI-thread safe—or could be configured as such. Timers such as `System.Windows.Forms.Timer`, `System.Windows.Threading.DispatcherTimer`, and `System.Timers.Timer` (if configured appropriately) are UI-thread friendly. Others, such as `System.Threading.Timer`, are optimized for performance.

ADVANCED/BEGINNER TOPIC

Controlling the COM Threading Model with the STAThreadAttribute

With COM, four different apartment-threading models determine the threading rules relating to calls between COM objects. Fortunately, these rules—and the complexity that accompanied them—have disappeared from .NET as long as the program invokes no COM components. The general approach to handling COM interoperability issues is to place all .NET components within the main, single-threaded apartment by decorating a process's `Main` method with the `System.STAThreadAttribute`. This approach means it is not necessary to cross apartment boundaries to invoke the majority of COM components. Furthermore, apartment initialization does not occur unless a COM interop call is made. The caveat to this approach is that all other threads (including those of `Task`) will default to using a multithreaded apartment (MTA). In turn, care needs to be taken when invoking COM components from other threads besides the main one.

COM interop is not necessarily an explicit action by the developer. Microsoft implemented many of the components within the Microsoft .NET Framework by creating a runtime callable wrapper (RCW) rather than rewriting all of the COM functionality within managed code. As a result, COM calls are often made unknowingly. To ensure that these calls are always made from a single-threaded apartment, it is generally a good practice to decorate the main method of all Windows Forms executables with the `System.STAThreadAttribute`.

Summary

In this chapter, we looked at various synchronization mechanisms and saw how a variety of classes are available to protect against race conditions. Coverage included the `lock` keyword, which leverages `System.Threading.Monitor` under the covers. Other synchronization classes include `System.Threading.Interlocked`, `System.Threading.Mutext`, `System.Threading.WaitHandle`, reset events, semaphores, and the concurrent collection classes.

In spite of all the progress made in improving multithreaded programming between early versions of .NET and today, synchronization of multithreaded programming remains complicated, with numerous pitfalls awaiting the unwary developer. To avoid these sand traps, several best practices have been identified, including consistently acquiring synchronization targets in the same order and wrapping static members with synchronization logic.

Before closing the chapter, we considered the `Task.Delay()` method, a .NET 4.5–introduced API for implementing a timer based on TAP.

The next chapter investigates another complex .NET technology: that of marshaling calls out of .NET and into unmanaged code using P/Invoke. In addition, it introduces a concept known as unsafe code, which C# uses to access memory pointers directly, as unmanaged code does (e.g., C++).

23

Platform Interoperability and Unsafe Code

C# has great capabilities, especially when you consider that the underlying framework is entirely managed. Sometimes, however, you need to escape out of all the safety that C# provides and step back into the world of memory addresses and pointers. C# supports this action in two significant ways. The first option is to go through Platform Invoke (P/Invoke) and calls into APIs exposed by unmanaged dynamic link libraries (DLLs). The second way is through **unsafe code**, which enables access to memory pointers and addresses.

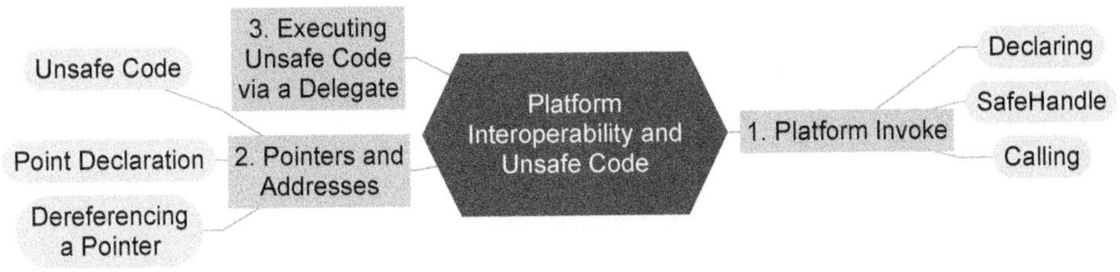

The majority of the chapter discusses interoperability with unmanaged code and the use of unsafe code. This discussion culminates with a small program that determines the processor ID of a computer. The code requires that you do the following:

1. Call into an operating system DLL and request allocation of a portion of memory for executing instructions.
2. Write some assembler instructions into the allocated area.
3. Inject an address location into the assembler instructions.
4. Execute the assembler code.

Aside from the P/Invoke and unsafe constructs covered here, the complete listing demonstrates the full power of C# and the fact that the capabilities of unmanaged code are still accessible from C# and managed code.

Platform Invoke

Whether a developer is trying to call a library of existing unmanaged code, accessing unmanaged code in the operating system not exposed in any managed API, or trying to achieve maximum performance for an algorithm by avoiding the runtime overhead of type checking and garbage collection, at some point there must be a call into unmanaged code. The Common Language Infrastructure (CLI) provides this capability through P/Invoke. With P/Invoke, you can make API calls into exported functions of unmanaged DLLs.

The APIs invoked in this section are Windows APIs. Although the same APIs are not available on other platforms, developers can still use P/Invoke for APIs native to their operating systems or for calls into their own DLLs. The guidelines and syntax are the same.

Declaring External Functions

Once the target function is identified, the next step of P/Invoke is to declare the function with managed code. Just as with all regular methods that belong to a class, you need to declare the targeted API within the context of a class, but by using the `extern` modifier. Listing 23.1 demonstrates how to do this.

In this case, the class is `VirtualMemoryManager`, because it will contain functions associated with managing memory. (This particular function is available directly off the System.Diagnostics.Processor class, so there is no need to

LISTING 23.1: Declaring an External Method

```
using System;
using System.Runtime.InteropServices;
public class VirtualMemoryManager
{
    [DllImport("kernel32.dll", EntryPoint = "GetCurrentProcess")]
    internal static extern IntPtr GetCurrentProcessHandle();
}
```

declare it in real code.) Note that the method returns an IntPtr; this type is explained in the next section.

The extern methods never include any body and are (almost) always static. Instead of a method body, the DllImport attribute, which accompanies the method declaration, points to the implementation. At a minimum, the attribute needs the name of the DLL that defines the function. The runtime determines the function name from the method name, although you can override this default by using the EntryPoint named parameter to provide the function name. (The .NET framework will automatically attempt calls to the Unicode [...W] or ASCII [...A] API version.)

In this case, the external function, GetCurrentProcess(), retrieves a pseudohandle for the current process that you will use in the call for virtual memory allocation. Here's the unmanaged declaration:

```
HANDLE GetCurrentProcess();
```

Parameter Data Types

Assuming the developer has identified the targeted DLL and exported function, the most difficult step is identifying or creating the managed data types that correspond to the unmanaged types in the external function.[1] Listing 23.2 shows a more difficult API.

Listing 23.2: The `VirtualAllocEx()` API

```
LPVOID VirtualAllocEx(
    HANDLE hProcess,          // The handle to a process. The
                              // function allocates memory within
                              // the virtual address space of this
                              // process.
    LPVOID lpAddress,         // The pointer that specifies a
                              // desired starting address for the
                              // region of pages that you want to
                              // allocate. If lpAddress is NULL,
                              // the function determines where to
                              // allocate the region.
    SIZE_T dwSize,            // The size of the region of memory to
                              // allocate, in bytes. If lpAddress
                              // is NULL, the function rounds dwSize
                              // up to the next page boundary.
    DWORD flAllocationType,   // The type of memory allocation
    DWORD flProtect);         // The type of memory allocation
```

`VirtualAllocEx()` allocates virtual memory that the operating system specifically designates for execution or data. To call it, you need corresponding definitions in managed code for each data type; although common in Win32 programming, `HANDLE`, `LPVOID`, `SIZE_T`, and `DWORD` are undefined in the CLI managed code. The declaration in C# for `VirtualAllocEx()`, therefore, is shown in Listing 23.3.

One distinct characteristic of managed code is that primitive data types such as `int` do not change their size on the basis of the processor. Whether the processor is 32 or 64 bits, `int` is always 32 bits. In unmanaged code, however, memory pointers

1. One particularly helpful resource for declaring Win32 APIs is https://github.com/microsoft/CsWin32. It provides a great starting point for many APIs, helping you avoid some of the subtle problems that can arise when coding an external API call from scratch.

will vary depending on the processor. Therefore, instead of mapping types such as

Listing 23.3: Declaring the `VirtualAllocEx()` API in C#

```
using System;
using System.Runtime.InteropServices;
public class VirtualMemoryManager
{
    [DllImport("kernel32.dll")]
    internal static extern IntPtr GetCurrentProcess();

    [DllImport("kernel32.dll", SetLastError = true)]
    private static extern IntPtr VirtualAllocEx(
        IntPtr hProcess,
        IntPtr lpAddress,
        IntPtr dwSize,
        AllocationType flAllocationType,
        uint flProtect);
}
```

`HANDLE` and `LPVOID` simply to `int`s, you need to map to `System.IntPtr`, whose size will vary depending on the processor memory layout. This example also uses an `AllocationType` enum, which we discuss in the section "Simplifying API Calls with Wrappers" later in this chapter.

An interesting point to note about Listing 23.3 is that `IntPtr` is useful for more than just pointers—that is, it is useful for other things such as quantities. `IntPtr` does not mean just "pointer stored in an integer"; it also means "integer that is the size of a pointer." An `IntPtr` need not contain a pointer but simply needs to contain something the size of a pointer. Lots of things are the size of a pointer but are not actually pointers.

Begin 9.0

Native sized integers

Begin 11.0

C# 9.0 introduced new contextual keywords, `nint` and `nunit` that represent native machine-size integers. These are both signed integers that will either be 32 or 64 bits depending on the running process. Internally `nint` and `nuint` are implemented with `System.IntPtr` and `System.UIntPtr`. In C# 11 these are updated to simply be aliases for the types they represent.

End 9.0

End 11.0

Using ref Rather Than Pointers

Frequently, unmanaged code uses pointers for pass-by-reference parameters. In these cases, P/Invoke doesn't require that you map the data type to a pointer in managed code. Instead, you map the corresponding parameters to `ref` (or `out`, depending on whether the parameter is `in/out` or just `out`). In Listing 23.4, `lpflOldProtect`, whose data type is `PDWORD`, returns the "pointer to a variable that receives the previous access protection of the first page in the specified region of pages."[2]

LISTING 23.4: Using `ref` and `out` Rather Than Pointers

```
public class VirtualMemoryManager
{
    // ...
    [DllImport("kernel32.dll", SetLastError = true)]
    static extern bool VirtualProtectEx(
        IntPtr hProcess, IntPtr lpAddress,
        IntPtr dwSize, uint flNewProtect,
        ref uint lpflOldProtect);
}
```

Although `lpflOldProtect` is documented as `[out]` (even though the signature doesn't enforce it), the description also mentions that the parameter must point to a valid variable and not `NULL`. This inconsistency is confusing but commonly encountered. The guideline is to use `ref` rather than `out` for P/Invoke type parameters, since the callee can always ignore the data passed with `ref`, but the converse will not necessarily succeed.

The other parameters are virtually the same as `VirtualAllocEx()` except that `lpAddress` is the address returned from `VirtualAllocEx()`. In addition, `flNewProtect` specifies the exact type of memory protection: page execute, page read-only, and so on.

2. MSDN documentation.

Using `StructLayoutAttribute` for Sequential Layout

Some APIs involve types that have no corresponding managed type. Calling these types requires redeclaration of the type in managed code. You declare the unmanaged `COLORREF` struct, for example, in managed code (see Listing 23.5).

Listing 23.5: Declaring Types from Unmanaged Structs

```
[StructLayout(LayoutKind.Sequential)]
struct ColorRef
{
    public byte Red;
    public byte Green;
    public byte Blue;
    // Turn off the warning about not accessing Unused
gma warning disable 414
    private byte Unused;
gma warning restore 414

    public ColorRef(byte red, byte green, byte blue)
    {
        Blue = blue;
        Green = green;
        Red = red;
        Unused = 0;
    }
}
```

Various Microsoft Windows color APIs use `COLORREF` to represent RGB colors (i.e., levels of red, green, and blue).

The key in the Listing 23.5 declaration is `StructLayoutAttribute`. By default, managed code can optimize the memory layouts of types, so layouts may not be sequential from one field to the next. To force sequential layouts so that a type maps directly and can be copied bit for bit (blitted) from managed to unmanaged code, and vice versa, you add the `StructLayoutAttribute` with the `LayoutKind.Sequential` enum value. (This is also useful when writing data to and from filestreams where a sequential layout may be expected.)

Since the unmanaged (C++) definition for `struct` does not map to the C# definition, there is no direct mapping of unmanaged struct to managed struct. Instead, developers should follow the usual C# guidelines about whether the type should behave like a value or a reference type, and whether the size is small (approximately less than 16 bytes).

Begin 12.0

Inline Arrays

Often it can be helpful to declare struct types as buffers. With C# 12.0 structs can be decorated so that they can be used as a fixed size array. Inline arrays are implicitly convertible to `Span<T>` or `ReadOnlySpan<T>` as an easy way to interact with the inline array. You can also directly access the elements in the inline array with a familiar indexer syntax, including ranges and index for reading and writing elements. To create an inline array, declare a struct with a single field and decorated with the `System.Runtime.CompilerServices.InlineArrayAttribute` specifying the size of the inline array in the attribute.

End 12.0

Skip Initializing Locals

Begin 9.0

Since C# 1.0, local variables have been initialized to zero values. However, in some high-performance situations, these zero initialized values are then overridden. C# 9.0 introduced a new `SkipLocalsInitAttribute`. This attribute will result in the compiler not outputting the `localsinit` CIL flag. The result is that locals may not be zero initialized. Accessing uninitialized data is discouraged because the behavior is undefined.

Error Handling

End 9.0

One inconvenient aspect of Win32 API programming is the fact that the APIs frequently report errors in inconsistent ways. For example, some APIs return a value (`0`, `1`, `false`, and so on) to indicate an error, whereas others set an `out` parameter in some way. Furthermore, the details of what went wrong require additional calls to the `GetLastError()` API and then an additional call to `FormatMessage()` to retrieve an error message corresponding to the error. In summary, Win32 error reporting in unmanaged code seldom occurs via exceptions.

Fortunately, the P/Invoke designers provided a mechanism for error handling. To enable it, if the `SetLastError` named parameter of the `DllImport` attribute is `true`, it is possible to instantiate a `System.ComponentModel`

.Win32Exception() that is automatically initialized with the Win32 error data immediately following the P/Invoke call (see Listing 23.6).

Listing 23.6: Win32 Error Handling

```
public class VirtualMemoryManager
{
    [DllImport("kernel32.dll", SetLastError = true)]
    private static extern IntPtr VirtualAllocEx(
        IntPtr hProcess,
        IntPtr lpAddress,
        IntPtr dwSize,
        AllocationType flAllocationType,
        uint flProtect);

    // ...
    [DllImport("kernel32.dll", SetLastError = true)]
    static extern bool VirtualProtectEx(
        IntPtr hProcess, IntPtr lpAddress,
        IntPtr dwSize, uint flNewProtect,
        ref uint lpflOldProtect);

    [Flags]
    private enum AllocationType : uint
    {
        // ...
    }

    [Flags]
    private enum ProtectionOptions
    {
        // ...
    }

    [Flags]
    private enum MemoryFreeType
    {
        // ...
    }

    public static IntPtr AllocExecutionBlock(
        int size, IntPtr hProcess)
    {
        IntPtr codeBytesPtr;
        codeBytesPtr = VirtualAllocEx(
            hProcess, IntPtr.Zero,
```

```
            (IntPtr)size,
            AllocationType.Reserve | AllocationType.Commit,
            (uint)ProtectionOptions.PageExecuteReadWrite);

        if (codeBytesPtr == IntPtr.Zero)
        {
            throw new System.ComponentModel.Win32Exception();
        }

        uint lpflOldProtect = 0;
        if (!VirtualProtectEx(
            hProcess, codeBytesPtr,
            (IntPtr)size,
            (uint)ProtectionOptions.PageExecuteReadWrite,
            ref lpflOldProtect))
        {
            throw new System.ComponentModel.Win32Exception();
        }
        return codeBytesPtr;
    }

    public static IntPtr AllocExecutionBlock(int size)
    {
        return AllocExecutionBlock(
            size, GetCurrentProcessHandle());
    }

    // ...
}
```

This code enables developers to provide the custom error checking that each API uses while still reporting the error in a standard manner.

Listing 23.1 and Listing 23.3 declared the P/Invoke methods as internal or private. Except for the simplest of APIs, wrapping methods in public wrappers that reduce the complexity of the P/Invoke API calls is a good guideline that increases API usability and moves toward object-oriented type structure. The `AllocExecutionBlock()` declaration in Listing 23.6 provides a good example of this approach.

Guidelines

DO create public managed wrappers around unmanaged methods that use the conventions of managed code, such as structured exception handling.

Using SafeHandle

Frequently, P/Invoke involves a resource, such as a handle, that code needs to clean up after using. Instead of requiring developers to remember this step is necessary and manually code it each time, it is helpful to provide a class that implements `IDisposable` and a finalizer. In Listing 23.7, for example, the address returned after `VirtualAllocEx()` and `VirtualProtectEx()` requires a follow-up call to `VirtualFreeEx()`. To provide built-in support for this process, you define a `VirtualMemoryPtr` class that derives from `System.Runtime.InteropServices.SafeHandle`.

Listing 23.7: Managed Resources Using SafeHandle

```
public class VirtualMemoryPtr :
  System.Runtime.InteropServices.SafeHandle
{
    public VirtualMemoryPtr(int memorySize) :
        base(IntPtr.Zero, true)
    {
        _ProcessHandle =
            VirtualMemoryManager.GetCurrentProcessHandle();
        _MemorySize = (IntPtr)memorySize;
        _AllocatedPointer =
            VirtualMemoryManager.AllocExecutionBlock(
            memorySize, ProcessHandle);
        _Disposed = false;
    }

    public readonly IntPtr _AllocatedPointer;
    private readonly IntPtr _ProcessHandle;
    private readonly IntPtr _MemorySize;
    private bool _Disposed;

    public static implicit operator IntPtr(
        VirtualMemoryPtr virtualMemoryPointer)
```

```
    {
        return virtualMemoryPointer.AllocatedPointer;
    }

    // SafeHandle abstract member
    public override bool IsInvalid
    {
        get
        {
            return _Disposed;
        }
    }

    // SafeHandle abstract member
    protected override bool ReleaseHandle()
    {
        if (!_Disposed)
        {
            _Disposed = true;
            GC.SuppressFinalize(this);
            VirtualMemoryManager.VirtualFreeEx(_ProcessHandle,
                _AllocatedPointer, _MemorySize);
        }
        return true;
    }
}
```

`System.Runtime.InteropServices.SafeHandle` includes the abstract members `IsInvalid` and `ReleaseHandle()`. You place your cleanup code in the latter; the former indicates whether this code has executed yet.

With `VirtualMemoryPtr`, you can allocate memory simply by instantiating the type and specifying the needed memory allocation.

Calling External Functions

Once you declare the P/Invoke functions, you invoke them just as you would any other class member. The key, however, is that the imported DLL must be in the path, including the executable directory, so that it can be successfully loaded. Listing 23.6 and Listing 23.7 demonstrate this approach. However, they rely on some constants.

Since `flAllocationType` and `flProtect` are flags, it is a good practice to provide constants or enums for each. Instead of expecting the caller to define these constants or enums, encapsulation suggests that you provide them as part of the API declaration, as shown in Listing 23.8.

LISTING 23.8: Encapsulating the APIs Together

```
public class VirtualMemoryManager
{
    // ...

    /// <summary>
    /// The type of memory allocation. This parameter must
    /// contain one of the following values.
    /// </summary>
    [Flags]
    private enum AllocationType : uint
    {
        /// <summary>
        /// Allocates physical storage in memory or in the
        /// paging file on disk for the specified reserved
        /// memory pages. The function initializes the memory
        /// to zero.
        /// </summary>
        Commit = 0x1000,
        /// <summary>
        /// Reserves a range of the process's virtual address
        /// space without allocating any actual physical
        /// storage in memory or in the paging file on disk.
        /// </summary>
        Reserve = 0x2000,
        /// <summary>
        /// Indicates that data in the memory range specified by
        /// lpAddress and dwSize is no longer of interest. The
        /// pages should not be read from or written to the
        /// paging file. However, the memory block will be used
        /// again later, so it should not be decommitted. This
        /// value cannot be used with any other value.
        /// </summary>
        Reset = 0x80000,
        /// <summary>
        /// Allocates physical memory with read-write access.
        /// This value is solely for use with Address Windowing
        /// Extensions (AWE) memory.
        /// </summary>
        Physical = 0x400000,
```

```
        /// <summary>
        /// Allocates memory at the highest possible address.
        /// </summary>
        TopDown = 0x100000,
    }

    /// <summary>
    /// The memory protection for the region of pages to be
    /// allocated.
    /// </summary>
    [Flags]
    private enum ProtectionOptions : uint
    {
        /// <summary>
        /// Enables execute access to the committed region of
        /// pages. An attempt to read or write to the committed
        /// region results in an access violation.
        /// </summary>
        Execute = 0x10,
        /// <summary>
        /// Enables execute and read access to the committed
        /// region of pages. An attempt to write to the
        /// committed region results in an access violation.
        /// </summary>
        PageExecuteRead = 0x20,
        /// <summary>
        /// Enables execute, read, and write access to the
        /// committed region of pages.
        /// </summary>
        PageExecuteReadWrite = 0x40,
        // ...
    }

    /// <summary>
    /// The type of free operation.
    /// </summary>
    [Flags]
    private enum MemoryFreeType : uint
    {
        /// <summary>
        /// Decommits the specified region of committed pages.
        /// After the operation, the pages are in the reserved
        /// state.
        /// </summary>
        Decommit = 0x4000,
        /// <summary>
        /// Releases the specified region of pages. After this
```

```
        /// operation, the pages are in the free state.
        /// </summary>
        Release = 0x8000
    }

    // ...
}
```

The advantage of enums is that they group together the various values. Furthermore, they can limit the scope to nothing else besides these values.

Simplifying API Calls with Wrappers

Whether they are focused on error handling, structs, or constant values, one goal of effective API developers is to provide a simplified managed API that wraps the underlying Win32 API. For example, Listing 23.9 overloads `VirtualFreeEx()` with public versions that simplify the call.

Listing 23.9: Wrapping the Underlying API

```
public class VirtualMemoryManager
{
    // ...

    [DllImport("kernel32.dll", SetLastError = true)]
    static extern bool VirtualFreeEx(
        IntPtr hProcess, IntPtr lpAddress,
        IntPtr dwSize, IntPtr dwFreeType);
    public static bool VirtualFreeEx(
        IntPtr hProcess, IntPtr lpAddress,
        IntPtr dwSize)
    {
        bool result = VirtualFreeEx(
            hProcess, lpAddress, dwSize,
            (IntPtr)MemoryFreeType.Decommit);
        if (!result)
        {
            throw new System.ComponentModel.Win32Exception();
        }
        return result;
    }
    public static bool VirtualFreeEx(
        IntPtr lpAddress, IntPtr dwSize)
    {
```

```
            return VirtualFreeEx(
                GetCurrentProcessHandle(), lpAddress, dwSize);
        }

        [DllImport("kernel32", SetLastError = true)]
        static extern IntPtr VirtualAllocEx(
            IntPtr hProcess,
            IntPtr lpAddress,
            IntPtr dwSize,
            AllocationType flAllocationType,
            uint flProtect);

        // ...
    }
```

Function Pointers Map to Delegates

One last key point related to P/Invoke is that function pointers in unmanaged code map to delegates in managed code. To set up a timer, for example, you would provide a function pointer that the timer could call back on, once it had expired. Specifically, you would pass a delegate instance that matches the signature of the callback.

Begin 11.0

C# 11 introduced an additional construct for storing pointers to functions. These function pointers can provide a performance improvement over using delegates to invoke methods. These are only available in unsafe code which is covered in more detail later in this chapter.

End 11.0

Guidelines

Given the idiosyncrasies of P/Invoke, there are several guidelines to aid in the process of writing such code.

Guidelines

DO NOT unnecessarily replicate existing managed classes that already perform the function of the unmanaged API.

DO declare `extern` methods as private or internal.

DO provide public wrapper methods that use managed conventions such as structured exception handling, use of enums for special values, and so on.

DO simplify the wrapper methods by choosing default values for unnecessary parameters.

DO use the `SetLastErrorAttribute` on `Windows` to turn APIs that use `SetLastError` error codes into methods that throw `Win32Exception`.

DO extend `SafeHandle` or implement `IDisposable` and create a finalizer to ensure that unmanaged resources can be cleaned up effectively.

DO use delegate types that match the signature of the desired method when an unmanaged API requires a function pointer.

DO use `ref` parameters rather than pointer types when possible.

Pointers and Addresses

On occasion, developers may want to access and work with memory, and with pointers to memory locations, directly. This is necessary, for example, for certain operating system interactions as well as with certain types of time-critical algorithms. To support this capability, C# requires use of the unsafe code construct.

Unsafe Code

One of C#'s great features is the fact that it is strongly typed and supports type checking throughout the runtime execution. What makes this feature especially beneficial is that it is possible to circumvent this support and manipulate memory and addresses directly. You would do so when working with memory-mapped devices, for example, or if you wanted to implement time-critical algorithms. The key is to designate a portion of the code as unsafe.

Unsafe code is an explicit code block and compilation option, as shown in Listing 23.10. The `unsafe` modifier has no effect on the generated CIL code itself, but rather is a directive to the compiler to permit pointer and address manipulation within the unsafe block. Furthermore, *unsafe* does not imply *unmanaged.*

You can use `unsafe` as a modifier to the type or to specific members within the type.

Listing 23.10: Designating a Method for Unsafe Code

```
public class Program
{
    unsafe static int Main(string[] args)
    {
        // ...
    }
}
```

In addition, C# allows `unsafe` as a statement that flags a code block to allow unsafe code (see Listing 23.11).

Listing 23.11: Designating a Code Block for Unsafe Code

```
public class Program
{
    static int Main(string[] args)
    {
        unsafe
        {
            // ...
        }
    }
}
```

Code within the `unsafe` block can include unsafe constructs such as pointers.

> **NOTE**
>
> It is necessary to explicitly indicate to the compiler that unsafe code is supported.

When you write unsafe code, your code becomes vulnerable to the possibility of buffer overflows and similar outcomes that may potentially expose security holes. For this reason, it is necessary to explicitly notify the compiler that unsafe code occurs. To accomplish this, set `AllowUnsafeBlocks` to `true` in your CSPROJ file, as shown in Listing 23.12. Alternatively, you can pass the property on the command line when running `dotnet build` (see Output 23.1). Or, if invoking the C# compiler directly, you need the `/unsafe` switch (see Output 23.2).

Listing 23.12: Invalid Referent Type Example

```
<Project Sdk = "Microsoft.NET.Sdk" >
  <PropertyGroup>
    <OutputType>Exe</OutputType>
    <TargetFramework>netcoreapp1.0</TargetFramework>
    <ProductName>Chapter20</ProductName>
    <WarningLevel>2</WarningLevel>
    <AllowUnsafeBlocks>True</AllowUnsafeBlocks>
  </PropertyGroup>
  <Import Project = "..\Versioning.targets"/>
  <ItemGroup>
    <ProjectReference Include="..\SharedCode\SharedCode.csproj"/>
  </ItemGroup>
</Project>
```

Output 23.1

```
dotnet build /property:AllowUnsafeBlocks=True
```

Output 23.2

```
csc.exe /unsafe Program.cs
```

With Visual Studio, you can activate this feature by checking the Allow Unsafe Code checkbox from the Build tab of the Project Properties window.

The `/unsafe` switch enables you to directly manipulate memory and execute instructions that are unmanaged. Requiring `/unsafe`, therefore, makes explicit any exposure to potential security vulnerabilities that such code might introduce. With great power comes great responsibility.

Pointer Declaration

Now that you have marked a code block as unsafe, it is time to look at how to write unsafe code. First, unsafe code allows the declaration of a pointer. Consider the following example:

```
byte* pData;
```

Assuming `pData` is not `null`, its value points to a location that contains one or more sequential `bytes`; the value of `pData` represents the memory address of the bytes. The type specified before the * is the **referent type**—that is, the type located where the value of the pointer refers. In this example, pData is the pointer and byte is the referent type, as shown in Figure 23.1.

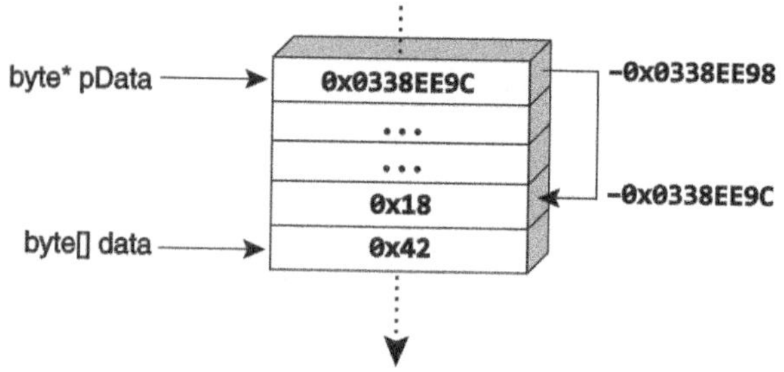

FIGURE 23.1: Pointers contain the address of the data

Because pointers are simply integers that happen to refer to a memory address, they are not subject to garbage collection. C# does not allow referent types other than **unmanaged types**, which are types that are not reference types, are not generics, and do not contain reference types. Therefore, the following command is not valid:

```
string* pMessage;
```

Likewise, this command is not valid:

```
ServiceStatus* pStatus;
```

where ServiceStatus is defined as shown in Listing 23.13. The problem, once again, is that ServiceStatus includes a string field.

LISTING 23.13: Invalid Referent Type Example

```
struct ServiceStatus
{
    int State;
    string Description;  // Description is a reference type
}
```

Language Contrast: C/C++—Pointer Declaration

In C/C++, multiple pointers within the same declaration are declared as follows:

```
int *p1, *p2;
```

Notice the `*` on `p2`; this makes `p2` an `int*` rather than an `int`. In contrast, C# always places the `*` with the data type:

```
int* p1, p2;
```

The result is two variables of type `int*`. The syntax matches that of declaring multiple arrays in a single statement:

```
int[] array1, array2;
```

Pointers are an entirely new category of type. Unlike structs, enums, and classes, pointers don't ultimately derive from `System.Object` and are not even convertible to `System.Object`. Instead, they are convertible (explicitly) to `System.IntPtr` (which can be converted to `System.Object`).

In addition to custom structs that contain only unmanaged types, valid referent types include enums, predefined value types (`sbyte`, `byte`, `short`, `ushort`, `int`, `uint`, `long`, `ulong`, `char`, `float`, `double`, `decimal`, and `bool`), and pointer types (such as `byte**`). Lastly, valid syntax includes `void*` pointers, which represent pointers to an unknown type.

Assigning a Pointer

Once code defines a pointer, it needs to assign a value before accessing it. Just like reference types, pointers can hold the value `null`, which is their default value. The value stored by the pointer is the address of a location. Therefore, to assign the pointer, you must first retrieve the address of the data.

You could explicitly cast an `int` or a `long` into a pointer, but this rarely occurs without a means of determining the address of a particular data value at execution time. Instead, you need to use the address operator (`&`) to retrieve the address of the value type:

```
byte* pData = &bytes[0]; // Compile error
```

The problem is that in a managed environment, data can move, thereby invalidating the address. The resulting error message will be "You can only take the address of [an] unfixed expression inside a fixed statement initializer." In this case, the byte referenced appears within an array, and an array is a reference type (a movable type). Reference types appear on the heap and are subject to garbage collection or relocation. A similar problem occurs when referring to a value type field on a movable type:

```
int* a = &"message".Length;
```

Either way, assigning an address of some data requires that the following criteria are met:

- The data must be classified as a variable.
- The data must be an unmanaged type.
- The variable needs to be classified as fixed, not movable.

If the data is an unmanaged variable type but is not fixed, use the `fixed` statement to fix a movable variable.

Fixing Data

To retrieve the address of a movable data item, it is necessary to fix, or pin, the data, as demonstrated in Listing 23.14.

Listing 23.14: Fixed Statement

```
byte[] bytes = new byte[24];
fixed (byte* pData = &bytes[0]) //pData = bytes also allowed
{
  // ...
}
```

Within the code block of a `fixed` statement, the assigned data will not move. In this example, `bytes` will remain at the same address, at least until the end of the `fixed` statement.

The `fixed` statement requires the declaration of the pointer variable within its scope. This avoids accessing the variable outside the `fixed` statement, when the data is no longer fixed. However, as a programmer, you are responsible for ensuring that you do not assign the pointer to another variable that survives beyond the scope of the `fixed` statement—possibly in an API call, for example. Unsafe code is called "unsafe" for a reason; you must ensure that you use the pointers safely, rather than relying on the runtime to enforce safety on your behalf. Similarly, using `ref` or `out` parameters will be problematic for data that will not survive beyond the method call.

Since a string is an invalid referent type, it would appear to be invalid to define pointers to strings. However, as in C++, internally a string is a pointer to the first character of an array of characters, and it is possible to declare pointers to characters using `char*`. Therefore, C# allows for declaring a pointer of type `char*` and assigning it to a string within a `fixed` statement. The `fixed` statement prevents the movement of the string during the life of the pointer. Similarly, it allows any movable type that supports an implicit conversion to a pointer of another type, given a fixed statement.

You can replace the verbose assignment of `&bytes[0]` with the abbreviated `bytes`, as shown in Listing 23.15.

LISTING 23.15: A `fixed` Statement without Address or Array Indexer

```
byte[] bytes = new byte[24];
fixed (byte* pData = bytes)
{
    // ...
}
```

Depending on the frequency and time needed for their execution, `fixed` statements may have the potential to cause fragmentation in the heap because the garbage collector cannot compact fixed objects. To reduce this problem, the best practice is to pin blocks early in the execution and to pin fewer large blocks rather than many small blocks. Unfortunately, this preference must be tempered with the practice of pinning as little as possible for as short a time as possible, so as to minimize the chance that a collection will happen during the time that the data is pinned. To some extent, .NET 2.0 reduces this problem through its inclusion of some additional fragmentation-aware code.

Potentially you might need to fix an object in place in one method body and have it remain fixed until another method is called; this is not possible with the `fixed` statement. If you are in this unfortunate situation, you can use methods on the `GCHandle` object to fix an object in place indefinitely. You should do so only if it is absolutely necessary, however; fixing an object for a long time makes it highly likely that the garbage collector will be unable to efficiently compact memory.

Allocating on the Stack

You should use the `fixed` statement on an array to prevent the garbage collector from moving the data. However, an alternative is to allocate the array on the call stack. Stack allocated data is not subject to garbage collection or to the finalizer patterns that accompany it. Like referent types, the requirement is that the `stackalloc` data is an array of unmanaged types. For example, instead of allocating an array of bytes on the heap, you can place it onto the call stack, as shown in Listing 23.16.

Listing 23.16: Allocating Data on the Call Stack

```
byte* bytes = stackalloc byte[42];
```

Because the data type is an array of unmanaged types, the runtime can allocate a fixed buffer size for the array and then restore that buffer once the pointer goes out of scope. Specifically, it allocates `sizeof(T) * E`, where `E` is the array size and `T` is the referent type. Given the requirement of using `stackalloc` only on an array of unmanaged types, the runtime restores the buffer back to the system by simply unwinding the stack, thereby eliminating the complexities of iterating over the f-reachable queue (see the "Garbage Collection" section and discussion of finalization in Chapter 10) and compacting reachable data. Thus, there is no way to explicitly free `stackalloc` data.

The stack is a precious resource. Although it is small, running out of stack space will have a big effect—namely, the program will crash. For this reason, you should make every effort to avoid running out stack space. If a program does run out of stack space, the best thing that can happen is for the program to shut down/crash immediately. Generally, programs have less than 1MB of stack space (and possibly a lot less). Therefore, take great care to avoid allocating arbitrarily sized buffers on the stack.

Dereferencing a Pointer

Accessing the data stored in a variable of a type referred to by a pointer requires that you dereference the pointer, placing the indirection operator prior to the expression. For example, `byte data = *pData;` dereferences the location of the `byte` referred to by `pData` and produces a variable of type `byte`. The variable provides read/write access to the single `byte` at that location.

Using this principle in unsafe code allows the unorthodox behavior of modifying the "immutable" string, as shown in Listing 23.17 with Output 23.3. In no way is this strategy recommended, even though it does expose the potential of low-level memory manipulation.

LISTING 23.17: Modifying an Immutable String

```
string text = "S5280ft";
Console.Write("{0} = ", text);
unsafe // Requires /unsafe switch
{
    fixed(char* pText = text)
    {
        char* p = pText;
        *++p = 'm';
        *++p = 'i';
        *++p = 'l';
        *++p = 'e';
        *++p = ' ';
        *++p = ' ';
    }
}
Console.WriteLine(text);
```

OUTPUT 23.3

```
S5280ft = Smile
```

In this case, you take the original address and increment it by the size of the referent type (`sizeof(char)`), using the pre-increment operator. Next, you dereference the address using the indirection operator and then assign the location with a different character. Similarly, using the + and – operators on a pointer changes the address by the * `sizeof(T)` operand, where T is the referent type.

The comparison operators (==, !=, <, >, <=, and >=) also work to compare pointers. Thus, their use effectively translates to a comparison of address location values.

One restriction on the dereferencing operator is the inability to dereference a `void*`. The `void*` data type represents a pointer to an unknown type. Since the data type is unknown, it can't be dereferenced to produce a variable. Instead, to access the data referenced by a `void*`, you must convert it to another pointer type and then dereference the latter type.

You can achieve the same behavior as implemented in Listing 23.17 by using the index operator rather than the indirection operator (see Listing 23.18 with Output 23.4).

Listing 23.18: Modifying an Immutable String with the Index Operator in Unsafe Code

```
string text = "S5280ft";
Console.Write("{0} = ", text);
unsafe // Requires /unsafe switch
{
    fixed(char* pText = text)
    {
        pText[1] = 'm';
        pText[2] = 'i';
        pText[3] = 'l';
        pText[4] = 'e';
        pText[5] = ' ';
        pText[6] = ' ';
    }
}
Console.WriteLine(text);
```

Output 23.4

```
S5280ft = Smile
```

Modifications such as those in Listing 23.17 and Listing 23.18 can lead to unexpected behavior. For example, if you reassigned `text` to `"S5280ft"` following the `Console.WriteLine()` statement and then redisplayed `text`, the output would still be `Smile` because the address of two equal string literals is optimized to one string literal referenced by both variables. In spite of the apparent assignment

```
text = "S5280ft";
```

after the unsafe code in Listing 23.17, the internals of the string assignment are an address assignment of the modified `"S5280ft"` location, so `text` is never set to the intended value.

Accessing the Member of a Referent Type

Dereferencing a pointer produces a variable of the pointer's underlying type. You can then access the members of the underlying type using the member access dot operator in the usual way. However, the rules of operator precedence require that `*x.y` means `*(x.y)`, which is probably not what you intended. If `x` is a pointer, the correct code is `(*x).y`, which is an unpleasant syntax. To make it easier to access members of a dereferenced pointer, C# provides a special member access operator: `x->y` is a shorthand for `(*x).y`, as shown in Listing 23.19 with Output 23.5.

Listing 23.19: Directly Accessing a Referent Type's Members

```
unsafe
{
    Angle angle = new(30, 18, 0);
    Angle* pAngle = &angle;
    System.Console.WriteLine("{0}° {1}' {2}\"",
        pAngle->Hours, pAngle->Minutes, pAngle->Seconds);
}
```

Output 23.5

```
30° 18' 0
```

Executing Unsafe Code via a Delegate

As promised at the beginning of this chapter, we finish up with a full working example of what is likely the most "unsafe" thing you can do in C#: obtain a pointer to a block of memory, fill it with the bytes of machine code, make a function pointer that refers to the new code, and invoke it. In this example, we use assembly code to determine the processor ID. If run on a Windows machine, it prints the processor ID. Listing 23.20 shows how to do it (results shown in Output 23.6).

Listing 23.20: Designating a Block for Unsafe Code

```
using System;
using System.Runtime.InteropServices;
using System.Text;

public class Program
{
    public unsafe static int Main()
    {
        if (RuntimeInformation.IsOSPlatform(OSPlatform.Windows))
        {
            unsafe
            {
                byte[] codeBytes = new byte[] {
                0x49, 0x89, 0xd8,       // mov    %rbx,%r8
                0x49, 0x89, 0xc9,       // mov    %rcx,%r9
                0x48, 0x31, 0xc0,       // xor    %rax,%rax
                0x0f, 0xa2,             // cpuid
                0x4c, 0x89, 0xc8,       // mov    %r9,%rax
                0x89, 0x18,             // mov    %ebx,0x0(%rax)
                0x89, 0x50, 0x04,       // mov    %edx,0x4(%rax)
                0x89, 0x48, 0x08,       // mov    %ecx,0x8(%rax)
                0x4c, 0x89, 0xc3,       // mov    %r8,%rbx
                0xc3                    // retq
                };

                Buffer buffer = new();
                using (VirtualMemoryPtr codeBytesPtr =
                    new(codeBytes.Length))
                {
                    Marshal.Copy(
                        codeBytes, 0,
                        codeBytesPtr, codeBytes.Length);

                    delegate*<byte*, void> method = (delegate*<byte*,
```

```
↪void>)(IntPtr)codeBytesPtr;
                    method(&buffer[0]);
                }
                Console.Write("Processor Id: ");
                char[] chars = new char[Buffer.Length];
                Encoding.ASCII.GetChars(buffer, chars);
                Console.WriteLine(chars);
            } // unsafe
        }
        else
        {
            Console.WriteLine("This sample is only valid for Windows");
        }
        return 0;
    }
}

[System.Runtime.CompilerServices.InlineArrayAttribute(Length)]
public struct Buffer
{
    public const int Length = 10;

    private byte _element0;
}
```

Output 23.6

```
Processor Id: GenuineIntel
```

Summary

As demonstrated throughout this book, C# offers great power, flexibility, consistency, and a fantastic structure. This chapter highlighted the ability of C# programs to perform very low-level machine-code operations.

Before we end the book, Chapter 24 briefly describes the underlying execution framework and shifts the focus from the C# language to the broader context in which C# programs execute.

24

The Common Language Infrastructure

One of the first items that C# programmers encounter beyond the syntax is the context under which a C# program executes. This chapter discusses the underpinnings of how C# handles memory allocation and de-allocation, type checking, interoperability with other languages, cross-platform execution, and support for programming metadata. In other words, this chapter investigates the Common Language Infrastructure on which C# relies both at compile time and during execution. It covers the execution engine that governs a C# program at runtime and considers how C# fits into a broader set of languages that are governed by the same execution engine. Because of C#'s close ties with this infrastructure, most of the features that come with the infrastructure are made available to C#.

Defining the Common Language Infrastructure

Instead of generating instructions that a processor can interpret directly, the C# compiler generates instructions in an intermediate language, the Common Intermediate Language (CIL). A second compilation step then occurs, generally at execution time, that converts the CIL to machine code that the processor can understand. Conversion to machine code is still not sufficient for code execution, however. It is also necessary for a C# program to execute under the context of an agent. The agent responsible for managing the execution of a C# program is the Virtual Execution System (VES), more casually referred to as the runtime. (Note that the runtime in this context does not refer to a specific time, such as execution time;

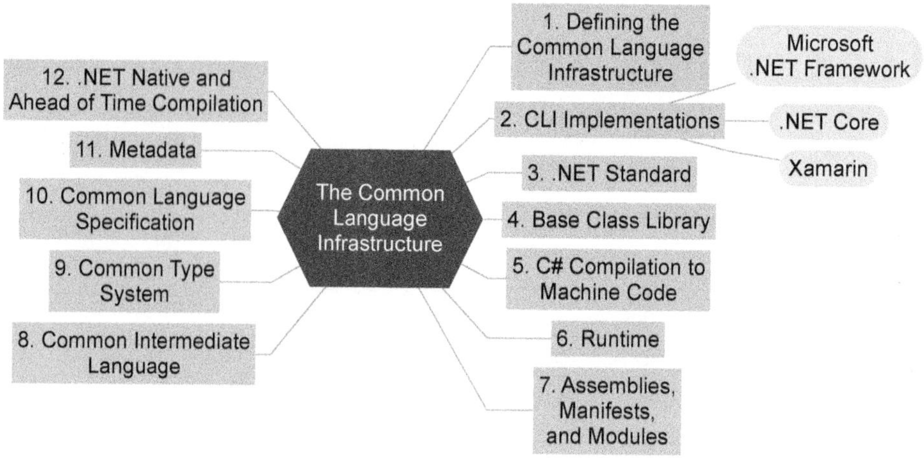

rather, the runtime—the VES—is an agent responsible for managing the execution of a C# program.) The runtime is responsible for loading and running programs and providing additional services (security, garbage collection, and so on) to the program as it executes.

The specifications for the CIL and the runtime are contained within an international standard known as the **Common Language Infrastructure (CLI)**.[1] The CLI is a key specification for understanding the context in which a C# program executes and how it can seamlessly interact with other programs and libraries, even when they are written in other languages. Note that the CLI does not prescribe the implementation for the standard but rather identifies the requirements for how a CLI framework should behave once it conforms to the standard. This provides CLI implementers with the flexibility to innovate where necessary while still providing enough structure that programs created by one CLI implementation can execute on a different implementation and even on a different operating system.

---

1. Throughout the chapter, CLI refers to Common Language Infrastructure rather than command-line interface as in dotnet CLI.

NOTE

Note the similarity between the CIL and CLI acronyms and the names they stand for. Distinguishing between them now will help you avoid confusion later.

Contained within the CLI standard are specifications for the following:

- The Virtual Execution System
- The Common Intermediate Language
- The Common Type System
- The Common Language Specification
- Metadata
- The framework

This chapter broadens your view of C# to include the CLI, which is critical to how C# programs operate and interact with programs and with the operating system.

CLI Implementations

The primary implementations of the CLI today are next generation .NET, which runs on Windows, Linux and Mac OS; the .NET Framework for Windows; and .NET Multi-platform App UI (MAUI), which is intended as a general cross-platform solution including iOS, macOS, and Android applications. Each implementation of the CLI includes a C# compiler and a set of framework class libraries. The version of C# supported by each, as well as the exact set of classes in the libraries, varies considerably, and many implementations are now only of historical interest. Table 24.1 describes these implementations.

TABLE 24.1: Implementations of the CLI

Compiler	Description
.NET	After .NET Core version 3.1, the next release was .NET 5. Version number 4 was skipped to avoid any confusion with existing .NET Framework versions. It is cross platform running on Microsoft Windows, macOS, and Linux. It supports desktop, service, and cloud applications.
.NET Multi-platform App UI (MAUI)	MAUI was the successor to Xamarin, allowing cross platform native applications to be written in Microsoft Windows, iOS, macOS, and Android. Its tooling allows for a single code base to be used for all applications, enabling a high degree of code reuse.
Blazor	Blazor supports running .NET code within a browser. It offers various hosting models, including Server, WebAssembly, and Hybrid models. See https://learn.microsoft.com/aspnet/core/blazor/hosting-models for more details. WebAssembly is an open standard that allows executing byte code within a web browser. See https://webassembly.org/ for more details.
.NET Core/CoreCLR	The .NET Core project, as the name implies, contains the core functionality common to a new implementation of .NET. It is an open source and platform-portable rewrite of the .NET Framework designed for high-performance applications. The CoreCLR is the implementation of the CLR for this project. It encompasses versions up through .NET Core 3.1 and has been released for Windows, macOS, Linux, FreeBSD, and NetBSD. However, some of the APIs, such as WPF, only work on Windows. See https://github.com/dotnet/coreclr for more details.
Microsoft .NET Framework	This traditional (and first) version of the CLR is for creating applications that run on Windows. It includes support for Windows Presentation Foundation (WPF), Windows Forms, and ASP.NET. It uses the .NET Framework Base Class Library (BCL).
Mono	An open source, cross-platform implementation of the CLI for many UNIX-based operating systems, mobile operating systems such as Android, and game consoles such as PlayStation and Xbox.

Table 24.1: Implementations of the CLI (continued)

Compiler	Description
Xamarin	A set of development tools and platform-portable .NET libraries as well as an implementation of the CLR that helps developers create applications that run on Microsoft Windows, iOS, macOS, and Android platforms with a very high degree of code reuse. Xamarin uses the Mono BCL. Xamarin reached end of support in May of 2024.
Microsoft Silverlight	A legacy cross-platform implementation of the CLI intended for creating browser-based web client applications. Microsoft stopped developing Silverlight in 2013.
.NET Compact Framework	A legacy trimmed-down implementation of the .NET Framework designed to run on PDAs, phones, and Xbox 360. The XNA library and tools for developing Xbox 360 applications are based on the Compact Framework 2.0 release; Microsoft stopped development of XNA in 2013.
.NET Micro Framework	Microsoft's open source implementation of the CLI for devices so resource constrained that they cannot run the compact framework.
DotGNU Portable.NET	This effort to create a cross-platform implementation of the CLI was decommissioned in 2012.
Shared Source CLI (Rotor)	Between 2001 and 2006, Microsoft released shared-source reference implementations of the CLI licensed for noncommercial use.

While the list is extensive considering the work required to implement the CLI, just three frameworks are the most relevant going forward.

Microsoft .NET Framework

The Microsoft .NET Framework was the first .NET CLI implementation (released in February 2000). As such, it is the most mature framework and has the largest API set. It supports building web, console, and Microsoft Windows client applications. The biggest limitation of the .NET Framework is that it runs on Microsoft Windows only —in fact, it is bundled with Microsoft Windows. Numerous sub-frameworks are included with the Microsoft .NET Framework; the most prominent are described here:

- **.NET Framework Base Class Library (BCL):** Provides types representing the built-in CLI data types, which include support for file IO, fundamental collections classes, custom attributes, string manipulation, and more. The BCL provides the definition for each of the C# native types such as `int` and `string`.
- **ASP.NET:** Used to build websites and web-based APIs. This framework has formed the foundation of Microsoft-based websites since its release in 2002. With the introduction of .NET Core in 2016, ASP.NET provides operating system portability along with significant performance improvements and an updated API with greater pattern consistency.
- **Windows Presentation Foundation (WPF):** A graphical user interface framework used to build rich UI applications that run on Microsoft Windows. WPF provides not only a set of UI components but also a declarative language, called **eXtensible Application Markup Language (XAML)**, that enables a hierarchical definition of an application's user interface.

You will frequently hear the Microsoft .NET Framework referred to simply as the .NET Framework. Notice the capital F, which distinguishes it from a generic implementation of the CLI and the term .NET framework.

.NET Core

.NET Core is the cross-platform implementation of the .NET CLI going forward. Furthermore, .NET Core is an open-source rewrite of the .NET Framework, with a focus on high performance and cross-platform compatibility.

.NET Core consists of the .NET Core Runtime (Core CLR), .NET Core framework libraries, and a set of Dotnet command-line tools that can be used to create and build all available application scenarios. The combination of these components is included in the .NET Core SDK. If you've followed along with this book's examples, you've already used .NET Core and the Dotnet tools.

The .NET Core API is compatible with existing .NET Framework, Xamarin, and Mono implementations via .NET Standard, which is discussed in further detail later in the chapter.

The current focus of .NET Core is to build high-performant and portable console applications as well as to serve as the .NET Foundation for ASP.NET Core and Windows 10 Universal Windows Platform (UWP) applications. Additional frameworks are emerging from .NET Core as more and more operating systems are supported.

.NET Multi-platform App UI (MAUI)

This cross-platform development tool includes application UI development support for Microsoft Windows, Android, macOS, and iOS. What makes MAUI especially powerful is that a single code base can be used to produce platform-native user interfaces on each of the operating systems supported.

.NET Standard

Historically, it has been quite difficult to write a library of C# code that can be used on multiple operating systems or even different .NET frameworks on the same operating system. The problem was that the framework APIs on each framework had different classes available (and/or methods in those classes). The .NET Standard solves this issue by defining a common set of .NET APIs that each framework must implement to be compliant with a specified version of the .NET Standard. This uniformity ensures that developers have a consistent set of APIs available to them across each .NET framework that is compliant with the .NET Standard version they target.

For more information, including the mapping of .NET framework implementations and their versions to their corresponding .NET Standard version, see http://itl.tc/NETStandard.

Base Class Library

In addition to providing a runtime environment in which CIL code can execute, the CLI defines a core set of class libraries that programs may employ, called the Base Class Library. The class libraries contained in the BCL provide foundational types and APIs, allowing programs to interact with the runtime and underlying operating system in a consistent manner. The BCL includes support for collections, simple file access, some security, fundamental data types (string, among others), streams, and the like.

Similarly, a Microsoft-specific library called the **Framework Class Library (FCL)** includes support for rich client user interfaces, web user interfaces, database access, distributed communication, and more.

C# Compilation to Machine Code

The HelloWorld program listing in Chapter 1 is obviously C# code, and you compiled it for execution using the C# compiler. However, the processor still cannot directly interpret compiled C# code. An additional compilation step is required to convert the result of C# compilation into machine code. Furthermore, the execution requires the involvement of an agent that adds more services to the C# program—services that it was not necessary to code for explicitly.

All computer languages define syntax and semantics for programming. Since languages such as C and C++ compile to machine code, the platform for these languages is the underlying operating system and machine instruction set, be it Microsoft Windows, Linux, macOS, or something else. In contrast, with languages such as C#, the underlying context is the runtime (or VES).

CIL is what the C# compiler produces after compiling. It is termed a *common intermediate language* because an additional step is required to transform the CIL into something that processors can understand. Figure 24.1 shows the process.

In other words, C# compilation requires two steps:

1. Conversion from C# to CIL by the C# compiler

2. Conversion from CIL to instructions that the processor can execute

The runtime understands CIL statements and compiles them to machine code. Generally, a **component** within the runtime performs this compilation from CIL to machine code. This component is the **just-in-time (JIT) compiler**, and **jitting** can occur when the program is installed or executed. Most CLI implementations favor execution-time compilation of the CIL, but the CLI does not specify when the compilation needs to occur. In fact, the CLI even allows the CIL to be interpreted rather than compiled, in the same way that many scripting languages work. In addition, .NET includes a tool called `NGEN` that enables compilation to machine code

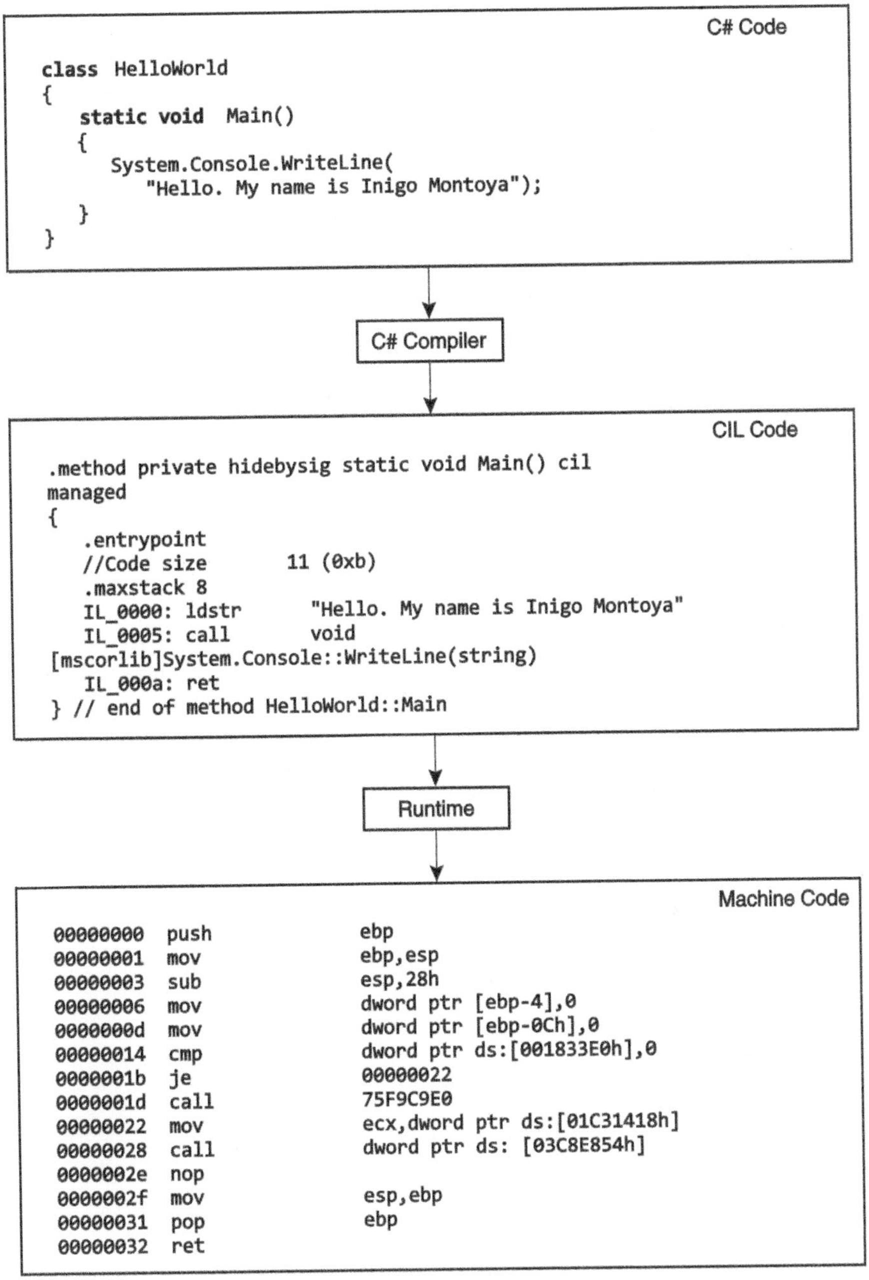

FIGURE 24.1: Compiling C# to machine code

prior to running the program. This pre-execution-time compilation needs to take place on the computer on which the program will be executing because it will evaluate the machine characteristics (processor, memory, and so on) as part of its effort to generate more efficient code. The advantage of using `NGEN` at installation (or at any time prior to execution) is that you can reduce the need for the jitter to run at startup, thereby decreasing startup time.

As of Visual Studio 2015 and later, the C# compiler also supports .NET native compilation, whereby the C# code is compiled into native machine code when creating a deployed version of the application, much like using the `NGEN` tool. Universal Windows Applications make use of this feature.

Runtime

Even after the runtime converts the CIL code to machine code and starts to execute it, it continues to maintain control of the execution. The code that executes under the context of an agent such as the runtime is managed code, and the process of executing under control of the runtime is managed execution. The control over execution transfers to the data; this makes it managed data because memory for the data is automatically allocated and de-allocated by the runtime.

Somewhat inconsistently, the term *Common Language Runtime* is not technically a generic term that is part of the CLI. Rather, CLR is the Microsoft-specific implementation of the runtime for the .NET framework. Regardless, CLR is casually used as a generic term for *runtime,* and the technically accurate term, *Virtual Execution System,* is seldom used outside the context of the CLI specification.

Because an agent controls program execution, it is possible to inject additional services into a program, even though programmers did not explicitly code for them. Managed code, therefore, provides information to allow these services to be attached. Among other items, managed code enables the location of metadata about a type member, exception handling, access to security information, and the capability to walk the stack. The remainder of this section includes a description of some additional services made available via the runtime and managed execution. The CLI does not explicitly require all of them, but the established CLI frameworks have an implementation of each.

Garbage Collection

Garbage collection is the process of automatically de-allocating memory according to the program's needs. It represents a significant programming problem for languages that don't have an automated system for performing this cleanup. Without the garbage collector, programmers must remember to always free any memory allocations they make. Forgetting to do so, or doing so repeatedly for the same memory allocation, can introduce memory leaks or corruption into the program—something exacerbated by long-running programs such as web servers. Because of the runtime's built-in support for garbage collection, programmers targeting runtime execution can focus on adding program features rather than on the "plumbing" related to memory management.

Language Contrast: C++—Deterministic Destruction

The exact mechanics for how the garbage collector works are not part of the CLI specification; therefore, each implementation can take a slightly different approach. (In fact, garbage collection is one item not explicitly required by the CLI.) One key concept with which C++ programmers may need to become familiar is the notion that garbage-collected objects are not necessarily collected **deterministically** (at well-defined, compile-time–known locations). In fact, objects can be garbage-collected anytime between when they are last accessed and when the program shuts down. This includes collection prior to falling out of scope and collection well after an object instance is accessible by the code.

The garbage collector takes responsibility only for handling memory management; that is, it does not provide an automated system for managing resources unrelated to memory. Therefore, if an explicit action to free a resource (other than memory) is required, programmers using that resource should utilize special CLI-compatible programming patterns that will aid in the cleanup of those resources (see Chapter 10).

BEGINNER TOPIC

Garbage Collection on .NET

For those reading this chapter out of order, most implementations of the CLI use a generational, compacting, mark-and-sweep–based algorithm to reclaim memory. It is "generational" because objects that have lived for only a short period will be cleaned up sooner than objects that have already survived garbage collection sweeps because they were still in use. This convention conforms to the general pattern of memory allocation, in which objects that have been around longer will continue to outlive objects that have only recently been instantiated.

Additionally, the .NET garbage collector uses a mark-and-sweep algorithm. During each garbage collection execution, it marks objects that are to be de-allocated and compacts together the objects that remain so that there is no "dirty" space between them. The use of compression to fill in the space left by de-allocated objects often results in faster instantiation of new objects (than is possible with unmanaged code), because it is not necessary to search through memory to locate space for a new allocation. Compression also decreases the chance of paging because more objects are located in the same page, which improves performance as well.

The garbage collector takes into consideration the resources on the machine and the demand on those resources at execution time. For example, if memory on the computer is still largely untapped, the garbage collector is less likely to run and take time to clean up those resources. This optimization is rarely taken by execution environments and languages that are not based on garbage collection.

BEGINNER TOPIC

Type Safety

Similarly, if you are reading this chapter out of order, you may not be aware as yet that one of the key advantages offered by the runtime is checking conversions between types, known as **type checking**. Via type checking, the runtime prevents programmers from unintentionally introducing invalid casts that can lead to buffer overrun vulnerabilities. Such vulnerabilities are one of the most common means of breaking into a computer system—and having the runtime automatically prevent these holes from opening is a significant gain.[2] Type checking provided by the runtime ensures the following:

- Both the variables and the data that the variables refer to are typed, and the type of the variable is compatible with the type of the data to which it refers.
- It is possible to locally analyze a type (without analyzing all of the code in which the type is used) to determine which permissions will be required to execute that type's members.
- Each type has a compile-time–defined set of methods and the data they contain. The runtime enforces rules about which classes can access those methods and data. Methods marked as "private," for example, are accessible only by the containing type.

ADVANCED TOPIC

Circumventing Encapsulation and Access Modifiers

Given appropriate permissions, it is possible to circumvent encapsulation and access modifiers via a mechanism known as **reflection**. Reflection provides late binding by enabling support for browsing through a type's members, looking up the names of particular constructs within an object's metadata, and invoking the type's members.

Platform Portability

C# programs are platform-portable, supporting execution across different operating systems (cross-platform support)—that is, C# programs are capable of running on multiple operating systems and executing on different CLI implementations. Portability in this context is not limited to recompiling source code for each platform, but rather a single CLI module compiled for one framework can run on any CLI-compatible framework without needing to be recompiled. This portability occurs

2. Assuming you are not the unscrupulous type who is looking for such vulnerabilities.

because the work of porting the code lies in the hands of the runtime implementation rather than the application developer (thanks to the .NET Standard). The restriction is, of course, that no platform-specific APIs can be used in your cross-platform code. When developing a cross-platform application, developers can package, or refactor, common code into cross-platform–compatible libraries and then call the libraries from platform-specific code to reduce the total amount of code required to support cross-platform applications.

Performance

Many programmers accustomed to writing unmanaged code will correctly point out that managed environments impose overhead on applications, no matter how simple they are. The trade-off is one of increased development productivity and reduced bugs in managed code versus runtime performance. The same dichotomy emerged as programming went from assembler to higher-level languages such as C, and from structured programming to object-oriented development. In the majority of scenarios, development productivity wins out, especially as the speed and reduced price of hardware surpass the demands of applications. Time spent on architectural design is much more likely to yield big performance gains than the complexities of low-level development. In the climate of security holes caused by buffer overruns, managed execution is even more compelling.

Undoubtedly, certain development scenarios (e.g., device drivers) may not yet fit with managed execution. However, as managed execution increases in capability and sophistication, many of these performance considerations will likely vanish. Unmanaged execution will then be reserved for development where precise control or circumvention of the runtime is deemed necessary.[3]

Furthermore, the runtime introduces several factors that can contribute to improved performance over native compilation. For example, because translation to machine code takes place on the destination machine, the resultant compiled code matches the processor and memory layout of that machine, resulting in performance

3. Indeed, Microsoft has indicated that managed development will be the predominant means of writing applications for its Windows platform in the future, even for those applications that are integrated with the operating system.

gains generally not leveraged by non-jitted languages. Also, the runtime is able to respond to execution conditions that direct compilation to machine code rarely takes into account. If, for example, the box has more memory than is required, unmanaged languages will still de-allocate their memory at deterministic, compile-time–defined execution points in the code. Alternatively, JIT-compiled languages will need to de-allocate memory only when it is running low or when the program is shutting down. Even though jitting can add a compile step to the execution process, code efficiencies that a jitter can insert may lead to improved performance rivaling that of programs compiled directly to machine code. Ultimately, CLI programs are not necessarily faster than non-CLI programs, but their performance is competitive.

Assemblies, Manifests, and Modules

Included in the CLI is the specification of the CIL output from a source language compiler, usually an assembly. In addition to the CIL instructions themselves, an assembly includes a manifest that is made up of the following components:

- The types that an assembly defines and imports
- Version information about the assembly itself
- Additional files the assembly depends on
- Security permissions for the assembly

The manifest is essentially a header to the assembly, providing all the information about what an assembly is composed of, along with the information that uniquely identifies it.

Assemblies can be class libraries or the executables themselves, and one assembly can reference other assemblies (which, in turn, can reference more assemblies), thereby establishing an application composed of many components rather than existing as one large, monolithic program. This is an important feature that modern programming frameworks take for granted, because it significantly improves maintainability and allows a single component to be shared across multiple programs.

In addition to the manifest, an assembly contains the CIL code within one or more modules. Generally, the assembly and the manifest are combined into a single file, as was the case with `HelloWorld.exe` in Chapter 1. However, it is possible to place modules into their own separate files and then use an assembly linker (`al.exe`) to create an assembly file that includes a manifest referencing each module.[4] This approach not only provides another means of breaking a program into components but also enables the development of one assembly using multiple source languages.

Casually, the terms *module* and *assembly* are somewhat interchangeable. However, the term *assembly* is predominant when talking about CLI-compatible programs or libraries. Figure 24.2 depicts the various component terms.

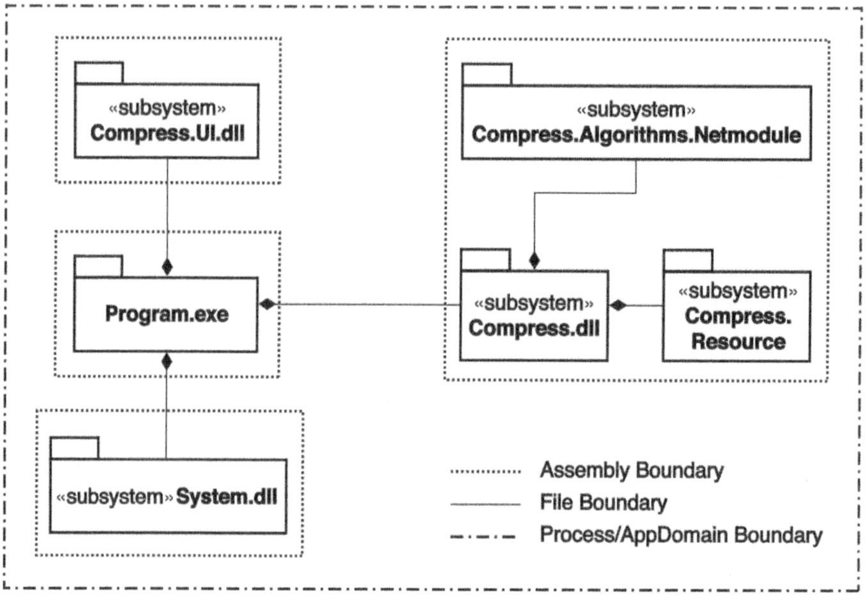

FIGURE 24.2: Assemblies with the modules and files they reference

4. This is partly because one of the primary CLI IDEs, Visual Studio .NET, lacks functionality for working with assemblies composed of multiple modules. Current implementations of Visual Studio .NET do not have integrated tools for building multimodule assemblies, and when they use such assemblies, IntelliSense does not fully function.

Note that both assemblies and modules can also reference files such as resource files that have been localized to a particular language. Although it is rare, two different assemblies can reference the same module or file.

Even though an assembly can include multiple modules and files, the entire group of files has only one version number, which is placed in the assembly manifest. Therefore, the smallest versionable component within an application is the assembly, even if that assembly is composed of multiple files. If you change any of the referenced files—even to release a patch—without updating the assembly manifest, you will violate the integrity of the manifest and the entire assembly itself. As a result, assemblies form the logical construct of a component or unit of deployment.

> **NOTE**
>
> Assemblies—not the individual modules that compose them—form the smallest unit that can be versioned and installed.

Even though an assembly (the logical construct) could consist of multiple modules, most assemblies contain only one. Furthermore, Microsoft now provides an `ILMerge.exe` utility for combining multiple modules and their manifests into a single file assembly.

Because the manifest includes a reference to all the files an assembly depends on, it is possible to use the manifest to determine an assembly's dependencies. Furthermore, at execution time, the runtime needs to examine only the manifest to determine which files it requires. Only tool vendors distributing libraries shared by multiple applications (e.g., Microsoft) need to register those files at deployment time. This makes deployment significantly easier. Often, deployment of a CLI-based application is referred to as **xcopy deployment**, after the Windows `xcopy` command that simply copies files to a selected destination.

Language Contrast: COM DLL Registration

Unlike Microsoft's COM files of the past, CLI assemblies rarely require any type of registration. Instead, it is possible to deploy applications by copying all the files that compose a program into a particular directory and then executing the program.

Common Intermediate Language

In keeping with the Common Language Infrastructure name, another important feature of the CIL and the CLI is to support the interaction of multiple languages within the same application (instead of portability of source code across multiple operating systems). As a result, the CIL is the intermediate language not only for C# but also for many other languages, including Visual Basic .NET, the Java-like language J#, some incantations of Smalltalk, C++, and a host of others (more than 20 at the time of this writing, including versions of COBOL and FORTRAN). Languages that compile to the CIL are termed source languages, and each has a custom compiler that converts the source language to the CIL. Once compiled to the CIL, the source language is insignificant. This powerful feature enables the development of libraries by different development groups across multiple organizations, without concern for the language choice of a particular group. Thus, the CIL enables programming language interoperability as well as operating system portability.

NOTE

A powerful feature of the CLI is its support for multiple languages. This support enables the creation of programs using multiple languages and the accessibility of libraries written in one language from code written in a different language.

Common Type System

Regardless of the programming language, the resultant program operates internally on data types; therefore, the CLI includes the Common Type System (CTS). The CTS defines how types are structured and laid out in memory, as well as the concepts and behaviors that surround types. It includes type manipulation directives alongside the information about the data stored within the type. The CTS standard applies to how types appear and behave at the external boundary of a language because the purpose of the CTS is to achieve interoperability between languages. It is the responsibility of the runtime at execution time to enforce the contracts established by the CTS.

Within the CTS, types are classified into two categories:

- **Values** are bit patterns used to represent basic types, such as integers and characters, as well as more complex data in the form of structures. Each value type corresponds to a separate type designation not stored within the bits themselves. The separate type designation refers to the type definition that provides the meaning of each bit within the value and the operations that the value supports.
- **Objects** contain within them the object's type designation. (This helps in enabling type checking.) Objects have identity that makes each instance unique. Furthermore, objects have slots that can store other types (either values or object references). Unlike with values, changing the contents of a slot does not change the identity of the object.

These two categories of types translate directly to C# syntax that provides a means of declaring each type.

Common Language Specification

Since the language integration advantages provided by the CTS generally outweigh the costs of implementing it, the majority of source languages support the CTS. However, there is also a subset of CTS language conformance called the Common Language Specification (CLS), whose focus is on library implementations. The CLS is intended for library developers and provides them with standards for writing libraries that are accessible from the majority of source languages, regardless of whether the source languages using the library are CTS-compliant. It is called the Common Language Specification because it is intended to also encourage CLI languages to provide a means of creating interoperable libraries, or libraries that are accessible from other languages.

For example, although it is perfectly reasonable for a language to provide support for an unsigned integer, such a type is not included as part of the CLS. Therefore, developers implementing a class library should not externally expose unsigned integers because doing so would cause the library to be less accessible from CLS-compliant source languages that do not support unsigned integers. Ideally, then, any libraries that are to be accessible from multiple languages should conform to the CLS. Note that the CLS is not concerned with types that are not exposed externally to the assembly.

Also note that it is possible to have the compiler issue a warning when you create an API that is not CLS-compliant. To accomplish this, you use the assembly attribute `System.CLSCompliant` and specify a value of `true` for the parameter.

Metadata

In addition to execution instructions, CIL code includes metadata about the types and files included in a program. The metadata includes the following items:

- A description of each type within a program or class library
- The manifest information containing data about the program itself, along with the libraries it depends on
- Custom attributes embedded in the code, providing additional information about the constructs that the attributes decorate

The metadata is not a cursory, nonessential add-on to the CIL, but rather represents a core component of the CLI implementation. It provides the representation and the behavior information about a type and includes location information about which assembly contains a particular type definition. It plays a key role in saving data from the compiler and making it accessible at execution time to debuggers and the runtime. This data not only is available in the CIL code but also is accessible during machine code execution so that the runtime can continue to make any necessary type checks.

Metadata provides a mechanism for the runtime to handle a mixture of native and managed code execution. Also, it increases code and execution robustness because it smooths the migration from one library version to the next, replacing compile-time–defined binding with a load-time implementation.

All header information about a library and its dependencies is found in a portion of the metadata known as the manifest. As a result, the manifest portion of the metadata enables developers to determine a module's dependencies, including information about particular versions of the dependencies and signatures indicating who created the module. At execution time, the runtime uses the manifest to determine which dependent libraries to load, whether the libraries or the main program has been tampered with, and whether assemblies are missing.

The metadata also contains **custom attributes** that may decorate the code. Attributes provide additional metadata about CIL instructions that are accessible via the program at execution time.

Metadata is available at execution time by a mechanism known as **reflection**. With reflection, it is possible to look up a type or its member at execution time and then invoke that member or determine whether a construct is decorated with a particular attribute. This provides for **late binding**, in which the system determines which code to execute at execution time rather than at compile time. Reflection can even be used for generating documentation by iterating through metadata and copying it into a help document of some kind (see Chapter 18).

.NET Native and Ahead of Time Compilation

The .NET Native feature creates a platform-specific executable. This is referred to as ahead of time (AOT) compilation.

.NET Native allows programmers to continue to code in C# while achieving native code performance and faster startup times by eliminating the need to JIT compile code. When .NET Native compiles an application, the .NET FCL is statically linked to the application; .NET Framework runtime components optimized for static pre-compilation are included as well. These specially built components are optimized for .NET Native and provide improved performance over the standard .NET runtime. The compilation step does not change your application in any way. You are free to use all the constructs and APIs of .NET, as well as depend on managed memory and memory cleanup, since .NET Native will include all components of the .NET Framework in your executable.

Summary

This chapter described many new terms and acronyms that are important for understanding the context under which C# programs run. The preponderance of three-letter acronyms can be confusing, so Table 24.2 summarizes the terms and acronyms that are part of the CLI.

TABLE 24.2: Common C#-Related Acronyms

Acronym	Definition	Description
.NET	None	Microsoft's implementation of the entire CLI stack. Includes the CLR, CIL, and various languages, all of which are CLS-compliant.
BCL	Base Class Library	The portion of the CLI specification that defines the collection, threading, console, and other base classes necessary to build virtually all programs.
C#	None	A programming language. Separate from the CLI standard is a C# Language Specification, also ratified by the ECMA and ISO standards bodies.
CIL (IL)	Common Intermediate Language	The language of the CLI specification that defines the instructions for the code executable on implementations of the CLI. It is sometimes also referred to as IL or Microsoft IL (MSIL) to distinguish it from other intermediate languages. (To indicate that it is a standard broader than Microsoft, CIL is preferred over MSIL and even IL.)
CLI	Common Language Infrastructure	The specification that defines the intermediate language, base classes, and behavioral characteristics that enable implementers to create Virtual Execution Systems and compilers in which source languages are interoperable on top of a common execution environment.

TABLE 24.2: Common C#-Related Acronyms (continued)

Acronym	Definition	Description
CLR	Common Language Runtime	Microsoft's implementation of the runtime, as defined in the CLI specification.
CLS	Common Language Specification	The portion of the CLI specification that defines the core subset of features that source languages *must* support to be executable on runtimes implemented according to the CLI specification.
CTS	Common Type System	A standard generally implemented by CLI-compliant languages that defines the representation and behavior of types that the language exposes visibly outside a module. It includes concepts for how types can be combined to form new types.
FCL	.NET Framework Class Library	The class library that makes up Microsoft's .NET Framework. It includes Microsoft's implementation of the BCL as well as a large library of classes for such things as web development, distributed communication, database access, and rich client user interface development, among others.
VES (runtime)	Virtual Execution System	An agent that manages the execution of a program that is compiled for the CLI.

Index

Symbols

B

C

J

N

O

S

W

X

Y

Index of 8.0 Topics

N

P

R

S

T

U

Index of 9.0 Topics

Index of 10.0 Topics

Index of 11.0 Topics

IntelliTect

IntelliTect uses best-practice application life-cycle management to deliver quality software solutions on time, on scope, and within budget. IntelliTect specializes in the following services:

- Software development consulting, implementation, and training using state-of-the-art platforms including C#, .NET, TypeScript, SQL Server, Oracle, Azure DevOps, and cloud services such as Azure, Amazon Web Services, and the Google Cloud Platform.
- Conducting software architecture workshops tailored to its client's needs. Engagements can include strategic design, architecture roadmaps, technology selections, security assessments, scope definition, and solution deployment blueprints.
- Efficiently collaborating with companies to provide enterprise content management (ECM) services on Office365/SharePoint, including consulting, training, deployment, intranet portals, and custom application development.
- Developing cloud, BizTalk, and SQL Server Integration Services (SSIS) solutions or integrating or migrating large enterprise applications and business-to-business transactions. Cloud solutions include technologies such as Azure Data Factory, Logic Apps, Azure Functions, AWS Lambdas, and Application Services. BizTalk integrations include the use of line-of-business adapters and the Enterprise Service Bus (ESB).

IntelliTect personnel include a Microsoft Regional Director and Microsoft MVPs. Team members serve on numerous Microsoft advisory boards, publish frequently, and present at conferences including DevSum, Update, and VSLive.

The IntelliTect team is committed to devoting a significant portion of the company's profits to the fight against extreme poverty around the world. Their goal is to give freedom to those without hope through their partnership with organizations fighting to eliminate poverty and injustice both locally and worldwide.